# NONDESCRIPTIVE MEANING AND REFERENCE

# Nondescriptive Meaning and Reference

*An Ideational Semantics*

WAYNE A. DAVIS

CLARENDON PRESS · OXFORD

# OXFORD
## UNIVERSITY PRESS

Great Clarendon Street, Oxford OX2 6DP

Oxford University Press is a department of the University of Oxford.
It furthers the University's objective of excellence in research, scholarship,
and education by publishing worldwide in

Oxford New York

Auckland Cape Town Dar es Salaam Hong Kong Karachi
Kuala Lumpur Madrid Melbourne Mexico City Nairobi
New Delhi Shanghai Taipei Toronto

With offices in

Argentina Austria Brazil Chile Czech Republic France Greece
Guatemala Hungary Italy Japan Poland Portugal Singapore
South Korea Switzerland Thailand Turkey Ukraine Vietnam

Oxford is a registered trade mark of Oxford University Press
in the UK and in certain other countries

Published in the United States
by Oxford University Press Inc., New York

British Library Cataloguing in Publication Data

Data available

Library of Congress Cataloging in Publication Data

Data available

Typeset by SPI Publisher Services, Pondicherry, India
Printed in Great Britain
on acid-free paper by
Biddles Ltd, King's Lynn, Norfolk

ISBN 0-19-9261652   978-0-19-926165-9

1 3 5 7 9 10 8 6 4 2

*Dedicated to our son John*
*on the occasion of his eighteenth birthday*

# Preface

The expression theory is the thesis that meaning consists in the expression of thoughts, their component ideas, or other mental states. In *Meaning, Expression, and Thought*, I set out the general theory, argued for its truth, showed its superiority to alternative theories of meaning, and replied to common objections. Much remains to be done, however. This work will move the theory further to completion by treating two interrelated sets of topics: reference and nondescriptive meaning. I have explained what it is for speakers and words to refer in terms of the expression of ideas. I will here defend this approach by exploring the vague connection of reference with predication, and reviewing the difficulties of alternative approaches, both descriptivist and causal. I will show how the expression theory can account for the meaning of names, and the distinctive way in which their meaning determines their reference. I will show that my account of names does not preclude the use of a possible worlds or situation semantics to systematize their formal referential properties, and how referential semantics can be pursued within an ideational framework. I will briefly examine interjections, syncategorematic terms, pejorative terms, and other cases that have long been seen as difficult for both ideational and referential theories of meaning. I will take up the other main category of terms with nondescriptive meaning in a subsequent book, *Indexicals*.

The treatment of special cases that might otherwise appear *ad hoc* will be seen to be the application of general principles. Part I is therefore a concise exposition of the theory developed at length in *Meaning, Expression, and Thought*. It can serve as a brief introduction to the theory for those who have not read the previous book, or a brief review for those who have. Those for whom *Meaning, Expression, and Thought* is fresh in mind may proceed from Chapter 1 'Introduction' to Chapter 6, 'Nondescriptive Meaning', taking in §3.9 'Atomic Ideas', which is expanded, and plays a particularly important role in the foundations for Chapter 6 and Part III.

As in *Meaning, Expression, and Thought*, my interest lies as much in the nature of the mental states we use words to express as it does in meaning and reference. Studies in the foundations of semantics are important not only because of the light they shed on semantics, but because of what we learn about the mind.

The first drafts of the chapters of this book were written in about 1994, together with the chapters of *Meaning, Expression, and Thought*. Since then, I have been refining the theory and completing my review of this large and growing body of research. I have benefited from comments I have received from Thomas Bartelborth, Matthew Burstein, Nathaniel Goldberg, John Hawthorne, Mark Heller, Christoph Jäger, Steve Kuhn, Mark Lance, Adrienne Lehrer, Georg Meggle, Andrew Milne, Ram Netta, Christopher Peacocke, Joseph Rahill, Stephen Rieber, Georges Rey, Jennifer Saul, Mark Seibel, Cara Spencer, Dan Sperber, Michael Slote, and Linda Wetzel. I am grateful to the editor, Peter Momtchiloff, not only for support but for sound advice. I am particularly indebted to Mitchell Green, and the reviewers for Oxford University Press, for many pages of detailed comments. Last, but certainly not least, I thank my wife, Kathryn Olesko, for more than thirty years of intellectual stimulation and love.

*Washington, DC*
*October 2004*

# Contents

## Part II: Reference

# Part I

# The Expression Theory of Meaning

# I
# Introduction

We will begin with a brief overview of the three parts of this work. Part I briefly sets out the expression theory of meaning, and then extends it to four categories of terms with nondescriptive meaning. Part II provides an analysis of reference, defining speaker reference in terms of expression and intention, and begins examining the relationship between word meaning and word reference. Part III shows that the expression theory handles proper names with ease, and is superior to extant rivals.

## 1.1 THE EXPRESSION THEORY OF MEANING

The fundamental fact on which the expression theory is based is that people can think, and have beliefs, desires, intentions, and other propositional attitudes. Thought, in the sense we focus on, is distinct from belief. We can think the thought that Germany was victorious in World War II even when we do not believe or desire that it was, and we can believe or desire that the Allies were victorious even when we are not thinking the thought that they were. Thinking plays a distinct and essential role in action and emotion. A man cannot intentionally turn off the stove, for example, unless he thinks about turning off the stove at the appropriate time. Tautologically, we think thoughts. The thought that the sky is blue is a type of event that has occurred and will occur to people all over the world. Thinking is the occurrence of thoughts. All the other propositional attitudes are relations to these event types. While the syntactic properties of thoughts are most important in accounting for meaning, thoughts also have associative or connectionist properties, which play a key role, for example, in the process of understanding speech and writing.

The fundamental fact on which the compositionality of meaning is based is that thoughts are complex events. They have parts. Compound thoughts have other thoughts as parts, but even simple thoughts have parts. We use the terms 'idea' and 'concept' interchangeably and exclusively for thoughts and those thought parts that make a difference to the qualitative character and attitudinal status of the thoughts containing them. The idea of water is such a thought part, which occurs in the thought that water is wet as well as the thought that there is little water in the desert. To think of water is for that idea to occur to us. Ideas in this sense are neither sensory images (perception-like complexes of sensations) nor conceptions (systems of belief about something). As a useful analogy, we can say that thoughts are sentence-like mental representations. Ideas stand to thoughts roughly as words stand to sentences. But thoughts are not literally sentences, and thinking is not a relation to sentences. In particular, while the object or content of an idea is similar in some respects to the meaning of a word, there are critical differences. For an idea to have the content *water* is for it to be the idea of water. The content of an idea is thus an intrinsic, essential property: it makes no sense to suppose that the idea of water should change its content, or to ask how it acquired this content. Ideas are 'individuated' by their content. The meaning of the word 'water', in contrast, is something that word acquired at a certain point in the history of the English language, and may well change in the future. Words can have more than one meaning, and different words can have the same meaning. Having an object or content is an intentional property, not a relation, despite grammatical appearances. 'Santa Claus is the object of the idea of Santa Claus' is true even though the idea cannot stand in any relation to Santa because Santa does not exist. The idea of water differs in content from the idea of $H_2O$, moreover, despite the fact that water and $H_2O$ are the same substance. What it is to be thinking of water, and how we acquire the ability to think of it, are important questions. But they are not linguistic issues. The answers are in all probability largely neurophysiological.

Given the importance to us of referring to ideas, we will pay special attention to indexical descriptions like 'the idea of water' or 'the thought that water is wet' (or alternatively, 'the idea *"water"* ' and 'the thought *"water* is wet" '). On my view, we use such expressions to refer deictically to the ideas expressed by the words following 'of' or 'that'. We express certain ideas when we use 'water' or 'water is wet' in these contexts, and we are introspectively aware of the ideas expressed. Those ideas are the referents of 'the idea of water' and 'the thought that water is wet' respectively. Such ideo-reflexive reference is as rigid and direct as deictic reference generally. (I will treat ideo-reflexive phrases in more depth in *Indexicals*.)

Thoughts are private. We often know what other people are thinking, but we cannot see, hear, smell, taste, or feel their thoughts in the way that we can see their hair, hear their words, or feel their temperature. We know our own thoughts by introspection. Because we wish to make our mental states known to others, or simply because we want to, we often provide observable indications of the ideas occurring to us. To do this in a certain way is to express the ideas. In general, to express a mental state is to do something with the intention of providing an undisguised indication that we are in that state, one that is not a feigned unintentional indication. While implying involves indirect expression, speaker meaning involves the direct expression of ideas, beliefs, and other mental states. A speaker means "Theodore Roosevelt was an unmarried man" by 'Roosevelt was a bachelor' iff the speaker directly expressed the thought that Theodore Roosevelt was an unmarried man by uttering that sentence. As is natural given its importance in our lives, we have many specialized terms for the expression of ideas. A woman refers to Theodore Roosevelt provided she verbally expresses the idea of Theodore Roosevelt, directly or indirectly. Mentioning Roosevelt requires use of a word that refers to him. A man communicates a thought to a woman only if he expresses the thought and she recognizes that he expressed it. Telling and informing require more specific intentions.

Like other acts, the expression of ideas can be conventional or unconventional. An action is conventional if it is a socially useful and self-perpetuating but arbitrary regularity. As a first approximation, word meaning is conventional speaker meaning. The word 'vixen' means "female fox" because it is conventional for speakers to use 'vixen' to mean "female fox". Communication is the common interest that primarily sustains linguistic conventions. In addition to conventions governing the use of individual words, there are also conventions to use certain word structures to express particular idea structures. Noun phrases of the form 'N Ver' mean either "Ver of Ns" or "N that Vs" because it is conventional to use expressions of the form 'N Ver' both to express ideas of the form "Ver of Ns" and to express ideas of the form "N that Vs". Consequently 'female inspector' means either "inspector of females" or "female that inspects". These construction conventions make possible a recursive definition of word meaning. The base clause assigns meanings to individual words, dead metaphors, and the like on the basis of what people conventionally mean by them. The recursion clause assigns meanings to phrases, clauses, and sentences on the basis of the meanings of the component words and the conventions pairing word structures with idea structures. The recursion clause assigns meanings to novel expressions for which there are no special conventions because they have never been used.

This definition of word meaning must be relativized to living languages. Languages in general are systems of modes of expression, which pair expressions with ideas or other mental states. Living languages are those that depend on the conventional usage of an evolving lineage of speakers. A natural language is discovered and named when a group of speakers is isolated with a distinctive way of expressing ideas. As the conventions perpetuate themselves over time, they are passed to new members of the speech community. Since conventions are seldom perfect regularities, they can change over time. Previously unconventional uses can spread and become conventional. What words mean in a living language today is determined by the conventional usage of the linguistic descendants of prior users. Languages die when use becomes too uncommon to perpetuate itself. In artificial languages, words mean what they do as a result of stipulation rather than convention. And in idiolects, words mean what they do because of personal practices of the individual.

Ideational theories have been thought to be materially inadequate because some meaningful terms do not express ideas (e.g., syncategorematic terms), or cannot be fully explained in terms of the expression of ideas (e.g., pejorative terms). I will argue that in fact syncategorematic terms do express thought parts. But I accept the general point that meaning does not consist exclusively in the expression of ideas. We will here look more closely at the mental states other than ideas that interjections, pejorative terms, and terms with conventional implicatures express.

Traditional ideational theories have been burdened with the assumption that ideas must be images of some sort. It is true that meaning cannot be defined in terms of images, but we define ideas not as images but as thought parts. Thinking is distinct from inner speech and the imagery that accompanies it. Other mentalistic theories have tried without success to define meaning in terms of conceptions—systems of belief—which are concepts in a different sense. Speakers with very different conceptions of man may nevertheless mean the same thing by 'man'. Many mentalistic theories have erred by saying that meanings *are* ideas. Such an identification is not essential to ideational theories, however, and I have argued against it.

One of the most influential objections to ideational theories is that they are regressive or circular in some way because ideational content is either a type of meaning itself, or something that must be defined in terms of meaning. This too is a mistake. The meanings of words are properties of words, which are dependent on conventions or other external factors. The contents of ideas are intrinsic, identifying properties of ideas. A subsidiary objection is that ideational theories are incomplete because they do not say what ideas are or provide a theory of content for them. But every theory is incomplete in that it does not define its primitive terms, or explain everything. A referential theory of meaning that identifies the meaning of the word 'quark' with the set of quarks cannot be faulted for failing to tell us what quarks or sets are. There is no more reason to require that an ideational theory of meaning must tell us what it is for people to think. The objection that ideational theories are incomplete because they do not account for truth and reference will be addressed by showing how these subjects can be treated within an ideational semantics.

## 1.2  REFERENCE

Thoughts and ideas are mental representations. The idea of water represents water, and the thought that water is wet represents water as being wet. When what an idea represents exists, we call what it represents the extension of the idea. The word 'water' refers to water because water is the extension of the idea the word expresses. The sentence 'water is wet' is true because the thought it expresses is true. In general, the referential properties of words are determined by the extensions of the ideas they express. As important as word reference and truth is, it cannot be equated with meaning. For we find words with the same reference but different meanings ('water', 'H$_2$O') and words with a meaning but no reference at all ('Santa Claus'). This is possible because what different ideas represent may turn out to be identical, and because we can think of things that do not exist. In an ideational semantics, words are assigned to ideas. The extensional properties of ideas can be set out recursively by providing a generative theory of ideas, assigning extensions to atomic ideas, and formulating the rules whereby the extension of a complex idea is determined by the extensions of its components. The same can be done for intensions, characters, and other 'semantic values'.

Unlike word reference, speaker reference is an intentional notion in Brentano's sense. We can and often do refer to things that do not exist. We will critically examine the arguments of Donnellan and others for thinking otherwise, and review the many defects in causal theories of reference. We will see that the standard externalist conclusions drawn from the Twin Earth examples are invalid, such as that speaker reference is not determined by intention. While 'S referred to Φ' and other psychological statements do have a transparent interpretation, we will generally be focusing on their opaque interpretation.

### 1.3 NAMES AND NONDESCRIPTIVE MEANING

Standard proper names have been hard cases for theories of meaning because of the groundless assumption that if names have any meaning at all beyond their reference, they must have a *descriptive* meaning. Kripkean arguments against the description theory show that names do not have descriptive meanings. Frege's and Russell's problems show that the meaning of a name cannot be identified with its reference. Some Millians have attempted to explain away apparent failures of substitutivity as illusions based on implicatures. We will see that such explanations are unsuccessful, and are no help with Russell's problem. The proper conclusion to draw is that standard names have nondescriptive senses.

The expression theory has no difficulty with names. The word 'Aristotle' is meaningful because it is conventionally used to express the idea of Aristotle. 'Santa Claus' is meaningful because it expresses the idea of Santa Claus, even though Santa does not exist. 'Cary Grant' and 'Archibald Leach' differ in meaning because the ideas they express are different despite the fact that Cary Grant and Archibald Leach are in fact the same person.

Names are 'directly referential' in the sense that their reference is not determined by any descriptive concept. The extension of a name concept is determined directly by its content and not by the extensions of its components. What the arguments against the description theory show is that the ideas expressed by proper names are atomic or basic. There must be some ideas that do not have other ideas as parts. The evidence showing that names are not synonymous with any descriptive phrases can be easily accounted for by the hypothesis that names express some of the atomic ideas. There is no more reason to insist that nominal concepts must contain descriptive concepts than there is to insist that descriptive concepts must contain nominal concepts. There appear to be at least four categories of atomic or basic concepts, expressed respectively by names, descriptive general terms, syncategorematic terms like logical particles, and pronouns. Three of the four categories have nondescriptive meaning.

The fact that names with different meanings can nonetheless have the same reference means that identity statements made using them can be true without being logical or epistemic necessities. We will show how standard arguments that the necessity of identity is a logical truth go astray, and how a possible worlds semantics for names can be developed without it. We will show too how a formal semantics can be provided within both ideational and situational frameworks.

## 1.4 THE GRICEAN PROGRAM

The expression theory thus realizes Grice's program of defining word meaning in terms of speaker meaning, and speaker meaning in terms of speaker intention. By defining speaker meaning in terms of evidential meaning as well as intention, and focusing on thoughts and ideas rather than beliefs, exploiting their complexity, it avoids the problems Grice and his followers encountered. The theory is simultaneously a use theory and an ideational theory, intentionalist and conventionalist, while avoiding the traditional flaws of these approaches. The expression theory accounts fully for the referential properties of expressions without identifying meaning with reference. The theory has the strength of Fregean approaches without their descriptivist bias. It has the virtues of Millian approaches without their referentialist shortcomings. The expression theory explains fundamental linguistic concepts in terms of elementary psychological concepts, and thus contributes to the systematization of our knowledge of the mind. As is normal in cognitive science, or any other field of intellectual inquiry, many important questions remain to be answered. But the expression theory is, I believe, the most viable foundational theory of meaning.

# 2

# Thoughts

The thesis that meaning consists in the expression of ideas is generally true when an idea is defined as a thought or thought part, and a thought is understood to be a particular type of mental event. A thought in this sense is not an act of belief, although it may be an object of belief, other propositional attitudes, or nonpropositional attitudes. Thoughts, I maintain, are cognitively and motivationally neutral, abstract, generatively constructed representations with truth values and sentence-like constituent structures. Thinking a thought is one of the fundamental propositional attitudes. The goal of this chapter is to introduce this cogitative sense of thought. We will compare and contrast it with belief, distinguish thoughts from sentences, identify propositions with one type of thought, and establish that thoughts have constituents, including subpropositional constituents.[1]

## 2.1 THOUGHT VERSUS BELIEF

The word 'thought' is at least doubly ambiguous. Like 'belief', 'desire', and 'intention', it suffers from the *act–object ambiguity*. 'S's thought that it will rain' can refer either to what S thinks, or to S's act of thinking it. What S thinks, the 'object' of his thought, is in this example simply the proposition that it will rain (§2.5). We will be equally concerned with the act of thinking and its objects. In addition, 'thought' is like 'meaning' in displaying the *cognitive–cogitative ambiguity*. 'Thought' can mean either *believing* or *occurrent thinking*, or their respective objects. We will use 'thought' in its cogitative sense to denote occurrent thinking and its objects.

Compare the following:

(1) S thinks that p.
(2) S is thinking the thought that p.

Form (1) means that S believes that p. (2) means that the thought that p is occurring to S. (2) does not entail (1). Right now I am thinking the thought that Berlin is the capital of France. Now that I have told you what I am thinking, I am sure you are thinking the same thought. But I do not think that Berlin is the capital of France, and I am sure you do not either.

Moreover, (1) does not entail (2): S may think (i.e., believe) that 5 is prime even though he is not at the moment thinking about numbers. I may assert that my wife thinks 5 is prime, for example, without knowing what she is doing or thinking about at the moment. Indeed, my statement will be true even if she is asleep or unconscious. Only if my wife suffers a rather total memory loss will I have to retract the statement that she believes that 5 is prime.

Forms (1) and (2) have different contraries and implications. At least in ordinary circumstances, it is not possible for S to think that p at the very same time that S thinks that not-p. But it is not the least extraordinary for S to be thinking the thought that p while also thinking the thought that not-p. This occurs, for example, when S thinks "It is tautological that p or not-p". It is of course possible for S to think that p at one time and think that not-p at a later time. It follows in that case that S has changed his mind. From the fact that S is thinking the thought that p at one time and the thought that not-p at a later time, it does not follow that S has changed his mind about anything, although it is certainly true that something has changed in his mind.

The fact that beliefs need not be occurrent is often expressed by saying that belief is a *'dispositional' state*. The act of thinking expressed in (2), in contrast, is an *occurrence*, an *act* or *event*. In this respect, thinking is more like saying or uttering than believing is. That is, (2) differs from (1) in implying that *something is going on*, and in being an appropriate answer to *'What is S doing?'* Like statements, and unlike beliefs, it makes sense of occurrent thoughts to ask *'Precisely when and where did S think that thought?'* or *'How often did S do it?'* Beliefs are said to be occurrent when the proposition believed is an object of occurrent thought as well as of belief. Thus Kathy has believed that $2 + 2 = 4$ since she was about four years old, but has only occurrently believed that proposition on those occasions on which she was also thinking the thought that $2 + 2 = 4$.

Both (1) and (2) can occur in *oratio recta* form:

(3) S thinks "p".
(4) S is thinking the thought "p".

As a free-standing declarative sentence, (3) always has the cognitive sense. 'John thinks "Berlin is the capital of France"' means "John believes that Berlin is the capital of France". But in certain subordinate clauses, (3) is ambiguous. Consider: *If John thinks "Tomorrow is Saturday" during the math exam, then he is not concentrating.* This conditional is likely to be true in one sense (where the antecedent describes him as having a certain occurrent thought), false in another (where the antecedent describes him as having a certain belief).

In either sense, 'think' is like 'believe' in that its sentence-complement need not in any sense be a 'direct quote'. Replacing 'p' in any of these forms with a strictly synonymous sentence will not change the truth value of the statement. There is no difference between thinking "Jimmy didn't win" and "Jimmy did not win", even though there is a clear difference between uttering or saying 'Jimmy didn't win' as opposed to 'Jimmy did not win'. Consequently, when we translate (1) through (4) into another language, the complement 'p' gets translated as well as the rest of the sentence. We might try to summarize this point by saying that thinking the thought that p resembles believing that p in being a *propositional* rather than *sentential* attitude (see §2.4). But this formulation is not quite general enough. When it has the cognitive sense, 'think' like 'believe' must be followed by a declarative sentence. But in its cogitative sense, 'think' is like 'say' in that its complement can be a quoted interrogative or imperative sentence. As a free-standing sentence expressing belief, 'Bill thinks "Is it going to rain?"' is as ungrammatical as 'Bill believes "Is it going to rain?"' But in the cogitative sense, Bob may think "Will Mary sing?" or "Mary, sing!" just as well as he can think "Mary will sing". If John thinks "Will Mary go out with me?" during the math exam, then he is definitely not concentrating. So whereas the objects of belief are restricted to propositions, the objects of occurrent thought include nonpropositional thoughts (§6.1).

Thinking and believing are alike in being *intrinsic properties*, those whose acquisition or loss implies a real change in the object. If Bob is thinking the thought that the sky is blue at one moment, and not thinking it the next, then Bob has changed. Occurrent thought is also like belief in being '*private*': we can introspect our own beliefs and thoughts, but they are not observable with any of the five senses. We can observe that someone is 'thinking out loud'. But what we hear are his words, not his thoughts. To say that beliefs and thoughts are private is not to say that they are unknowable to others. We can recognize both on the basis of verbal and other behavior.

Occurrent thought differs from belief in *not having degrees*. Whereas we can believe in God *more* at one moment than at another, there is no analog for thinking. We can, though, measure the *frequency, duration*, and *latency* of a thought, and the degree of *association* of two thoughts. For instance, we can determine how often Steve thinks about being a millionaire, and how long he thinks about being one on a particular occasion. We can also measure how long it takes him to think of the Russian word for 'millionaire' after we ask him, and how often he thinks about being a millionaire when he thinks about his monthly mortgage. It makes sense to ask how long it takes to think something in a way it makes no sense to ask how long it takes to believe something. While we do not have the technical means to measure precisely how long a thought takes, we can say that it takes very little time. For we know that thoughts can occur to us 'suddenly', and 'flash' through our mind. Some are 'fleeting'. These vague quantitative terms do not apply to belief.

Voluntary actions depend on thoughts as well as beliefs, but in different ways. Beliefs combine with desires in a familiar manner to determine what we do. I may go to the supermarket, for example, because I want to buy milk and believe that I can buy milk if I go to the supermarket. The contents of these states form my reasons for acting. The likelihood that I go to the supermarket, moreover, is directly related to how much I want milk and to how certain I am that I can buy milk if I go. Thought, in contrast, is a necessary condition for voluntary action whose content is not a motive. *Forgetfulness*, *absentmindedness*, and *distraction* are major causes of failure to act. No matter how much I want milk, or believe that I can buy milk in the supermarket, I will not go to the supermarket, at least not on purpose, unless it occurs to me to do so.[2] The likelihood that I will go is directly related to the likelihood that I will think about going at the appropriate moment, which is directly related to the probability that I will think associated thoughts, such as the thought that I am out of milk, or the thought that I will go to the drugstore next door to the supermarket. The likelihood of my thinking about going to the supermarket is also directly related to how much I want to go ('Objects of desire tend to be on our minds'), which is directly related to how much I want milk and believe I can get it at the supermarket. It would ordinarily be misleading to say that I went to the supermarket because I thought of going, just as it would be misleading to say that a match lit because there is oxygen about. But if the other critical necessary conditions of action are evidently satisfied, and this one was iffy, such a causal statement would be quite in order. All of this is true even though going to the supermarket is in no sense my reason for going to the supermarket.

Thought also plays an important and distinctive *role in emotion*. Given two people who believe that they are in dire financial straits, the one who dwells more on the problem will tend to be more miserable than the one who can get his mind off it. We have greater *voluntary control* over thought than belief. While we cannot start thinking about a topic at will, the desire to continue thinking about it is generally effective in bringing about that result, although the ability to concentrate varies from person to person and time to time. Thoughts differ markedly from beliefs in both their *causes* and the criteria for their *rational assessment*. We typically believe what we do because we have reasons for our belief, which consist in the evidence we have for the proposition we believe. The rationality of the belief depends on how good our reasons are from an epistemological standpoint. Thoughts, in contrast, often just pop into our mind. There is nothing irrational about this, although it would be highly irrational if our beliefs arose in the same way. Equally often, thoughts are prompted by events that do not constitute reasons, as when hearing a report that the drought continues in Florida reminds me that I left the sprinkler on. We have reasons for thinking things only to the extent that our thoughts are voluntary, and in that case the reasons we have are reasons for action rather than reasons for belief.

I have been emphasizing the independence of belief and thought, the fact that we can think a proposition without believing it, and vice versa. Their independence is not complete, however. First of all, the well-known fact that our beliefs depend on our reasons for belief needs to be supplemented by the realization that our beliefs also depend on the occurrence of those reasons. A physician who cannot keep all the symptoms in mind at once might not be able to form a stable diagnosis. I believe that forgetfulness, absentmindedness, and distraction are more common causes of inconsistency than irrationality. Second, some propositions cannot be believed without being thought (e.g., the proposition that it is noon *now*), and some propositions cannot be thought without being believed (e.g., the proposition that 2 is not both prime and not prime). Third, I have argued that S believes any proposition only if he is *able to* think it, and actually *has* thought it.

**2.1 Postulate:** *S believes P only if P is able to occur, and has occurred, to S.*

I call this the *first law of occurrence*, although the second clause is controversial. A similar principle holds for disbelief, desire, and aversion, and all other propositional attitudes. It may be that Tom *would* believe that grizzly bears run faster than box turtles. But we cannot say that Tom *does* believe this if it has never occurred to him that grizzlies run faster than box turtles. As one piece of evidence, observe that 'Tom believes it, but it has never occurred to him' sounds as self-contradictory as 'Tom knows it, but doesn't believe it'.[3]

## 2.2 THINKING AS THE OCCURRENCE OF THOUGHTS

We will select as primitive the term 'thought' in the cogitative, objective sense—the sense in which it is a general term denoting the thought that the sky is blue, the thought "Will Mary sing?", and so on. The thought "p" for any sentence 'p', and the thought that p, for any indicative sentence 'p', are thoughts. Thoughts in this sense are *events*, specifically *mental* events. Thoughts are the sorts of events that occur to people or other intelligent beings, and any being to which a thought occurs *ipso facto* has a mind. For a thought to occur is for some thinking to take place. Thoughts in this sense are event-*types*, however, rather than event-tokens. 'The thought that the sky is blue' denotes a type or kind of event, occurring to many people at different times. Given that thoughts are event-types, the act of thought can be defined in terms of their occurrence.

**2.2  Definition:** *S is thinking T iff T is a thought (-type) occurring to S.*

While it will not be important for us, 'thought' is like many other common nouns in having a closely related sense in which it denotes tokens. Suppose Tom, Dick, and Harry are all thinking "The sky is blue". If I ask 'How many thoughts are being thought?' I would most commonly be asking how many thought-types are being thought, and the answer would be 'One'. But I might be asking how many thought-tokens are being thought; in that case the answer would be 'Three'. (Compare: 'How many letters are used on this page?') The type sense of 'thought' may be taken as primitive. That is, a thought-token can be defined as a token of a thought-type. Any attempt to reverse the conceptual order and define a thought-type as one whose occurrences are thought-tokens is problematic. For any set of thought-tokens are tokens of more than one type. For example, every thought-token is a token of the type *mental event, event,* and *token.* Furthermore, some thought-types may never have been tokened. Unless I indicate otherwise, 'thought' is to be interpreted as 'thought-type' below.

Since different people can grasp the same thought, Frege concluded that thoughts are abstract objects distinct from mental states. This makes a mystery of what it is to grasp a thought, and of how thoughts can influence behavior.[4] Thoughts are abstract, on my view, but only because they are *mental event types.* For you to think the thought that the sky is blue is for that mental event type to occur to you. Frege wrongly assumed that 'mental state' denotes only tokens, and took images to be the paradigm case. The fact that 'thinking consists in a relation to an objective entity' is no grounds for denying that thinking is an 'inner mental process' when the objective entity is a mental event type and the relation is occurrence.[5] While it makes no sense to say of some abstract objects that they have causes and effects (e.g., numbers, geometric lines, sets, units of measure, temporal relations, logical properties), it makes perfect sense to say that event types do (such as homicide, reckless driving, anger, war, hyperventilation, and the fire alarm). In general, to say that an event type has certain causes and effects is to claim that tokens of the type have causes and effects of those types.

How do types differ from other abstract objects? We can distinguish types from abstract objects like numbers by observing that types are *universals,* which have tokens or instances. Types differ from properties and sets in that *the properties of a type are typically properties of its tokens.*[6] The word 'true' has one syllable, as do its tokens. Since the thought that John is a man is singular, so are its tokens. The properties of properties, in contrast, are typically not properties of the things that instantiate them (red is a primary color, and apples are red, but apples are not primary colors). And the properties of sets (such as their cardinality and membership) are generally not properties of their members. Types also *occur in other types.* Thus in addition to having countless tokens (individual hydrogen atoms), the hydrogen atom occurs in countless molecules such as water and peroxide. The word 'sings' occurs in the sentence 'John sings'. And the thought that today is Sunday occurs in the thought that if yesterday was Saturday then today is Sunday (§2.6). Types of events not only occur in more complex events, they also *occur in places, at times*, and *to people*. Thus the thought that the Super Bowl is on may occur to John at 7:00 pm in Los Angeles, just as hunger or exhaustion may.

Frege's view that thoughts exist eternally and necessarily[7] may seem absurd on its face. For surely thoughts cannot exist unless there is someone to think them, and thinking beings are contingent, having existed for only a fraction of the time the universe has existed? However, the principle that thoughts cannot exist without a thinker is tautological only when we are referring to thought *tokens*. Frege, however, was concerned with thought *types*, which are a kind of abstract object. In that sense, there are many thoughts no one has ever thought, and there may well be thoughts no one ever thinks. In the same sense, since there is an infinite range of colors, there are colors no object has ever had, or is ever likely to have. There is an infinite number of sentences that will never get tokened. Frege was particularly concerned with truth, logic, and mathematics. Since the thought that $2 + 2 = 4$ is a mathematical truth, we seem compelled to conclude that it is true at all times and in all possible worlds. The thought was as true a billion years ago as it is today. The assumption that thoughts exist eternally is fully consistent with the fact that we can often date the time when a thought first *arose*. For a thought to arise is for it to be thought for the first time. The Platonist who treats biological species as eternally existing abstract objects can similarly acknowledge that species originate and become extinct. For that concerns when the species is instantiated for the first and last time. The issue of whether types exist eternally and necessarily is a major part of the venerable problem of universals. We will assume that universals exist eternally in all possible worlds, but this assumption is not critical for the development of the theory. The weaker assumption that thought-types may exist even when they are not tokened will be essential for some developments.

## 2.3 THINKING OF OBJECTS

In the cognitive sense, 'think' must be followed by a complete sentence, typically preceded by 'that'. In the cogitative sense, the quoted expression need not be a complete sentence. Thus *Mary was thinking "After Caesar came, he"—and then she died* is grammatical and may be true. In the same sense, 'think' most often occurs with 'about' or 'of', which must be followed by a noun ('Mary'), noun phrase ('brown cows'), gerund ('going home'), or nominalization ('Mary's loving Jack') that may serve as a direct or indirect object. We will use '$\Phi$' as a place-holder for such terms, which we call '*object nominals*'.

(5)  S is thinking of (about) $\Phi$.
(6)  S is thinking of $\Phi$ as $\Psi$.

In both formulas, 'thinking' is synonymous with 'conceiving'. (6) says that S is thinking the thought that $\Phi$ is $\Psi$, with no implication that S believes this. (5) will be true if *any* statement of form (6) is true. That is, (5) holds if (4) ('S is thinking the thought that p') is true for some thought "p" about $\Phi$. Thus John is thinking of Mary if some thought about Mary is occurring to John. He may be thinking the thought that Mary is pretty, that he loves Mary, that Jane is taller than Mary, and so on, again with no implication of belief.

Thoughts are complex, with components that occur together in certain relationships when the thoughts occur. We use the terms *idea* and *concept* to denote the components. The thought that Mary should be president is about Mary because it contains the idea of Mary. In general, *a thought is about $\Phi$ iff it contains the idea of $\Phi$*. Now a complex event occurs if, and only if, all of its components occur, and occur in the right relationships. It follows that if John thinks of Mary, then the idea of Mary has to occur to John (Theorem 2.8). The fact that the idea of Mary occurs to John does not logically entail that any thought containing that idea occurs to John, although it does appear to be true that ideas occur only as parts of thoughts. Whether this is universally true or not, it would be self-contradictory to say that the idea of Mary is occurring to John but John is not thinking of Mary. So we can define thinking of objects in terms of the occurrence of ideas.

2.3  **Definition:** *S is thinking of (about) $\Phi$ iff the idea of $\Phi$ is occurring to S.*

Both sides of Definition 2.3 have opaque and transparent interpretations (§2.8). The formula holds on both interpretations, as long as both sides are interpreted in the same way. We will be focusing on the opaque interpretation, on which thinking of the morning star implies thinking of it *as* the morning star. What must occur to S is the specific idea "the morning star".

Context (5) differs markedly from (7), which lacks the preposition 'of' or 'about'.

(7)  S is thinking $\Phi$.

In (7), '$\Phi$' can be replaced by a restricted range of nouns and noun phrases, including singular terms like 'the thought that John loves Mary', quoted sentences like "'John loves Mary'", indefinite descriptions like 'a thought about Mary', names like 'Newton's third law', or the variable T with thoughts in its domain. '$\Phi$' may not be replaced by a gerund, a nominalized sentence, or a proper name of anything other than a proposition or thought. Expression (7) is a genuine relational predicate, which entails the existence of Φ. Indeed, (7) is a fully extensional context. In contrast, (5) is an intentional context, whose truth does not entail the existence of Φ (even on its transparent interpretation). Thinking *about Pegasus* does not entail that Pegasus exists. All it entails is the existence of the *idea* of Pegasus. Thinking *the thought that Pegasus is a flying horse*, in contrast, entails the existence of that thought. Thoughts must exist for people to think them.

Confusion can arise from the fact that 'Φ' may be said to denote the *'object of thought'* in both (5) and (7). Thus, if John is thinking the thought that Pegasus had wings, then we can say both that the thought that Pegasus had wings is the object of John's thought (because that is what he is thinking) and that Pegasus is the object of John's thought (because that is what John is thinking of). To avoid equivocation, I will use *'relational object of thought'* to denote *what S is thinking*, that is, *the thought S is thinking*. I will use *'intentional object of thought'* to denote *what S is thinking of*. Relational objects of thought are genuine objects, the things over which the second variable in the relational predicate 'S is thinking T' ranges. If T is a relational object of S's thought, then T must exist. Moreover, if T = T′, then T′ must also be a relational object of S's thought. Intentional objects of thought, in contrast, cannot be treated as genuine objects on pain of Meinongian absurdities. Pegasus can be an object of thought even though Pegasus does not exist. And the cube root of 8 need not be the object of John's thought even though the square root of 4 is. 'S is thinking of Φ' and 'Φ is the object of S's thought' should not be treated as expressing a relation between Φ and S or his thought (§8.5). They should just be treated as descriptions of S and what S is thinking.

Note that 'S is thinking *about the thought that p*' is an instance of (5), not of (7) or (2). For Bill to think about the thought that smoking causes cancer, it is not enough for him to think "Smoking causes cancer". He has to think some second-order thought about that thought, such as "The thought that smoking causes cancer is widely believed but still controversial". Thinking a thought T does not entail thinking about T on pain of an infinite regress.

## 2.4 SENTENCES VERSUS THOUGHTS

There are many important similarities between sentences and thoughts. Both are *representations*. The thought "The sky is blue" and the sentence 'The sky is blue' are both about the sky and both represent the fact that the sky is blue. Sentences and thoughts are both capable of being *true or false*, sentences in virtue of their *meanings*, thoughts in virtue of their *contents*. Sentences and thoughts are both *attitudinally neutral* representations. The subject that produces them may or may not believe that they are true, may or may not desire that they be true, and so on. Such representations are *abstract* in a way that pictorial or iconic representations are not. A portrait of President Washington that represents him as having false teeth will also represent him as having countless other characteristics: a smile or frown, open or closed eyes, long or short hair, and so on. The sentence 'President Washington had false teeth' represents only the fact that Washington had false teeth, in contrast, and the same goes for the thought that sentence expresses.

Sentences and thoughts are not only *structured*, they both have a *phrase* or *constituent* structure. Just as a sentence is an expression consisting of expressions, so a thought is an idea consisting of ideas (§2.6). Both have *systematic, generative* structure (§9.5): different thoughts and sentences may have the same constituents in different relationships, or different constituents in the same relationship; moreover, an infinity of different thoughts and sentences can be generated from a finite number of unstructured components and structural relationships. What a complex expression or idea represents depends on what its components represent and their mode of combination. Finally, the *compositionality* of natural language semantics means that the idea expressed by one linguistic unit—whether it be a word, phrase, clause, or sentence—is generally a constituent of the ideas expressed by larger linguistic units containing it (§5.6). Thus the idea expressed by the word 'Mary' is a constituent of the idea expressed by the phrase 'loves Mary', which is a constituent of the thought expressed by the sentence 'John loves Mary'. Compositionality means that the structures of sentences and thoughts are similar not only in kind, but also in detail. Indeed, their structures are *isomorphic* to a high degree.

In short, thoughts are like sentences in being attitudinally neutral, abstract, generatively constructed representations with truth values and highly isomorphic constituent structures. Thinking resembles inner speech in consisting of the occurrence of sentence-like mental representations.

When employed with caution, the sentential analogy provides a useful characterization of thought. Philosophers, linguists, and psychologists have often claimed not just analogy but identity. Many introspectionist psychologists treated thought as inner speech (§3.2). Many contemporary cognitive scientists characterize thoughts as 'sentences in the language of thought'. And the logical positivists treated propositions and thoughts as 'logical constructions' out of sentences, reducing talk about propositions to talk about sets of synonymous sentences. It is critical to understanding the nature of both thought and language to recognize that *thoughts are not sentences*. Sentences are used to assert, order, amuse, and so on; thoughts are not. Sentences can be written or spoken, and it is reasonable to identify them with sequences of sounds or letters, or types of such. Thoughts are not composed of sounds or letters. Thoughts are mental events, and thinking is their occurrence. Sentences are not mental events, and their occurrence does not constitute thinking. We speak of sentences as being ambiguous or unambiguous, and as being synonymous with, translations of, or paraphrases of, other sentences. These terms do not apply to thoughts.

The most important facts establishing that thoughts cannot be identified with the sentences expressing them are the following. *The relationship between sentences and the thoughts they express is not one-to-one, but many-many.* Thus 'Bill's accuser is mad' and 'The accuser of Bill is mad' are different sentences that express one thought, and the same goes for 'It is raining' and 'Il pleut'. And one ambiguous sentence like 'Kissing girls never hurt me' can be used to express several different thoughts. These same examples show in addition that *thoughts are grammar and language independent.*[8] The sentences of any given natural language express particular thoughts in virtue of the conventions constituting that language (see Chapter 5). As languages change, the sentences of the language may come to express different thoughts. Given that it depends on variable factors such as convention, *any relationship between sentences and thoughts is contingent.* As a consequence, even though thought content and sentence meaning are similar properties, *sentences have their meaning contingently, by convention or stipulation; thoughts have their content essentially, by nature.* The sentence 'Grass grows' could have meant "Snow falls", but the thought "Grass grows" could not have had the content "Snow falls". The power of stipulation is regularly used to enrich languages. When new phenomena are named, we are able to express thoughts that were previously inexpressible in that language. This gives rise to another respect in which thoughts are language independent: *at any given time, many thoughts are inexpressible in any existing language.*[9] Thus the thought that solid-state televisions are electronic is true and has always been true. But it was inexpressible in ancient Greek or any other language of that period. Since it is reasonable to assume that human beings will continue to discover new phenomena, we can infer that there are also thoughts inexpressible in any language existing today. When these propositions are thought, language will be modified to express them. More controversially, it is plausible that infants and animals have thoughts that will never be precisely expressed in any language, assuming that language remains restricted to older humans.

Given the distinction between thoughts and sentences, it follows that *thinking cannot be characterized as a relation to sentences.*[10] From the fact that S thinks the thought that the ball is red, it does follow that S is related in a certain way to the sentence 'The ball is red'. Our standard *oratio recta* and *oratio obliqua* methods of ascribing thoughts exploit this relationship. Thus we may say 'S is thinking "The ball is red".' But the implied relationship is neither essential nor fundamental to thinking. For the relationship presupposes the existence of the sentence, whereas thinking the thought does not. And the connection depends on the meaning of the sentence, which could have been different. If 'red' had meant "blue", then a person who thinks the thought that the ball is red would be related in the indicated way to 'The ball is blue' rather than 'The ball is red'. (In that case, of course, we would say 'He is thinking the thought that the ball is blue' rather than 'He is thinking the thought that it is red'.) Ambiguous sentences show, moreover, that reference to an interpretation, which determines the thought expressed by the sentence, will be necessary to determine which relation to a sentence is implied by a thought statement. Under one interpretation, S may stand in the indicated relation to 'Mary slept on the bank'; on another, S may not. This makes it clear that it is the thought expressed that is important, not the sentence that happens to express it. Finally, since there might be a proposition that is not expressible in any existing language, it is possible for a person to think something even though he is not related in the indicated way to any sentence. This is a possibility, of course, that I cannot illustrate.

### 2.5   Propositions as Thoughts

'Proposition' has long been a term of art for philosophers and logicians. It is often taken to mean *interpreted declarative sentence, set of possible worlds,* or *situation.* We will use 'proposition' instead in the sense in which it denotes a *relational object of belief or disbelief.* The proposition that the sky is blue is *what we believe* when we believe that the sky is blue. Tautologically, to believe that p is to believe the proposition that p. Propositions in this sense, I have argued,[11] are thoughts. What we are thinking when we think the thought that the sky is blue is exactly the same as what we believe when we believe that the sky is blue. *Thinking the thought that p* is the same process as *conceiving the proposition that p.* Expressing the thought that p is the same property as expressing the proposition that p.

While all propositions are thoughts in this sense, not all thoughts are properly called propositions. One can think "Will it rain?", but that thought does not count as a proposition. The thought "Will it rain?" is not the sort of thought that can be believed or disbelieved. Some thoughts cannot be believed or disbelieved because they are too complex, or because we do not have the requisite concepts, or because the evidence compels us to suspend judgment. The reason the thought "Will it rain?" cannot be believed or disbelieved, in contrast, is that it does not have the right kind of structure. The thought is 'interrogative', we shall say, rather than 'declarative'. Propositions are declarative thoughts.

2.4   **Definition:** *T is a proposition iff T is a declarative thought (-type).*

In describing thoughts as declarative, we are not assuming that thoughts are sentences, nor are we saying that declarative thoughts have the same structure as declarative sentences. We are assuming that declarative sentences express thoughts with a common and distinctive structural feature, and are using the term 'declarative' in a second sense to denote that feature. Propositions are thoughts with that feature.

Propositions are often defined as thoughts *capable of being true or false*. Whereas the thought "It will rain" is true or false, the thought "Will it rain?" cannot be so evaluated. This definition is approximately correct, but is problematic for two reasons. First, on the Strawsonian view of presupposition I accept, propositions with necessarily false presuppositions like "The prime number between 3 and 5 is bald" are not capable of being true or false. Second, propositions like "This sentence is false" are 'paradoxical'. Since the assumption that they are either true or false leads to a contradiction, we have to conclude that they cannot be either. Both thoughts we have mentioned count as propositions on Definition 2.4, because they have a declarative structure. Both consist of a subject concept combined with a predicate concept. As a result, someone could foolishly believe that the prime number between 3 and 5 is bald, and that 'This sentence is false' is true.

The term 'declarative' could be defined for thoughts within a Tarski-style theory of thought structure of the sort sketched in §9.5, in several ways. We could define a declarative thought as one that is not bound by the interrogative or imperative operators (§6.1). Alternatively, we could define a declarative thought recursively as a subject-predicate thought, any disjunction or conjunction of declarative thoughts, and so on. While it is important for us to note that some but not all thoughts are propositions, we do not need to define the term 'declarative'. So we shall leave it primitive.

Let '$p_i$' be a declarative sentence expressing proposition i. Since propositions are thoughts, and thoughts are ideas, the generalization of Definition 3.10 tells us that we can refer to i as *the idea, thought, or proposition that $p_i$*. All sentences of the following form are true.

2.5 **Theorem:** *The proposition (thought, idea) that $p_i = i$, provided i is a proposition.*

This principle implies that sentences of form (8) (and cognate sentences with 'thought' or 'idea' in place of 'proposition') are true in every context in which "the proposition expressed by 'p' " in its predicate is used to refer to the proposition expressed by 'p' in its subject.

(8) The proposition that p = the proposition expressed by 'p'.

As explained in §3.7, the singular terms flanking the identity sign in (8) are not synonymous. The expression on the right at most fixes the reference, not the sense, of the expression on the left. A speaker uttering 'the proposition that grass is green' is not referring to a sentence. He *uses* the sentence 'grass is green', but does not *mention* it. The speaker uses that sentence to express the thought that grass is green in the process of using the whole expression 'the proposition that grass is green' to refer to the thought thus expressed.[12] The reference to the proposition is thus more demonstrative than descriptive. The function of the sentence is not to serve as an object of reference, but to introduce the proposition to be mentioned into the context. As a consequence, when we translate expressions of the form 'the proposition that p' into another language, we translate 'p' as well as 'the proposition that'. When we translate "the proposition expressed by 'p' ", we do not translate 'p' but leave it in English. Furthermore, 'the proposition that grass is green' is a rigid designator, referring to the same proposition in every world, even worlds in which 'grass is green' does not express the proposition that grass is green. "The proposition expressed by 'grass is green' ", in contrast, is a non-rigid designator, and does not express the proposition that grass is green in a world in which 'grass is green' means that snow is purple. Sentences of form (8) are thus like "I am the person uttering 'I' ", which is true in every context in which 'I' is used deictically, but does not express a necessary truth in any context.

A consequence of Theorem 2.6 formulates the familiar principle that sentence-synonymy is the criterion of propositional identity.

2.6   **Theorem:***The proposition that $p_i$ = the proposition that $q_j$ iff $i = j$.*

That is, the identity asserted by the sentence on the left of 2.6 is true provided the two subordinate clauses are used with the same meaning on that occasion. When '5 > 4' is used to mean "Five is greater than four", 'The proposition that 5 > 4 is identical to the proposition that five is greater than four' is true. Indeed, it seems evident that sentences of the form 'the proposition that p' are semantically regular, so that their meaning is determined by the meanings of their components. The form appears to be neither an idiom nor metalinguistic. In that case, instances with synonymous sentences in place of 'p' should have the same meaning, and thus the same reference.

In what has come to be known as the Mates objection,[13] Putnam (1954) argued against this principle on the grounds that sentences such as (9) and (10) are not synonymous, and need not have the same truth values, even though 'eye-doctor' and 'oculist' are synonyms.

(9)   Henry believes (the proposition) that all eye-doctors are eye-doctors.
(10)  Henry believes (the proposition) that all eye-doctors are oculists.

But given that 'eye-doctors' and 'oculists' are synonyms, this should not be possible if 2.6 were true. For in that case, 'the proposition that all eye-doctors are oculists' and 'the proposition that all eye-doctors are eye-doctors' should denote the same proposition. I have argued that the Mates objection is inconclusive.[14] First, when we think of (10) as asserting a falsehood even though we are assuming that 'eye-doctor' and 'oculist' are synonyms, it is most natural for us to be interpreting it metalinguistically or quotationally. When used metalinguistically, what (10) says is that Henry believes that eye-doctors *are called 'oculists'*. In that case, there is no reason to expect that (9) and (10) have the same truth value. We often use object-language formulations in everyday language when we intend our claim to be metalinguistic, particularly when a term is relatively unfamiliar, as when we say of a dog-lover 'He does not know what a chien is', meaning thereby that he does not know that dogs are called 'chien' in French, not that he does not know what a dog is. Second, while it may be evident that 'eye-doctor' and 'oculist' are *near* synonyms, it is not obvious that they are *exact* synonyms, as Theorem 2.6 requires. Whether two words are synonymous in a natural language is not something that is self-evident or knowable on the basis of introspection. Indeed, if in fact competent speakers of English judge that (10) might be false in situations in which (9) is true, even when (10) is not interpreted metalinguistically, then that would constitute evidence that 'eye-doctor' and 'oculist' are not exact synonyms. Finally, when we interchange equally familiar terms that are clearly exact synonyms, such as '5' and 'five', or 'premise' and 'premiss', we have no temptation to think that the pairs corresponding to (9) and (10) are inequivalent. This is particularly true when we *stipulate* the meaning of a term. If we stipulate that 'ruk' is to mean "eye-doctor", then it makes no sense for us to say 'Henry believes that all ruks are ruks, but he does not believe that all ruks are eye-doctors', particularly if Henry has never heard the word 'ruk' before (which makes a metalinguistic interpretation implausible).

## 2.6   THE CONSTITUENCY THESIS

In describing the analogy between sentences and thoughts, we said that both have constituent structures. Just as the sentence 'Cleveland won and Detroit lost' contains the sentences 'Cleveland won' and 'Detroit lost' as components, so the thought that Cleveland won and Detroit lost has the thought that Cleveland won and the thought that Detroit lost as components. These thoughts in turn have the ideas "Cleveland", "Detroit", "winning", and "losing" as components. This *constituency thesis* for thoughts is one of our most important principles.

### 2.7   Postulate: *Thoughts have parts.*

Since the constituency thesis is neither self-evident nor uncontroversial,[15] we need to present a compelling case for it.

We must first be clear about what the constituency thesis does and does not say. Since the occurrence of a complex event entails the occurrence of all its parts, the constituency thesis together with the definition of ideas as thought parts (Definition 3.1) entails what I call the *second law of occurrence*.

2.8   **Theorem:** *A thought occurs to S only if all ideas composing that thought occur to S.*

Hence John thinks the thought that Cleveland won and Detroit lost only if John thinks the thought that Cleveland won, and only if John thinks of Detroit. The converse of the second law fails, however, and is not a consequence of the constituency thesis. In order for the thought that Cleveland won and Detroit lost to occur to John, rather than the thought that Cleveland lost and Detroit won, the ideas "Cleveland", "Detroit", "won", and "lost" must occur in the right structural relationships.

As Theorem 2.8 should make clear, we are using 'part' and cognate terms in their *mereological* sense. The term 'containment' has long been applied to propositions to denote the logical consequences of the proposition. The thought that Cleveland won is contained both logically and mereologically in the thought that Cleveland won and Detroit lost. But the logical consequences of a proposition are not generally its parts, and its parts are not generally logical consequences. The thought that Detroit is larger than Cleveland entails that Cleveland is not larger than Detroit; but the latter is not a part of the former. And the thought that Cleveland won is a part of the thought that Cleveland or Detroit won; but the latter does not entail the former. The entailment relations among thoughts may in part be a consequence of their internal structure. But the observation that one thought is entailed by another does not suffice to show that they have any internal structure.[16]

The constituency thesis should be understood as the claim that every thought has two or more proper parts. This entails that the parts of a thought are *distinct*—that is, not identical with each other. But it does not entail that thought parts are either *discrete* or *separable*. North and South Carolina are distinct geographical parts of the United States, but they are not discrete parts since no space separates them. They might be separable by some tectonic process, but that is not implied by the claim that they are distinguishable. There is some reason to believe that proper thought parts cannot exist except as parts of thoughts. It is hard to find cases in which the idea of Detroit occurs to us, for example, without some thought about Detroit occurring to us.

The constituency thesis similarly says nothing about the *sort* of parts thoughts have. In particular, the thesis does not say that ideas are *spatial* or even *temporal* parts of thoughts. Mental events do not appear to introspection to be spatially extended, but the hypothesis that a thought is a two- or three-dimensional neural process cannot be rejected on the basis of introspection alone. The structure of a thought is in some respects like the nonspatial structure of a musical *chord*. For while trains of thought are temporally extended, with one thought occurring after another, the ideas comprising an individual thought appear introspectively to occur simultaneously rather than seriatim. There are other possibilities. For example, in addition to written sentences (in which words are spatial parts) and spoken sentences (in which words are temporal parts), there are 'abstract' sentences which can occur either as written or as spoken, and so in which words are neither spatial nor temporal parts. A thought might thus be a *concatenation* of its constituents, a *sequence*—something that can be represented by ordered n-tuple. However, like chemical molecules or musical chords, thoughts seem too complex to be described as simple linear arrangements of concepts. In observing that the relationship between ideas and thoughts is like that between words and sentences, we can only claim an analogy and not an identity. The modes of containment might be different.

As sentences and molecules illustrate, the part-whole relationship applies to both types and tokens, but has somewhat different properties in the two cases. For example, the rule that wholes are identical iff their parts are identical holds only for tokens. 'John loves Mary' and 'Mary loves John' are two different sentences composed of exactly the same words. Tokens of the two sentences will necessarily contain different tokens of the words, but the sentence-types themselves contain exactly the same three word-types. Isomers, similarly, are chemical compounds that have the same atoms but different structures. In general, the identity of a complex type depends not just on the identities of its components, but also on the relationships among its components. Whether we are dealing with types or tokens, different relationships among the components produce different compounds.

The constituency thesis is not self-evident, and cannot be established on the basis of introspection alone. In this respect, it is like the thesis that water has constituents. The principal evidence for the constituency thesis lies in the fact that it provides a simple explanation of *observed co-occurrences*. We can observe on the basis of introspection that when we think thought E, for example, we are also thinking C and D.

C   The thought that Cleveland won.
D   The thought that Detroit lost.
E   The thought that if Cleveland won then Detroit lost.
F   The thought that if Detroit lost then Cleveland won.

The body of data of this type is readily available and enormous. It is simply explained by the hypothesis that the apparently complex thought is actually composed of the thoughts always observed to occur with it.

Other hypotheses do not explain the co-occurrence data nearly as well. One is the *feature thesis*, according to which what the constituency thesis takes to be parts of a thought are actually its properties or attributes.[17] If C and D were features of E, that would explain why C and D were observed whenever E is observed. But this hypothesis is a category mistake. C and D are thoughts, which are events rather than features. The properties of an event occurring to S are not themselves occurring to S.

A much better hypothesis is that the putative components of a thought are merely *correlated* with it in one way or another. A plausible thesis along these lines is the *connectionist thesis*, according to which the alleged parts of a thought are actually associated thoughts it *activates*. On the connectionist thesis, we observe C and D whenever we think E because E *activates* C and D. The fact that the brain is a neural network is often cited in favor of connectionism.[18] But the brain is also a mereological structure. So the two hypotheses are equal in gross neurophysiological plausibility.

The constituency hypothesis is superior to the connectionist in having greater *simplicity* and *explanatory power*. The connectionist thesis is more complex than the constituency thesis in two ways. First, the fact that one idea activates another itself requires explanation, whereas the fact that one idea is part of another does not. In particular, the connectionist needs to explain why it is that E *always* activates C and D. Activation is generally a stochastic process. So to assume otherwise without explanation is *ad hoc*. The hypothesis that C and D are parts of E, on the other hand, provides a simple explanation. Indeed, the constituency thesis also accounts for the modal fact that E *cannot* occur without C and D, something not predicted by the connectionist thesis. It makes no sense to suppose that someone is thinking "If Cleveland won then Detroit lost" without thinking "Detroit lost", but only the constituency thesis tells us why. Second, if one idea activates others, the sum of those other ideas is an entity separate from the activating idea. On the constituency thesis, in contrast, the sum of C and D (and any other components E might have) is not an *additional* entity; E *is* the sum of its parts. The fact that C and D are parts of E, furthermore, is not something it is necessary or possible to explain, any more than we can or must explain why the sentence 'Snow is white' contains the word 'Snow'. We can ask why *particular* H and O molecules come together to form an $H_2O$ molecule. But it makes no sense to ask why $H_2O$—the type—contains H and O.

The constituency thesis explains many other facts left unexplained by the connectionist thesis:

### Introspective Integration

When the thought that if Cleveland won then Detroit lost occurs to us, the thought that Cleveland won occurs to us, as does the thought that Detroit lost and the concept of implication. Despite its having distinguishable components, we seem to be aware of just one unified thought process. Contrast this with a case in which we are listening to a piece of music while wondering who won. Suppose we are thinking "That is an oboe" (G) while thinking "If Cleveland won then Detroit lost". Introspectively, there seem to be two separate thought processes going on simultaneously but coincidentally. The fact that E and F are occurring as part of a single complex thought F in the first case, while G and F are not occurring as part of any single thought in the second, explains the difference between the two cases. On the connectionist thesis, in contrast, the occurrence of E is also something going on over and above the occurrence of C and D. So no explanation is provided of the difference between the two cases. Even though the thought "The flag is at half mast" activates the thought "Someone died", the two thoughts do not appear to form one unified process when they co-occur. The same goes for the idea of salt and the idea of pepper.

### Similarity Relations

The constituency hypothesis also provides a simple explanation of various similarity relations. Why are E and F similar, and why are both about Cleveland? The fact that E and F both have the thought that Cleveland won as a component provides a simple explanation. The sentences 'If Cleveland won then Detroit lost' and 'If Detroit lost then Cleveland won' are similar for similar reasons. The thesis that occurrences of E and F are correlated with occurrences of C does not imply that E and F are similar in any significant way or that they are about the same things. The thought that the flag is at half mast resembles the thought that someone died in only the most general respects.

### Systematic Relations

More significantly still, the constituency thesis explains why occurrences of the apparent components of a thought are related in certain ways when the thought occurs, and not otherwise. The thought that Cleveland won (C) and the thought that Detroit lost (D) are related in one way when the thought that if Cleveland won then Detroit lost (E) occurs to us, and in a different way when the thought that if Detroit lost then Cleveland won (F) occurs to us. C and D both occur when either E or F occurs. But the occurrences of C and D switch roles in relation to each other in the two cases. C is the antecedent of the conditional in one and the consequent in the other. D occurs in F where C occurs in E. In other words, the apparent components of thoughts satisfy the ideational analogues of the *movement* and *substitution tests* used to show that sentences have phrase structure (O'Grady *et al.* 1993: 165). These facts are easily explained on the constituency hypothesis: C and D occur in certain relationships when thought E occurs because E *is* a compound consisting of those ideas related in certain ways. No explanation is provided on the hypothesis that E is a separate thought correlated with C and D. Consider an analogy. The hypothesis that the first chord of Beethoven's *Moonlight* sonata is correlated with the occurrence of three notes, two C♯'s and a G♯, would not explain why the two C♯'s are always one octave apart, or why the G♯ is always one fifth above the higher C♯. The hypothesis that the first chord of the *Moonlight* sonata consists of those three notes in that relation does.[19]

## Referential Dependencies

There are many referential dependencies among thoughts and ideas, where by 'reference' I mean "extension".[20] The extension of the thought "John loves Mary", for example, depends on the extension of the ideas of John, Mary, and loving. The thought that John loves Mary is true iff the ordered pair consisting of the extension of the idea of John and the extension of the idea of Mary is in the extension of the idea of loving. The existence of such a dependency is not at all surprising on the constituency thesis, given the general dependence of the properties of a whole on the properties of its parts, and given the similarities in representational content explained by the constituency thesis. Such referential dependencies are not explained by correlations among thoughts and ideas. For example, the thought that Hitler invaded Russia is associated with the ideas of Stalin and Churchill even though the extension of the former is not a function of the extensions of the latter.

## Compositionality

The correlation thesis leaves similarly unexplained the fact that sentences have a compositional semantics, which is readily explained on the constituency thesis. On both the constituency thesis and the correlation thesis, it is possible to provide a semantics according to which the meaning of a compound sentence is a *function* of the meanings of its putative components. The rule that when '$S_1$' expresses $P_1$ and '$S_2$' expresses $P_2$, '$S_1$ or $S_2$' expresses $P_3$ tells us that the meaning of '$S_1$ or $S_2$' is a function of the meanings of '$S_1$' and '$S_2$', even if $P_3$ is not composed of $P_1$ and $P_2$. The rule would be satisfied even if $P_1$ were the proposition that Cleveland won, $P_2$ the proposition that Detroit won, and $P_3$ the proposition that grass is green. Despite the functional relationship, that rule provides no account or explanation of the fact that the meaning of '$S_1$ or $S_2$' is related in an intimate way to the meanings of '$S_1$' and '$S_2$'. For example, we have no account of the fact that '$S_1$ or $S_2$' is about the same things that '$S_1$' and '$S_2$' are about, that '$S_1$ or $S_2$' is true if and only if '$S_1$' or '$S_2$' is true, and so on. On the correlation hypothesis, we could of course postulate that $P_3$ is about the things that $P_1$ and $P_2$ are about, and so on. But we would have no explanation of the truth of such postulates. They would describe mere coincidences. On the constituency thesis, in contrast, we can say that $P_3$ is about the same things that $P_1$ and $P_2$ are about because $P_3$ *is* the disjunction of $P_1$ and $P_2$ (that is, because $P_3$ is a complex entity consisting of $P_1$, $P_2$, and the concept of disjunction in certain relationships). In short, only the constituency hypothesis makes a true compositional semantics possible.[21]

## Phrase-Structure Syntax

The natural language unit used to express thoughts is the sentence. In English, and every other known language, sentences have a phrase structure. Sentences are not random sequences of words. The words are organized into a hierarchical structure of phrases. The correlation thesis provides no explanation for the basic fact that we use phrase-structured symbols to express our thoughts. If the thought that John loves Mary were really separate and distinct from, yet correlated with, the ideas of John, Mary, and loving, then we could just as well use an *unordered* quadruple AJML to express the thought and its associated ideas, where A expresses the thought that John loves Mary, J the idea of John, M the idea of Mary, and L the idea of loving. To say that the quadruple is unordered is to say that AJML, LJAM, JMAL, and so on, would all be synonymous and interchangeable with each other. On the other hand, if the thought that John loves Mary were literally composed of the ideas of John, Mary, and loving, then it would be more efficient and informative to express the thought using a symbol whose structure reflects the structure of the thought. The demands on memory would be much lower. Given that the number of thoughts we can think is potentially infinite, and that we rarely use the same sentence twice, a language would be unlearnable without a phrase structure syntax that enables a recursive scheme for generating all sentences from a finite lexicon and grammar, and a parallel recursive scheme for assigning thoughts to the sentences on the basis of an assignment of ideas to the words in the lexicon. And that will be possible only if each thought were identical with a unique combination of basic ideas. A mere correlation between the thoughts and the idea combinations would not suffice. The correlation could not be learned because the list of thoughts is infinite, and new sentences will present new idea combinations.[22]

Note finally that constituency is a special feature of thought. There are conclusive arguments against the constituency thesis for belief, desire, and other propositional attitudes. For example, it cannot be maintained that the belief that if Cleveland won then Detroit lost contains the belief that Cleveland won. For the implied 'co-occurrence' relations do not exist. People who have the former belief need not have the latter. Belief is systematic. But the systematicity of belief is due to the systematicity of its propositional objects, which are thoughts.[23]

## 2.7 SUBPROPOSITIONAL CONSTITUENTS

We have established that *there are such things as thought parts*. We need to go even further, however. It is widely maintained that even if compound thoughts are composed of other thoughts, simple thoughts are indivisible they are 'minimal units of mental action' and 'syntactically unstructured'.[24] On this view, the constituent structure of thoughts would resemble that of the formulae of propositional logic, in which the atomic constants are propositional, rather than quantification theory (with its individual constants, predicate constants, and quantifiers) or English (with its nouns, verbs, and adjectives). Simple thoughts are defined as those not composed of other thoughts. If *all* thoughts have constituents, which is the intended interpretation of Postulate 2.7, then simple thoughts must have constituents that are not thoughts. If simple thoughts have such constituents, then all thoughts do. To complete our defense of the constituency thesis, therefore, we must establish that *thoughts have constituents that are not themselves thoughts*. We will describe such components as *subpropositional* and call them *ideas* or *concepts*.

If we assume that expressions like 'the idea of John' and 'the idea of loving' are regular referential phrases denoting mental events that are not thoughts, then the evidence presented in the previous sections shows that their referents are better construed as constituents of various thoughts than as mere correlates. The constituency hypothesis is simpler, and provides a better explanation of the co-occurrence and other data. It may not be as obvious, however, that the ideas of John, Mary, and loving are events as it is that a related thought is. The hypothesis that subpropositional ideas are features rather than components of thoughts provides a good explanation of introspective integration (when the thought that John loves Mary occurs to us, a single event occurs with many features) and co-occurrence (the ideas of John, loving, and Mary occur to us when the thought that John loves Mary occurs to us because the ideas are features of the thought). But the feature thesis provides shallower explanations of some of the data, and none of others. For example, the feature theorist can account for the similarity of the thought that John loves Mary and the thought that Mary loves John: both have the same three features. But the feature theorist will have no explanation as to why these thoughts have common features. The constituency theory says they have common features because they have common components. It might be thought that the constituency theory has no advantage on this score, since something is unexplained on both theories. But when the constituents of something are essential to its identity, they do not need to be explained. We cannot ask 'Why does the thought that John loves Mary contain the idea of John?' any more than we can ask 'Why does $H_2O$ contain hydrogen?' Since thoughts have no internal structure on the feature thesis, it provides no explanation of the systematic relations among occurrences of similar thoughts, or the fact that sentences expressing simple thoughts have a phrase-structure syntax.

We will conclude with a more direct argument that thoughts have subpropositional components. Consider the thoughts expressed by the following sentences:

(11) It is not the case that Cleveland won.
(12) It is probable that Cleveland won.
(13) It is too bad that Cleveland won.

The arguments of §2.6 show that these thoughts have the thought that Cleveland won as a component. Since the thought that Cleveland won is not identical to any of these thoughts, it must be a *proper* part of them. That can only be the case if they have some *other* components. They do not appear to have any other thoughts as components. So the extra components must be subpropositional ideas. The feature theorist would have to maintain that the thought that it is too bad that Cleveland won and the thought that Cleveland won are *separate* thoughts, which have most, but not all, features in common, and which are such that the first never occurs without the second. But then the arguments against the correlation thesis become arguments against the feature theory. The feature theory does not explain why the three thoughts all occur with the thought Cleveland won, why they are similar, or why there appears to be a unified thought process in each case.

Consider next the following expressions:

(14) Cleveland won.
(15) Cleveland won Tuesday.
(16) Tuesday.

Reading sentences (14) and (15) makes us conceive complete thoughts. The arguments of §2.6 show that the thought (14) makes us conceive is a constituent of the thought (15) makes us conceive. The argument of the previous paragraph shows that the thought (15) makes us conceive has an additional subpropositional component beyond the component (14) makes us conceive. Now, reading word (16) also makes us conceive something. Indeed, it makes us think of Tuesday. That is something we think of when we think the thought expressed by (15) but not when we think the thought expressed by (14). It is thus natural to suggest that the idea (16) makes us conceive is at least one of the extra constituents that makes the idea expressed by (15) more complex than that expressed by (14). On the feature theory, reading (16) either does not make us conceive any idea, or it makes us conceive a thought with a distinctive feature. Either way, the feature theory cannot maintain that (16) expresses the extra component differentiating (15) from (14). To account fully for the compositionality of semantics, and the systematic relations among thoughts, we must postulate that thoughts have subpropositional components.

## 2.8   OPACITY AND TRANSPARENCY

Nearly all psychological language is subject to an ambiguity that can lead to mistakes if we are not vigilant. Imagine Oedipus on his wedding night, and consider the following.

> (17)  Oedipus is thinking of his mother.

On the *opaque* interpretation, this statement is false. Oedipus would not realize until much later that Jocasta was really his mother, with tragic results. If he had been thinking of his mother, in this sense, on his wedding night, Oedipus would have been displaying more evidence of the Freudian complex named after him than he actually did in the myth. The tragedy of Oedipus cannot be understood unless we think of him as *acquiring* the belief, long after his wedding to Jocasta, that she was in fact his mother. There is also a *transparent* interpretation of (17), however, on which it is true because Jocasta was in fact Oedipus's mother. This interpretation would be most natural if we were guardian angels or secret service agents instructed to keep track of Oedipus's mother. On the opaque interpretation, but not the transparent, (17) entails (18):

> (18)  Oedipus is thinking of his mother as his mother.

(18) is false on his wedding night, when he was thinking of his mother as his wife. Note that in (18), the first occurrence of 'his mother' is given the transparent interpretation, while the second occurrence has the opaque interpretation.

The opaque interpretation is more natural for us reading the Oedipus story. We cannot understand why Oedipus put his eyes out, for example, unless we know that he had not all along been thinking of Jocasta as his mother. There are other cases in which the transparent interpretation is more natural.[25] Suppose our teenage son tells me he wants to go skydiving. I might report this to my wife as follows:

(19) John is thinking of doing something very dangerous.

On the opaque interpretation, (19) may well be false. Given a teenager's lack of concern for risk, John may not think of skydiving as at all dangerous. But I would have intended (19) to mean that *what John is thinking of doing is very dangerous*. And that will be true if my assessment of the risks of skydiving is correct. We definitely have this sense in mind if we cite (19) to justify prohibiting John from skydiving. In general, on the opaque interpretation of 'S is thinking of Φ', 'Φ' is intended to convey how the *subject* conceptualizes the object of thought, whereas on the transparent interpretation it is intended to convey how the *speaker* conceptualizes it. Only on the opaque interpretation can the state expressed by a psychological description be recognized by introspection alone. The fact that Oedipus would insist that he was not thinking of his mother is evidence against the truth of (17) only on its opaque interpretation. For whether it is true transparently depends on whether in fact Jocasta is his mother, which is something external that cannot be introspected.

Despite having different truth conditions, the opaque and transparent senses of any psychological claim are closely related conceptually, with the opaque sense being primary. A statement of what someone is thinking of is true in the transparent sense in virtue of the fact that a statement of the same form is true in the opaque sense. That is, whenever 'S is thinking of Φ' is intended in the transparent sense, it will always be possible to find or introduce a term 'Φ'' making the following *transparent-to-opaque reduction formula* true:

(20) 'S is thinking of Φ' is true in the transparent sense because (i) Φ' is Φ and (ii) 'S is thinking of Φ'' is true in the opaque sense.

Thus 'Oedipus is thinking of his mother' is true in the transparent sense because 'Oedipus is thinking of Jocasta' is true in the opaque sense, and because Jocasta is in fact Oedipus's wife. Clause (i) entails that the transparent interpretation is subject to the substitutivity of identity. Since Oedipus's mother is also the mother of Antigone (who was not born when Oedipus married Jocasta), (17) entails that 'Oedipus is thinking of Antigone's mother' is also true in the transparent sense. No such inference is valid on the opaque interpretation of (17). Any term *co-extensive* with 'Φ'' will describe what S is thinking of in the transparent sense, but only terms *synonymous* with '$\Phi''$' will describe what S is thinking of in the opaque sense (cf. §2.5). '*Latitudinarians*' hold that 'S is thinking of $\Phi$' is true in the transparent sense iff for *any* term '$\Phi''$', 'S is thinking of $\Phi''$' and '$\Phi' = \Phi$' are both true.[26] Others maintain, on the contrary, that in order for the reduction formula to be true, '$\Phi''$' must be demonstrative or at least rigid.[27] This issue will not be important for us because we will be focusing on the opaque interpretation. That is, whenever possible, we will intend psychological claims to be fully opaque, unless we explicitly indicate otherwise.

## 2.9 QUANTIFYING IN

In Definition 2.3, S *is thinking of* $\Phi$ *iff the idea of* $\Phi$ *is occurring to S*, the Greek letter '$\Phi$' is a *substitutional variable*, with an implicit universal substitutional quantifier. Definition 2.3 asserts that all substitution instances of the given form are true. Hence Definition 2.3 entails all of the following for any S.

(21) S is thinking of the sky iff the idea of the sky is occurring to S.
(22) S is thinking of his mother iff the idea of his mother is occurring to S.
(23) S is thinking of the square root of 4 iff the idea of the square root of 4 is occurring to S.

In each of these instances, all occurrences of the terms replacing '$\Phi$' are to be given the fully opaque interpretation. Definition 2.3 does not entail a statement like (24), which is false on the intended opaque interpretation even though the square root of 4 is the cube root of 8.

(24) S is thinking of the square root of 4 iff the idea of the cube root of 8 is occurring to S.

Definition 2.3 does not yield (24) because no *uniform* substitution will produce it. That is, to generate (24) from Definition 2.3, different terms with different meanings must be substituted for the different occurrences of '$\Phi$' in the formula.

Whenever we use *individual variables* or *constants*, we will intend them to be governed by the rules of quantification theory. Hence if 'k' is an individual constant, '$\Sigma(k)$' will be subject to existential instantiation and the substitutivity of identity. That is, '$\Sigma(k)$' will entail '$\exists x \Sigma(x)$' and '$\Sigma(j)$' if $j = k$. This means that any context containing an individual variable or constant must be given a transparent interpretation, even if the context is normally opaque, because it is governed by a psychological verb. Since we will on several occasions use individual variables in theoretical formulations to state generalizations linking opaque contexts to transparent contexts, we need to specify exactly how we are going to be interpreting sentences like 'S is thinking of k' and 'S is thinking of x' when 'k' is a constant and 'x' a variable. We stipulate that these contexts are to be given a latitudinarian interpretation. That is, we will count 'S is thinking of k' as true iff there is some term 'Φ' for which 'S is thinking of Φ' and 'Φ = k' are both true. We will similarly count 'S is thinking of x' as true of some object k iff 'S is thinking of Φ' and 'Φ = k' is true for some 'Φ'. Thus if Bob is thinking about the morning star, and the morning star happens to be Mars, then we will count 'Bob is thinking of m' as true when 'm' is a constant referring to Mars, even if Bob believes that the morning star is Venus rather than Mars. And we will count 'Bob is thinking of x' as satisfied by Mars in the same case. In general, we will adopt the following convention for quantifying in.

2.9 **Convention**: *A normally opaque context 'Σ[x]' containing an individual variable 'x' should be understood as true of y iff 'Σ[Φ]' is true for some 'Φ' such that 'Φ = y' is true. And 'Σ[k]' is to count as true iff 'Σ[Φ]' and 'Φ = k' are both true for some 'Φ', when 'k' is an individual constant.*[28]

We will generally use Roman letters as individual variables, and Greek letters as substitutional variables. Thus the occurrences of 'Φ' in Definition 7.1 are opaque, and the occurrences of 'S' are transparent. Exceptions to the Greco-Roman rule include 'p' and 'q', which are so standardly used as placeholders for sentences rather than as individual variables that the chances of misunderstanding are minimal. When these are used to form that-clauses of propositional attitude ascriptions, they should be understood as opaque contexts.

It should be noted that given Convention 2.9, '∃x(S believes that x is F)' is not equivalent to 'S believes that something is F' as the latter is conventionally interpreted in English when the belief context is opaque. For example, if Johnny believes that Santa brought the presents, then 'Johnny believes that someone brought the presents' is true, but '∃x(Johnny believes that x brought the presents)' is false. The latter is false because '∃x(x = Santa)' is false. 'Johnny believes that someone brought the presents' is true because some substitution instance of 'Johnny believes that Φ brought the presents' is true, that in which 'Santa' replaces 'Φ'.

NOTES

[1] This chapter is a summary of Chapters 12 through 14 in *Meaning, Expression, and Thought*. Fuller explanations, arguments, and references to the literature can be found there.

[2] Given that they occur so automatically, habitual actions might appear to be an exception. We do not pay attention to the actions we are performing when they are done purely out of

habit. If we do think about the actions before we perform them, the thoughts are subconscious, occurring too quickly to be noticed. It is therefore possible to maintain that no thought is occurring at all. But it is just as possible to maintain that the action was not intentional. Habitual action is typically not the carrying out of an intention formed a significant time in advance of the action. If there is an intention, it is subconscious, arising and vanishing too quickly to be noticed. This is not the place to marshal the evidence, but I believe that habitual actions are the result of both thought and intention.

[3] The first law of occurrence does fail when 'S believes P' is interpreted transparently rather than opaquely (see §2.8). On this interpretation, believing P only entails thinking P or some proposition that implies P. See §12.6 of *Meaning, Expression, and Thought* for a full defense of this principle.

[4] Frege 1897: 145. See also James 1890: 294; Husserl 1900: §1.4.31; Bloomfield 1933: 143; Ryle 1949: 295–6; Gale 1967: 500; Katz 1972: 38–9; Hacking 1975: 49–52; Evans 1982: 104, fn. 24; Cresswell 1985: 56; Allan 1986: 88, 139; Carruthers 1989: 14, 77, 87–8, 90–2; Chierchia and McConnell-Ginet 1990: 58; Schiffer 1990: 260–1; Nelson 1992: 52–3; and Peacocke 1992: 99; 1997a; 2000. Compare and contrast Fodor 1998a: 17–20.

[5] The objective relation view does not entail that thinking involves *viewing* thoughts in any sense, or having something in the mind '*aimed at*' the thought (Frege 1918: 26), which would make thinking mysterious.

[6] This characteristic of types and many of the others described in this paragraph are observed by Linda Wetzel in *Of Types and Tokens* (forthcoming).

[7] See, for example, Frege 1884: vi; 1897: 135–8, 148; 1918: 17, 25, 27–8. Contrast Carruthers 1989: Ch. 9; Bealer 1993b: 26–8. Frege allowed that thoughts exist at all times, but preferred to say that they are 'timeless'.

[8] In saying that thoughts are grammar independent, I mean of course that they are independent of the '*surface*' or constituent structure of any sentence expressing it. The relationship between thoughts and 'deep structure' may be closer, depending on the exact definition of deep structure, which varies from linguist to linguist. On one view, the structure of the thought expressed by a sentence *is* its deep structure. Furthermore, in claiming that thoughts are language independent, I do not mean to deny that there are many causal and other empirical relationships between the thoughts or beliefs an individual possesses and the language he or she learns.

[9] Cf. Weiskrantz 1988; 1997; Lance and O'Leary-Hawthorne 1997: §7.6 Contrast Hartnack 1972: 551; Schiffer 1987a; and Dummett 1993: 10–11.

[10] Compare and contrast Carnap 1947: §14; Church 1950; 1951; 1956b; Pap 1955; 1957; Chisholm 1958; Quine 1960: 219; Kneale and Kneale 1962: 604–8; Hunt 1962: 13; Davidson 1968; 1975: 167; Sellars 1969: 104; Hartnack 1972: 546; Danto 1975: 16; Loar 1976b: 147; 1981: Ch. 7; 1987: 180; Wettstein 1976; Field 1978; P. S. Churchland 1980; Fodor 1981: 187–203; Schiffer 1982: 139–45; 1987a: Ch. 5; Stich 1983: 38–40, 73–88; Lycan 1985: 87; Katz 1986a: 68–71; Richard 1989: 326–8; Fodor and Lepore 1992: 139–42; Dummett 1993: Ch. 2; Lance and O'Leary-Hawthorne 1997: §7.6; and J. G. Moore 1999a. See also §3.4 below.

[11] *Meaning, Expression, and Thought*, §13.3.

[12] This differs markedly from Frege's view that the sentence in a that-clause has an oblique sense on which it refers to the proposition that is its customary sense (see *Meaning, Expression, and Thought*, §20.2). See *ibid* §13.4 for a critical discussion of Davidson's and Forbes's views.

[13] See Scheffler 1955; Quine 1960: 202–3; Burge 1978; Linsky 1983: 33–9; Boër 1986: 93; Loar 1987: 180; Fodor 1989: 66–8; 1998a: 16–17; Richard 1989: 328; Tomberlin 1991: 241; Crimmins 1992: 26; Nelson 1992; Bealer 1993a: 19; Taschek 1995b: 73–4. Contrast Moore 1942; Mates 1950; Church 1954; Carnap 1954; Sellars 1955; Pap 1955, 1957; Lakoff 1971a: 282; Katz 1972: 267–74; Yagisawa 1984; Soames 1987a: 123–5; Crane 1991: §6; Fodor 1994: 112; Horwich 1998a: §3.24.

[14] *Meaning, Expression, and Thought*, §13.6. See also Rieber 1997b.

[15] For affirmations, see Leibniz 1709: 7.1; Frege 1897: 143, 150, 253; 1919; 1923: 55–7; Geach 1957a: Ch. 14; McCawley 1968; 1994 ('generative semantics'); Fodor 1975; 1981; 1998a ('the language of thought'); Lyons 1977 ('componential analysis'); Peacocke 1983: 62–4; 1986: 1–2, 15, 63; Cocchiarella 1984: 334–5; 2002; Jackendoff 1989; Crimmins 1992: Ch. 3; Gillett 1992: 12; and Fitch 1993: 471. For denials, see James 1890: 276–8; 603; Loar 1981: §9.1; Dennett 1982: 91; Marconi 1990: 86; Ryle 1951; 1958; Geach 1957: Ch. 14; Evans 1982: 101; Peacocke 1983: Ch. 8; 1986: 63, 114; van Gelder 1990; 1991; Clark 1991. Some *say* that thoughts have parts, but give the claim a non-literal meaning; see Frege 1923: 55; Dummett 1993: 7–8; Bealer 1993a: 22, 30; Peacocke 1983: 208, 212; 1986: 114; 1992: 118; 1997a: 20–1.

[16] See *Meaning, Expression, and Thought*, §14.5. Also Frege 1884: 101; Fodor 1981: 299–301; 1998a: 88–9, 108–12; Katz 1986b: Ch. 5; 1990; Fodor and Lepore 1992: 49. Contrast Descartes 1641b: 54; Arnauld 1662: 51; Leibniz 1676: 283; 1709: §2.2.1; §2.6; Kant 1787: 48; Peacocke 1986: 63; Mates 1986: 60–1, 87 (discussing Leibniz); Gillett 1992: 15.

[17] Cf. Frege 1923: 55; Evans 1982: 108 fn 31; van Gelder 1990; 1991a; Peacocke 1992: 105–24; Bealer 1993a: 22. The related theory that what appears to be a part of a thought is instead a *genus* is duly considered in *Meaning, Expression, and Thought* (§14.2), and fares no better.

[18] See Churchland and Churchland 1983; McClelland, Rumelhart, and Hinton 1986: 10; Dennett 1986: 66–7; Bechtel 1988: 30, 39–40, 50–2; van Gelder 1991b: 56; Ramsey, Stich, and Garon 1991; Davies 1991: 250–1, 254–5; Macdonald and Macdonald 1995: xiv. Contrast Bechtel 1988: 30–6; 46–50; 53–5; Lycan 1990: 202, 278; Sterelny 1990: §§8.2–8.3; Boden 1991; Garson 1991.

[19] The systematicity of thought provides evidence for constituency in the same way. Whereas I focus on actual occurrences in the text, 'systematicity' refers to the fact that thinking one thought implies an *ability* to think other thoughts related to it in certain ways, ways that resemble the systematic syntactic relations among sentences. See Fodor 1987: 147–53; 1998a: 97–100. See also Evans 1982: 103–4 (the 'generality constraint'); Fodor and Pylyshyn 1988: §3.2; Sterelny 1990: 24–5; Davies 1991: 239–44; Schiffer 1994; Rey 1995: 213; and *Meaning, Expression, and Thought*, §14.2. Contrast Cummins (1996) and A. Clark (1991).

[20] See Fodor and Pylyshyn 1988: §3.3; Crane 1990. Contrast Schiffer 1994.

[21] See *Meaning, Expression, and Thought*, §14.2, for limitations of purely functional definitions of compositionality.

[22] This argument, of course, derives from Davidson 1967, although his 'semantic values' were truth and reference rather than thoughts and ideas. See also Lycan 1984: 19 and Fodor 1987: 150.

[23] See *Meaning, Expression, and Thought*, §14.5. Contrast Barwise and Perry 1983: 242; Crimmins and Perry 1989; Crimmins 1992; and especially Fodor 1987: 135–54.

[24] Lance and O'Leary-Hawthorne 1997: 357 and Peacocke 1983: 211, respectively. See also Geach 1957a: Ch. 14; Evans 1982: 101; Peacocke 1983: 62–3, 209–10. Contrast Frege 1919: 254.

[25] Cf. Berg 1988, 1998. Berg questions whether sentences like (17) are properly described as ambiguous, and suggests that the opaque interpretation should be explained as a pragmatic implicature. We will consider this question directly in Chapter 11. For most purposes, it will not matter whether the different interpretations are described as senses or implicatures, as long as they are distinguished.

[26] See Noonan 1984: 218, E. Sosa 1995, and McKinsey 1999: 528. See also triadic relation theorists who think that 'S is thinking of Φ' is true iff S is thinking of the referent of 'Φ' under *some* 'mode of presentation'. Cf. Salmon 1990: 230, 246; Frances 1998b: 344.

[27] Kaplan 1969; 1989: 606; Sosa 1970: 887; Loar 1972: fn. 6; 1976a: 368; Chisholm 1976: 168–70; Donnellan 1977; Schiffer 1978: 173, 202–3; 1981: 50–1, 86; Perry 1979: 620; Lewis

1979a: 539; 1981: 117–18; Fitch 1987: 126; R. M. Adams 1989: 36–7; Crimmins 1992: 171–9; 1995a: 476; Kvart 1994: 292; Feit 2000: 42.

[28] This formulation of the convention corrects for an inadequacy in principle 6.3 of *Meaning, Expression, and Thought*.

# 3
# Ideas

Having defended the assumption that thoughts have constituents, we will now formally define ideas as thoughts or cognitive parts of thoughts, and set out their basic properties. Of particular importance later will be the distinction between atomic and complex concepts, and the ideo-reflexive method of referring to ideas.[1]

## 3.1 DEFINITION

We presented evidence in Chapter 2 that ideas are parts rather than features or correlates of thoughts. We did not argue for the converse thesis that all thought parts are ideas. Atomic ideas, by definition, do not have other ideas as parts (§3.9). That leaves open the possibility that atomic ideas, and the thoughts containing them, have parts other than ideas. There are no *known* thought parts other than ideas. But there is abundant evidence for the view that mental events are neurophysiological processes. Any neural process is bound to have spatial or temporal parts too small to be mental events themselves.

Given that thoughts may have parts other than ideas, our definition of 'idea' should specify which thought parts the term denotes. We will specify those parts on which the qualitative, intentional, semantic, and attitudinal properties of a thought depend, which we call *cognitive* thought parts. In any given position in a thought, different ideas can occur. The thought that Berlin is the capital of France is identical structurally to the thought that Paris is the capital of France, except that the former has the idea of Berlin where the latter has the idea of Paris. Because of this difference in component ideas, the thoughts contrast in at least four important respects.

(i) *Qualitative character*: Thinking the thought that Berlin is the capital is a different conscious experience from thinking the thought that Paris is the capital.

(ii) *Intentional content*: One thought is about Berlin, the other Paris. One represents Berlin as the capital, the other represents Paris as the capital.

(iii) *Semantic properties*: One thought is true, the other false. The thoughts have different entailments and incompatibilities. The contrast between the idea of Paris and the idea of the capital of France makes the thought that Paris is the capital of France a contingent truth, whereas the thought that Paris is Paris is a logical truth.

(iv) *Attitudinal status*: The proposition that Paris is the capital of France is something I believe, while the proposition that Berlin is the capital is something I disbelieve. That Berlin is the capital of France might well have been something Kaiser Wilhelm desired, preferring that to Paris's being the capital.

It appears that thoughts differing in one of these four respects differ in all of them. I believe any thought part incapable of making a cognitive difference would not properly be called an idea. We will therefore define ideas as cognitive thought parts.

3.1   **Definition**: *Ideas (concepts) are thoughts or cognitive parts thereof.*

The terms 'idea' and 'concept' have other meanings in English, and have been used to mean many different things in philosophy and psychology, including universals (Husserl), sensory images (Hume), objects of thought (Descartes), senses (Katz), conceptions or belief systems (many contemporary psychologists), and mental representations generally (Brentano). Definition 3.1 defines the only sense in which Definition 2.3 holds: *S is thinking of Φ iff the idea of Φ occurs to S.* Definition 3.1 also defines the only sense for which it is generally true that what a word means is determined by the idea it expresses (Chapter 5).[2]

We will use the terms 'idea' and 'concept' interchangeably, even though they have somewhat different connotations and patterns of usage in standard English. There is a tendency to reserve both terms for *proper* parts of thoughts, those that are not themselves thoughts. But we will allow that it is proper to refer to the idea or concept that man evolved from the apes, which is a proposition. There is a marked tendency in philosophy and psychology to use 'concept' only for *general* as opposed to *singular* concepts, to speak, for example, of the concept of man but not of the concept of Socrates. Hence concepts are often identified as mental representations of *universals* or *categories*, and defined by their role in *classification*. But the proposition that Socrates is a man has at least two parts, and we will call both 'concepts'. Since we can think about Socrates, we have to have the concept of Socrates (see §2.3, §13.2). General and singular concepts differ in important ways, but do share many properties. For example, recognizing that an object is Venus involves a singular concept just as recognizing that an object is a planet involves a general concept. Identification is just as important a cognitive process as classification. A pertinent similarity for us, of course, is that both singular and general thought parts are expressed by words.

Depending on whether 'thought' is taken to denote types or tokens, Definition 3.1 defines the type or token sense for 'idea' and 'concept' (§2.2). As with 'thought,' however, we will be focusing on ideas as event *types*. In particular, an expression of the form 'the idea of Φ' will always be used as a singular term referring to a unique idea-type. 'The idea of Venus' refers to one constituent of the thought that Venus is a planet, which is also a constituent of the thought that Venus is closer to the Sun than Mars, and occurs twice in the thought that Venus is the same size as Venus. Millions of people have this concept, even though none of its tokens occurs to more than one person. When different people think the thought that Venus is a planet, there are different tokens of the idea that is the subject concept of that thought.

As we are using the term, concepts are word-like mental representations. But concepts are not words. Ideas differ from words just as much as thoughts differ from sentences (§2.4). Words contain letters or speech sounds, and belong to particular languages. Concepts do not. Words express concepts but concepts do not express words. Many different words may express the same concept ('premise', 'premiss', 'premisa', 'prémisse'), and one word may express many concepts ('bank'). And at any given time, many concepts are not expressed by any words. This is particularly true for at least a brief period of time after a new object or species is discovered. Finally, the content of an idea is an essential property, while word meanings are contingent. The idea of red could not have been the idea of blue, even though the word 'red' might have meant *blue*.

## 3.2 IMAGES

Ideas in our sense (thought parts) need to be carefully distinguished from *sensory images*.[3] The idea of Φ is neither the image of Φ nor the inner speech word 'Φ' (which is the image of the word 'Φ'). Concepts and images are similar in many respects. The concept of a horse and an image of a horse, for example, are mental events that occur to us from time to time. Both in some way represent horses. Both are typically parts of larger wholes: the idea of a horse might occur as part of the thought that a horse is jumping over a fence, and an image of a horse might occur as part of an image of a horse jumping over a fence. Having the concept of a horse, moreover, is highly correlated with the ability to form an image of a horse. Both images and concepts have intentional objects. I can think of Pegasus, and form an image of him, even though Pegasus does not exist. Both images and ideas, finally, are introspectible mental events. I can tell introspectively whether I am thinking of a horse as surely as I can tell whether I am forming an image of a horse.

Despite these similarities, there are many differences.

(1) The fundamental difference is that images unlike ideas are composed of sensations. As a result, images are localizable and particularized in ways ideas are not. My image of a horse may be in the middle of my visual field, and must be an image of a horse of a particular color. The concept of a horse does not occur in a visual field, and is not itself the concept of a brown or other colored horse. Images can be faint or vivid, terms that do not apply to concepts.

(2) People have concepts of things they do not, and sometimes cannot, form images of. Since we can think of thousand-sided figures and numbers, we have concepts of them. But for different reasons, we cannot form images of thousand-sided figures or numbers. Even when we can form an image of the thing, we can think of it without doing so, as when we are reading out loud. Conversely, people could form images of a satellite (the Moon) long before they had the concept of a satellite.

(3) Concepts and images differ in the way they correspond to reality, or fail to. An image of a horse may be 'anatomically correct', 'distorted', or 'upside down'. These terms do not apply to the concept of a horse. The concept of a horse 'applies' to horses, and the concept that horses evolved is 'true'. These terms do not apply to images.

All the similarities between thoughts and sentences noted in §2.4 hold for concepts and inner speech words. Indeed, inner speech words are more like concepts in many respects. Both are mental representations. Both thinking and inner speech are structured, and both are subject to voluntary control. Both are introspectible events that are not publicly observable, in marked contrast to external speech. Finally, there is at least a strong connection between thought and inner speech. The thought that it will rain typically occurs to us when the sentence 'It is raining' (or something equivalent) occurs in our inner speech. Conversely, we typically say to ourselves 'It is raining' when we think "It is raining".

Despite these similarities, thought is distinct from inner speech.

(1) The correlation between thought and inner speech is far from perfect. Inner speech can occur without thought, as when a woman utters a meaningless sentence to herself, or a sentence in a language she does not understand. There can also be thinking without inner speech, as when a subject uses visual images. And a person who is trying to fit a piece into a puzzle by trial and error is thinking all the time about where the piece goes, but does not have to be continuously saying to herself 'Where does it go?' There is abundant evidence that children think before they have learned a language, and that other animals think even though they are incapable of learning a language (see e.g. Wieskrantz 1997). In the tip-of-the-tongue phenomenon we think of a man without being able to recall his name. And there is

evidence that certain forms of aphasia garble inner speech without affecting thought (Humphrey 1951: 251).

(2) The facts distinguishing thoughts from sentences and words from concepts also prove that ideation is distinct from inner speech even when we think in words to ourselves. For example, subjects who say 'It is raining' and 'Il pleut' have different inner speech even though they are thinking the same thought. And two subjects who utter the sentence 'Kissing girls never hurt me' to themselves have the same inner speech, but may be thinking very different thoughts.

(3) What the subject is thinking in those words is the occurrent factor that *determines* what the inner speech means and refers to. The inner speech words have their meaning and reference contingently; the ideas they express have their content essentially.

(4) Finally, inner speech is an episodic, serial process, whereas ideation appears to be a continuous, parallel process. The components of a thought do not occur to us one after another, and do not appear to 'take time'. We appear to think of many things at the same time, even though we have only one stream of inner speech.

### 3.3   CONCEPTION AND CONCEPTIONS

Definition 2.2 says that S is thinking T iff T is a thought occurring to S. The requirement that T be a thought is essential. For only propositions or other thoughts can be relational objects of thinking; yet thoughts are not the only event-types that occur to us. We have observed that ideas other than thoughts—subpropositional concepts—also occur to us. So do nonrepresentational mental events such as pain, and nonmental events such as heart attacks. While we do not speak of thinking subpropositional ideas or concepts, we do speak of *conceiving* them. We conceive any concept or idea when it occurs to us.

3.2   **Definition:** *S is conceiving C iff C is a concept (idea) occurring to S.*

Since thoughts are a kind of idea, conceiving is a genus of which thinking is a species. Paralleling the definition of thinking of Φ (Definition 2.3), we have:

3.3   **Definition:** *S is conceiving of Φ iff S is conceiving the concept of Φ.*

To conceive of the sky is to conceive the concept of the sky. Definition 3.3 holds even when the referent of 'Φ' is itself a concept: to conceive of the concept of the sky is to conceive the concept of the concept of the sky. Note, though, that conceiving *the concept* of the sky is different from conceiving *of* the concept of the sky. Similarly, conceiving of the sky is an ordinary event (since we have the concept of the sky), whereas conceiving the sky is impossible (since the sky is not itself a concept[4]).

We observed in §2.1 that while 'thinking the thought that p' denotes the simple occurrence of the proposition that p, 'thinking that p' means believing that p. The verb 'conceive' has the same ambiguity. Without implying belief, it can be used to express the act of conceiving subpropositional concepts, as in 'S is conceiving of $\Phi$', or propositional concepts, as in 'S is conceiving of $\Phi$ as $\Psi$', which means 'S is thinking of $\Phi$ as $\Psi$'. Thus while reading *Animal Farm,* I was conceiving of pigs as more intelligent than people; and when I watch *Psycho*, I end up conceiving of Tony Perkins as a murderer. It does not follow that I ever believed pigs to be intelligent, or Perkins to be a murderer. But 'conceive' can also be used to express belief. To say that unlike Ptolemy, Copernicus conceived of the Earth as moving is normally to say that Copernicus believed that the Earth moves.

The noun 'conception' also has both cognitive and cogitative senses. It can be used to designate the act of conceiving concepts, an act which implies neither belief nor disbelief (Definition 3.4). But 'conception' can also be used cognitively as in (1) and (2).

(1)  On S's conception (concept), $\Phi$ is $\Psi$.
(2)  S has a conception (concept) of $\Phi$.

Sentence form (2) means that S has some beliefs about $\Phi$, and (1) specifies a particular belief S has. The cognitive sense of 'conception' may be adequately defined for our purposes as a *centered belief system*, a system of beliefs with a common subject. *S's conception of $\Phi$ consists of S's beliefs about $\Phi$.*[5] 'Concept', 'idea', and 'notion' all mean belief system in conventional English when preceded by a possessive. When preceded by the definite article, these terms all denote thought parts. Thus *Ptolemy's* concept of Earth and *the* concept of Earth are very different things. Ptolemy's concept of Earth consists of what he believed about Earth, and so contains the proposition that Earth stands still but not the proposition that Earth moves. The concept of Earth is not an object of belief at all, and is part of both the proposition that Earth stands still and the proposition that Earth moves. *John's* idea of happiness may be unique (no one else has the same beliefs about happiness) even though *the* idea of happiness is ubiquitous (the idea crosses everyone's mind from time to time). And Hilary's concept of an elm tree may be pretty much the same as his concept of a beech tree ("a big, deciduous tree grown in the eastern U.S."), even though the concept of an elm is not the same as the concept of a beech, and even though Hilary has both concepts (if he did not have both, he could not know that elm trees are not beech trees, that only the former are properly called 'elm trees', and so on). In accordance with Definition 3.1, we will always use the terms 'concept' and 'idea' to mean *thought part* (proper or improper), reserving 'conception' for either a *centered belief system* or the act of *conceiving*.[6]

The principle that an idea (concept) cannot occur to us unless all of its components do (generalization of Theorem 2.8) does not apply to conceptions. Being systems of belief, conceptions are not event-types. They are possessed, but do not occur to a subject. We could define 'occurrent conception' by analogy with 'occurrent belief', but then we would find that our conceptions of things are invariably too complex to be occurrent. Important parts of the conception may be occurrent, but never the whole conception. When thinking about astronomy, for example, it may occur to me that Earth moves around the Sun. When thinking about geology, it may occur to me that the surface of Earth is subject to continental drift. When thinking about language, it may occur to me that Earth is properly referred to by the impersonal pronoun 'it'. On very few occasions will all three parts of my conception of Earth be simultaneously occurrent. Using the terminology of psychologists, we may say that a conception is *activated* when some but not all of the beliefs in the conception are occurrent. In accordance with the laws of association, activation will tend to spread from one component of a conception to another. The principle that the components of a concept must occur whenever the concept occurs is a consequence of general mereological principles, not the laws of association.

Concepts and conceptions have different kinds of *structures*. The structure of something is defined by the relationships among its parts. As we observed in §2.6, concepts have a *phrase structure*. The relationships defining the structure of a concept resemble the relationships among words in a phrase, clause, or sentence. The relationships defining the structure of a conception are like relationships among the sentences expressing a *theory*, and include entailment, incompatibility, and confirmation. Unlike the sentences in a paragraph or story, the beliefs in a conception do not have a sequential order. Conceptions, we might say, have an *inferential system structure*. Deductive systems, like Euclidean geometry, are the most clearly understood types of inferential system. The elements of conceptions more generally can be related inductively as well as deductively. Conceptions also have an *associational system* or *prototype structure*. Parts have a tendency to activate other parts, and these links define a structure.

Whereas concepts are expressed by individual words, phrases, or sentences, it requires systems of sentences—theories—to express conceptions.

### 3.4 POSSESSION

'Having' a belief is the same as believing the belief, and 'having' a thought is the same as thinking it. To 'have an idea' is to conceive it. In its most common sense, however, *having a concept* must be distinguished from *conceiving a concept.* We have countless concepts we are not currently conceiving. I have had the concept of neutrons since grade school. But I have conceived of them only on selected occasions since then, and was not conceiving of neutrons five minutes ago. Thus conceiving a concept is an occurrence, and concepts themselves are types of occurrences. Having a concept, in contrast, is a 'disposition', specifically, an ability.

3.4   **Definition:** *S has concept C iff S has conceived C and is still capable of conceiving C.*

It follows that S has any concept that is occurring to him at the moment. For if it is occurring to him, then he has conceived it and is obviously capable of conceiving it. To have a concept that is not occurring at the moment is to have a previously activated ability to conceive it, that is, the persistent ability to reconceive it. To have the concept of cats is to have the ability to think again of cats. The sense of 'ability' intended in Definition 3.6 is *first potentiality* rather than second—the sense in which someone who has learned to play the piano is able to play, while one who is merely able to learn to play is not. The retention of a concept is presumably a memory process.

An immediate corollary of Definition 3.4 given Definitions 2.3 and 3.2 is that *S has the concept of Φ only if S has the ability to think of Φ.*[7] The converse of this corollary fails, however.[8] When 'Φ' is a complex concept, people have the ability to conceive the concept of Φ as long as they have all its components and have conceived other concepts with the same structure.[9] But they do not have the concept until it has occurred to them. Thus no one had the concept *grue* until Goodman (1955: Ch. 3) introduced it, even though nearly everyone had the ability to think of being green if examined before a certain time and blue otherwise. Having the ability to think of Φ does seem sufficient for concept possession when 'Φ' is an atomic concept (§3.9), though, because it appears that people have the ability to conceive atomic concepts only when they have actually occurred. There appears to be a *third law of occurrence,* therefore, that applies specifically to atomic concepts.

The second law of occurrence states that a thought occurs to S only if all constituent ideas occur to S (Theorem 2.8). Definition 3.6 therefore entails:

3.5   **Theorem:** *S is thinking P only if S has all concepts contained in P.*

Aristotle could not think the thought that neutrons are subatomic particles because he did not have the concept of a neutron. The converse fails. I have had all the concepts contained in 'The Moon is made of chocolate mousse' for some time. But to my knowledge I have never thought that thought before. The most we can say along these lines is that possession of all the concepts in P gives us the *ability* to think P, provided that other things, such as excessive 'length' or complexity, do not prevent it. Theorem 3.5 is concerned specifically with occurrent thought. A similar principle holds for all propositional attitudes. Thus the first law of occurrence (Postulate 2.1) entails:

3.6 **Theorem**: *S believes P only if S has all the concepts contained in P.*

The two clauses of the first law of occurrence form the definition of concept possession. Since propositions are thoughts and thoughts are concepts, the first law can be reformulated as saying that S believes P only if S has P itself. Theorem 3.6 follows in virtue of the principle that having a complex concept entails having its components.

Nominalists have attempted to define possession of the concept of Φ as the ability to understand the word 'Φ.'[10] However, an Eskimo may have the concept of a dog without knowing a word of English, and there is good evidence that a one-year-old has the concept before understanding any words. People can discover a new species before there is any word for it. The ability to use and understand words depends on the ability to conceive concepts, but is a more specialized ability.

As we are using the terms, concepts are thought parts whereas conceptions are belief systems. To have a particular conception of Φ is to have a particular set of beliefs about Φ. Having a conception of Φ is definitely sufficient for having the concept of Φ, by Theorem 3.6. For S has a belief about Φ only if S believes a proposition containing the concept of Φ. But it is not obvious that having a conception of Φ is necessary for having the concept of Φ. It is generally true, of course, that people with a concept of something have a number of beliefs about it. It is hard to imagine anyone with the concept of a cat who does not believe at least that cats are cats, and that a cat either is or is not black.[11] But it is logically possible that people should have a psychological disorder that leaves them able to think thoughts without being able to have beliefs. It is also conceivable that coming to believe any proposition no matter how obvious requires at least some time (even if measured in nanoseconds) during which the thought is processed in the way that results in belief or disbelief. But the only way having a conception of Φ could be necessary to have the concept of Φ, given that thinking any proposition about Φ in any conception entails having the concept of Φ, would be if the propositions were believed just as soon as they were thought. Instantaneous belief may be possible, but it should not be a consequence of the definition of having a concept. Having a conception of Φ is more plausibly necessary for the stronger relations of *understanding* and *mastering* a concept. Unlike having a concept, which is all-or-nothing, understanding a concept varies in degree, depending on how much we know about its object. It also appears to be as context dependent as knowing what a Φ is.

### 3.5  ACQUISITION

We are said to *acquire* or *form* a concept when we change from
non-possession to possession.

3.7   **Definition**: *S acquired (formed) concept C at t iff S possessed C at t but
not before.*

Acquisition coincides with an initial occurrence marking the beginning of a
period of possession, during which the concept may or may not reoccur.
Thus 'forming a concept' (which implies its initial occurrence) has a more
specific meaning than 'conceiving a concept' (its occurrence or reoccur-
rence). Although it is logically possible to lose a concept and then reacquire
it, we normally form a concept just once, when it first occurs to us. In the
normal case, a concept acquired at t has never been possessed before t. In
every case, there must be some period of non-possession ending at t. Several
processes result in the formation of concepts: observation or abstraction,
communication, constructive thought, and abstractive thought.

### Observation

We may acquire the concept of a platypus simply by seeing platypuses in the
zoo, or by seeing pictures of them in a book. We may acquire the concept of
an afterimage by being aware of one introspectively. Observing an object
often causes us to think about it even though we have never thought about it
before. This process is traditionally called *abstraction*,[12] a usage we will
follow without thereby endorsing traditional theories about how abstraction
works. Note well that as long as a woman is not blind, she can *see a platypus*
before she has the concept of a platypus, although she cannot beforehand see
*that* something is a platypus or see something *as* a platypus.[13]

### Communication

We may acquire the concept of a wombat by hearing other people talk about
wombats, or by reading about wombats. This may occur even though we do
not pick up enough information to visualize or define wombats. Communication was presumably ignored in classical discussions of concept formation
because it is not an original source of concepts among human beings generally. Before a concept can be communicated to others, it has to be acquired
by someone through another process. But communication is responsible for
a large portion of any individual's stock of concepts. The fact that communication dramatically expands the range of our thoughts is one of the
fundamental advantages of social living.

## Constructive Thought

We may acquire the concept of a winged earthworm by simply imagining one—by mentally 'putting together' the concepts of wings and earthworms. The imagination may be sensory, or purely conceptual. As an example of the latter, I might mentally combine the concept of a prime number with that of a number less than 10 to conceive of a prime number less than 10. I might coin the term 'first order prime' to denote such a number. If I continue to define 'second', 'third', and 'fourth order' prime numbers in terms of 100, 1,000, 10,000, and so on, I might then wonder whether the number of prime numbers increases or decreases with their order. The constructive thought resulting in possession of a new concept may itself result from communication. If a speaker expresses a complex concept the hearer did not possess, the hearer may acquire the concept when she grasps what the speaker meant. The process of combining concepts to get new concepts is often described as 'definition'. But definition involves either the assignment of concepts to words, or the expression of concepts in words. Hence there are two key differences between definition and constructive thought: the defined concept must exist in the definer's mind before the act of definition; and constructive thought need not involve words.

## Abstractive Thought

Once some concepts have been acquired, it is possible to acquire others by abstraction without the use of observation. Thus a person could acquire the concept of a raptor by thinking of hawks, falcons, owls, and osprey, and contrasting them with robins, sparrows, pigeons, and ostriches, without at the time seeing, hearing, or otherwise observing any birds. In this case, the subject would acquire the general concept of a raptor as a result of thinking of particular raptors. Occurrences of particular concepts cause formation of a more general concept. It is possible that abstractive thought is simply a special case of constructive thought. This would turn out to be true, for example, if thinking of hawks, falcons, and owls caused the subject to focus on their talons, hooked beaks, and carnivorous habit, and if the concept of a raptor were analyzable as the concept of a carnivorous bird with talons and hooked beaks. But as the arguments of Putnam, Fodor, and others have made clear, it is doubtful that the concept is definable in this way (see §3.9). Whereas constructive thought invariably produces *complex* concepts, abstraction generally produces *atomic* concepts, and communication often does.

Since concept possession requires both an ability and its exercise, there are two ways to acquire a concept, depending on whether the ability is acquired before it is first exercised, or at the same time. In the case of atomic concepts produced by abstraction or communication (e.g., "platypus"), the ability to think of the novel object appears to be acquired at the same time the concept is acquired. In the case of complex concepts formed through constructive thought, the ability to think of the object may be acquired long before the concept is acquired, as the example of grue makes clear.

Fodor and others have asked why it is that observations of cats lead people to form the concept of a cat, rather than say the concept of a chordate or jellyfish.[14] The common assumption is that the explanation has to cite intervening psychological processes, such as the formation of hypotheses about cats. But acquiring the concept of a cat cannot be explained in terms of the formation of hypotheses about cats, because that process itself presupposes possession of the concept of a cat (Theorems 3.5, 3.6). Moreover, a similar question would arise: why is it that observations of cats lead people to formulate hypotheses about cats, rather than chordates or jellyfish?

There are two ways to answer such questions. We can specify how the mechanism works, or how humans came to have it. Since the ability to form concepts through abstraction, like the ability to respond rationally to evidence, is an inherited trait, it presumably resulted from evolution, through natural selection. It is plausible that we came to have the ability to respond rationally to evidence because we were better able to survive with it than without it. The same goes for the disposition to acquire the concept of red on seeing red objects rather than on hearing blue whales. Surely we would not be as successful as a species if perceiving objects in our environment did not give us the concepts that enable us to think about them, and consequently to form beliefs and desires about them. Nor would we be as successful, I should think, if perception produced concepts randomly, with no connection between what is perceived and what is conceived of. The question 'How did humans come to have the ability to form the concept of cats in the presence of cats?' seems highly analogous to 'How did humans come to have the ability to see cats when cats are present?' No *a priori* philosophical argument could undermine the answer 'through evolution' to both.[15]

As for how abstraction works, little is known about the process other than the initial and final stages. In the paradigm case, the initial cause is observing Φ, and the final result is acquiring the concept of Φ. In other cases, the initial cause is observing pictures of Φ, or thinking of particular instances of Φ. Even though the details remain to be identified, we do know that the process occurs, and that it is distinct from other processes by which we acquire mental abilities or states. It is possible, furthermore, that the intermediate stages are not psychological events. If there is any process at all by which mind and body interact, it has to have a 'brute-causal' stage at which a nonmental event causes a mental event directly, with no intermediate mental events. That is, there must be some *basic psychophysical processes*. Plausible examples are the process by which red objects cause sensations of red, and deep cuts pain (sensation); the process by which the intention to raise one's arm causes one to raise one's arm (volition); the process by which anxiety causes perspiration (emotion); and that by which food deprivation causes a desire for food (appetition). There is no reason to think that we can provide a psychological explanation for any of these processes. On the contrary, it seems that the only way to understand them is by examining their neuro-physiological basis and evolutionary origin.

Abstraction appears to have psychological conditions as well as brute-causal elements. Selective attention is surely involved. A child who acquires the concept of a Corvette by observing one must be attending to the Corvette and not exclusively to the car's wheels or color or position. Furthermore, there is reason to believe that, like communication, abstraction generally involves some belief formation, or at least some thoughts about the object perceived.[16] It is plausible, for example, that an individual S acquires the concept of a cat when observing some object only if S first forms the belief that the object is a distinct kind of animal—that is, an animal different in kind from other animals S knows. It is similarly plausible that S acquires the concept *tabby* when observing the same object only if S first forms the belief that it is a distinct kind of cat. Then acquisition of *cat* would require prior possession of *animal*, and acquisition of *tabby* would presuppose possession of *cat*. However, the formation of a concept cannot use the very concept that is to be but has not yet been acquired. Acquisition of *emu* may depend on prior possession of *animal*, but cannot possibly depend on prior acquisi-tion of *emu*. And on pain of an infinite regress, the acquisition of some concepts through abstraction must not depend on beliefs involving concepts acquired through abstraction.

In these respects, forming a concept differs markedly from learning the meaning of a word. When we learn the meaning of 'tabby' ostensively, as when someone points to a tabby and says 'That is a tabby', we perceive and think about the word 'tabby'. We also have to conceive the concept of a tabby, and learn that it is expressed by the word, which involves forming a belief about both. We might have possessed the concept beforehand, or just acquired it through abstraction. There is no hint of regress here because it is obvious that perceiving and thinking about a word does not require already knowing the meaning of the word.

## 3.6 ASSOCIATION

Once concepts have been acquired, they can become *associated*. The idea of automobiles is strongly associated with the idea of gasoline in most people, but not with the idea of wings. Thinking of automobiles tends to make people think of gasoline, but not of wings. Association is a causal relation among ideas involving memory. Two ideas are associated if *the occurrence of one tends to cause occurrence of the other in a particular way*. Specifically, the object of one must have a tendency to *remind* a person of the object of the other.

3.8   **Definition:** *Ideas A and B are associated iff A tends to activate B and/or B tends to activate A.*

English has a subsidiary convention whereby we can mean that ideas are associated by saying that their objects are associated. Thus 'salt is associated with pepper' means that the ideas of salt and pepper activate each other. Association is a highly relative phenomenon, varying with the individual or group, time, and context. Thus trains and steam engines were much more strongly associated in the nineteenth century than they are today, while the reverse holds for trains and diesel engines. Connectionist networks provide good mathematical models for the dynamics of associated ideas. Realistic neurophysiological models can be provided by assuming that the occurrence of an idea is the activation of a neural structure, with synaptic connections between structures being the mechanism by which one idea activates another.

As observed in Chapter 2, we can use our knowledge of associations to predict, explain, and control behavior. As a trivial but obvious example, if we realize that Bill has forgotten to buy pepper, we can help by saying 'Salt!' We often help students answer a question by dropping hints. Marketers make it their business to expand and exploit their knowledge of standard associations. Writers select words carefully for their connotations, which are things associated with but not meant by the words. Education is important not only for instilling a system of beliefs, but also for creating a set of associations whereby relevant facts are recalled to mind when they are useful.

Association psychologists gave association a bad name by trying impossibly to reduce all psychological laws to the laws of association, and by trying to treat all relations among ideas as associations. Their classification of the relation between a complex concept and its components as 'simultaneous association' is a classic example of the Procrustean bed. Unfortunately, these mistakes are still made today by some connectionists.[17] So it is worth noting that the idea of a red ball contains the idea of a ball, but these two ideas cannot be associated in the sense defined by Definition 3.8. Given the asymmetry of the causal relation, the occurrence of a complex event cannot cause its own components to occur. And by the second law of occurrence, it is impossible for a complex idea to occur without its components occurring, whereas associated ideas often fail to activate each other.

### 3.7 IDEO-REFLEXIVE REFERENCE

*Referring to* an idea and *expressing* it are different semantic acts. To express an idea is to do something as an indication that it is occurring to us (§4.5). To refer to an idea is to express the idea *of that idea* (§7.1). We express the idea of horses without referring to it when we say 'Secretariat and Sea Biscuit were magnificent horses'. We refer to the idea of horses when we say 'The idea *horses* is occurring to me now'. In the first case, we are talking about horses; in the second, we are talking about the idea of horses. As this example illustrates, natural languages have productive rules by which we can refer to an idea by using in certain contexts a word that expresses the idea.[18] 'The idea *horses*' refers to the idea that 'horses' expresses. I call this the *ideo-reflexive* use of words. The rules of ideo-reflexive usage enable the word-idea pairings determined by a language to serve two different purposes, and thereby increase the efficiency of the language as a means of expression.

In written English, we commonly use italics or quotation marks to set off ideo-reflexive use. Cognitive scientists have begun using small caps. In spoken English we typically use a distinctive intonation. But we often leave ideo-reflexive use unmarked, to be inferred from the context. Thus in all the sentences in (3), the first occurrence of the word 'red' is used metalinguistically, to refer to itself. The second occurrence is used ideo-reflexively, as part of a noun phrase that refers to the idea it expresses.

(3) The word 'red' expresses the idea 'red'.
   The word *red* expresses the idea *red*.
   The word 'red' expresses the idea *red*.
   The word red expresses the idea red.
   'Red' expresses the idea 'red'.
   'Red' expresses the idea RED.

In a work like this one, in which we will be referring constantly to both words and ideas—often in the same sentence—it can be confusing to use the same marks for both metalinguistic and ideo-reflexive usage. Many philosophers and logicians trained on the idea that quotation is always used to form the name of the word quoted regard the use of quotation marks to set off ideo-reflexive usage as erroneous or improper. Using a distinctive font like small caps is clear, but tolerable only in small quantities. If a phrase is italicized to mark ideo-reflexive usage, then it cannot be italicized for emphasis. To avoid these problems, I will use distinctive angular quotation marks to set off ideo-reflexive usage, and regular curved quotation marks for metalinguistic reference. For added contrast, single quotes will be used wherever possible for metalinguistic reference and double quotes for ideo-reflexive. Thus I will write:

(4) The word 'red' expresses the idea "red".

One significant syntactic and semantic difference between metalinguistic and ideo-reflexive quotation, in my view, is that whereas metalinguistic quotation is used to form singular terms, ideo-reflexive quotation is used to form syncategorematic terms. We will be treating noun phrases like 'the idea "red" ' as a singular term, but not ' "red" ' all by itself. The latter functions like an adjective rather than a name. Thus none of our definitions will assign referents or extensions to expressions of the form ' "e" '. (As usual, regular curved quotation marks will also be used as scare quotes and for direct quotation. And both types of quotation marks will be used as corner quotes when the expression quoted represents a form and contains place-holders, as in Convention 2.9.)

I will use 'μ' as a place-holder for *oratio recta* expressions used ideo-reflexively after 'idea' and cognate terms. Table 3.1 illustrates some of the main forms of ideo-reflexive use. Row three indicates, for example, that in the expression 'idea *plane*', the instance of 'μ' is the noun 'plane', which has been italicized to indicate ideo-reflexive usage.

A complete sentence can occur unmarked after 'idea' only with the subordinating conjunction 'that', thereby shifting to *oratio obliqua*, as in 'the idea that John won'.

Like 'red' and 'plane', most words are ambiguous, and therefore express more than one idea in English. On any occasion on which 'the idea "red" ' is used, however, the word 'red' is used with a particular meaning. 'The idea "red" ' is used to refer to the idea which 'red' expresses on that occasion. Thus when we are talking about colors, 'the idea "red" ' designates the idea of being the color red. When we are talking about political orientations, the same phrase refers to the idea of being a communist. A word e expresses an idea i on an occasion provided two conditions obtain: the speaker is using e to express i on that occasion; and e expresses i in the language the speaker is using on that occasion (see §5.3).

In general: *on any occasion of use, 'the idea "μ" ' refers to the idea expressed by 'μ' on that occasion, if there is one*. Expressions of the form 'the idea "μ" ' are indexical descriptions used deictically. A substitution instance of 'the idea "μ" ' has the referent it has because the speaker is aware of the idea expressed by 'μ' on that occasion. 'Ideo-reflexive' indexi-

**Table 3.1**  Conventions for Ideo-reflexive reference

| *idea "μ"* | μ | *idea "μ"* | μ |
| --- | --- | --- | --- |
| idea "plane" | plane | idea "John won" | John won |
| idea "plane" | plane | idea "John won" | John won |
| idea *plane* | plane | idea *John won* | John won |
| idea plane | plane | | |

cality thus resembles the more familiar 'token-reflexive' form in that the speaker refers to something present that is related to the word used, differing in what is presented and the way it is related to the word used.

To capture the rule governing 'the idea $"\mu"$ ' formally, we need to index '$\mu$' with variables and constants standing for ideas or other expressibles. That is, we need to use place-holders of the form '$\mu_i$', which stand for linguistic units expressing a particular idea i at the place '$\mu_i$' occupies in a formula. If $a$ is the idea of an airplane, then 'idea $"plane"$ ' is a substitution instance of 'idea $"\mu_a"$ ' only if 'plane' expresses the idea of an airplane in that instance. If $c$ is the idea of a carpenter's wood plane, then 'idea $"plane"$ ' is a substitution instance of 'idea $"\mu_c"$ ' only if 'plane' expresses the idea of a wood plane in that instance. 'Idea $"airplane"$ ' could not be a substitution instance of 'idea $"\mu_c"$ ' unless we are using a code of some sort. With these conventions in hand, we can use the following schema to define expressions of the form 'the idea $"\mu"$ '.

3.9  **Definition**: *The idea $"\mu_i" = i$, provided i is an idea.*

When '$\mu$' does not express an idea, 'the idea $"\mu"$ ' has no referent. Thus 'the idea $"ouch"$ ' has no referent because what the word 'ouch' expresses is a sensation rather than an idea. 'The idea $"borogrove"$ ' has no referent because the nonsense word 'borogrove' does not express anything. Definition 3.9 tells us that 'The idea $"plane"$ is the idea of an airplane' is true when the occurrence of 'plane' therein expresses the idea of an airplane. It would be false if 'plane' there meant $"wood plane"$. Definition 3.9 can be extended in obvious ways to cover terms referring ideo-reflexively to specific *types* of idea as well, such as 'the *thought* $"\mu_i"$ ' and 'the *proposition* $"\mu_i"$ '.

Definition 3.9 tells us what 'the idea $"\mu"$ ' designates in the actual world. When generalized to all possible worlds, the definition would say that *given any world w, the idea $"\mu_i" = i$ in w*. Expressions of the form 'the idea $"\mu"$ ' are *rigid designators*. On any occasion of use, they designate the same idea in all possible worlds. Whenever 'the idea $"red"$ ' is used, it rigidly designates *that idea*, the one the word 'red' actually expresses on that occasion. If English were different, so that 'red' had a different meaning, then 'red' would express a different idea, an idea other than the idea of red; 'the idea $"red"$ ' would refer to that other idea. The idea $"red"$ would remain the same, although a different phrase would designate it. It would remain the idea $"red"$ even though in the hypothetical variant of English it would not be designated by the phrase 'the idea $"red"$ '. This can be very confusing, for speakers of the imagined variant of English would say (and should say), ' 'Red' expresses the idea $"red"$ ', just as we do. The agreement would be verbal, however. Since their language would be different from ours, they would be talking about a different idea than we do when we use the sentence. Expressions like 'The idea "red" ' are thus indexical in the same way 'I' and 'here' are.[19] On different occasions of use, these expressions are used to rigidly designate different objects.

Definition 3.9 implies that sentences like (5) are true in every context in which "the idea expressed by 'plane' " in its predicate is used to refer to the idea expressed by 'plane' in its subject.

(5) The idea "plane" is the idea expressed by 'plane'.

This is true when the first occurrence of 'plane' is used to express the idea of an airplane, and "the idea expressed by 'plane' " is used to refer to that idea. It similarly follows that "The idea "plane" is the idea expressed by 'plane' *on this occasion*" is true whenever 'this occasion' refers to the very occasion on which that sentence is being uttered. Definition 3.9 does not imply that 'the idea "plane" ' and "the idea expressed by 'plane' " are *synonymous*. They are not. First, when speakers use 'the idea "plane" ' in ordinary usage, they are *using* the word 'plane' but they are not talking *about* that word. In contrast, speakers are talking about the word 'plane' when using "the idea expressed by 'plane' ". Second, (5) could be used to say something false. The speaker could be using the definite description in the predicate of (5) to refer to the idea expressed by 'plane' in some contextually salient place other than the subject of (5) itself. The speaker might be pointing at an occurrence in a book, where 'plane' means "tool for planing wood" while he is using it to mean "airplane". The speaker could also use "the idea expressed by 'plane' " in its unrestricted Russellian sense. In that case, (5) is either false or neither true nor false due to failure of the uniqueness presupposition. Since 'plane' is ambiguous, "the idea expressed by 'plane' " does not have a unique referent. Third, (5) never expresses a necessary truth. The idea "plane" need not be expressed by 'plane' in English at all, and need not be the idea expressed by 'plane' on any particular occasion. The singular term in the subject of (5) is a rigid designator; the singular term in the predicate is non-rigid. Substitution instances of (5) thus resemble 'Here is the place where I am', which is true in every context in which 'Here' and 'I' are used deictically, but is not analytic and does not express a necessary truth in any context. Because (5) is about the word 'plane', can be used to say something false, and never expresses a necessary truth, it cannot be listed as a theorem. Nonetheless, Definition 3.9 does account for why (5) is true in every context on its most natural interpretation.

Note well that quotation has different functions on the two sides of 'is expressed by' in (5). Only on the right does quotation form the name of the word quoted. On the left, the quotation marks emphasize that a word is being used ideo-reflexively. Hence 'the word' or 'the letter sequence' can be inserted redundantly before the occurrence of " 'plane' " on the right (the idea "plane" is the idea expressed by *the word* 'plane'). But inserting 'the word' or 'the letter sequence' in front of the occurrence of ' "w" ' on the left either produces nonsense or changes the sense dramatically. "The idea the word 'plane' " is hard to interpret, and can only be used to refer to the idea of the word 'plane', which is not expressed by the word 'plane'.

Definition 3.9 defines the *oratio recta* way of referring to ideas by displaying the words that express them, which can be used with any type of linguistic expression. When an idea is expressed by words in certain grammatical categories, local conventions using *oratio obliqua* are more common. For example, let 'ρ' stand for any pronoun-free declarative sentence expressing a proposition, which is defined in §2.5 as a declarative thought. The idea "ρ" can be referred to as the idea *that ρ*.

3.10  **Definition:** *The idea that ρ =the idea "ρ".*

Thus the idea that man evolved from the apes is the idea "Man evolved from the apes". Instances of 'the idea "ρ" ' in turn are defined by Definition 3.9. It follows that the idea that $ρ_i = i$, when i is a proposition. Like 'the idea "ρ" ', 'the idea that ρ' is a rigid designator. 'The idea that the sky is red' designates the same proposition even in a world in which 'The sky is red' expresses a different proposition. Definition 3.10 can also be generalized to cover specific types of ideas, yielding results like Theorem 2.5.

The reason for restricting 'ρ' to *pronoun-free* declarative sentences is that pronouns behave differently in *oratio recta* and *oratio obliqua*. There are two differences. First, the reference is generally different. For example, 'The idea "I am a man" occurred to S' says that S was thinking about himself. But 'The idea that I am a man occurred to S' says that S was thinking about me. It does not matter in either case who S is. Second, pronouns are partially transparent in that-clauses, but completely opaque in the corresponding *oratio recta* form (see §7.7). 'S is thinking the thought that I am a man' does not specify how S is thinking of me. That is, it does not specify the particular subject concept of the thought S is thinking; all it tells us is that the extension of the concept is me. 'S is thinking the thought "I am a man" ', in contrast, does specify how S is thinking of himself. It specifies that the subject concept of S's thought is specifically his self-concept.[20] The restriction on 'ρ' is thus consistent with our general focus on the opaque interpretation of propositional attitude statements.

We introduced the term *object nominals* to denote the class of nouns, noun phrases, gerunds, and nominalizations that can occur as direct or indirect objects (§2.3), and use 'Φ' as a place-holder for them. Let us introduce 'φ' as a place-holder for the more specific class of *pronoun-free* nominals given an *opaque* interpretation. The idea "φ" can be referred to as the idea *of φ*. The idea of green is the idea "green", the idea of grass is the idea "grass", the idea of Mars is the idea "Mars", and so on.

3.11   **Definition:** *The idea of φ = the idea "φ".*

As in the case of that-clauses, pronouns behave differently in these two contexts. The phrase 'the idea "me" ' is non-indexical, and designates the self-concept in every context. The phrase 'the idea of me' is indexical, and in every context denotes some concept whose extension is the speaker.[21] Transparent descriptions behave differently too: 'The idea of water is the idea of a liquid' is true on a transparent interpretation of the predicate, but false on the intended opaque interpretation. Similarly, if 'idea of Aristotle' is interpreted as meaning "idea whose extension is Aristotle", then the ideas "Plato's star pupil" and "Alexander's most famous teacher" count as ideas of Aristotle as does the idea "Aristotle". But only the third is the referent of 'the idea of Aristotle' when that phrase is given the opaque interpretation that is our standard (see §7.7). Note carefully that the idea "grass" is the idea *of grass*, not the idea *of 'grass'*.[22] A Chinese person may have the idea of grass—which is the idea we English speakers customarily use 'grass' to express—without having the idea of the English word 'grass'.

   When the ideas we wish to refer to are expressed by words other than object nominals, the prepositional phrase construction cannot be used directly. Nevertheless, we often do use the construction with cognate nominals to produce a term whose reference is the idea expressed by the root of the nominal. When 'A' is a suitable adjective, we often refer to the idea it expresses as the idea *of A-ness* or the idea *of A-ity*. (If 'A' doubles as a noun, we can also refer to it as the idea *of A*.) We thus use 'The idea of circularity' to refer to the idea expressed by 'circular'. When 'V' is a verb, we often refer to the idea it expresses as the idea *of V-ing*. The idea expressed by 'walk' is called the idea of walking. When 'p' is an indicative sentence, we may refer to the idea it expresses as the idea *of NOM(p)*, where 'NOM(p)' stands for the nominalization of p. For example, the idea "Mary sang" might be referred to as the idea of Mary's singing. As a result, when 'φ' is derived from a root form, 'the idea of φ' is ambiguous in English. For example, 'the idea of circularity' can be used to refer to the idea expressed by either the subject or the predicate of 'circularity is circular'. That is, 'the idea of circularity' can denote either the idea "circularity" or the idea "circular".

   Since the *oratio recta* form 'the idea "μ" ' is universally applicable, it is unnecessary for us to provide a definition that covers all instances of 'the idea of φ' in English. The special case defined by Definition 3.11 is enough for all our purposes, and together with Definition 3.10 suffices to indicate how the *oratio obliqua* form of ideo-reflexive reference works.

### 3.8  OBJECTS AND CONTENTS

Descartes, Arnauld, Locke, Leibniz, and others often defined ideas as *objects* rather than *parts* of thought.[23] That is, they defined an idea as *what a thought is of* or *about*. On this definition, the Sun is an idea, because it is something I am thinking of. Few philosophers or psychologists have been able to stick consistently to this 'Cartesian' definition, because it leads to statements that are absurd if 'idea' has anything like its conventional sense. Given the Cartesian definition, for example, we have to either deny that ideas are mind-dependent (because the Sun is not), or affirm that physical objects are mind-dependent (because they are ideas). We would have to say that some ideas are millions of miles away from any thinking beings, and are massive balls of hydrogen gas—or deny that the Sun is. What we can legitimately say is that the objects of thought are the *objects* of the ideas they contain. That is, on our definition of 'idea', a thought is of what the ideas composing it are of (Definition 2.3). But it makes no sense to say that an idea *is* what it is *of* (unless it is somehow of itself; but 'the idea of itself' does not appear to have a referent). I believe Cartesians were led to their definition by the fact that a sentence like 'the Sun is an idea' is true when its subject term is interpreted ideo-reflexively. And its subject term refers to the object of an idea on its standard interpretation. So there was an equivocation.

The Cartesian definition is implied by the conceptualist solution to the traditional problem of universals. Philosophers from Plato onward have observed that all individual men have in common the property of being a man, or equivalently, that all are instances of mankind. Properties and kinds are therefore called universals, and the metaphysical questions concern their existence and nature. The conceptualist maintains that universals are concepts, and therefore exist in the mind. Thus when reflecting on the signification of general words like 'horse' and 'white', Locke argues that 'the abstract idea for which the name stands, and the essence of the species, is one and the same' (1690: §3.3.12). Conceptualism can seem very natural given that we use the devices of quotation and italics to refer to both the properties and the concepts expressed by general terms. Thus it might well appear that we are referring to the same thing when we refer to the property *white* and the concept *white*. But we are not. The property of being white is possessed by pieces of chalk and paper—by anything that is white. The concept of being white is not possessed by pieces of chalk or paper, since they cannot think. To possess the concept of being white is not to be a white thing, but to be able to think of white things.

In their own fall from semantic innocence, neo-Fregeans take ideas to be *parts of thought contents*. On this approach, the thought that the sky is red is the content, *that the sky is red*. Part of that content is the content, *the sky*, which is identified with the concept of the sky. It is possible that neo-Fregeans are simply using 'the content that p' in an unconventional way to mean "the thought that p". In that case, their definition of ideas is equivalent to the one we have adopted (assuming only cognitive parts count). But as ordinarily interpreted, the content of a thought is not the thought itself, but at best an identifying property of the thought—something the thought *has*, not something the thought *is*. In another sense, the content of a thought is a mere intentional object, which cannot be said to have parts. Thought contents in either sense are not things that occur to people. In fact, in conventional English, an expression like 'the content that the sky is red' is ungrammatical and uninterpretable unless we hear a comma pause after 'content', or equivalently, hear 'the sky is red' as italicized or quoted, making it analogous to 'the mayor, John Doe'.

I believe that the terms 'object' and 'content' when applied to subpropositional ideas are fully defined by the following schemas.

3.12   **Definition:** *The content of i is "μ" iff i = the idea "μ".*

3.13   **Definition:** *i has the content "μ" iff i = the idea "μ".*

3.14   **Definition:** *The object of i is φ iff i = the idea of φ.*

3.15   **Definition:** *i has φ as its object iff i = the idea of φ.*[24]

Thus we say that the idea of the sky has the content "the sky", and that its content is "the sky". The sky is its object. 'The content "the sky" ' can be interpreted either as a nonreferential term, or as a term referring to an identifying property of the idea. As we saw in §3.7, 'the idea "μ" ' is an ideo-reflexive singular term used to refer to the idea expressed by 'μ'. In this usage, 'μ' and 'φ' themselves are not functioning as singular terms referring to i, nor to any entity related to i called its object or content. To interpret them that way is to misunderstand ideo-reflexive reference.[25] The same goes for the occurrences of 'μ' and 'φ' in the locutions on the left side of the above definitions, which say nothing more than the expressions on the right. I will place no theoretical weight on the notion of the content or object of an idea.

The search for a 'theory of content' that has become a central preoccupation of philosophers of mind is, I believe, misguided. To ask what the conditions are in virtue of which the idea i has its content is to ask what makes i be i. This question can only be answered, I believe, if i is complex. In that case, the answer specifies the components of i and the way they are put together in i. Since every theory of content on offer cites objects and conditions that are external to i, they are bound to fail. These claims will be explained and defended in §3.9 and §8.5.

### 3.9 ATOMIC IDEAS

We distinguish 'atomic' from 'complex' ideas in the usual way:

3.16 **Definition**: *An idea is complex if it contains other ideas as parts; otherwise it is atomic (simple).*

A familiar type of *reductio ad absurdum* argument shows that ideas cannot all be complex.

3.17 **Postulate.** *Some ideas are atomic.*

Some ideas must be atomic because otherwise there would be an infinite regress or circle of ideas. There cannot be a circle, because 'x is (proper) part of y' is an order relation: transitive, asymmetric, and irreflexive. If there were a circle, then some idea would be part of a part of a part ... of a part of itself. By transitivity, it would be a part of itself, violating irreflexivity. There cannot be an infinite regress either. If there were, then the parts of any idea would have to have ideas as parts, and those ideas would have to have ideas as parts, and so on *ad infinitum*. Every thought and idea of even the least intelligent and mature person would have to be infinitely complex. But this is absurd given that human experience and cognition are finite and limited.[26]

Given that every thought is composed of at least two other ideas, it follows that thoughts are not simple ideas. This means that only subpropositional ideas are atomic. If a subpropositional idea is complex, then it is in principle *definable*, and definable in the strictest sense. If idea i is composed of ideas j and k, then there at least could be terms 'I', 'J', and 'K' expressing those ideas in such a way that 'I' means "JK". The qualification 'in principle' is necessary because the languages available to us need not have the requisite words and constructions. When I say that a term is definable in the strictest sense, I mean that the definiens and definiendum are not only co-extensive but synonymous: they have the same meaning because they express the same idea. It is plausible that 'vixen' expresses a complex idea because it is plausible that 'vixen' means "female fox". That is, a vixen is definable as a female fox, and the definition 'A vixen is a female fox' is not just true but analytic. Psychologists refer to the thesis that all concepts are definable as the *classical theory*.

A term or idea that is not defined in a given system is said to be *primitive*. Atomic ideas are primitive in an absolute sense: they cannot be analytically defined in any system. The argument that some ideas must be simple has the same logic as the familiar argument proving that in any system of definitions, some terms must be undefinable or primitive. The thesis that not every word is definable holds for 'semantic' or 'analytic' definitions, in which the definiens is a complex expression synonymous with the definiendum.[27] If every word were definable, then there would have to be either an infinite regress of definitions, or a circle. Since there are only a finite number of simple words (those that do not contain other words as parts), there cannot be an infinite regress. There cannot be a circle of analytic definitions given that the definiendum means what the definiens does, and that the meaning of the definiens is determined compositionally by the meanings of its components. If there were a circle, then the definiendum would have to be synonymous with some complex expression containing itself as a proper part. Then the definiendum would have to mean a proper part of what it means, which is an impossibility.

It will not generally be important for us whether any particular subpropositional idea or class thereof is simple or complex. We will conclude in Part III, though, that standard proper names are not definable in English or other natural languages, making it plausible that names express atomic ideas. Fodor generalizes this conclusion to the extreme, arguing that 'all or most lexical concepts have no internal structure'.[28] A 'lexical' concept is one that is expressed by a semantically unstructured word in a given natural language. Thus the concepts "cat" and "brother" are lexical in English, in contrast to "feline animal" and "male sibling", which are phrasal. Fodor bases his lexical primitiveness thesis on the sort of evidence Putnam marshaled against Katz concerning the definability of terms like 'brother' and 'cat'. There is at least as much reason to think that 'sibling' means "brother or sister" as there is to think that 'brother' means "male sibling". Actually, there is more, because young children seem to acquire the concept of a brother before they acquire the concept of a sibling. As for cats, we could conceivably have discovered that they are Martian robots and not animals at all. Fodor also points to the inability of generative semanticists to provide successful analytic definitions of terms such as 'kill', and the failure of epistemologists to define 'know' despite a massive effort. It is well known that 'To kill is to cause to die' and 'Knowledge is true justified belief', for example, are too broad.[29] Attempts to strengthen the definitions tend to either produce circularity or introduce material that is not known or intended by most people who use the terms 'kill' or 'know'. Others point to the difficulty of defining everyday concepts like "cup" or "game". While Fodor presumably intends his generalization to hold for all natural languages, and not just English, it is nonetheless a contingent thesis about languages, with no fundamental implications about the nature of the mind. Fodor believes the lexical primitiveness thesis has deep psychological significance because he concludes from it that a large number of any normal human being's concepts are innate. But this conclusion depends on a false premise about concept acquisition.[30]

Margolis and Laurence (1999) note that despite Fodor's advocacy, 'conceptual atomism' is sometimes met with 'stark incredulity'. Part of the resistance, I suspect, is due to an equivocation on 'concept'. The term often means *"conception"*, which denotes a type of belief system (§3.3). Our conceptions of cats, brothers, and games are fantastically complex. As we can easily tell by introspection, for example, it is part of our conception of cats that they are four-legged, furry animals that meow and sleep a lot when adult. It surely makes no sense to say that a conception—that is, a belief system—has no parts. Images too are complex. They arguably have atomic parts of their own, called 'sensations'. But sensations are not themselves images. We are using 'concept' and 'idea' to mean *"cognitive thought part"* rather than *"conception"* or *"image"*. What the argument for Postulate 3.17 proves is that thoughts must have some cognitive parts that do not themselves have cognitive parts.

Rey (1994: 191) suggests that the classical theory has the advantage over atomism because it provides an account of conceptual competence.

> If competence doesn't consist in a grasp of a definition, what makes it true on this view that someone has one concept rather than another? What makes it true that a child or an adult has the concept [cause], or [knowledge], if she can't define it?
>
> (Rey 1994: 191)

Definition is an action involving *words*. To define the concept of a vixen is to say something like 'A vixen is a female fox.' One cannot grasp a definition unless one understands the words used, and one cannot do that without having the concepts expressed by the words, including the concept being defined. Having those concepts does not consist in grasping the definition, or in being able to define anything. Learning the definition of a term may enable us to use the *term* by telling us what concept the term expresses. But we could never learn the definition unless we already had the ability to conceive that concept.

It is more plausible to claim that a child has the concept of a vixen only if the child knows that a vixen is a female fox, which says nothing about words. The child knows a definition in that the child knows a proposition that states or implies necessary and sufficient conditions for an object to be a vixen. Possessing a concept cannot *consist in* knowing a definition in this sense, however. For if it did, then possessing one concept would entail possessing an infinite regress of concepts and knowing an infinite regress of definitions. One cannot know or believe *any* proposition without having all the concepts contained in the proposition. Having the concept of a vixen (i.e., of a female fox) is a precondition of having any propositional attitude about vixens. Hence knowing something about vixens cannot *make it true* that one has the concept of a vixen. In sum, the classical theory does nothing to explain how someone is able to think of something, or what it is to think of something.

Margolis and Laurence believe that a concept has to have structure because they take concepts to be theoretical entities postulated to explain the process of categorizing.

How can lexical concepts have no structure at all? If they are atoms, wouldn't that rob them of any explanatory power? After all, in other theories, it's a concept's structure that is implicated in accounts of categorization, acquisition, and all the other phenomena that theories of concepts are usually taken to address.

(Margolis and Laurence 1999: 60)

Psychologists use 'categorization' to denote a belief-forming process. A subject S categorizes an object *a* as *P* when the subject forms the belief that *a* is *P* as a result of observing *a*. How does S determine, for example, that the sign on this corner is a stop sign? Typically, by observing that it is a red, octagonal sign with the word 'STOP' on it in white.

(6)  The sign is red.
(7)  The sign is octagonal.
(8)  The sign has 'STOP' in white.
(9)  Stop signs are red, octagonal signs with 'STOP' in white.
(10)  ∴ The sign is a stop sign.

One possible explanation is that observing the sign causes S to form the belief that it is red (6), the belief that it is octagonal (7), and so on for each of the observable features of the sign. These perceptual beliefs combine with the standing general belief that stop signs are red, octagonal signs with 'STOP' in white (9) to form premises from which S deduces the conclusion that the sign on this corner is a stop sign (10).[31] Note that the whole explanation is in terms of *beliefs*. The general belief (9) is a central element of our common conception of stop signs whether the concept of a stop sign is simple or complex. That is, people believe (9) whether it is an analytic definition or an empirical generalization.

What explanatory role do concepts play when they are defined as thought parts? Their essential role in the present case is to enable S to think the things S comes to believe. The concept of a stop sign is a part of propositions (9) and (10). These propositions are the conclusion and the major premise of the inference that was the categorization process. Without the concept, S could not think about stop signs or form beliefs about them. Without beliefs, there would be no categorization. Atomic concepts are cognitively basic in an important sense: they are the ultimate mental components out of which all thoughts and ideas are composed.[32]

There is a second role the concept of a stop sign might play in the categorization process. If the concept were analyzable as the concept "red, octagonal sign with 'STOP' in white" (or something to that effect), then proposition (9) would be analytic, and thus presumably self-evident. This would provide an explanation of why the subject believes (9), thus deepening the explanation of the categorization process. But alternative explanations of that belief are readily imaginable. S may have acquired the belief from books or parents, or from experience by induction.

If any categorization process had to be inferential with a self-evident major premise that is an analysis of the predicate concept applied in the process, then categorization would be impossible because it would require an infinite regress of categorizations. How did the subject categorize the sign as red? That is, how did the subject arrive at premise (6)? If it was because the subject categorized the sign as F (where "F" is part of the definition of 'red'), then we must ask how the subject categorized the sign as F. If it was because the subject categorized the sign as G (where "G" is part of the definition of 'F'), then we must ask how the subject categorized the sign as G. Etcetera *ad infinitum. Inferential categorization is not possible unless some categorization is noninferential.* This point holds as well when the inferences are inductions from prototypes as when they are deductions from analyses. At some point, perception must have the ability to cause us to apply some concepts to particulars directly, without first causing us to apply other concepts.

Margolis and Laurence go on to say that a conceptual atomist must at least provide a theory of how the reference of unstructured terms is determined. Boghossian makes the point more colorfully in an argument for externalism.

One of the principal considerations has to do with how thin the concept associated with a natural kind term would have to be, if we removed the information associated with its extension. For let us ask this: What can we plausibly insist upon up front is packed into the concept of a natural kind, say, to use Putnam's famous example, the concept cat? Furriness? Having four legs? Meowing? Not even the concept animal, Putnam argued, could be thought of as built into the concept cat (cats might turn out to be robots) . . . If we insisted that narrow contents are thinkable contents, then we would have to conclude that most of our thoughts about natural kinds are virtually blank and so don't determine, in and of themselves, any sort of determinate truth conditions for themselves.                    (Boghossian 1998b: 256)

Let us assume that Putnam's examples show that no other concepts are packed into the concept of a cat. Assume, that is, that the concept of a cat is atomic, and therefore does not contain the concepts of furriness, four-leggedness, or even animality. Does it follow that the concept is 'virtually blank' in the sense that it does not determine any truth conditions? Hardly. Tautologically, the concept of a cat applies to an object if and only if it is a cat. Hence the thought "Morris is a cat" is true iff Morris is a cat. It is because the thought "Morris is a cat" contains the concept of a cat as its predicate concept rather than the concept of a dog that the truth of the thought depends on Morris being a cat rather than a dog. The truth conditions of a thought are a consequence of the concepts it is composed of and the way they are related in the thought. The explanation of truth conditions is thus another part of the explanatory power of concepts. Even if they explained no psychological phenomena, concepts would still have an explanatory role.

If a concept were blank in the sense of having no content, then indeed it would not determine any truth conditions. But the fact that a concept has no content does not follow from the fact that it is atomic. Definitions 3.12 and 3.13 apply whether i is atomic or complex. Furthermore, it would be incoherent to maintain that only complex concepts have content. For that would have the absurd implication that some concepts have no content, and that putting together a number of contentless concepts could somehow result in a concept with content. Complex concepts and atomic concepts are alike in that their extensions are determined by the facts together with their identities, or equivalently their contents. If i is the concept of a cat, then an object x is in the extension of i iff x is a cat. If i has the content "dog", then x is in the extension of i iff x is a dog. A complex concept differs in that it has components whose identities (or contents) determine its extension by determining its identity (content): the concept of a female cat applies to an object iff the concept's component concepts both apply. If the concept of a cat had no content, it could not determine the extension of the concept of a female cat. Since every concept has content, the claim that a concept has content only if it has components would lead to the impossible conclusion that every concept contains other concepts, *ad infinitum*.

Atomic concepts have one special property: since they have no cognitive components, no such components *make* them have the content they do. Does anything make an atomic concept have its content? By Definition 3.13, what makes a concept i have the content "μ" is that i is identical to the concept "μ". This holds whether i is atomic or complex. The interesting question is whether anything makes a concept be the concept "μ". Given that the concept "μ" is an event-type, an equivalent question is whether something makes event-tokens be occurrences of the concept "μ". If having property Δ made i be the concept "μ," then an event token would be an occurrence of the concept "μ" iff the token possessed Δ. In the same way, the property Δ would tell us what makes it the case that a subject is conceiving the concept "μ" rather than some other concept.

There appear to be three ways to answer a question of the form 'What makes A be B?' We can give the *definition*, *composition*, or *explanation* of B.

(11) *Definition*: What makes Mount Everest the tallest mountain? It is taller than any other mountain.

(12) *Composition*: What make this liquid water? It is composed of $H_2O$ molecules.

(13) *Explanation*: What makes radium dangerous? It is radioactive.

What makes this move a mistake? It allows your opponent to take your queen.

What makes this move illegal? It violates the rule that pawns cannot move backwards.

What makes 'Someone is president' true? The fact that George Bush is president.

When 'B' picks out a concept descriptively, then a definitional or causal answer is possible to the question 'What makes A be B?' For example, if we ask 'What makes the concept of God *Frank's favorite concept?*' we can answer by noting that it is the concept that occurs to Frank most frequently (definitional), or by noting that Frank is preoccupied with religious issues (explanatory). When 'B' is an ideo-reflexive term, however, its referent is not picked out descriptively. Like typical rigid designators, 'the concept "$\mu$"' does not have descriptive content that can serve as a definition (§3.7). So no definitional answer is possible. When 'B' is a nondescriptive term that designates A rigidly, the property of being B is an intrinsic, essential characteristic. In that case, no causal or explanatory answer is possible to the question 'What makes A be B?' either. Nothing *external* makes something be the concept "red". That means that 'What makes i be the concept "$\mu$"?' can only be answered compositionally. By definition, atomic concepts do not have other concepts as parts. So if the concept "red" is atomic, then what makes it that concept is not that it has certain cognitive parts. Consequently, if there is any answer to the question 'What makes an atomic concept have a particular content?' then the answer will have to specify noncognitive parts.

Given the evidence for materialism and the neurophysiological basis of mental phenomena, it is plausible that concepts are neural event-types. In that case, what makes a concept have a particular content is that it consists of certain neural processes. If the concept "red" is a neurophysiological process, then thinking of red consists in having that process occur in us. To discover what that process is, we have to study what goes on in the brain when people think of red. Since we do not yet know much about the neurophysiological basis of ideation, however, we are not now in a position to give neurophysiological answers to the question of what makes an atomic concept be the concept it is. And there is no guarantee that we will ever discover the correct answer. There is no *a priori* assurance that scientists will ever gather the evidence necessary to answer an empirical question.[33]

Given that the evidence for materialism is not yet complete, we are also not in a position to say for sure that the question we are raising has any answer. I believe there are many cases in which 'What makes A be B?' has no answer. Consider:

> (14) What makes me today the same person as me yesterday?
> (15) What makes Aristotle Aristotle?
> (16) What makes this that? (where I am pointing at the same object in two ways)
> (17) What makes this identical to itself?

It seems increasingly likely as we go down this list that *nothing* makes the things identical. They 'just are'. It is possible, then, that nothing makes a concept be the concept "red". It may be that all we can say is that it just is what it is. In that case, nothing will make an atomic concept be the concept it is.

Our inability to say now, or perhaps ever, what makes an atomic concept be that concept will not prevent us from answering any of the foundational questions about meaning that we set out to answer in this work. None of our issues depend on being able to say what it is to be a particular atomic concept. It is enough that we know the concept exists, and can tell when it occurs to ourselves or others. Competing theories of meaning will raise their own unanswered and possibly unanswerable questions. The fact that we may not be able to say what makes the concept of Aristotle be that concept does no more damage to the ideational theory than the fact that we may not be able to say what makes Aristotle be Aristotle does to the referential theory of meaning.

## NOTES

[1] This chapter is a summary of Chs. 15–19, and §7.6, of *Meaning, Expression, and Thought*. §3.9 of this chapter, however, is an expansion of §15.2 of the earlier book.

[2] Concepts cannot be defined as *belief parts* unless we are talking about objects of belief rather than acts of believing. The objects of belief are propositions, identified with thoughts in §2.5. So the claim that concepts are parts of beliefs in this sense is nearly equivalent to the claim that they are parts of thoughts. But the propositional attitude of belief does not have parts, as we mentioned in §2.6. Compare and contrast Barwise and Perry 1983: 242, Crimmins 1992: Ch. 3, and Horwich 1998a: 44.

[3] For further discussion of the relationship between images and thoughts, see James 1890: Ch. 18; Ryle 1951; 1958; Humphrey 1951: Chs. 2–4; Ginnane 1960: 387; Aune 1967a: 102; Fodor 1975: 174–95; Blackburn 1984: 47; Stillings *et al.* 1987: 36–48, 449–50; and *Meaning, Expression, and Thought*: §19.2, §19.3.

[4] Nor an invention. There is a related sense in which Edison conceived the phonograph but not the sky.

[5] There is a question as to whether a subject's conception of something contains *all* his beliefs about it, or omits unimportant ones.

[6] Woodfield (1991: 549; 1997: 83–4) defines the concept–conception distinction similarly, although he describes concepts as 'classificatory norms'. Katz's (1972: 450–2; 1977a) 'dictionaries' and 'encyclopedias' may be viewed as formal representations of concepts and conceptions, respectively. Perry (1990: 18–19) distinguishes between 'notions' and 'files', the latter consisting of a number of beliefs with a common notion. Higginbotham (1998) draws a related distinction between the concept of Φ and S's conception of *the concept*. S's conception of the concept of Φ consists of S's beliefs about the concept, such as that it applies to Φ. Many authors conflate the two senses. For a recent example, see Bilgrami 1992; compare pages 6 and 11.

[7] Definition 3.4 thus captures what is attractive in Evans's (1982: 104) view, without the undesirable consequences of maintaining that concepts *are* abilities. See also Price 1953: 276–7; Geach 1957a: 12–15; Kenny 1963: Ch. 10; E. Sosa 1991; Fitch 1993: 470–1; Millikan 1998b: 530–1, 537. Contrast Fodor 1998a: 125, fn. 6. Abilities cannot occur to us or be constituents of occurrent thoughts.

[8] Contrast Fodor 1998a: 3; 1998b: 11; Moya 1998: 245.

[9] Evans (1982: 103–4) dubbed this 'The Generality Constraint'. Cf. Fodor's (1987: 151) notion of the 'systematicity' of thought, discussed in §2.6. See also Davies 1991: 239–40; Peacocke 1992: §2.1. Contrast Leibniz 1676: 281.

[10] Cf. Berkeley 1710: 2nd edn., §27, 140, 142; Reid 1785: 193, 431, 523; Geach 1957a: 12–13, 16; Aaron 1967: 196–7; Woodfield 1997: 94; Philipse 1994: 234. Contrast Humphrey 1951: Ch. 8; Price 1953: 313–6, 344–6; Heath 1967: 179; Hamlyn 1971: 6; McGinn 1997: 102; and Vendler 1977: 58.

[11] Compare and contrast Bealer 1998a: 272.

[12] Cf. Aristotle *De Anima*: 431b15; Aquinas *Commentary on De Anima*: Lns III.10.54–63; *Treatise on Man*: Art. I.79.3; Locke 1690: §§3.3.6–11; Reid 1785: Ch. 5.3; Mill 1879: Ch. 4.2; James 1890: Ch. 1.12; Joseph 1916: 34–5; Humphrey 1951: 265–78; Price 1953: 38–9, 215; Rand 1969: 15. Contrast Geach 1957a: Chs. 6–11; Carruthers 1992: 54ff.

[13] See Dretske 1969. Contrast Sellars 1963: 176; Carruthers 1992: 55; Fodor 1998a: 136, fn. 10.

[14] Fodor 1981: 281; 1998a: 127–9, 139; Sterelny 1989: 129; 1990: 113, 116; Cowie 1999: 86–9, 93–4, 99–100, 111, 115.

[15] Contrast Fodor 1994: 19–20; 1998a: 129 and Cowie 1999: 103, also 86–9, 93–4, 111.

[16] Cf. Geach 1957a: 28; Hacking 1975: 64; Sterelny 1989: 129–39; Loar 1991; Fodor 1998a: 124–5.

[17] See, e.g., Stillings *et al.*, 1995: 27–32, on 'propositional networks'.

[18] Cf. Kneale and Kneale 1962: 585; Woodfield 1982: 281; Crimmins 1992: 163–6; Horwich 1998a: 26; Soames 2002: 137–40. Compare and contrast Sellars 1963: §7; 1979: Ch. 4; Davidson 1968; Peacocke 1975: §4; Lycan 1981, 1985; Böer and Lycan 1986: Chs. 3–4; Forbes 1993; Heal 1997: 638–9.

[19] I will develop this point in *Indexicals*.

[20] I explain and defend this claim in *Indexicals*.

[21] Let it also be understood that an instance of 'φ' has narrow scope if it is a quantifier. 'The idea of something is the idea "something" ' is ambiguous, and is true only when 'something' has narrow scope.

[22] Contrast Alston 1964a: 24–5; Crimmins 1989: 291.

[23] Descartes 1641: 9–10, 52; Arnauld 1641: 87, 106; 1683: Chs. 5–7; Locke 1690: 'Introduction', §8; §2.1.1; Leibniz 1709: §2.1. See also Berkeley 1710: §§1.7, 1.38, 1.89, 1.140, 1.142; J. Mill 1829: 264; Joseph 1916: 21–2; Humphrey 1951: 274, 315; Urmson 1967: 119; Quillian 1968: 227; Collins and Loftus 1975: 408–10; Burge 1979b: 537; Marconi 1990; and Bradshaw 1991: 422–3. Contrast Gassendi 1641: 157; Reid 1785: §2.4.2; James 1890: 461; and Husserl 1900: 355.

²⁴ As specified in §3.7, 'φ' is a place-holder for pronoun-free object nominals. 'The idea of φ' does not have an opaque interpretation when 'φ' contains pronouns. Definitions 3.12 and 3.13 hold as well when i is a thought. But '=' must be changed to 'contains' in Definitions 3.14 and 3.15.

²⁵ This error was Frege's well-known fall from semantic innocence.

²⁶ Cf. Husserl 1900: 494. M. Green objected that if this argument were good, that would imply that we could not comprehend a non-well-founded set (a set violating the axiom of foundation). But there are two critical differences that make the argument valid for wholes but not for sets. First, unlike 'x is part of y', the relation 'x is a member of y' is nontransitive. Second, sets are not human events, and so are not subject to human limitations.

²⁷ Contrast Goldstein 1986, who argues that every term could be defined without specifying what kind of definition he has in mind. I survey the varieties of definition in Davis 1986: §10.4.

²⁸ Fodor 1981: 279, emphasis deleted. See also Wittgenstein 1953: §65–67; Putnam 1970a; 1973; 1975; Fodor 1975: 124–56; 1987: 161; 1994: Chs. 2–3; 1998a: Chs. 3, 4, 5A; Fodor *et al.* 1980; Smith and Medin 1981: 2–3; Ch. 3; Lakoff 1987; E. E. Smith 1988: 21; Sterelny 1989: §5; Margolis 1998: §3; Millikan 1998b; Margolis and Laurence 1999: §2. Contrast Katz and Fodor 1963; Katz 1964a; 1972; 1974; 1977; Schank and Abelson 1977: §1.4; Jackendoff 1989: 96; Wierzbicka 1992a. For an introduction, see Lyons 1977: §9.9 and Chierchia and McConnell-Ginet 1990: 350–66. In casual statements, Fodor sometimes says that *most concepts* are unstructured (1981: 283; 1998a: 13ff; see also Margolis and Laurence 1999: 10). Without the 'lexical' qualifier, this claim is unsustainable given that there is an infinite number of concepts.

²⁹ Fodor (1998a: 71) also cites Quine's argument that there is no analytic-synthetic distinction given that no one has been able to provide a 'serious and un-question-begging' definition of the distinction. But this would prove much more than Fodor wants, since Quine's conclusion entails that even 'unmarried males are unmarried' is not analytic, and that phrasal concepts are atomic too. Moreover, parallel reasoning should lead Fodor to the conclusion that 'analytic' is simply a typical lexical concept.

³⁰ See *Meaning, Expression, and Thought*, §17.2.

³¹ There are other possible explanations. If (9) is taken to express a general rule with exceptions, then the inference can be construed as an induction using the statistical syllogism. Or it can be construed as an inference to the best explanation with (10) viewed as explaining (6)–(8), and (9) being an empirical covering law.

³² The term 'basic-level' has acquired a technical sense in cognitive psychology, meaning 'the level at which human beings interact with their environments most effectively and process and store and communicate information most efficiently' (Lakoff 1989: 107). See also R. Brown 1958; Rosch 1978; Lakoff 1987: 31–8; 46–54; E. E. Smith 1988: 30–1; Millikan 1998. It is an open question whether all basic-level concepts in Lakoff's sense are atomic (*triangle* suggests otherwise), or whether all non-basic concepts in Lakoff's sense are complex (*animal* suggests otherwise).

³³ The argument of this paragraph is given more fully in *Meaning, Expression, and Thought*, §23.2.

# 4

## Speaker Meaning and Expression

According to the expression theory, meaning consists in the expression of ideas or other mental states. We have explained one of the key terms in this thesis, namely 'ideas'. Now we need to define 'expression'. Before we can do this, we need to observe that 'means' and 'expresses' are both ambiguous, meaning different things when said of speakers or words. Following H. P. Grice, we will define the word senses of these terms in terms of their speaker senses, and their speaker senses in terms of intention. This chapter presents the definitions of speaker meaning and expression. We will not offer Grice's own definitions, however, since he mistakenly assumed that speaker meaning was the attempt to communicate. Since there are many cases in which people mean something without being concerned to communicate, Grice's definition is subject to numerous counterexamples. We will say instead that to express an idea or other mental state is to provide a publicly observable indication of its occurrence, in a certain way. Communication requires not only meaning but understanding—interpretation as well as expression. Indicating, we will note, is a close relative of a nonsemantic sense of meaning, which Grice labeled 'natural' meaning.[1]

### 4.1   SPEAKER, WORD, AND EVIDENTIAL MEANING

Like most important and commonly used terms, 'means' has a large set of meanings, some closely related and others quite distinct. The three most important senses for us are represented in the following sentences.

(1) Ice means a temperature drop. (*evidential meaning*)
(2) 'Ice' means "frozen water". (*word meaning*)
(3) By 'ice', S means "I.C.E. (Inter-City Express)". (*speaker meaning*)

Sentence (1) says that ice *indicates* and *provides evidence of* a drop in temperature, which is true because the causal connection between temperature and ice enables us to infer the latter from the former. Since 'indicate' and 'provide evidence of' are close synonyms of 'mean' in examples like (1), I refer to this sense of meaning as *evidential meaning*. 'Indicate' and 'provide evidence of' are not even rough synonyms of 'mean' in (2) or (3). They do not tell us what we can infer from the word 'ice' or the speaker, and do not imply that there is anything like a causal relationship between the word 'ice' and the two phrases or the concepts they express. I use *word meaning* for the sense of meaning illustrated by (2), since in this sense the verb 'means' takes a subject referring to things like words. I use *speaker meaning*, similarly, for the sense of meaning illustrated by (3), since in this sense the verb 'means' takes a subject referring to an individual who has spoken, or has done something similar such as writing or gesturing. Note that 'means' is interchangeable with 'has the meaning', and is able to take an adverbial qualifier specifying a language only in (2). Evidential signifiers are signs, expressions, or symptoms *of* what they signify, while symbolic signifiers are signs, expressions, or symbols *for* what they signify. Thus ice is a sign of, not for, a temperature drop, and '+' is a sign for, not of, addition. Speakers are generally not signs of any sort.[2]

The discipline of semantics is concerned with both word and speaker meaning, but not evidential meaning. Both forms of semantic meaning depend on intelligent action and intention. Neither (2) nor (3) would be true unless someone had used the word 'ice' for certain purposes. Evidential meaning, in contrast, does not generally depend on intention or intelligent action of any form. (1) could be true even if human beings or other intelligent agents had never evolved on the planet. People are required to interpret or use the evidence provided, but indications need not be interpreted to exist.

It is natural to suspect that word meaning is the more fundamental semantic notion, and that 'S means "m"' is simply short for something like 'S used a word that means "m"'. I call this the *naive analysis* of speaker meaning, because a little reflection suffices to show that it is false.

(4) S means "m" by e iff S used e and e means "m".[3]

Codes, nonce words, technical stipulations, figures of speech (metaphor, simile, irony, hyperbole, metonymy, etc.), ellipses, shorthand expressions, and pronouns constitute a large and vital part of language. They are all cases in which what a word means differs from what a particular speaker means by it. Thus (3) may be true as well as (2) because S invented an acronym. Similarly, if Bill makes a common mistake and says 'Dr. Johnson is an entomologist' meaning that she is an etymologist, then Bill means "etymologist" by 'entomologist' even though 'entomologist' does not mean "etymologist". And from the fact that the ambiguous word 'broom' has the meaning *Cytisus scoparius*, it does not follow that this is what Aunt Hilda meant by it.

I argue that speaker meaning is the more fundamental semantic notion. For a brief characterization, we may say that "'Ice' means "frozen water"" is roughly equivalent to "Speakers conventionally mean "frozen water" by 'ice'". Chapter 5 develops a more accurate definition along this line.

In sentences like (2) and (3), the quotation marks to the left of 'means' are metalinguistic: the grammatical subject of these sentences refers to a word, the word 'ice'. The quotation marks to the right of 'means' function differently. They refer not to the words quoted, but to what the quoted words mean. Thus when (2) and (3) are translated into other languages, the quoted expressions on the right get translated, but not 'ice'. If the grammatical subject of (2) were translated, for example, the resulting statement would not give the meaning of the English word 'ice'. It is important to recognize that (2) does not mean the same thing as (5), in which both sets of quotation marks are used metalinguistically.

(5) 'Ice' means the same thing as 'frozen water'.

Sentence (5) is true, of course. But it would remain true, for example, if English changed so that both 'ice' and 'frozen water' meant 'fake jewelry'. In that case, though, (2) would be false: 'ice' would no longer mean "frozen water". Similarly, a foreigner can know that 'ice' means the same as 'frozen water' without knowing that 'ice' means "frozen water". Knowing that two words mean the same is possible without knowing what either means. I argue that both word and speaker meaning can be defined in terms of the expression of ideas (or other mental states). On this view, the quotation marks after 'means' in (2) and (3) are functioning ideo-reflexively. So I will use the distinctive angular quotes introduced in Chapter 3, writing " 'ice' means "frozen water" " for (2).

We will not be concerned with the subtle distinctions among semantic signifiers marked by the terms 'sign', 'signal', 'symbol', 'word', and so on. For we are interested in meaning, and all of them mean what they do in the same sense. For example, 'ice' is properly characterized as a word, but not as a sign. Its translation into American Sign Language, on the other hand, is properly characterized as a sign but not as a word. Nevertheless, both are signifiers, and both mean "frozen water". We will use *expression* neutrally for the broad class of symbolic, non-agentive signifiers.

Grice (1957) used 'natural meaning' for evidential meaning, and classified both word and speaker meaning as 'nonnatural meaning'. Grice's usage, however, is confusing in light of the venerable distinction between *natural* and *conventional signs*. Hobbes introduced the distinction as follows.

Signs however are customarily called *the antecedents of consequences and the consequences of antecedents, since we generally experience them in a similar way preceding or following one another in a similar fashion.* For example, a dense cloud is a sign of consequent rain and rain a sign of an antecedent cloud, for the reason that we know from experience that there is rarely a dense cloud without consequent rain, and never rain without an antecedent cloud. Of signs, however, some are natural of which type we have just discussed an example. Others are conventional, namely, those which are applied of our own accord; of this type are: a bush hung for signifying that wine is for sale, a stone for signifying the boundaries of a field, and human vocal sounds connected in a certain way for signifying the thoughts and motions of the mind.

(Hobbes 1655: §2.3)[4]

Hobbes's distinction applies only to evidential signs, his main concern. So even Hobbes's conventional signs mean what they do in Grice's 'natural' sense. The fact that John said 'It is raining' may mean (i.e., indicate) that John is thinking the thought that it is raining. But John's utterance is a conventional sign of the thought rather than a natural sign. For English sentences are artificial, and indicate what they do in virtue of certain conventions. Note well that while utterances of 'It is raining' signify *evidentially* the thought that it is raining, the sentence signifies *symbolically* that it is raining. Convention is involved in both relationships, but in different ways. The same may hold when the signified and signifier are identical, as when a turn signal signifies a turn both evidentially and symbolically.

'Means' can be replaced by 'signifies' in (1)–(3), but not in other contexts.

(6) S means to say 'ice'. (*intention*)
(7) S means what he says. (*seriousness*)

Sentence (6) concerns what S intends to say, and hence may be true even though, due to a slip of the tongue, or a speech impediment, S actually says 'ace'. In the same sense, one may mean to win, or to get rich. Note that S may mean to say 'ice' even though he does not mean "ice", as when (3) is true. Conversely, S may mean "ice" without intending to say 'ice', as when S uses a synonym or a foreign language. Sentence (7)—or more simply 'S means it'—claims that S's utterance is intentional, literal, and serious. Hence when S says 'The water is ice', (7) may be false because he is exaggerating or joking, even when he means "The water is frozen" rather than "The water consists of diamonds". Meaning it is compatible with lying, however.[5] Indeed, a witness would not be guilty of perjury if she did not mean it when she said that the defendant was with her all night. Before the prosecutor charges perjury, he must be sure the witness meant exactly what she said.

In the process of defining speaker meaning, we will also define speaker implication and expression. All three depend on the speaker's intentions. They depend specifically, I shall argue, on what the speaker intends his actions to indicate about his beliefs and other mental states, in the evidential sense of indication. All three allow insincerity, when the speaker lacks the indicated mental state. What words mean, imply, or express depends not on any particular speaker's intentions, but rather on conventional usage and the rules of the language, which are determined by the intentions of prior speakers of the language. Evidential meaning, implication, and expression do not in general depend on intentions at all, and so exist outside the realm of intelligent, language-using creatures. The analyses I shall present, therefore, will show that all five senses of meaning we have distinguished have intricate interconnections.

## 4.2 Cogitative versus Cognitive Meaning

Schiffer (1972: 2–3) showed that there are even two kinds of speaker meaning.

> (8) By (the expression) e, S meant "p". (*cogitative speaker meaning*)
> (9) By (saying or doing) e, S meant that p. (*cognitive speaker meaning*)

Typically, when a speaker means "It is raining" by an expression, he means that it is raining by uttering it, and vice versa. But these forms do not mean the same thing and are not equivalent. One difference is that in (8) any meaningful expression can replace 'p', whereas in (9) only declarative sentences can replace 'p'. Thus S can *mean* "a female fox", "Go to the store!" and "Is that a canary?" as well as "Today is Sunday". But among these, S can only mean *that* today is Sunday. 'S meant that a female fox', for example, is ill-formed and unintelligible. Even with declarative sentences, (8) and (9) may have different truth values in a number of cases.

*Fiction*: Robert Harris meant "The Führer sent a V-3 rocket to explode in the skies over New York in 1946" by something he wrote in *Fatherland*, but did not mean that such a thing ever happened.

*Irony*: A man may have meant that the weather is lousy by saying 'Beautiful day!' even though he did not mean "The weather is lousy" by that sentence.

*Parts of compound sentences*: A speaker who says 'If I won the lottery, I am a millionaire' would normally mean "I won the lottery" by the antecedent of the conditional he uttered. But he would normally not mean by uttering it that he won.

We will see many more cases in which these forms diverge as we go along.

The most important difference is that (9) says that S used e to *express the belief* that p, while (8) only says that S used e to express the *idea* or *thought* "p" (§2.1). Accordingly, I say that (9) expresses *cognitive* speaker meaning, while (8) expresses *cogitative* speaker meaning. Harris expressed the thought, not the belief, that Hitler fired a V-3 at New York. To the extent that an author is expressing beliefs in a literary work, it ceases to be a work of fiction. We use interrogative and imperative sentences to express thoughts—nonpropositional thoughts (§2.5)—but not beliefs. And we use individual words to express subpropositional ideas, but not beliefs.

A subtle difference is that the parenthetical insertions in (8) and (9) cannot be switched without either impropriety or a change of meaning. The novelist meant "The Führer sent a V-3 rocket to explode in the skies over New York

in 1946" *by the expression* 'The Führer ...', not *by saying* 'The Führer ...'.
On the other hand, S meant that Charlie is obese by saying 'Charlie is a sea
elephant', not by the expression 'Charlie is a sea elephant'. The term 'expression' here can be replaced by something more specific like 'words' and
'sentence', or by cognate terms like 'signal', 'sign', and 'gesture'. And 'saying' can be replaced by 'uttering', 'writing', 'declaring', 'signing', and so on.

Finally, the fact that (8) is *oratio recta* while (9) is *oratio obliqua* means
that we have to adjust for indexicals. When Steve said 'I cut myself', he
meant *that he cut himself*, assuming that he was using English normally. He
did not mean *that I cut myself*, since Steve cannot use the first person
pronoun to talk about me. But by the sentence 'I cut myself', Steve meant
"I cut myself" *not* "he cut himself".[6]

## 4.3   Cognitive Meaning and Implication

Cognitive speaker meaning has both an inclusive and an exclusive sense. In
the latter, meaning *excludes* implying. By 'It is necessary that 2+2=4' we
imply but do not mean that 2+2 equals 4. We mean rather than imply that
2+2 necessarily equals 4. By 'Bob's son is a thief', we mean rather than imply
that he is. We may imply but not mean: that Bob has a son; that Bob's son is
morally reprehensible; that we can back up our claim; and so on. Finally, a
student who says 'I have to study' in response to 'Do you want to go to the
movies?' implies, but does not mean, that he does not want to go. He means
rather than implies that he has to study.[7]

Implying that p also entails expressing the belief that p. When a student
says 'I have to study', he expresses both the belief that he has to study and the
belief that he does not want to go to the movies. Indeed, he expresses
the latter belief *by* expressing the former. Let us say that S *directly*
expresses the belief that p provided S expresses the belief that p but not
by expressing another belief. S expresses a belief *indirectly* if he does so by
expressing another belief. Then we use 'It is necessary that 2+2=4' to
directly express the belief that 2+2 necessarily equals 4, and to indirectly
express the belief that 2+2 equals 4. Whereas meaning in the exclusive sense
requires direct expression, implication requires indirect expression. Indeed,
meaning and implication are mutually exclusive and jointly exhaustive
species of expression.

In its inclusive sense, meaning *includes* implying, and involves the expression of belief either directly or indirectly. It would be natural in many
contexts to describe the student as having meant that he did not want to
go when he said 'I have to study'. When the subtle direct–indirect distinction
is unimportant, it would be impertinent to insist that the student implied,
but did not mean, that he did not want to go. The term 'means' is thus like
'animal', which has a general sense in which it applies to humans, and a

more specific sense in which it does not. 'Implies', in contrast, always connotes indirectness of expression.

Having noted the inclusive sense of 'means', we will henceforth focus on the exclusive. We will accordingly formulate our definitions as follows:

**4.1 Definition:** *S means that p iff S directly expresses the belief that p.*

**4.2 Definition:** *S implies that p iff S indirectly expresses the belief that p.*

The relationships we have defined can be illustrated by comparing and contrasting the standard uses of the following:

(10) It will rain.
(11) It will rain, I believe.
(12) I believe that it will rain.

All three sentences can be used to express both the belief that it will rain (R) and the belief that one believes it will rain (B). But the user of (10) typically expresses B by expressing R. Hence he means that it will rain, and implies that he believes it will rain. The typical user of (12), in contrast, expresses R by expressing B, and accordingly means that he believes it will rain, and implies that it will rain. The user of (11) does not express R by expressing B, nor B by expressing R. Hence he means both that it will rain and that he believes that it will rain. When the speaker uses (10) to express R but not B, then he neither means nor implies that he believes it will rain.[8]

What S means in the exclusive sense generally coincides with what S *said*.[9] In using (10), for example, we imply but do not say that we believe it will rain; what we say is that it will rain. In using (12), we imply but do not say that it will rain; what we say is that we believe it will rain. Exceptions arise when the speaker says something by mistake, either through a slip of the tongue or through linguistic ignorance. If Bill says 'Dr. Johnson is an etymologist', either because he thinks that 'etymologist' means "entomologist (insect scientist)", or because he intended to say 'entomologist' but the wrong word came out, then Bill said that Dr. Johnson is an etymologist ("word scientist") even though he neither meant nor implied this. He meant that Dr. Johnson is an entomologist even though he neither said nor implied that. What a speaker says is more closely connected to what his words mean than what he either meant or implied. *Asserting* that p requires both saying and meaning that p.

### 4.4 COGITATIVE SPEAKER MEANING (EXCLUSIVE)

In the cogitative form, 'mean' also has both an inclusive and an exclusive sense, although 'implied' has no cognate cogitative sense. Whether 'By (the expression) e, S meant "p"' has the exclusive or inclusive sense depends on whether 'the expression' (or a cognate term) is present or absent. In the exclusive sense, we can say that by *the sentence* 'Rockefeller is in hock', Steve meant "Rockefeller is in debt", not "Rockefeller is in great financial shape". In the inclusive sense, we can say that S meant "Rockefeller is in debt" by 'Rockefeller is in hock', and thereby meant "Rockefeller is in great financial shape". Pronouns and ellipses provide further examples. In the inclusive sense, Tanya might well mean "Edberg won the US Open" by 'He won'. But Tanya would not mean "Edberg won the US Open" by *the sentence* 'He won' unless she were speaking in a code. What speakers normally mean by the sentence 'He won' is just 'He won'. Whereas the exclusive sense is more closely tied to word meaning, the inclusive is closer to speaker reference (§7.3).

As in the cognitive case, the difference between the inclusive and exclusive senses depends on whether the expression may be indirect or not. We will focus on the exclusive sense. Let 'p' stand for a pronoun-free declarative sentence expressing a proposition. For this range of substitution instances, the definition of cogitative meaning goes like Definition 4.1, with thought replacing belief. Thoughts, of course, are ideas (Definition 3.1).

4.3  **Theorem**: *By (the expression) e S means "p" iff S directly expresses the idea or thought that p by producing e.*

Theorem 4.3 follows from Definitions 4.4, 3.9, and 3.10. When Steve uses 'Rockefeller is in hock' ironically, he expresses both the thought that Rockefeller is in debt *and* the thought that Rockefeller is in great financial shape. But he expresses the latter thought *by* expressing the former. So by the sentence 'Rockefeller is in hock', Steve meant "Rockefeller is in debt", not "Rockefeller is in great financial shape". In contrast, suppose Tanya is using a code in which 'hock' means "great financial shape", so that by the sentence 'Rockefeller is in hock' she means "Rockefeller is in great financial shape". Then Tanya is not using irony. This shows that irony is not simply the use of a sentence to mean the opposite of what the sentence means conventionally. Rather, irony is the use of a sentence to express one proposition directly in order to express a contrary proposition indirectly, so that cognitive speaker meaning is the opposite of cogitative (in the exclusive senses). The belief expressed is the opposite of what the speaker means by the sentence. Thus, if Tanya were to speak ironically in her code, she could use 'Rockefeller is in hock' to mean that Rockefeller is in debt!

The difference between 'dead' and 'live' metaphors turns on whether the speaker's thought is expressed indirectly. In a live metaphor like 'Charlie is a sea elephant', the speaker expresses the thought that Charlie is obese by expressing the thought that he is a certain sort of especially blubbery seal.

Hence S meant "Charlie is a certain sort of seal" rather than "Charlie is obese" by the sentence 'Charlie is a sea elephant'. When using a dead metaphor like 'There is a fork in the road', the speaker expresses the thought that there is a bifurcation in the road but not by expressing the thought that there is a pronged utensil in the road. The idea of such a utensil generally does not even cross the speaker's mind. Hence S means "There is a bifurcation in the road" rather than "There is a pronged utensil" by the words I uttered.

Even in the exclusive sense, cognitive speaker meaning allows more indirection than cogitative. As a result, direct expression must be defined more strictly for thought than for belief if Definition 4.1 and Theorem 4.3 are to give the correct results. A *belief* is expressed directly, we will say, if it is not expressed by expressing any other *belief*. This allows the belief to be expressed by expressing a mental state other than belief, such as thought. In the case of irony, as we have seen, Steve expressed the belief, and meant, that Rockefeller is in great financial shape by expressing the thought that he is in debt. A *thought* is expressed directly, in contrast, if it is not expressed by expressing any other *mental state*. Suppose that S answers 'Ow!' when asked 'How do you feel?' S expressed both the thought and the belief that he is in pain by expressing pain. Then by our stipulation, S expressed the belief directly, and the thought indirectly. Hence Theorem 4.3 correctly rules that S did not mean "I am in pain" by the one-word sentence 'Ow!' And Definition 4.1 correctly rules that S did mean that he is in pain by saying it. In Ziff's (1967) irritable academic example, George was compelled to take a moronic test designed to establish sanity. In response to 'What would you say if you were asked to identify yourself?' George replies 'Ugh ugh blugh blugh'. George expressed irritation and thereby expressed both the thought and the belief that the test is stupid. Since George directly expressed that belief, Definition 4.1 rules that George meant that the test was stupid. Since George did not directly express the thought, Theorem 4.3 rules that George did not mean "The test is stupid" by the words 'Ugh ugh blugh blugh'.

We have focused on instances of (8) in which 'p' is replaced by a declarative sentence. While the cognitive form (9) has no other instances, 'p' can be replaced by any grammatical and meaningful unit in the cogitative form (8). When 'p' is an interrogative, imperative, or performative sentence, we can still say that S means "p" provided S directly expressed a thought, the thought "p". But the thought in this case will be *nonpropositional* (§§2.5, 6.1). Thus S may directly express the thought "What time is it?" when he says '¿Que hora est?' The switch to the *oratio recta* mode of reference to the thoughts also allows sentences with pronouns to be accommodated. S means "I am sick" in virtue of expressing the thought "I am sick", which is the thought that he himself is sick, not the thought that I (Wayne Davis) am sick.

Finally, subsentential expressions can also replace 'p' in (8). Thus S means "female fox" in virtue of expressing the idea "female fox".

Since the practice of using 'p' to stand for declarative sentences is so well entrenched, we will switch to the variable '$\mu$' when we wish to allow subsentential and nondeclarative instances. Thus Theorem 4.3 can be generalized further to say that S meant "$\mu$" provided S directly expressed the *idea* (or *concept*) "$\mu$". The same range of expressions can follow 'means' as can follow 'idea' or 'concept'(see Table 3.1), and are used ideo-reflexively in both places (§3.7). Recall that '$\mu_i$' stands for instances of '$\mu$' that express i on that occasion. If f is the idea of a female fox, then 'means "vixen"' is a substitution instance of 'means "$\mu_f$"' on a given occasion only if 'vixen' expresses the idea of a female fox on that occasion. 'Means "female fox"' is also a substitution instance of 'means "$\mu_f$,"' assuming that 'female fox' has its salient English sense. If s is the idea of a shrewish woman, then 'means "vixen"' is a substitution instance of 'means "$\mu_s$"' on a given occasion only if 'vixen' expresses the idea of a shrewish woman on that occasion. 'Means "female fox"' could not be a substitution instance of 'means "$\mu_s$"' unless we are using a code of some sort. We can now use the following schema to define cogitative speaker meaning.

4.4   **Definition:** *By (the expression) e S means "$\mu_i$" iff S directly expresses i by producing e.*[10]

Thus Steve means "debt" by 'hock' iff Steve directly expressed the idea "debt" by producing 'hock', and so on for all replacements for the place-holder '$\mu_i$'. 'Directly' is defined for 'idea' as for thought: an idea is expressed directly provided it is not expressed by expressing any other mental state. It will be noticed that the meaning of the subscript in Definition 4.4 was given in terms of what a word expresses on a given occasion of use. No circularity results from this, since what a word expresses on an occasion, like speaker meaning and word meaning, is defined in terms of speaker expression, not speaker meaning (§5.3).

In the vast majority of cases, a speaker means something by an expression because he uses it to express an idea, and words mean something because they express ideas. But there are exceptions. Consider the standard use of an *interjection*, such as 'Ouch!' There is a marked semantic difference between 'Ouch!' and 'I am in pain!' even though both are used to express pain. If S expresses pain by saying 'I am in pain', he does so *by* expressing an idea, namely, the idea that he is in pain. But when S says 'Ouch!' in the typical manner, he appears to be expressing pain directly. He is normally not expressing the idea that he is in pain. There is, moreover, no other idea that he expressed directly. It is not true that S meant "Ouch!" iff S expressed the idea "Ouch!" Although S did mean "Ouch!", there is no such idea.

Definition 4.4 has been formulated to allow nonideational speaker meaning. We selected the letter 'i' as our variable because in the typical case what is expressed is an idea. But we have not stipulated that the range of 'i' is restricted to ideas. Definition 4.4 can perfectly well hold when i is some other type of mental state. Thus it might well be true that a Frenchman means "Ouch!" by 'Aïe!' because he used 'Aïe!' to express pain. I will argue later that things are more complicated than this, but the conclusion that 'Ouch!' has nonideational meaning will stand. Interjections, pejorative terms, and other cases of nonideational meaning will be discussed further in Chapter 6.

We are using the letter 'e' as the variable ranging over potential signifiers because linguistic expressions are its typical value. But 'e' should be interpreted without restriction as a general individual variable. It ranges over any action or object which an agent might or might not use to express something. We will similarly use the word 'produce' quite generally, so that we can be said to produce any gesture, hand signal, facial expression, noise, and mark by which we might mean something, as well as written or spoken words. We can produce e by saying, writing, performing, presenting, or making e.

### 4.5 EXPRESSION

Expression is like meaning in having speaker, word, and evidential senses, related in roughly the same ways. The first and most obvious difference concerns the subject to which the predicate 'express' applies. In the speaker sense, the term applies to a person or other animate object, and does so in virtue of the person's saying or doing something. In the other two senses, the term 'express' applies to inanimate objects like words or facial expressions, and not in virtue of their doing or saying anything themselves. Second, 'x expressed fear' entails 'x expressed *himself*' in the speaker sense, but words and facial expressions cannot express themselves. Third, 'x expresses fear' entails 'x is an expression' only in the non-speaker senses. The look on S's face is an expression, and the word 'fear' is another sort of expression. But S himself is not an expression in any sense, although his utterance of 'I'm afraid' may be an expression of fear in the evidential sense. The further distinction between word and evidential expression is marked by 'of' and 'for'. An utterance or a fearful look is an expression *of* fear, whereas the word 'fear' is an expression *for* fear.

A theoretically important difference concerns intentionality. To express fear in the speaker sense is to do something intentionally. Looks and words, on the other hand, cannot act intentionally. More significantly, facial expressions of emotion are typically involuntary manifestations of the emotion. And what the words in any language express is not dependent on the intentions of any particular speaker.

There are many connections between what words express and what speakers use the words to express. Thus the word 'fear' expresses the idea of fear because speakers of English have conventionally used the word to express that idea. And I may use the word 'fear' to express the idea of fear because that is what the word expresses. But speaker expression and word expression often differ radically. By a suitable stipulation, Steve could use the word 'fear' to express the idea of happiness. And many English sentences express thoughts even though no one has ever actually used the sentences to express those thoughts. Because individual usage can differ from conventional usage, languages change over time as new uses catch on, and old uses become archaic.

I will introduce the definition of speaker expression by focusing on the special case of expressing ideas. Definition 4.6 will have the following consequence.

4.5 **Theorem**: *S expresses idea i iff S performs an observable act as an indication of i, without thereby covertly simulating an unintentional indication of i.*

The key idea is that whether S expresses the idea "airplane" or "wood plane" when S utters 'plane' depends on whether S *intends* his utterance to be an *indication* of the idea of an airplane, or of the idea of a wood plane. The utterance of 'entomology' is normally an indication that the speaker is thinking of the study of insects. But if S misspeaks, and intends his utterance to be a sign that he is thinking of the study of word origins, then S expressed the idea "etymology" despite what 'entomology' means. Similarly, the act of buying car insurance is an extremely good indication that the agent is thinking the thought that there is a risk of an accident. But the purchase is seldom, if ever, intended as an indication that that or any other thought is occurring to the agent. So it would be highly unusual if the speaker expressed the thought "There is a risk of an accident" by buying insurance.

Expression requires doing something that is publicly observable. No matter what it indicates, or is intended to indicate, saying something *to oneself* does not count as *expressing oneself*. It might, though, if people someday acquire the ability to 'read minds', at least to the extent of detecting inner speech.

Providing an indication of the thoughts one is thinking need not be the speaker's *main* or *primary* intention. And there is no requirement that the speaker's intentions result from deliberation or self-reflection. People generally speak, and express their thoughts, with remarkable spontaneity.

The prohibition clause excludes certain cases in which the speaker provides an observable indication of a thought but cannot be said to have expressed the thought. Thus suppose Stu tastes a new dish prepared by a friend, and immediately contorts his face and spits it out in an attempt to perfectly fake a reflexive response and make his friend think he found the dish to be awful. He is simulating an unintentional response to foul-tasting food. His simulation is covert in the sense that Stu is not letting his friend know that his response is a simulation. Because the simulation is disguised, we cannot say that Stu has expressed the thought that the food is awful. If Stu gave the same act as an answer to the question 'How is the food?' then the simulation would be overt, and Stu would count as having expressed the thought that the food is awful. The prohibition clause will not be important in any of the developments below.

Theorem 4.5 can be generalized into a definition of speaker expression as follows. Let '$\Psi$' stand for terms expressing introspectively applicable concepts.

4.6 **Definition:** *S expresses $\Psi$ iff S performs an observable act as an indication of occurrent $\Psi$ without thereby covertly simulating an unintentional indication of $\Psi$.*[11]

Since thoughts are necessarily occurrent, to provide an indication of a thought is to provide an indication that it is occurring to us. The same goes for sensations like pain and emotions like fear. But belief and other propositional attitudes need not be occurrent. We can believe that penguins swim even when it is not occurring to us that penguins swim. Nevertheless, we cannot express this belief without expressing the thought that penguins swim. Definition 4.6 secures this result by requiring that the speaker intend to provide an indication that he is occurrently believing that penguins swim, that he both believes and is thinking that proposition. Terms that do not meet the restriction on '$\Psi$' include 'the knowledge that p' and 'an unconscious desire for $\Phi$'. We can provide indications that we have them, but we cannot be said to express knowledge or unconscious desires. The definition accommodates the expression of propositions given our definition of propositions as thoughts.

Definition 4.6 holds straightforwardly for emotions such as joy and fear, and distinguishes expression from evincing and coping.[12] Evincing an emotion, as when we turn red in anger, differs from expressing one in being an involuntary effect of the emotion. Coping is intentional behavior, but is aimed at dealing with the object of the emotion in some way, or at controlling the emotion itself. The definition also accounts for the distinction between emotive and descriptive expression.[13] A woman who says 'You bastard!' expresses anger but not the belief that she is angry, while one who says 'I am angry' expresses anger *by* expressing the belief that she is angry. Definition 4.6 allows insincere expression because one can provide an indication that one has a mental state that in fact one does not have, as when one lies or feigns anger.[14] The expressive act cannot, in such cases, be either a manifestation or an evidential expression, of the state.

Definitions 4.1 and 4.6 imply, of course, that S means that p only if S undisguisedly conveyed the occurrent belief that p, where 'undisguisedly' abbreviates the no covert simulation clause. Since the exclusive sense of speaker meaning requires direct expression, we have:

4.7 **Theorem:** *S meant that p by (producing) e iff S produced e as a direct and undisguised indication that he occurrently believes p.*

According to Grice's (1957) classic analysis, meaning that p is defined as intending to produce the belief that p in one's audience by means of recognition of intention.[15] To mean that the sky is blue, on Grice's view, I have to intend to make you believe that the sky is blue by getting you to recognize that I have that intention. Grice's analysis is much too strong, and numerous counterexamples can be found in the voluminous literature.[16] A student can mean that World War II ended in 1945 without intending to produce that belief in the teacher. Someone who sends an unsigned note to the police can mean that he is going to kill the children he has kidnaped unless his terms are met, without intending the police to recognize who he is or what his real intentions are. Most radically, people can speak and mean things without having an audience that can recognize anything. People often talk to their babies, and the dead, and mean what they say. The fundamental defect of the Gricean analysis is that it is *audience-oriented*. Many speech acts do require an audience, such as *communicating*, *telling*, and *informing*. We cannot tell, for example, unless we tell someone, and cannot communicate unless we communicate something to someone. But meaning, implying, and expressing are different, as are saying, signaling, and indicating. 'S meant something' does not require, or even allow, completion by 'to . . . .'. Meaning cannot be identified with the attempt to communicate, even though communication is the social function that sustains the conventions that create word meaning in living languages (see Chapter 5). On my view, cognitive speaker meaning is the attempt to produce an indication of belief, in a certain way. Since indicators do not require an audience, the real or perceived absence of one does not prevent meaningful speech. While we might occasionally wonder why, speakers without audiences sometimes do make sounds intended to indicate beliefs. Husserl's (1900: 279) view that an indication is necessarily an indication *to* someone is false. A patient's symptoms may indicate that he has Lyme disease even though no one realizes that they do.

## 4.6 COMMUNICATION

Given Grice's assumption that meaning is the attempt to communicate, his definition of speaker meaning implies that to communicate the belief that p is to produce the belief that p in one's audience by means of recognition of intention. While the shift to communication eliminates many problems, the Gricean analysis is still too strong. S can communicate a belief to A: even though A's recognition that S intends to produce that belief plays no role in its production, as when shouting 'I am here' in a crowd; without producing it in any way, as when accusing one's spouse of lying or proclaiming one's innocence in the face of incriminating evidence; and while producing exactly the opposite belief in A, as in cases of countersuggestion and extreme mistrust. The Gricean analysis of communication is also too weak. We can make A believe something by sending her a message that we know she will misinterpret.

For S to communicate the belief that p to A, A must recognize that S means or implies p. That is, A must understand S. Whether A goes on to believe p or anything else, and how A arrives at her belief if she does, is irrelevant to whether communication has occurred.[17] Our definition of communication will yield 4.8 as a theorem.

4.8    **Theorem**: *S communicates the belief that p to A iff S means (or implies) that p and is understood by A.*

Besides our beliefs, we can communicate our thoughts, desires, intentions, hopes, fears, and emotions—anything we can express. The novelist who writes 'A V-3 exploded over New York' was not communicating a belief because he was writing fiction. He did, however, *express the thought* that a V-3 exploded over New York, as his readers recognized. By yelling 'Yahoo!', S can spontaneously communicate his happiness without communicating the belief that he is happy. As the *American Heritage Dictionary* puts it, communication is *'effective expression'*. To communicate is to express oneself in such a way that one is understood. To generalize 4.8, let 'M' be an individual variable ranging over 'pure' mental states, including the belief that $2 + 2 = 4$, but not the knowledge that $2 + 2 = 4$ (which entails a fact about numbers as well as a belief) or John's belief that $2 + 2 = 4$ (which entails that John has the belief).

4.9    **Definition**: *S communicates M to A iff S does something by which S expresses M and from which A recognizes that S is expressing M.*

Definition 4.9 allows that S may communicate something to A without even trying to; indeed, while trying not to. Consequently, A need not recognize, or even believe, that S intends to communicate anything to her, as when S sends a secret radio transmission that is intercepted, or insults A in a language he mistakenly believes A does not understand.[18] This feature of our analysis may appear implausible; S cannot be described as having *communicated with* A in either case. But communicating *with* A involves more than merely communicating something *to* A.

Griceans have emphasized the '*overtness*' of communication.[19] The requirement that S intend the audience to recognize his intentions was designed to express part of this feature. While almost as inessential for communicating something to an audience as for meaning, overtness does seem required for communicating with an audience. The above examples suggest, though, that communication *with* A requires *intentionally* communicating something *to* A.

4.10   **Definition**: *S communicates with A iff S intentionally communicates something to A.*

Given Definition 4.9, this would imply that communicating with A entails intending A to recognize what one means, which is partly a matter of what one intends. Since communicating with A is stronger than communicating something to A, the suggestion that the former requires intending to do the latter does not produce a circular analysis, entail an infinite regress of intentions, or make the intention to communicate in any way 'reflexive'.

It is often suggested that to communicate something is to *transmit* it to someone else.[20] The transmission model certainly fits electronic communication, in which a sender transmits an electronic signal to a receiver. The transmission idea also applies to the markedly different sense in which people communicate diseases, as well as that in which actions or other events communicate information. If S communicates a disease to A, A gets the disease from S. And the sound of the engine communicates to the mechanic the information that the valves need adjustment only if the sound carries that information and the mechanic gets the information from the sound.[21] The transmission idea even fits the communication of thoughts by speakers. When a speaker communicates the thought that it is a nice day, he has the thought and expresses it, typically in words. The hearer hears the words, 'decodes' them, and winds up having the thought herself.

The transmission model loses all plausibility, however, when we examine the communication by speakers of mental states other than occurrent thought. Imagine a known liar telling you that your son cheated. The liar communicated the belief that your son cheated. Yet he did not have the belief to begin with (since he was lying), and you did not end up with it (since you knew he was lying). So transmission of a belief is not necessary for communication. It is also insufficient. My belief that it will rain may cause me to carry an umbrella, which causes you to inform your husband that it will rain. It does not follow that I communicated to you the belief that it will rain. Transmission is similarly irrelevant to the communication of desires, intentions, and emotions. The special character of the case of thought is due to the impossibility of expressing a thought without thinking that thought. With some exceptions for indexical thoughts, the same goes for recognizing that someone else is expressing a thought. It is very easy, in contrast, to express a belief, desire, or emotion (or recognize that another is doing so) without having that belief, desire, or emotion.

Informing is a special case of communication in which the speaker transmits knowledge and information to the hearer. The communication of information to a speaker does not result in informing the speaker unless the hearer comes to accept the information as true. Informing involves causing the informed to acquire knowledge. It is thus possible to communicate the same information over and over again, whereas it is not possible to inform the same person over and over again (unless she is very forgetful). More specifically still, S informed A that p only if A learned that p from the fact that S intended to communicate the information that p to A. Of all the semantic acts we have looked at, informing best fits the Gricean analysis.[22]

Even though we have distinguished speaker meaning from communication, we will nonetheless go on to affirm in Chapter 5 that communication plays an important role in word meaning, as the common interest that sustains the conventions in virtue of which words have meaning. The use of words to express certain ideas is conventional, moreover, only when they are conventionally used to communicate them. So the idea that word meaning in living languages depends on communication in some way will be upheld.

## Notes

[1] This chapter summarizes Chapters 2 through 5 of *Meaning, Expression, and Thought*.

[2] Evidential signifiers are Peirce's 'indexes', symbolic signifiers his 'symbols'. See Peirce 1931–35: 2.247, 2.248, 2.307; Burks 1949; and Alston 1964a: 55–6. Cf. Meinong 1910: 23 and Husserl 1900: 269–73. The third element of Peirce's famous trichotomy were not speakers but 'icons', illustrated by schematic diagrams and pictures. We will ignore icons because they cannot be said to mean or signify what they represent.

[3] Cf. Black 1972–3: §7; Dummett 1973: 149; McKinsey 1978: 191–2; Harrison 1980: 193; Skulsky 1986: 593; Pettit 1987: 729; Laurence 1996: 285–6, 292–6. Contrast H. H. Clark 1983, 1993.

[4] See also Augustine *On Christian Doctrine*, Chs. 2.1–2.2; Arnauld 1662: 47; and Reid 1764: §4.2, §5.3.

[5] I am indebted here to Mark Siebel and Christian Plunze.

[6] This was observed by S. Davis 1994 in the case of word meaning. I discuss this property of certain indexicals in *Indexicals*.

[7] 'Indirect speech acts' (Austin 1962: 129; Searle 1969: 65; 1979: 30–57; Tormey 1971: 70; Holdcroft 1978: 61–3; Carr 1978a; Fasold 1990: 152–7; Chierchia and McConnell-Ginet 1990: 161) provide numerous examples of the contrast between meaning and implication, as do 'presuppositions' (Bach and Harnish 1979: 155–72), other 'implicatures' (Grice 1975; Martinich 1984a: Ch. 4; Chierchia and McConnell-Ginet 1990: 187–203; Davis 1998), and the referential use of definite descriptions (McKinsey 1978: 177).

[8] Cf. M. S. Green 2000. And see below, §6.4. There are additional contrasts, of course. For example, (10) is typically used to express certainty about rain, while (11) is typically used to express uncertainty; (12) may be used without implying certainty or uncertainty about rain.

[9] Cf. Neale's (1992: 520) tentative exegesis of Grice's notion of the 'total signification' of an utterance. In at least one place, Grice does explicitly state that S's saying that p entails S's meaning that p (1989: 87). He suggests the view in 1968: 227–9 and 1989: 120–1 without endorsing it, and omitted even the suggestion from the original version of 'Utterer's Meaning and Intention' (1969a). See also Neale (1992: 554). I am indebted to Jennifer Saul for bringing these passages in Grice to my attention. See Saul 2001, 2002.

[10] As explained more fully in §2.9, '$\mu_i$' is a substitutional variable in Definition 4.4, whereas 'e' and 'i' are individual variables. All three are bound by implicit universal quantifiers of the appropriate type: substitutional for '$\mu_i$', objectual for 'e' and 'i'. A substitution instance of a form containing '$\mu_i$' is obtained by uniformly replacing '$\mu_i$' with any of its permissible substituends: any English expression expressing i, or a constant stipulated to express i.

[11] As explained in §2.8, we are taking '$\Psi$' to occupy an *opaque* context on both sides of Definition 4.6. But either side can be given a transparent interpretation. Thus if S has expressed the belief that God exists, then there is a sense in which S has expressed Frank's favorite belief. Definition 4.6 can appear to fail if we equivocate and give one side an opaque interpretation and the other a transparent interpretation.

[12] Cf. Benson 1967: 339–40; Koch 1983; and Davis 1988: §4.

[13] This is discussed by Meinong 1910: 25–7; Alston 1965; Benson 1967: 336, 338, 347–9; O. H. Green 1970: 563–5; Tormey 1971: 7; Black 1972–73: 262–3; and Wierzbicka 1992b: 162–3. See also §6.3.

[14] 'S expressed *his* belief that p' differs from 'S expressed *the* belief that p' in presupposing that S does believe that p. The former should be interpreted as meaning something like "S expressed the belief that p (which he possesses)".

[15] See Grice 1957, 1968, 1969a, 1982, 1986, 1989. For a precursor, see Hart 1952: 62. Grice's basic approach has been picked up by Strawson 1964, 1971; Stampe 1968; Patton and Stampe 1969; Searle 1969, 1979; 1983, 1986; Armstrong 1971; Bennett 1971, 1973, 1976; Schiffer 1972, 1982, 1987a, 1992; Facione 1972, 1973; Walker 1975: 155; Kempson 1975: 138; Holdcroft 1978; Platts 1979; Schwarz 1979: xxxi–iv; Loar 1976a, 1976b, 1981; Martinich 1984; Blackburn 1984; Suppes 1986; Avramides 1989; 1997: §§6–7; Chierchia and McConnell-Ginet 1990: 148–57; Neale 1992: §5; Meggle 1997. The Gricean approach has been taken in somewhat different directions in Lewis 1969; Vendler 1972: 62–3; Schwarz 1979: Chs. 2–4; Bach and Harnish 1979; Hungerland and Vick 1981; Kemmerling 1986; Sperber and Wilson 1986; Recanati 1986, 1987; Bach 1987a, 1987b, 1994a, 1994b; Devitt and Sterelny 1987: §7.4; Bertolet 1987; Thomason 1990: 342–4; Schiffrin 1994; S. Neale 1997: 429; and Christensen 1997: 506. A similar view was developed by Anton Marty (1908), a student of Brentano. See Liedtke 1990.

[16] See *Meaning, Expression, and Thought*, Ch. 4, for a full survey, and for discussion of the few extant alternatives to the Gricean approach.

[17] Cf. Black 1972: 270–1; Schiffer 1972: 121; Fodor 1975: 103–8; Bach and Harnish 1979: 23, 31, 154; Martinich 1984: 19; Searle 1986: 212–18; Recanati 1986: 239; and Forbes 1989a: 469.

[18] Contrast Bach and Harnish 1979: xv–xvi; Taylor 1980: 299; McDowell 1980: 130; Martinich 1984: 19; Davidson 1986: 169; Recanati 1987: 32; and Christensen 1997: 507. Compare and contrast Gilbert 1996: 251.

[19] Cf. Strawson 1964: 446–7, 454, 460; Bach and Harnish 1979: 5–8, 84–5, 152–4; McDowell 1980: 128–30; Blackburn 1984: 114–18; Martinich 1984: 115–22; Sperber and Wilson 1986: 30–1, 60–1; Kemmerling 1986: 147; Recanati 1986: 226–34, 238–9; Bertolet 1987: 205; and Avramides 1989: 50–5. See also §4.5 above.

[20] See, for example, *Webster's Encyclopedic Unabridged Dictionary*; Augustine *On Christian Doctrine*: Ch. 2.2; Bentham 1843: 329; Katz 1966: 98, 103–4; Bennett 1971: 1–2; 1976: 127–71; Barwise and Perry 1983: 120; Martinich 1984: 10; as well as Sperber and Wilson's (1986:

Ch.1) exposition and critique of the 'Code Model', Schiffrin's (1994: Ch. 11) discussion of three models of communication, and Tormey's (1971) discussion of the 'expression theory' in art. Contrast Bach 1994b: 11; Peacocke 1997: 15.

[21] See Dretske 1981.

[22] I define informing, distinguishing it from telling, communicating, and meaning, in Davis 1999.

# 5
# Word Meaning

Having defined speaker meaning in terms of expression, and expression in terms of intention and indication, we now turn our attention to defining word meaning in terms of speaker meaning and expression. We will first look at what a language is, since words mean different things in different languages. We will then provide a recursive definition of word meaning, or equivalently, word expression. In the basic case, individual words and idioms have meaning because of what they are conventionally used to mean. The key is to look at conventions governing cogitative rather than cognitive speaker meaning, and abandoning the thesis that word meaning has to be defined in terms of sentence meaning. The recursion clause is provided by the fact that word structures are conventionally used to express certain idea structures, which is the basis of compositionality. Finally, we will look at the way in which what words mean today in living languages is dependent on the conventions that evolve from those of prior users of the language, and at how words get their meaning in artificial languages.[1]

## 5.1 LANGUAGES

David Lewis (1975) distinguished *languages* from *language*. Languages are things like French, German, and English. French is *a* language, but is not language itself. Language is a human activity, in which languages are used. It includes speech, writing, and other types of symbol use. While linguists and philosophers sometimes debate as to which is primary, it should be clear that languages and language are complementary subjects.[2] The most important fact about languages for us is that word meaning may vary from language to language. 'Cap' means "cap" in English, "cape" in French. 'Coeur' means in French what 'heart' means in English.

Given the view that meaning consists in the expression of ideas and other mental states, it is natural to suggest that languages are ordered n-tuples whose first elements are expressions and whose second elements are ideas. While such relations provide a good *model* of languages, they cannot be identified with languages themselves. For one thing, the converse relation, whose first elements are ideas and second elements expressions, provides an equally good model, but there is no reason to think that one rather than the other is the language. We can say that languages are *systematic ways of expressing ideas and other mental states.* To learn, teach, use, or create a language is to learn, teach, use or create a systematic way of expressing ideas. Languages arise and change as systems of expression arise and change.

I use 'mode of expression' as a technical term to denote *the use of a particular expression to express a particular idea or other mental state.* A mode of expression is direct or indirect depending on whether the idea is expressed directly or indirectly. Modes of expression are not only ways of expressing ideas but also ways of using expressions. Expressing the idea of red by using 'red' is as much a way of using 'red' as it is a way of expressing the idea of red. For every mode of expression there is a unique ordered pair whose first element is an expression and second element an idea (or other mental element). Hence ⟨the word 'red', the idea ″red″⟩ represents a mode of expression.[3] Whereas ⟨e,i⟩ and ⟨i,e⟩ are different ordered pairs, using e to express i and expressing i by using e are one and the same mode of expression. Languages may now be defined as systems of modes of expression.

5.1  **Definition**: *A language L is any system of modes of expression.*

Since a mode of expression can be represented by an ordered pair ⟨e,i⟩, a language can be represented by a language model. The set of expression-idea pairs representing a natural language is not a *function*, because of the phenomenon of ambiguity. 'Bank' is ambiguous in English because it means several different things—that is, it expresses more than one idea.[4] Each mode of expression ⟨e,i⟩ in a language L represents a *rule* specifying that it is permissible in L to use e to express i and mean $″\mu_i″$. Indeed, we could use sets of such rules as our language state models, with only a loss of some convenience.[5]

The concept of a mode of expression is defined in terms of *speaker* expression. A mode of expression is a way of expressing an idea or other mental state, that is, a way for a speaker to express something. We define word expression in terms of speaker expression by defining it in terms of mode of expression. Let 'e' and 'i' be general individual variables. The former will generally occur in formulas where terms referring to expressions would occur, and the latter where terms referring to ideas would occur, but we will not stipulate a restrictive range for these variables.

5.2  **Definition**: *e expresses i in L iff using e to directly express i is one mode of expression in L.*

While Definition 5.2 does define word expression in terms of speaker expression, it does not answer the fundamental question which began our inquiry. It sheds no light, for example, on what it is for the word 'red' to express the idea "red" in English. Definition 5.2 does tell us that to answer the fundamental question, we need to identify what makes it true that the use of 'red' to directly express the idea of red is one mode of expression in English. We will answer that question in the remainder of this chapter.

In English, 'express' is ambiguous when applied to words and other expressions. There is an inclusive sense in which 'vixen' expresses the idea of a fox and the idea of a female, as well as the idea of a female fox. And there is a stronger, exclusive sense in which 'vixen' expresses only the idea of a female fox. In the exclusive sense, it is 'fox' rather than 'vixen' that expresses the idea of a fox. Definition 5.2 defines the exclusive sense of word expression, and that is the one we will use throughout.

It is customary to refer to L, the language we are studying, as the *object language*. The language we are using to describe L is the *metalanguage*. The metalanguage in this work is obviously English—augmented by technical terms and modified by restrictive stipulations. The object language will usually be English, but not always. When there is no explicit reference to a language, the implicit reference is to the language that is the contextually indicated object of discussion.

5.3   **Definition**: *e expresses i iff e expresses i in the object language.*

In other words, 'e expresses i' *simpliciter* makes an indexical reference to the language under discussion. Hence we say "'Hood' expresses the idea of the engine covering", with no explicit reference to a language, when we wish to say that 'hood' expresses the idea of the engine covering in the language we are talking about. The statement is accordingly true when the object language is American English, false when it is British English. This holds whether American English is our metalanguage, or British English.

In defining languages as systems of expression, I am not denying that words are used to perform actions other than expression. It is undeniable, for example, that 'Hello!' is used to greet people and 'Go home!' to order people home. 'It is going to rain' is used to assert, predict, and warn that it is going to rain. What I am assuming is that in all such cases, we use words to perform actions by using them to directly express ideas or other mental states. It would be easy enough to define languages as modes of use, the bulk of which are modes of expression. But while theoretical options are available, I believe expression is the fundamental form of language use. Reasons for believing this even in the case of words like 'Hello!' will be presented in Chapter 6.

Natural languages exhibit great *variation* at any given time, and have distinct regional and social varieties called *dialects*. Thus American English and British English are dialects of English. In addition to differences in spelling and pronunciation, hundreds of words have different meanings in the two dialects, such as 'bonnet' and 'hood'. Black American English and Midwestern American English differ in grammar as well, with sentences like 'He thinking about it' and 'The teachers don't be knowing the problems' acceptable in the former but not the latter (Fasold 1990: 208). Chinese has dialects such as Cantonese and Mandarin that are mutually unintelligible except in writing.

It should be emphasized that dialects are themselves languages: 'is a dialect of' expresses a relation between two languages. Both American English and English are systems assigning meanings to expressions. Furthermore, I use the term 'dialect' descriptively, to denote any variant of a given language, with no connotation that the variant is in any way substandard. Given Definition 5.1, the relation between a language and its dialects is the relation between a system and its subsystems, that is, between a whole and its parts. The use of 'hood' to mean "top of a car" is part of British English but not American English, while the use of 'hood' to mean "engine covering" is part of American English but not British English. The set-theoretical model of a language is the *union* of the models of all its dialects, which are its model's *subsets*. The ordered pair ⟨'hood', the idea of the top of a car⟩ is in the model representing British English but not American English, while ⟨'hood', the idea of the engine covering⟩ is in the model representing American English but not British. Both are in the model representing English.

British English and American English are not dialects of each other. Instead, they are dialects of a common and more inclusive language. Two languages *overlap* to the extent that they share ways of expressing ideas. American English and British English overlap almost completely, while Cantonese and Mandarin Chinese overlap only in writing. It is important to note that there need be no *linguistic* reason why one language is considered a dialect of a second rather than a third. For example, Low German is a dialect of German despite being more similar linguistically to certain dialects of Dutch than to some other dialects of German.[6] It is also hard to see much difference between dialects and *styles* or *registers*, except that one and the same individual switches from style to style as the occasion demands, no matter what dialect he or she speaks (Labov 1970: Ch. 3). There are numerous differences in pronunciation, vocabulary, and grammar depending on whether the style is formal or informal. 'Going to' is pronounced 'gonna', contractions and slang are permitted, and 'tick off' is used to mean "make angry", only in informal English. Styles are situational rather than regional or class variations.

Languages are also capable of *change*, which is variation over time. They are temporally extended systems. Natural languages change constantly (if slowly) with regard to vocabulary, grammar, and meaning. They have an origin, and eventually evolve into other languages or become extinct. Between the eleventh and fourteenth centuries, the distinction between the nominative and the oblique cases disappeared in French, and the final 's' came to be the mark of the plural (Lyons 1971: 47). At one time 'I've' meant "female horse" in French, later 'cavale' had this meaning, and today 'jument' does. 'Jument' at one time meant "pack horse" before coming to mean "female horse" (Anttila 1989: 134). Words are constantly added to one language by 'borrowing' them from neighboring languages, or from classical sources such as Latin or Greek. The etymology of a word traces its origins. According to *Webster's Encyclopedic Unabridged Dictionary*, the modern English word 'disease' came from the Old English 'disese', which derived from the Old French 'disaise' ('dis' + 'ease'). More globally, Old English changed into Middle English. French, Italian, Spanish, Portuguese, and Romanian all descended from Latin. Language *families*, such as the Romance languages just mentioned, are groups of languages with a common origin, as are dialects of a language.

While languages change, and wholes change their parts, sets of ordered pairs do not. Sets of expression-idea pairings therefore model *language states* rather than languages. Languages as temporally extended systems may be modeled by *functions from times (or time intervals) to language state models*. The description of languages at a particular time is called 'synchronic' description, and is the task of descriptive linguistics. The description of languages as they change over time is called 'diachronic' description, and is the subject of historical linguistics. Genetic, or comparative, linguistics studies the evolution of similar languages from common ancestors.

Finally, languages exhibit 'modal variation'. Natural languages *might have been different* from the way they actually are; they might have evolved in a different way. Thus language models must be functions from times *and possible worlds* to sets of expression-idea pairings. Definition 5.2 should be understood as having an implicit quantification over times and possible worlds. That is, 5.2 is short for *e expresses i in L(t,w) iff using e to directly express i is one mode of expression in L(t,w)*. Other references to L in this chapter should be understood similarly. We will normally be concerned with the present time and the actual world.

## 5.2   WORD MEANING AND EXPRESSION

What a word means in a language can be defined in terms of what it expresses in that language. As in Chapters 2 and 3, let '$\mu$' be a place-holder for the ideo-reflexive expressions that can follow 'means' and 'idea' (see Table 3.1). Let '$\mu_i$' be a more specific place-holder standing for linguistic units expressing i at the place '$\mu_i$' occupies in a formula. Definition 5.4 uses these conventions to define word meaning in terms of expression.

5.4 **Definition:** *e means "$\mu_i$" (in L) iff e expresses i (in L)*.

Thus a word *means* "red" in English iff it *expresses the idea* "red" in English. 'Rot' means "red" in German because it expresses the idea of red in German. 'C'est rouge' means "That is red" in French because 'C'est rouge' expresses the idea (thought, proposition) "That is red" in French.

Definition 5.4 is intended to hold when the parenthetical material is absent as well as when it is present, so it follows that what an expression means *simpliciter* is what it means in the object language. Thus *'Rot' means "red"* must be counted as false when we are describing English, even though 'rot' means "red" in German. When German is the object language, the same sentence is true. Of course, since the metalanguage usually is the object language—we are normally most interested in the properties of the language we are using—it is also true that 'e means "$\mu$"' is normally true when e expresses the idea "$\mu$" in the metalanguage.

We can go on to say that two expressions mean the same thing in a language (they are *synonymous*) if the language assigns them the same idea, and that one word means two different things (it is *ambiguous*) if the language assigns it two different ideas. The word means something, has a meaning, and is *meaningful*, if it expresses something. *The meaning of e is "$\mu$"* if "$\mu$" is what e means, i.e. if the idea "$\mu$" is expressed by e. We say that the meaning of 'rot' is "red", for example, because 'rot' means "red". The meaning of e is a compositional function of the meaning of its parts if the idea expressed by e is composed of the ideas expressed by its parts (§5.6). None of this requires holding that ideas are meanings, or that 'means' is a relational predicate. When e means "$\mu$", the meaning e *has* can be identified with the feature e has of meaning "$\mu$". Given Definition 5.4, meaning "$\mu_i$" is the property of expressing i. Hence the meaning "rot" has is not the idea it expresses, but the feature it has of expressing that idea. Like the word 'content' applied to ideas, 'meaning' and its synonym 'sense' thus have something akin to the act-object ambiguity. In either sense, however, *it is a category mistake to say that ideas are meanings or senses.*[7] Thought parts are neither what words mean nor properties of words. The most we can do is identify what words mean (meanings in the object sense) with the content of ideas (in the parallel sense). Thus "female fox" is what 'vixen' means, and it is the content of the idea "vixen".

We are focusing on the overwhelmingly typical case in which words have meaning because they express ideas. As in the case of speaker meaning (§4.4), interjections are exceptions. Definition 5.4 holds even for nonideational meaning because we have not stipulated that 'i' must denote an idea. *'Aïe!' means "Ouch!" in French* is true as long as 'Aïe!' expresses the mental state in French that we are using 'Ouch!' to express in English. While 'Ouch!' does not express an idea, it is used to express at least one mental state, namely pain. Interjections will be discussed more fully in §6.3.

### 5.3   APPLIED WORD MEANING

The notion of what a word means *here*, or *on a given occasion*, is distinct from, though related to, that of what a word means in a given language.[8] Roughly put, the meaning of an expression on a given occasion is the sense the speaker intended it to have on that occasion. More accurately, applied word meaning is the coincidence of linguistic word meaning and cogitative speaker meaning.

5.5   **Definition**: *e means "μ" on o iff (i) S means "μ" by e on o, and (ii) e means "μ" in the language S is using on o.*

Suppose S is using English on the occasion we are interested in, and says 'John bought a car', meaning "automobile" rather than "rail car" by 'car'. Later, S says 'The locomotive is pulling thirty cars', meaning "rail car" rather than "automobile". The next day, S transmits 'Five cars arrived' in a secret code in which 'car' means "light cruiser", so that he means "Five light cruisers arrived". Then on the first occasion, 'car' meant "automobile", on the second occasion it meant "rail car", and on the third it meant "light cruiser".

Typically, when e means "μ" on a given occasion, the speaker intended e to mean "μ" on that occasion (cf. Wilson and Sperber 1981: 156). But 'S intended e to mean "μ" on o' cannot replace 'S means "μ" by e on o' without rendering Definition 5.5 circular. Such a replacement would also make the definition too strong, for a word may well mean something on a given occasion even though the speaker is too young or to unreflective to have acquired the concept of applied word meaning.

We say that an ambiguous expression is *ambiguous on a given occasion* when the speaker means both things (*double entendre*), or when we cannot figure out what the speaker meant. If Steve said 'I bought a car at Sheehy Ford', and it is perfectly clear that Steve meant "automobile" by 'car', then the word was not ambiguous on that occasion even though it is ambiguous in English. Definition 5.5 entails that a word has no meaning on a given occasion if the word means nothing in the language S is using (as when he utters a nonsense word), or if the speaker means nothing by it (as when he is just testing his voice). A special case of the latter arises when a word is not even used on an occasion. We might be able to conjecture what the word 'plane' *would* have meant on an occasion if someone *had* used it, but the claim that it *does* mean something then implies that the speaker did use it. "What does 'plane' mean on this line?" has a presupposition that can be rejected by observing that it does not occur on that line.

Words often have different meanings in different languages. Definition 5.5 says that the relevant language is the one the speaker is *using* on the given occasion. To use a language, the speaker must be using some words of the language, and using them to mean what they mean in the language. A speaker who does not utter a word of English is not using English. He may understand English, and have the ability to use it; but he is not actually using it himself. The speaker must use the words and constructions to express what they express in the language. A person who says things like 'Ball if saw and' is using English words but not speaking English. A cryptographer who said 'The cat is on the mat', but meant "Enemy submarines have surfaced", used an English sentence but did not use English. Using a language does not require the speaker to use the whole language, and could not given human finitude and the productivity of languages. On the contrary, the speaker might use only one word of the language. Thus S can use Spanish by answering 'Dos' to the question 'How many brothers do you have?' It is also unnecessary for the speaker to use words *exclusively* from the language he is using, or to use them exclusively to express what they mean in that language. Speakers of English frequently introduce new words (often borrowed from another language), or give existing English words new meanings. Until the words 'catch on', they are not part of English. Bilingual speakers, or those still learning English, may dot their speech with words from another language, such as Spanish. Even competent users of a language occasionally misspeak, using the language incorrectly. So the most that can be required is that the speaker's expression-idea pairings be *predominantly* from the language. This means that the concept of using a language has at least one element of vagueness.

Let us stipulate that S *conforms* to L when S uses expressions and constructions predominantly from L, and uses them predominantly to mean cogitatively what they mean in L. A speaker is using English even when speaking metaphorically, because what the speaker means cogitatively coincides with word meaning even though cognitively he means something different (§4.2). If S conforms to L, then S will automatically conform to all languages containing L, but uses only a small number of those languages. For example, if S is conforming to English, then S is also conforming to the combination of English and Hopi. Yet it is doubtful that any English speaker has ever used such a combination. What is missing, I believe, is another layer of intentionality. While S conformed to the union of Hopi and English, he did not do so on purpose. Normal people never think of the combination of English and Hopi, and would not try to conform to it even if they did.[9] I believe that intentionally conforming to a language constitutes using it.

5.6 **Definition:** *S uses L iff S intentionally conforms to L.*[10]

In other words, S used L iff it is generally true that S used e to express i (or mean $"\mu_i"$) *because* e expresses i (or means $"\mu_i"$) in L. It follows that S cannot use a language without having *learned* or *constructed* it. For S would not

then be able to form the intention to conform to it. It similarly follows that S
*knows* the language, or at least some of it.


### 5.4    BASIC WORD MEANING

We now turn to the principal foundational question we have posed: what
makes it true that a word has the meaning it has? Given the framework we
have adopted, this is equivalent to the following questions: What makes it
true that the word expresses what it does? That is, in virtue of what is the use
of a word to directly express something part of the language? We seek the
answer for expressions in general, not just individual spoken words.

Words are intrinsically meaningless. There is something about language
users that makes it true that words have the meanings they do. It is not at all
obvious, however, just which facts about individuals determine what words
mean in a language. Grice (1957: 385) proposed that word meaning is
determined by cognitive speaker meaning. His basic idea was the following:

(1) Expression e means that p iff people use e to mean that p.[11]

Given the definitions of speaker meaning and expression provided above,
this says that e means that p iff people use e to express the belief that p, that
is, to produce thereby an indication of the belief that p, without pretense.
Grice's was thus endorsing the doctrine that '*meaning is use*'. While Wittgenstein (1953) and Austin (1962) used this slogan to reject the idea that
meaning consists in the expression of mental states, Grice embraced it. The
Gricean analysis is a particular version of the use theory, in which the
illocutionary act selected as constitutive of word meaning is the expression
of belief.

The Gricean analysis has many defects. For starters, (1) is incomplete as a
theory of meaning because it only tells us whether or not an expression
means *that* something is the case. Hence (1) cannot assign appropriate
meanings to subsentential expressions, including *morphemes* ('non-',
'hyper-', '-able'), individual *words* ('The', 'cat', 'is', 'uncatlike'), *phrases*
('the cat', 'on the mat'), and *clauses* ('that the birds sing', 'when the sky
clears'). The Gricean analysis correctly rules that subsentential expressions
do not mean that p for any 'p'. For people do not use them to mean that
anything is the case. For the same reason, though, (1) does not have the
resources to tell us positively what '-able', 'cat', and 'when the sky clears' do
mean.

Rather than rejecting (1) entirely, or finding illocutionary acts that
subsentential units are used to perform, Griceans adopted the *primacy of
sentence meaning*, the thesis that *the meaning of words is derived from
the meaning of sentences*.[12] More specifically, Griceans believed that subsentential units get any meaning they have entirely from the fact that they are

parts of meaningful sentences, and searched for definitions that would assign meanings to individual words solely on the basis of the meanings of the sentences in which they appear. Griceans essentially treated (1) as a partial definition, to be completed by a definition of word meaning in terms of sentence meaning.

I have argued that the sentential primacy thesis is unfounded and false.[13] First, few independent arguments for the thesis have been presented, and they are unsound. One popular argument, for example, uses the premise that only sentences can be used to perform 'complete' speech acts. But individual words can be used to express ideas, refer to objects, ascribe properties, and so on. Another argument uses the premise that we learn the meaning of words from their role in sentences. Whether this epistemological premise is true or not, the metaphysical conclusion that the meaning of words is derived from the meaning of sentences does not follow. Second, the sentential primacy thesis conflicts with the well-established thesis of compositionality, according to which the meaning of a sentence is determined by the meanings of its components. Sentences mean what they do because of what their component words mean. Given the asymmetry of explanatory relationships, the meanings of words cannot derive from the meanings of sentences containing them if those sentences have their meanings because of what their component words mean. Third, the few attempts that have been made to define subunit meaning in terms of sentence meaning have been very wide of the mark. Fourth, it is easy to describe languages, some with great expressive power, in which the assignment of meanings to sentences does not determine a unique assignment of meanings to words. There are too many subunits given the number of sentences. There is no reason to think that English is different in this respect. Finally, the Gricean has no criterion for determining, just on the basis of the meanings of the sentences, which subunits have meanings and which do not.

Even where it applies, to sentences, the Gricean analysis is defective.[14] People often use 'That's great!' to mean that it is the very opposite of great. Yet 'That's great!' does not mean that it is the very opposite of great. The Gricean analysis thus wrongly turns figurative use into literal meaning. The Gricean analysis also confuses generalized implicatures with meanings. For example, people often use 'Some S are P' to imply "Not all S are P". But this is not part of the meaning of 'Some S are P'. Moreover, an expression e might be used only in science fiction stories. Then people never use e to mean *that* anything is the case, in which event e means nothing according to the Gricean analysis. So the Gricean analysis wrongly turns exclusively fictional use into nonsense. The same goes for nondeclarative sentences and dependent clauses. Finally, since 'He sings' means "He sings", the Gricean analysis entails that speakers conventionally use 'He sings' to mean that he sings. That sounds fine. Unfortunately, *meaning that he sings* denotes different actions on different occasions. When S is referring to Pavarotti, he means that *Pavarotti* sings. When S is referring to Glenn Gould, he means that *Glenn Gould* sings. There is no one belief people commonly use 'He sings' to express (or produce in others). The converse defect is even clearer. People often use 'He sings' to mean that Pavarotti sings. But 'He sings' does not mean *"Pavarotti sings"*.

The five problems with the Gricean analysis—figurative use, generalized implicature, fictional use, pronouns, and subsentential meaning—can be solved at one stroke by shifting to *cogitative* speaker meaning. As explained in Chapter 4, people use 'That's great!' to mean cogitatively *"That is great!"* while meaning cognitively that it is the very opposite of great. I presume that no one has ever used 'Man was establishing his first base on the Moon' to express a *belief* that man was establishing his first base on the Moon. But people have used the sentence to mean that (Arthur C. Clarke did in *2001: A Space Odyssey*). *Meaning "He sings"* is a single action that people commonly use 'He sings' to perform (as is expressing a certain complex idea—see *Indexicals*). By performing this action, people sometimes express the belief that Pavarotti sings, sometimes the belief that Gould sings, and so on *ad infinitum*. Finally, people use 'vixen' to mean something, viz., *"female fox"*, even though they do not use 'vixen' to mean *that* anything is the case.

When cogitative meaning replaces cognitive in (1), the result says that expression e means *"μ"* iff people use e to mean *"μ"*. This does not rely on the primacy of sentence-part meaning any more than it relies on the primacy of sentence meaning. It says that the meaning of words in general, sentences as well as their parts, is determined by what people use them to mean.

Despite its considerable advantages over the Gricean original, the cogitative formulation is still much too weak. People often confuse 'entomologist' and 'etymologist'. As a result, people often mistakenly use 'etymologist' to mean *"entomologist"*. It does not follow that 'etymologist' means *"entomologist"*.[15] Similarly, if a group used 'scarlet' in a code to mean a battleship, their usage would not affect the meaning of that English word at all. At the level of sentences, it is quite possible for an English sentence like 'The fox chased the whale into the bullpen' to be used only by actors testing their voices, or spies using codes, so that it is never used to mean what it actually means in English. In general, what a word means is not influenced by what particular speakers happen to mean by it, a phenomenon sometimes called the *autonomy* of word meaning.[16]

This problem can be avoided by insisting that word meaning is *conventional* speaker meaning, where a convention is an *arbitrary social practice* or *custom* (see §5.5).[17] Codes are deliberate departures from convention. And while many people do use 'etymologist' to mean *"entomologist"*, their usage is unconventional. It is not 'the practice'. If a linguistic mistake became conventional, it would no longer count as a mistake: the language would have changed. Usage of sentences to test one's voice, or by spies in a code, are clearly unconventional uses. I refer to the thesis that word meaning is conventional cogitative speaker meaning as the *basic neo-Gricean analysis*.

(2) e means "μ" iff it is conventional for people to use e to mean "μ".[18]

When 'μ$_i$' stands for words expressing i, this can be reformulated as saying that *e means "μ$_i$" iff it is conventional for people to use e to directly express idea or other mental state i* (see §5.2).

The neo-Gricean analysis correctly allows that *all* speakers of a language could misuse a word on occasion. For the fact that all people do something at a particular time does not entail that it is conventional to do so. A convention is more than a momentary, accidental regularity in action. The neo-Gricean analysis also enables us to explain why, despite the autonomy of word meaning, speaker meaning is the more fundamental phenomenon. It often happens, for example, that an individual uses an expression with a new sense, or uses a completely new expression. It is only when this usage 'catches on', and becomes conventional, that the word acquires a (new) sense.

The neo-Gricean analysis avoids what I call the *explanation problem* with the Gricean.[19] If an expression means "μ", it is not merely a coincidence that people use it to mean the same thing, namely, "μ". Speakers mean "μ" *because* that is what the word means. If the Gricean analysis told us what it is for an expression to mean something, it would contradict the irreflexivity of explanation to claim that speakers mean "μ" because the word means "μ". It would say: the fact that people use e to mean "μ" is explained by the fact that people use e to mean "μ", which is absurd. There is no absurdity in the claim that people use e to mean "μ" because it is conventional to do so. Collectively and individually, we do use the word 'true' to mean "true" at least in part because it is conventional to do so. Our usage resulted from the convention, and the convention gives us a good reason for our usage.

What I have called the neo-Gricean analysis focuses on the *production* of e, saying that e means "μ" provided people conventionally *use e to mean "μ"*. But there is also a strong connection between word meaning and *interpretation*. Expression e means "μ" only if people are conventionally *taken to mean "μ" by e*.[20] Taking people to mean "female fox" by 'vixen' is as customary as using 'vixen' to mean "female fox". In general:

5.7   **Postulate:** *It is conventional for people to mean "μ" by e iff it is conventional for people to be taken to mean "μ" by e.*[21]

The claim that meaning "μ" implies being taken to mean "μ" is false: people are misinterpreted all too often. What 5.7 asserts is that a convention governing meaning implies a convention governing interpretation, and vice versa. This is not a necessary truth, although it is hard to imagine a case in which it fails. The equivalence is true in virtue of the contingent yet fundamental fact that *the common interest primarily sustaining linguistic conventions is communication.* While there are exceptions to the rule, as we emphasized in earlier chapters, speakers *normally* wish to communicate, and hearers normally want them to succeed. Speakers therefore need to use words in ways that will enable them to be understood, and hearers need to take speakers to mean what they mean. If it were conventional for people to use 'vixen' to mean "female fox", but not for people to take others to mean "female fox" by 'vixen', people would fail to communicate, and the convention would not sustain itself.

The convention of using 'vixen' to mean "female fox" is similarly connected to the convention of taking *the word* 'vixen' to mean "female fox" and the convention of using 'vixen' to *communicate* the idea of a female fox and *produce* it in others. And when these conventions prevail, the use of 'vixen' will be a *conventional indication* of the idea of a female fox.

## 5.5　Conventions

It is often said that conventions are *agreements*.[22] Indeed, in one sense, the word 'convention' denotes an international agreement, and in another denotes formal meetings designed to secure agreements. But in the sense we are concerned with, most conventions, including linguistic conventions, are not and did not result from agreements. It is hard to even imagine the first language arising by agreement. Linguistic conventions do occasionally arise from agreements, as when scientific congresses succeed in standardizing terminology. But other origins are much more common, as when a metaphor dies or a stipulative definition catches on.

A good definition of convention for our purposes can be derived from an informal characterization given by David Lewis that echoed a famous passage in Hume (1739: 490).

> Conventions are regularities in action, or in action and belief, which are arbitrary but perpetuate themselves because they serve some sort of common interest. Past conformity breeds future conformity because it gives one a reason to go on conforming; but there is some alternative regularity which could have served instead, and would have perpetuated itself in the same way if only it had got started.
>
> (Lewis 1975: 4–5)

This characterization perfectly fits Lewis's paradigm example of driving on the right. It also fits linguistic conventions. It is conventional to use 'plane' to mean "airplane": people regularly use the word this way; the regularity serves a common interest, namely communication; the regularity sustains itself in part because it gives people a reason to continue using the word that way; and the regularity is arbitrary, in that we could just as well have used 'aero' or 'avion' to mean "airplane". We will therefore adopt a modification of Lewis's gloss as our definition.[23]

5.8   **Definition:** *A convention is a regularity that is socially useful, self-perpetuating, and arbitrary.*

Our primary goal in offering this definition is not to analyze the English word 'convention', although I think the fit is quite good, but to characterize and name the social factor that turns speaker meaning into word meaning.

  In order for an action to be *socially useful*, it is necessary but not sufficient that it serve the interests of individual members of the group. The interest may not be universal, but it does need to be *common* and *widespread*. The interest must also be *mutual* or *collective*, something that people generally want not only for themselves but for others or for society as a whole. In the clearest cases, individuals are motivated to coordinate their actions for a common goal. Thus people regularly drive on the right in America because drivers have a common and mutual interest in avoiding head-on collisions. Languages are socially useful because they serve a common and collective interest in *communication*. That is the sociobiological function of language. Because people individually and collectively wish to communicate, they need to coordinate their actions. Speakers need to use a language their audience will understand. Because people understand the language they use, speakers are generally better off using the language their audience uses. It is not nearly as important which language speakers and hearers use as long as it is the same language.

  Conventions are *self-perpetuating* in special ways. There are at least six mechanisms by which social practices are reinforced and sustained: *precedent, association, habit, enculturation, normative force,* and *social pressure.*

### (i) Precedent

Given the common interest served by a convention, the fact that people have conformed to the regularity in the past gives people a good reason to continue conforming, as Lewis observed. Previous conformity thus serves as a precedent. The very fact that Americans have used English before is a good reason for Americans to use English now. A community with one language is easier to communicate in than one with many languages. More importantly, the fact that Americans have used English before gives Americans a reason to expect that their current audience will understand English now. Dictionaries represent a way in which precedent operates indirectly. Lexicographers base their entries on citations of past usage. Current users consult dictionaries as authorities on current usage. In both ways, the fact that others before me have used the word 'true' to mean "true" gives me a good reason to do so now. The reasons provided are seldom *conclusive* in any sense, but they do lead Americans to continue using English.

## (ii) Association

The regular use of a word to express an idea results in a mental association between the word and the thing meant, so that images and perceptions of the word call up the idea of the thing, and vice versa (see §3.6). The more often the two are paired, the stronger their association. The association between the word and a meaning together with knowledge of the precedent connecting them commonly makes that use of the word *salient*, and thus more likely to be noticed as an alternative and selected.[24]

## (iii) Habit

Regular action leads to a habit in each individual, which is reinforced by subsequent actions done out of that habit. At an early age, English speakers develop the habit of using the word 'red' to mean "red". They also develop the habit of interpreting the word 'red' as meaning "red". The fact that an individual habitually conforms to such a complex set of regularities in a flexible, creative, and purposive manner implies that the individual has some sort of knowledge or internal representation of the regularities, as Chomsky (e.g., 1965: Ch. 1) and his followers have stressed. Other evidence suggests that linguistic habits have a specialized neural basis (e.g. Laurence 1996: 284–92).

## (iv) Enculturation

Language is passed on as a *tradition* in the process of enculturation.[25] Because adult Americans use English, American children learn English. Children learn it natively at home, are taught it in school, and pick it up from their peers. Adults who join the group learn the conventions from old members. The transmission of a language during child rearing is facilitated by features not found in other traditions. For example, the set of speech sounds that an individual is capable of perceiving and producing is influenced by the set of speech sounds that he or she heard as a child. While the use of one word rather than another to mean something is often a conscious, reflective process, guided by known precedents, conscious decisions to follow precedents appear to play only a small role in linguistic enculturation.[26]

## (v) Normative Force

Conventions also serve as *generally accepted standards of correctness.*[27] The left side of the road is considered the right side to drive on in England, the wrong side in America. When I find, as I often do, that I have used 'their' to mean "there", I do not just regard my action as unusual or accidental; I consider it to be a mistake. The more closely I monitor and control my writing, the less often I make the mistake. Conventional regularities are thus generally accepted *rules* or *norms*, by which agents judge and guide their actions. Conventions are more than statistical regularities: they are *de jure* rules 'in force' in the community.

## (vi) Social Pressure

Conventions are partly sustained by social pressure. People use conventional norms not only to guide their own behavior, but to criticize or correct the behavior of others. Children are praised and otherwise rewarded for learning to speak and write properly. Adults who do not speak correctly may be shunned or denied jobs. Change is often greeted negatively as corruption— until, of course, the change becomes fully conventional. Editors alter manuscripts, sometimes against the author's will, to make them conform to conventional usage. Manuscripts departing too much from convention are simply rejected. Social pressure is seldom perfectly consistent. There are many cases in which a common linguistic usage is accepted by most users of the language but rejected by some.

Because conventional actions are regularities that perpetuate themselves in the six ways we have discussed, *the fact that an action is conventional can explain why people perform it* (§5.4). People drive on the right today because it is conventional to do so. They drive on the right today because the fact that people have done so before gives them a good reason to do so today, because they have been taught to drive on the right, and so on. In the same way, people use the word 'red' to mean "red" today because it is conventional to do so. Normative forces and social pressures, along with the force of precedence, association, and habit, lead people to use 'red' to mean "red" today.

Conventions are *arbitrary* in that there is another possible regularity in action that could have served the same common interest, and would have perpetuated itself in the same ways if only it had gotten started. The arbitrariness of symbols stands in marked contrast to the statistical or causal character of indexes and the representational character of icons.[28] There is nothing in the nature of the human mind, the word 'hood,' or the idea of an engine covering, in virtue of which one expresses the other. Hence 'hood' could just as well mean *"tire"*, and the idea of an engine covering could just as well be expressed by 'hatch' or 'torp'. The American interest in communication would have been served equally well by Spanish. If Americans spoke Spanish, that would give Americans a good reason to continue speaking Spanish. American children would learn Spanish because adults use it. And Americans would criticize each other for speaking Spanish incorrectly.

For our purposes, a *regularity* should be defined as *a common way of doing things*. 'Dog' is regularly used to express the idea of a dog in America. The use of 'dog' to express the idea of a dog is both a common way of using the word and the common way of expressing the idea. If W is the conventional way of doing A, then W is 'the way A is done'. Definition 5.8 can therefore be reformulated as follows: *A conventional way of doing things is one that is common, socially useful, self-perpetuating, and arbitrary.* An action *is* a convention only if it is common *today*, meaning not 'this day', but 'these days'. A regularity over the recent past suffices. It is conventional in America today to use the word 'decagon' to mean *"ten-sided polygon"*. This may be so because it has regularly been used that way in the last few years or decades, even if no one happens to use that word this week. The boundary of 'the present time' is of course vague. There may be no precise point in time at which we can begin to say 'people no longer do things that way'. But when it is true, then it is no longer conventional to do things that way. It is no longer our practice.[29] The fact that 'the present time' is vague entails that lexicographic decisions as to whether words have lost certain meanings will inevitably be uncertain even when the evidence is complete.

The word 'common' is vague in another way, since there is no precise percentage $r$ such that a way of doing something is common in a population iff more than $r$% of the population do it that way. This is a second reason why lexicographers have to agonize over when a new usage is frequent enough to be included in their dictionaries, and when an old usage has declined sufficiently to be labeled 'obsolete' or dropped altogether. *Pace* Lewis, conventions need not be universal or near universal regularities, and linguistic conventions generally are not.[30] In some cases, such as driving on the right, a regularity will be socially useful provided it is the *only* common way of doing things. But in other cases, such as language, the mutual interest may be served by several common ways of doing things. The general interest in communication is served quite well even though 'plane' and 'airplane' are both commonly used to express the idea of an airplane, and even though 'plane' is commonly used to express both the idea of an airplane and that of a certain tool. It is consequently not the case that, by convention, people use 'plane' *only when* they mean *"airplane"*, nor *whenever* they mean *"airplane"*.

Somewhat paradoxically, there may be a common way of doing something uncommon. How common a way W of doing A is is determined by the *relative* frequency of W *given* A, not the absolute frequency of W. For example, Americans seldom use the word 'googol' or express the idea of $10^{100}$. Nevertheless, using the word 'googol' to express the idea of $10^{100}$ is both a common way of using that word and a common way of expressing that idea. Similarly, many words are considered profane, vulgar, obscene, offensive, or taboo. Their use is therefore unconventional. It is nevertheless conventional to use the abhorrent words to express certain ideas. There is a common way of expressing ideas it is improper to express. Similarly, the usage of 'ain't' is nonstandard. But when it is used, it is almost universally used to mean "am not". There is a common way of using words it is improper to use. 'Archaic' words like 'affright' are rarely used nowadays, and considered old-fashioned. Nevertheless, when 'affright' is used, it is usually used to mean "frighten" or "fright". The fact that it is only the way we express ideas that is conventional, not their expression itself, holds even in the case of commonly expressed ideas. People commonly express the idea of food, for example, but this action is neither arbitrary nor self-perpetuating in the right way. The fact that many people before me have expressed the idea of food is a negligible reason for me to express it when I am hungry. The Gricean analysis should be understood as requiring that *using e to mean "μ"* is a conventional way of both *using e* and *meaning "μ"*.

We observed that conventional rules serve as generally accepted standards of correctness. Whether we are dealing with linguistic or nonlinguistic conventions, the members of a population in which an action is conventional generally believe the action to be right and proper. The criticism occasioned by violations of the norm and rewards by conformity are social pressures acting to conserve the convention. Embarrassment and pride play a similar role within the individual.

The arbitrariness of a convention is sometimes obscured by its normativeness.[31] The arbitrariness of linguistic conventions in particular is so salient that many linguists find their normative force hard to defend. How can it be objectively correct or proper to use words one way rather than another if the choice is arbitrary? We can begin answering this question by noting that a *regularity in action* may be arbitrary when a *particular choice of action* conforming to the regularity is not. It is the general use of 'red' to mean "red" that is arbitrary. What makes this practice arbitrary is the existence of other possible regularities that would have been just as useful to society. In contrast, *my* use of 'red' to mean "red" is not at all arbitrary. The fact that I want to be easily understood, together with the fact that my audience speaks English, normally gives me a conclusive reason to use 'red' rather than 'blue' to mean "red".

Furthermore, judging speech to be correct or incorrect is like judging a musical performance to be correct or incorrect. A particular sequence of notes, say C-C-E-E-G-G-E, will be objectively correct if I am trying to play Haydn's *Surprise Symphony*, incorrect if I am trying to play *Twinkle Twinkle Little Star* (C-C-G-G-A-A-G), despite the similarity of the melodies. Similarly, using 'rot' to mean "red" is correct if I am trying to speak German, and incorrect if I am trying to speak English. Using 'red' to mean "blue" may even be correct, if I am using a code I have stipulated. In general, a musical performance is correct provided the musician performs the sequence of notes that defines the work he or she is trying to perform. A speech performance is correct provided the speaker uses 'modes of expression' defining the language he or she is trying to use (§5.3). Conventional usage is the proper standard of correct English usage if the neo-Gricean analysis is correct, because conventional usage determines what words mean in English. Linguistic correctness is thus as objective as it is relative.[32]

## 5.6   COMPOSITIONAL WORD MEANING

According to the neo-Gricean analysis presented in §5.4, word meaning is conventional cogitative speaker meaning. That is, what an expression means is determined by what idea people conventionally use it to directly express. This thesis works very well for individual words, stock phrases, dead metaphors, and idioms. 'Green' means "green" only because it is conventional for English speakers to use the word 'green' to mean "green". The phrase 'kicked the bucket' means "died" only because people conventionally use it to mean that. The basic neo-Gricean analysis does not, however, account for the *constructive* and *recursive* character of the semantic rules of a language.[33] That is, the analysis does not account for *compositionality*, the way in which the meaning of a complex word, phrase, clause, or sentence is normally determined by the meanings of its components.[34] The deficiency of the neo-Gricean analysis can be seen most starkly by reflecting on the fact that every natural language contains a large—indeed infinite—number of meaningful sentences that have never in fact been uttered. Some are too long or convoluted ever to be uttered. Furthermore, whereas the finite stock of words in a language are generally used over and over again, it is unusual for the very same sentence to be used twice. If a meaningful sentence has been used no more than once, however, then it is not conventional for people to use it for anything (§5.5). So the neo-Gricean analysis wrongly entails that the sentence has no meaning.

Even when we confine our attention to sentences that are used repeatedly, these may have meanings that people seldom if ever intend. Consider (3):

(3) He gave him hell.

It is conventional to use (3) to mean "He gave him a tongue-lashing", even though its literal meaning is "He gave him the place where sinners go". So the neo-Gricean analysis rules that (3) means the former but not the latter. Yet (3) has both meanings in English. It *can* be understood as having its literal meaning. And sometimes it *must* be interpreted that way, as in 'God's brother Theo gets everything he asks for; Theo asked God for the place where sinners go; therefore, He gave him hell'. An exercise like this may change the way we 'hear' a sentence of English, but it does not change the English language. It did not just create a new sense for (3).[35]

We can preserve the neo-Gricean analysis for the cases in which it is accurate, while broadening our definition to accommodate compositionality and productivity, by using (2) as the *base clause* of a recursive definition. This clause gives the meaning of the smallest meaningful units in the language, as well as the idiomatic meaning of noncompositional word combinations.[36] An analogue of the neo-Gricean analysis can be used to define the meaning of the basic grammatical constructions used in the language, providing the *recursion clause*. A phrase of the form 'N Ver' means "person who Vs Ns" rather than "Ver who is an N" because it is conventional for speakers to use such phrases to mean the former rather than the latter. We can now say that the conventions of English assign meanings directly to 'girl' and 'watcher' and to the construction 'N Ver'. These conventions indirectly assign the meaning "Person who watches girls" to 'girl watcher'.[37]

We used 'N Ver' and 'something that Vs Ns' to represent certain *expression structures*. We also used them ideo-reflexively to represent certain *idea structures*. An idea structure is defined by relationships that two or more ideas may stand in. Complex ideas have that structure when they contain two or more ideas standing in the indicated relationships. A sentence structure is similarly defined by relationships that words in a sentence may stand in. For formal purposes, it is convenient to use functions to represent structures. A familiar example is the propositional function of quantification theory, which in some treatments represents a sentence form that results in a sentence when names or individual constants are substituted for individual variables. Thus the sentence form 'x is a composer', whose substitution instances are 'Brahms is a composer', 'Chopin is a composer', 'Dvořák is a composer', and so on, can be represented by the function $C(x)$—or $Cx$ for short—whose domain is the set of individual constants or names and whose range is the set of sentences combining them with the predicate 'is a composer'. In general, let $E[x_1, x_2, \ldots, x_n]$ designate a function from a number of expressions to a complex expression that contains them. The form 'N Ver' corresponds to the function $E_1[N, Ver]$. The related form 'Ver of Ns' is represented by the function $E_2[N, Ver]$, whose range contains 'lover of cats', 'hater of dogs', 'player of violins', and so on. As the 'of' indicates in

**Table 5.1**   Expression Structure Functions

| N | Ver | $E_1[N, Ver]$ | $E_2[N, Ver]$ |
|---|-----|---------------|---------------|
| cat | love | cat lover | lover of cats |
| dog | hate | dog hater | hater of dogs |
| violin | play | violin player | player of violins |
| etc. | | | |

this simple example, there is no requirement that $e_1, e_2, \ldots, e_n$ be the only components of $E[e_1, e_2, \ldots, e_n]$.

Let $I[i_1, i_2, \ldots, i_n]$ designate a function from a number of ideas to a complex idea with a particular structure containing $i_1, i_2, \ldots$, and $i_n$. We will use $i(e_i)$ to designate the idea the speaker directly expressed by $e_i$ when using $E[e_1, e_2, \ldots, e_n]$. Thus it is conventional for English speakers to use both

**Table 5.2**   Idea Structure Functions

| i(N) | i(Ver) | I[i(N), i(Ver)] |
|------|--------|-----------------|
| i(*cat*) | i(*lover*) | i(*person who loves cats*) |
| i(*dog*) | i(*hater*) | i(*person who hates dogs*) |
| i(*violin*) | i(*player*) | i(*person who plays the violin*) |
| etc. | | |

$E_1[N, Ver]$ and $E_2[N, Ver]$ to express $I[i(N), i(Ver)]$ as in Table 5.2. We can use these functions to provide a recursive definition for word expression.

(4) Expression e expresses i iff (i) people conventionally use e to directly express i; or (ii) people conventionally use $E[x_1, x_2, \ldots, x_n]$ to directly express $I[i(x_1), i(x_2), \ldots, i(x_n)]$, where $e = E[e_1, e_2, \ldots, e_n]$ is grammatical, $i = I[i(e_1), i(e_2), \ldots, i(e_n)]$, and $i(e_i)$ is the idea expressed by $e_i$ for all i from 1 to n.

Clause (ii) tells us that 'aardvark lover' expresses the idea "person who loves aardvarks" because people conventionally use $E[N, Ver]$ to directly express $I[i(N), i(Ver)]$, use 'aardvark' to directly express the idea "aardvark", and use 'lover' to directly express the idea "lover".

Commonly used compounds such as 'cat lover' satisfy clause (i) as well as clause (ii). But expressions like 'aardvark lover', which are rarely if ever used, will satisfy clause (ii) but not (i). 'Kicked the bucket' gets its idiomatic meaning "died" from clause (i) and its literal meaning "struck the bucket with a foot" from (ii). 'Cooked one's goose' is not a pure idiom but a regular instance of the ambiguous construction 'cooked N's goose'. 'Cooked Aristotle's goose', in either its literal or its idiomatic sense, cannot get its meaning from clause (i) because it has probably never been used. But expressions of the form 'cooked N's goose' are conventionally used to express the idea structure "ruined N's chances" as well as "heated N's goose for eating". So 'cooked one's goose' and 'cooked Aristotle's goose' get their meanings from clause (ii).

With complex expressions like (5), we can work our way up recursively from the simplest components to the whole compound.

    (5) Bill ate purple spaghetti with a titanium tea cup.

For example, 'spaghetti' is a commonly used word, and so is assigned a meaning by (i). Expressions of the form 'purple N' are commonly used to express ideas of a certain structure. Given the meaning already assigned to 'spaghetti', clause (ii) assigns a meaning to 'purple spaghetti'. Expressions of the form 'ate NP' are commonly used to express ideas of a certain structure. Given the meaning already assigned to 'purple spaghetti', clause (ii) assigns a meaning to 'ate purple spaghetti'. And so on. Formulation (4) thus shows how, and to what extent, the meaning of a sentence, or other grammatical compound, depends on the meanings of the words making it up.

As the examples we have been using illustrate, there is no requirement that the structure of $I[i(e_1),i(e_2),\ldots,i(e_n)]$ be isomorphic to the structure of $E[e_1,e_2,\ldots,e_n]$.[38] The structure of the phrase 'aardvark lover' is its *surface structure*. The structure of the idea "person who loves aardvarks" could naturally be termed the *deep structure* associated with 'aardvark lover'. Three common linguistic phenomena prove that the structure of the idea expressed by a compound expression may diverge from the structure of the expression. First, complex phrases with different surface structures may express the same ideas, as 'aardvark lover', 'lover of aardvarks', and 'person who loves aardvarks' illustrate. Second, expressions with no surface structure may express structured ideas. Thus 'vixen' expresses the idea of a female fox, and statement constants in propositional logic are used to express complete thoughts of unlimited complexity. Third, complex phrases are often amphibolous: ambiguous in ways that do not result simply from ambiguities in their components. Thus 'Russian teacher' can mean "teacher of Russian" or "teacher who is Russian". And 'flying planes' can mean "the act of flying planes" or "planes that are flying".

Some expression structures do not have a conventional usage even though more specific structures do. Consider, for example, the general structure 'ADJ N' consisting of an adjective followed by a noun. Is it conventional to use expressions of this form to express the idea "N that is ADJ"? That depends on whether the adjective is 'regular'. We recognize that when adjectives like 'red', 'large', 'good', and 'fat' are combined with nouns, the result is conventionally used to express the idea "N that is ADJ". But when the adjectives are like 'phony', 'former', 'would be', and 'nominal', the

*Word Meaning*

combination is not conventionally used to express the idea "Noun that is ADJ". Whereas an old Vermeer is a Vermeer that is old, a phony Vermeer is not a Vermeer, and so cannot be a Vermeer that is phony. The conventions governing the two adjective categories $ADJ_r$ and $ADJ_i$ are different. Expressions of the form '$ADJ_r N$' are conventionally used to express ideas of the form "Noun that is $ADJ_r$". There is no general convention governing the use of expressions of the form '$ADJ_i N$'. Instead, the conventions vary with the adjective. For example, 'phony N' is conventionally used to express the idea "object that purports to be N but is not". And 'former N' is conventionally used to express the idea "object that used to be N but is no longer".

The requirement that $E[e_1, e_2, \ldots, e_n]$ be *grammatical* prevents the recursion clause of (4) from assigning meanings to some ungrammatical compounds. It is conventional to use expressions of the form 'A-er' to mean "more A", or more properly, "greater in A-ness", as in 'higher', 'faster', and 'farther'. But 'gooder' does not mean "greater in goodness" in English, even though it is an expression of the form 'A-er'. For while we know how to interpret it when mistakenly used, 'gooder' is not a grammatical English word, and so does not mean anything in English. No grammaticality restriction is needed on the base clause. Conventional usage of a letter or sound sequence, no matter how irregular, makes it an expression of the language and gives it a meaning. The English plural noun 'alumni' is a good example.

We will refer to (4) as the *recursive neo-Gricean analysis*. It explicitly defines word expression in terms of speaker expression, and implicitly defines word meaning given Definition 5.4: *e means "$\mu_i$" iff e expresses i*.[39] For short, the recursive neo-Gricean analysis may be characterized as saying that word meaning (expression) is *constructive conventional cogitative speaker meaning (expression)*. The recursive neo-Gricean analysis allows it to be true in general that the meaning of an individual word is its contribution to the meaning of sentences containing it. The analysis also allows it to be true in general that the meaning of a sentence is the product of the meanings of the individual words making it up and the way they are put together. But the recursive neo-Gricean analysis allows exceptions to both rules, and uses neither to define linguistic meaning.

## 5.7 LIVING LANGUAGES

We began the chapter by noting that word meaning is relative to a language. 'Bonnet' means "hood of a car" in British English, but not in American English. The full formula we seek to define is:

(6) e means "$\mu$" in L. (*linguistic word meaning*)

The relativity of word meaning to languages may be obscured by the fact that *e means "$\mu$"*, without a linguistic reference, is not understood as an incomplete utterance. That is because it is interpreted with a tacit reference to the object language (cf. Definition 5.3). When we are talking about English, *'gourmand' means "greedy"* describes what 'gourmand' means *in English*, and is false. When we are talking about French, the sentence correctly describes what 'gourmand' means in French.

Conventions vary from one community to another. It is conventional for the French to use the word 'gourmand' to mean "greedy", but not for Americans. We must replace *people* with a more specific term in the neo-Gricean analysis. How do we identify the group of people whose conventions determine what e means in L? It is natural to suggest that the relevant group is the *users of L*. Thus 'bonnet' means "hood" in British English, but not in American English, because it is conventional for people who use British English to use 'bonnet' to mean "hood", but not for people who use American English. While such a revision of the recursive neo-Gricean analysis is true in all the cases we have considered so far, it is problematic as an *analysis* of word meaning or expression due to circularity. We have defined what it is for a speaker to use a language in terms of what the words mean in that language (Definition 5.6). So we cannot now define what words mean in a language in terms of the users of that language. The problem transcends our particular system of definitions. In general, what words mean in English depends on conventions among users of English. How can we identify the users of English except as those who use English words to mean what they mean in English? This is one problem Grice never saw.

The proposed revision of the recursive neo-Gricean analysis has a further limitation: it holds only for *living* languages. Extinct languages are no longer used at all. And in newly constructed artificial languages, words mean what they are stipulated to mean, whether they are used or not. The word meanings may be stipulated directly, as L. L. Zamenhof did in constructing Esperanto. Or the meanings can be generated from a living language by a stipulated rule. Consider Morse English, the language that is like English except for the fact that the expression elements are the transcriptions into Morse code of the spoken and written expressions of English. Thus in Morse English, '− −• − − −' means "go". I assume that no one has ever used the Morse code sequence spelling out 'zaptiah' (−−•• •− •−−• − •• •− ••••), or stipulated a meaning for it. The sequence still means "Turkish policeman" in Morse English.

Living languages are used conventionally, but that is not their only defining property. The railroad industry used semaphore signals consisting of a row of lights mounted on posts to indicate how switches on the track are set. The semaphore system is a simple language, and was used conventionally. But it was not a living language. A group of people with different native languages who all happen to have learned C. K. Ogden's Basic English may well come to use it to communicate among themselves. Even if it became conventional to use Basic English in this way, that would not necessarily make it living.

Why wouldn't an artificial language count as a living language even when it is the conventional language of some community? I do not believe the answer is simply that the language had its origin in an act of construction. The fantastic discovery that someone had constructed, say, Basque (a language whose origins are uncertain), should not lead us to conclude that Basque is not a living language. Or suppose the Army began teaching Huron, an extinct American Indian language, so that it could be used to encrypt secret messages. That would not necessarily bring Huron back to life. The correct answer, I believe, is that the nature of a still-born or dead language does not *depend on* the conventions of its users even when it is used conventionally. The language is fixed by stipulation or past usage. Even if there is a perfect correlation between what words mean in the language and what speakers mean by those words, word meaning does not depend on speaker meaning.

Consider the difference between Morse code and the pronunciation rules of a natural language. The code invented by Samuel Morse pairs sequences of dots and dashes with sequences of letters. Even though it is used conventionally in a number of communities, the correspondence constituting the code is fixed, an external standard consciously learned and consulted in the process of coding and decoding messages. Pronunciation rules, in contrast, and the orthographic rules that are their inverse, vary considerably as conventions vary. The correspondence between letters and speech sounds was presumably stipulated at some point in the distant past, but it is now dependent on convention. People learn the correspondence from other users, and minor differences can and do accumulate from time to time and place to place, resulting in accents. The alphabetic writing system is a living symbol system. Morse code is not.

Two exceptions that prove the rule are Esperanto and American Sign Language (ASL). Esperanto was an artificial language, invented by Zamenhof in 1887. But its use spread around the world, and has even been handed down in some families as a first language for three generations. The pronunciation, vocabulary, and syntax has evolved, so that Colloquial Esperanto now differs from Zamenhof's Esperanto.[40] A more important and complex example is provided by the various sign languages that evolved from the system of signed French constructed by Abbé de l'Epée in the eighteenth century to teach deaf students. His system was taken to America by Thomas Gallaudet and Laurent Clerc, who established the first American school for the deaf. Others introduced the system around the world. Since the communities were isolated, de l'Epée's artificial language evolved differently in different places. In a result common among pidgins and Creoles, the lexicon of de l'Epée's system was used with the basic grammar of the local, pre-existing sign languages. French Sign Language and American Sign Language are now mutually unintelligible languages learned as first languages by large numbers of the congenitally deaf.[41]

We need, then, to augment the definition of living languages as conventional languages with a clause stating the dependence of the states of L on the conventions of the community using L. Just such a clause is provided by the recursive neo-Gricean analysis. We also need to recognize that the group of users of a natural language is temporally extended, changing over time. If U is the group, let U(t) be the set consisting of all members of U at t.[42] With these two changes, our definition is complete.

5.9 **Definition:** *L is a living language at t iff some group U is such that at t: (i) L(t) is used conventionally by members of U(t) to communicate with one another; (ii) L(t) depends on the conventions in U(t), consisting of all modes of expression $\langle e,i \rangle$ such that it is conventional for members of U(t) either to use e to directly express i, or to use $E[x_1,x_2,\ldots,x_n]$ to directly express $I[i(x_1),i(x_2),\ldots,i(x_n)]$ where $e = E[e_1,e_2,\ldots,e_n]$ is a grammatical expression of L(t), $i = I[i_1,i_2,\ldots,i_n]$, and $e_i$ expresses $i_i$ in L(t) for all i from 1 to n.*

Clause (i) implies that L(t) changes from $\lambda_i$ to $\lambda_f$ during $\Delta t$ iff the members of U changed from using $\lambda_i$ to using $\lambda_f$ during $\Delta t$. Clause (ii) has a similar implication. Two different sorts of conventions are mentioned in Definition 5.9 as definitive of living languages. Clause (i) requires a *global* convention to use the whole language (state) L(t). Clause (ii) requires *local* conventions to use and interpret each word, idiom, and construction in L(t). The two sorts of conventions go together naturally, but are logically independent. Definition 5.9 entails that the recursive neo-Gricean analysis holds for living languages like English.

5.10 **Theorem:** *If L is a living language, then e expresses i in L iff (i) the people on whom L depends use e conventionally to directly express i; or (ii) they use $E[x_1,x_2,\ldots,x_n]$ conventionally to directly express $I[i(x_1),i(x_2),\ldots,i(x_n)]$, where $e = E[e_1,e_2,\ldots,e_n]$ is a grammatical expression of L, $i = I[i_1,i_2,\ldots,i_n]$, and $e_i$ expresses $i_i$ in L for all i from 1 to n.*

Basically, a language is living only if the recursive neo-Gricean analysis holds for it relative to a certain group of people, whose semantic-act conventions define the language.

Theorem 5.10 defines word expression for living languages. Given the connection between meaning and expression (Definition 5.4), it tells us what it is for words in a living language to have meaning. Theorem 5.10 entails, for example, that 'vixen' means *"female fox"* in English because the language users on whom English depends use 'vixen' to mean *"female fox"*. This is not circular, even though the people on whom English depends are users of English, and users of English are those who use 'vixen' to mean *"female fox"*. Theorem 5.10 is noncircular because of the convention dependence of living languages. The people on whom English depends are identified in terms of their historical relations to prior users—as people whose linguistic conventions descended from those of prior speakers of English. Since the prior users can be identified without knowing that their descendants now use 'vixen' to mean *"female fox"*, no circularity arises.

Given the self-perpetuating character of conventions, the group on which a language depends is a *lineage*, consisting of the *original* speakers of the language and their linguistic *descendants*. A new living language is discovered and named when a group of people is found with a previously unknown set of semantic conventions. The referent of the name is fixed by a description like 'the language this community uses'. The community's own name for its language may be fixed by a description like 'the language we speak'. We determine what expressions of the language mean by observing actual current usage, and figuring out what it is conventional for speakers to express. The conventions defining the modes of expression of the language in the future are those that evolve from the conventions of the original group in the ways described in §5.5. The people on whom the language depends are those whose conventions descend from those of the original group.[43] The people on whom L depended in earlier times were those whose semantic-act conventions evolved into those of the group relative to whom the reference of 'L' was fixed. Since 'L' and 'the people on whom L depends' are not defined in terms of particular modes of expression, there is no circularity in the claim that what an expression means in L is determined by the meaning conventions found in the people on whom L depends.

As a consequence, every subsequent state of a natural language results indirectly and in part from the practices of the original group of speakers. When we consider how a natural language would have evolved under different conditions, we must consider what the line of descendants would have been under those conditions. The line of linguistic descendants will be confined to biological descendants only when the group remains extremely isolated. Normally, the biological descendants teach their language to immigrants, who pass the new language on to their offspring, in a repeating cycle. Conversely, emigration removes many biological descendants from the linguistic lineage.

As with biological species, the boundaries of a living natural language are not generally fixed by the concept of a natural, living language. Nothing in the concept of a language, for example, tells us where exactly we should place the boundary between Old English and Middle English, and nothing stops us from distinguishing Early Modern English (pre-1800) from Late Modern English. The latter are 'different languages' in the sense that they are not numerically identical, even if they are not 'different languages' in the stronger sense requiring significant qualitative differences. The distinction between languages or dialects can be made on the basis of geographic or political differences as well as linguistic differences (cf. German versus Dutch). A language *dies* (or becomes *extinct*), however, when it either ceases to be conventionally used or ceases to be convention-dependent. Language death is generally a gradual process, unless the entire population of users dies suddenly, as in the case of Tasmanian, whose speakers all died of disease or were killed between 1803 and 1876.

Nearly all living languages are natural languages. Whereas artificial languages are invented, natural languages are discovered. Natural languages are found in the natural world, and are not merely objects of human conception. A natural language, moreover, is generally *used 'naturally'* in the sense that some people use it spontaneously, effortlessly, unselfconsciously, automatically, and habitually. Its use is *second nature*. Indeed, a natural language is generally used naturally because it is the *native language* of the speakers. Until they become dead or extinct, natural languages are passed on from one generation to the next in the first few years of life as part of the normal maturation process. Because all languages must be learned, and different people learn different languages depending on their native environment, even natural languages are not *innate*. Only the capacity to learn a language is innate.

An artificial language is one that was stipulated by some individual or group. It consists at least initially of all the expression-idea pairings linked by the stipulations of that individual or group. When more than one individual is involved, the stipulation constitutes an *agreement*. Whereas word meaning is established by convention in living natural languages, it is established by stipulation or agreement in most artificial languages. The case of Esperanto shows that artificial languages might come alive and evolve. If the change should become so extensive that few, if any, of the originally stipulated modes of expression were part of the language, then I believe it would no longer qualify as an artificial language. A natural language would have been born. ASL and FSL surely qualify as natural languages.

## 5.8 IDIOLECTS

Grice (1968: 226) observed that locution (7) differs both from 'S means "$\mu$"
by e' and 'e means "$\mu$"', while having affinities with both. I call it *idiolectic word meaning*.

(7) e means "$\mu$" for S. (*idiolectic word meaning*)

Idiolectic meaning is a form of word meaning, but differs from linguistic word meaning: if S regularly uses a code in which 'sunshine' means "cocaine", then 'sunshine' means "cocaine" for S even though 'sunshine' has a different meaning in English. Idiolectic meaning depends on the individual speaker, but differs from speaker meaning in requiring a certain type of regularity over time: if I suffer a slip of the tongue when I say 'erotic', I may have meant "erratic". But 'erotic' does not mean "erratic" for me because I do not *customarily* use the word 'erotic' to mean "erratic". I did on this occasion, but only by mistake.

Whereas linguistic word meaning is established by convention or stipulation, idiolectic meaning is mainly established by individual custom. Conventions are *social customs* (or *practices*): regularities in action among many people, which are arbitrary but serve a common interest and transmit themselves from individual to individual and generation to generation. *Individual customs* (or *practices*), in contrast, are *regularities over time in the voluntary actions of one individual, which are arbitrary but useful for that individual and self-perpetuating.* An individual custom is a regular way an individual has of doing something, which serves that individual's purposes. The regularity is self-perpetuating in the way habits are. Moreover, the individual considers that manner of doing things the correct way. And the fact that he has acted that way in the past gives him a good reason to continue doing so. Finally, individual customs are arbitrary in the same way group customs are: there is another regular way of doing things that would serve the same purposes, and would perpetuate itself in the same way.[44]

## NOTES

[1] This chapter is a summary of Chs. 7–11 of *Meaning, Expression, and Thought*.

[2] See Bentham 1843: 298; Fodor and Katz 1964: 1–19; Searle 1969: 18–19; R. Harris 1980: 22–32; Leech 1983: esp. Ch. 1; Avramides 1989: 6. Contrast Harrison 1980: 165–7 and Mey 1993: §1.3.

[3] My 'mode of expression' thus resembles Saussure's (1916: 67) 'sign' (the 'combination' of a signifier and a signified) and the notion of 'symbol as sign together with sense' that Carruthers (1989: Ch. 4) attributes to Wittgenstein.

[4] A system is a combination of elements, but not every combination is a system. So Definition 5.1 does not imply that every arbitrary assemblage of modes of expression counts as a language. To constitute a system, there must be some unifying, structural features relating the elements combined. In the case of natural languages, the fact that all expressions are sequences of a small set of speech sounds or letters is one of many unifying features. Since the systematic nature of languages is not essential to the fact that words have meaning in them, we will ignore it.

[5] Alternatively, a language can be modeled by a set of rules (comprising a 'grammar') that generate all and only the material rules of the language, as suggested by Katz (1966: 100–5, 112).

[6] Lyons 1971: 35; Anttila 1989: 182–3, 289–9; Vogelin *et al.* 1988: 659ff; and J. M. Y. Simpson 1994: 1895.

[7] Cf. *Meaning, Expression, and Thought*, §21.1. Contrast Arnauld 1662: 90; Reid 1785: 394, 477; James 1890: 472; Frege 1892a: 43; 1918: 4–5; Husserl 1900: 284–6; 327; Hampshire

1939: 5, 19; Russell 1940: 219; Humphrey 1951: 42; Church 1951; Quine 1959: 200; 1961a: 21–2; Kneale and Kneale 1962: 497–602; Alston 1964a: 11–12, 20; Katz 1966: 154–5; 177–85; 1972: 37–9; 1977a: 5; Hamlyn 1967b: 140; Quillian 1968: 223; Hacking 1975: 19, 43–4; Lyons 1977: 254, 316; Devitt 1981: §§5.1, 5.5; D. W. Smith 1981: 102–3, 106; McGinn 1982: 217; Peacocke 1986: 116; 1996: 441; 1997a: 22–3; Devitt and Sterelny 1987: 56; Jackendoff 1989: 73; Recanati 1990: 705; Fodor and Lepore 1992: 221; Böer 1995: 353–9; Künne 1997; Fodor 1998a: 2; Boghossian 1998a: 199; Horwich 1998a: 4, 20, 98. Many have argued that meanings are not things of any sort, which holds only for the object sense of 'meaning'. See Ryle 1957: 256, 262–3, 295; Sellars 1958: 224–5; 1963: vii; Austin 1961: §I; Cartwright 1962: 101–2. Alston 1963b; 1964a: 20–2; 1967: 237; Heath 1967: 178–9; Stampe 1968: §§1–7; Hungerland and Vick 1981: 72; Cresswell 1985: 56; Schiffer 1987a: 265–6; Chierchia and McConnell-Ginet 1990: 15; Nelson 1992: 14; Horwich 1998a: 8–19.

[8] Cf. Grice 1968: 1969a; Kripke 1977; and Yu 1979: 272, 279. See also Katz and Fodor's (1963: 487–8) distinction between what words mean 'in a setting' from what they mean 'in isolation', and Bach and Harnish's (1979: 20–3) notion of 'operative meaning'. 'Occasion meaning' would have been an excellent name for applied word meaning, except for the fact that Grice (1968; 1969a) used that term to denote speaker meaning, which also varies from occasion to occasion. Katz (1977a: 14) and others conflate applied meaning and speaker meaning.

[9] Cf. the distinction between 'fitting' a rule and being 'guided' by it, developed by Quine (1972: 442), Rosenberg (1974: 31), and others. See also Lewis 1975; 1992 and O'Leary-Hawthorne 1990; 1993.

[10] Given the use of the individual variable 'L' in the normally opaque context created by 'intentionally', Definition 5.6 says that a speaker who is using the language with the largest vocabulary must be trying to conform to that language, but need not think of it as the language with the largest vocabulary (§2.9). He must think of the language under some description, but not under any particular description. Cf. Lewis 1969: 50.

[11] Cf. Meinong 1910: 29–33; Chisholm 1958: 239; Stampe 1968: 165–74; Patten and Stampe 1969: 7; Schiffer 1972: 7; 1982: 123; Bennett 1976: 8; and Evans 1973: 300.

[12] Cf. Grice 1969a: 148–50; Schiffer 1972: 6, 166; 1987a: 92, 214–16; Bennett 1976: 16–22, 212–21, 272–6, 280–4; Loar 1976a: §1; 1981: §9.9; Blackburn 1984: 24, 129, 180; and Avramides 1989: 4–5. See also Bentham 1816: 188; 1843: 322; Frege 1884: §60; Ryle 1957: 248–9; Ziff 1960: 44–5, 141, 151 fn. 2, 160–1; Austin 1961; Alston 1963a; 408–10; 1964a: 36–9; 1971: 35–6; 1974: 33; 1977: 17; 1994: 48, 31; 2000; Wiggins 1965: 56; Kretzmann 1967: 390 (describing Destutt De Tracy); Davidson 1967: 451, 454; 1973: 127; 1977: 220; Armstrong 1971: 428; Danto 1975: 13–15; McDowell 1978: 308–9; Harrison 1980: 193–6; Hungerland and Vick 1981: 47, 58, 66, 135 (describing Hobbes); Chierchia and McConnell-Ginet 1990: 61–2, 152, 349; Vanderveken 1990: 7; Neale 1992: 555, fn. 68; Brandom 1994: 79–84; Hugly and Sayward 1995. Compare and contrast Dummett 1973: 3–4; 1976: 72, 76 and Peacocke 1986: 63–4. Contrast Dummett 1956: 592; Grice 1968: 129–31.

[13] *Meaning, Expression, and Thought*, §8.4.

[14] Cf. Cartwright 1962: 92–5; Schiffer 1972: 119–20; Loar 1976b; 1981: 256–7; Carr 1978a; Posner 1980: 169–80; Blackburn 1984: 118, 123–5; Landau 1984: 215–16; Chierchia and McConnell-Ginet 1990: 153–4; Neale 1992: 553–4; S. Davis 1994.

[15] Cf. Ziff 1960: 22–4; Cartwright 1962: 95; Chomsky 1965: 3; Stampe 1968: 171; Follett 1970: 4–6, 24; Alston 1974: 19; Tsohatzidis 1994: 2; Love 1994: 779. Contrast Newman 1962: 437 and Hall 1962: 434 ('The function of grammars and dictionaries is to tell . . . what people actually do when they talk and write'), who, I suspect, were simply overstating their case.

[16] Cf. Locke 1690: §3.2.8; Leibniz 1709: §§3.1–3.2; Ziff 1960: 22–4; Follett 1970: 4–6; Harrison 1980: Ch. 1; Davidson 1983: 274–9; and Avramides 1989: 74. Compare and contrast M. S. Green 1997.

[17] See Grice 1989: 298; Neale 1992: 553; Avramides 1997: 80. In 1968: 127, Grice revised his original tentative analysis by adding a proviso that foreshadowed the self-perpetuation condition of the definition of convention (§5.5).

[18] Compare and contrast Leonard 1929: 21–6, Ch. 9; Schiffer 1972: 154; 1982: 123; 1987a: 12; Loux 1974: 4; Fodor 1975: 106; 1998a: 9; Bennett 1976: 10, 16–17, 213; Cummins 1979: 352; Harrison 1980: 183–9; H. H. Clark 1983: 316; Blackburn 1984: 90, 112–13; Emmett 1988: 79–80; and Tsohatzidis 1994: 2–3. As we have seen, Alston (1964a: 43–4; 1974: 17–20; 1977: 29; 1994: 45; 2000) championed the view that words have meaning because they are governed by rules, while specifying a different set of rules. Contrast Sellars 1969: 115.

[19] Cf. Alston 1965: 21, fn. 1; Sellars 1969: 112; Schiffer 1972: 13; Kempson 1975: 141; Bennett 1976: 8, 10; Biro 1979: 242; Yu 1979: 284; Platts 1979: 89–91; Harrison 1980: 167; Blackburn 1984: 90; Millikan 1984: 4–5; and Devitt and Sterelny 1987: 124–8. Contrast Smith *et al.* 1952: 284.

[20] Cf. Hungerland and Vick 1981: 69 on Hobbes; and Husserl 1900: 277, 302, 309. See also Laurence's (1996: 282–4) claim that the semantic properties of utterances are inherited from those of the mental representations they are associated with in language processing.

[21] Cf. Hockett's notion of 'interchangeability', one of the 'design features' he presumed to be universal and distinctive of human languages: 'any speaker of a language is in principle also a hearer, and is theoretically capable of saying anything he is able to understand when someone says it' (1958: 578).

[22] The *locus classicus* is Hermogenes in Plato's *Cratylus* (383b). See also Reid 1764: 32; Whorf 1956: 213; and Schein and Stewart 1996: viii. Hume (1739: 490) called conventions 'agreements' while denying that they are 'promises'. Gilbert (1996: 110) describes conventions as 'quasi-agreements', saying that 'it is as if they agreed'.

[23] Lewis's official formulations were much stronger, with requirements that fail for most linguistic conventions. See *Meaning, Expression, and Thought*, Ch. 9.

[24] Cf. Schelling 1960: 57, 67, 91; Lewis 1969: 35–6; Schiffer 1972: 145–8; Ullmann-Margalit 1977: 83–4; and Gilbert 1996: Ch. 1.

[25] Cf. Hockett 1958: 579–80; 1966: 11 and Asher 1994: 876.

[26] Labov 1970: Ch. 2; Rickford 1992: 226–7; Laurence 1996: 291–2.

[27] Cf. Quintilian *Institutio Oratoria*: 72–3; Locke 1690:§3.2.8, Priestley 1762: 136–9, 184; Leonard 1929: Chs. 1–2, 9–10; Fries 1940: Ch. 1; D. V. Smith *et al.* 1952: Ch. 12; Alston 1964a: 41–4; 1964b: 57–8; 1974: 19, 25; Lewis 1969: 97–107; Rosenberg 1974: 43–5; Ullmann-Margalit 1977: 12–13; 85–93, 96; Kripke 1982: 89–95; Blackburn 1984: 83; Landau 1984: Ch. 5; Fasold 1990: Chs. 7–8; O'Grady *et al.* 1993: 12; Gilbert 1996: 78–86, 107–12; Lance and O'Leary-Hawthorne 1997: Ch. 3; and Yagisawa 1998: 449. Contrast Ziff 1960: 30–1, 34–8.

[28] Cf. Peirce 1931–35: vol. II; Ziff 1960: 25–6, 57–8; Alston 1964a: Ch. 3; 1974: 19, 25; Bennett 1976: 14, 149; and Anttila 1989: 12.

[29] Contrast Gilbert 1996: 73–4.

[30] Universality or near universality is assumed by Arnauld 1662: 90; Grice 1968: 232–3; Schiffer 1972: 128–9, 136, 154, 156; 1987a: 250–1; Walker 1975: 169; Kempson 1975: 150–2; Bennett 1976: 213; Bach and Harnish 1979: 108–10, 189–95; Yu 1979: 282–5; Loar 1981: 256; Davies 1987: 717; S. Russell 1987: 730ff; Avramides 1989: 68; Chierchia and McConnell-Ginet 1990: 153; Contrast: R. Harris 1980: 104–5; Gilbert 1996: Chs. 3–4.

[31] See e.g. Gilbert 1996: 69–70.

[32] Correct usage, furthermore, is not necessarily *true* usage. If I say 'President Bush is a bachelor', I am using 'bachelor' correctly as long as by it I mean "unmarried male". But while my use of 'bachelor' is correct English, my statement that Bush is a bachelor is incorrect, that is, false. We can use sentences correctly to express beliefs that happen to be false.

[33] Cf. Geach 1957: 12; Ziff 1960: 59–62; 1964: 391; 1967: 6; Fodor and Katz 1964: 11; Davidson 1967: 79; Rosenberg 1974: 3, 30; Chomsky 1975: 74–5; Grandy 1977: 135–6; Searle

1979: 156; Platts 1979: 89; Cummins 1979: 350; Harrison 1980: 190–6; Loar 1981: 256; Blackburn 1984: 10–18, 35–6, 127–33; Hornstein 1984: 123; Schiffer 1987a: Chs. 7–8; Avramides 1989: 4–13; Chierchia and McConnell-Ginet 1990: 6–7, 152; Katz 1987: 171; Grandy 1990; Horwich 1998a: §3.9. Contrast Fodor 1998a: 9.

[34] I defend compositionality against recent objections in §10.6 of *Meaning, Expression, and Thought*.

[35] Cf. Stillings *et al.*, 1995: 373. Contrast Katz and Fodor 1963: 496–8; Grice 1968: 127; Neale 1992: 553–4.

[36] Cruse (1986: Ch. 2) and A. P. Cowie (1994) survey the broad range of 'ready-made memorized combinations'.

[37] Cf. Ziff 1960: 61–2; Katz and Fodor 1963: 482, 493, 503–16; Katz 1964b: 520; 1972; Schiffer 1972: 161–2; Evans 1973: 303; Blackburn 1984: 133; Horwich 1998a: Ch. 7. Contrast Schiffer 1987a: 251.

[38] Contrast Horwich 1998a: 163–4, 180.

[39] Alternatively, we can derive from (4) a principle defining word meaning directly in terms of conventional speaker meaning. See *Meaning, Expression, and Thought*, §10.3.

[40] Sources: Forster 1982; Large 1985; Anttila 1989: 176; Jordan 1992; Janton 1993: Ch. 4; Wells 1994.

[41] Sources: Woodward 1978; Deuchar 1984: 2–3; Wilbur 1987: 228–9, 251; Fischer 1993: 20–1; Radutsky 1993: 242–8; Schein and Stewart 1996: 18; *Encyclopedia Britannica Micropedia* 1997: 796.

[42] The group is 'modally extended' too: the membership of the group might have been different, and would have been if certain conditions had been different. But we will focus on the actual world.

[43] The people on whom L depends need not comprise the entire set of users of L; see *Meaning, Expression, and Thought*, §11.3.

[44] Idiolectic meaning is defined in *Meaning, Expression, and Thought*, §11.7.

# 6

## Nondescriptive Meaning

This book will focus on names, which have been problematic in semantics because they have *nondescriptive meaning*. We will begin with a brief look at other cases of nondescriptive meaning, including interjections, syncategorematic terms, words with conventional implicatures, and nondeclarative sentences. While descriptive meaning has been the paradigm case for most theories of meaning, nondescriptive meaning is equally important and comes in many varieties. No theory of meaning can deny its existence or ignore it. My goal is to show how the expression theory can account for the different kinds of nondescriptive meaning.

### 6.1 NONDECLARATIVE SENTENCES

If a sentence is meaningless, then it expresses no proposition. The inverse fails: not every meaningful sentence expresses a proposition. Only *declarative* sentences express propositions. Compare the following:

(1) Everybody will stop.
Will everybody stop?
Everybody stop!

These three sentences are meaningful. Moreover, they differ in meaning. The declarative sentence expresses the proposition that everybody will stop. The interrogative and imperative sentences are nondescriptive because they do not express propositions: they do not express objects of belief or disbelief or subjects of truth or falsity. Nevertheless, the nondeclarative sentences do express thoughts. *Not all thoughts are propositions.* The thought "Will everybody stop?" is not a proposition, but it does occur to people in the same way the thought "Everybody will stop" occurs to people. I might think "Everybody stop!" when it is time to begin a musical performance. In cartoons, nondeclarative sentences occur in 'thought bubbles' as freely as declaratives. Wilson and Sperber (1988: 100) noticed that nonpropositional thoughts can be attributed in free direct or indirect speech.[1] Their example was: *John sighed. Would she never speak?* And reports of some complex mental states entail nonpropositional thoughts, such as *Mary wondered, 'Will he marry me?'*

It is natural to use the adjectives 'declarative', 'interrogative', and 'imperative' to classify thoughts as well as the sentences that express them. In these terms, propositions are declarative thoughts (Definition 2.4). This should not lead us to identify nondeclarative thoughts with sentences. The thought "Will everybody stop?" differs from the sentence 'Will everybody stop?' in all the ways detailed above for declarative thoughts and sentences (§2.4): the thought is language independent. The principle that *a sentence expresses a thought only if it is meaningful* holds for imperative and interrogative as well as declarative sentences. It is also holds for all three moods that *meaningful sentences express the same thought iff they have the same meaning* (cf. §5.2). Thus the three sentences in (1) express different thoughts given that they have different meanings. 'Everybody will stop?' and 'Everybody'll stop?' express the same thought given that they have the same meaning. The fact that the three sentences in (2) express the same thoughts as the corresponding sentences in (1) shows that the punctuation marks alone—or in speech, intonation—can convey the difference in meaning.

(2) Everybody will stop.
    Everybody will stop?
    Everybody will stop![2]

Definition 3.9 similarly implies that whether 'p' is declarative or not, *"The thought "p" is the thought expressed by 'p'"* is true in every context in which "the thought expressed by 'p'" in its predicate is used to refer to the thought expressed by 'p' in its subject. The thought "Will everybody stop?" is the thought expressed by the sentence 'Will everybody stop?' Recall that we cannot use 'the thought that ...' to refer ideo-reflexively to nondeclarative thoughts, because 'that' requires a declarative sentence. Since nondeclarative sentences are ungrammatical in that-clauses, we must use direct speech or free indirect speech to refer to or ascribe nondeclarative thoughts, as when I observed above that the thought "Will everybody stop?" differs from the thought "Everybody will stop".

It is also possible to use the nouns 'statement', 'question', and 'command' to classify the three kinds of thoughts. But we will reserve these terms for *speech acts*. A speech act is the 'locutionary' act of uttering words, or an 'illocutionary' act like the stating, asking, ordering, and requesting that a person does by uttering words.[3] Uttering the sentence 'Will everybody stop?' is a speech act, as is expressing the thought "Will everybody stop?". When we perform these actions, we can either *ask whether everybody will stop*, or *ask everybody to stop*. To do the former is to ask a question, to do the latter is to make a request. We can make the same request by uttering the imperative sentence 'Everybody stop!' and expressing an imperative thought, or even by uttering the declarative sentence 'Everybody will stop now' and expressing a proposition. We can ask the same question using the declarative sentence

'Everybody will stop' with proper intonation, as well as by using the performative 'I ask you whether everybody will stop'. There is no essential connection between sentence mood and speech act type,[4] and the thoughts can occur without performing any speech acts at all.

Even though the thoughts expressed by the interrogative and imperative sentences in (1) differ from the thought expressed by the declarative sentence, the three thoughts are clearly related. Indeed, it seems clear that the declarative thought is in some way the 'root' of the interrogative and imperative thoughts. A man cannot think *"Will everybody stop?"* or *"Everybody stop!"* unless the thought that everybody will stop occurs to him. He need not believe that everyone will stop, of course, but he must be thinking of everyone stopping. (This point is particularly clear when expressed using the sentences in (2).) The converse fails: someone who is merely imagining everyone stopping, for example, is thinking the declarative thought but not the interrogative or the imperative. The simplest way to account for these co-occurrence relations is to regard interrogative and imperative thoughts as compound thoughts, which contain a declarative thought as a component (cf. §2.6). Indeed, we will treat nondeclarative thoughts as negations and modal statements are treated in propositional logic. Consider:

(3)  Not everybody will stop.
     Everybody must stop.

These are treated as compound propositions whose single component is the proposition that everybody will stop. If 'E' designates the proposition that everybody will stop, '−E' designates its negation and '□E' the modal statement. We can in the same way use '?E' to designate the interrogative thought *"Will everybody stop?"* and '!E' the imperative thought *"Everybody stop!"*[5] Hence ? and ! are operators like − and □. There is one significant disanalogy: whereas the negation and modal operators convert propositions into compound propositions, the question and command operators convert propositions into compound thoughts that are not propositions. Thus whereas −P and □P are potential objects of belief, ?P and !P are not. Similarly, P stands in a simple logical relationship to −P (the truth value of −P is completely determined by the truth value of P), and in a more complex logical relationship to □P (the truth value of □P is determined by the truth value of P in some but not all cases). But ?P and !P do not stand in any logical relationship to P. For whereas −P and □P are true or false, ?P and !P have no truth value. Hence ? and ! are operators, but not logical operators. We might call them *mood operators*.[6]

It is possible to define semantic predicates applicable to ?P and !P in terms of the truth value of their root. Thus we can stipulate that !P is *satisfied*, and that ?P *has a positive answer*, iff P is true.[7] 'Unsatisfied' and 'has a negative answer' can be defined similarly in terms of the falsity of P. The thought expressed by a wh-interrogative like 'Who will stop?' would thus have neither a positive nor a negative answer since the root thought would be neither true nor false. We can derive theorems such as that the satisfaction of !(P&Q) entails the satisfaction of !P, and that the truth of □P entails that ?P has a positive answer. While the issue could be left open, I believe that logical operators and connectives like negation and conjunction cannot apply to anything but propositions, so that whereas !−P exists, −!P does not.[8] If such compound nondeclarative thoughts do exist, it is unclear how satisfaction and other semantic values would be defined for them. Other semantic properties can be defined in terms of satisfaction or having a positive answer. For example, we might stipulate that !P is *correct* if it is obligatory or right that !P be satisfied. It would be an open question as to whether the logic of correctness is isomorphic to that of satisfaction.

Intensions and other 'semantic values' can be defined for nondeclarative thoughts using either a possible worlds or a situation semantics (see Chapter 14). In the former, the intension for !P could be the set of all possible worlds in which !P is satisfied, and the intension for ?P the set of all worlds in which ?P has a positive answer. Such intensions could not be identified with meanings, since nondeclarative sentences such as 'Make a triangle!', 'Make a polygon whose angles add up to 180°!', and 'Will you make a triangle?' would all have the same intension despite differing substantially in meaning.[9] The same goes for 'Disobey this order!' and 'Is he both male and not male?' In the sort of ideational semantics I am developing, these sentences differ in meaning because the thoughts they express are different, despite having the same intension (cf. Chapter 9).

We have noted that the mood operators are not logical operators: they convert propositions into thoughts without truth values. We can add that mood operators are nonrepresentational concepts. They are thought parts that do not represent any objects or properties of objects, and thus have no extension or denotation. Mood operators do have a psychological function. The three kinds of thoughts are involved in different mental states. Only declarative thoughts can be objects of belief or disbelief. Imperative thoughts are involved in willing, while interrogative thoughts are involved in wondering. Furthermore, P, !P, and ?P have different connectionist properties. The mood operators *prime* different associations (see §3.6). The interrogative thought "Will John call home?" is much more likely to call up thoughts of reasons for or against John calling home, and the evidence for and against his doing so, than the thought "John, call home!" The imperative thought, in contrast, is much more likely to call up thoughts of the ways and means for John to call home, and the consequences of his calling home. The declarative thought "John will call home" is just as likely to call up thoughts of means and consequences as thoughts of reasons and evidence, and seems more likely to call up thoughts that recently or frequently co-occurred with it.

We might summarize these differences metaphorically by saying that the imperative operator marks thoughts for action, while the interrogative operator marks thoughts for investigation.[10]

## Attempts to Reduce the Moods

The fact that corresponding declarative, interrogative, and imperative sentences differ in meaning does not suffice to establish that there are three different thought moods. Many have tried to define the interrogative operator in terms of the imperative operator, which would imply that every interrogative sentence could be translated into a synonymous imperative sentence.[11] Åqvist (1972) proposed, for example, that 'Will everybody stop?' means "Let it turn out that I know whether everybody stops!" This identification provides for an interesting logical system, but is not credible as a semantic analysis. It is true that people who ask a question typically want to know the answer, and typically ask the question in order to prompt someone to inform them. Thus typical users could achieve some of their goals by using 'Let it turn out that I know whether everybody stops!' instead of 'Will everybody stop?' But this instrumental fact is not enough to make the two sentences synonymous. If the fact that one is interrogative and the other imperative does not suffice to show a difference in meaning, note that one calls for an answer and the other does not. The request could be satisfied, in fact, without anyone giving an answer or saying anything, since there are other ways of coming to know things. And the addressee could answer the question correctly without satisfying the request because the speaker does not believe the addressee. Moreover, 'Will the universe expand forever? No one will ever know' and 'Has Alan been unfaithful? I don't want to know' may not be typical uses of interrogatives. But they are not linguistically, logically, or pragmatically deviant. Their proposed translations are. For 'Let it turn out that I know whether p' conflicts in different ways with 'I don't want to know whether p' and 'No one will ever know whether p'. The addressee in the familiar guessing game would hardly know what to do if 'What hand is it in?' were replaced by the allegedly synonymous 'Let it turn out that I know what hand it is in!'

Lewis and Lewis's (1975) theory that interrogatives are synonymous with imperatives of the form 'Tell me truly whether p!' is much better,[12] but is also implausible as a claim of literal synonymy. 'Yes' is an appropriate answer to the question but not to the request. 'What is in the box? Don't tell me!' is an intelligible combination, but 'Tell me truly what is in the box. Don't tell me' is flatly contradictory. Similarly, 'I don't expect anyone to tell me the answer, but what is the meaning of life?' is not at all paradoxical, while 'I don't expect anyone to tell me the answer, but tell me the correct answer!' is incoherent. 'Is anything true?' is a plausible way of starting a philosophical paper on truth. But 'Tell me truly whether anything is true!' would seem self-refuting. 'Tell me truly whether the Pope is Catholic!' could not be used to give an affirmative answer in place of the classic rhetorical question. An interrogative can also be used to express doubt or concern without expecting an answer (e.g., 'Is he going to make it?' said to no one in particular of someone late for a meeting).

Other attempts to reduce one mood to another face similar difficulties.[13] The best known is J. R. Ross's (1970) 'performative hypothesis', which implies that any nondeclarative sentence has the meaning of a declarative sentence with a performative verb.[14] Thus 'Will everybody stop?' is equated with 'I ask you whether everybody will stop'. The fact that the interrogative sentence is typically used to ask the question that the performative is used to ask does not establish a synonymy. The interrogative sentence may be used with its literal meaning to do something other than ask a question, for example, such as to command or request everyone to stop. The performative cannot be so used. When the interrogative is used to ask a question, 'Yes' is an appropriate response, but it is not an appropriate response to the declarative. The declarative is true when seriously uttered, but truth does not apply to interrogatives. The declarative mentions me and you, but the interrogative does not. "He wondered 'Will everybody stop?'" is well formed and meaningful, but "He wondered 'I ask you whether everybody will stop'" is neither. Finally, what reason could there be for the performative hypothesis to be correct for interrogatives and imperatives but not for declaratives? But if the theory were applied to declaratives, it would seem to imply that 'Everybody will stop' is synonymous with 'I state that everybody will stop', which is particularly implausible since the two sentences have different truth conditions. Moreover, the theory further implies that both are synonymous with 'I state that I state that everybody will stop', and so on *ad infinitum*.[15]

## The Force Theory of Mood

I have accounted for the difference in meaning attributable to sentence mood in terms of a difference in the thoughts expressed. Nondeclarative sentences express nonpropositional thoughts. The most common approach, however, works exclusively with propositional thoughts, and seeks to explain the differences in meaning due to mood in terms of the different speech acts that sentences of different moods are used to perform.[16] This approach may seem more economical, given that any theory has to acknowledge that declarative sentences are used to make statements, interrogative sentences are used to ask questions, and imperatives sentences are used to give orders. Sentences of different moods are thus said to differ in *force*. The force theory of mood maintains that the three sentences in (1) are similar in meaning because they all express the proposition that everybody will stop, but differ in whether they are used to make a statement, ask a question, or give an order. The force theory is very congenial with the ideational approach I am developing. The main difference is that the force theory uses a broader range of illocutionary speech acts to define meaning, with a narrower range of thoughts. In addition to the expression of declarative thoughts, it defines meaning in terms of stating, asking, and ordering.

One problem with the force theory, however, is that nondeclarative sentences should have truth values if they express propositions. But 'true' and 'false' do not apply to interrogatives or imperatives. To see another problem, consider an ambiguous sentence like:

(4) Workers Unite!

This is most naturally interpreted as an imperative. But it can also be interpreted as a declarative (think of it as a headline). Phenomenologically, the ambiguity of (4) seems just like standard lexical or syntactical ambiguities, such as that of:

(5) No singing teachers allowed.

This expresses two different thoughts, one about teachers of singing, the other about teachers who are singing. In contrast, (5) differs significantly from (6).

(6) If you don't, you will suffer.

This can be 'heard as' a simple prediction, or as a threat. But that does not make (6) ambiguous.[17] Heard as either prediction or threat, (6) is heard as expressing the same proposition. On the force theory, however, (4) is like (6) rather than (5): it expresses one proposition, and can be used to either make a statement or issue a directive. The force theory does not have the resources to distinguish between (4) and (6), and so must erroneously say either that (6) is ambiguous or that (4) is not.

The most insuperable difficulty with the force theory is that sentences can be used with their conventional meaning but without the force that is typical of the mood. Speakers can use 'Everybody will stop' literally without stating that everybody will stop when they are: telling a story; using it ideo-reflexively; using it as the antecedent of a conditional; just joking; speaking metaphorically; and even ordering everyone to stop. Speakers can use 'Will everybody stop?' with its literal meaning but without asking whether everybody will stop when they are: telling a story; using it ideo-reflexively; speaking metaphorically; and commanding everyone to stop. Imperatives can be used with their literal meaning but without being used to give orders when they are used to grant permission ('Come in'), give directions ('Turn left at the first light'), or excuse oneself ('Excuse me, please'); or when used as the consequent of a conditional ('If you want security, buy bonds'), or ideo-reflexively ("He thought, 'Don't do it!'").[18] Some force theorists observe that we can know what a sentence means if we know that it can be used to express a particular proposition with a given force (see e.g. Hare 1970: 17). That may be, but it does not follow that to have that meaning is in part to have that force, any more than it follows that to be female is in part to be pregnant given that we can infer that an individual is female from the fact that she is pregnant.

The impression that the force theory is simpler than the nonpropositional thought theory is an illusion, moreover. First, we have direct, introspective evidence that thinking the thought "Everybody will stop" differs from thinking the thought "Will everybody stop?". So the differences in thought have to be acknowledged too, and they cannot be accounted for in terms of mere differences in inner speech (§2.4). Second, we need to explain what it is to state that everybody will stop, and how that speech act differs from asking everybody to stop and asking whether everybody will stop. We also need to explain what it is for *speakers* to mean "p!" as opposed to "p?" or "p" (cf. Chapter 4). We cannot account for the difference in speech act or speaker meaning in terms of the difference in sentence meaning if the difference in sentence meaning has been explained in terms of the difference in speech act or speaker meaning. Besides, as we saw above, speakers can ask questions without using an interrogative sentence, as when they say 'I ask you whether everybody will stop'. And speakers can issue a directive without using an imperative, by saying 'Everybody will stop, *now!*'.

On my view, the difference in speech act type is partly due to the difference in mood of the thought expressed. It seems evident that S counts as asking whether everybody will stop only when S is thinking, and expressing the thought, "Will everybody stop?" S counts as ordering everyone to stop only when thinking "Everybody stop!" S counts as stating that everyone will stop only if that thought is occurring to him without a mood operator. The standard view, however, is that the difference in speech act type is to be explained in terms of *other* mental states of the speaker. One suggestion proposes that S is asking whether p iff S expresses the proposition that p with *the intention of getting someone to tell him whether or not p*. This analysis has all the defects of the Lewises' theory and more. First, S need have no such intention. S might want to answer the question himself, for example. Or S may be asking the question rhetorically. Second, S may express the proposition in order to get someone to tell him its truth value without asking any questions. For example, S might be just toying with a subordinate 'yes-man', saying 'Profits are going to increase this year, in my judgement. Tell me your opinion.' We cannot change 'tell' to 'inform' in the proposed analysis, since S might ask a question for which he already knows the answer. Nor will it do to say that S is asking whether p iff S expresses the proposition that p while *expressing a desire to know whether that proposition is true*. For he would express both if he said 'I do in fact want to know whether everybody will stop', without asking whether everybody will stop. Moreover, there is no evident absurdity in saying 'Did I pass? I don't want to know.' Exam questions, rhetorical questions, expository questions, and the like are common examples in which the indicated desire is not expressed. The same questions undermine Lyons's (1977: 755) proposal that S asked whether p only if S *expressed doubt whether p*, along with the variant that substitutes *indicating that he wonders* for expressing doubt.

Similar analyses have been proposed for imperatives. Some suggest, for example, that to mean ʺDo ϕ!ʺ is to express the proposition that you will do ϕ while *attempting to get you to do ϕ*, or while *expressing the desire that you do ϕ*. But consider a case of countersuggestion. If a teenager is trying to decide what to wear to the dance, her mother might say 'Wear the red dress!' knowing that will encourage her daughter *not* to wear it. A colonel might order her men to carry out an order that she vehemently disagrees with and is actively trying to subvert. Or she might give an order she hopes they will disobey so that she can punish them. A prisoner who is being forced to tell his captors how to operate the machinery might reluctantly say 'Turn this switch on first'. He would mean ʺTurn this switch firstʺ, but would not be expressing the desire that his captors do what he is telling them to do. Or suppose my son says that he is going to work as a lifeguard rather than attend college. If I express my frustration by saying 'Throw away your life if you want', I will not be expressing a desire that he throw away his life if he wants, nor trying to persuade him to. Similarly, suppose you tell me that one of your best students missed a point on her final exam. I might say, ironically, 'Flunk her!' Then I meant ʺFail her!ʺ by the expression I used. But I was not attempting to get you to fail her, nor expressing a desire that you should. Conversely, speakers can express the desire that you do something, and thereby try to get you to do it, without meaning ʺDo A!ʺ by anything. If my wife says she will plant whatever I want, and I say 'I would like it if you planted azaleas', I did not mean ʺPlant azaleas!ʺ by what I said.

Blakemore (1992: 117) says that '*telling to* is analyzed in terms of the communication of a thought which is entertained as a description of a state of affairs that is potential and desirable'.[19] But if Ripken hits a long ball, I might say 'It's out of here!'—communicating a thought I entertain as a description of a potential and desirable state of affairs—without telling the ball or anything else to do anything. And if I say and mean 'Bush's defeat is both achievable and desirable', then I have expressed the beliefs Wilson and Sperber (1988: 83–7) required, but did not mean ʺDefeat Bush!ʺ In general, it seems clear that the only mental state and speech act common in all cases of interrogative and imperative meaning is thought and its expression.

## The Characteristic Force–Mood Connection

I have argued that there is no *necessary connection*, or *perfect correlation*, between mood and force. It is nonetheless undeniable that declarative sentences are *characteristically* used to express belief and make statements; that interrogative sentences are characteristically used to express wondering and a desire for information, and to ask questions; and that imperative sentences are characteristically used to express desire and will, and give orders.[20] See Table 6.1.

Why does this connection exist in English and other natural languages? On the mood operator theory I have proposed, this is a significant, empirical question. The three sentence moods are distinguished by the type of thought they are conventionally used to express, and the thoughts are differentiated by the presence or absence of the mood operators. It is logically possible that the type of sentence used to express propositions is typically used to express desire, for example, so that if σ is used to express the proposition that p, then uttering σ in unmarked contexts would express the desire that p. The sentence used to express imperative thoughts might similarly be used to express belief, so that if σ expresses p!, then uttering σ in unmarked contexts would express the belief that p. So why is mood and force connected the way it actually is?

On the force theory of mood, in contrast, asking why declarative sentences are used to make statements in natural languages is like asking why vixens are female in zoos. It is simply analytic that declarative sentences are those with the grammatical mood that is characteristically used to express belief and make statements, while interrogative sentences are those with the grammatical mood that is characteristically used to express wondering and a desire for information and to ask questions. The connection between mood and force is logical, not empirical. Things could not be otherwise.

Table 6.1   The characteristic force–mood connection

| Mood | Mental states expressed | Speech acts performed |
| --- | --- | --- |
| Declarative | Believing, knowing | Stating, saying, informing, reporting, or predicting that p |
| Interrogative | Wondering, desiring to know | Asking, questioning, or inquiring whether p |
| Imperative | Desiring, willing | Ordering, commanding, directing, asking, instructing, or telling A to φ |

The force theory is thus simpler than the mood operator theory in one respect: something that needs to be explained on the mood operator theory does not require explanation on the force theory. But I believe the force theory is too simple: the connection between mood and force could be otherwise. Imagine the following use of English. A declarative sentence 'p' is conventionally used to express the *thought* that p, but never by itself to express the *belief* that p, or to *state* that p. To state and express the belief that p, speakers use the performative sentence 'I hereby state that p'. Thus if I wanted to state that it is going to rain, I would never say 'It is going to rain'; I would have to say 'I hereby state that it is going to rain'. If I simply said 'It is going to rain', hearers would assume that I am just as likely to have expressed something I am merely imagining or considering as something that I believe. The imagined change in the use of English breaks the standard connection between declarative sentences and the act of declaring. But the alteration does not imply any change in the syntax or semantics of English.

More radical alternatives are possible. In addition to what we previously imagined, speakers might come to express the belief that p by using the interrogative sentence 'p?' If they utter an interrogative without any head or hand motion, the question is rhetorical. If speakers accompany the utterance with a nodding of the head, then they express the belief that p. A thumbs up may replace the head nod, and head-shaking or thumbs down may be used to convey disbelief. Then speakers could use 'Is it going to rain?' in two ways to express the belief that it is going to rain. Competent speakers would consider 'S asked whether it is going to rain' and 'S meant "It is going to rain" by the words used' as false in such cases, while counting 'S meant "Is it going to rain?"' as true. When speakers want to ask genuine questions, let us suppose, they use the performative sentence 'I hereby ask whether p'. When they want information, they request it using imperatives, saying something like 'Please tell me whether p'. This alternative possibility severs the standard connection between interrogative sentences and the asking of questions. The resulting practice seems much less efficient. But again, the change does not imply any change in the syntax or semantics of English.

How can we account for the connection between force and mood if we assume that declarative, interrogative, and imperative sentences differ in meaning because they express different thoughts? My hypothesis is that the answer lies in the natural connection between the thoughts expressed and the other mental states expressed, and between those mental states and the speech acts performed. Declarative sentences are those that express declarative thoughts, that is, propositions (Definition 2.4). Propositions are the objects of belief. Stating that p involves expressing the belief that p, and requires that the proposition that p is occurring to the speaker without a mood operator.[21] Saying that p has the same occurrence requirement, but is more general because it involves either expressing the belief that p or pretending to believe that p. The other speech acts associated with the declarative mood are all specific ways of stating or saying that p. For example, informing implies not just belief but knowledge, which is also a relation to declarative thoughts. The connection between propositions, believing, and stating is 'natural' in the sense that it does not depend on any human conventions or actions. It is what I have elsewhere called an 'antecedent relation' that makes one practice seem uniquely right and fitting even though alternatives are possible (see Davis 1998: §6.5). The natural connection between propositions, believing, and stating makes it natural to use the sentences that express propositions to perform the further illocutionary acts of expressing beliefs and making statements. The use is so natural that it hardly seems arbitrary. Indeed, the connection strikes many as analytic, with no possible alternatives.

Interrogative sentences are used to express interrogative thoughts, which are involved in wondering. Wondering whether it is going to rain involves thinking the interrogative thought "Is it going to rain?" Wondering whether p also involves desiring to know whether p. Asking whether p, in turn, entails either expressing wonder whether p, or pretending to wonder. Given these antecedent relations, it is natural to use the sentences that express interrogative thoughts to perform the further illocutionary act of asking questions.

The speech acts of ordering, commanding, directing, requesting, and so on all involve either providing an indication that one wills and therefore desires something, or acting as if one willed and desired it. I treat desire as a relation between subjects and propositions. But I think desire could be treated as a relation between subjects and imperative thoughts. Indeed, we could easily stipulate that S desires !P iff S desires P. But this connection between desire and imperative propositions would clearly not provide any reason for finding it more natural to use imperative rather than declarative sentences to express desire. I believe willing, on the other hand, requires thinking an imperative thought. To will one's leg to move, we must be thinking "Leg, move!" Willing A to φ also entails desiring A to φ. Merely thinking an imperative thought is not enough for willing, however. If I will my leg to move, I must want it to move. So the directive force is connected with desire and imperative thoughts because both are involved in willing.[22]

It is my hypothesis, then, the various practices that connect mood and force arose and perpetuated themselves because the antecedent relation between thought mood, mental states, and speech acts makes it natural to use sentences expressing thoughts of a particular mood to express the connected mental states and perform the connected speech acts. Alternative practices are possible, but not as natural. But because of the antecedent relations, the practices are not completely arbitrary, as are those that connect certain audiovisual patterns with concepts. Given how natural the connection is, it is not surprising that the practices described in Table 6.1 are common to many languages. I have offered a similar hypothesis as to why certain implicature conventions are widespread in natural languages (Davis 1998: §6.6).

Does the force–mood correspondence hold for *all* languages? It is hard to say because of the well-known difficulties of translation. Sadock and Zwicky (1985), for example, surveyed 32 languages from a wide range of families, and found that all had at least three syntactically distinct classes of sentences, one characteristically used to make statements and express belief, one used to do things like make requests and give commands, and the third used to ask questions and seek information. Following their sources, they translate these into English as declaratives, imperatives, and interrogatives, respectively. Given the connection between mood and force in English and other well-known languages, these are certainly reasonable translations. Not enough information is provided, however, to rule out the possibility that some of the language communities break the characteristic mood–force connection in the ways imagined above. Since Sadock and Zwicky took the force theory of mood for granted, they did not raise the critical questions. So at least in my mind, the question of the universality of the mood–force correspondence is open.

The recognition of mood operators that convert propositions into non-propositional thoughts does not account for all the distinctive semantic features of nondeclarative sentences. I will show in *Indexicals*, for example, how indexical concepts are involved in the thoughts expressed by wh-questions. Furthermore, the notion of an appositive thought compound introduced in §6.4 is needed to account for the distinctive presuppositions or presumptions of negative and disjunctive interrogatives.[23] A negative interrogative like *Isn't Jack coming?* does not appear to express either $?-P$ or $-?P$. For its positive answer is given by *Yes, Jack is coming*, the same as for the corresponding positive question *Is Jack coming?* The negative question seems to differ in presuming that Jack is expected to come. A disjunctive interrogative like *Is Jack or Jill coming?* is ambiguous. It can express the disjunctive interrogative thought $?(JvM)$, in which case the answer is 'Yes' if the disjunction 'Jack or Jill is coming' is true, and 'No' otherwise. But more commonly a disjunctive interrogative expresses a wh-question with the presupposition that the answer is one of the two alternatives presented. Thus the question about Jack or Jill would express the thought *"Who is coming?"* while presupposing that the correct answer is either 'Jack' or 'Jill'. 'No' is not a possible answer. 'Neither' and 'Both are coming' reject the question as defective. It is natural to suggest that the disjunctive interrogative expresses $?Jv?M$. But we do not appear to have thoughts of this form, and do not know what would constitute a correct answer, if indeed such a disjunction would have an answer. Stressing elements of an interrogative sentence may also introduce presuppositions. Thus *Did <u>Jack</u> kiss Jill in the* *park?* presupposes that someone kissed Jill in the park, while *Did Jack kiss Jill in the park?* presupposes that Jack did something to Jill in the park. Without stress, neither is presupposed. Similarly, *How many died?* differs from *How many died?* in presuming that some did die. But stress has a similar effect on declarative sentences.

The purpose of this section was limited to showing that the expression theory of meaning can provide a promising account of the nondescriptive meaning of interrogative and imperative sentences by recognizing the existence of nonpropositional thoughts. Both nonpropositional thoughts and nondeclarative sentence meaning warrant further study.

## 6.2 SYNCATEGOREMATIC TERMS

Terms like 'when', 'if', and 'every' have long seemed problematic for ideational theories because it is thought they do not express ideas.[24] Such terms are classified as *syncategorematic*: they can occur with categorematic terms, but cannot themselves appear as subject or predicate terms in a categorical proposition. Those that can, like 'John', 'man', and 'walks', are called *categorematic* terms. Syncategorematic terms do not apply to any category of thing: nothing is denoted by 'when' the way John is denoted by 'John', men by 'man', and walking things by 'walks'. We cannot point to anything and say 'That is (a) when' or 'That when(s)'. We may justly conclude that syncategorematic terms do not express descriptive concepts, and thus have nondescriptive meaning. These facts do not suffice, however, to show that syncategorematic terms do not express ideas. Sentences also fail to apply to things the way 'John', 'man', and 'walks' do, for example, and yet clearly do express ideas.

Locke (1690: 3.7.1) was forced to the conclusion that 'when' did not express an idea because he followed Descartes in defining an idea as an object of thought, something we are thinking of (see §3.8). The root of the problem for Cartesians is that when asked what the idea expressed by 'when' is the idea *of*, it is difficult to answer. We cannot answer 'the idea of when', as James (1890: 245–56) urged. In contexts like (7), 'of' must be followed by a noun, noun phrase, or gerund, otherwise the resulting phrase is ungrammatical.

(7) The idea of ____.
    The concept of ____.
    The thought of ____.

If we try to use (7) to refer to the idea expressed by 'when', we are forced to fill the blank with a related nominal such as 'when something happened'. But 'The idea of when something happened' is most naturally interpreted as designating the idea expressed by the whole phrase 'when something happened' rather than the idea expressed by the syncategorematic term 'when'.

For an unambiguous reference, we must use *oratio recta* and refer to *the idea "when"* (Definition 3.11). Note that we cannot refer to the idea expressed by 'when' as the idea *of* 'when', as Alston (1964a: 24–5) tried to. While "the idea of 'when'" is fully grammatical, it refers to the idea of the four-letter word itself rather than the idea expressed by the word.

Since we define an idea as a thought or thought part, the difficulty of saying what the idea is of provides no reason to deny that 'when' expresses an idea. For there is no reason to think that every proper or improper constituent of a thought can be referred to unambiguously using the *oratio obliqua* forms in (7). It is just as impossible to say what the ideas expressed by sentences are of as it is to say what the ideas expressed by syncategorematic terms are of. Furthermore, there is no reason to think that every proper part of a thought is such that a word expressing it would make sense in (7). Indeed, verbs cannot appear in (7) either. If we try to put 'walk' in, we are forced to nominalize it. 'The idea of walking' is grammatical, but not 'The idea of walks'. Strictly speaking, 'the idea of walking' refers to the idea expressed by 'walking' as in 'John is walking' rather than the idea expressed by 'walks' in the non-equivalent 'John walks'. The correct way to refer to that idea is by using the *oratio recta* form 'the idea "walks"'.

To determine whether syncategorematic terms express ideas, we need to determine whether they express constituents of thoughts. Compare the following sentences.

> (8) Jack kissed Jill when the moon came out.
> Jack kissed Jill if the moon came out.
> Jack kissed Jill because the moon came out.
> Jack kissed Jill, unless the moon came out.
> Jack kissed Jill, so the moon came out.

We know that these sentences express similar but different thoughts. Moreover, it seems undeniable that 'when' signifies the distinguishing feature of the thought expressed by the first sentence, while 'if' signifies the distinguishing feature of what is expressed by the second sentence. In contrast, the number of letters in these sentences does not signify any feature of the thoughts the sentences express. Nor does the presence or absence of the comma. The hypothesis that what distinguishes these five thoughts is the possession of five different components, and that these components are expressed by the words 'when', 'if', 'because', 'unless', and 'so' explains all the available data quite well. This postulate is no less plausible than the hypothesis that the thought that the moon came out differs from the thought that the moon went in because the two thoughts contain different components in the predicate position, which are expressed by 'came out' and 'went in' respectively.

Locke's hypothesis was that 'particles' signify 'the *connexion* that the mind gives to ideas, or to propositions, one with another'.[25] On this hypothesis, we might propose that the two thoughts expressed by 'Jack kissed Jill' and 'The moon came out' can occur in at least five different relationships, and that the five compound thoughts expressed above differ only in the way the two simple thoughts are connected, not in having different components. For an analogy, isomers like $CH_3OCH_3$ and $CH_3CH_2OH$ differ not in their component atoms but in which components are bonded together, and in the spatial relations among the bonded components. Locke's thesis is thus an example of the feature thesis (§2.6), in which the relevant features are certain *structural relationships* among ideas. The feature thesis can be ruled out as a general account of the evidence suggesting that thoughts have constituents, because some of the apparent constituents are themselves ideas occurring to the thinker. But in the case of syncategorematic terms, the suggestion that they do not express ideas at all is not obviously false. So the feature theory cannot be rejected for syncategorematic terms on the same grounds without begging the question.

Borrowing an idea from modern compositional semantics, Locke could say alternatively that 'when' expresses not an idea, but an *ideational function*, a function from ideas to compound ideas containing them. Locke could have focused on ideational functions taking two or more ideas to a compound idea in which they have a distinctive relationship. But the ideational function notion can apply even when there is no apparent connection for the syncategorematic term to signify. Locke could then adopt Ockham's account of the 'signification' of nonrelational modifiers.

Thus the syncategorematic word 'every' does not signify any fixed thing, but when added to 'man' it makes the term 'man' stand for all men actually, or with confused distributive *supposito*. When added, however, to 'stone', it makes the term 'stone' stand for all stones; and when added to 'whiteness', it makes it stand for all occurrences of whiteness. As with this syncategorematic word 'every', so with others, although the different syncategorematic words have different tasks, as will be shown further below

Should some quibbler say that the word 'every' is significant and consequently it signifies something, we answer that it is called significant, not because it signifies something determinately but only because it makes something else signify or represent or stand for something, as we explained before.

(Ockham, *Summa Logicae* I: §3)[26]

It is not true that 'every' makes the term 'man' signify anything other than what it signifies in other contexts. The term 'man' expresses the idea of man and denotes men whether it is preceded by 'every' or 'no' or taken in isolation. In modern terminology, the extension of 'man' is the same in 'No man is an animal' as in 'Every man is an animal'. What 'every' does affect is the meaning of phrases containing it. Because of the difference in meaning between 'every' and 'no', the whole phrase 'every man' has a different meaning from 'no man'. But that provides no more reason to think that 'every' makes 'man' signify all men than it provides for thinking that 'man' makes 'every' signify all men. The relation between 'every' and 'man' is not even like the relation between 'hot' and 'dog', which mean one thing in contexts in which they occur separately, but typically mean something very different when they occur together in 'I had a hot dog for lunch'. This meaning of 'hot dog' is not determined compositionally by the meanings of 'hot' and 'dog' (see §5.6). What Ockham could have said is that 'every' signifies a function that takes the idea "N" and yields the related idea "every N".

Even though Locke's hypothesis would entail that not every meaningful word expresses an idea, when ideas are defined as thought parts, it would not contradict any of the principles of the theory I have been developing. Definitions 3.9 and 5.4, for example, imply that e means "$\mu_i$" iff e expresses the idea "$\mu_i$" *provided i is an idea*. The proviso allows for a class of exceptions to the rule that the meaning of an expression is determined by the idea it expresses. Interjections like 'Hello!' were cited in §5.2 as expressions that plausibly express mental states other than ideas, an idea that will be developed in §6.3. Interjections are covered by the more general principle that what an expression means is determined by the mental state expressed, a formulation that covers Locke's connection hypothesis as well. Locke's hypothesis would merely expand the number of cases of nonideational meaning. Since the mental states Locke cites are connections or relations among ideas, his hypothesis revises a detail in, rather than the essence of, ideational theories. It is completely compatible with the expression theory.

While Locke's connection hypothesis fits well within the general ideational framework, there does not appear to be any evidence favoring it over the constituent hypothesis. It might be thought that the connection hypothesis is more parsimonious. But ontological economy provides no basis for preferring the postulation of additional types of structural relationships over that of additional types of constituents. On the contrary, the constituent hypothesis provides an explanation of why the propositional components of the five thoughts in (8) stand in different relationships. They stand in different relationships because they are connected by different components. The connection hypothesis postulates connections, but does not tell us what it is for thoughts to be connected in these ways, or why two thoughts are connected in one way rather than another. It is true that the constituent hypothesis does not explain why the thoughts have the constituents they do, but this is not something that needs to be explained. As noted in §2.6, the fact that a thought has the constituents it has is no more in need of explanation than the fact that a molecule has the constituents it has.

The constituent thesis also has greater analogical support. Meaningful words that are known not to express ideas, such as interjections, are the exception rather than the rule. Given that the vast majority of words express ideas, the hypothesis that syncategorematic words do too should be accepted in the absence of specific evidence to the contrary. The connection hypothesis is a possibility, to be sure, but it has no direct support. On the contrary, there is a marked intuitive difference between what a word like 'when' expresses and what a symbol carrying purely structural information like commas and periods express. The placement of the comma in sentences like 'Jack will visit Europe and Asia, or Africa' and 'Jack will visit Europe, and Asia or Africa' indicates how the constituents of the thoughts expressed are related. The punctuation marks seem to have a different kind of meaning from the connectives 'and' and 'or'.

The final reason favoring the constituent hypothesis is more direct. Reflect on what you conceive when you read each of the following expressions.

  (9) Jack kissed Jill
  (10) Jack kissed Jill when
  (11) Jack kissed Jill when the moon came out

Introspection should reveal that each expression makes you conceive something more complex than the previous. What (10) makes us conceive contains what (9) makes us conceive, and is contained in what (11) makes us conceive. The reading of 'when' in (10) makes something occur to us that does not occur when we read (9), but which does occur when we read (11). What (10) makes us conceive, furthermore, is not a complete thought, in contrast to what (9) or (11) makes us conceive. I, for one, wish the thought to be completed: 'When *what?*' I wonder. Locke's hypothesis that 'when' signifies a structural relationship among thoughts rather than a thought part can account for the difference between (9) and (11), but not for the differences between them and (10). (Ockham's hypothesis has a similar difficulty with the 'when' in (10).) The hypothesis that 'when' expresses a distinct thought part accounts for both. Similar evidence, of course, was provided for categorematic terms in §2.6.[27]

What do we know about the constituents that differentiate the thoughts in (8), other than the fact that they exist? We know that they are distinct from each other, and from the other concepts contained in the thoughts in (8). We know that they are propositional connectives, and are expressed by certain words. Given that the propositions in (8) have different truth conditions, and differ only in which of these constituents they contain, we can attribute the difference in truth conditions to the difference in constituents. So we know what their contribution is to the truth conditions of the thoughts. Given this knowledge, we can assign intensions of various sorts to the connectives (Chapters 9 and 14). Negatively, we know that the constituents do not represent objects or actions the way the other constituents of the thoughts in (8) do, and thus do not have extensions.

Syncategorematic terms differ from categorematic terms in having nondescriptive meaning. They do not represent individuals, properties, or states of affairs, and consequently do not have any reference (or extension). They do not express thoughts, or concepts of objects. In other respects, however, syncategorematic terms are like categorematic terms. They belong to recognized parts of speech, and have a sense. Their meaning contributes compositionally to the meanings of any phrase or clause they appear in. And on my view, syncategorematic terms are like other terms in that they are meaningful because they express parts of thoughts.

It is commonly claimed, however, that syncategorematic terms have no meaning 'of their own' or 'by themselves'. I take this to entail that *their meaning is somehow dependent on or derived from what compounds they appear in mean*.[28] According to Husserl (1900: 499–500), for example, Anton Marty inferred this from the fact that *syncategorematic terms do not express presentations or judgments, but are parts of expressions that do.* Marty's premise is certainly true. But his terms does not follow. The conclusion concedes that syncategorematic terms do have meanings. Together with the premise that syncategorematic terms do not express presentations or judgments, it follows that having a meaning cannot consist in expressing presentations or judgments. So if the additional premise that syncategorematic terms are parts of complexes that express presentations or judgments implied that they do not have meaning 'by themselves', then it should just as well imply that categorematic terms do not have meanings by themselves. Neither conclusion follows, though. For the principle of compositionality is compatible with Marty's premise, but not his conclusion. Compositionality implies that the meaning of a syntactically complex expression is determined by what its components mean and the way they are compounded. But if the syncategorematic terms in (8) did not have their meanings independently of what the other terms in the sentences mean, then the meanings of the sentences in (8) would not be determined compositionally by the meanings of their components. And the ambiguity of *Jack kissed Jill since the moon came out* could not be attributed to the ambiguity of 'since' ('after' versus 'because'). It is obvious that the meanings of the categorematic terms in (8) together with its syntactic structure do not enable us to infer the meanings of the syncategorematic terms. For the five syncategorematic terms all have different meanings. Furthermore, the meanings of those five terms are not dependent in any way on the other terms in (8). For as Husserl (1900: 502) observed, the syncategorematic terms in (8) can have the same meaning in sentences containing none of those other terms.

We might be able to infer what a syncategorematic term means from our knowledge of what the categorematic terms in a sentence mean together with our knowledge of what proposition the sentence as a whole expresses. But this ability is compatible with the thesis that the syncategorematic term has its meaning independently of what the categorematic terms mean. Indeed, it is hard to see how we could infer what the syncategorematic terms in (8) mean without inferring that they express some parts (or features) of the expressed propositions that the categorical terms do not express. Imagine a code based on English in which 'kissed' means "kicked" and 'moon' means "sun", and in which each sentence must contain a nonsense syllable somewhere whose only function is to confuse code-breakers. Then (12) is a sentence in this code.

(12) Jack kissed Jill when bluh the moon came out.

We know that (12) expresses the proposition that Jack kicked Jill when the sun came out. But we can not infer that 'when bluh' has any meaning.

Read (1994: 4452) defines syncategorematic terms as those that '*have no meaning of their own, but have meaning only in the contribution they make to the meaning of a whole proposition by being added to categorematic terms*'.[29] But if a term has no meaning of its own, it has nothing to contribute to the meanings of sentences it appears in. The word 'bluh' makes no contribution to the meaning of (12). Nor does the word 'borrow' any meaning not its own from any of the other terms in the sentence. If we know that inserting 'tilp' between two sentences produces a sentence expressing the conjunction of the propositions expressed by those sentences, then we know what 'tilp' contributes to the meaning of a sentence. But then we also know that 'tilp' has a meaning of its own: it means "and".

Husserl (1990: IV) too said that the meaning of syncategorematic terms is '*incomplete*' and '*non-independent*'. His reason was also that syncategorematic terms do not name or describe things. In what way is the meaning of a term that names or describes complete and independent? And why do terms that do not name or describe 'need supplementation'? It might seem as if Husserl's claims were motivated by the referential theory of meaning. But if that theory were correct, it would follow not that syncategorematic terms have incomplete or dependent meanings, but that they have no meanings at all (§10.2). In one place, Husserl (1900: 499) says that syncategorematic terms are 'incomplete expressions of presentations' and 'incomplete expressions of judgments'. But 'and' does not express a presentation or judgment at all. It is part of many complexes that do express presentations (e.g., 'the pens and pencils on the table') or judgments (e.g., 'The weather is hot and humid'). But that is no reason to say that the meaning of 'and' is in any way incomplete. If it were, then we could just as well describe as incomplete the meaning of a noun phrase (because it is incomplete as an expression of a thought) or subject-predicate sentence (because it is incomplete as an expression of a complex thought).

Husserl's (1900: 502, 506) clearest explanation was that the meanings of sentences and categorematic terms are 'complete' and 'independent' because the thoughts or thought parts they express are able to exist alone, separate from other thoughts and thought parts. The meaning of a syncategorematic term, in contrast, is 'incomplete' and 'non-independent' because the thought part it expresses cannot exist alone, but only as part of a more comprehensive whole. Husserl is therefore characterizing the meaning of a syncategorematic term itself, not the way it is possessed. That is, Husserl is not claiming that the possession of meaning by syncategorematic terms is in any way dependent on what compounds containing those terms mean. Instead, he is characterizing the meaning that syncategorematic terms independently possess in terms of the nature of the thought parts they express. The claim that a word like 'and' has non-independent meaning consequently does not imply that we cannot understand it when it occurs in isolation. The most Husserl's claim implies is that when we understand 'and' in isolation, the concept we recognize that it expresses must be occurring to us as part of some thought that the word itself does not express (Husserl 1900: 509).

It is not clear, however, that the thought parts expressed by categorematic terms are any more capable of occurring separate from thoughts and other thought parts than those expressed by syncategorematic terms. Indeed, I have taken pains to argue that the thesis that thoughts have parts does not entail that the parts can exist independently of the thoughts.[30] For there are reasons to believe that proper thought parts always do occur as parts of thoughts. It is difficult, if not impossible, to think of Iraq, for example, without thinking something about Iraq. If Husserl's claim is about the mere logical possibility of separate occurrence (cf. 1900: 443, 445), then it can be accepted. But in that sense, it is unclear that either sort of concept cannot exist alone. The question Husserl has raised about the concepts expressed by syncategorematic terms is interesting, but it does not bear on the adequacy of ideational theories of meaning.

## 6.3 Interjections

I have offered interjections as clear exceptions to the rule that meaning consists in the expression of ideas. For example, 'Ouch!' does not express a thought or part of a thought. It makes no sense to say that someone is thinking the thought *"Ouch!"* And except in quotation and the like, 'Ouch!' does not combine with other expressions to express a thought. Paratactic compounds like 'Ouch! That hurts' do express thoughts, but only because the other component does. The interjection does not serve to modify in any way the thought expressed by the rest of the construction.[31] Even though an utterance of 'Ouch!' conventionally indicates that the speaker is in pain, there is no sense in which 'Ouch!' is semantically equivalent to 'I am in pain'.[32] Because interjections do not express ideas, they do not represent anything, and have no reference.[33] 'Ouch!' does not even represent or refer to pain, or the objects that cause it. *A fortiori*, interjections do not express beliefs, or anything with a truth value. Interjections cannot be used to lie, although they can be used artfully in attempts to deceive. The characteristic syntactic independence of interjections[34] is another consequence of their having nonideational meaning. For the syntactic structure of phrases and sentences is a consequence of the fact that they express thoughts and ideas, which themselves have constituent structure. The phonological independence of interjections (the fact that they often contain speech sounds not found in other word classes)[35] is also not surprising, given that they do not enter into construction with the vast bulk of the language.

Defenders of a purely ideational theory of meaning could try to maintain that interjections simply do not have a meaning. Indeed, there is some evidence that 'means' and 'meaning' do not apply to interjections. If a man stubs his toe and says 'Ouch!' it would be odd for anyone to ask 'What did he mean by that?' And whether asked or not, the statement 'He meant "Ouch"?' would be highly unusual. The question 'What does 'Ouch!' mean?' also seems unnatural, as does the suggestion that 'Ouch!' means (or does not mean) "Ow!" It would be especially strained to ask what 'Ouch!' means on a particular occasion. We are more likely to say something like this: "'Ouch!' does not meaning anything, really, it just the thing people say when experiencing a sudden pain."

However, the suggestion that interjections are not meaningful, or that they have a meaning but do not mean anything, is untenable (cf. Chapter 10). 'Ouch!' differs markedly from an expression like '%#@&!' which might be used in a comic strip in place of an interjection, or from combinations like 'ammnpqprrt' which are not used at all. It is particularly clear that interjections are words of English and apparently all other natural languages, and that their mode of use is part of what constitutes the language. What accounts for the oddity of the above questions and statements about the meaning of interjections? We can cite several factors.

(i) 'Ouch!' is one of the few unambiguous words of English, and nearly every English speaker knows what it means. If we change object languages, the same questions might well be in order. It would be natural for an English speaker to ask what 'Aïe!' means in French, and the correct answer is that 'Aïe!' means "Ouch!" If a German speaker says 'Auf Wiedersehen!', an English speaker might naturally wonder what he meant by that, and the answer would usually be 'He meant "Good bye!"' And in devising a code, a woman might stipulate that 'Marshmallow%' means "Ouch!", 'Daisy%'

means "Damn!", and so on. She can then lard her transmissions with exclamations as appropriate. We may even need to infer that an English speaker meant "Good bye!" if he was speaking with his mouth full.

(ii) An interjection like 'Darn!' is ambiguous, since it can also be used as an imperative ordering someone to commence mending. It is perfectly appropriate to wonder whether 'Darn!' means "Damn!" or "Mend!" on a particular occasion. The sentence 'God, I wish you would answer my letters' is ambiguous, because the 'God' can be interpreted as either a vocative or an interjection (Downing 1969: 576).

(iii) 'What did he mean by that?' is always out of place with interjections when it is asking about cognitive speaker meaning (§4.2). Given that interjections do not express beliefs, we can never say "By 'Ouch!' S meant *that* something is the case", unless S was speaking figuratively in some way.

(iv) 'What does that mean?' is always out of place with interjections when it is asking for a definition. Given that interjections do not express ideas, we cannot define them.

(v) Finally, both the statement that people mean different things by 'Ouch!' and 'Ow!' and the statement that they mean the same thing must be rejected if the inclusive sense of cogitative speaker meaning is intended (§7.3). In that sense, meaning Φ entails referring to and expressing the idea of Φ, and thus does not apply to interjections.

Interjections present no fundamental threat to the expression theory because it seems evident that interjections are meaningful in virtue of being used to express *something*. We say that 'Aïe!' and 'Ouch!' mean the same thing because they are used to express the same mental state in the same circumstances. 'Ouch!' and 'Aïe!' are used to express pain, specifically sudden pain that is neither too minor nor too serious. So is 'Ow!', unless it is moaned, in which case it can express chronic or intense pain. The intensity of the pain expressed varies with stress and the intensity of utterance (Cruse 1986: 282). 'Damn!' and 'Shit!' can be used to express sudden, moderate pain too, but they can equally well be used to express annoyance, anger, frustration, or disappointment. 'Wow!' is used to express amazement, or pleasant surprise. 'Aha!' is used to express the characteristic emotional impact of sudden insight, triumph, or contempt. 'Hello!' expresses friendly regard on meeting someone; 'Good bye!' expresses the same on departure. And so on. Dictionaries thus define interjections as 'a class of words expressing emotion', evidently construing 'emotion' broadly.[36] These practices are every bit as conventional as the use of nouns, verbs, and adjectives to express ideas. And the use of interjections to express emotions is clearly related to their meaning. These facts make it seem evident that *the meaning of an interjection consists in its expressing emotions.*

This emotion theory of interjection meaning is natural and plausible, and fits well with the expression theory of meaning I have developed. I nonetheless believe the hypothesis is false. I do not deny that interjections are used to express 'emotions,' nor that such conventions are related to their meaning. What I believe we must reject is the foundational claim that the meaning of an interjection *consists in* the expression of emotions. There are two reasons to reject the emotion theory. First, the emotion theory correctly rules that 'Ouch!' differs in meaning from 'Ah!' because they are used to express different mental states—pain in the one case, pleasure in the other. But then the theory would also seem to rule incorrectly that 'Shit!' is ambiguous, since it is used on different occasions to express different emotions. The theory would also seem to rule incorrectly that 'Shit!' means "Ouch!" on those occasions in which 'Shit!' is used to express sudden pain. Since 'Shit!' has the same meaning whether it is used to express pain or annoyance, its having that meaning must consist in something other than the expression of pain or the expression of annoyance.

Second, the emotion theory cannot account for the fact that interjections have at least four different uses. The *emotive* or *exclamatory* use is the one we have been discussing. But interjections are also used *semantically*, *figuratively*, and *fictionally*. See (13) through (16).

(13) *Exclamatory*: Damn! [Said upon learning that one's team lost the game.]

(14) *Figurative*: Damn! [Said ironically upon learning that things turned out even better than expected.]

(15) *Fictional*: Damn! [Said by the narrator in a novel.]

(16) *Semantic*: 'Verdammt!' means "Damn!"

In the figurative case, the speaker is using 'Damn!' to express the opposite of the emotion it usually expresses.[37] In the semantic case, the speaker is not using 'Damn!' to express an emotion at all. The author is not using 'Damn!' to indicate that *he* is experiencing an emotion in the fiction case, but rather to make the narrator express emotion in the novel.[38] Yet in all four cases, the speaker is using the word with its conventional meaning. In the cogitative sense, the speaker means the same thing by the word 'Damn!' in the figurative, fictional, and semantic cases as he does in the exclamatory case. The word consequently has the same meaning on all four occasions. If the speaker meant "Condemn to hell!" by 'Damn!' in (16), then he would be making a different, although equally true, claim about 'Verdammt!', which has the same ambiguity in German that it has in English. If a speaker said "'Verdammt!' means "Darn!"" he would be politely expressing a near truth if he used 'Darn!' with the meaning that is salient here, but would be expressing a patent falsehood if he meant "Mend!" The speaker would also be saying something false about 'Verdammt' if he were using a code in which 'means' means "means" but 'Damn!' means "Hooray!"

It is particularly important to note that if the emotion theory of interjection meaning were true, the ideo-reflexive analysis of 'means "$\mu$"' (Definition 5.4) would fail when '$\mu$' is an interjection. The difficulty is not simply that the term '*ideo*-reflexive' would be inappropriate in the case of nonideational meaning. Nothing in Definition 5.4 requires that i be an idea. The variable 'i' stands for anything, although 'e expresses i' will be true only when i is something that can be expressed. The problem is that on the emotion theory, a statement like (16) would have to assert that 'Verdammt' expresses pain, anger, annoyance, and so on. But 'Damn!' does not express any of these states where it occurs in (16). So if the emotion theory were true, 'e means "Damn!"' could not be true in virtue of the fact that e expresses what 'Damn!' is used to express in 'e means "Damn!"'.

The emotion theory of interjections is thus led astray by focusing exclusively on the exclamatory use of interjections. To account for all uses, we must hypothesize that the mental event-type whose expression constitutes the meaning of a given interjection has the following properties.

(i) The event is idea-like, but is not a thought or thought part. The occurrence of the event does not constitute thinking of something.

(ii) We indicate that the event is occurring whenever we use an interjection with the given meaning. 'Damn!' expresses the same event-type in (13) through (16), and 'Verdammt' expresses it in German.

(iii) Whether we *hear* 'Damn!' *as* an interjection rather than as an imperative in "'Verdammt' means "Damn!"'" depends on whether an event of this kind is occurring to us rather than an imperative thought.

(iv) Occurrences of the event can be connected in a distinctive fashion to a range of nonrepresentational mental states like pain, annoyance, amazement, and friendly regard. The nature of the event-type determines the particular range of emotions it connects with. The use of an interjection is exclamatory when it expresses an event so connected with an emotion. A noun, verb, or phrase is used as an interjection when the idea it expresses is similarly connected with an emotion, as in General McAuliffe's famous exclamation 'Nuts!' at Bastogne during the Battle of the Bulge. In such cases, the speaker uses the noun or verb to express an emotion as well as the idea directly expressed by the word. I call the mental event-type expressed by interjections an *interject*.

An interesting hypothesis is that the event-type expressed by an interjection contains as a proper part the idea expressed by its root. The suggestion is that 'Shit!' expresses a nonidea that contains the idea "shit". We might postulate that the exclamation point expresses an operator that converts an idea into an interject. This hypothesis would obviously fail for 'Ouch!'

and 'Wow!' whose roots do not express any idea. Moreover, the hypothesis would seem to falsely predict that 'Shit!' and 'Excrement!' as well as 'Fuck!' and 'Fornicate!' should be synonymous interjections. We may choose one expletive rather than another because of the meaning of its root, and the interjection may have originated historically from metaphorical use of the root (Wilkins 1992: 130–1), but we do not seem to mean "shit" by 'shit' when we say 'Shit!' except in the rare case in which we use 'Shit!' to mean something like "Behold, it is shit!" or "Take a crap!"[39]

## 6.4 CONVENTIONAL IMPLICATURES

A problem for any use theory is to distinguish meaning from what Grice (1975) called 'implicature'.[40] A speaker *implicates* that p iff he means or implies that p without saying that p, and does so by saying something else. If Ann asks Bob 'Where can I get some gasoline?' Bob might reply 'There is a station around the corner', implying that Ann can get gasoline at the station around the corner. Then he expressed that belief, and meant this in the inclusive sense of speaker meaning (§4.3). But Bob did not *say* that Ann can get gasoline at the station around the corner, because that is not what the sentence he used meant. So Bob 'implicated' this. Figurative usage is another case in which implicatures arise. Speakers who use 'That's great!' ironically implicate, but do not say, that it is the very opposite of great.

Grice went on to distinguish *conversational* from *conventional* implicatures. Bob's implicature is conversational, because it is generated in some way from the conversational context, not just from the meanings of the words he used. Bob could have used 'There is a station around the corner' without having implied that Ann could get gasoline there. This would not have been a cooperative thing for Bob to do, since he would have misled Ann into thinking that she could. But Bob would have been using proper English; he would not have made any linguistic mistakes. Moreover, he could perfectly well have said 'There is a station around the corner but it is closed', in which case he would not even have implicated that Ann could get gasoline there. Grice would say that the but-clause *canceled* the implicature. In contrast, someone who says 'Jack is sick, so he should rest' normally implicates that Jack's being sick implies that he should rest. This implicature is said to be conventional because it arises in some way from the conventional meaning of 'so', and cannot be canceled. A speaker who says 'Jack is sick, so he should rest, but his being sick does not imply that he should rest' has not exactly contradicted himself. Yet his but-clause undermines his use of 'so'. 'Negro' and 'Nigger' have both been used to implicate that people are inferior. But while the implicature depends on the particular speaker and context in the first case, and can be canceled, the implicature is part of the meaning of the second, and is not cancelable. What makes a term pejorative is that it has a negative conventional implicature.[41]

As in the case of 'means', 'expresses', and 'implies', 'implicates' can be applied to *sentences* as well as *speakers*. A sentence implicates, roughly, what speakers using the sentence with its regular meaning would commonly use it to implicate. Despite what Bob implicated in his response to Ann, the sentence Bob used does not itself implicate "Ann can get gasoline at the station". Generally, the use of 'There's a station around the corner' would not suggest that the hearer can get gasoline there, and its use would not be misleading if the speaker thought the station had no gasoline, or was closed. Indeed, the speaker may have been talking about a train station. In contrast, (17)(a) itself implicates (17)(b).

> (17) (a) Jack is sick, so he should rest.
> (b) Jack's being sick implies that he should rest.

A speaker could not properly use (17)(a) without implicating (17)(b). And (18)(a) implicates (18)(b):

> (18) (a) Some died.
> (b) Not all died.

For speakers commonly implicate "Not all died" when using 'Some died'. In the case of (18), the implicature is conversational, and can be canceled. 'Some died, but not all did' is not contradictory or linguistically odd in any way.

I have argued elsewhere (Davis 1998) that even conversational implicatures depend on conventions when we are talking about sentence rather than speaker implicatures. The sentence form 'Some S are P' is commonly used to implicate that not all S are P, and is regularly so interpreted. This practice meets all the conditions for something to be conventional. The regularity is socially useful, contributing as it does to communication. Speakers who implicate that not all S are P communicate the thought that not all S are P when their implication is recognized. The regularity is self-perpetuating: the fact that speakers before us have used 'Some S are P' to implicate "Not all S are P" gives us a good reason to do so ourselves; the habit of using the sentence to express the thought, and the association between the two, are both reinforced each time 'Some S are P' is used to implicate "Not all S are P"; and the practice is transmitted from one generation to the next as language is learned. Lastly, the regularity is arbitrary. We could have used 'Some S are P' to implicate "It is not the case that 50% of all S are P" or "Perhaps all S are P" or "It is an open question whether all S are P". Or we could have used 'Some S are P' with no implicature at all about stronger propositions, the way we use 'At least 99% of all S are P'. The arbitrariness of conversational implicature conventions conflicts with the Gricean assumption that conversational implicatures are 'calculable' from and 'determined' by contextual factors together with general psychosocial principles, namely, the cooperative principle and associated maxims. I have argued directly against these claims in the work cited.

The conventionality of sentence implicatures creates the following problem for the theory that word meaning is the conventional expression of an idea or other mental state. Given the implicature convention noted above, 'Some S are P' is conventionally used to express the belief and therefore the thought that not all S are P. So why doesn't 'Some S are P' *mean* "Not all S are P"? Why doesn't 'Some S are P' have "Not all S are P" as at least part of its meaning? The fact that 'Some S are P' is not always used with its customary implicature is not the answer. For the usage conventions underlying word meaning are almost invariably nonuniversal (§5.5). The correct answer, I believe, lies in the *indirection* that is characteristic of implicature. Speakers who use 'Some died' to express the thought that not all died do so *by* expressing the thought that some died. Hence even though they use 'Some died' to mean in the inclusive sense that not all died, they do not mean "Not all died" by the sentence 'Some died'. We have an instance of *cognitive* speaker meaning here, but not *cogitative*; *expression* but not *direct expression*. In moving from the Gricean to the neo-Gricean analysis of word meaning, we moved from using cognitive speaker meaning and the expression of belief to cogitative speaker meaning and the direct expression of thought. We did so in order to rule out figurative usage and rule in fictional uses, indexicals, and subsentential meaning (§5.4).

The worry we have just addressed is that the refined Gricean analysis might be too broad, counting what is conventionally conversationally implicated as part of what an expression means. The solution to this problem creates a new one. How can the analysis account for the meaning of expressions with what Grice called conventional implicatures, which are nonconversational? If what is conventionally implicated is indirectly expressed, then how can it be part of the meaning of the expressions? How could it be directly expressed without being part of what is said? If a conventional implicature is part of what is said, as Bach (1999) suggests, why isn't it a standard truth condition of the whole utterance? The worry this time is that the theory is too narrow, excluding part of the content of 'so', 'but', and similar locutions.

There is an alternative way of formulating the problem. If 'p, so q' is used to *indirectly* express the thought that 'p' implies 'q', then what is the thought (or thoughts) we *directly* express? What is the thought we use 'p, so q' to express by which we express the further thought that if p then q? It is not the conjunctive thought "p and q". For in that case 'p, so q' would express a proposition, and would be true or false depending on the truth values of 'p' and 'q'. Moreover, it is hard to see how we could express the thought "if p then q" by expressing the thought "p and q", unless we are in a special context. The base of the implicature cannot simply be the sequence of thoughts ⟨"p", "q"⟩ either. The sentence 'It is Friday; it will snow' expresses the right sequence of propositions but is not synonymous with 'It is Friday, so it will snow', and does not conventionally implicate "That it is Friday implies that it will snow". Similarly, 'p but q' differs from 'p and q' in that only the former implicates that the truth of 'q' may be unexpected or surprising given the truth of 'p'.[42] So if 'p but q' simply expressed the thought "p and q", then its meaning would in no way generate its implicature.

One hypothesis is that words have conventional implicatures because part of their meaning is nonideational.[43] Words have nonideational meaning in virtue of being conventionally used to directly express mental states other than ideas, or to directly perform actions other than expression. This hypothesis fits many of the facts. Sentences of the form 'p so q' are used to express not only the thoughts "p" and "q", but also the *inference* from "p" to "q".[44] Because the inference from "p" to "q" is valid only if "p" implies "q", we would expect 'p so q' to have the implicature noted above. Similarly, 'but' is used to *warn* or *alert* the audience that an idea is coming that may be unexpected or surprising given the ideas that have just been expressed. Its function is partly performative.[45] 'But' does not simply express the state of surprise. Consider one of my own uses of 'but'.

Thus 'nigger' is like 'black' and 'colored person' in expressing the idea of a Negro. But 'nigger' differs radically from the other two terms in expressing an extremely negative attitude toward Negroes.

I was not expressing surprise here. Both facts have been well known to me for some time, and I see no incompatibility between them. I used 'but' there because I wanted to signal that I was going to move from describing similarities between the terms to describing differences. I intuitively felt that the reader might expect me to go on in the same way, so I provided a transition marker. Because we use 'p but q' to warn our audience in this way, the form should implicate that it may be unexpected or surprising for us to say that q given that we have just said that p. The fact that we felt the need to mark this transition indicates that we believe the implicated proposition.

'Moreover' and 'furthermore' have a similar but different function. These are used to signal that the speaker is going to make further claims in support of the point he has just been making.[46] Speakers who utter 'p; furthermore q' imply that 'p and q' is stronger than 'p' alone. It would thus be odd for someone to say 'All men are greedy; moreover, some men are greedy' or 'Jack is taller than Jim; moreover Jim is shorter than Jack'.

It is therefore plausible that words have conventional implicatures because they are used to perform acts other than expressing ideas. Nevertheless, the nonideational meaning hypothesis does not square with all the data.

There are several cases in which words like 'so' and 'but' are used with their standard meanings but not to perform the other actions that are distinctive of them (cf. §6.3).

*Fiction.* If the author of a novel has the narrator say 'The lights are out, so no one is home', the author is expressing the thought that 'The lights are out' implies 'No one is home'. But there is no indication that the *author* is making that inference. The author is not even pretending to make an inference. Instead, the author is making it true that the *narrator* is so inferring in the novel. Similarly, if the author has the narrator say 'She is a woman, but she can read', the author is not using 'but' to warn the reader that 'She can read' may be unexpected given 'She is a woman'. Instead, the author is trying to portray the attitude of the narrator.

*Indirect discourse.* If I say 'Jack is thinking "The lights are out, so no one is home",' I am indicating that Jack believes the first proposition implies the second, not that I do.

*Semantic uses.* The 'but' in " 'Mais' means "but" " is not used to issue any warnings.

One hypothesis that can account for all the uses of words with conventional nonconversational implicatures is that they are used to directly express certain kinds of complex thoughts. Consider (19):

(19) Washington, a Virginian, owned slaves.[47]

A speaker who uses (19) implies that Washington was a Virginian, but does not say that Washington was a Virginian.[48] This implicature is conventional, as indicated by its noncancelability. A sentence like (19) with an appositive phrase is used to directly express what I call an *appositional thought*. Someone can think "Washington, a Virginian, owned slaves". This thought is not simply the conjunction "Washington was a Virginian and owned slaves", nor is it just the thought pair "Washington was a Virginian. Washington owned slaves." Appositional thoughts have a structure consisting of a *main thought* plus a *subordinate thought* in apposition to it.[49] I believe that in tokens of the appositional thought expressed by (19), the tokens of its main and subordinate thoughts share the same subject-concept token. When the subordinate thought is true, the compound is true or false depending on its main component. Thus (19) is true, while 'Washington, a Virginian, owned cars', is false. When the subordinate clause is false, the compound is *defective*. In that case, it is unclear whether the compound has a truth value. I think we would be inclined to count 'Washington, a Floridian, owned cars' as false, but not to count 'Washington, a Floridian, owned slaves' as true or false (cf. Grice 1981: §3). In a nontechnical sense, it is correct to say that an appositional thought *presupposes* the truth of its subordinate thought. Sentence (19) presupposes, but does not assert, that Washington was a Virginian. Whether the presuppositions of appositional thoughts have the same properties as the presuppositions introduced by definite descriptions—or more generally, whether they satisfy the definitions of various technical notions of presupposition—is an open question.

When sentences expressing appositional thoughts are embedded in negations, conjunctions, disjunctions, or conditionals, the resulting sentence expresses an appositional thought whose subordinate thought (or thoughts) is the subordinate thought expressed by its components and whose main thought is the indicated logical compound of the main thoughts expressed by its components. Thus 'It is not the case that Washington, a Virginian, owned slaves' expresses an appositional thought whose main thought is "It is not the case that Washington owned slaves", and whose subordinate thought is "Washington was a Virginian". And 'If Washington, a Virginian, owned slaves, then Jefferson, another Virginian, would have been appalled', expresses an appositional thought in which the main thought is "If Washington owned slaves, then Jefferson would have been appalled", and in which there are two subordinate thoughts, "Washington was a Virginian" and "Jefferson was another Virginian". When sentences expressing appositional thoughts are the subordinate clauses in propositional attitude statements, the result is amphibolous. 'S believes that Washington, a Virginian, owned slaves' can express either: i) an appositional thought in which the main thought is "S believes that Washington owned slaves" and the subordinate thought is "Washington was a Virginian"; or ii) a nonappositional thought in which S is represented as believing the appositional thought expressed by (19). Interpretation ii) can be expressed unambiguously by 'S believes "Washington, a Virginian, owned slaves".' Interpretation i) can be expressed unambiguously by using square brackets to insert a speaker's comment: 'S believes that Washington [a Virginian] owned slaves'.

I suggest that '*p but q*' expresses an appositional thought in which the main thought is "*p and q*", and the subordinate thought is something like *the fact or statement that q may be unexpected or surprising given the fact or statement that p.* In the case of 'Hillary Clinton is female but literate', the speaker might believe that literacy may be unexpected in a female for any number of reasons: the belief that most females are illiterate, that someone recently said most females are illiterate, that Clinton's name was on a list of people who were supposedly both female and illiterate, and so on (cf. Bach 1999: 346). In the case of 'I'm not supposed to say anything, but it is my wife's birthday', it would most likely be the statement that it is his wife's birthday that he thinks might be surprising given that he was not supposed to say anything, not the mere fact that it is her birthday.

The hypothesis that 'but' is used to express appositional thoughts explains why 'Hillary Clinton is female but literate' is defective in a way that 'Hillary Clinton is female and literate' is not. It also explains why 'It is not the case that Hillary Clinton is female but literate' presupposes the same thing that

'Hillary Clinton is female but literate' does, namely, that Clinton's being literate is somehow unexpected or surprising given that she is female. 'Bubba believes that Hillary Clinton is female but literate' has the expected amphiboly, implying either that Bubba is sexist or that the speaker is.

When the appositional thought "p but q" occurs, the component thoughts share occurrences of thoughts "p" and "q". The word 'but' expresses the complex thought part that combines with two propositions to form an appositional thought of the form "p but q" (cf. §6.2). 'But' expresses this thought part in fictional, semantic, and indirect discourse uses as well as in direct discourse. A speaker who uses 'p but q' assertively in direct discourse typically warns or signals that 'q' may be unexpected given 'p' by expressing that concept.

Similarly, I suggest that '*p so q*' expresses an appositional thought with *two* main thoughts, "*p*" and "*q*", and with the subordinate thought "p" implies "q". Since the appositional thought expressed by 'p so q' has two main thoughts, it is not a proposition (cf. §2.5). It is assessed as valid or invalid rather than true or false. Given the connection between implication and inference, a speaker who uses 'p so q' assertively in direct discourse expresses an inference from 'p' to 'q' by expressing the subordinate thought expressed by 'p so q'. 'But' and 'so' generate implicatures, and are used to express certain mental states and perform certain actions because they are used to directly express certain thought parts.

## NOTES

[1] See Greenbaum 1996: 361–2.

[2] The exclamation point can also be used, of course, to express amazement instead of an imperative thought. The two uses are associated with slightly different intonation patterns. According to Sadock and Zwicky (1985: 158, 166, 182), mood is conveyed lexically in some languages, such as Tagalog, Welsh, and Greenlandic.

[3] See Austin 1962; Alston 1964b; Searle 1965; 1969.

[4] For comprehensive evidence of this fact, see Leech 1983: §5.5; Davies 1986: Ch. 2; Hamblin 1987: Ch. 1; Wilson and Sperber 1988.

[5] A simple imperative like 'Stop!' is second-personal and future-tensed (see, e.g., Han 2000: 139 ff), so the root thought is "You will stop". In English, an imperative with a definite, singular, third-person subject has a vocative element as well (Downing 1969: 577–8; Hamblin 1987: 51 ff). Thus what 'Mary, sing!' expresses is not exactly the imperative transform of the thought "Mary will sing". When the third-person noun is general, as in (1), however, or indefinite, it is not vocative (Downing 1969). Hofstadter and McKinsey 1939 would use 'Let everybody stop!' to express !E (cf. Hamblin 1987: 59). But English sentences of the form 'Let p' still seem to have 'you' as their implicit subject (even if the referent is the personified 'forces that be'); thus we must say 'Let *yourself* sing!' rather than 'Let *you* sing!' And 'Let Mary sing!' asks someone to *allow* Mary to sing, contrasting in meaning with other imperatives, such as '*Make* Mary sing!'

[6] Cf. A. Ross 1944: 33; Stenius 1967; McGinn 1977: 308; Loar 1981: 222; Pendlebury 1986; Han 2000. Contrast Schmerling 1982: 209–10; and Hamblin 1987: 108–11, whose criticisms are based on a number of assumptions independent of the basic thesis. Compare and contrast

Katz 1977b: 11; also Hare (1949; 1952; 1970), and following him Kenny (1963: 222 ff) and Chierchia and McConnell-Ginet (1990: 164–5), who proposed that corresponding declarative, interrogative, and imperative sentences expressed something in common (the 'phrastic') and something different (the 'neustic'), without telling us what either is. There is a suggestion that 'Everyone will stop' means "Everyone's stopping—it is the case", while 'Everyone stop!' means "Everyone's stopping—make it the case". But such formulations are not exact synonyms, and do not advance the inquiry since their 'neustics' are declarative and imperative respectively.

  [7] See Hofstadter and McKinsey 1939; Dummett 1973: 303; McGinn 1977: 308–9; Katz 1977b: xiv, 4, 120; Kuhn 1984: 171–2; Huntley 1984: 103; Hamblin 1987: Ch. 4.

  [8] See Han 2000: §5.3.4. Contrast A. Ross 1944; Huntley 1984: 113–14; Dummett 1973: 315–6, 328–48. Wilson and Sperber (1988: 99) claim that 'The omotic languages of Southern Ethiopia have both indicative and imperative interrogatives—that is, interrogatives with an imperative verb, which expect an imperative answer.' Such compounds might express ?!P. For something that fits Wilson and Sperber's description in English, consider imperatives with interrogative intonation: 'John: Everybody stop? Mary: Yes, everybody stop!' But there is some reason to believe that imperative sentences are being used here to express propositions in which the main verb is 'should'. This can be seen by thinking about the conditions for something being a positive answer, and by noting that the implicit subject in 'John: Buy milk? Mary: Yes, buy milk!' is the first-person rather than the second-person pronoun.

  [9] The 'propositional approach' that identifies a question with the set of correct answers in effect equates meanings with intensions. See Hiż 1978: xv; Kiefer 1983: 1; Harrah 2001: §2.

  [10] It might be suggested that P, !P, and ?P have different 'directions of fit', with P the mind–world direction, and !P the world–mind direction; cf. Kenny 1963: 216 ff; Anscombe 1975: §32; Searle 1979: 1–27; 1983: 7–9; M. Smith 1987: §§6–7; Allan 1994: 2541. ?P might be said to have a mind–mind direction of fit, calling for the thinker to think the answer. It is the wrong question if the answer does not provide the information needed. However, while believing P, willing !P, and wondering ?P can meaningfully be said to have these directions of fit, I do not think 'direction of fit' can be defined for the thoughts themselves. For example, while we might expect a man who believes that Mars has rings to change his mind to conform to the facts, we would not want a man who disbelieves that Mars has rings to change. Yet both propositional attitudes have the same propositional object. Similarly, the propositional objects of believing that Bush will prevail and desiring that Bush prevail are the same even though the propositional attitudes have different directions of fit.

  [11] For a review, see Harrah 2001: §5.

  [12] See also Hare 1949: 24; Bell 1975; Åqvist 1983; Keifer 1983: 3; Sadock and Zwicky 1985: 155; Harrah 2001: 33. Contrast Hoepelman 1983: 198–9; Wilson and Sperber 1988: 92–3.

  [13] Hoepelman (1983: 207) equates an interrogative 'p?' with a very different declarative, namely, 'It is the question whether p' or 'It is indeterminate whether p'. Russell (1940: 26–7) once suggested that declaratives were really implicit imperatives. And Bohnert (1945) proposed that the imperative 'Do φ!' is equivalent to 'Either you φ or q', where 'q' describes a 'penalty'. Davidson (1979: 119–21) proposed that a nondeclarative sentence is synonymous with a *sequence* of declarative sentences, one saying that the other has imperative or interrogative force. Contrast Hare 1952: 5 ff.

  [14] See also McCawley 1968; Downing 1969; Sadock 1974; Lewis 1976: 207–12; Harris 1978; Allan 1994: 2541; Jackson and Pettit 1998: 248–9. Contrast Katz 1977b: 38–49; Kuhn 1984; Chierchia and McConnell-Ginet 1990: 184–7.

  [15] Ross (1970: 251–2) sought to avoid the regress problem by noting that when declaratives embed, they do not have performative force. Instead of solving the problem, however, the cited fact constitutes a problem in itself, since the embedded and non-embedded declaratives have the same meaning.

[16] Cf. Hobbes 1655: Ch. 3, §1; Frege 1918: 7; Hare 1949; 1952; 1970; Lewis 1969: 186; Searle 1969: §2.4; Dummett 1973: 302–7; Gordon and Lakoff 1975; McDowell 1976: 44; Lyons 1977: Ch. 16; Bach and Harnish 1979: 10, 47; Davies 1981: Ch.1; Leech 1983: 33; Sadock and Zwicky 1985: 155–6, 160, 178; Fraser 1988: 217; and Chierchia and McConnell-Ginet 1990: 163–70. Compare and contrast Frege 1892b: 68; McGinn 1977: 303; Katz 1977b: Ch. 1; Holdcroft 1978: 79; Davidson 1979: 110–14; Schmerling 1982: 210–11; Levinson 1983; Pendlebury 1986; Wilson and Sperber 1988; Vanderveken 1990: 8, 11; Chierchia and McConnell-Ginet 1990: 173–4, 186; Blakemore 1992: 110–18; Tsohatzidis 1994: 1–5; Han 2000: 162. Some Fregeans (e.g., Dummett) say that sentences of different moods have the same 'sense' as long as they express the same (root) proposition. Sense and force are thus different components of meaning. As we are using the terms, however, 'sense' is a synonym for 'meaning', and sentences with the same sense are synonymous. It is patent that the three sentences in (1) are not synonymous.

[17] Cf. Levinson 1983; Sadock and Zwicky 1985: 192; and Chierchia and McConnell-Ginet 1990: 106.

[18] Katz (1977b: 14–15, 120) attempts to distinguish the moods in terms of the speech acts they would be used to perform in the 'null context', 'where the context of an utterance contributes nothing to its meaning'. This is confused. By 'its meaning', Katz has to mean the sentence's meaning on a particular occasion, since context never contributes anything to sentence meaning in the language. But the speaker contributes something to applied meaning on any occasion. So there are no null contexts, and if there were, no speech acts would be performed.

[19] Cf. M. Huntley 1984; E. Davies 1986: 56; Wilson and Sperber 1988: 83–7.

[20] Cf. Stenius 1967: 254–74; Davidson 1979: 116; Sadock and Zwicky 1985: 160; Wilson and Sperber 1988: 82; Allan 1994: 2541.

[21] The occurrence requirement accounts for why asking a rhetorical question does not count as stating anything even though it does count as expressing a belief.

[22] Compare and contrast Kenny 1963: 238–9; Huntley 1984: 110–11.

[23] Cf. Prior and Prior 1955: 44–55; Bolinger 1978; Harris 1978; Hajičová 1983; Hoepelman 1983; Sadock and Zwicky 1985: §3.3; Wilson and Sperber 1988: 94. I am using 'presuppose' and 'presume' here interchangeably in a nontechnical sense.

[24] Cf. Locke 1690: 3.7.1; Arnauld and Lancelot 1660: Ch. 2.13; James 1890: 245–56; Quillian 1968: 232, 249; Bennett 1971: 3; and Vendler 1972: 135. Contrast Ockham *Summa Logicae I*: §3; Husserl 1900: IV; Geach 1957: Ch. 7; Katz 1966: 185; Ashworth 1982; Lampert 1992. Compare and contrast Mill 1879: §1.1.2.

[25] Cf. Lampert 1992, who appears to mistakenly attribute the Lockean view to Husserl.

[26] See also Boehner 1964: xxxi. Contrast Ashworth 1982: 61–2.

[27] For an example of further evidence that might settle the issue, suppose it is found that idea $A$ is correlated with neural structure X, and idea $B$ is correlated with neural structure Y. Suppose in addition that (i) the neural structure Z correlated with idea $A$ *when* $B$ contains a third substructure in addition to X and Y, which substructure is also found in the neural structures correlated with ideas $C$ *when* $D$, $E$ *when* $F$, etc. Or suppose in addition that (ii) the neural structure Z correlated with idea $A$ *when* $B$ only has X and Y as components, but these components are connected differently in Z than in Z', which is the structure associated with idea $A$ *if* $B$. Then (i) would support the constituent hypothesis, (ii) the structural relation hypothesis.

[28] Cf. William of Sherwood as described in Sirridge 1974; and *Encarta World English Dictionary* 1999.

[29] See also Katz 1964b: 761. After giving this definition, Katz says that the meaning of a syncategorematic term depends on the meanings of the categorematic terms it occurs with. None of the syncategorematic terms in (8) satisfy this description. Henry of Ghent similarly said

that syncategorematic terms 'have a signification whose definiteness they derive from those [words] that are adjoined to them' (Kretzmann 1982: 213).

³⁰ See §2.6 above, and §14.1 of *Meaning, Expression, and Thought*.

³¹ Cf. Peterson 1999.

³² Contrast Ameka 1992: 109–10; Wilkins 1992: 120, 128, 136, 148–50; Wierzbicka 1992b: 162; Jackson and Pettit 1998.

³³ Some interjections do have *addressees*, and express attitudes toward them, such as 'Hello!'

³⁴ 'From a formal point of view, an interjection is typically defined as a lexical form which (a) conventionally constitutes a non-elliptical utterance by itself, (b) does not enter into construction with other word classes, (c) does not take inflectional or derivational affixes and (d) is monomorphic' (Ameka 1994: 1712). See also Jespersen 1921: 415; Wilkins 1992: 124–31. James 1978 discusses uses of interjections ('say', 'well') that cannot stand alone, and points out distributional limits that follow from their meaning. Note that while (a) may be true only of interjections in natural languages, it is easy to devise cases in which single words express complete thoughts. And in propositional logic, single letters ('statement constants') are used as complete sentences.

³⁵ Jespersen 1921: 415; Ameka 1992: 105–6; 1994: 1712; Wilkins 1992: 135, 147; Rhodes 1992.

³⁶ See, for example, *Webster's Third New International Dictionary, Unabridged* (1981); *The Random House Dictionary of the English Language, Unabridged Edition* (1983); and Meidner 1994. *The American Heritage Dictionary of the English Language* (1969) defines 'interjection' in terms of 'exclamation', and 'exclaim' in terms of 'emotion or surprise'. Jespersen 1921: 415 characterized interjections as 'abrupt expressions for sudden sensations and emotions'. And Cruse (1986: 284) implies that they convey 'emotions or attitudes'. These characterizations are all too narrow. Ameka 1992, 1994; Rhodes 1992; and Taavitsainen 1995: 439 err in the other direction, defining interjections in terms of the expression of 'mental states or reactions', or 'internal states, comments, and 'something to the interlocutor''. Since the only important point for us is that at least some interjections express mental states other than ideas, we need not pursue the difficult issue of precisely defining 'interjection'. Note too that while the utterance of some interjections constitutes an evidential expression of emotion, the utterance of others does not and may be insincere, especially when it is socially expected (see §4.5).

³⁷ Cases in which the speaker is pretending to swear, and thus feigning displeasure, is not a case of figurative use. Think instead of its use in something like 'Damn, it's really too bad you have to go to Hawaii for two weeks', used ironically.

³⁸ The semantic case is not mere quotation: (16) is not equivalent to "'Verdammt!' means the same as 'Damn!'" The quotation marks around 'Damn!' in (16) are ideo-reflexive, not meta-linguistic. See §3.7.

³⁹ I will compare interjections to indexicals in *Indexicals*.

⁴⁰ Neale 1992: 555–6 wistfully expressed disappointment that Grice made no progress on this 'urgent' problem. See also Frege 1892b: 73–4; 1918: 9; Cohen 1971; Kempson 1975; Kartunnen and Peters 1979; Grice 1981: §3; 1989; Levinson 1983: §3.2.3; Rieber 1997a; Davis 1998; Authier 1998; and Bach 1999.

⁴¹ Bach 1999 tries to show that what Grice and others call conventional implicatures are really part of what is said (cf. Kempson 1975; Jackson and Pettit 1998). The term 'say' can be used more or less strictly, but I do not believe it can stretch far enough to apply in the given examples. See also Lycan 1991, who argues that 'even' introduces truth conditions, while Kartunnen and Peters 1979: 12, Bennett 1982, Barker 2000, Francescotti 1995, and Authier 1998 argue that it introduces conventional implicature. See also Jackson and Pettit 1998.

⁴² The standard claim that 'p but q' implicates that 'p' *contrasts with* 'q' is not quite right. 'It is hot but dry' would be a natural thing to say in a Washington DC summer, while 'It is hot but humid' would be most odd. In Death Valley, things would be reversed. Yet heat does not

*contrast* with dryness any more (or less) than it contrasts with humidity. There is a contrast in this case, but it is between the meteorological conjunction claimed (heat and dryness) and the conjunction normally found (heat and humidity). Compare and contrast Bach 1999: 342.

[43] Cf. Cruse 1986: 270–82.

[44] Sometimes 'p so q' is used to *explain* 'q' in terms of 'p'. Cf. Grice 1989: 362; Rieber 1997a: 53.

[45] Rieber (1997a) suggests that 'but' is performative in a different way. On his view, 'p but q' means 'p and (I suggest that this contrasts) q'. Rieber's analysis falsely predicts that when we say 'It is hot but dry', we have *said parenthetically* that we suggest something. On the hypothesis under discussion, we suggest or signal but do not say even parenthetically what we do. We act but do not represent our action. Cf. Bach 1999 on both issues.

[46] Grice 1968: 122; Levinson 1983: 128; Bach 1999: 342, 356–60. See also McKinsey 1999: 532–3. Bach provides an extensive classification of such 'utterance modifiers'. He claims that they generate no implicatures, which seems false.

[47] Compare and contrast Peterson 1999: §6.3; Bach 1999: 345–50; M. Green 2000: §3.4; Asher 2000.

[48] If the speaker does count as saying this (à la Bach 1999), he does so in a different, less explicit way than that in which he says that Washington owned slaves. While 'implicate' is defined in terms of 'say', 'imply', and 'mean' are not. Hence nothing hinges for us on the proper application of 'say'.

[49] Cf. Corazza 2002: 317–19. Peterson 1999: 240–5 argues that appositives are juxtapositions, and that the latter are 'non-syntagmatic'—that is, do not 'form a single grammatical construction'. But then he notes that 'The key *semantic* characteristic of apposition is that the juxtaposed items are referentially equivalent.' There is an *implication* that they are equivalent, perhaps. But that indicates that the juxtaposed items express components of a thought in the 'deep structure' of the sentence even though they do not form a unit in its surface structure.

# Part II

# Reference

# 7

## Reference and Expression

The principal goal of the next two chapters is to examine what it is for a speaker to refer to something. We will define speaker reference in terms of expression, which has already been defined in terms of intention and evidential indication. Along the way, we will relate referring to meaning, mentioning, and the inclusive sense of cogitative meaning. Some vagueness of the concepts to be defined, and a host of ambiguities, make it difficult to offer a nonstipulative definition with complete confidence. The distinction between opaque and transparent interpretations of sentences of the form 'S is referring to **Φ**' will be especially important, along with the referential–attributive distinction.

We are studying reference for at least two reasons. First, it is one of the defining characteristics of names that they are used to refer. Second, meaning—particularly the meaning of names—is often identified with reference. We need to see as clearly as possible why referential theories of meaning are false. The notion of reference involved in this theory is word reference, however, not speaker reference. We will define word reference in terms of speaker reference in Chapter 9.[1]

### 7.1 SPEAKER REFERENCE

Speaker reference differs as markedly from word reference[2] as speaker meaning differs from word meaning. When Sam said 'Canada's capital', he may have been referring to Toronto even though the words he uttered refer to Ottawa. This difference between word reference and speaker reference may have occurred because of a false belief about which city is the capital of Canada, a false belief about what 'capital' means, or a verbal slip. Alternatively, the divergence may have been intentional, as when Sam is using a code, speaking loosely or figuratively, acquiescing in someone else's unconventional usage, or conveying his feelings about which city should be the Canadian capital. The dependence of speaker reference on the speaker's intentions and of word reference on linguistic conventions parallels what we set out in Chapters 4 and 5 for speaker and word meaning.

We use '**Φ**' as a place-holder for all terms that can grammatically fill the blank in formulas like 'S referred to ___' or 'S is thinking of ___'. These are *object nominals*: nouns, noun phrases, gerunds, and nominalizations that can appear as direct or indirect objects (§2.3). I believe speaker reference can be defined as follows.

**7.1    Definition:** *S refers to **Φ** iff S verbally expresses the idea of **Φ**.*

Referring to something differs from merely thinking about it in requiring expression.[3] If we ask 'Is he referring to anyone?', we have to answer 'No' if the man is just sitting silently, no matter who he is thinking of. Unlike cogitative speaker meaning, speaker reference does not require *direct* expression.[4] If Sam referred to Toronto as Canada's capital from an erroneous belief about Canada rather than a linguistic mistake, then S did not mean "Toronto" by the phrase 'Canada's capital'. For S expressed the idea of Toronto *indirectly*, by expressing the idea of Canada's capital. Or suppose Terry employs a figure of speech and says 'Mozart is practicing', meaning that Bob's son is. Then Terry referred to Bob's son, but he did not mean "Bob's son" by 'Mozart' because he did not express the idea of Bob's son directly. Since it allows indirect expression, speaker reference is more akin to the *inclusive* sense of cogitative meaning, rather than the exclusive sense we have focused on (see §4.4).

Speaker reference differs in another way from speaker meaning in requiring that the speaker *says something* in the broad sense that includes writing and signing.[5] S must use a language, code, or symbol system containing words or word-like elements (see §5.1). Suppose a policeman points at John, indicating that John is to pull over. Then the officer meant John, but did not refer to John. The reason the policeman's act does not count as referring is not simply that he did not use a natural language. We can refer to people in Morse code, American Sign Language, private codes, or artificial languages. The officer failed to refer because he did not use any system of signs with the appropriate syntactic structure.

## 7.2    REFERENCE AND PREDICATION

Many would argue that Definition 7.1 is too broad, citing a variety of cases that involve a lack of predication one way or another. I shall argue that while there is some evidence suggesting that predication is necessary for reference, the balance of the evidence supports the definition given.

Ziff (1960: 83) claimed that someone may be referring to Spenser when saying (2) but not (1).

(1) The author of the *Faerie Queene* was Spenser.
(2) Spenser lived in Ireland.

I think it is more natural to say 'The speaker referred to Spenser' after (2) rather than (1). But there is abundant evidence that the speaker is correctly described as referring to Spenser in both cases. For example, if asked 'Did the speaker ever refer to Spenser in any way?', we would have to answer 'Yes'. And the question 'Was the speaker referring to Edmund Spenser, the poet, or Earl Spenser, Princess Diana's father?' is perfectly appropriate, the expected answer being 'Edmund'.

Suppose S is asked 'Who won?' and answers 'John'. Or suppose S blows his referee's whistle, yells 'John!', and points at the penalty box. Strictly speaking, S did not predicate anything of John in these cases. In the first case, the context supplied the predicate, as it were. In the second, a nonverbal action did. Ziff (1960: 84) reported that it 'seems somehow repugnant' to say that S referred to John in such cases.[6] I certainly find it less natural to say that S referred to John than I do to say that S meant John. On the other hand, if someone queried 'When John was asked 'Who won?', did he refer to anyone?', I would find it even more repugnant to answer 'No one'. It would be very natural, furthermore, for someone to ask 'Which John was he referring to?' Moreover, if John walked into the room and asked 'Are you referring to me?' S would have to say 'Yes'. Finally, since S clearly 'named' John as the winner, it is hard to see why we should not say that he referred to John.

Consider the title character's famous last word in *Citizen Kane*, the enigmatic 'Rosebud'. When the movie is over, it is clear that Kane expressed the idea of Rosebud, his childhood sled, even though he did not express any particular thought about Rosebud. I find 'Kane referred to Rosebud on his deathbed' something of an overstatement. Yet I would have to answer 'Yes' if someone asked whether Kane had ever referred to Rosebud in any way. Or imagine that what Kane said on his deathbed was his estranged wife's name. She later asks those who were present, 'Did he mention me at all before he died?' Those at Kane's bedside would surely have to answer 'Yes'. Yet it would seem contradictory to maintain that Kane mentioned someone without referring to her.

When President Reagan said 'We must remember that we always have a duty to protect the lives of American citizens abroad', he was *alluding* to Grenada. Most philosophers would outright deny that the President referred to Grenada.[7] In some cases, perhaps, this is because the President did not use any expression that itself refers to Grenada; but we are concerned with speaker reference now, not word reference. If asked 'Did Reagan refer to Grenada in his talk?', I myself would not be inclined to say simply 'Yes'. Instead, I would say something like 'Well, not really. He alluded to it, though.' On the other hand, it is impossible to deny that the President made an *oblique reference* to Grenada. The dictionaries I have consulted all define allusion as a type of reference.

Suppose Don says 'John's father is a mafia don'. Clearly, Don referred to John's father. Did Don also refer to John? I am inclined to say 'Yes', and to observe that Don referred to John's father by referring to John. But if someone asked, 'Who was Don referring to?', I would answer 'John's father', not 'John', or 'both John and his father'. This seems explicable, however, on the assumption that the question is interpreted as asking about Don's *principal* reference. The questioner presumably wanted to know who Don referred to *as a mafia don*. If the prosecuting attorney asked 'Did Don ever refer to John?', one would have to answer 'Yes'. And if John had told Don never to refer to him in public, John could justly complain. Even Ziff (1960: 84) would grant that Don 'made a reference' to John. Don can be described as mentioning John, talking about him, and telling something he knows about John, all of which seem to entail that Don was referring to John.

Finally, some cases with no predication are quite clear. For example, a recording company entitled a CD 'Early Byrd'. Since 'Byrd' is not exactly a household name in music, and has a homonym in the very familiar line 'The early bird gets the worm', one radio announcer felt compelled to note that 'They are referring to William Byrd, an early English composer'.

As we have seen, there is plenty of evidence that 'S refers to **Φ**' is often true when S is not predicating anything of **Φ**. How can we explain our reluctance to assert 'S refers to **Φ**' in such cases? One hypothesis that fits the evidence is that 'S refers to **Φ**' *implicates* that S is non-obliquely referring to and predicating something of **Φ**. This implicature can be canceled in various ways, as by adding the adverb 'obliquely', or by talking about a title.

## 7.3   COGITATIVE SPEAKER MEANING (INCLUSIVE)

As we have noted, speaker reference resembles the inclusive sense of cogitative meaning distinguished from the exclusive in §4.4. We have focused on the *oratio recta* form (3), since our main interest is in the exclusive sense of cogitative meaning, which cannot otherwise be expressed. But the inclusive sense can also be expressed using form (4), which I believe is the *oratio obliqua* form corresponding to (3), and which most closely resembles 'S refers to **Φ**' grammatically.[8] Compare:

(3)  By e, S meant "m".
(4)  When S said e, S meant m.

As is usual in ideo-reflexive contexts (§3.7), these forms differ when e is a pronoun. For example, suppose S uses 'me' in the normal way. Then we must use *S meant "me"* or *S meant himself*, rather than *S meant "himself"* or *S meant me*, which have very different meanings. Similarly, if we want our answer in form (3), we will ask "*What* did S mean by 'My old lady'?" If we want form (4), we will ask '*Who* did S mean?' The major difference between (3) and (4) is that 'm' is restricted to object nominals in (4) but not in (3).[9] Thus *S meant "if"* may be true, but *S meant if* is ungrammatical. Finally, (4) differs from (3) in having no exclusive sense. The fact that Sam expressed the idea of Toronto by expressing the idea of Canada's capital does not entail that 'Sam meant Toronto' is false in any sense. However, when 'm' is restricted to object nominals, and we focus on the inclusive sense of (3), the two forms appear to have the same truth conditions (adjusting for pronouns). Thus when Sam used 'Canada's capital', *Sam meant Toronto*, with no quotation marks around 'Toronto', will be true if and only if *S meant "Toronto"* is true in the inclusive sense. The difference appears to be grammatically but not semantically significant, in marked contrast to the difference between *S meant "p"* and *S meant that p* when 'p' is an indicative sentence (see §4.2).

Strawson (1986: 251) asked us to imagine that S says to his host, 'Your brother is charming'. Unbeknownst to S, the host has two brothers; one is charming (Dick) and the other was at the party (Larry). While the host took S to mean his charming brother, S actually meant the one at the party. Strawson then said: 'Philosophical debate may arise over the question what reference, if any, the speaker has actually made, what proposition, if any, he has actually asserted (i.e., over what—whatever he *meant* to say—he has *actually* said).' Now people often say one thing and mean another, as when S slips and says 'Jane is erotic' when he meant that she is erratic. Then S said that Jane is erotic even though he did not mean to say this. But the relationship between 'meaning that p' and 'saying that p' is very different from the relationship between 'meaning Φ' and 'referring to Φ'. There might be some question as to whether the speaker's *words* referred to Larry. But if S meant Larry, then I do not believe there can be any doubt that the *speaker* referred to Larry.

Meaning Φ does differ from referring to Φ, however. As noted in §7.1, reference requires verbal expression. When the policeman points at you, indicating that you are to pull over, he means you even though his action does not count as referring to you. Furthermore, reference is associated with predication in a way meaning is not (see §7.2). Kane clearly meant Rosebud by his final utterance, even though he said nothing about it.

In another respect, meaning is more restrictive. When Reagan said, 'We must remember that we always have a duty to defend American lives abroad', he may have been referring obliquely to Grenada. But it is clearly incorrect to say that he meant Grenada. It is possible to mean what one is alluding to, however. Suppose that Sue is asked who the sixteenth president was. She might answer by saying 'Four score and seven years ago...', meaning Lincoln. What is distinctive about the Lincoln case, I believe, is that the speaker was expressing a thought about the object alluded to. Sue did so by using 'Four score...' to express the idea of Lincoln. Sue was able to do this because she had been asked who the sixteenth president was. In the Grenada case, Reagan may have used 'We must remember...' to express the idea of Grenada, but he was not in the process of expressing any thoughts containing that idea. Meaning $\Phi$ does not always require expressing a thought about $\Phi$, though, as the Rosebud case shows. In that case, the speaker was not expressing ideas by allusion. What the inclusive sense of cogitative meaning appears to exclude is allusion without thought expression. Expressing this idea positively yields the following definition, which holds in all the cases I have considered.

7.2   **Definition:** *S means $\Phi$ iff S expresses the idea of $\Phi$ without using allusion, unless S is in the process of expressing a thought about $\Phi$.*

It follows from Definition 7.2 that S meant $\Phi$ *if* S referred to $\Phi$ without using allusion, as when S expresses the idea of $\Phi$ directly or metaphorically, or by using a description one believes to be uniquely satisfied by $\Phi$. The attempt to give a definition of allusion will be left to another occasion. Having observed that meaning $\Phi$ allows some but not all types of indirect expression, I am content to indicate roughly the type excluded.

## 7.4   MENTIONING

*Mentioning* is stricter than both referring and meaning. Mentioning resembles referring in requiring verbal expression. The policeman meant you when he waved you over, but did not mention you. Mentioning differs from both meaning and referring in excluding oblique reference. As *Webster's Encyclopedic Unabridged Dictionary* puts it, to mention something is to refer to it 'clearly, specifically, and explicitly'. Reagan clearly did not mention Grenada when he said 'We have a duty to protect American lives abroad', and Sam did not mention Toronto when he used 'Canada's capital'. Reference is oblique, I suggest, when the speaker's reference diverges from the reference of the words he or she uses. The phrase Reagan used to allude to Grenada, namely, 'a duty to protect Americans living abroad', does not itself refer to Grenada. Similarly, 'Canada's capital' does not refer to Toronto. Hence mentioning something requires the coincidence of word reference and speaker reference.

Chastain (1975) observed that a speaker can use an indefinite description to refer to a particular person. Thus a teacher who says 'A certain member of this class cheated' may be referring to Jenny.[10] Chastain's claim has been disputed because indefinite descriptions themselves do not refer to particular individuals. But all this shows is that the teacher did not *mention* Jenny. Indeed, the teacher may have chosen this mode of expression precisely to avoid mentioning her.

Suppose S says 'The bank is a mess', referring to Citibank during a discussion of its Latin American loans. Then S mentioned Citibank. While he referred to it correctly and literally, there still appears to be a divergence of word and speaker reference. For 'The bank' does not refer specifically to Citibank. The phrase does refer to Citibank *here* or *on this occasion*, however. What needs to coincide with the speaker reference in mentioning must therefore be the 'applied reference' of the words S uses rather than the reference of the words themselves.[11] An expression refers to **Φ** on a given occasion only if the speaker used it correctly and literally[12] to refer to **Φ**. The fact that applied reference is determined in part by speaker reference produces no circularity, for we are using the notion of applied reference to define mentioning rather than referring.

7.3 **Definition**: *S mentions **Φ** iff S expresses the idea of **Φ** by using an expression that refers to **Φ** on that occasion.*

If S expressed the idea of **Φ** in this way, then S expressed the idea verbally. So Definitions 7.1 and 7.3 straightforwardly entail that *if S mentioned **Φ** then S referred to **Φ***. Moreover, if S expressed the idea of **Φ** by correctly using an expression that refers to **Φ**, then S did not express that idea by allusion. Hence Definitions 7.2 and 7.3 imply that *if S mentioned **Φ** then S meant **Φ***. The converse implications fail, as desired.

## 7.5 GRAMMATICAL EQUIVOCATIONS

I have focused almost exclusively on meaning, mentioning, and referring to **Φ** for the case in which '**Φ**' is a proper name or pronoun. Nevertheless, I believe the definitions hold for all object nominals. Focusing on the case in which '**Φ**' is a proper name has enabled us to avoid a number of potentially misleading equivocations. Most of the unclarity of 'S refers to **Φ**' and its cousins I ascribe to the ambiguities discussed in this and the next two sections. The rest I attribute to the general association of reference with predication.

As is customary, when a variable or place-holder appears more than once as '**Φ**' does in Definition 7.1, it must be replaced *uniformly*. This means not only that the same expression must replace it everywhere, but also that the expression replacing it must have the same sense and reference wherever it occurs. We cannot argue that Definition 7.1 is too broad on the grounds that when a man says 'I colored the car gold', he expresses the idea of gold (meaning the color) without referring to gold (meaning the metal). In other cases, however, the senses are more closely related, and the equivocation occurs at a deeper level, so it might well be missed. Consider:

(5) Mary kissed John's brother.
(6) The pitcher is John's brother.[13]

(6) is ambiguous, and can be interpreted as expressing either an identity statement or a simple predication. On the identity interpretation, (6) tells us who the pitcher is by saying that he is identical to a certain person, namely John's brother. On the predication interpretation, (6) does not tell us who the pitcher is, for it says only that the pitcher is related in a certain way to John, namely, as a brother. On the identity interpretation of (6), 'John's brother' is a *singular term* referring to one particular brother of John, and thus has the same interpretation it has in (5). But on the predication interpretation, 'John's brother' is a *general* term, denoting any brother of John. 'And the catcher is too' after (6) on the predication interpretation would in no way imply that the pitcher and catcher are the same person. In contrast, 'And Jane did too' after (5) would imply that Mary and Jane kissed the same person. If we are not careful we might think that Definition 7.1 is too broad on the grounds that a speaker uttering (6) expresses the idea of John's brother but does not refer to John's brother. However, 'S refers to John's brother' is false only when 'John's brother' is interpreted as a singular term. If it is given the same interpretation in 'S expressed the idea of John's brother', that is false too. So unless we equivocate, the predication interpretation of (6) does not present a counterexample to Definition 7.1.

When '$\Phi$' is *quantifier*, we find the familiar *scope-ambiguity*. For example, 'something' is normally used not to specify the object of reference, but to say that there is an object of reference. That is, 'S referred to something' is normally interpreted as meaning "There is something S referred to" (in which the quantifier has wide scope) rather than "What S referred to was something" (in which it has narrow scope). Definition 7.1 holds in either case, as long as the definiens is taken in the parallel sense. 'S expressed the idea of something' should be interpreted as meaning "There is an idea S expressed" in the former case, or "S expressed the idea *something*" in the latter. There is a similar ambiguity when '$\Phi$' is negative. 'S referred to nothing' is most naturally interpreted as meaning "There is nothing that S was referring to" rather than "What S was referring to was nothing". The definiens 'S expressed the idea of nothing' is similarly ambiguous, but more naturally means "S expressed the idea *nothing*" than "S did not express any idea". So unless we are careful to give 'nothing' the same scope in both the definiens and the definiendum, Definition 7.1 will appear false.

## 7.6 THE REFERENTIAL–ATTRIBUTIVE DISTINCTION

There is a more problematic ambiguity when '$\Phi$' is a *definite description*. Let us stipulate that when Sam said 'The president is tall', Sam was referring to Al Gore rather than George Bush. Now consider this question: was Sam also referring to the president? According to Definition 7.1, the answer depends on the answer to another question: did Sam express the idea of the president?

When we add that Sam thinks Al Gore rather than George Bush is the president, we may conclude that the idea of the president is different from the idea of either Al Gore or George Bush and was expressed by Sam. This conclusion holds, however, only on the *attributive* interpretation of 'the president'. It is also possible to interpret the phrase *referentially*.[14] Indeed, since *we* know that George Bush is the president, it would be most natural for us to use 'Was Sam referring to the president?' to ask whether Sam was referring to George Bush. And the answer to that question is 'No'. I myself find it most natural to interpret 'the president' referentially in 'Was Sam referring to the president?' and attributively in 'Did Sam express the idea of the president?' Hence I find it natural to answer the first question 'No' and the second 'Yes'. When I do this, Definition 7.1 seems too broad. But when the term replacing 'Φ' is interpreted the same way in both places, Definition 7.1 is confirmed. If 'the president' is taken attributively in both places, 'Sam referred to the president' and 'Sam expressed the idea of the president' are both true. If the same phrase is taken referentially in both places, both statements are false.

The terminology used to mark this distinction is unfortunate, since it suggests that descriptions used attributively are not used to refer to anything, an erroneous view Donnellan (1966: esp. 291) seems to have held.[15] S was certainly referring to Smith's murderer when he said 'Smith's murderer, whoever he is, is insane'. If we were asked 'Who was S referring to?', we could not answer 'No one'. It is even true that S was referring to *someone in particular,* viz., Smith's murderer. The fact that S did not know who Smith's murderer was is irrelevant. The fact that S was not *also* referring to Smith's murderer *under another description* makes S's usage attributive rather than referential. But it does not prevent him from having referred to someone.[16]

## 7.7 THE OPAQUE–TRANSPARENT DISTINCTION

The opaque–transparent distinction (§2.8) can also make Definition 7.1 seem false. Suppose Professor Jones says 'My transcendental refutation puts skepticism to rest once and for all', and a friend of mine asks, 'What is he referring to?' I might answer:

(7) He is referring to a big mistake.

Suppose I am right that Prof. Jones's refutation was a big mistake. Does it follow that Prof. Jones was referring to a mistake? That Prof. Jones expressed the idea of a mistake? On the most natural interpretation of the latter question—the opaque—the answer is 'No'. 'The idea of a mistake' normally denotes the idea expressed by the words 'a mistake', which is not an idea Prof. Jones expressed when he said 'My transcendental refutation'. But on the most natural interpretation of the former question—the transparent—the answer is 'Yes'. For what I clearly meant was 'The thing he is referring to is in fact a big mistake', which we are assuming is true. When both questions are given the same interpretation, however, the answer is the same, confirming Definition 7.1.

The opaque–transparent distinction cuts across the attributive–referential distinction.[17] Suppose Sam announces, 'The Canadian president is coming to my pool party'. To whom was Sam referring?

(8)  Sam was referring to the Canadian president.

There is a sense in which this answer is obviously correct, given what Sam said. On that interpretation of (8), 'the Canadian president' is attributive and its context is opaque: (8) says that Sam expressed the idea "the Canadian president". But there is also a sense in which we cannot use (8) without committing ourselves to the existence of the Canadian president. This is the transparent interpretation. When the context is transparent, 'the Canadian president' can be used either attributively (in which case (8) says that the person Sam was referring to happens to be the president of Canada) or referentially (in which case the speaker means that Sam was referring to a particular individual—Cretien, perhaps—whom the speaker takes to be president of Canada). The two distinctions are not completely independent, however. For there is no way for 'the Canadian president' to be used referentially in an opaque context. For if it is used referentially, then there is no implication that Sam was expressing the specific idea "the Canadian president". That is, there is no implication that Sam referred to the Canadian president *as* the Canadian president.

According to Burge, demonstrative reference shows that what S refers to is not determined by the content of the thought S expressed.

When Alfred refers to an apple, saying to himself 'That is wholesome,' what he refers to depends not just on the content of what he says or thinks, but on what apple is before him. Without altering the meaning of Alfred's utterance, the nature of his perceptual experiences, or his physical acts or dispositions, we could conceive an exchange of the actual apple for another one that is indistinguishable to Alfred. We would thereby conceive him as referring to something different and even as saying something with a different truth value.                          (1979b: 544)[18]

It is true that Alfred is referring to a different apple when the apple is switched. But it is also true that Alfred is thinking about a different apple. The reason is that 'the same apple' and 'a different apple' are interpreted in both contexts as *transparent* descriptions. In general, comparative nouns like '*the same object*' and '*a different object*' are conventionally interpreted as transparent descriptions when they replace 'Φ' in either the definiens or definiendum of Definition 7.1. What these examples show is not that reference is underdetermined by thought content, but rather that transparent descriptions of objects of both reference and thought are underdetermined by opaque descriptions. That is why the reduction formula (20) of §2.8 has two clauses.

An individual's thoughts are not limited to those that can be expressed conventionally in any particular language. Consequently, a speaker may refer to an object for which there is no word in the language we are using to describe the speaker. Inventions and discoveries make this abundantly clear, as do radically different cultures. More unusual, but hardly rare, is the case in which there are words in our language with the right extension but none with the right intension. That is, the language we are using may provide us with appropriate transparent descriptions of the speaker's referent, none of which are appropriate as opaque descriptions. A variant of Kripke's (1979) puzzle[19] illustrates this. Suppose Peter believes that there are two famous Americans named 'Ronald W. Reagan', one an actor, the other a president. When watching a movie, Peter says 'Reagan is nothing but a two-bit actor'. When watching a presidential address, he says 'Reagan is one of the greatest Americans who has ever lived'. It is easy to provide a transparent description of Peter's referent: he is referring to the same man in both cases, namely Ronald W. Reagan. But clearly, Peter is expressing different ideas on the two occasions. As a result, he is not contradicting himself or being irrational. Yet there are no words in the English language (or any idiolect we share with Peter) that express those ideas. So we have no conventional way of providing an opaque description of what Peter is referring to. The best we can do is improvise, saying that Peter is referring to Ronald Reagan *the actor* in the first case, and to Ronald Reagan *the president* in the second, noting that Peter thinks the actor and the president are different people. What we are doing cannot quite be described as 'disambiguating' the term 'Ronald Reagan'. For that name conventionally applies to the president and the actor in exactly the same sense. Nevertheless, the italicized phrases serve an analogous function.[20]

## Notes

[1] Chapters 7 to 9 are an expansion of Chapter 6 in *Meaning, Expression, and Thought*.

[2] This distinction has been clearly drawn in Kaplan 1973: 502–5; Kripke 1977; Fitch 1987: 8–11; Bertolet 1987; 1990: 46–58, 85–8; Jackson 1998. See also Linsky 1963 and Bach 1987a: 3–6, 39–40. Word reference is often called semantic or linguistic reference. Similar distinctions were drawn in §4.1 for meaning and §4.5 for expression.

[3] Contrast Kvart 1994: 94.

[4] Cf. McKinsey 1978: 177; and §4.3 above.

[5] Cf. Searle 1979: 142–3; Bertolet 1987: 203; 1990: 105, 108.

[6] Cf. Donnellan 1974: 16, discussed in Bertolet 1987: 200; 1990: 102–3, 111–13. See also Strawson 1950: 185–6; Ziff 1960: 84; Schwarz 1979: xxvi, 16–17, 21–2; and Bach 1987a: 51. Contrast Geach 1962: 52.

[7] Schwarz 1979: 22–6 appears to be an exception. This example is discussed in Bertolet 1987: 210–12, who attributes it to Donnellan.

⁸ Strawson (1950: 182) noticed the sense of meaning involved in (4) and distinguished it from word meaning, but did not analyze or relate it to the other forms of speaker meaning. Schiffer (1972: 112–13) and Bertolet (1990: 68–9) distinguish it from cogitative speaker meaning. But Schiffer took (4) to express speaker reference, and Bertolet overlooked the opaque/transparent distinction.

⁹ The words 'When S said e, S meant …' can be followed by a sentence. But then the sense is cognitive rather than cogitative, and reads as if a 'that' had been deleted.

¹⁰ See also Strawson 1950: 188, 193; Partee 1972: 419; Kripke 1977: 266; Bach 1987a: §12.2; and Cormack and Kempson 1991. Contrast Russell 1919: 212; Bertolet 1987: 212–17; 1990: 125–9.

¹¹ See Grice 1969a: 147–9; Kripke 1977: 262–3; also §9.1 below, and §5.3 above.

¹² If a parent uses 'King Tut' figuratively to refer to one of her children, then she did not mention King Tut on that occasion even though she did express the idea of King Tut.

¹³ Cf. Strawson 1950: 175; Fodor and Katz 1964: 10; Boër 1978: 180; and Kaplan 1978: 328.

¹⁴ See Arnauld 1662: 64; Donnellan 1966; Grice 1969b: 141; Peacocke 1975: 208; Kripke 1977; Boër 1978; Searle 1979: Ch. 6; Martinich 1979a; 1984: Ch. 10; Wettstein 1981; Salmon 1982; Fitch 1987: Ch. 1; Bach 1987a: Chs. 5–6; Recanati 1989a: 299–300; 1993: Ch. 15; Millikan 1990: 170–2; Bertolet 1990: §1.1; Cormack and Kempson 1991: 548; Neale 1992: 537–41; 1997; Elugardo 1997; Bezuidenhout 1997b; Reimer 1998a; 1998b; Berg 1999. Chastain 1975, Fodor and Sag 1982, Ludlow and Neale 1991, and Neale 1997 observe that indefinite descriptions (e.g., 'a student') and quantificational expressions (e.g., 'some student') similarly have two interpretations. *Nota bene:* I do not mean to imply that the phrase 'the F' itself is ambiguous, with both a referential and an attributive sense.

¹⁵ See also Russell 1905; Strawson 1950; Partee 1972: 424–5; Stalnaker 1972: 393–4; Vendler 1976: 43–4; Loar 1976a: 364, 366–7; Boër 1978. Contrast Stampe 1974: §5; Bach 1987a: 111, Fitch 1987: 30–1, Bertolet 1990: 10. Donnellan would have been correct, however, if attributive descriptions had a Russellian analysis, that is, if 'the F is G' meant "There is one and only one F and it is G".

¹⁶ Many of the things that Donnellan claimed to be distinctive of the referential use are not. For more such errors, see Searle 1979: Ch. 6; Martinich 1984: Ch. 10; Fitch 1987: Ch. 1; and Bach 1987a: Ch. 6.

¹⁷ Cf. Searle 1979: 151–3. Contrast Partee 1972: 415–20; Boër 1978: 184.

¹⁸ See also Fodor 1981: 236–7, 331; Peacocke 1981: 198; Burge 1982: 97–9, 107; Stich 1983: 65; Bach 1987a: 16; and my forthcoming *Indexicals*.

¹⁹ Kripke used Paderewski, who is not widely known these days. See §11.3 for a full discussion of Kripke's Puzzle.

²⁰ Cf. Over 1983. Loar argues that 'S believes that Reagan is a man' may be true in virtue of two *different* beliefs S has even when it is given a *univocal* reading (cf. Braun 1998: 578). This phenomenon is ubiquitous with transparent descriptions, impossible with opaque descriptions. The problem in the case at hand is that we have no conventional opaque descriptions. Carey 1991 argues for the converse possibility in which a subject expresses one concept where we make a distinction.

# 8

## Reference and Intention

I have defined speaker reference as the verbal expression of ideas, with expression being understood in terms of speaker intention. I will now show that this definition is superior to alternative analyses. I will defend the implication that speakers can refer to nonexistent objects, arguing for the intentionality of speaker reference and against the widespread assumption that it is a relation. In particular, I will enumerate many defects in the theory that reference is a species of causal relation. The intentions in virtue of which we refer to an object need not be causally connected to that object. Finally, I will defend the thesis that speaker reference is determined by intention against Twin Earth arguments. While Putnam's and Burge's startling conclusions about the dependence of meaning and mind on the external environment are almost universally accepted, I believe the arguments are fallacious.

### 8.1 ALTERNATIVE ANALYSES

Unlike cognitive speaker meaning and word reference, speaker reference has not been the subject of extensive analytical study. Most characterizations have been brief and informal, like Searle's.

The speaker refers to the object because and only because the object satisfies the Intentional content associated with the name.[1]                    (Searle 1983: 245)

Unfortunately, Searle did not specify *which* mode of association is definitive of reference. The specification cannot, of course, make use of the notion of speaker reference. And it surely cannot be the sort of classical association that links the contents "Nazi" and "blitzkrieg" with the name 'Hitler'. If Searle means the intentional content conventionally expressed by the name, then the definition is both too broad and too narrow, since speaker reference may diverge from word reference. If he means the intentional content the speaker used the name to express, then his definition is close to Definition 7.1. Jackson's (1998) examples suggest that he is thinking of the properties S takes to identify or define $\Phi$. That is, Jackson appears to think of the associated properties as the set of properties $\Delta$ satisfying the following condition: S believes that x is the referent of e iff x has all the properties in Δ. On this understanding of associated properties, Jackson's definition has many of the problems of the description theory of meaning, such as the problem of error (see Chapter 12). S may refer to Aristotle even though the properties S takes to identify Aristotle in fact identify someone else, or no one. This would happen if S mistakenly thought that Aristotle was the son of Plato.

Chierchia and McConnell-Ginet repeat a common formulation.

We can say that the *speaker's reference* of *Pavarotti* is Pavarotti if it is Pavarotti to whom the speaker intends to refer when uttering *Pavarotti*.[2]
(Chierchia and McConnell-Ginet 1990: 152)

This could not be regarded as a definition, on pain of explicit circularity. The notion of speaker reference appears in what would be the definiens. As a result, the definition does not tell us what it is to refer to something. In addition, it is not evident that a speaker must have the concept of reference in order to refer to something. It seems plausible that people acquire linguistic concepts like that of referring in part as a result of the experience of using a language to perform acts such as referring. Finally, many of the problems addressed in Chapter 4 arise here. For example, someone uttering 'The president is a republican' may intend to refer to Bush. But that does not make Bush the speaker reference of the whole sentence.

Kripke only sought to provide a rough differentiation between speaker and semantic reference.

We may tentatively define the speaker's referent of a designator to be that object which the speaker wishes to talk about, on a given occasion, and believes fulfills the conditions for being the semantic referent of the designator.[3]   (Kripke 1977: 264)

First, 'talking about Φ' is so similar in meaning to 'referring to Φ' that little illumination can be gained by defining the latter in terms of the former, unless the former has previously been defined in very different terms. Second, talking about Φ seems more strongly connected to predication than referring to Φ is. While it does seem correct to use 'talking about' in some of the cases of reference without predication described in §7.2, in others it seems prohibited. For example, the producers who entitled a CD 'Early Byrd' were not talking about William Byrd (nor presumably did they wish to), although they were referring to him. Third, Kripke's belief clause often fails. Metaphorical reference is one case in which S refers to something without believing that it is the semantic referent of the designator he used, as when referring to his wife Jane as his conscience. Elliptical reference is another. People with several brothers often refer to one of them as 'my brother' even when there is no contextual clue as to which brother is meant. Speakers in both cases nevertheless intend their utterances to indicate that they are thinking about a particular individual.

As we have noted, Grice devoted most of his attention to defining cognitive speaker meaning in terms of intention. His first and most influential formulation can be modified to suit referring to Φ by requiring the use of words, and by changing the intended effect on the audience from the belief that p to the idea of Φ, or equivalently, to thinking about Φ.

> (1) S refers to Φ iff S uses words with the intention of producing in some audience A the idea of Φ by means of recognition of intention.

Extant Gricean theories of reference replace the idea of Φ with more complex responses. Stine (1978) held that S must intend A to *identify Φ*, by which she means that A must be intended to 'pick out who it is S has in mind'.[4] Bertolet (1987; 1990: 89, 104–8) argues that S must intend to *direct A's attention to Φ*.[5] And Schwarz (1979: 17) proposes that S must intend A to *think that S thinks that Φ has some predicate*.[6] All three stress that the audience must be intended to respond in the indicated way as a result of recognizing the speaker's intention to produce that response.

These Gricean analyses of reference share the fundamental defects of Grice's definition of cognitive meaning (see §4.5). I will focus on (1) to avoid duplication. First, S may refer to something without having an intended audience, or without intending to produce the idea of Φ, or any other effect, in the audience if S has one. S can refer to Φ in private, or while speaking to someone who is dead or unconscious. When S does have a living and intelligent audience, S can deliberately use a language his audience does not understand. And even when S's audience does understand the language, S might say 'The sun is shining' knowing full well that his audience is already thinking about the sun. Moreover, S might say 'The president will speak at 9:00', knowing that his audience will think of the president of the United States, even though S is referring to the president of the university. The knowledge and even hope that our audience will misinterpret us does not prevent us from meaning or referring to something. Finally, S may be referring to Jane when he says 'Too bad you can't see her', despite knowing that his audience cannot determine who he is referring to.

Second, S need not intend his audience to recognize his intentions, even when S has an audience. The examples above show this, as does the case in which I write an unsigned note to Alan. Finally, recognition of the speaker's intentions cannot play a causal role even when the idea of Φ is produced in the audience. For it is impossible for A to identify what S wants her to think about without already thinking about it. At best, the audience's recognition of S's intention would be a reason for the audience to *continue* thinking about Φ. But the speaker need not intend such a thing. To refer to Φ, it suffices for S to verbally *express* the idea of Φ. To do this, S must intend his utterance to be a sign that he is thinking of Φ. S need not intend anyone else to properly interpret that sign, or respond in any way to it.

Because of both the audience requirement and the recognition requirement, the Gricean analysis is better suited to analyzing the triadic predicate *S refers A to Φ* than the dyadic predicate *S refers to Φ*. One doctor may refer a patient to another. I may refer you to a passage on page 25. And a lawyer might refer the jury to certain pieces of evidence. '*Direct*' is a near synonym of 'refer' in the triadic predicate but not the dyadic. To refer (direct) A to something, it is not enough for a speaker simply to refer to (mean, mention) the other doctor, passage, or evidence. A doctor who advises his patient to see Dr. Jones in a language his patient does not understand will have referred to Dr. Jones. But he will not have referred his patient (or anyone else) to Dr. Jones. To refer A to Φ, S must not only try to get A to take some action but also choose suitable means. Moreover, the action S must intend A to perform is the act of *referring to Φ for information, advice, etc.* This sort of reference is not a speech act, and is not closely related to meaning. A rough synonym of 'refer to Φ' here is *consult Φ*. Since consulting Φ implies directing one's attention to Φ, Bertolet's version of the Gricean analysis would seem most promising as an analysis of referring A to Φ. Since 'S refers A to Φ' differs markedly from 'S refers to Φ' in the linguistic sense we are interested in, we will pay no more attention to it.[7]

The causal theory of reference, even more popular than the Gricean approach, will be discussed in §8.3 and §8.4.

### 8.2   INTENTIONALITY

We distinguished the opaque interpretation of psychological descriptions from the transparent in §2.8. On the intended *opaque* interpretation, 'S expressed the idea of Φ' is not subject to the substitutivity of identity in the Φ position. The idea of Φ may differ from the idea of Φ', enabling us to express one without expressing the other, even when Φ = Φ'. Furthermore, we can express the idea of Φ even though Φ does not exist. That is, 'S expressed the idea of Φ' is not subject to existential instantiation in the Φ position. The failure of substitutivity and especially of existential instantiation make it evident that objects of ideas are *intentional objects* in Brentano's sense.[8] 'S expressed the idea of Φ' describes a relation between S and an idea, not between S and Φ.

Speaker reference and meaning also have intentional objects on their opaque interpretation. Adults as well as children refer to mythical creatures like Pegasus. The most pedantic realist can refer to mythical characters in order to deny their existence. We do not need to believe in God to acknowledge that religious people often make reference to God. As for the failure of substitutivity, suppose S takes Jack Stevenson to be a reputable banker, and John Smith to be a ruthless drug lord. Suppose further that when S said

'Jack is a fine man', S was referring to Jack Stevenson. It does not follow that S was referring to John Smith when he said this even if in fact 'John Smith' is just an alias for Jack Stevenson. Despite its grammatical form, 'S referred to Φ' does not describe a true relation between S and Φ.[9]

When 'S referred to Φ' and 'S expressed the idea of Φ' are interpreted *transparently*, the Φ position is subject to the substitutivity of identity. But it is still an intentional context, since existence is not presupposed or implied. If 'Johnny is referring to Santa Claus' is true on the opaque interpretation, then 'Johnny is referring to a make-believe character' will be true on the transparent interpretation, as will 'Johnny is referring to the object of Suzie's dreams' if she is dreaming of Santa Claus. The truth of these statements does not imply that make-believe characters or the objects of Suzie's dreams exist. Note that on its opaque interpretation, 'Johnny is referring to a make-believe character' is false: since Johnny believes Santa Claus is real, he is certainly not expressing the idea *"make-believe character"*.[10] 'Johnny is referring to the object of Suzie's dreams' is false too on its opaque interpretation, since he is not expressing the idea *"object of Suzie's dreams"*.

The idea that people *cannot* refer to nonexistent objects has received much discussion and an amazing amount of support. A notable example is Donnellan.[11]

Among a number of puzzles mentioned by Russell, two stand out as more important than others.... The second puzzle is the topic of this paper. In a large number of situations speakers apparently refer to the nonexistent. The most obvious example of this is, perhaps, the use of singular terms in negative existence statements—for example, ... *"Robin Hood did not exist."* The problem is, of course, well known and ancient in origin: such statements seem to refer to something only to say about it that it does not exist. How can one say something about what does not exist?

(Donnellan 1974: 3)

Where is the puzzle? We can obviously think about Robin Hood, as we are doing now. Since we can think about him, we can talk about him. In particular, we can say that he did not really exist. The mere fact that we are thinking and talking about Robin Hood does not prove that he exists. If the alleged 'problem' is well known, so is the 'solution': meaning and related concepts have *intentional* objects, which must be objects of thought but need not exist in reality. Speaker reference is one of those related concepts. Just as I can think about, expect, want, hunt for, or dread things that do not in fact exist, so I can refer to them.

Because 'S refers to Φ' and 'S is thinking about Φ' do not describe *relations* between S and Φ, the following argument is valid but unsound.

Statements of the form 'S refers to Φ' have the logical form 'Rab.' But '∃x(x = a)' follows logically from 'Rab' in quantification theory. Hence 'S refers to Φ' entails '∃x(x = Φ)).'

The first premise of this argument is plausible because English subject-verb-object sentences can generally be symbolized 'Rab'. But this principle is not a law of logic, but a rule of thumb for the application of logic. Such rules have numerous exceptions since surface structural similarities sometimes conceal deep structural differences. The surface structure of sentences like 'S wants Φ', 'S expects Φ', and 'S is hallucinating Φ' makes it appear that they have the same logical form as 'S hits Φ'. But our understanding of the meaning of such sentences tells us that there are important logical differences. 'S refers to Φ' is another one of these exceptions.

Whereas *speaker* reference is opaque and intentional, *word* reference is transparent and relational. Since Mt. Everest is the tallest mountain, 'the tallest mountain' refers to Mt. Everest. Mt. Everest is the referent or extension of that phrase. To say that 'the golden mountain' does not refer to anything is just to say that there is no such thing as the golden mountain. This phrase has no referent. A referring term is therefore one that can appropriately be represented by an individual constant serving as an argument of a predicate in classical quantification theory. Since 'Fa ∴ ∃Fx' is a valid inference in quantification theory, the constant 'a' must denote an existent object. Similarly, since 'a = b ∴ Fa ≡ Fb' is valid in quantification theory, any context in which an individual constant appears must be extensional. A key question in the application of quantification theory then is: which terms in a natural language are referring terms, in this sense? That is, which can be represented by individual constants serving as arguments of predicates?

We will be concerned with word reference later (§9.1). We are concerned now with the sense of reference expressed by sentences of the form 'S referred to Φ' in standard English. We are interested in this sense of reference because it is similar to, yet different from, speaker meaning. Moreover, referring in this sense is something we use names to do. The importance of this concept of reference can be measured by the frequency with which we ask in daily life 'Who is S referring to?' The answer typically determines the answer to other questions. For example, S made a true statement when S uttered 'Robin Hood did not really exist' only if S was referring to Robin Hood rather than, say, Franklin D. Roosevelt. And S displayed a knowledge of literature when he said 'Tom was a ladies' man' provided S was referring to Tom Jones rather Tom Sawyer. Our assessment of everything from S's grammar to his sanity may depend on what he is referring to in the sense we are concerned with. In particular, what actions we predict on the basis of S's utterances depends on what S is referring to. Suppose S says 'I am going to photograph Santa Claus'. We can predict straight away that S is going to fail if he is a child referring to the 'real' Santa Claus, in a way we could not if S were an adult referring to the Macy's Santa. To know what S will do in order to carry out the intention S is expressing in the former case, we must know what S believes about Santa Claus, such as whether he invariably comes down the chimney on Christmas Eve night. If we stipulate that 'S refers to Φ' is to be interpreted relationally rather than intentionally, we will just have to introduce another intentional term (such as Quine's 'purports to refer') to make the required discriminations.

How can we argue against Donnellan's assumption that 'S referred to Φ' on its conventional interpretation is relational? We may appeal first to our linguistic intuitions. A statement like 'Sam was referring to the Canadian president' does not automatically strike us as false, the way a statement like 'Sam was looking at the Canadian president' would. And a statement like 'S was referring to something that isn't there' does not seem self-contradictory in the way 'S is touching something that isn't there' does. Finally, an argument like 'Socrates may not have been a real person, so I cannot be sure I am talking about him' seems fallacious and curiously self-defeating, in marked contrast to 'There may be no golden eagles in this part of the country, so I cannot be sure I saw one.' Even Donnellan should agree with these observations about linguistic intuition, since he grants that people certainly *appear* to refer to nonexistent objects.

Second, we may appeal to the linguistic usage of competent speakers who are not trying to describe reference. Suppose Bill is on trial for murder. David is in the witness stand. The prosecuting attorney asks 'And then what did Bill do?' David answers 'He shot Harry's wife'. At this point, the defense attorney takes over, asking 'Is Harry married?' David could hardly say 'No'. If he did, the defense attorney would hop all over him: 'If Harry is not married, why did you tell us that Bill shot his wife? Are you aware of the penalty for perjury?' If David instead answered 'Yes', and the defense attorney could prove otherwise, David's testimony would be discredited unless it could be established that David was referring to a real woman when he said 'Bill shot Harry's wife'. In contrast, suppose the prosecutor asked 'And then who did Bill refer to?', to which David answered 'Harry's wife'. If the defense attorney again asked 'Is Harry married?' David could perfectly well answer 'No' or 'I have no idea'. Such a response would not elicit surprise or charges of perjury. Nor would the defense attorney insist that David correct or reformulate his statement that Bill referred to Harry's wife. Indeed, the last thing I would expect the defense attorney to say is this: 'Surely you meant only that Bill *tried but failed* to refer to Harry's wife?' If he did, the only response I could imagine David making is 'Huh?'

Third, we can look at our epistemological practices. Our claims about what we ourselves are referring to are accorded the same sort of first-person, introspective 'privilege' that our claims about what we mean or what we are thinking about receive. They stand in marked contrast to our claims about what someone else is referring to or thinking about. 'How do you know you are referring to Homer' would be answered in the same way as 'How do you know you are thinking of Homer'—'By introspection'. If a woman who says 'Homer wrote the *Iliad*' is asked 'Who are you referring to?', she would never answer 'I cannot be sure because my evidence is incomplete'. But if referring to Homer, like seeing Homer, were possible only if Homer really existed, then the woman could not know whom she was referring to without having historical evidence about the distant past. If the evidence that Santa Claus is a mythical figure showed that we are not referring to Santa Claus, then we could never know that we have told our children that Santa does not really exist.[12]

Crimmins (1998) has suggested that in using sentences like 'Santa Claus does not exist', we are engaging in 'semantic pretense'.[13]

One is pretending (or at least alluding to a pretense) that one can refer to a thing with a certain kind of use of the name 'Santa', in order to *disavow* such uses; one's statement is true just in case such uses do not refer. One very attractive feature of these accounts, as Walton and Evans emphasize, is that they capture the semantic phenomenology of such uses of empty names: they *feel* just like ordinary uses of referring names. This is respected by taking the use of the name, within the pretense, to *be* an ordinary use of a referring name.                    (Crimmins 1998: 33)

The use of an empty term like 'Santa Claus' in a negative existence claim is not phenomenologically *identical* to the ordinary use of a referring term like 'George Bush'. For we *take* the latter to have a referent, but not the former. But the uses are similar in some respects. On my view, one introspectible respect in which the two uses are alike is that we use both to refer to something. Crimmins cannot say this because he holds the common view that we cannot refer to nonexistent objects. Crimmins claims that his pretense theory accounts for the felt similarity, but it does not. For pretending to do something feels markedly different from doing it. I know introspectively whether I am in pain or only making as if to be in pain. I do not believe I am engaging in pretense when I assert that Santa Claus does not exist any more than when I assert that George Bush does exist. We do of course pretend that Santa Claus exists when we have young children. But negative existence claims are in no way dependent on such pretense.

If, when saying 'Santa Claus does not exist', it is only *as if* I am referring to Santa Claus, then it is at most *as if* I have asserted that Santa does not exist. If I am actually referring to something else—a plastic toy, perhaps, or a mode of presentation, as Crimmins suggests—then what I am actually saying is that this other thing does not exist. If I am actually referring to nothing, then I am not actually making a statement. Crimmins says that 'speaking about modes of presentation as if we were speaking about the objects presented is something that we do spontaneously and naturally' (1998: 24). But when I say 'Santa Claus does not exist', I emphatically do not think that I am speaking about a mode of presentation. I am talking about Santa Claus, and denying that he exists. I am not even making as if to deny that a mode of presentation of Santa Claus exists. Crimmins seems to assume that in order to deny that Santa Claus exists, we need to pretend that he does. Aside from the fact that this seems patently untrue, why is pretending something about nonexistent objects any easier than referring to them?

For an example of a case where we do engage in something like semantic pretense, look at the figure of speech discussed in §14.4. If I say of a model of the solar system 'Jupiter is out of place', I am making as if to refer to Jupiter, but I am actually referring to the ball representing Jupiter. Nothing like this seems to be going on in the case of serious negative existence claims.

Donnellan grants that people *appear* to make references to nonexistent objects. Why did he conclude that this appearance is an illusion? One reason can be found in his example of the man carrying a walking stick.

There is finally the case in which there is nothing at all where I thought there was a man with a walking stick; and perhaps here we have a genuine failure to refer at all, even though the description was used for the purpose of referring.... I cannot say of anything, "That is what I was referring to, though I now see that it's not a man carrying a walking stick." (Donnellan 1966: 296)

It does not follow that he did not refer to anything. On the contrary, he referred to something that does not exist, viz., the man he thought he saw carrying a walking stick. Referring to something that does not exist differs as much from referring to nothing or not referring as thinking about something that does not exist differs from thinking about nothing or not thinking. It is just as absurd to conclude that Donnellan was not referring to anything as it would be to conclude that someone who wants a 6,000-square-foot new house priced less than $100,000 in a prestigious Washington neighborhood does not want anything.

Donnellan appears to have been misled by the special character of de- monstrative pronouns, which may carry an existence presupposition even in intentional contexts.[14] While we can truly say 'He wants a cheap 6000- square-foot house in Washington' without committing ourselves to the existence of such a house, we cannot point to a house and say 'He wants *that*' without presupposing that *that* exists. This is why we cannot say of anything '*That* is what Donnellan was referring to' or '*That* is what he is thinking of' when Donnellan is hallucinating.

Evans (1982: Ch. 6) seems to have concluded that the speaker isn't even thinking in such cases. But that is absurd. While we cannot say of anything 'S is thinking of *that*' or 'S is referring to *that*', there are other ways to describe what S is thinking and referring to. Whereas demonstratives typically pre- suppose existence after 'to' and 'of' and in *oratio obliqua* contexts, they typically do not in *oratio recta* contexts. Thus, if we are given that S is hallucinating the Holy Grail, we can say 'S is thinking "That is the Holy Grail"', without committing ourselves to a real referent for 'that'. We can also say that S is thinking the thought that S could sincerely express by saying 'That is the Holy Grail'. Furthermore, we often use *that* and other pronouns without presupposing existence when we are pointing to a picture and referring not to the picture but to what it is a picture of. Thus I might point at a painting of the Holy Grail, and say truly 'S wants *that*' or 'S is referring to *that*', referring not to the painting, but to the Holy Grail. This does not commit me in any way to the existence of the Holy Grail. We can also use 'that' anaphorically without presupposing existence. Thus I might say 'That is what S was referring to' after Jane says 'According to medieval legend, the Holy Grail was a cup with magical powers because it was used by Jesus at the Last Supper.' Finally, we can always use terms other than demonstratives. S was referring to, and thinking about: something that does not exist, something S was hallucinating, a man S thought he saw carrying a walking stick. All of these entail that S was thinking and referring.

I believe the fundamental reason Donnellan denied the possibility of reference to nonexistent objects was to avoid the conclusion of an argument Russell attributed to Meinong.

It is argued, e.g. by Meinong, that [A] we can speak about "the golden mountain," "the round square," and so on; [B] we can make true propositions of which these are the subjects; hence [C] they must have some kind of logical being, since [D] otherwise the propositions in which they occur would be meaningless. In such theories, it seems to me, there is a failure of that feeling for reality which ought to be preserved even in the most abstract studies.                                        (Russell 1919: 213)

The abhorrent conclusion here is [C], which I would be as loathe as Russell to accept. There are no golden mountains, and there could not be any round squares. But our concern is [A], which does not seem to entail [C] at all. We may grant that [A] entails [B]. For if we can talk about Φ, then *either* 'Φ exists' *or* 'Φ does not exist' must be true. And Φ is the subject of both of these propositions. But [C] does not follow from [B]. Many true statements about Φ do not entail that Φ exists, such as the statement that Φ does not exist. *A fortiori*, the fact that we can speak about Φ does not entail the truth of any proposition that entails the existence of Φ, such as a statement predicating a property of Φ. We can freely affirm both that *people can refer to nonexistent objects* and that *properties cannot be truly predicated of what does not exist*.[15] The latter principle is not contradicted by the former any more than it is contradicted by the fact that people can think about, want, and have beliefs about nonexistent objects. We simply need to make clear that 'Johnny referred to Santa Claus' does not predicate a property of Santa Claus. Hence this sentence can be true even though Santa does not exist, whereas a sentence like 'Santa weighs 250 pounds' cannot be true if it is interpreted as predicating a property of Santa.[16]

The abhorrent conclusion [C] in the Meinongian argument does not follow from [A] without [D]. Donnellan accepts [D] because he holds *both* of the following:

(2) Understanding a sentence entails grasping the proposition expressed.

(3) The proposition expressed by a sentence of the form 'S is P' is an ordered pair consisting of the *object* S and the *predicate* 'P'.

On such a view of propositions, true sentences like 'Sherlock Holmes is a fictitious character' do not express propositions.[17] Hence by (2) they cannot be understood. Since the sentence *can* be understood by almost any speaker of English, one of these two principles must be false. While Donnellan (1974) refers to (3) as the 'natural' theory of propositions, it is anything but natural when conjoined with the theory of understanding represented by (2). A better theory of propositions to pair with (2) is that the proposition expressed by a sentence is the *thought* it expresses. Since 'Sherlock Holmes never existed' expresses a clear and easily grasped thought, the sentence can be easily understood. It is not my point here to argue that this alternative definition of 'proposition' is correct (cf. §2.5). We can accept (3) as the definition of a technical term. But then (2) needs to be assessed when 'proposition' is interpreted according to (3). When it is, (2) must be rejected as obviously false. Any argument based on (2) and (3) either has a false premise or commits the fallacy of equivocation.

It is possible to reformulate the Meinongian argument without using the term 'proposition'.

(4) If we can refer to an object, then we can make a statement about it that is at least meaningful.

(5) A statement about nothing is a meaningless statement.

(6) A statement is about something only if that object exists.

(7) Therefore, we cannot refer to nonexistent objects.

In this formulation, the equivocation is on 'about'. On the ordinary interpretation of 'about', its objects are intentional and need not exist. 'S made a statement about the mythical golden mountain' does not describe an obvious impossibility the way 'S climbed the mythical golden mountain' does. A parent who says to his child, 'This is a story about Babar' can without the slightest contradiction answer 'No' when the child asks whether Babar is real. Making a statement about a nonexistent being in this sense is very different from making a statement about nothing. Only the latter sort of statement can be described as nonsensical. Like many philosophers today, however, Russell (e.g., 1905: 205) used 'about' relationally. On this interpretation, 'The King of France is bald' is not about anything, since there is no King of France. But in this relational sense, a meaningful statement *can* be about nothing. 'The King of France is bald' is meaningful even though there is no King of France. *Only if we equivocate on 'about' can a puzzle be generated.* While each premise in the reformulated argument is true on one interpretation of 'about', on neither interpretation are all three true. If 'about' is interpreted intentionally, (4) and (5) are plausible but (6) is false. If 'about' is interpreted relationally, (6) is true but (4) and (5) are false.[18] Henceforth, I shall continue to use 'about' in its standard, intentional interpretation.

I have presented evidence that 'S refers to $\Phi$' is an intentional context, and have shown that arguments designed to support the conclusion that it is relational are fallacious. Even if I were wrong, the definition of speaker reference I have presented would require little or no revision. *If* there is any good reason to think that people cannot refer to nonexistent objects, then there should also be a good reason to think that people cannot think about, or express ideas of, nonexistent objects. So Definition 7.1 (and its generalization) may still be maintained. To refute Definition 7.1, in other words, someone would have to show that referring to $\Phi$ and expressing the idea of $\Phi$ *differ* in that only the latter has an intentional object. *If* that could be shown, moreover, Definition 7.1 could easily be corrected by adding 'and $\Phi$ exists' to the definiens.

## 8.3   CAUSAL THEORIES

The most influential theory of reference is the *causal theory*. Donnellan provided a rough characterization.

When a speaker uses a name intending to refer to an individual and predicate something of it, successful reference will occur when there is an individual that enters into the historically correct explanation of who it is that the speaker intended to predicate something of. That individual will then be the referent.

(Donnellan 1974: 16)

The first problem is to distill out a definition. That S intends to refer to $\Phi$ cannot be a defining condition of S referring to $\Phi$, on pain of circularity. I take Donnellan to be proposing that in every logically possible world, *S refers to $\Phi$ iff $\Phi$ enters into the historically correct explanation of who it is that S intends to predicate something of.* This formulation is much too broad, as Donnellan (1974: 18) was well aware. My parents entered into the historically correct explanation of who it is that I intend to predicate something of when I say 'My brother loves hockey'. But I was not referring to my parents. Donnellan (1974: 16) indicated by example the specific way in which $\Phi$ must connect with S's intention. I would put it this way:

S must intend to predicate something of $\Phi$ because $S_1$ intended to predicate something of $\Phi$, who did so because ... $S_n$ intended to predicate something of $\Phi$, who did so because he perceived $\Phi$. To use Donnellan's example, when S referred to Socrates, S intended to predicate something of Socrates because S read about Socrates; the authors of the books S read intended to predicate something of Socrates because they read Plato's dialogues; Plato intended to predicate something of Socrates because he knew Socrates.[19]

Standard formulations of the causal condition focus on a chain of utterances rather than a chain of intentions: S used a name he picked up from $S_1$ who picked it up from ... $S_n$ who 'baptized' $\Phi$.[20] These formulations give the wrong referent when the intentions with which speakers use the name shift along the chain. As Evans (1973: 300) observed, we use the name 'Madagascar' as we do because Marco Polo used it that way. But he picked up the word indirectly from African natives, who unbeknownst to him used the word to refer to part of the mainland rather than the island.[21] Naming a baby 'after' someone presents similar problems. The standard formulation fails to provide the correct reference when names change over time or from language to language. For example, the name Aristotle was given at birth was similar to but not identical to 'Aristotle'. The fact that any use of a name has many causes is another problem. When Pizarro stood on a cliff and named the Pacific, his utterance of the name was caused by: the Pacific, the South Pacific, and a certain bay in the South Pacific; light coming off the Pacific, retinal activity caused by that light, and so on. Standard formulations do not tell us why 'The Pacific' refers to the whole ocean, and not any of these parts or effects thereof.[22] Standard formulations also founder on the existence of ambiguity. Suppose Bill names both his son and his dog 'Sym'. His neighbors pick up the name. Standard formulations seem to imply that every time Bill's neighbors use the name 'Sym', they are referring to both Bill's son and Bill's dog.[23] Donnellan's formulation in terms of a chain of intentions avoids these problems with the standard formulation.

A central defect of any causal theory is that $\Phi$ itself need not be part of the causal chain in virtue of which S refers to $\Phi$.[24] We can refer to the largest fish in the sea or the contents of a hermetically sealed box even though there is no causal chain leading from them to us. We can refer to future objects (such as tomorrow's sunrise) even though they cannot be part of the historical explanation of any current event. We can introduce a name now after a prediction of the future, as in the following passage.

Recent calculations by astronomers have shown that in about 500 million years, the asteroid belt will coalesce into a single medium sized planet. Let us call this planet 'Hera.' Hera will orbit the sun between Mars and Jupiter, and will be visible to the naked eye.[25]

Finally, we can refer by name or definite description to numbers even though they are abstract, and to Pegasus even though he does not even exist.

The fundamental flaw in Donnellan's theory is its very emphasis on the *causes* of the speaker's intentions. Let us suppose that *S intended to predicate something of Socrates*, and as a result said 'Socrates was snub-nosed'. To determine who S was referring to, Donnellan says, we must look at the chain of causes leading to S's intention. But let us suppose that Socrates was in no way involved in the explanation. Suppose, say, that Socrates never existed, and that S's intention had no explanation at all. Would it follow that S did not refer to Socrates? How could it, given the initial stipulation that S intended to predicate something specifically *of Socrates*? That is, once we are *given* an intention to predicate something of Socrates (or to provide an indication that one is thinking of Socrates), the causal origins of the intention are irrelevant to whether or not S referred to Socrates.

If we strip the historical relation clause from Donnellan's analysis, we are left with a definition much like Kripke's: *S refers to Φ iff S uses a name with the intention of predicating something of Φ*. This definition is fairly close to the truth, but has two defects. First, as with talking about Φ, predicating something of Φ is too close a synonym of referring to Φ to provide an illuminating analysis. Second, I have argued in §7.2 that reference is possible without the intent to predicate, as in cases of oblique reference and incomplete sentences.

I believe causal factors have this much relevance: one is currently *thinking about* Φ only if one's current mental state has the right sort of history. If S had never acquired the concept of Socrates, for example, S could not now be thinking about Socrates. Nor could S do so if S had acquired the concept but suffered a complete memory loss in the meantime. This holds true at least contingently whether Φ is a historical figure like Socrates, a future event like tomorrow's sunrise, an unproven object like the Loch Ness monster, or a completely fictitious character like a Pegasus.

It follows that *S is referring to Φ only if S's current mental state has the right history*. What we have seen, though, is that Φ itself need not enter into this history, and that this history need not be mentioned in a definition of referring. There is no *logical* incoherence in the claim that someone is thinking about Socrates who is not causally connected with Socrates in any way. There is no contradiction in the claim that God did not acquire any of His concepts. The origins of many of the concepts we possess are unknown. Homer and the Loch Ness monster provide familiar examples. Even if having originated in the perception of their object is empirically essential to these concepts, we do not know that it is.

It is true in some special cases that *S is referring to Φ only if S's current mental state is causally connected to Φ*. This plausibly holds, for example, when 'Φ' is 'Socrates'. It is plausible that the concept of Socrates is occurring to S only if S's current mental state is causally connected to Socrates. I am thinking of Socrates now in part because a long chain of predecessors did beginning roughly with Plato, who thought of Socrates because he perceived him. We know something about all people known to think about Socrates that connects them to Socrates, such as their reading Plato, or hearing lectures about Socrates. Consequently there is no *real* possibility of a person thinking about Socrates who is not plugged into that causal network. The idea of Socrates is an event-type which had its origin in the perception of Socrates. On some definitions, the relationship between referring to Socrates and being connected to Socrates is plausibly a 'natural' or 'metaphysical' necessity (§15.1).[26] But it is not a logical necessity, and is not something we know *a priori*. The concept of Socrates could be like the concept of the Loch Ness monster. The empirical connection between reference and causation in these cases will have no bearing on the issues we discuss.

### 8.4  Consequences for Skepticism

As we observed in §8.2, we standardly accord individuals' claims about what they are referring to the same introspective privilege as their claims about what they intend, which fits well with intentionalist accounts of referring. An unacceptable implication of the causal theory as an analysis of reference (in the opaque sense) is that what we are referring to cannot be known by introspection, and may be highly uncertain.[27] Whether Socrates existed, and initiated an appropriate causal chain, are historical matters, for which my evidence is indirect and limited. The causal theory therefore implies, absurdly, that I cannot be sure I am referring to Socrates when I say this. On the causal theory, 'S is referring to Φ' is much like 'X is a photograph of Φ', which entails that Φ bears a certain causal relation to X. Since Socrates lived thousands of years before the invention of photography, we can easily dismiss anyone's claim to have a photograph of Socrates. And to the extent that we are doubtful that the Loch Ness monster really exists, we must be doubtful that any picture is a photograph of it. We can know introspectively that something *seems* to be a photograph of the monster, but not that it *is*. If the causal theory of reference were correct, we would have to be equally doubtful that we are referring to the Loch Ness monster when we say this. A causal theory of *word* reference would not be as implausible. For we often do not know what words refer to, and never know by introspection. To the extent that we are doubtful that there is a Loch Ness monster, we are doubtful that 'the Loch Ness monster' has a referent, and we cannot know whether it does by introspection.

Burge (1988: 654) correctly denies that knowing that p requires knowing of each condition for having such knowledge that it is satisfied. For example, people can know by vision that a ball is red without knowing that their optic nerve is functioning properly. They must be justified in believing that the ball is red, but need not know that they are justified. Hence knowing that p does not entail knowing the very fact that one knows that p. These observations are irrelevant to the issue at hand, however. To successfully defend the compatibility of the causal theory with self-knowledge, Burge would have to deny a different and highly plausible principle, namely epistemic closure: knowing that p requires knowing things that are obviously entailed by the proposition that p.[28] Just as we cannot know that a photograph is of the Loch Ness monster without knowing that the monster exists, and was causally connected to the photograph, so, if the causal theory were true, we could not know that we are referring to the Loch Ness monster without knowing that it exists, and was causally responsible for our thoughts.

Following Burge (1988: 656–8), Gibbons (1996: 291–3) argues that externalist theories of content do allow introspective self-knowledge. Such theories generalize the causal theory of reference to mental states generally, holding that what it is for a mental state to be about something is for the state to have the right sort of causal connection with the object. A key premise in the Burge-Gibbons argument is:

> (8) If your thinking about something is conscious, it must cause a higher order belief to the effect that you are thinking about it.[29]

Necessarily, beliefs caused in this way are true. However, the sense of 'about' for which the causal theory holds would have to be relational. But Gibbons's principle of introspection is plausible only for the intentional sense of 'about' (§8.2). Using subscripts to disambiguate, Gibbons's claim that introspection is a process in which thinking about$_r$ x causes one to believe that one is thinking about$_r$ x contradicts his own claim that 'Introspection … only affords access to the intrinsic properties of thoughts'(291). Whereas being about$_i$ something is an intrinsic property of thoughts, being about$_r$ something is relational property. Because I know that Pegasus does not exist, I will not believe that I am thinking about$_r$ Pegasus even when I am thinking about$_i$ Pegasus. Similarly, even if I am in fact thinking about$_r$ the Loch Ness monster, I will not believe that I am doing so if I do not believe that the creature exists. Indeed, I might incorrectly believe that I am not thinking about$_r$ it.

More importantly, the question we are addressing is not whether the causal theory allows *beliefs* about our mental states, but whether such beliefs can constitute *direct introspective knowledge* (Brueckner 1990: 449). How could they if having particular mental states entails things we cannot know through introspection? Even though I do believe that I am thinking about$_r$ Homer, I cannot know that I am thinking about$_r$ Homer unless I know that Homer was a real person. This is true even if thinking about$_r$ Homer caused me to believe that I am. The fact that a belief is true is not enough for it to be justified. Gibbons (1996: 292) argues that beliefs about our own mental states are justified because they are produced by a reliable process, described by (8). But as we observed, (8) is false for the relational sense of thinking about something. Thinking about$_r\Phi$ does not reliably cause us to believe that we are thinking about$_r\Phi$. For whether we are thinking about$_r\Phi$ is not accessible to introspection, and cannot be known without having evidence that x exists and bears the right causal relations to our thought.

Burge (1996: 96) relies on the premise that 'There is no way for one to make a mistake about the content of one's present-tensed thought in the relevant cases', which he infers from the following principle:

(9) Thinking the thought that one is thinking about something entails thinking about it.

Burge defends (9) on the grounds that the thought that p itself is part of the thought that we are thinking the thought that p, relying presumably on the second law of occurrence (Theorem 2.8). I accept (9) but deny Burge's constituency thesis: the thought that one is thinking T contains a representation of T, not T itself. What makes (9) true is the fact that ideo-reflexive representations of T cannot occur unless T occurs (see §3.7). If Burge's externalism were true, moreover, (9) would be false. To see this, note that because Pegasus does not exist, it is not possible for anyone to think about$_r$ Pegasus, where 'r' marks the relational sense of 'about'. That does not entail, though, that it is impossible to think the thought that one is thinking about$_r$ Pegasus. We are thinking that second-order thought now even though we are not thinking about$_r$ Pegasus. We might well mistakenly believe that we are thinking about$_r$ Pegasus if we know introspectively that we are thinking about$_i$ Pegasus, and believe erroneously that that thought is about$_r$ Pegasus. We might believe that if we foolishly believed that we had actually seen Pegasus.

Macdonald (1998) has tried to defend externalist theories of content by developing an observational model of introspection. She claims that we can know directly that an object is brown through sense-perception because it is presented to us *as* brown. Macdonald (1998: 134) gives the same explanation for introspection: '[i] A subject S typically thinks about her own intentional states *as* states of particular contentful types.... [ii] S's intentional states are of the contentful types that they appear to be.' But the very problem is that if externalism were true, intrinsically identical states could differ in content. Being intrinsically indistinguishable, such states would appear the same to introspection. Consider thoughts of Socrates. According to the causal theory, there could be intrinsically indistinguishable thoughts that are not of Socrates because they were not caused ultimately by Socrates. We could not tell the difference by introspection.

To see where Macdonald's explanation goes awry, let us grant that there is a sense in which [i] is true. Our thoughts of Socrates are presented to us specifically as thoughts of Socrates. The problem is that in this sense, [ii] would be false if externalism were true. To take an analogy, there is certainly a sense in which a photograph of Elvis is typically presented to us as a photograph of Elvis. But in this sense, photographs of Elvis look-a-likes may also present themselves to us as photographs of Elvis. Because whether a photo is of Elvis rather than a look-a-like depends on who caused the photo, the mere fact that something presents itself as a photo of Elvis in this sense does not enable us to know that it is a photo of Elvis. There is another sense, moreover, in which nothing can present itself as a photo specifically of Elvis because photos of Elvis do not appear any different than photos of Elvis look-a-likes. Thoughts of$_r$ Socrates do not present themselves specifically as thoughts of$_r$ Socrates. In this sense, Macdonald's [i] would be false if externalism were true. Externalism is incompatible with the joint truth of [i] and [ii].

Whereas the causal theory leads to skepticism where we least expect it, some have used it to provide arguments against skepticism that seem too good to be true. The causal theory erroneously implies that we can know facts about the external world solely on the basis of knowledge of our own mind.[30] Witness Putnam's (1981) famous 'brain in the vat' argument. Putnam asks us to imagine that a brain was removed from the body, before birth say, and connected to a computer and life-support system in such a way that its neural inputs are identical to those it would have received had it been connected normally to the person's sense-organs, blood vessels, afferent nerves, and so on. In the present state of technology, such a scenario is fantastically far-fetched. Nevertheless, the case seems logically, physically, and psychologically possible. That is, the scenario contradicts no known laws of logic, physics, or psychology. Now, given that the brain in the vat receives the same inputs it would have had if it were normally embodied, it seems undeniable that the person would end up with the same thoughts he would have had in normal conditions. The sensory experience that would lead a normal person to think "My hand is before me" should lead the person whose brain is in the vat to think "My hand is before me". This possibility has led many epistemologists to conclude that we cannot really know that we have a hand.

If the causal theory of content were correct, however, then the vatted brain could not be thinking the same thoughts as a normal person because the distal causes of its thoughts are different. This led Putnam to conclude that we could not possibly be brains in vats, *pace* the skeptic.

(10) We can think the thought that we are a brain in a vat.
(11) If we were a brain in a vat, we could not think that we were.
(12) So, we could not be a brain in a vat.

The first premise is obviously true, given that we are thinking that thought now. Devitt and Sterelny set out the argument for the second premise.

It is an application of the causal theory of reference. Ultimately reference is determined not by what is in the head but by appropriate causal links to objects. A brain in a vat is not appropriately linked to any object; it lacks the perceptual links that are necessary for reference. None of its thoughts are *about* anything. So, though the words 'I am a brain in a vat' could run through its mind, that would not amount to thinking that it was a brain in a vat.[31]                                   (Devitt and Sterelny 1987: 207)

I think the second premise is false. We can think about Pegasus, phlogiston, and the twelfth planet in the solar system even though they do not exist (see §8.2). We can think about tomorrow even though we are not perceptually linked to tomorrow. A psychiatric patient might think that she is pregnant, and that the baby inside her is moving, even if she is completely deluded. Perceptual links are present in some cases of reference, but not all.[32]

Of course, if 'about' is taken in a sufficiently strong relational sense, so that thinking 'about' Φ entails that one's thought is causally connected with Φ in the standard way, then it would be trivially true that a vatted brain could not be thinking 'about' brains or vats. This is not enough to make Putnam's argument sound, though, for the first premise does not entail that we are thinking 'about' brains or vats *in this sense*. If we stipulate that (10) is to have such an implication, then it could not be accepted without begging the question against the skeptic. For in that sense, we could not know on the basis of introspection alone that *we* are actually thinking 'about' brains or vats. Acceptance of (10) would require prior knowledge that our ideas of brains and vats originated in the perception of brains and vats in the standard way, knowledge the skeptic denies we possess. Interpreting the argument in this way therefore makes it valid but question-begging.[33]

## 8.5  The 'Connection' between Thought and Object

It should not be thought that I am siding with the 'description theory', according to which we can think about things, and hence refer to them, only if we have in mind some 'identifying' description. Description theorists maintain that we can think of or refer to Aristotle only if we have in mind some description like 'The eldest son of Nichomachus' or 'The most famous student of Plato' that is uniquely true of Aristotle, and would enable us to identify him. I argue at length in Part III that this is false.

My rejection of both leading theories is likely to elicit the following objection:

You deny that S is thinking of **Φ** in virtue of any causal connection between S and **Φ**, or of some identifying description of **Φ** S has in mind. What then connects S's thought to **Φ**?[34]

I believe the question is misguided. It has a false presupposition. First, as I have emphasized, on the opaque interpretation we are focusing on, '*S is thinking of Φ*' *is not a relational predicate*. It does not state that S or S's thought stands in a certain relationship to **Φ**. This is proven by two facts: (i) 'S is thinking of **Φ**' and '**Φ** = **Φ**'' do not jointly entail 'S is thinking of **Φ**''; and (ii) 'S is thinking of **Φ**' does not entail the existence of **Φ**. It is for these reasons that 'S is thinking of **Φ**' cannot be symbolized *TsΦ* in classical quantification theory. I have used the unusual symbol '**Φ**' as a place-holder for the terms that can fill the blank in 'S is thinking of ___' partly as a reminder that it is not an individual variable, and cannot be bound by a standard objectual quantifier (§2.9). Since 'S is thinking of **Φ**' is not a relational predicate, it makes no sense to ask what *connects* S or S's thought with **Φ**. For a connection is a relationship. There may of course be many relationships between S and **Φ**, and some of these may even be the cause of S's thinking of **Φ**. But 'S is thinking of **Φ**' does not assert the existence of any of these relationships. Hence none of them *make it true* that S is thinking of **Φ**.

On my view, what makes 'S is thinking of **Φ**' true is the fact that the idea of **Φ** is occurring to S. What makes a thought be a thought about **Φ** is the fact that it contains the idea of **Φ**. 'What then connects the idea to the thing it is the idea of?' This query has the same faulty presupposition as the first question above. Since 'C is the idea of **Φ**' does not express a relationship between C and **Φ**, it does not imply that anything *connects* C to **Φ**.

A similar question may be pressed without presupposing relationality: 'What makes the idea of **Φ** be *of* **Φ**?' In virtue of what does an idea have the content or object "**Φ**"? As discussed in §3.8, for an idea to have the intentional content "**Φ**" is for it to *be* the idea of **Φ**. In some cases, we can explain what makes an idea have the object it has. For example, the idea of the most famous student of Plato has that object because it contains the idea of Plato, the idea of a student, the idea "most famous", and so on, all related in a particular way. Complex ideas are the sum of their parts, and have the objects they do because of the objects of their parts and the way the parts are put together. Atomic ideas do not have other ideas as parts. So they are not individuated the same way complex ideas are. If atomic ideas do have parts, they are not psychological, and we do not know of them by introspection. Only sophisticated empirical research will tell if atomic ideas are neurophysiological complexes. If they are, then 'What makes the idea of red be of red?' will be like 'What makes water be $H_2O$?' We can say that what makes water $H_2O$ is the fact that a water molecule consists of two atoms of hydrogen and one atom of oxygen. But if we now ask, 'What makes a water molecule consist of two atoms of hydrogen and one of oxygen?', we will have asked an unanswerable question. All we can say is 'That's just what a water molecule is'. The question is just as unanswerable as 'What makes Aristotle be Aristotle?' or 'What makes Wayne Davis me?'

Philosophers who insist on an answer to 'What makes the idea of $\Phi$ be of $\Phi$?' normally presuppose either that *there are no simple ideas*, or that *ideas have their objects in virtue of external factors*. Both presuppositions are false. We argued in §3.9 that every idea could not be complex any more than every term could be definable. Chapter 13 will present evidence that the ideas expressed by standard proper names are atomic ideas. Nothing *external* to any idea makes it *be* the idea it is. For an idea to be of this or that is for it to be the idea it is. Hence nothing external makes an idea be of $\Phi$.

In contrast, whether a photograph P is of O depends on something external to P, namely, its relation to O. P had to be the product of a particular causal process initiated by O. Hence it makes perfectly good sense to ask what makes a photograph of Elvis be of Elvis. 'P is a photograph of O' asserts a genuine relation between P and O, one that need not obtain. We might have a photograph intrinsically indistinguishable from a photograph of Elvis that is nevertheless not of Elvis. And the reason may be that the photograph was produced when someone took a picture of the winner of the Elvis look-alike contest. Grammar aside, 'idea of $\Phi$' differs from 'photograph of O' in fundamental ways.

We can easily define *a* relationship between ideas and objects. Consider the set of ordered pairs containing ⟨The idea of Aristotle, Aristotle⟩, ⟨The idea of Napoleon, Napoleon⟩, ⟨The idea of triangularity, triangularity⟩, and so on. Let 'i is an idea *re* x' be true iff ⟨i, x⟩ is a member of that set. The relation just defined is the *extension function* ex{i} = x for ideas, which assigns to each idea i its referent or 'semantic value' x (if it has one). We can go on to stipulate that 'S is thinking *re* x' is true iff an idea *re* x is occurring to S; that 'S is referring *re* x' is true iff S is linguistically expressing an idea *re* x; and so on. It makes sense to ask 'What makes the idea of Aristotle an idea *re* Aristotle?' The answer is 'The very fact that that idea is the idea of Aristotle, together with the fact that Aristotle exists'. Similarly, 'What makes the idea of the morning star an idea *re* Venus?' can be answered 'Because the morning star is Venus'. The idea of the evening star is a different idea *re* Venus, because Venus is the evening star too. The idea of Pegasus is not *re* anything because Pegasus, and consequently the ordered pair ⟨The idea of Pegasus, Pegasus⟩, does not exist. The idea of Aristotle is not an idea *re* Plato because the idea of Aristotle is not the idea of anything which in fact is Plato. Note, however, that this 'idea *re*' relation is not what is expressed by 'idea of' in conventional English. The idea of Pegasus is tautologically of Pegasus.

The fact that an idea is *re* an object will generally be a contingent fact about the idea. An idea *re* Homer could well exist and retain its identity even if Homer did not exist. In that case, the idea would no longer be *re* Homer, although it might still be the idea of Homer. What explains why i is an idea *re* an existing object x is simply the identities of i and x. Specifically, i is *re* x provided i is *of* **Φ** for some description '**Φ**' that denotes x. An idea i is not *re* x in virtue of any causal relationship between i and x or anything like one. This will remain true even if we find some way of picking out all the right ordered pairs ⟨i,x⟩ (neurophysiologically, say) without mentioning what any of the ideas are ideas of.

I have argued that 'What makes the thought of **Φ** be of **Φ**?' is unanswerable to the extent that it falsely presupposes that something external to the thought connects it to its intentional object. Schiffer (1987a: 173–4, 270) rejects similar questions, such as 'What is it to think of **Φ**?' or 'What makes it true that S is thinking of **Φ**?' But these questions are significantly different. It is more than conceivable that to think of **Φ** is to be in a particular neural state. Similarly, while it makes no sense to ask what makes water be water, it makes perfectly good sense to ask what it is for something to be water. The answer is that to be water is to be $H_2O$. So, in denying that we can say what connects a thought to its object, I am not denying that we can explain what it is to have a thought with a certain object.

Devitt (1990: 99) would object that before we accept that thinking of **Φ** *is* a neural state, we have to explain how it *could be* a neural state. It is certainly true that A is B only if A could be B: 'p' entails '$\diamond$p'. But there is no reason whatsoever to insist that we have to be able to explain how A could be B before we show that A is B. Indeed, it is self-evident that every object is itself. Yet it seems almost as evident that it is impossible to 'explain how' an object could be itself. It is easy to think of the sort of evidence that would show water to be $H_2O$. But we draw a complete blank when asked to explain how water could be $H_2O$, at least if we are being asked to do something other than show that water is $H_2O$. So an inability to explain how thoughts could be neural states is no reason to deny that they are.

## 8.6   The Twin Earth Case

Putnam argued that reference is determined not by intentions, but by factors that are completely independent of the mental state of the speaker. Putnam asked us to imagine that everyone on Earth has a twin on an isolated planet called Twin Earth. Twin Earthlings are generally just like Earthlings, having the same sensory experiences, using the same words, and engaging in the same behavior. Let this premise be [A].

Suppose, now, that [B] the rivers and lakes on Twin Earth are filled with a liquid that superficially resembles water, but which is *not* $H_2O$. Then [C] the word 'water' as used on Twin Earth refers *not* to water but to this other liquid (say XYZ). Yet [D] there is no relevant difference in the mental state of Twin Earth speakers and speakers on Earth (in, say, 1750) which could account for this difference in reference. [E] The reference is different because the *stuff* is different. [F] The mental state by itself, in isolation from the whole situation, does not fix the reference.[35]

(Putnam 1981: 22–3)

It is implicit in [B], I shall assume, that the liquid on Twin Earth is not water, although (*pace* Putnam) this does not follow by logic alone from the stipulation that the liquid is not $H_2O$. 'Water is $H_2O$' is not a logical truth, but a scientific generalization established empirically. Water could have turned out to be HO, as John Dalton thought. Only experimental analysis showed that there were two atoms of hydrogen for every oxygen atom rather than one. Let us call the liquid XYZ on Twin Earth 'twin water'.

Whether it concerns speaker or word reference, the conclusion of the Twin Earth argument does not follow. The stipulation that the liquid on Twin Earth is twin water, and that the Twin Earthlings are behaviorally indistinguishable from Earthlings, *entails nothing* about the mental state of the people on Twin Earth. Adding that the Twin Earthlings' sensory experiences are the same as ours entails nothing about their thoughts, beliefs, desires, intentions, hopes, or fears. Nothing in [A] or [B] tells us with necessity what the Twin Earth people believe the liquid to be, for example. They could believe falsely that the stuff is water, or correctly that it is twin water. They (or their descendants) could even believe falsely that water is XYZ rather than $H_2O$. Premise [A] similarly leaves it open whether the Twin Earth people are thinking of water or of twin water when they say the word 'water' out loud or to themselves.

According to Schiffer (1987a: 36), 'Twin earth is simply a fanciful way of making a plain point': in order to have beliefs about water, 'one must have had some sort of contact, direct or indirect', with water. It does seem true that all our beliefs about water are the direct or indirect result of human contact with water. People acquire the concept by observation and abstraction (§3.5). But there is no *logical* necessity here at all (see §8.3). It would be no more self-contradictory to say 'Descartes believed water is wet, but in fact there never was any water' than it would be to say 'Joseph Priestley believed that phlogiston was a chemical, but in fact there never was any phlogiston'. Indeed, the latter statement is true. *Believing* that my glass contains water contrasts markedly in this respect with *knowing* that it does. So the hypothesis that the Twin Earthlings are like Earthlings in having beliefs about water is at least a logical possibility. Arguments from environmental and behavioral premises to psychological conclusions are never *deductively* valid. Arguments from premises about purely sensory experiences to conclusions about propositional attitudes are similarly defeasible.

## Different Twin Earth Cases

We therefore have two logically possible cases to consider: in (I), Twin Earthlings have the same concepts, thoughts, beliefs, and intentions as we do. In (II), they do not. As usual, we are concerned with the *opaque* sense of psychological descriptions.

(I) *If* the Twin Earth people are *exactly* like their Earth counterparts *psychologically*, as is sometimes stipulated, and as [D] seems to assume, then they must believe that the liquid in rivers and lakes is *water*, and must use 'water' with the intention of indicating that they are thinking of water.[36] For that is what Earthlings believe and intend. Beliefs and intentions are mental states. So any differences in beliefs and intentions would constitute psychological differences. In this case, surely, the Twin Earthlings are also like Earthlings in meaning "water" and referring to water when they use 'water'. The truth value of what the Twin Earthlings believe and assert would be different, of course, but that is not a purely psychological matter. Similarly, the *extension* of the word 'water' would differ on Twin Earth, being empty. The word would have no referent because there is no water on Twin Earth.

Even though "Twin Earthlings use 'water' to refer to XYZ" is in this case false on the *opaque* reading (on which we are focusing), it will be true on the *transparent* reading. For we Earthlings also use 'water' with the intention of indicating (indirectly) that we are thinking of *that stuff* (pointing), of *the liquid in rivers and streams*, and so on. That is, we not only use 'water' to refer directly to water, we also use it to refer indirectly to that stuff, to the liquid in rivers and streams, and so on. Since we are assuming that the Twin Earthlings are exactly like us psychologically, they must also use 'water' indirectly to refer to that stuff, and to the liquid in rivers and streams. Since the liquid in rivers and streams on Twin Earth is in fact XYZ, it follows that "Twin Earthlings also use 'water' to refer to XYZ" is true when this is interpreted transparently. In this sense, their thinking of and referring to XYZ and our thinking of and referring to $H_2O$ do not differ psychologically. Their referring to water is not incompatible with their referring to XYZ in this sense even on the assumption that XYZ is not water. Again, John Dalton referred to both water and HO, even though water is not HO. Note also that while 'What Twin Earthlings are referring to is water' is true on one interpretation (as a transformation of 'Twin Earthlings are referring to water' in the opaque sense), it is false on another (when 'what Twin Earthlings are referring to' is used to refer to the stuff in rivers and streams on Twin Earth).

(II) On the other hand, *if* the Twin Earthlings use 'The liquid in rivers and streams is water' as an indication of their belief that the liquid is twin water, as would be indicated by the ultimate cause of their behavior, then surely they are referring to twin water when they use 'water'.[37] This should be true even as an opaque description of their referent. The extension of the word 'water' on Twin Earth would again differ from its extension on Earth, but this time for a different reason: its extension on Twin Earth would include all the XYZ lying about. The truth value of what Twin Earthlings assert would sometimes be different (as when uttering 'Water is $H_2O$') while sometimes being the same ('Water is wet', 'This is water').

Many philosophers who say that Earthlings and Twin Earthlings differ in this way in what they believe, think, and refer to also say that they are in the same mental state. This has led some to distinguish between 'narrow content' (in virtue of which the states are the same) and 'broad content' (in virtue of which they are different). If this is a claim about belief, thought, and reference in the *opaque* sense, then the position is incoherent. If in the opaque sense Earthlings believe that something is water and Twin Earthlings do not, then *ipso facto* they are in different mental states. A coherent position is that the Earthlings and Twin Earthlings believe, think, and refer to the same thing in the opaque sense, but different things in the transparent sense. This position falls under case (I), however, not case (II). If case (I) is the correct description, then Twin Earthlings refer transparently to twin water, but Earthlings do not. This difference is not purely psychological however. For in the transparent sense, what they refer to differs only because what they are both referring to in the opaque sense (the liquid in rivers and streams) differs.

(II') This case is like (II) in assuming that the Twin Earthlings do not use 'water' to indicate that they are thinking of water, and in assuming that the extension of the concept they use 'water' to express includes all the XYZ lying around. The subtle difference is that they do not have the concept of twin water either. They have some concept $\chi$ that differs from any concept we have, despite having the functional role of our concepts of water and twin water, and despite having the extension of our concept of twin water. In this case, 'Twin Earthlings are thinking of twin water' is true, but as a *transparent* description only. The novelty of (II') is that, by hypothesis, we are incapable of giving an opaque description of what they are thinking of. We know some important facts about their concept $\chi$, such as that they use the word 'water' to express it. But since we do not have concept $\chi$, we cannot fill in the blank in 'The Twin Earthling's concept $\chi$ is the concept of ____' in a way that will produce a statement true as an opaque as opposed to transparent description. They can, of course, by using the word 'water'. But what 'water' means in their language is at least slightly different from what it means in ours. I believe it follows straightforwardly that 'Twin Earthlings are referring to twin water' is true in this case, but only in the transparent sense. Since we do not have the concept χ, we cannot give an opaque description of what they are referring to.

(I') In describing the case in which Earthlings and their twins are exactly the same psychologically, I assumed that 'water' expresses a *purely descriptive* concept. We get a variant of case (I) by assuming that 'water' expresses an *indexical* concept, one that denotes $H_2O$ on Earth and XYZ on Twin Earth.[38] This assumes that 'water' means something like "this liquid" or "the water-like liquid around here", allowing 'Water is plentiful' to be true on both planets. In this case we must abandon Putnam's claim that 'water' has a different *meaning* on Twin Earth. Only the *reference* varies. "Twin Earth speakers use 'water' to refer to XYZ" will be false on the opaque interpretation, but true on the transparent. "Twin Earth speakers use 'water' to refer to water" will have only the transparent interpretation if 'water' is indexical. On that interpretation the sentence will be false on Earth but true on Twin Earth. Case (I') is thus like (II') in that we cannot give an opaque description of what speakers are referring to. We can provide an opaque description of a speaker's propositional attitudes in case (I'), though, using direct discourse. 'Earthlings and Twin Earthlings both think "Water is wet"' is true on this view.

I believe the hypothesis that 'water' is an indexical term is linguistically untenable. An indexical term is one whose referent varies from context to context even when it is used with the same meaning. 'This liquid' is clearly indexical. I can use it now to refer to the liquid my attention is focused on, namely coffee. It is easy to imagine someone using 'this liquid' with the same meaning to refer to a different liquid they are pointing to. But if we imagine someone using 'water' with its conventional meaning, that is, to mean "water", we have to imagine them referring to water. This is true even if we imagine 'Water is not $H_2O$' uttered on Twin Earth. If the speaker used 'water' to mean the same thing we do, namely "water", then the speaker has made the false statement that water is not $H_2O$. Note that while we automatically hear (13) as true because of the indexicality of 'me', we cannot hear (14) in the same way.

(13) The Twin Earthling meant "me" by 'me', but was not referring to me.

(14) The Twin Earthling meant "water" by 'water', but was not referring to water.

'Water' behaves differently from any clear indexical for which the difference between Earth and Twin Earth as the context of utterance would make a difference to the reference of the term. Suppose, for example, that an Earth man fills a container with water and seals it. Every day thereafter he examines the container and says correctly 'The container is still filled with water'. One day he is transported to Twin Earth without noticing anything different.

As usual, he says 'The container is still filled with water'. Since he is expressing the same thought as before and the liquid in the container has not changed, his statement on Twin Earth should also be true. But if 'water' meant something like "the water-like liquid prevalent in *this* place", indicating the planet he is currently on, then his statements would become false after the switch.

The switching problem can be reduced by hypothesizing that 'water' expresses an indexical concept with a more stable referent. For example, if what our transported Earth man means each day is "The container is still filled with the water-like liquid that has typically caused *me and my compatriots* to use the term 'water' ", then what he says will be as true after he is transplanted as before. But eventually, when he has lived on Twin Earth long enough to be considered a Twin Earthling, his daily pronouncements will begin to be false. Yet if what he means each day is "The container is still filled with water", then what he says should remain true until the contents of the container are changed. The suggested analysis wrongly implies that whether my utterance of 'The container still contains water' is true depends on who my compatriots happen to be. As a consequence, it also wrongly implies that I cannot tell just by look, feel, smell, and taste that my glass is filled with water. I would have to have the historical knowledge that the same liquid has caused me and my compatriots to use the term 'water'. The epistemic problem becomes most severe if one tries to avoid the slow-switching problem by construing 'compatriot' so that it always denotes my 'original' compatriots. The suggested analysis would also make it impossible for anyone to think about water who had never heard of the English word 'water' or did not have the concept of a compatriot.

Finally, any indexical analysis would make familiar skeptical lines of reasoning literally incoherent.

Appearances often deceive us. We believe there is a lot of water around here on Earth, but maybe we are wrong. Perhaps all our experiments were in error, and the stuff we always thought was water is really alcohol or peroxide. What typically causes us to use the word 'water' is really not water.

This skeptical hypothesis is absurd, of course, but not incoherent. Yet if 'water' *meant* something like "the water-like liquid which has typically caused us to use the word 'water' ", then this skeptical proposition would be literally self-contradictory. The skeptic would be suggesting that what typically causes us to use the word 'water' is really not what typically causes us to use the word 'water'. Causal theorists have rightly stressed the similarities between proper names and natural kind terms. In §10.6 and §12.4, we will look in more detail at indexical analyses of proper names, and see that they fail for the same sorts of reasons.

## Are Twin Earthlings Thinking About Water?

Now, having noted that any inference will be nondemonstrative, what should we believe about the Twin Earthlings' mental states? Are they the same as ours (case I) or different (case II)? The question is difficult, because it has been stipulated that our evidence conflicts. Normally, people with the same sensory stimulation and behavioral responses have the same mental states. And normally, people who use a word like 'water' are thinking about the thing or kind of thing that ultimately caused their usage in the familiar way. The former fact would lead to the conclusion that Twin Earthlings are thinking about water. The latter fact would lead to the conclusion that they are thinking about twin water (or conceiving the opaquely inexpressible concept $\chi$ described in II'). Without further evidence, I do not believe that either conclusion can be drawn with any confidence.

It is often added to premise [A] that the Twin Earthlings are not only behaviorally identical to Earthlings, but neurophysiologically identical as well. That evidence, I believe, would tip the scale in favor of the conclusion that the Twin Earthlings have the same mental states we do. For there is considerable evidence that 'pure' mental states are neurophysiological. But again, any inference here would be inductive, and somewhat doubtful for three reasons. First, the normally reliable indicators have been hypothesized to conflict. Second, I do not believe the case describes an empirical possibility.[39] Water looks, tastes, smells, and behaves as it does because it is composed of two atoms of hydrogen combined with one atom of oxygen. Since neurons contain water, they also behave the way they do because of the chemical composition of water. It is unclear what weight we should give to the empirical evidence for physicalism when it is combined with an assumption that is empirically impossible. Third, I do not believe we are yet in a position to confidently rule out the possibility that mental states have a neurophysiological basis without being neurophysiological states (cf. Braun 1991b). For example, the state of seeing a dagger has a neurophysiological basis, but it is not itself a neurophysiological state. A state that is neurophysiologically identical may not count as seeing a dagger because no dagger is involved. The independence of thought, belief, and desire from one's current environment makes them unlike seeing a dagger. But we conceded above that S is thinking about or referring to $\Phi$ only if S's current mental state has the right history. This may be because the neurophysiological state associated with thinking about $\Phi$ only results from those causes. Or it may be that that state only counts as thinking about $\Phi$ when it results from those causes.

In §8.3 and §8.4, I argued against the thesis that referring to $\Phi$ logically entails being in a state that traces its origin causally to $\Phi$. A more defensible version of the causal theory claims that referring to $\Phi$ is only naturally or empirically connected to being related to Φ by a causal chain. While this empirical form of the causal theory could not be true in general, it is plausible for concepts acquired on the basis of observation or abstraction, such as the concepts of Socrates and water (§3.5). Many objections no longer hold. For example, the empirical form of the causal theory does not imply that introspective knowledge of mental states is impossible. While knowledge may be closed under obvious logical entailment, it is far from closed under empirical connection (cf. McKinsey 1991; McLaughlin and Tye 1998). If we assumed an empirical form of the causal theory of concepts, according to which having its source in Φ is empirically connected to being the concept of Φ, would that tip the scale back in favor of the conclusion that Twin Earthlings have different concepts, thoughts, and propositional attitudes? I do not think so. I submit that the empirical connection between male sex organs and the Y chromosome is as strong as any between the concept of water and water. Yet suppose that on Twin Earth, half the population have organs anatomically, physiologically, and functionally indistinguishable from male sex organs on Earth, but which result from having a Z chromosome rather than the Y chromosome. Should we say that Twin Earthlings do not have male sex organs because their organs have a different genetic source? I think we should conclude from the anatomic, physiological, and functional identity that male sex organs result from the Z chromosome on Twin Earth. It might be suggested that the concept case differs from the sex organ case in that having their origins in one chromosome rather than another is not what makes something be a male or female sex organ. But the Twin Earth argument is supposed to prove that concepts are individuated by their origins. To presuppose that fact in defending the argument would beg the question. The marked semantic difference between 'concept of water' and 'photograph of water' is independent evidence against the assumption that concepts are individuated by causal relations to their referents.

## *Is XYZ Water?*

Most philosophers have inferred that Twin Earthlings do not have the same mental states as Earthlings because the source of these states is not water. I have assumed until now that XYZ is not water in order to assess the validity of Putnam's argument. But this premise is itself questionable. It is almost as hard to decide whether the liquid on Twin Earth is a different kind of water or merely an isomorph of water as it is to decide what Twin Earthlings believe it to be, and for similar reasons.[40] The proposition that water is $H_2O$ is a scientific hypothesis that has been established inductively on the basis of empirical evidence. 'Water is XYZ' is logically consistent for any chemical compound XYZ. If a substance with microstructure XYZ were discovered that looked, tasted, smelled, felt, and behaved just like water, logic alone would not *necessitate* either the conclusion that it was water or the conclusion that it was not water. Scientists could conclude that the hypothesis that all water is $H_2O$ was erroneous, since some XYZ water has been discovered. Or they could retain the hypothesis that all water is $H_2O$ by concluding that XYZ is not water. The decision that the sample of XYZ is or is not water is *logically* independent of the decision that it is or is not $H_2O$. If it were not, the claim that water is $H_2O$ would be a logical truth rather than an empirical hypothesis, and we could no more have discovered through experimental analysis that water is $H_2O$ than we could have discovered through experimental analysis that salt water contains salt. It is not clear what to say about the case because our normally reliable indicators (microstructure and perception) have been hypothesized to conflict.

Putnam assumed that since XYZ and $H_2O$ have different atomic structures, they could not both be water. This consideration cannot be sufficient to settle the issue. The term 'petroleum' applies to a diverse set of thick oily liquids containing a mixture of different hydrocarbons, including propane ($C_3H_8$), butane ($C_4H_{10}$), pentane ($C_5H_{12}$), hexane ($C_6H_{14}$), heptane ($C_7H_{16}$), octane ($C_8H_{18}$), and so on. 'Alcohol' applies to methanol ($CH_3OH$) as well as ethanol ($C_2H_5OH$). In fact, all samples of water on Earth contain small portions of heavy water—deuterium oxide ($D_2O$)—which contains an isotope of hydrogen. Is heavy water not water because it has a different microstructure? Or is it water because it tastes, smells, looks, and feels like water? We have actually concluded that heavy water is water even though it differs in atomic structure from ordinary water. Why should we not similarly conclude that XYZ is extraordinary water? Indeed, nothing in Putnam's stipulations prevents XYZ from being $D_2O$.

## Conclusion

I see little in the Twin Earth cases but another demonstration of two familiar facts: (i) scientific hypotheses in psychology and elsewhere are not logically entailed by the objective evidence; and (ii) it is hard to make clear judgments about counterfactual hypotheses when they are incompletely specified and our normal standards of evidence lead to conflicting conclusions.

This sort of uncertainty, however, does not extend to the claim that reference is determined by intention. If we conclude that the Twin Earthlings are thinking about water when they use 'water', then we must also conclude that they are referring to water. If we conclude that they are thinking about twin water, then that is what they are referring to. If they are expressing a concept we do not possess, then we can only say what they are referring to transparently. Proper analysis of Putnam's thought experiment confirms, rather than refutes, the proposition that the speaker's reference depends on the speaker's intentions. The conclusion that reference does not depend on 'what is in the head' depends either on ignoring the fact that thoughts, beliefs, desires, and intentions are 'in the head' if anything is,[41] or on committing the fallacy of equivocation in giving opaque descriptions of intentions and transparent descriptions of referents.

We will return to the Twin Earth case in §13.9, where it provides an argument against conceptual descriptivism, the psychological thesis underlying the description theory. The case also shows the falsity of the strongest form of functionalism, according to which mental states can be functionally defined in such a way that the defining conditions are *logically* necessary and sufficient for the state being defined. The famous 'inverted spectrum' case provides an alternative refutation of 'logical functionalism', one starring nonintentional states.

## NOTES

[1] Cf. Evans 1973: 303: '*in general* a speaker intends to refer to the item that is the dominant source of his associated body of information'; and Jackson 1998.

[2] Cf. Fodor 1975: 182; McKinsey 1978: 191–2; and Schiffer 1992: 515. Contrast Wettstein 1991: 71.

[3] Cf. MacKay 1968: 198: 'Referring is making knowable what we are talking about *by way of* using an expression which correctly describes the object in question.' See also Evans 1982: 311.

[4] See also Donnellan 1966: 285; Searle 1969: 95; Vendler 1976: 36; Wettstein 1991: 70–9; Evans 1982: 311; Martinich 1979b; 1984: 161–2; Strawson 1986: 249–50; and Bach 1987a: 52. Contrast Bertolet 1990: 103–5.

[5] Cf. Evans 1982: 316–17.

[6] Cf. Schiffer 1981: 73–6.

[7] Both Martinich (1984: 161–2) and Bach (1987a: 40, 52) offer Gricean analyses of 'S refers A to R' in chapters whose aim is to clarify referring to R. See also Vendler's (1976: 39) assertion that success or failure of the act of reference depends on the hearer's 'uptake'.

[8] Cf. Brentano 1874; Husserl 1900: 352; Chisholm 1955–6; Quine 1960: §45; and Dennett 1969. Intentional objects are characteristically *indeterminate* too. For example, the idea of an F is not the idea of any particular F. Hence when the detective announces 'A woman killed the victim', he may have referred to a woman without referring to any particular woman.

[9] Cf. Reid 1785: 4.2; Goodman 1952: 70; Ziff 1960: 84–5; Linsky 1963: 83–6; Campbell 1968; McKinsey 1978: §3; D. W. Smith 1982a: 198–9; Martinich 1984: 154. Contrast Vendler 1976: 37–8; Stampe 1979: 84; Perry 1980: 318; Pylyshyn 1980: 159; Schiffer 1981: 90; 1990: 256; Yourgrau 1990: 97; Nelson 1992: 155; and the causal theorists cited in fns. 20, 21, and 27 below.

[10] Cf. Castañeda 1977: 177–8.

[11] See also Cartwright 1963; Searle 1969: 77; Plantinga 1974: Chs. 7–8; Schiffer 1978; 1981: 88; Schwarz 1979: 17–19; Putnam 1981; Devitt 1981: Ch. 6; Evans 1982; Bertolet 1984b; Wettstein 1984b; Bach 1987a: 119–20; 195–8; Boër 1989; Chisholm 1990; Crimmins 1998: 33. The *locus classicus* is Plato's *Sophist* 237b–239b. Contrast Stroll 1998: 531.

[12] Similar epistemological objections against causal theories will be discussed in §8.4.

[13] See also Chisholm 1981: 74; Evans 1982, 1985: 74–9; Walton 1990, 1993.

[14] Cf. Burge 1977: §2; Castañeda 1977: 180; Fodor 1981: 237; and Forbes 1987. Contrast Bach 1987a: 205–6.

[15] Contrast Devitt 1981: xii: 'If we do not view reference as an objective relationship to the world, we cannot view truth as a property a sentence has in virtue of an objective correspondence to the world.' See also Martinich 1984: vii.

[16] We can even hold that someone who says 'Sherlock Holmes was a detective' is referring to Sherlock Holmes and making *a* true statement without denying that predication presupposes existence. For we can insist that the speaker is *also* implicitly referring in some way to the *story* of Sherlock Holmes and predicating a property of it. Cf. Devitt 1981: Ch. 6 and Bertolet 1984b: 418–19.

[17] Cf. Russell 1905: 210; Kaplan 1978: 319–20; Dennett 1982: 74, 87; Fitch 1987: Ch. 5; Bach 1987a: 120; and Braun 1993. See also §14.2 below.

[18] Similar equivocations are required in Cartwright's (1963) formulation of the problem of negative existential statements. Cf. Putnam 1981: 27–8; Yourgrau 1986: 97–103; and Plato's *Sophist*.

[19] Kvart (1994) would require in addition that S *knows* that Φ is a cause of his intention to predicate something of Φ.

[20] Donnellan 1972: 373; Kripke 1972: 298–303, 330–1; Field 1972: 287; Devitt 1974; 1981: 20, 25, 33, 64; Kaplan 1977: 559; Stampe 1979: 84; Unger 1983: 2; Devitt and Sterelny 1987: Ch. 4; Teichmann 1991: 196; and Nelson 1992: §§8.1, 8.6, 9.2–9.4. Compare and contrast Stalnaker 1997: 544, 546.

[21] See Kripke 1972: 768; Hacking 1975: 150; Chastain 1975; Linsky 1977: 107–10; Ziff 1977; Katz 1977a: 121–2; McKinsey 1978; Stampe 1979: 95–9; Searle 1983: 237, 245; Martinich 1984:188–9; Lance 1984: 340–1; McKinsey 1984: 498; Fodor 1987: 100; Devitt and Sterelny 1987: 62–3; and McDermott 1988: 229.

[22] See Devitt and Sterelny's (1987: §4.4, §5.3) '*qua* problem'; Katz's (1977b: 69–73) case of 'Jack the Ripper' (why doesn't the name designate the scissors he used?); and Loar's (1981: 233) 'Quinean reference schemes'.

[23] McKinsey 1978: §2; Castañeda 1989: 49; Devitt 1974: 189; 1981: 32–6; Stich 1983: 96–7, 145–7; Devitt and Sterelny 1987: 59; Crimmins and Perry 1989: 690, fn. 8; Bertolet 1990: 93–5.

[24] Cf. Kripke 1972: 349, fn. 42; Burge 1973: 436; Evans 1973: 299, 302, 304; McKinsey 1978: §4; 1984: 498–501; Putnam 1981: 52; Searle 1983: 235, 241; Lance 1984: 338; Chastain 1975; Devitt and Sterelny 1987: 61; Fodor 1987: 101; Sterelny 1990: §6.2; Wettstein 1991: 73; and Rosenberg 1993: 517. Contrast Harman 1973: §4.4; Devitt 1981: 79, 133; Lycan 1985: 87; Maloney 1989: Ch. 6; Fodor 1990b: 326; Sterelny 1990: Ch. 6: Fitch 1990; Teichmann 1991; McKay 1994: 298; McGinn 1997: 80.

[25] Soames's (2002: 92) argument against names of future objects is based on the premise that we cannot name an object unless we are 'acquainted' with it, which is false even for past or present objects.

[26] Cf. McGinn 1989: 35–6, 47–8; McKinsey 1991; McLaughlin and Tye 1998.

[27] Cf. Kaplan 1977: 559, fn. 78; McKinsey 1978: §4; 1991; 1994: 306–7; 2002; Ingber 1979: 728; Searle 1983: 249; Devitt 1981: 20, 33, 78–9, 131; Evans 1982: Ch. 4; Stalnaker 1993: 300. Devitt's extension of his theory to the 'language of thought' even implies that we generally cannot know who we are thinking about! Cf. Maloney 1989: 204–5, Fitch 1990: 692. See also the general discussion of whether externalism is compatible with privileged access in Burge 1988; Heil 1988; Boghossian 1989; 1997a, 1998a, 1998b; Brueckner 1990; Ludlow 1995; Gibbons 1996; Yablo 1998; Corbí 1998; Moya 1998; Heal 1998.

[28] Cf. McKinsey 2002: 207. The sorts of cases that have prompted Dretske (1970), Nozick (1981), and others to deny epistemic closure are controversial and very different, involving far-fetched skeptical hypotheses of dubious relevance (such as that we are brains in vats). See also Cohen 1986; 1988; Burge 1988: 654–5; Brueckner 1990:448, 450; Falvey and Owens 1994: 114; DeRose 1995.

[29] See also Burge 1988: 656; 1996: 96 and Heil 1988.

[30] Cf. McKinsey 1991, 2002; Boghossian 1997a.

[31] Cf. Ludwig 1992: §3, §6; Falvey and Owens 1994: 132–3.

[32] As Steinitz (1994: §2) suggested, even the causal theorist might reject Putnam's second premise by allowing a broader range of *indirect* causal relations to suffice for mental reference.

[33] Cf. Brueckner 1986; Ludwig 1992: §§4, 7, 8. The question is similarly begged if one uses the principle of essential origins to argue that since the idea of a brain had its origin in the normal perception of brains, nothing could be that idea unless people had normal perceptual capacities.

[34] Cf. Searle 1969: 87; Vendler 1976: 37–8; Harman 1977; Schiffer 1978: 189; 1982: 130–1; 1987a: 6–7; Field 1978: 53; Stampe 1979: 84; Ingber 1979: 728; Devitt 1981: 78–9, 83; 1990: 83, 94; Putnam 1981: 1–5; Dennett 1982; Evans 1982: 76–9, 284–5; 1985: 79; Blackburn 1984: 72; McKinsey 1984: 498; Fodor 1987: Ch. 4; 1990a: Ch. 2; Devitt and Sterelny 1987: 124–6; Fitch 1987: 114; 1990; Avramides 1989: 3–5; Crimmins and Perry 1989: 690; Chisholm 1990; Yourgrau 1990; Sterelny 1990: Ch. 6; Castañeda 1990c; Crimmins 1992: §3.3; Nelson 1992: 155; Stalnaker 1997: 545–6; and a reviewer. Contrast Horwich (1998a: 21–30, Ch. 4).

[35] See also Putnam 1973: 1975; Dennett 1982: 11; Pendlebury 1990: 536.

[36] Many appear to have overlooked this point. See Putnam 1973: 309; 1981: 22–3; Burge 1979b: fn. 2; Salmon 1981: 67; Dennett 1982: 11; Barwise and Perry 1983: 84; Unger 1983: 25–6; Fodor 1987: Ch. 2; Devitt and Sterelny 1987: 52, 69–70, 165–7; Schweizer 1991: 270; Stalnaker 1993: 298–9. Bilgrami (1992) is one who seems to opt for (I). Falvey and Owens (1994: 111) claim only that the twins' 'qualitative' mental states are identical, erroneously assuming that thinking of something is not 'qualitative'.

[37] Cf. Burge 1979b: esp. 540, 556, 559; 1982: 101, 107–11; 1988: 652; Dennett 1982: 12; Stich 1983: 61–2; Fodor 1987: 27–30; 1994: Ch. 2; Schiffer 1987a: 35–36; Loar 1988: 569; Stalnaker 1989; 1993: 298–9; Owens 1989: 296–7, 303; Braun 1991b: 375–6; Gauker 1994: Ch. 3; Gibbons 1996; McGinn 1997: 75; Lance and O'Leary-Hawthorne 1997: Ch. 1; McLaughlin 1995; Heil 1995; Tye 1998: 80. Compare and contrast Unger 1983: 26–7; Crane 1991; Falvey and Owens 1994: 104, 109; Aydede 1997, esp. 454.

[38] Putnam 1975:148–52; Fodor 1981: 247; 1987: Ch. 2, esp. 45–7; Barwise and Perry 1983: 84; Boër and Lycan 1986: 53–4; McDermott 1988: 230; Pendlebury 1990: 536; E. Sosa 1991: 186–7; 1993: 326–8; Crane 1991: 12; Fodor and Lepore 1992: 167–9; Fitch 1993: 475; McGinn 1997: 75; Tye 1998; Heal 1998; Moya 1998: 248. Contrast Mellor 1977: 302, 305–6; Fodor 1981: 246–7; Burge 1982: 103–7; Stalnaker 1989; Crane 1991: 13–14.

[39] Cf. Fodor 1994: 28–9; Garcia-Carpintero 1994: 126, 130–1, 133. Many are confident that other twin cases can be described that are empirically possible; see, e.g., Burge 1982: 102 ('aluminum', 'elm'); Stich 1983: 60–1 ('Ike'); Schiffer 1987a: 35–6 ('cat'). Doubts can be raised about all their cases. I am not sanguine about our ability to determine empirical possibilities from the armchair.

[40] Cf. Zemach 1976; Mellor 1977: 303; Farrell 1981: 143–4; Fodor 1981: 248–9; Donnellan 1983; Cassam 1986; Crane 1991: 10; Putnam 1992: 442–3. See also Barnett 2000, who argues that water could conceivably be only one form of $H_2O$, just as sand is only one form of $SiO_2$ (others being glass and quartz). Compare and contrast Unger 1983: 26–7, 30.

[41] Cf. Falvey and Owens 1994: 110; Wettstein 1991: 152: "Not only does the reference of an utterance not depend upon one's cognitive fix but the reference of one's silent thought similarly does not depend upon 'what is in the head'." But surely, (1) the 'reference' of a thought depends on the identity of that thought, and (2) silent thinking is something 'in the head'.

# 9
# Meaning and Reference

The most widely accepted meaning theories take as their inspiration the fact that language is used to talk about the people, places, and things in the world, and to state the truth about them. This is one of the most important and central functions of language. Referential theories of meaning go beyond these undeniable facts to identify the meaning of an expression with its reference to things in the world rather than its expression of ideas in the mind. In terms of the familiar 'triangle of signification' (Fig. 9.1), ideational theories locate meaning in the language–mind link. Referential theories locate it in the language–world link. Extensionalist versions of the referential theory focus on objects in the actual world and sets thereof, while intensionalist versions consider other possible worlds and/or universals (properties, relations, etc.).

In this chapter, 'reference' means *word* reference. Unlike speaker reference, which is intentional, word reference denotes a relationship between words and things, or the things so related to the words. We will first define word reference in terms of the expression of ideas. The identities of the ideas expressed, together with the identities of things in the world, determine what words refer to.

I will review the basic facts which show that the referential properties of language are not meaning itself, but a consequence of meaning. The goal is to round out the defense of the expression theory of meaning by showing how it avoids problems with a leading group of competitors, and to complete the exposition of the theory by indicating the place of reference therein. Ideational theories need not ignore reference, or minimize its importance, even though they treat it as a consequence of meaning rather than meaning itself. (Analogy: Atomic theories of matter that take the valence of a molecule to be a consequence of the number of electrons and protons it contains do not thereby downgrade the importance of valence in chemistry or physics.)

I will not attempt an exhaustive survey. Some objections can be avoided by complicating the referential theory in ways that destroy the simple picture that motivated the theory in the first place. None of the alterations, I believe, can avoid variations on all the objections. A comprehensive review would thus yield little marginal gain.

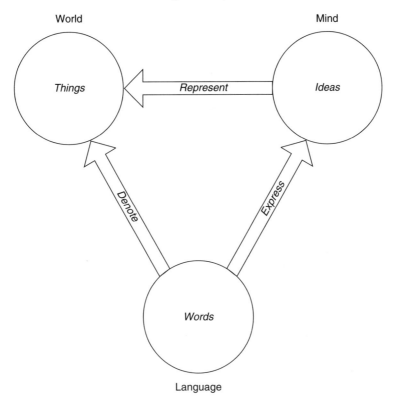

**Fig. 9.1**   The triangle of signification

Among the most popular referential theories are those that seek to understand meaning in terms of truth conditions. The most influential, arguably, is the Davidsonian. Davidson used a Tarski-style axiomatization for languages to describe the compositionality of language. Frege's problem still arises. Furthermore, no consistent axiomatization can handle ambiguity without referring explicitly to senses. So the Davidsonian approach cannot provide a foundational theory of meaning. The truth-theoretic properties of language are not meaning itself, but consequences of meaning.

To show how the truth-theoretic properties can be treated in an ideational theory, I will sketch a generative theory of thought, with rudimentary phrase structure rules and Tarskian reference rules. Thoughts, not sentences, are the primary objects of a Tarskian truth theory. I will not attempt a complete and rigorous treatment of the referential properties of language within an ideational theory. That would involve us in large bodies of evidence that shed little light on the fundamental nature of meaning, and in theoretical complexities that arise for any formal semantics. Some issues will be pursued in greater depth when we turn to the specialized topic of names.

## 9.1  WORD REFERENCE

According to Definition 5.4, the concept of word meaning is defined as follows: *e means* $\mu_i$ *iff e expresses i*. Word reference differs from word meaning in several respects. First, only words expressing *ideas* have referents. Words like 'Ouch' are meaningful, but do not refer to anything. Second, 'refers to' must grammatically be followed by object nominals, for which our place-holders are '$\Phi$' and '$\phi$'. This means that only terms expressing ideas expressible by object nominals have referents. Sentences and syncategorematic terms do not refer to things. Third, 'refers' applies only to *verbal* (word-like) expressions (see §7.1). Finally, word reference is transparent and fully relational, subject to both the substitutivity of identity and existential instantiation. 'The 43rd president' refers to George W. Bush because he is the 43rd president. We do not yet know who if anyone 'the 70th president' refers to. And 'the 1st female president in the twentieth century' does not refer to anyone. In this respect, word reference also differs markedly from speaker reference, which is opaque (§2.8) and intentional (§8.2).

By making these modifications to Definition 5.4, we can say that *e refers to* $\Phi$ *iff (i)* $\Phi$ *exists and (ii) for some* $\Phi' = \Phi$, *e verbally expresses the idea of* $\Phi'$. Thus 'Clinton' refers to William Jefferson Clinton because it is a word expressing the idea of William Jefferson Clinton, who is a real person. 'The 1st female president in the twentieth century' does not refer to anyone despite the fact that it expresses the idea of the 1st female president of the twentieth century because there was no such person. '$\Phi$ exists' is to be interpreted tenselessly, so that it is true if $\Phi$ exists now, existed in the past, or will exist in the future. Thus 'Socrates' refers to Socrates even though Socrates no longer exists. The name will not stop referring to Socrates until English changes. Using the convention discussed in §2.9 governing the use of quantificational variables in normally opaque contexts, we can define word reference as follows:

9.1   **Definition:** *e refers to x (in L) iff e verbally expresses the idea of x (in L).*

Equivalently, we can say that e refers to x iff *e verbally expresses some i such that* ex{i} = x, where ex{i} is the extension function for ideas (§8.5).[1]

We saw above that Definition 3.9 explains why *'The idea "$\Phi$" is the idea expressed by '$\Phi$''* is true in every context in which "the idea expressed by '$\Phi$'" in its predicate is used to refer to the idea expressed by '$\Phi$' in its subject. Together with this, Definition 9.1 explains why instances of the 'disquotation formula' (1) are true in any context in which the speaker is talking about English and is using a pronoun-free object nominal 'ɸ' in one of its conventional senses. Thus we can truly say that 'Venus' refers to Venus, '2' to 2, and so on.[2]

(1) 'ɸ' refers to ɸ, provided ɸ exists.

Formula (1) is not a theorem, however, and can be used to assert a falsehood. Thus "'One billion' refers to one billion" is false if I am using British English (in which 'billion' means "million million") to describe American English (in which 'billion' means "thousand million"). This is a mistake I am sure at least some Britons have made when reading the American financial papers.

## 9.2   REFERENTIAL THEORIES OF MEANING

The expressions of a language fall into a variety of syntactic categories, members of which have very different sorts of meanings and referential properties. Let us consider three: singular terms, general terms, and sentences.

### Singular Terms

Since 'The 35th president' means "The 35th chief executive officer of the US", it is used to talk about the 35th chief executive officer of the US, who happens to be John F. Kennedy. The 35th chief executive officer himself is the referent of 'the 35th president', by Definition 9.1. The referent of a singular term is also known as its *extension*. Different forms of the referential theory focus on different referential properties. On extensionalist versions of the referential theory, the meaning of a singular term is identified with its referent, or the relational property of having that referent. On intensionalist versions of the referential theory, the meaning of a singular term is identified with a function from possible worlds to extensions, the property defining that function, or functions from contexts to such functions or properties. The meaning of 'the 35th president' might be represented by the function whose value in the actual world is John F. Kennedy, and whose value in a world in which Nixon defeated Kennedy is Nixon.

### General Terms

General terms do not have a referent as defined by Definition 9.1. We can say in conventional English that 'cat' refers to cats. But cats are not a single object, and cannot be considered a value of the individual variable 'x'. If we tried to identify the meaning of a general term with what it refers to in this colloquial sense, we would have to say that 'cat' has millions of meanings. The referential theory would thus end up confusing generality with ambiguity. To avoid this problem, referential theorists focus on the *set* of all cats. Even though there are millions of cats, there is just one set containing them all. We cannot say that the general term 'cat' refers to that set, however. What does refer to that set is the singular term 'the set of all cats'.

To avoid these semantic problems, referential theorists use the technical terms 'extension' and 'intension'. The extension of a general term is stipulated to be the set of objects it applies to. The extension of 'cat' is the set of all cats. Extensionalist theories identify the meaning of a general term with its extension, or with the relational property of having that extension. Intensionalist theories identify the meaning of a general term with a function from possible worlds to the extension of the term in that world, the property defining such a function, or functions from contexts to such functions or properties. The second selection gives us the familiar idea that the meaning of 'cat' is the property it expresses, namely, the property of being a cat. Referents, extensions, and intensions may all be considered different kinds of reference.

## Sentences

The extension of a declarative sentence is its truth value. (Analogues of truth values are selected for interrogatives and imperatives; see §6.1.) The technical term 'extension' is imperative here, since it is highly unnatural to think of a sentence as 'referring' to its truth value. Extensionalist approaches are not pursued since there are only two truth values. Intensionalist theories define the meaning of a sentence in terms of its 'truth conditions', conceived as either: the set of all possible worlds in which the sentence is true (or equivalently, a function from possible worlds to truth values); or: the state of affairs that would make the sentence true (an ordered n-tuple of objects and properties); or a function from contexts to truth conditions.

In general, the referential theorist seeks to define the reference of terms and sentences in such a way that the reference of a sentence can be stated as a function of the reference of its parts. The extensionalist, for example, can say that the extension of a singular subject-predicate sentence is truth iff the extension of the subject is contained in the extension of the predicate. The situation semanticist can say that a sentence is true provided the state of affairs obtains that consists of the ordered pair whose first member is the referent of the subject term and whose second member is the referent of the predicate term. In this way, the referential theorist attempts to account for the compositionality of meaning (see §5.6).

Referential theories that *identify* meanings with referents succumb to *'Cartwright's problem'* (named in honor of R. Cartwright 1962). By Leibniz's Law of Identity, such a theory would be true only if meanings and referents have all the same properties. But while the referent of 'the president' has hair, the meaning of the expression does not. Meanings are not the sorts of things that can be hairy. Cartwright's problem can be minimized or avoided by identifying meanings with suitable properties of words, such as their *having* referents.

To show that the referential theory is false, we must establish that despite the importance of the referential properties of language, they are not constitutive of meaning. The principal defects of referential theories were identified by Russell (1910–11) and Frege (1892b). *Russell's problem* is that *meaningful words may have no reference.* Thus 'Pegasus' is a meaningful term, as is 'the twelfth planet', despite the fact that there is no object in the actual world to which either term applies. The problem is not simply that Pegasus does not exist now, but that there never was and never will be such a thing. 'The largest prime number between 2 and 3' cannot possibly have a referent. Russell's problem is not confined to singular terms. A general term like 'member of the set of all sets that are not members of themselves' is meaningful, but cannot have an extension, as Russell's familiar proof shows.[3] The problem is not that the set of objects to which the term applies is empty, but that there is no such set (not even the empty set). A parallel proof shows that 'property that is not a property of itself' does not express any property. Interjections like 'Wow!' do not even purport to have a referential function.

*Frege's problem* is that *words with the same reference may have different meanings.* 'The morning star' and 'the evening star' have different meanings, the former meaning "the last heavenly body visible in the morning", and the latter meaning "the first one visible in the evening". The terms nevertheless refer to the same object, namely Venus. 'The square root of 4' and 'The cube root of 8' differ significantly in meaning but have the same referent in all possible worlds. And since water is $H_2O$, it would seem that the property of being water is identical with the property of being $H_2O$.[4] Nevertheless, 'water' and '$H_2O$' are far from synonymous. Many forms of the referential theory predict erroneously that sentences expressing logically equivalent propositions have the same meaning because they are true in all the same worlds (e.g., 'Not-p', 'Not-not-not p', '2 = 2 and not-p'), and that sentences expressing logical falsehoods come out having either no meaning, or the same meaning, because they are all true in no worlds (e.g., '2 > 3', 'Triangles have four sides').

In short, Frege's and Russell's problems entail that the relationship between meanings and referents is not one-to-one, as referential theories require. They entail in addition that whereas word reference is a genuine relation between words and things, meaning is an intentional phenomenon, not a relation between words and things (recall §8.2). These problems will be developed more fully in Chapter 10. We will see in Chapter 11 that recent attempts to dissolve them are unsuccessful.

*Vagueness* presents another way in which meanings and referents fail to be isomorphic. A term is vague in a given sense if there are some cases in which there is no way to decide except arbitrarily whether the term applies or not. Thus 'green' is vague because there are certain colors that can equally well be characterized by 'greenish blue' as by 'bluish green'. The difficulty is not lack of information about the color, but lack of definiteness in the meaning. 'Atlantic' and 'Pacific' are vague because there is no precise boundary line separating the two oceans. There are some points on the Earth at which it is impossible to decide non-arbitrarily whether we are in the Pacific or the Atlantic. Nearly every term in a natural language is vague in some respect. It is natural to say that it is unclear what the referent of a term is to the extent that it is vague. But on the referential theory, that would imply that it is unclear what the meaning of the term is. Yet we know that 'the Atlantic' differs in meaning from any more precise term. To maintain a one-one correspondence between meanings and referents, it seems that the referential theorist must postulate questionable objects, such as sets that neither do nor do not contain certain shades of blue-green.[5] Vagueness, we might say, is another mark of the intentional.

A further problem with the idea that reference exhausts meaning has not, to my knowledge, been noticed before. The key is Fine's observation that 'for Frege, the referent and the sense of a term might coincide, as in 'the sense of this term'' (1989: 227). I call these *'Fine terms'*. Consider the following true sentence:

> (2) The meaning of the noun phrase to the left of the second occurrence of 'differs from' in this sentence differs from the meaning of the noun phrase to the right of its second occurrence.

Sentence (2) is true, and provides two examples of terms whose referents are their meanings. But Fine terms are highly unusual. We can hardly claim that all meaningful terms are like them. Furthermore, even though Fine terms conform to the letter of the referential theory, they violate its spirit. The referential theory is intended to tell us what meanings are. But the theory tells us nothing about what those meanings are to which Fine terms refer. We need a nonreferential theory of meaning before we can identify the referents of certain terms.

The final problem arises from Frege's observation that reference *depends on* meaning. 'The 35th president' refers to John F. Kennedy because of the meaning of the term together with the history of the world. If either had been different, the referent would have been different. The referent of a Fine term depends on its meaning in both ways. The dependence of reference on meaning is incompatible with the referential theory given that dependence is an asymmetric relation, while identity is symmetric. The meaning of a word cannot be identified with its having a referent, if its having that referent depends on its having that meaning.

The expression theory provides a natural solution to all the problems of the referential theories. 'The morning star' and 'the evening star' have different meanings because they express different ideas, one containing the idea "morning", the other containing the idea "evening". Similarly, even though 'Pegasus' does not have a referent, it does express an idea. The idea of Pegasus occurs to us whenever we think of Pegasus.[6] Cartwright's problem arises for ideational theories that identify meanings with ideas. For ideas have properties that meanings lack, such as the property of occurring to people. But Cartwright's problem is avoided by expression theories that identify meaning with the property of expressing an idea.[7] There is no circularity in saying that a Fine term refers to its meaning when meaning is identified with expressing an idea.

No analog of Russell's paradox arises on the expression theory. The general term 'idea that is not an idea of itself' is meaningful, and true of every idea. *The idea of an idea that is not an idea of itself* is straightforwardly *not* an idea of itself, which in no way entails that it *is* an idea of itself. What it is an idea *of* is just *an idea that is not an idea of itself* (§3.8). It may help to observe here that *the idea of an idea* is not an idea of itself even though it is an idea. For it is not *the idea of the idea of an idea*. It should also be noted that whereas 'x is a member of y' and 'x is a property of y' are genuine relational predicates, 'x is an idea of $\Phi$' is intentional in the $\Phi$ position. It can be interpreted transparently, but we are interpreting it opaquely (§2.8). Hence 'x is an idea of $\Phi$' cannot be represented by a dyadic predicate like 'Ix$\Phi$' in quantification theory. So for a second reason, a contradictory formula like 'I$\iota$ iff –I $\iota$' cannot be derived from the assumption that 'idea that is not an idea of itself' expresses an idea, namely $\iota$, the idea of an idea that is not an idea of itself.[8]

A version of Russell's paradox can be used to show that not all ideas have extensions. That is, we can show that for some idea i, there is no such thing as ex{i}. Most ideas do have extensions, although they might be empty. The extension of the idea of a cat is the set of all cats. The extension of the idea of a centaur is empty. In general, the extension of the idea of an F is the set of all Fs, if there is such a set. We cannot show that $\iota$ lacks an extension. Indeed, as explained above, it seems clear that $\iota \in$ ex{$\iota$}. But let '$\chi$' designate *the idea of an idea that is not in its own extension*. If we assume that the extension function is defined for $\chi$, we get trouble. For if ex{$\chi$} exists, then we must conclude that $\chi \in$ ex{$\chi$} iff $\chi \notin$ ex{$\chi$}. Since this is a contradiction, the assumption that ex{$\chi$} exists must be false. Why isn't ex{i} defined for $\chi$?

Because the formula used to define ex{i} does not suffice to tell us for every object x whether or not x is in ex{$\chi$}. In particular, the formula does not tell us whether $\chi$ is in ex{$\chi$}. By definition, $\chi$ is in the extension of $\chi$ iff $\chi$ is an idea that is not in its own extension. To determine whether the definiens is true, we have to already know whether the definiendum is true. Since the formula is circular when applied to $\chi$, it does not suffice to define ex{$\chi$}. The fact that ex{$\chi$} fails to exist does not lead to the faulty prediction that the phrase 'an idea that is not in its own extension' is meaningless. For an expression is meaningful on the expression theory provided it expresses an idea. What led to a Russellian contradiction was not the assumption that 'an idea that is not in its own extension' expresses an idea, but rather the assumption that this idea had an extension. The meaningfulness of a term on the expression theory does not depend on its having an extension, or on its expressing an idea that has an extension. The fact that the phrase 'an idea that is not in its own extension' lacks an extension is, however, a problem for the referential theory—another instance of Russell's problem.

There is another way in which the referential theory leads dialectically to an ideational theory. It begins by asking '*What makes it true that words have the referents they do?*' Why is 'Grass is green' true iff grass is green, when it could just as well have been true iff snow is blue? Why is 'The car has no bonnet' true in British English iff the car has no top, but not in American English? The questions are pressing because of the lack of any intrinsic connection between words and sentences on the one hand and objects and states of affairs on the other. Clearly, the sequence of words 'Grass' $\frown$ 'is' $\frown$ 'green' has the truth conditions it does because speakers use those words and their structure in a certain way. To provide a complete theory of meaning, therefore, a referential theory must be supplemented with a use theory.[9] Once use-factors are acknowledged, however, the isomorphism, vagueness, and dependence problems can be avoided by defining meanings in terms of use rather than reference. I have already argued, of course, that the most promising use theory is the expression theory.

One of the strengths of a referential theory is the ease with which it yields the platitude that the meaning of a sentence is determined by the meaning of its parts. For example, the truth condition for 'Bush is Republican' can be stated as follows: the sentence is true iff the object to which the subject term applies (George Bush) is a member of the set of objects to which the predicate term applies (the set of Republicans). This strength of the referential theory is not sacrificed by switching to the expression theory. For the expression theory has the same virtue. The idea expressed by 'Bush is a Republican' is the thought in which the idea expressed by 'Bush' is the subject-concept and the idea expressed by 'is a Republican' is the predicate concept. Hence the meaning of the sentence is determined by the meanings of its components. As we saw in §5.6, however, functional dependence does not exhaust the notion of compositionality. The ideational theory can say that what a sentence expresses is literally *composed* of what its parts express. But on many referential theories, sentence references are not composed of word references (e.g., possible worlds semantics). And all referential theories have difficulty with sentences like 'The twelfth planet is a member of the Russell set' because their components do not have referents (cf. §14.2). Even in this case, however, the thought expressed by the sentence consists of the ideas expressed by its subject and predicate. Only the expression theory, in sum, provides a complete account of the compositionality of semantics.

## 9.3   THE DAVIDSONIAN THEORY

One of the most influential forms of the referential theory maintains that meaning consists in truth conditions. The *truth conditions* of a sentence are conditions which are necessary and sufficient for it to be true. To understand a sentence, on this view, is to know its truth conditions. Frege's problem shows that this is at best a simplification. A woman who knows (3) knows necessary and sufficient conditions for the truth of '2 is the cube root of 8'.

(3)   '2 is the cube root of 8' is true iff 2 is the square root of 4.

But such knowledge does not suffice for her to know what '2 is the cube root of 8' means. Compatible with what she knows, she could also believe that '2 is the cube root of 8' *means* "2 is the square root of 4". But if that is what she believes, she is mistaken, and does not fully understand English.[10]

Davidson (1967) adds that understanding a sentence requires not just knowing its truth conditions, but also knowing the reference of its components, and knowing how the truth conditions of the sentence are determined by the reference of its components.[11] While this helps with the example at hand, all we need to do is change to a technical variant of English in which 'cate' means "the cube root of 8" and 'skor' means "the square root of 4". Then '2 is cate' and '2 is skor' have the same truth conditions, and are composed in the same way out of components with the same reference. Nevertheless, the two sentences differ in meaning, and anyone who understood '2 is cate' to mean "2 is skor" would misunderstand it. The familiar examples of 'Hesperus' and 'Phosphorus', or 'Superman' and 'Clark Kent', present the same problem. In general, Davidson's suggestion fails for sentences that differ in meaning only because certain unstructured or idiomatic components differ in meaning despite having the same reference.[12]

Davidson later required the additional knowledge that the truth condition statement follow from a Tarski-style axiomatization for the language.[13] Davidson specifically had in mind a concise set of axioms yielding as a theorem a true sentence of the form 'e is true iff p' for each sentence e in the object language. This requirement cannot be necessary for understanding a sentence, however, since the overwhelming majority of competent speakers have no idea what a Tarski-style axiomatization is. Furthermore, no consistent axiomatization will adequately handle ambiguity without referring to senses. Consider, for example, the amphibolous (4), which is true in one sense, false in another.

(4) The number of planets is three times two plus one.

No consistent Tarski-style axiomatization will yield both of the following as theorems, since they jointly entail that $9 = 7$.

(5) (4) is true iff $n = 3 \times (2 + 1)$.
(6) (4) is true iff $n = (3 \times 2) + 1$.

Nevertheless, (5) is true in one sense of (4), and (6) is true in another. It is natural to make (5) and (6) consistent by inserting *in one sense* after 'true' (see §9.4). But this move is not open to Davidson, who is trying to make no use of meanings in his theory of meaning (1967: 83). If senses are mentioned in this way, the theory would no longer be able to tell us what senses are.

Tarski thought ambiguity made a formal treatment of natural languages impossible. But Davidson dismissed the problem with the claim that 'As long as ambiguity does not affect grammatical form, and can be translated, ambiguity for ambiguity, into the meta-language, a truth definition will not tell us any lies' (1967: 86). Davidson seems content with the fact his requirements can be satisfied by (7):

(7) (4) is true iff the number of planets is three times two plus one.

But (7) can hardly be said to give us either the meaning or the truth conditions of (4), and knowledge that (7) is a theorem of our theory of truth would not enable us to understand (4) as used by any speaker of the language. Nor can a theory that yielded only (7) give any account of the ambiguity of (4). And it would have the odd result that (4) entails neither (5) nor (6), nor their disjunction.

Frege's puzzle also shows that the knowledge Davidson requires is not sufficient for understanding a sentence. A speaker might realize, for example, that (3) follows from a Tarski-style axiomatization. For (3) *does* follow as a theorem from *some* such axiomatization, if we may assume that (8) follows:

(8) '2 is the cube root of 8' is true iff 2 is the cube root of 8.

For (3) follows from (8) by elementary arithmetic. Consider also:

(9) '2 is the cube root of 8' is true iff both 2 is the cube root of 8 and $\tau$,

where '$\tau$' is either an elementary logical truth (e.g., 'grass either is or is not green') or an axiom or theorem of the system (e.g., "x satisfies 'x is red' iff x is red"). Any deductive system having (8) as a theorem will have (9) as a theorem. Finally, consider a Tarski-style axiomatization **A** of the kind Davidson hopes for, which generates T-sentences of the form 'e is true iff p' as theorems only when e means "p". Now consider the axiomatization **A'** that results from adding one new axiom to **A**, namely:

(10) 'Ammonia is poisonous' is true iff $NH_3$ is poisonous.

**A'** is a finite, recursive specification of truth conditions meeting all of Davidson's formal conditions if **A** is. Given any true but nonanalytic sentence like (10), there will always be *a* finite, recursive axiomatization yielding it as a theorem if there are any such axiomatizations, although no one finite axiomatization will yield all such sentences as theorems. It is hard to see how Davidson could avoid this problem by tightening up his 'formal constraints' without making it impossible to handle idioms.

Davidson's (1967: 83–4) 'radical' response to Frege's puzzle was that if the meaning of a sentence does differ in this way from what is captured by a truth theory, 'then there would not, I think, be anything essential to the idea of meaning that remained to be captured'. But while understanding the difference may not be essential for certain purposes, it is certainly essential for understanding what it is for words to mean something. And that is what we are trying to understand. Elsewhere, Davidson (1974: 154) says that 'the idea that each word and sentence has a definite meaning, cannot be invoked in describing the goal of a successful theory'. But if this is true, it only confirms that Davidson's goal is not to provide a theory of meaning. Words and sentences *do* have definite meanings, and *our* goal is to discover what it is for words and sentences to have particular meanings.

The 'moderate' Davidsonian response is to hold that a 'T-sentence' gives the meaning of the sentence mentioned on the left only if its relationship to the sentence used on the right satisfies certain 'empirical constraints on translation'.[14] This yields a format for defining meaning I call the *Davidsonian Schema*.

(11) e means "p" iff (i) e is true iff p and (ii) e and 'p' satisfy the constraints on translation.

If such a definition is not to be blatantly circular, the constraints will have to be specified. Otherwise, (11) will simply say that e means "p" iff...and e satisfies the conditions for having the same meaning as 'p'. While Davidson never gave a detailed specification of the constraints, he did indicate the following.

Typical of the sort of evidence available then would be the following: a speaker holds
'Es schneit' true when and only when it is snowing.                    (Davidson 1974: 458)

If this were the empirical constraint, then Davidson's schema would fail in
both directions. *Left-to-right*: a generalization like 'e is held true when and
only when p' will rarely if ever be true either for an individual or a community. Most sentences are ambiguous, and could be held true under different
circumstances; any sentence can be used ironically, in which case it will be
held true in the opposite circumstances; and so on. Another problem is that
speakers are often wrong about the facts. So sometimes, due to a faulty
report or perception, a speaker will hold 'Es schneit' true when it is not
snowing, and vice versa. *Right-to-left*: the fact that S holds e true under
certain circumstances will not enable us to decide between the alternative
translations that (ii) is supposed to discriminate among. For example, if S
holds 'Es schneit' true when and only when it is snowing, then S will also
hold the sentence true when and only when it is both snowing and either
raining or not raining. The celebrated 'Principle of Charity', is no help in this
connection at all. Since '2 is the square root of 4' and '2 is the cube root of 8'
are both true, the desire to maximize the number of truths affirmed by
speakers will have no bearing on the decision to translate any given sentence
as meaning one rather than the other.

McDowell's writings suggest two constraints: *e can be used to say that p*;
or: *knowing that e is true iff p suffices to understand utterances of e*. The
former is materially inadequate. 'He did' can be used to say that John broke
the vase, but does not mean that John broke the vase. Both would seem to
make (11) circular. It is hard to see how 'say that p' in the relevant illocutionary sense can be defined without reference to what the words used mean.
Similarly, the relevant sense of understanding is understanding the *meaning*
of utterances of e, rather than their etiology, say. Furthermore, the only
utterances of e such knowledge would enable us to understand are those
on the occasion of which e *means "p"*. Knowing that 'Sally is a vixen' is true
iff Sally is a female fox does not enable us to understand utterances of 'Sally
is a vixen' when it means that she is a shrewish woman. Finally, given
that clause (i) does not suffice by itself to define meaning, it is unclear
how knowledge of (i) could suffice to understand what *any* utterances of e
*mean*.

It should not be thought that the lacuna in (11) is minor, as if the truth
condition clause comes close to defining meaning all by itself, except for a
small detail. The difference in meaning between the sentence mentioned and
the sentence used in (3) is large and obvious. Moreover, there is an infinitely
large set of sentences that differ from those as much or more in meaning
despite having the same truth conditions. And countless equivalence classes
of sentences possess the same property (having the same truth conditions

while differing in meaning) even though their subject matter differs. Finally, similarities and differences in these unspecified respects may outweigh similarities and differences in truth conditions as determinants of similarity of meaning. This can be seen by considering (12)–(14).

(12) 2 is the square root of 4.
(13) 2 is the cube root of 4.
(14) 2 is the cube root of 8.

Sentence (12) differs *less* in meaning from (13) than it differs in meaning from (14). This is so despite the fact that (12) has the same truth conditions as (14), while differing in truth value from (13).

No matter how the translation constraints are eventually defined, it seems clear that the resulting theory, if at all adequate as a theory of meaning, will not be a referential theory. Indeed, I see no reason why the theory should not be completed by incorporating the central principle of the expression theory. We get a much better theory out of the Davidsonian schema by specifying the constraint on translation as follows: *translate e as 'p' iff e and 'p' are used to express the same idea.*[15] This ideational constraint is completely empirical, and seems to be observed wherever possible by actual translators. No competent translator would be indifferent as to whether to render a French sentence as (12) or (14). The ideational constraint is compatible with the Principle of Charity. And the fact that the ideational criterion makes use of the notion of ideation, which is 'mentalistic', 'intensional', and so on, should be acceptable to Davidson (see 1976: 38). His 'hold true' constraint is thoroughly mentalistic.

One interesting property of an ideational completion of the Davidsonian schema is that *the translation clause implies the truth condition clause if the latter is consistent.*[16] Because 'Il pleut' and 'It is raining' are used to express the same thought, it follows that 'Il pleut' is true iff it is raining. I see nothing objectionable in this feature. The fact that the referential properties of expressions are derived makes them no less important.

## 9.4 TRUTH AND IDEATION

On the expression theory, the referential properties of expressions, along with their logical properties, are derived from those of the ideas they express.[17] We will focus on sentences and truth conditions.

9.1 **Definition:** $e_i$ *is true iff i is true.*

The symbol '$e_i$' is an individual quantificational variable ranging over expressions *interpreted as expressing i*. Truth values and truth conditions cannot be assigned to sentences *simpliciter*, but only to sentences *in a given sense*. For example, 'Sam is a vixen' is true in one sense iff the idea that Sam is a female fox is true. But in another sense, the very same sentence is true iff the idea that Sam is a shrewish woman is true. In a code, the sentence may be true iff the idea that the spy is listening is true. Definition 9.1 thus says that the truth conditions of a sentence on a given interpretation are the truth conditions of the idea expressed on that interpretation. Interpreted as expressing the idea that Sam is a female fox, the sentence 'Sam is a vixen' is true iff the idea that Sam is a female fox is true.

The case of 'Sam is a vixen' in English shows that we cannot generally replace reference to an interpretation by reference to a language. That is, we cannot generally specify truth conditions for 'e is true *in L*' when, as is typically the case, e is ambiguous in L. However, just as the reference to a language is conventionally omitted when it is understood to be the object language, so the reference to an interpretation is conventionally omitted when it is understood in the context. A particular interpretation is always so understood when e is used to refer ideo-reflexively to the idea i according to the rules discussed in §3.7. Reference to an interpretation is thus *practically* unnecessary on *'Sam is a female fox' is true iff the idea that Sam is a female fox is true*, because we are understood to be referring on the left of the biconditional to the very sense with which we are using the sentence on the right. Thus *'p' is true iff the idea that p is true* is understood as equivalent to *'$p_i$' is true iff the idea that $p_i$ is true* where 'i' is used on the left to refer explicitly to an interpretation, and on the right to restrict the range of substitution instances of 'p' to those in which it is used with that same interpretation.

The idea that Sam is a female fox is true, of course, iff Sam is a female fox. This fact does not follow from Definition 9.1, which says nothing at all about Sam. Instead, the fact is an instance of a Tarskian definition schema that I shall call simply the *truth postulate*. All of its substitution instances are true.

**9.2  Postulate:** *i is true iff $p_i$, provided i is a nonparadoxical proposition.*

The proviso that i be a proposition is obvious, because subpropositional concepts and nonpropositional thoughts cannot be described as true or false. It makes no sense to say that the concept ″blue″ is true, nor the thought ″Will it rain?″

The proviso that the proposition be nonparadoxical is necessary to avoid the contradictions of the semantic paradoxes. Paradoxical propositions are those which cannot have any truth value because if they did they would have contradictory truth values. A sentence like 'This sentence is false' is meaningful, and does express an idea. The idea it expresses counts as a proposition on Definition 2.4 because it is the sort of thought that can be believed or disbelieved. But the proposition that sentence expresses must be neither true nor false because either assumption would lead to the contradictory conclusion that the proposition is both true and not true (and that it is true iff not true). The truth postulate does apply to propositions whose presuppositions are false, such as 'The present king of France is bald'. While such propositions are in fact neither true nor false, on my view, they are not paradoxical, and would have a consistent truth value if those presuppositions were satisfied. There are no possible conditions under which paradoxical propositions are true or false.

As long as paradoxicality is characterized as above in terms of truth and falsity, the proviso would make Postulate 9.2 circular as an analysis of what truth is. Nevertheless, the truth postulate is like a definition schema in that its substitution instances do tell us what it is for any expressible idea with a truth value to be true. An instance tells us not only a necessary and sufficient condition for the truth of an idea, but the conditions *in virtue of which* it would be true. For the idea that Sam is a female fox to be true is for Sam to be a female fox. While such instances of the truth postulate are necessarily true and self-evident, they are not at all vacuous or trivial. For they describe a relationship between two different states of affairs. They describe thoughts as having one property (truth) just in case other things have different properties. The *thought* that the sky is blue is *true* provided *the sky* is *blue*. Furthermore, the truth postulate has instances that are contingent and unobvious. The postulate implies that the thought occurring to me at 10:05 was true iff the sky is blue, because the thought occurring to me then happened to be the thought that the sky is blue. The truth postulate provides only a partial definition schema, it should be noted, because it only specifies truth conditions for ideas expressible in the language we are using. Given that we can express any idea we can conceive by expanding our metalanguage if necessary, the scope of the postulate is limited only by our ability to think.

Because the truth postulate identifies the state of affairs in the world that makes an idea true or false, it specifies the 'content' of the idea in the objective, relational sense sometimes given this term (see §3.8 and §8.5). The postulate does not tell us what it is for the idea that p to be the idea that p. The truth postulate relies on the fact that we use sentences to express particular thoughts, which represent the truth conditions for sentences interpreted as expressing those thoughts. Postulate 9.2 would be circular if, with the truth conditionalist, we had defined meaning and expression in terms of truth. So another advantage of the expression theory of meaning is that it enables us to specify what it is for an unlimited range of ideas to be true.

Definition 9.1 and Postulate 9.2 jointly imply that $e_i$ is *true iff* $p_i$, provided i is a nonparadoxical proposition. When e is 'p' itself, which is understood to be expressing i, then we get '$p_i$' is *true iff* $p_i$, the most familiar version

of the Tarski 'Convention T', with the interpretation indexes explicit.[18]
A further permutation based on Definition 5.4 and Theorem 2.5 yields
something akin to the Davidsonian schema (§9.3): *$e_i$ means that p iff (i) $e_i$*
*is true iff p, and (ii) $e_i$ expresses i = the proposition that p.* Clause (i) is
redundant when i is nonparadoxical, because it is implied by clause (ii).
Clause (ii) in turn is equivalent to '$e_i$ means that p' by Definition 5.4 and
Theorem 2.5.

## 9.5   Tarskian Truth Theories for Thoughts

The truth conditions of thoughts can also be specified in terms of the
referential properties of their components by a Tarski-style recursive theory.
Briefly, such a theory provides a structural description of thoughts and ideas,
an assignment of referents to simple ideas, rules assigning referents to
complex ideas (including thoughts) given the referents of the atomic ideas
composing them, and finally, rules assigning truth conditions to complex
thoughts on the basis of the truth conditions of the thoughts composing
them. The Davidsonian, of course, proposes doing this directly for sentences. But the surface structure of natural language sentences invariably
fails to mirror the logical structure of what is expressed by the sentence.
Only when an artificial and highly regimented language is constructed,
whose surface form does reflect the structure of the thoughts expressed,
can a truth theory be constructed for sentences. But then such a theory can
easily be transformed into an explicit theory of truth for thoughts. And even
in ideal languages, sentences have the truth conditions they do because of the
thoughts they express. Hence thoughts, not sentences, are the *primary*
objects of a Tarskian theory of truth.

The structure of thoughts and ideas can be described by a set of phrase
structure rules,[19] such as the following.

### 9.3   Rudimentary phrase structure rules for thoughts

|   |   |   |
|---|---|---|
| 1. | $T \rightarrow PT, NT$ | (Thoughts can be propositional or nonproposi-tional thoughts.) |
| 2. | $PT \rightarrow PRED$ (*SUB*) | (Propositional thoughts can be composed of a subject concept and a monadic predicate con-cept.) |
| 3. | $PT \rightarrow MC(PT)$ | (Propositional thoughts can be composed of a monadic propositional connective concept and a propositional thought.) |
| 4. | $PT \rightarrow (PT)DC(PT)$ | (Propositional thoughts can be composed of a dyadic propositional connective concept and two propositional thoughts.) |

5. $NT \rightarrow NC(PT)$    (Nonpropositional thoughts can be composed of a monadic nonpropositional connective concept and a propositional thought.)

6. $MC \rightarrow -, +$    (Monadic propositional connective concepts can be the negation connective concept or the affirmation connective concept.)

7. $DC \rightarrow \&, v$    (Dyadic connective concepts can be the conjunction or disjunction connective concepts.)

8. $NC \rightarrow ?, !$    (Nonpropositional connective concepts can be the interrogative connective concept or the imperative connective concept.)

9. $PRED \rightarrow M, F$    (Monadic predicate concepts may be the concept of being male or the concept of being female.)

10. $SUB \rightarrow j, m$    (Subject concepts may be the concept of John or the concept of Mary.)

Despite the fact that these sample rules generate only a small fraction of the thoughts even the most limited humans are capable of thinking, they do generate an infinite number of thoughts and assign them structures, as in (15) and Fig. 9.2.

(15)
1. T
2. PT                                            From 9.3.1
3. MC(PT)                       From 9.3.3
4. MC[(PT)DC(PT)]       From 9.3.4
5. MC{[PRED(SUB)]DC[ PRED(SUB)]}   From 9.3.2
6. MC{[PRED(SUB)]v[ PRED(SUB)]}   From 9.3.7
7. +{[PRED(SUB)]v[ PRED(SUB)]}   From 9.3.6
8. +[M(SUB)vF(SUB)]         From 9.3.9
9. +[M(j)vF(j)]              From 9.3.10

Since each line of (15) is obtained from the preceding line by one or more applications of the phrase structure rules in 9.3, the higher lines represent increasingly abstract levels of structure of the last. The thought whose structure is depicted in (15) would be expressed in English by the sentence '*It is the case that John is either male or female*'. Note that a string like '+[M(j)vF(j)]' is a *name* in the theory of thought represented by 9.3, not a sentence. It is an abbreviation for a singular term like 'the thought whose components are +...', not for a declarative sentence like 'It is the case that....' '+[M(j)vF(j)]' is thus similar to a chemical name like '$H_2O$', except that '+[N(j)vF(j)]' represents the arrangement of the atomic constituents, and not just their numbers.

The output (i.e., final line) of the phrase structure rules in 9.3 could provide the input to an 'encoding' grammar for a particular language,

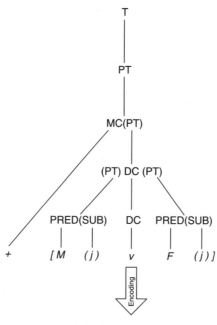

Fig. 9.2   Phrase structure analysis of a thought assigned to a sentence

whose output is a set of sentences in that language (see §5.1). On a theory of this type, the 'deep structure' or 'logical structure' of a sentence is not determined by its 'surface structure'—the way in which the sentence is composed of its parts. Instead, the deep structure is the constituent structure of the thought expressed by that sentence. In Fig. 9.2, the deep structure is above the 'encoding' arrow, the surface structure below. Such an encoding grammar would be complete only if the phrase structure rules for thoughts generated all thoughts expressible in that language. To some extent, the set of thoughts expressible in one natural language differs from that expressible in any other natural language. If a 'universal theory of thought' could be formulated, capable of generating structural descriptions of all thinkable or expressible thoughts, that one theory could provide the input for the grammars for every language. Even if a completely universal theory of thought is for some reason unattainable, theoretical simplification would result by using one theory for more than one language.

Recursive rules assigning referents on the basis of structure to all the thoughts described by the rules in 9.3 are formulated in 9.4. The extension of idea i is symbolized 'ex{i}'.

## 9.4    Rudimentary reference rules

(1)  *ex{j} = John.*
(2)  *ex{m} = Mary.*
(3)  *ex{M} = {x:x is male}.*
(4)  *ex{F} = {x:x is female}.*
(5)  *ex{PRED(SUB)} = T iff ex{SUB} ∈ ex{PRED}.*
(6)  *ex{PRED(SUB)} = F iff ex{SUB} ∉ ex{PRED}.*
(7)  *ex{−PT} = T iff ex{PT} = F.*
(8)  *ex{−PT} = F iff ex{PT} = T.*
(9)  *ex{+PT} = ex{PT}.*
(10)  *ex{PT&PT′} = T iff ex{PT} and ex{PT′} = T.*
(11)  *ex{PT&PT′} = F iff ex{PT} or ex{PT′} = F.*
(12)  *ex{PT∨PT′} = T iff ex{PT} or ex{PT′} = T.*
(13)  *ex{PT∨PT′} = F iff ex{PT} and ex{PT′} = F.*

The symbols 'T' and 'F', of course, stand for the two truth values. Hence *i is true iff ex{i} = T.* According to these rules, the idea described in (15) is true iff it is the case that John is either male or female, which is the correct truth condition for that idea. In light of Definition 9.1, the rules assign the same truth condition to the sentence 'It is the case that John is either male or female' on its intended interpretation. Using the symbols of Rule 9.4, Postulate 9.2 says that ex{i} = T iff $p_i$.

The first four referential rules can be generalized in familiar ways. For example, the first two are obtained from the following schema: *ex{c(N)} = N if N exists*, where 'N' is a proper name and c(N) is the concept of N. John is the extension of j *because* (i) John exists, and (ii) that concept is the concept of John. When N does not exist, ex{c(N)} may be left undefined, or assigned some arbitrary value, such as the empty set. The concept of Pegasus has no extension (or has the null-extension), since Pegasus does not exist. Similarly, the third and fourth rules are instances of: *ex{c(G)} = {x:x is G}*, where 'G' is a general term. This assigns the empty set to all terms like 'centaur', 'flying horse', and 'square circle' that apply to no existing things. When 'G' is a Russellian term, c(G) has no extension. Rule 9.4 leaves the extension function undefined for all connective concepts and nonpropositional thoughts.

We could also introduce an *intension* function in{i , w}, whose values for any idea i and world w is the extension of i in w.[20] Such rules would reveal an important difference between the concept "John F. Kennedy" and the concept "the President in 1962". Whereas in{c(JFK), w} is Kennedy for every world w in which Kennedy exists, in{c(the President in 1962),w} will be Kennedy for some worlds, Nixon for others. Once an intension function is introduced, the extension function can be defined in terms of it and the actual world @: *ex{i}= in{i,@}.* Given intension functions and phrase structure rules for thoughts, we could recursively define *structured* intension functions in the manner of Lewis (1972: §5) and Cresswell (1985).

The technical details of the rudimentary theory of truth sketched above are unimportant, as is its incompleteness. My purpose is merely to provide a concrete illustration of a general point: *Ideational theories of meaning need not ignore the referential properties of linguistic expressions, or preclude their proper treatment, even though they refuse to equate semantic properties with referential properties.* Ideational theories simply view the referential properties of language as derived, dependent on the meanings of the expressions in the language and the referential properties of the ideas they express.[21] This maneuver cannot be characterized as a mere shuffle, nor as the first step of an infinite regress. For unlike sentences, the truth conditions of thoughts follow from their intrinsic characteristics. Whereas the truth or falsity of the sentence 'grass is green' depends on the color of grass only because of the way the sentence is used or interpreted, the fact that the thought that grass is green is true iff grass is green is a necessary truth, and does not depend on the way the thought is interpreted. It is not even true that ideational theories minimize the importance of truth-or model-theoretic semantics. They merely relocate the primary subject of evaluation in such theories, from sentences and words to thoughts and ideas.

Truth- or model-theoretic semantics that make the primary bearers of referential properties symbols of some sort invariably assign to those symbols properties that no natural language expressions possess, such as univocity. They also have to ignore the fact that the meanings of countless natural language sentences are not complete enough to determine a truth-evaluable proposition; consider 'Bill needs three more units', which has a definite meaning, but cannot be evaluated for truth until we know 'units *of what?*' and 'needs *for what?*' More pertinently, the symbols to which the referential properties are assigned in such semantics invariably have constituent structures markedly unlike those of the natural language expressions whose meaning and reference are being studied. The fact that symbols are familiar objects does not eliminate the mystery of what they are supposed to represent in formal theories of this sort when presented as accounts of natural language semantics. The mystery can be dispelled by taking the symbols to represent the ideas expressed by natural language expressions. The perniciously stubborn belief that referential properties are the only semantic properties has led both to the hasty dismissal of ideational theories of meaning by logicians and formal semanticists like Lewis, and to the erroneous treatment of thoughts as 'sentences in the language of thought' by ideational theorists like Fodor.[22]

## NOTES

[1] I define the related notion of what a word refers to *on a particular occasion* in *Indexicals*.

[2] Compare and contrast Putnam (1981: 52) and Horwich (1998a: 114, 118, 120–3; 1998b), who have suggested that a theory of word reference would consist of nothing but such tautologies. Most would like a theory explaining *why* 'Φ' refers to Φ.

[3] See Quine 1963: 3, 36, and elsewhere.

[4] This underappreciated point was made forcefully by Wolterstorff 1960, and later by Putnam 1970a. See also Plantinga 1985: 350–3 and Peacocke 1992: 2. Contrast Linsky 1983: 29–30 and Higginbotham 1998: 153. See Soames (2002: Chs. 9–11) for a thorough discussion of sentences like 'Water is $H_2O$'.

[5] Zadeh (1983) and others have tried to handle vagueness within a referential framework by introducing 'fuzzy' sets. But even these are definite in ways that vague meanings are not.

[6] McDermott's 1988 theory, based on Lewis's 1970 functionalist theory of theoretical terms, may be viewed as a Fregean theory in which 'mode of presentation of X' is taken to be our *conception* of X rather than the *concept* of X (see §3.3). This avoids the Russellian problem with referential theories, but not the Fregean. Our conception of X will typically be identical to our conception of Y when the identity of X and Y is well established, even though the terms 'X' and 'Y' have different meanings, as 'water' and '$H_2O$' illustrate.

[7] See *Meaning, Expression, and Thought*, §21.1.

[8] Cf. Yourgrau 1990: 129.

[9] Cf. Field 1972: 281; Chierchia and McConnell-Ginet 1990: 81; Stalnaker 1997: 535; Siebel 2001: 249.

[10] Contrast Fodor 1990a: 111; Higginbotham 1998: 153.

[11] Cf. Hintikka 1969: 88–9; Lewis 1975: 19; Cresswell 1985; Schiffer 1987a: 115; Soames 1989: 200–1; Avramides 1989: 27–8; and Fodor and Lepore 1992: 63.

[12] Cf. Vermazen 1971; Loar 1976b: 141; Field 1978: 59, fn. 40; Hungerland and Vick 1981: 70–2; Fodor and Lepore 1992: Ch. 3.

[13] Tarski 1944. Cf. Hacking 1975: 140–4; Foster 1976: 17–18; Davidson 1973: 138; 1976; Evans and McDowell 1976: xiii–xv; Schiffer 1987a: 114–19; Larson and Segal 1995.

[14] Cf. Davidson 1973: 134–9; 1974: 150; 1975: 155; Lewis 1974b; Hacking 1975: 146–50, 154–5; Evans and McDowell 1976: xv, McDowell 1977; 1978: 306–8; McGinn 1982: 229, 239–40; Evans 1985: 72–5; Larson and Segal 1995: 182–4, 190; Sainsbury 2001: 214. Contrast Larson and Segal 1995: 186–7.

[15] Cf. McGinn 1982: 229, 239–40, who says that 'p' gives the meaning of e only when e and 'p' have 'the same cognitive role'.

[16] Inconsistency arises when the semantic paradoxes are generated. For example, if e is (L) and (L) is '(L) is not true', then e means "(L) is not true"; but no consistent deductive system will yield '(L) is true iff (L) is not true' as a theorem (see Chihara 1976). I believe Davidson's requirement that 'e' be a *structural description* of a sentence suffices to avoid the paradoxes.

[17] Cf. Frege 1918: 4; Loar 1981: 153; Schiffer 1981: §8; Boër and Lycan 1986: 56–7; Peacocke 1986: 4–6, 47, 62–4; Horwich 1998b: 371. Contrast Dummett 1993: 8–9.

[18] It may be necessary to recall here that 'e' is a variable ranging over expressions; it may be replaced by the name of a sentence, but not by a sentence. In contrast, the symbol 'p' is a place-holder for sentences, replaceable by sentences but not names of sentences.

[19] Cf. Husserl's (1900: IV, §13) notion of the 'laws of compounding of meanings', comprising the 'pure logico-grammatical theory of forms'.

[20] Or an object representing the extension: see Chapter 14.

[21] Cf. Katz 1977a: 38 and Carston 1988. Contrast Lewis (1969: 171): 'Katz takes [interpret-ations] to be expressions built out of symbols called 'semantic markers' which represent 'conceptual elements in the structure of a sense.' I find this account unsatisfactory, since it

leads to a semantic theory that leaves out such central semantic notions as truth and reference.'
See also Cresswell 1985: 27–8, 56–7; Devitt and Sterelny 1987: 28, 33, 102; Chierchia and
McConnell-Ginet 1990: 352, 430.

[22] See *Meaning, Expression, and Thought*, Ch. 20.

# Part III

# Names

# 10

# Millian Theories

Proper names are a large and important class of meaningful words for which the expression theory holds straightforwardly. The name 'Aristotle' means "Aristotle" because it expresses the idea of Aristotle, an idea everyone has who can think about Aristotle, the famous philosopher. A particular speaker means something different by 'Aristotle' if he or she uses it to express a different idea (that of Aristotle Onassis, perhaps, or that of a Mediterranean battle group if the speaker is using a naval code). With respect to the applicability of the expression theory, proper names do not differ from common names like 'man' or 'philosopher', except that the ideas they express are singular rather than general, and typically serve as subject concepts rather than predicate concepts. While some proper names have syntactic structure and a compositional meaning, standard proper names are like common nouns in being assigned meaning by the base clause of the recursive neo-Gricean analysis. 'Aristotle' is conventionally used to express the idea of Aristotle, just as 'man' is conventionally used to express the idea of man. We will conclude that standard proper names are like other syntactically unstructured terms introduced ostensively in a further respect: they express atomic or basic concepts, and thus have no semantic definitions. While the referent of any term is determined by its sense, a standard proper name is directly referential to the extent that the reference of the concept it expresses, and consequently its referent, is not determined compositionally by the reference of the components of that concept.

Despite the ease with which names are handled by the expression theory, standard names have widely been thought to be puzzling or exceptional from a semantic point of view. They have been called 'a hard problem for everybody'. Some respected scholars have even claimed that they are meaningless. Many feel compelled to accept intuitively unacceptable consequences of their theories because they see no alternative. Others have gone to desperate lengths to explain the problems away. We will see that the most popular theories are based on a false and groundless assumption, and that once this assumption is dispatched the puzzles vanish.

## 10.1   THE FREGE–MILL DICHOTOMY

What has impeded discussions of the semantics of proper names is a false dichotomy: *Either names have a descriptive meaning or they have no sense at all.* I call this the *Frege–Mill dichotomy.* The first alternative is Frege's way. The second is Mill's. Both are untenable. There must be, and are, alternatives. To demonstrate that the dichotomy is false, it largely suffices to review Russellian (§10.4) and Fregean (§10.5) arguments against the Millian theory and Kripkean arguments against the Fregean theory (Chapter 12). These need to be supplemented by linguistic evidence that names have meanings, and with a demonstration that recent versions of the description theory designed to avoid Kripkean arguments are untenable. We will see that defenses of Millianism based on pragmatics are unsuccessful. I believe the evidence presented is collectively conclusive. We should reject the dichotomy, and affirm that standard names have nondescriptive senses. We should also reject what might be called the *'classical corollary'* of the Frege–Mill dichotomy: *names are either definable or meaningless.* The evidence indicates standard names are semantic primitives, with unanalyzable senses.

I would view the main argument of Part III as belaboring the obvious except for the fact that so many eminent writers see no alternative to the Frege–Mill dichotomy.[1]

Kripke's examples prove too much, from our viewpoint, insofar as they can be used, as both Kripke and Putnam use them, to attack the claim that common nouns like 'cat' [have] meaning.                                                    (Katz 1977a: 23)

If this is right—if the idea that names have descriptive semantic content really has been discredited—then, given the alleged datum, one cannot identify the semantic contents of names either with their referents or with descriptive information that may vary from one coreferential name to another. It is not clear what alternatives remain. ... Thus we are left with a dilemma.                                   (Soames 2002: 14)

Most simply assert that the Fregean and Millian theories are the two leading approaches, and proceed to argue for one or the other without considering whether there are alternatives. The Millians seem compelled by the fact that the description theory is false. Thus the principal argument Soames (e.g., 2002: 101) uses to support Millianism is the fact that names do not have descriptive meaning. The Fregeans seem compelled by the falsity of Millianism. Thus one of the chief motivations for Searle's (1983: 244) descriptivist theory is its ability to explain substitutivity failures and negative existentials. The rational approach, I believe, is to accept the evidence against both Millianism and Fregeanism and take it together to establish that names have nondescriptive senses. Several independently plausible theories rejecting the dichotomy will be sketched in Chapter 13, and evidence for the superiority of an ideational theory will be presented. We will see that the expression theory I have developed as a general theory of meaning applies just as well to the nondescriptive meaning of names. Chapter 14 will show that our conclusions about names do not preclude powerful formal treatments of their semantics.

Three other corollaries of the dichotomy have also enjoyed wide support: the thesis that all concepts are purely or indexically descriptive; that propositions must be either 'purely descriptive' or 'singular' in Kaplan's sense; and that 'transworld identities' require descriptive conditions from which it can be deduced that an object in another possible world is a named individual. The metaphysical issues will be discussed in connection with possible worlds semantics (Chapter 14), and the cognitive issues in connection with ideational semantics (Chapter 13). We will explore the question of whether the ideas expressed by standard names are completely atomic, or contain a sortal component. I will show how possible worlds and situation semantics can handle proper names without taking either Mill's or Frege's way (Chapter 14). What blocks the adequate treatment of names in many formal semantics is their attempt to use the referents of the terms being studied as the model elements representing those referents in model structures. It is this artifact of standard models, not the formal frameworks themselves, that generates the conclusion that there are no contingent identities involving standard names. This part of the argument should be anything but obvious.

This chapter will focus on Millian theories, according to which names have no meaning, or no meaning beyond their reference. The most plausible versions are subject to the problems common to all referential theories of meaning (§9.2).

## 10.2  No Meaning

'A proper name is an unmeaning mark,' Mill (1897: §1.2) said, like the chalk line a burglar might make so that he can recognize a house later. While moderate forms of Millianism are possible (§10.4), many philosophers and linguists have embraced Mill's claim to the letter.[2] Despite many arguments advanced in its favor, the extreme view is completely untenable. I believe we have every reason to hold that names are meaningful in the same sense that other terms are meaningful. To begin, there is all the difference in the world between the following marks:

Brahms
S#2@tkks*

The first is meaningful, the second meaningless. We understand the first, but not the second. The first denotes a famous composer, the latter denotes nothing. The first is used to express the idea of Brahms, and thoughts about Brahms; the latter is not used to express anything. Proper names are employed in the characteristically human method of communication and expression. Together with other words, they are used to communicate and record vitally important information, and to express our beliefs, desires, intentions, and feelings. Proper names are employed in the process of making statements, giving orders, asking questions, making promises, and so on. Their usage is as systematic and conventional as that of other words, and just as determinative of the speech act performed. Like common names, proper names are used to make true or false statements, and give sentences containing them specific truth conditions. Proper names are among the very first words we master, and appear to be learned and remembered by the same psycholinguistic processes. The replacement of names of a recessive language by names from the dominant language is one step in the process of language death (Dressler 1996).

Of particular theoretical importance is the fact that just like other meaningful units, proper names enter into larger units whose meanings are predictable from and determined by the meanings of their components. Consider:

(1) Someone hates Roosevelt.
(2) Someone hates banks.

The meaning of (1) is dependent on the meaning of 'Roosevelt' in exactly the same way the meaning of (2) is dependent on the meaning of 'banks' (recall §5.6 and §2.6). Since 'Roosevelt' can mean either "Theodore Roosevelt" or "Franklin Roosevelt", (1) is ambiguous, just as (2) is ambiguous. In the manner characteristic of ambiguity, we can 'hear' both these sentences in different ways. A native speaker of Mongolian might fail to understand (1) solely because he did not understand the last word. We would similarly misunderstand a woman who uttered (1) if we took 'Roosevelt' to mean "Franklin Roosevelt" when she meant "Theodore Roosevelt". Finally, if we replaced the name with a meaningless mark like 'S#2@tkks*', the result would be a meaningless sentence.

Pairs of sentences otherwise alike except that one has 'Brahms' where the other has 'Bach' differ in meaning in the same ways. The names contrast 'paradigmatically' and are part of a 'semantic field' with a very simple semantic structure. Consider:

(3) Bach wrote four symphonies, Bach was German, ....
(4) Brahms wrote four symphonies, Brahms was German, ....

Given the difference in meaning between the first sentences in (3) and (4), the difference in meaning between the second sentences is completely predictable. The hypothesis that these sentences differ regularly in meaning because they contain different nonsense syllables has little to recommend it. The differences in meaning in (3) and (4) are as systematic as those in (5) and (6), which contain definite descriptions rather than names.

> (5) The Baroque composer wrote four symphonies, The Baroque composer was German,...
>
> (6) The Romantic composer wrote four symphonies, The Romantic composer was German,...

In general, the meaning of a subject-predicate sentence is a compositional function of the meaning of its subject. Whether the subject is a proper name or not is immaterial.

Sentences containing proper names have particular truth conditions. Those truth conditions are determined by the names they contain in the same way they are determined by the common nouns they contain, and can be formulated using T-sentences in the way Davidson popularized (§9.3). Thus 'x is the Atlantic' is true iff x is the Atlantic, just as 'x is an ocean' is true iff x is an ocean.[3] In general, for each sense of name 'N', we have a T-sentence of form (7):

> (7) 'x is N' is true iff x is N.

A Davidsonian should conclude straight away that proper names are as meaningful as common nouns. The fact that names can be ambiguous shows that this conclusion is hasty, but it is just as hasty for common nouns. Just as (2) has different truth conditions depending on the meaning of 'bank', so (1) has different truth conditions depending on the meaning of 'Roosevelt'. In one sense, (1) is true iff someone hates Franklin Roosevelt. In another, it is true iff someone hates Theodore Roosevelt.

Adjectives and pronouns can be formed from proper names in the same way they are formed from common nouns. Consider the following semantic proportions:

> (8) Brahmsian : Brahms :: reptilian : reptile.
> Bach's : Bach :: music's : music.

The meanings of the two adjectives in (8) are related in the same way to the two root nouns. The fact that one root noun is proper and the other common is irrelevant. If we were interested only in grammar, we might continue the series with ':: Blahgian : Blahg'. But since 'Blahg' is meaningless, so is 'Blahgian'. We would not be 'going on in the same way'. Similar comments apply to the possessives in (8), and to the convention whereby names are used without alteration as adjectives ('California girl', 'Earth man', 'Kennedy protégée') (Bolinger 1996). In short, significant semantic generalizations would be missed on the assumption that proper names are meaningless, or have meaning in a different sense from general terms. Put

another way, a wide variety of familiar and important semantic facts would
be hard to understand if we denied that names are like general terms in
having meaning.

There are various conventions whereby proper names can be used as
general rather than singular terms. Consider:

(9) He is a Roosevelt.

The word 'Roosevelt' has at least five markedly different senses in (9),
meaning (roughly): "person named 'Roosevelt'"; "person with the salient
features of Theodore Roosevelt (or Franklin)"; or "person in the family of
Theodore Roosevelt (or Franklin)".[4] On the latter two interpretations, (9)
has a compositional meaning that depends on the meaning of 'Roosevelt' as
a singular term. Note that I used proper names to give meanings for (8) in a
way that presupposes that those names are meaningful. The meaning of the
adjective 'Brahmsian' is similarly based on the meaning of 'Brahms' as a
singular term. As a linguistic exercise, you should try 'reading' (9) with
'Roosevelt' occurring as a singular term, and (1) with the same occurring
as a general term. You should find this impossible, at least without hearing it
as deviant and ungrammatical. We shall be concerned only with the meaning
of proper names as singular terms.

As evidence that proper names do not have meaning, Katz observed that a
question like (10 ) is quite standard, but not (11).[5]

(10) Who is Roosevelt?
(11) What does 'Roosevelt' mean?

However, our general preference for (10) over (11) does not entail, and
cannot be explained by, the hypothesis that (11) is semantically deviant or
meaningless. On the contrary, (11) has at least one trivially true answer,
namely: 'Roosevelt' means "Roosevelt". Lots of negative answers can be
given too: it does not mean "cow", "walk", or "happy". Positively informative
answers can be given when particular contexts are in question. The answer
might be, for example, that 'Roosevelt' means "Franklin Roosevelt" here,
and "Theodore Roosevelt" there. In contrast, we could not say that '7' means
"7" if '7' is the unmeaning chalk mark Mill's burglar makes. Furthermore,
contexts are readily imaginable in which (11) (or its translation into some
other language) would naturally be asked. Just visualize a group of fiftieth-
century historians, linguists, and cryptologists poring over recently
unearthed scraps of writing from the twentieth century containing inscrip-
tions like 'Roosevelt was the 32nd President of the United States'. A question
like "Does 'Roosevelt' mean anything, or is it a meaningless string of letters?"
is unusual for us only because the answer is so obvious. That answer
provides a very natural context in which to ask (11). Indeed, that is our
context in this section. Another natural use of (11) would be as a paraphrase

of 'What does the third word in (1) mean?' This question need not be retracted when it is discovered that the third word in (1) is a proper name, the way 'Who is the third person's husband?' would be if it were discovered that the third person is a three-year-old boy.

More directly, Katz argued that proper names do not have meaning because they do not have semantic properties or contribute to the semantic properties of the sentences in which they occur. As evidence, he claimed that proper names cannot be described as *ambiguous*.[6] It seems to me that (1) is as clear a case of ambiguity as there can be, and that the sentence is ambiguous because the last word in it is ambiguous. Because its last word can be taken in different ways, (1) can be 'heard' in different ways, and its grammaticality, truth value, and logical relations depend on which interpretation it is given. Like 'Men are men', 'Roosevelt is Roosevelt' expresses an analytic truth only if the terms are interpreted uniformly. Katz (2001: 147) asserts that names have multiple bearers instead of multiple senses. But there would be *two* different ways of reading (1) even if 'Roosevelt' had just *one* bearer (Franklin and Teddy being the same person) or *none* (both Roosevelts being myths of American history).

I take names to be sequences of sounds or letters. Other definitions of 'name' are common, of course, on which different people with the same name in my sense have different but homonymous names. While names on other definitions cannot be ambiguous, they still possess semantic properties, such as having nonsynonymous homonyms. The same goes for general terms. Whether the word 'ambiguous' properly expresses it or not, 'Roosevelt' has an important semantic property in common with 'bank', in virtue of which it has different truth conditions when interpreted in different ways.

Algeo (1973: 44–6) argued that names could not be described as either homonymous or polysemous without unacceptable practical and theoretical consequences. Specifically, reckoning names homonymous 'makes the vocabulary infinite and thus in principle indescribable'. Similarly,

Polysemy is no better as an explanation, for by it we must say that the word 'John' has as many meanings as there are, were, or will be persons so named. The vocabulary is still unlimited and indescribable because every proper name has a potentially infinite number of meanings. It is as though we should say that 'iris' has not just a few senses, ... but as many senses as there are individual flowers of the family Iridaceae. The consequence would be to make definition impossible. In either of these approaches, meaning is confused with reference, since there is assumed to be a one-to-one relationship between meanings and referents.          (Algeo 1973: 45–6)[7]

Despite its popularity, the argument is specious. First, it should be abundantly clear from Chapter 9 that I am not assuming any one-to-one correspondence between meaning and reference. Second, the claim that 'iris' has as many senses as there are individual irises is absurd because it embodies the sophomoric confusion of generality and ambiguity: while 'iris' applies to many individual irises (in either of its senses), it applies to them all in the same sense. The name 'John', in contrast, does not apply as a singular term to any two Johns in the same sense. 'This is John' is no more true of both John McEnroe and John Major in the same sense than 'This is an iris' is true of both a flower and an eye part in the same sense. Third, many infinite sets are readily describable, such as the set of integers and the set of numerals denoting them, not to mention the infinite sets of sentences described and analyzed by transformational grammars, Tarskian truth theories, and the like. Fourth, every general term has a *potentially* infinite number of meanings too. For example, there could well be a language in which 'light' meant "visible electromagnetic radiation" in optics, "light fixture" in the hardware industry, "means of lighting cigarettes" among smokers, "traffic light" among drivers, "weighing little" in mechanics, "low calorie" in the beer industry, "low fat" in the beef industry, and so on for any number of areas. There is surely a number n such that no noun actually has more than n meanings, but there is no n such that a noun could not have more than n meanings. The fact that if n is large enough no individual speaker could learn all its meanings is no more significant than the fact that no individual speaker knows the meaning of all words in any natural language. Fifth, while the number of meanings a name *could* have is unlimited, the number it *actually* has at any given time is finite. This would remain true even if every human being who has ever lived were named 'John'. Finally, it is hard to see why the claim that a name has many meanings would create any greater practical or theoretical consequences than Algeo's undeniable premise that names normally have many bearers.[8]

Proper names do not have *antonyms*. That is one set of semantic relations they do lack. This does not support the conclusion that names have no sense, however, as Katz (1986a: 77) claimed. For definite descriptions also lack antonyms despite having senses. Only general terms can be described as 'opposites'. Thus names lack antonyms because they have a particular kind of meaning—the meaning of a singular term.

The fact that proper names make a systematic contribution to the overall meanings of the sentences in which they appear leads Allerton (1987: 71–3) to insist that names do have a meaning. But he nevertheless denies that names have a meaning 'in the usual sense', by which he means 'language-internal semantic relations'.

[A name's meaning] is an isolated, unintegrated one, such that it cannot be related to the meanings of other words in terms of lexical relations.... [Proper names] cannot be understood by learning their relationships to other words (as described in diction-ary definitions, for instance).                              (Allerton 1987: 71)[9]

Allerton cites Lyons (1977: 219), who championed the structuralist principle that the sense of a term is constituted by the sense-relations it bears to all other units in the language. We need not question structuralism to rebut this argument. For names *do* have language-internal semantic relations. *Meaning contrast* is one, relating 'cat' to 'dog' as well as 'Brahms' to 'Bach'. Others are *synonymy* ('Brahms'/'Johannes Brahms'), *hypocorism* ('Bobby'/'Bob', 'doggy'/'dog'), the *nickname* relation ('Bill Clinton'/'William Clinton', 'Stu'/'Stuart'), *logical equivalence* ('Aristotle'/'the individual who is identical to Aristotle') and *subsumption* ('Aristotle'/'individual'). There are also distinctive semantic relationships between 'Brahmsian' and 'Brahms', 'Bachs' in its genetic sense as a plural common noun and 'Bach' in its sense as a proper name, 'Germany' as a proper name and 'German' as an adjective, and so on. Furthermore, 'Germany' and 'Aristotle' resemble 'the book' and 'this' semantically in a way that distinguishes all four from 'book', 'son', 'all', and 'or'. Roughly, the former all have a singular, referential meaning.

Synonymy, hypocorism, and the nickname relation even enable us to understand some proper names by learning their relationships to other words. Thus we can explain the meaning of the subject term in 'The Tigers were rained out' by saying that it means the same as 'The Detroit Tigers' there. Some names can be given definitions: May 9th =df the ninth day of May. Not all proper names can be learned by giving synonyms or definitions, obviously. But the same goes for general terms. To the best of my knowledge, 'blue' is not exactly synonymous with any other word or phrase in English. It does not follow that 'blue' has no meaning in the usual sense.

A final argument for the thesis that names have no meaning contains multiple confusions.

> The main reason why names are often said to have no meaning is this. In order to be denoted by an ordinary word, e.g., by a common name such as 'table', an object must possess certain characteristics associated with this word. Thus an object will not fall under the denotation of the word 'table' unless it has the characteristics of a table. I am not free to call any object I want a 'table': certain conditions have to be satisfied. But I am free to confer any proper name I want on my cat. I may call her 'Table' if I so wish (in so far as this is a proper name). (Recanati 1993: 136)[10]

First, Recanati appears to be arguing that names do not have meaning because they cannot be *defined*. This argument assumes what I called the classical corollary of the Frege–Mill dichotomy. But not all meaningful general terms can be defined either (see §3.9 and §13.1). It is dubious, in fact, that even 'table' can be given a strict, semantic definition. Just try to specify a noncircular set of characteristics that are logically necessary and sufficient for an object to be a table. Second, it is just as true that 'Aristotle' refers to an object only if it has the characteristics of Aristotle. For 'Aristotle' applies to an object iff that object *is*

*Aristotle*. This condition holds in all possible worlds. Similarly, 'table' applies to an object iff it *is a table*. The statement 'My coffee cup is Aristotle' is therefore just as false as 'My coffee cup is a table'. Third, Recanati's argument confuses the act of *introducing* a term with the act of *applying* a term, both of which can be referred to as 'calling'. I can call my cat any name I like in the sense that I can *give* her any name I want. We did not have to name our cat 'Samantha'; we could have named her 'Tasha' or even 'Table'. In the same way, we could *give* tables any name we want. We could introduce 'elbat' or even 'samantha' as a new term for tables by so stipulating. However, when I use 'A cat is a table' to make a statement rather than to stipulate a new use for 'table', I am applying a common name that was previously introduced and has an already established use. Whether 'table' correctly applies to a cat in that sense is in no way up to me. Similarly, if I use 'This cat is Aristotle' to make a statement rather than to stipulate a new use for 'Aristotle', I am applying a proper name that was previously introduced and has an already established use. Whether 'Aristotle' in that sense correctly applies to my cat is in no way up to me.

In a similar vein, Algeo (1973: 72–3) and Pendlebury (1990: 520–1) observed that I can classify a never before encountered individual as a cat but not as Pyewacket, and concluded that proper names differ from common nouns in requiring an act of bestowal. But while the noun 'cat' need not have been bestowed on a *particular* cat (the term being general), it did have to be bestowed on the *class* of cats. Rundle (1979: 81) thought the crucial contrast between common and proper nouns is that the use of a common noun is not determined by a 'given christening'. True, whether 'cat' applies to a never before seen animal does not depend on whether that animal is identical to the particular *individual* present when the noun 'cat' was introduced. But its application to a new animal does depend on whether that animal is of the same *kind* as that present when 'cat' was introduced. So all this difference amounts to is the fact that proper names are singular terms, common nouns are general. Furthermore, the *classification* of a newly encountered animal as a cat is analogous to the *reidentification* of a cat many years later as Pyewacket: neither is an act of bestowal, or in any way stipulative. Of course, it is dubious that the term 'cat' got its meaning when a single individual said "Let's call cats 'cats'". But it is equally dubious that proper names for the oceans, mountains, cities, and planets got their meaning from the actions of a single individual. That kind of 'bestowal' is not necessary for any term. But whether common or general, there had to be a first occasion on which the term was used with that meaning, and the term got its meaning when that usage became conventional (see Chapter 5). It should be noted that the name 'Aristotle' was not bestowed on Aristotle during his 'baptism'. His parents gave him an ancient Greek name, which evolved into the English 'Aristotle'. Finally, Rundle (1979: 72) observed that hearers can 'appreciate what a sentence is about, grasp the gist of the words, if we simply recognize the name as a name'. We might indeed count a woman as appreciating what the sentence 'Xavier Scharwenka used a mordent' meant even if she had never heard the name 'Xavier Scharwenka' before, as long as she knew it was a name, or more specifically the name of a composer. But we might similarly count her as grasping the gist of the words if she had never heard the noun 'mordent' before, as long as she knew it was a noun, or more specifically a musical term.

### 10.3   No Meaning in Natural Languages

Grant now that proper names are meaningful, that they mean something on given occasions, and that people mean something by them. A question remains: Are proper names meaningful *in natural languages*? Does 'Aristotle' mean anything *in English*? My wife and I used the word 'O-bar' to mean "granola bar" when we talked to our young son, a usage we picked up when he was just learning to speak. 'O-bar' thus means something in our common idiolect. Nevertheless, the word 'O-bar' has no meaning in English. So an affirmative answer to the question of whether proper names have meaning in natural languages does not follow from the fact that people use proper names to mean something, that the names mean something in their idiolects, and so on (see Chapter 5).

The remaining question has relatively little importance to philosophy or theoretical semantics. The conceptual issues that have puzzled philosophers about the nature of meaning arise just as well when we ask what people mean by their words, or what words mean in the idiolects of particular speakers or on given occasions of their use. Nevertheless, most linguists and philosophers of language are especially interested in natural language meaning. So let us press the question. Alston's argument is one best regarded as directed specifically against the claim that proper names have linguistic meaning.

> It is questionable whether proper names can be correctly said to have meaning. They are not assigned meanings in dictionaries. One who does not know what 'Fido' is the name of is not thereby deficient in his grasp of English in the way he would be if he did not know what 'dog' means. And the fact that 'Fido' is used in different circles as the name of a great many different dogs does not show that it has a great many different meanings or that it is a highly ambiguous word.
>
> (Alston 1964a: 12)[11]

I believe Alston is right about names like 'Fido'. For example, while my family uses the name 'Tasha' to denote our pet cat, 'Tasha' does not denote our pet cat in English. The name does not appear in my dictionary (*Webster's Encyclopedic Unabridged Dictionary*), and even if it did it would not have an entry like 'The pet cat of the Davis family', or anything of the sort. The most an English dictionary would have is 'Female given name, form of Natasha'. A speaker who does not know that 'Tasha' denotes our pet cat is not thereby ignorant of English even to the slightest extent. The fact that 'Tasha' is the familiar name of thousands of Natashas around the English-speaking world does not show that 'Tasha' is ambiguous in English.

But Alston seems wrong about names like 'Aristotle'. That name does have an entry in dictionaries. Mine says '384–322 BC, Greek philosopher; pupil of Plato; tutor of Alexander the Great'. It has multiple entries for 'Roosevelt'. The difference between 'Tasha' and 'Aristotle' is easy to explain. Words have a meaning in English only if their usage is conventional among speakers of English (see Chapter 5). While it is customary for the members of my family to use 'Tasha' to refer to our pet cat, the practice is not sufficiently widespread among speakers of English to count as a convention. Ditto for the general term 'O-bar'. The usage of 'Aristotle' to denote the philosopher, in contrast, is more widespread than the usage of most English words. True, 'dog' and 'cat' are used a lot more frequently. But a glance through the dictionary will turn up thousands of rarities like 'decemvirate', 'dechenite', and 'decibar'. Recanati (1993: 148–9) argued that even widely used proper names differ from general terms in being 'temporally local': 'their lifetime is shorter than that of an ordinary word'. But the names 'Aristotle', 'English', and 'Atlantic' have been in the English language much longer than 'floppy disk' or 'bazooka', and I predict will remain long after these general terms become obsolete.

Napoli (1997: 187) has argued that names are properly excluded from dictionaries because they are '*severally* pretty irrelevant to linguistic competence and cognition'. No named particular 'has a remarkable role in the structure of either knowledge or reality', he claims. While Napoli's premise may hold for names whose usage is too local to be conventional, it fails for widely used names. The referents of 'Earth', 'Hitler', and 'Einstein', for example, play a most significant role in the structure of both knowledge and reality, arguably much more important than the objects denoted by general terms like 'hoola hoop' and 'griffin'. A German speaker who does not know the English words for Aristotle and Germany would make a lot more mistakes than one who does not know the English word for a hauberk or a liang. A Mongolian who has not yet learned the English name for any of the countries, states, cities, languages, peoples, presidents, popes, generals, religions, gods, oceans, lakes, rivers, continents, islands, mountains, planets, stars, companies, universities, restaurants, sports teams, orchestras, composers, compositions, books, newspapers, magazines, scientists, or authors is *seriously* deficient in his grasp of English, and has a lot of language learning to do.

The case of numerals is less clear. English speakers conventionally use both the noun 'eight' and the numeral '8' to express the idea of the number eight. But whereas it is clearly correct to say that 'eight' means "eight" in English, it seems incorrect to say that '8' means "eight" *in English*.[12] It is possible that we are merely reacting to the false implicature that '8' means something else in languages other than English. But it seems equally incorrect to say that '8' means "eight" in English, French, German, and all other modern languages whose speakers use arabic numerals, which has no false implicature. Alston would note that dictionaries have entries for 'eight' but not '8'. But since dictionaries are alphabetical listings, that is not too surprising.[13] We might wonder, though, why dictionaries aren't alphanumeric listings if numerals have meanings in the language.

Looking at the definition of living languages that I developed in Chapter 5, one condition fails in the case numerals: the convention dependence clause. According to Definition 5.9, there must be some lineage of speakers U such that the expression–idea pairings in L depend on the conventions in U. L must change as the conventions in U change. The Arabic numeral lineage is distinct from the English lineage.[14] The Arabic numeral system appears to have originated in India or China in the third century BC, spreading to the Middle East by 700 AD. Fibonacci introduced it to Europeans in 1202. Since then its use has spread around the world. Old English arose in about 450 AD in Denmark and northern Germany, evolving from Germanic languages. While it became conventional among English speakers after 1202 to use the Arabic numeral system, the linguistic descendants of the original users of the Arabic numeral system now include the speakers of nearly all modern languages. '8' means "eight" in the Arabic numeral system because it is conventional in that broad group to use '8' to mean "eight". Even if English speakers began using '8' to mean "nine", that would not be enough to change the Arabic numeral system. In that case, however, it would seem correct to say that '8' means "nine" in the English form of the system. The relationship between the Roman numeral system and modern languages is very similar, except that it has undergone several stages of language death. Modern musical notation, which originated in Medieval Italy, is also very similar, except that it has evolved somewhat differently in different languages. Thus the *Harvard Brief Dictionary of Music* tells us that 'B-flat is called B in German' (Apel and Daniel 1960: 2) in order to explain why Schumann called a piece the 'Abegg Variations'.[15]

Ziff had an interesting argument against counting proper names as words in natural languages.

One may not know a single word of Chinese and yet know of Hsieh Ho. 'Hsieh Ho' is a Chinese proper name: is it a word or phrase in English? It would be odd to say so. If I say 'Are you familiar with Hsieh Ho's views on art?' I am speaking English: I am not speaking a combination of English and Chinese. Yet if 'Hsieh' and 'Ho' are words then they can only be words in Chinese and so I must be mistaken in supposing that I do not know a single word of Chinese and I must speak a combination of Chinese and English, which is absurd.                                                    (Ziff 1960: 86)

Unlike the English speaker who facetiously answers '*Si!*' when asked whether he is going to the bullfight, and is thereby speaking Spanish if only momentarily, Ziff was not trying to conform to Chinese when he uttered 'Hsieh Ho'. So according to Definition 5.6, the only natural language Ziff was using was English. 'Hsieh Ho' is not a word of English either, for the same reason 'Tasha' does not mean our cat in English. In contrast, whereas 'Peking' was once the English name for the Chinese capital city, the name 'Beijing' (preferred by the Chinese government) has pretty much replaced it in current English usage. The fact that in the course of using English Ziff was using words that are not words of English is not unusual, and was allowed for in our definition of language use. The use of a Chinese proper name in this way resembles the phenomenon of *borrowing*. When the first Frenchman borrowed the English word 'telephone' in the course of speaking French, he was not speaking English even for a second. His intentions are quite different from that of the Aristotle scholar who uses italicized Greek words because no English translation quite does justice to the original. For both proper and common names, it is conventional to borrow them only when the language one is speaking has no equivalent. The difference is that natural languages contain fewer proper names, and only a small percentage of those have equivalents in other languages. So borrowing is the norm with proper names whereas it is the exception with common names.

I attacked Alston's 'argument from lexicography' by attacking the truth of its premise, noting that some names have entries in some dictionaries. It is more instructive to question the validity of the argument. What appears in dictionaries depends on the beliefs and practices of lexicographers. If lexicographers excluded names from dictionaries on the grounds that names have no meaning, then the above evidence would suggest that their practices should be revised. In a fascinating historical study, Marconi (1990) observes that a major shift in lexicography occurred around 1700. Before that time, about two-thirds of all dictionaries had proper names of people, as opposed to one-third which lacked them. After 1700, the percentages roughly reversed. Today lexicographers generally exclude proper names of people. The question is, 'Why?' Marconi found that the linguistic reasons given by lexicographers are generally pretty obscure, and those clear enough to be assessed do not stand up to analysis (see also Algeo 1973: 75). Some reasons appear to be purely economic, such as the need for brevity and the existence of other sources like encyclopedias. Dictionaries that omit names of people may nonetheless contain names of countries, religions, oceans, and the like. Thus even my pocket English-German dictionary (*Langenscheidts Univer-*

*sal-Wörterbuch Englisch*) contains 'Atlantic/Atlantik', 'Asia/Asien', 'Austria/Österreich', and so on.

As far as Marconi could discern, the main reason for the shift in practice in 1700 was the rise of the belief that the purpose of dictionaries was to 'give the meaning' of terms, by providing either analytic definitions or suitable synonyms. If this were *the* purpose of dictionaries, then there would be a good reason for excluding *most* proper names. For as the failure of the description theory shows, standard names cannot be given analytic definitions (see Chapter 12). Furthermore, relatively few proper names have synonyms. 'Roosevelt' is an exception, being synonymous with 'Franklin Delano Roosevelt' in one sense and 'Theodore Roosevelt' in another. But the latter two names have no synonyms suitable for giving dictionary definitions.

It is dubious, however, that the purpose of a dictionary should be restricted to giving the meanings of words in the way indicated. Another valuable function is to identify and give concise information about their referents, which is what my dictionary did for 'Aristotle'. Such definitions have been termed 'cultural' rather than 'pure', and the dictionaries containing them 'encyclopedic' (Urdang 1996). Moreover, our general inability to analyze proper names extends to common nouns and other terms as well (§13.1). Hence dictionaries routinely describe referents rather than give meanings for general terms too. Thus the entry in my dictionary for 'gold' is 'a precious yellow metallic element, highly malleable and ductile, and free from liability to rust. *Symbol*: au. *at. wt.*: 196.967 . . .'. Finally, and most pertinently, the fact that we cannot *give* the meaning of a term does not mean that the term is meaningless. The meaningfulness of a word in a language does not depend on the existence of suitable synonyms, and it is well known that not every meaningful term can be defined.

### 10.4 NO SENSE: RUSSELL'S PROBLEM

So proper names do have meaning. This can be granted by the Millian who adopts the referential theory, identifying meaning with reference. It is granted by all parties that 'Brahms' refers to a famous composer. It should be granted that having a referent entails having a meaning. The moderate Millian holds that there is nothing more to the meaning of a proper name than its reference.[16] As it is often put, the sole semantic function of a name is to refer to its bearer. What the moderate Millian denies is that proper names have a *'sense'* that is something distinct from its reference. The radical Millian is an eliminativist ('Names have no meanings'). The moderate Millian is a reductive identity theorist ('Meaning for names is reference').

Some Millians infer that names have no sense from the premise that the sense of a term is a reference determining factor. From the falsity of the description theory or from the directly referential character of names (Chapter 12), it is concluded that there is no condition which an object must meet to be the referent of a proper name.[17] This conclusion is false. An object is the referent of 'John Stuart Mill' if and only if the object is John Stuart Mill, the famous nineteenth century philosopher. This is an instance of (7) above. Being John Stuart Mill is a very substantive condition an object must meet to be the referent of the name. 'Roosevelt' refers to an object in one sense only if the object is Franklin Roosevelt, and in another sense only if the object is Teddy Roosevelt. Names are no different from common nouns in this respect. An object is in the extension of 'cat' iff the object is a cat. This condition follows from the fact that 'cat' means "cat", just as the condition for 'John Stuart Mill' above follows from the fact that this name means "John Stuart Mill" rather than "Jeremy Bentham" or "cat" or nothing at all. Finally, as Devitt (1989a: 76) has emphasized, a name must have *some* property that determines its reference. Since the reference of a name is not an intrinsic or essential property, to hold otherwise is to claim that names refer by magic.

The referential theory is more plausible for standard names than definite descriptions, because names are not compositional compounds and have no descriptive content (Chapter 12). Since 'the superhumanly strong man with X-ray vision' and 'the seemingly weak bespectacled klutz that works with Lois Lane' have compositional meanings, and their components have different meanings, it is especially hard to maintain that they have the same meaning because they have the same referent, or that they are meaningless because they in fact have no referent.

One virtue of the Millian theory is that it provides a simple account of the rigidity of names.[18] If the meaning of a name is its reference, then as long as the name is used with the same meaning, it has to be used with the same reference. This must be true even when the name is used to make a claim that is evaluated with respect to other worlds.

Nevertheless, all the problems of the referential theory do arise even for names. We illustrated the vagueness problem with proper names in §9.2. For example, 'the Atlantic' is vague because it is indeterminate whether its referent includes certain regions bordering the Pacific. But the name differs in meaning from any more precise term that definitely does or does not apply to those regions. Reference is as dependent on meaning for names, moreover, as for definite descriptions. Thus whether 'Roosevelt' refers to the twenty-sixth or thirty-second president depends on whether it means "Theodore Roosevelt" or "Franklin Roosevelt". We will focus on Russell's problem in this section, and Frege's in the next.

Russell's problem is that *names can be meaningful even though they lack a referent*.[19] Witness 'Santa Claus', which does not apply to any object in the entire universe, past, present, or future. It can nevertheless be used in true sentences, which implies that it is meaningful. An example is following 'negative existential':

(12) Santa does not exist.

This sentence (in which 'does' is tenseless) does not suffer the curious fate of having a meaningless subject because it is true. If its subject were meaningless, the whole sentence would be meaningless, which would imply that it is not true after all. Conversely, the mere fact that 'God exists' is thoroughly meaningful does not prove its truth ('The Quick Ontological Argument').[20] And *pace* Evans (1985),[21] 'Santa Claus brings lots of presents' expresses a thought and belief that delights millions of youngsters every year. The arguments presented in §10.2 that names are meaningful apply just as well to 'vacuous' or 'empty' names. Thus truth conditions can be provided just as readily for sentences with empty name as for those with bearers. For example, (13) is true even though 'Santa' has no bearer. But it could not be true or false if 'Santa' were meaningless.

(13) 'Santa flies long distances' is true if and only if Santa flies long distances.

Similarly, the fact that a speaker knows that 'Santa Claus' applies to an object iff it is Santa Claus is good evidence that the speaker understands the term (Sainsbury 1999: 245–6; 2000: 57ff). The meaning of 'John believes in Santa Claus' is determined compositionally by the meanings of its components in the regular way, and differs in meaning from 'Johnny believes in the Tooth Fairy' because of the difference in meaning between 'Santa Claus' and 'the Tooth Fairy'.

Travis (1985) claims that there is a general 'stricture' on the use of names, requiring that the speaker know who he is talking about when using one. He further claims that nonreferring names should not be used, and that if they are used anyway, the speaker would not have said anything that could be true. So let me now make the following statement.

(14) My son John believed that Santa brought the Christmas presents when he was four.

Do I know who I am talking about? Of course: Santa Claus. That is who my son believed brought the Christmas presents. I know, of course, that Santa Claus does not exist, but John thought he did. We are all able to think the thought (14) expresses, and except for those hopelessly in the grip of Millianism, we recognize that it is likely to be true. It is because what (14) says is true that John was happy that he left cookies and milk on the coffee table in front of the fireplace, and did so again the next year. In contrast, the embedded sentence 'Santa brought the Christmas presents when he (John) was four' is not true, from which we can infer that John's belief was not true.

For an example of a sentence that violates Travis's stricture, consider (15), which contains a name I just made up.

(15) John believed that Anats brought the Christmas presents.

This is a sentence we should never use because we could not possibly have any idea who we were talking about. The sentence could express a thought if some real or fictional person were given the name 'Anats'. But since that is a completely meaningless sequence of letters, (15) expresses no thought and thus is neither true nor false. (15) does not ascribe any belief to John. The contrast between (14) and (15) could not be more striking. If Millianism were true, however, (14) should be as meaningless as (15).

Currie (1990: Ch. 4) has suggested a mixed view, according to which the meaning of a referring name is its reference, while the meaning of an empty name is given by a synonymous description.[22] But the objections to classical descriptivism apply even to empty names. First, consider 'Vulcan', which Leverrier introduced as the name of the planet he hypothesized to exist between Mercury and the sun in order to account for the observed perturbation in Mercury's orbit. Even in Leverrier's mouth, 'Vulcan might not have been between Mercury and the Sun' was not ambiguous the way it would be if 'Vulcan' meant "the planet between Mercury and the Sun". And for those of us who picked up the name from people who picked up the name from . . . Leverrier, 'If Vulcan exists, it is between Mercury and Mars' does not express a self-evident truth. We might mistakenly think Vulcan was supposed to be between Mercury and Venus. All of us, including Leverrier, might imagine that astronomers actually found Vulcan in the night sky about where Leverrier predicted, only to determine that what they observed actually orbited between Mercury and Venus, and accounted for only part of the perturbation of Mercury's orbit (Leverrier had miscalculated a bit). Second, fictional names like 'Santa Claus' and 'Sherlock Holmes' seem more similar to 'Aristotle' and 'Brahms' semantically than to descriptive names like 'World War II' or 'Chapter 1'. Fictional names, for example, are rigid: they denote the same object in all worlds in which they have a referent. A world in which Sherlock Holmes became a spy rather than a detective is still one in which Sherlock Holmes exists. Even if 'the F' would denote Sherlock Holmes if he existed, 'The F is G' is not *about* Sherlock Holmes in the same way 'Sherlock Holmes is G' is (cf. Miller 1975: 338). Third, Braun (1993: 454) observed that it seems intolerable to claim that 'Vulcan' in fact is synonymous with a description, but would have been a mere tag if only Vulcan had existed.[23] The problem is particularly acute with a name like 'God'. We can hardly claim that whether or not 'God' is synonymous with 'the perfect being' or some other description depends on whether or not it turns out that the name actually has a referent. The existence of a descriptive meaning does not seem contingent on existence claims in this way, and it is hard to see how it could be given that the reference of a term is determined in part by its meaning.

Adams, Fuller, and Stecker (1997) maintain that the meaning of a name is its bearer, and so conclude that vacuous names are meaningless. Nevertheless, following Braun (1993), Adams *et al.* maintain that sentences with vacuous names like 'Vulcan is small' do have meanings, and express something that can play an inferential role in thought. They have the meaning and 'information content' of open sentences or predicates, and what they express are 'incomplete' propositions, which have an empty subject slot.

> The semantics of 'Ivan Ilych got married' used within Tolstoy's novella is that of 'x got married' (where 'x' is a place holder for a referent in a structured entity that is an incomplete proposition).                    (Adams, Fuller, and Stecker 1997: 132)[24]

There are internal difficulties with this theory. First, the claim that 'Vulcan is small' has a meaning even though 'Vulcan' is meaningless entails that the meaning of a simple subject predicate sentence in English is not compositional—that a subject-predicate sentence magically gets a meaning despite having meaningless components. It would be better therefore to say not that 'Vulcan' is completely meaningless, but that it is a variable—that is, that it has the same meaning as 'x'. This seems patently false, however. Names function as constants, not variables. Second, since an open sentence like 'x does not exist' does not express something we can believe, it does not express something that can serve as the premise or conclusion of an inference.[25] The theory falsely predicts, moreover, that a sentence like 'Vulcan does not exist' does not have a truth value (because it has the meaning of an open sentence), and has the same meaning as 'Santa Claus does not exist'. Adams *et al.* (1997: 132, 145) concede that these results are 'surprising', and try to explain how sentences with the same meaning can nonetheless 'function' differently: they contain different names associated with different descriptions, and therefore 'pragmatically impart' different true sentences like 'The tenth planet does not exist' or 'The resident of the North Pole does not exist'. But these observations do not suffice to explain away our belief that 'Vulcan does not exist' itself is literally true and different in meaning from any statement about Santa Claus (see §11.4–11.6).

A separate challenge is to explain what an incomplete proposition is. Millians tend to be Russellians, who hold that propositions are n-tuples consisting of individuals and properties (or relations). If the meaning of a subject predicate sentence '*Ps*' is the n-tuple ⟨*s*, *being P*⟩ consisting of the referent of '*s*' and the property expressed by '*P*', then sentences with non-denoting names have no meanings. The n-tuple ⟨*s*, *being P*⟩ does not exist unless *s* exists. It is not that ⟨Vulcan, being a planet⟩ is 'gappy' or 'incomplete'. It does not exist at all.[26] Braun (1993: 462) postulates instead that the meaning of '*Ps*' is the n-tuple ⟨{*s*}, *being P*⟩ consisting of the set containing the referent of '*s*' and the property expressed by '*P*'. A proposition is incomplete for Braun if its first element is the empty set. The corresponding truth rule would say that ⟨{*s*}, *being P*⟩ is true iff the individual in {*s*} (not the set itself) has the property of being P. When {*s*} is empty, Braun's formulation makes incomplete propositions vacuously false. The negation '−*Ps*' is true iff '*Ps*' is false.

There is an element of arbitrariness in Braun's theory. Why should we maintain that 'Vulcan is a planet' expresses ⟨{}, *being P*⟩ rather than ⟨{{}}, *being P*⟩, ⟨{}, {*being P*}⟩, or ⟨*being P*, {}⟩? An arbitrary choice like this does not matter when we are doing formal semantics. There the only goal is to produce a mathematical model that correctly represents certain semantic features of expressions, such as how their truth values depend on the referents of their terms (cf.§14.5). But such an arbitrary choice is unacceptable in any foundational theory trying to say what meanings are, or what it is for expressions to have a meaning.[27]

Braun's rule correctly counts 'Vulcan does not exist' as true because it is the negation of 'Vulcan exists', which his rules count as false. But Braun's view incorrectly rules that 'Pegasus is a mythical object' and 'Vulcan was a figment of Leverrier's imagination' are both false rather than true. Braun's view would also seem to rule incorrectly that 'Vulcan exists' is not only false but necessarily false. For the empty set is necessarily empty. Hence the incomplete proposition expressed by 'Vulcan exists' is necessarily false. Technicalities aside, if 'Vulcan' is meaningless as Braun maintains, how can it pick out a possible object whose actual existence would make 'Vulcan exists' true? How does 'Vulcan exists' differ from 'Canvul exists'? Why should we maintain that one expresses an incomplete proposition while the other expresses no proposition at all? How can we account for the fact 'If it exists, Vulcan is a tenth planet' is true, while 'If it exists, Pegasus is a tenth planet' is false?

Finally, Braun's theory shares one of the most objectionable features of the Adams, Fuller, Stecker theory: it rules that 'Vulcan does not exist' has the same meaning as 'Santa Claus does not exist' because they both express the incomplete proposition ⟨{}, *existing*, NEG⟩. As Reimer (2001: 502ff) observed, Braun's theory does not account for the fact that 'Vulcan does not exist' expresses a thought *about* Vulcan rather than Pegasus. Furthermore, a sentence like 'If Vulcan exists, then the proposition that Vulcan exists is true' seems to express a self-evident logical truth. But if Braun's theory were correct, it would express a necessary falsehood. Braun observes that the difference in the 'cognitive significance' of the sentences could be explained by hypothesizing that they express different mental representations, with mental terms representing Santa Claus or Vulcan. But he does not explain why it would be preferable to insist that the sentences nevertheless have the same meaning rather than switching to the view that they have different meanings because they express different mental representations.

## 10.5   NO SENSE: FREGE'S PROBLEM

Frege's objection to referential theories of meaning is that terms may differ in meaning even though they have the same referent. Countless examples come to mind instantly, such as 'the square root of 4' and 'the cube root of 8', both of which refer to the number 2. Directed specifically against Millian theories, Frege's problem would be that *proper names may differ in meaning even though they name the same object*. In this case, examples do not flood in. Well-known names for the same thing like 'Beijing' and 'Peking', or 'Atlantic' and 'Atlantik', or 'Jack Kennedy' and 'John F. Kennedy', are plausibly synonymous. Philosophers often use 'Phosphorus' and 'Hesperus'. We know that the ancients used these as names of the morning star and the evening star respectively without realizing that they were one and the same. But we moderns do not use 'Phosphorus' and 'Hesperus' except as objects of historical or linguistic study. I myself can never remember which is which. I sometimes hear them as synonymous with 'the morning star' and 'the evening star', and sometimes as synonymous with 'Venus'. So they are not good examples of standard names with different senses.

Examples can readily be found, however, in cases where people have two or more identities. *Pseudonyms*, *screen names*, and *aliases* are often adopted to conceal one's identity. They could not serve this purpose if they were synonymous with one's given name. Examples include 'Mark Twain' for 'Samuel Clemens', 'Cary Grant' for 'Archie Leach', and "Carlos 'The Jackal'" for 'Ilich Ramirez Sanchez'. Most of us, however, cannot feel the full force of these examples because we did not know the referent as a private person and learned the second names as alternates for the first. It was only after hearing about Carlos's terrorist activities for years that we learned that his original name was 'Ilich Sanchez'. We can appreciate, however, that the CIA and other intelligence agencies knew who Carlos was, and later came to know who Ilich Sanchez was, before being able to establish that they were one and the same individual. And we are familiar with the sort of evidence the jury who convicted Ilich Sanchez of Carlos's murders had to use to make this identification. We know that before the identity was established, people were using both names with complete competence, but not as synonyms. Similarly, we can readily put ourselves in the position of people who knew Archie Leach well as a youngster, lost track of him for years, and later were surprised to learn that he became Cary Grant, the famous movie star.

It is hard to find actual cases like these in which all readers are in the position of Interpol or the childhood friends of Archie Leach. Such a case will arise the day Woodward and Bernstein reveal who Deep Throat is. Bob

Woodward and Carl Bernstein were the Washington Post reporters who broke the Watergate scandal in the 1970s. 'Deep Throat' is the name they gave to their secret informant high inside the Nixon administration, who provided key tips in the Watergate scandal. Deep Throat is undoubtedly a well-known public figure with a household name, perhaps Alexander Haig or even Henry Kissinger. We do not know what Deep Throat's 'real' name is. But we do know that it exists, and that it is not synonymous with 'Deep Throat'.

In some respects the most effective examples involve names of fictional characters, like 'Superman' and 'Clark Kent'. Here, everyone knows the relevant facts. In reality, the names have no referent. In the story, they refer to the same individual. The people in the story are fully competent with the names, applying both on the basis of visual recognition. But they do not realize that the names apply to the same individual, and so do not treat them as synonyms. We can use the well-known story to represent actual cases that are not common knowledge. Just as important is the fact that we do not use the names as synonyms in describing what goes on in the story. We use 'Lois Lane does not realize that Clark Kent is Superman' to describe one of its key elements. We cannot use 'Lois Lane does not realize that Clark Kent is Clark Kent' for that purpose.

Suppose the Millian were to insist that even 'Superman' and 'Clark Kent' have to have the same meaning given that they have the same referent. How could the sense theorist respond without simply begging the question? In the case of pairs like 'the square root of 4' and 'the cube root of 8', we can rely on the principle of compositionality, and argue that the descriptions have different meanings because their components '4' and '8', and 'square' and 'cube', have different meanings and references. Such an argument cannot be run when one or both of the expressions has no grammatical structure, as in the case of proper names. The sense theorist can first appeal to linguistic intuition. 'Superman' and 'Clark Kent' *seem* to be far from synonymous. They seem as different in meaning as 'the man from Krypton with super powers' and 'the klutsy reporter for the Daily Planet'. Without supplementary argument, however, the Millian is likely to charge that our intuitions have been infected by a theoretical commitment to the sense theory.

The sense theorist can supplement the appeal to intuition by relying again on the principle of compositionality, this time looking at compounds containing the coreferential names. The *principle of substitutivity of synonyms* says that substituting synonyms for synonyms in a compositional compound must leave the meaning of the compound unchanged. Thus we can observe that if 'water' were synonymous with '$H_2O$', then (16a) and (16b) should also be synonymous.

(16) (a) John Dalton believed that water is HO.
    (b) John Dalton believed that $H_2O$ is HO.

But we know that these differ in meaning because the first is true and the second is false. Sentence (16b) is false because the father of atomic chemistry knew that a molecule with one hydrogen atom was different from a molecule with two hydrogen atoms. Sentence (16a) is true because Dalton did not realize that in the gaseous state, oxygen atoms occur in pairs.[28] The same argument works with names. Consider:

(17) (a) Lois Lane believes that Clark Kent is Clark Kent.
(b) Lois Lane believes that Clark Kent is Superman.

We use these sentences to express very different thoughts. Sentence (17a) is true because Lois believes elementary tautologies. Sentence (17b) is false because Lois was fooled by Superman's Clark Kent disguise. Much of the Superman story would make no sense if (17b) were true. The Millian might object that the sentences in (17) do not actually have any truth values, refusing to take this fictional example to represent actual cases. But (17a) and (17b) do have different truth values in other possible worlds. And the same point can be made with the following, which have opposite truth values even in the actual world.

(18) (a) In the Superman story, Lois Lane believes Clark Kent is Clark Kent.
(b) In the Superman story, Lois Lane believes Clark Kent is Superman.

If 'Superman' and 'Clark Kent' were synonymous, then (18a) and (18b) should be synonymous. But one is true and the other false, so they must differ in meaning.

The semantic contrast between the members of the above pairs is no less evident than when co-referential definite descriptions, indexicals, or even common nouns appear in place of names.[29]

(19) (a) Lois Lane believes that her bespectacled co-worker is her bespectacled co-worker.
(b) Lois Lane believes that her bespectacled co-worker is the man with X-ray vision.

Just as the difference in meaning between the members of (19) can be attributed to the difference in meaning between 'her bespectacled co-worker' and 'the man with X-ray vision' (despite the fact that they have the same referent), so the difference in meaning between the sentences in (17) and (18) should be attributed to the difference in meaning between 'Clark Kent' and 'Superman'. Given our knowledge of the story, moreover, it seems evident that (19b) is false *because* (17b) is false. The argument here is *not* that (19) supports the conclusion that names have descriptive meanings. The point is that names are like descriptions in having meanings distinct from their referents. The Fregean theory errs in assimilating proper names too closely to definite descriptions (Chapter 12), but the Millian theory errs by making them too different.

The assumption that that-clauses are semantically regular, in the sense that the meaning of sentences containing them is determined compositionally by the meanings of its component words and the way they are put together, may of course be questioned. But compositionality is the norm in natural languages (§5.6), and there is no reason independent of the referential theory for denying that the sentences (17) are semantically regular. On the contrary, independent evidence supporting compositionality comes from substituting terms whose synonymy or non-synonymy is not in dispute. Replacing 'water' with 'oil' or 'steel' would change the meaning of (16a) in predictable ways. We have already observed that replacing 'her bespectacled co-worker' with the co-referential but nonsynonymous 'the man with X-ray eyes' changes the meaning of (19a) predictably. Similarly, the substitution of undisputed synonyms—such as '3 > 2' and 'Three is greater than two'—after 'S believes that' has no effect on meaning.

It is sometimes suggested that belief statements are in some way metalinguistic, so that (17a) and (17b) differ in meaning only because 'Superman' and 'Clark Kent' are different names.[30] But substitution of clear synonyms in belief contexts does not affect meaning in this way; try 'two' and '2', for example, or 'Dr. Smith' and 'Doctor Smith', or 'premise' and 'premiss'. Moreover, there is evidence that sense differs from reference even when only one name is involved. Ambiguous sentences like (20a) and (20b), for example, are contradictory only when 'Roosevelt' has the same meaning in both occurrences.

> (20) (a) George believes that Roosevelt was the 26th president.
> (b) George does not believe that Roosevelt was the 26th president.

It is not enough that 'Roosevelt' has the same referent on both occasions, as can be seen by imagining the fantastic discovery that Teddy Roosevelt went into hiding, took on a new identity, and emerged as the apparently much younger Franklin, thereby fulfilling his dream of a third term in office.[31]

Furthermore, belief contexts are not the only ones in which the substitution of co-referential names fails to produce synonymous sentences. Consider:

> (21) (a) It is self-evident (*a priori*, logically true) that Clark Kent is Clark Kent.
> (b) It is self-evident (*a priori*, logically true) that Clark Kent is Superman.
> (22) (a) Given Lois Lane's evidence, it is likely (certain, obvious) that Clark Kent is Clark Kent.
> (b) Given Lois Lane's evidence, it is likely (certain, obvious) that Clark Kent is Superman.

These pairs do not strike anyone as saying the same thing. With the possible exception of people trying to defend Millianism, or those fixated on the transparent interpretation of that-clauses, we take the (a) sentence in each pair to be true and the (b) sentence to be false.

Byrne and Thau (1996) defend the 'Hybrid View' according to which sentences containing co-referential names have the same meaning but express different beliefs. But once it is granted that *expression* can differ from *reference*, we get a better theory of *meaning* by identifying it with expression rather than reference. The alternative is not only needlessly counterintuitive, but curiously perplexing. It entails that we do not have the ability to produce a sentence that *means* exactly *what we believe*. The theory grants that believing that Clark Kent is Clark Kent is different from believing that Clark Kent is Superman. So why can't we use one sentence to mean exactly what we believe when we believe that Clark Kent is Clark Kent and another sentence to mean exactly what we believe when we believe that Clark Kent is Superman? That is, why can't we use one sentence to mean that Clark Kent is Clark Kent, and another to mean that Clark Kent is Superman? Indeed, is this not what the sentences 'Clark Kent is Clark Kent' and 'Clark Kent is Superman' *do* mean?

Most importantly, once it is granted that 'Clark Kent is Clark Kent' and 'Clark Kent is Superman' express different beliefs, there is a simple argument that 'Clark Kent' and 'Superman' differ in meaning.[32] The belief expressed by the first sentence is the belief that Clark Kent is Clark Kent, and the belief expressed by the second is the belief that Clark Kent is Superman. If these beliefs are different, then it is possible for Lois to have one without having the other. If Lois has the belief that Clark Kent is Clark Kent, then sentence (17a) is true. If she does not have the belief that Clark Kent is Superman, then sentence (17b) is false. Since it is possible for these sentences to differ in truth value in the same context, they must have different meanings. Given that they are compositional compounds, the difference in meaning of the sentences must be due to a difference in meaning between 'Clark Kent' and 'Superman'.

## 10.6 MODAL MILLIANISM

The moderate Millian theories we have considered so far are extensionalist, in that the meaning of a proper name is taken to be its extension. Modal forms of Millianism identify the meaning of a name with an *intension* or *character*. The intension of a proper name is defined as a function from possible worlds to the extension of the name in those worlds. Since 'Aristotle' refers to Aristotle in every possible world, the intension of 'Aristotle' is the constant function whose value is Aristotle for every possible world. The intension for a description like 'the teacher of Alexander' would be a variable function, whose value is Aristotle for the actual world, and Plato in a possible world in which Plato was the teacher of Alexander. The theory that the meaning of a definite description is its intension is not refuted by the fact that 'the golden mountain' is meaningful despite having no referent. For while there are no golden mountains in the actual world, golden mountains are possible. There is a possible world in which Mt. Everest is the golden mountain, and a world in which Mt. Blanc is. Hence the intension for 'the golden mountain' will be a function whose value is Mt. Everest in one world, Mt. Blanc in another, and which has no value for the actual world. The intension theory also seems to have no difficulty with referentless names like 'Pegasus.' For while Pegasus does not exist in the actual world, it does exist in other possible worlds. So it seems that the intension for 'Pegasus' would be the function whose value is Pegasus for any world in which Pegasus exists.

The apparent ability of modal Millianism to handle referentless names is an illusion. Without unrealistic existence and identity assumptions, intension functions whose values are the referents of the terms whose meanings are to be represented cannot account adequately for the intentionality of meaning. A *function* is a set of ordered pairs satisfying the constraint that whenever the first member (or *argument*) is the same, the second member (or *value*) is the same. An ordered pair exists only if its members exist. Consequently the value of any function must exist: *If $f(x) = a$, then $\exists y[f(x) = y]$.* Since Pegasus does not exist, it cannot be the value of any intension function for any of its arguments. When w is a possible world, '$f(w) = k$' represents more than the fact that k exists *in* w. It also entails that k exists. This implication is false when '$k$' is 'Pegasus.' Pegasus exists in many possible worlds, just as he exists in a familiar myth; but he does not exist. Pegasus is an imaginary creature, not a real horse. Any theory entailing that Pegasus exists (i.e., that $\exists x[x = \text{Pegasus}]$) is false and unworthy of serious scholarly attention. Some maintain that 'exists' is ambiguous, meaning "exists in the actual world" in one sense, and "exists in some possible world" in another. But there is no sense in which 'Pegasus exists' is true, or in which it follows from 'It is possible that Pegasus exists'.

Frege's puzzle is no less problematic for modal Millianism. The theory has some success with coextensive definite descriptions that differ in meaning. Even though 'the 35th president' and 'the president assassinated in Dallas' have the same referent in the actual world, they designate different people in different possible worlds. Hence the intensions of the descriptions are as different as their meanings. But modal Millianism cannot handle co-extensive proper names in the same way. The transitivity of identity entails that identical objects are the values of all the same functions: *If $f(x) = y$ and $y = z$, then $f(x) = z$.* Since Archie Leach is Cary Grant, any intension whose value is Archie Leach for a given argument is a function whose value is Cary Grant. Since 'Archie Leach' and 'Cary Grant' have the same intension despite differing in meaning, the meaning of a proper name cannot be identified with its intension. We will show in Chapter 14 how a possible world semantics can accommodate the intentionality of meaning. But that approach abandons the Millian assumption that the values of the intension functions are the extensions of the terms whose meaning is being represented.

Pelczar and Rainsbury (1998) identify the meaning of a name with a *character*, defined as a function from contexts to intensions. Kaplan (1977) showed that many features of the semantics of indexical terms can be handled by identifying their meaning with a variable character. Suppose I say 'I am a philosopher'. Since Wayne Davis uttered this sentence, it is true in any possible world iff Wayne Davis is a philosopher in that world. Hence the intension for 'I' on this occasion must be a constant function from possible worlds to Wayne Davis. This intension cannot be identified with the *meaning* of the indexical. For if William Clinton utters the same sentence with the very same meaning, the intension assigned to 'I' on that occasion would have to be the function from any possible world to William Clinton. The referents and intensions of indexicals vary from context to context, but their meanings do not. In Kaplan's framework, one thing that is constant in the case of indexicals is their character. The character for 'I' used deictically is taken to be a function from any context of utterance to the intension whose value is always the speaker in that context. On this approach, it is natural to assume that the character function for names like those for common nouns would be constant functions, since standard names are not indexical. Thus the character for 'Wayne Davis' would be a constant function from any context of utterance to the intension whose value at any world is Wayne Davis. You would make the same statement by saying 'Wayne Davis is a philosopher' as I would.

While standard character theory accounts nicely for the key difference between names and indexicals, it does not account fully for the semantics of names. The theory will not enable the Millian to account for the difference in meaning between 'Cary Grant' and 'Archie Leach'. For the character of both will be the constant function whose value in every context is the intension function whose value at any world is Cary Grant, i.e., Archie Leach. Pelczar and Rainsbury try to avoid Frege's puzzle by assigning names nonstandard character functions. They observe that names are like indexicals in that the same name may have different referents and intensions in different contexts.[33] In some contexts, 'Roosevelt' refers to Theodore Roosevelt. In others, it refers to Franklin Roosevelt. Kaplan maintained that names like 'Roosevelt' are ambiguous, so he assigned them one character for each meaning. For Kaplan, context determines which character is intended.[34]

Pelczar and Rainsbury maintain that names are indexical, so they assign just one character function to each name. Names differ from standard indexicals, on their view, because of the particular contextual factor that determines the reference of a name. The critical factor for them is the 'dubbing' that is 'in force' and 'prominent' for the name in any given context. In the case of 'Roosevelt', two dubbings include Teddy Roosevelt's parents naming Teddy at birth, and Franklin Roosevelt's parents naming Franklin at birth. Pelczar and Rainsbury say that 'a dubbing is *in force* in a given context if in that context the item that was dubbed in that dubbing bears the name it received in that dubbing'(1998: 294). Thus the original dubbing in which the name 'Madagascar' was given to the African mainland is no longer in force, but both dubbings of 'Roosevelt' are still in force. When two dubbings are in force, 'one of the competing dubbings must be brought to prominence in order to determine a unique referent for the name' (1998: 295). All they say about prominence is that features of the conversation are important factors. Pelczar and Rainsbury thus propose that 'Hesperus', 'Phosphorus', and 'Venus' differ in meaning because their characters are different. The character for 'Hesperus' assigns it the intension whose value is the planet Venus at any world when the dubbing of the evening star as 'Hesperus' is in force and prominent, and assigns it the intension whose value is a god when a different dubbing is prominently in force. The character for 'Venus' assigns it one intension when the planet's dubbing is prominently in force, and another when the goddess's dubbing is prominently in force. Let us refer to the sorts of functions Pelczar and Rainsbury assign to names as *PR-characters*, to distinguish them from the character functions Kaplan assigned to names.

We should first observe that possession of a PR-character does not make a term univocal or indexical. If it did, then we should have to conclude that common nouns like 'bank' are univocal and indexical, which would be absurd. Let us refer to the first use of a general term that subsequently becomes conventional as an 'introduction'. The introduction might be ostensive ("Let us call this sort of animal a 'kangaroo'"), verbal ("Let us call female foxes 'vixen'"), or implicit (people just start using 'ute' to mean "sports utility vehicle"). The content of a general term on any given occasion depends on which introduction is in force and prominent just as much as the content of a name depends on which dubbing is in force and prominent. Thus we can view 'bank' as having a variable character function that assigns it one intension (taking us from any world to commercial banks) when one introduction is prominent, a second intention (taking us from any world to river banks) when another introduction is prominent, and so on. Pelczar and Rainsbury claim that 'In contrast to indexicals, a non-indexical expression like 'excellent' does not depend in any way for its literal content upon extra-semantic features of its context of utterance' (1998: 305). There is no basis for this claim if their theory of names is correct.

In support of their theory that names are indexical, Pelczar and Rainsbury cite terms like 'Mom' and 'Dad'. These expressions are clearly indexical, in that their referent is determined by familial relationships to the speaker. They also behave in many respects like proper names. Another example is 'May 9th', which in the absence of a year specification refers to May 9th of *this year.* Thus there appears to be a class of *indexical names*, which forms a subclass of the logically descriptive names discussed in §12.1. But our focus is on *standard* names like 'Roosevelt' and 'Aristotle'. The referent of a standard proper name is not determined by contextual factors the way the referent of an indexical name is. The same goes for standard common names.

Standard names differ from indexicals in that the referent of a standard name on a given occasion is determined completely by the meaning of the name on that occasion together with the identities of objects in the world. Which meaning of any expression is operative on a particular occasion is determined completely by what the speaker means (§5.3). The referent of an indexical, in contrast, is determined by a third and independent contextual factor. If Bill used 'It rained today' deictically on June 10, 2004, and he meant "today" by 'today', then the indexical referred to June 10, 2004. This is the case even if Bill intended to refer to June 11. Nothing about the contexts in which the name 'Roosevelt' might be used determines what it refers to in the same speaker-independent way. If *I* mean "Franklin Roosevelt" by 'Roosevelt', then the *name* 'Roosevelt' refers to Franklin on that occasion. This will be true even if everyone else in the context is using the name to refer to Teddy Roosevelt. In this respect, names are just like ambiguous general terms. The fact that money and lending is being discussed is a clue that 'bank' denotes commercial banks on a given occasion. But whether it denotes commercial banks or river banks on that occasion is determined by what the speaker meant, and thus by the speaker's intentions.[35]

Whatever their possession implies about the univocity or indexicality of names, we cannot account for the meaning of names by assigning them PR-characters. First, one of the indices defining PR-characters is the set of dubbings 'in force' in a context. As we saw, to say that a dubbing is in force is to say that the individual dubbed bears the name assigned in the dubbing. But to say that an individual 'bears' a name is just to say that the name refers to that individual. As a result, Pelczar and Rainsbury's characters are not *reference determining factors*, and thus are not plausibly identified with meanings. PR-characters are functions that take a set of name referents as inputs and produce one of those referents as output.

Second, the Pelczar–Rainsbury theory rules that proper names like 'Germany' and 'Deutschland' could not have the same meaning. The character associated with the latter would not take us from any context to an intension whose value at every world is the little town in Iowa named 'Germany', and the character associated with the former would never take us from any context to an intension whose value at every world is a novel entitled 'Deutschland'. The theory would also rule that 'New York' never has the meaning of 'New York City'. These names would have different character functions because the former can refer to many things the latter cannot.

Third, the Pelczar–Rainsbury theory implies that every time a name is given to a new object, its meaning changes. But while naming a new movie 'Earth' may give that name a new meaning, the old meanings of the term did not change. As a result, 'Earth is the third planet' still has the meaning it had before even though it now has an additional meaning. The Pelczar–Rainsbury theory implies, incorrectly, that the sentence no longer means what it did before. The theory further implies that few if any people know the meaning of any name. For even widely known names like 'Aristotle' and 'Hitler' are borne by people, places and things that are not widely known. I doubt that anyone knows the PR-character of these names. At best we know part of the range of the functions. Given the millions of people bearing the name 'John', I believe it is humanly impossible for anyone to know its PR-character (contrast Pelczar and Rainsbury 1998: 297).

PR-characters could be construed as determinants of *applied* reference (see §5.3). The Pelczar–Rainsbury theory essentially says that what a name refers to on any occasion is that currently conventional referent whose dubbing is 'prominent' in that context. Thus 'Roosevelt' refers to Teddy Roosevelt in any context in which the bestowal of the name 'Roosevelt' on Teddy Roosevelt is prominent. People who use the name 'Roosevelt' today, however, seldom if ever think about the acts in which Teddy Roosevelt and Franklin Roosevelt were given their names. So the prominence of a dubbing cannot be a psychological factor like its being the focus of attention. Pelczar and Rainsbury (1998: 295) say that the dubbing of Teddy might be raised to prominence in a context by the fact that the 26th president is being discussed. But while such facts may be a *clue* to reference, they do not *determine* reference. Even if people have been discussing Theodore Roosevelt, a man could use the name 'Roosevelt' to mean Franklin. And if he did, that is who the name would refer to on that occasion. The contextual factor that determines which of all objects bearing a name is the referent on a given occasion is *what the speaker means* by the name. If by 'Roosevelt' S means "Franklin Roosevelt", then 'Roosevelt' refers to him on that occasion. However, even if PR-characters are determinants of applied reference, they cannot be identified with applied word meanings. For 'Roosevelt' has just one PR-character, even though it means "Theodore Roosevelt" on some occasions and "Franklin Roosevelt" on others.

Finally, whether it is taken as a theory of word meaning or applied word meaning, the Pelczar–Rainsbury character theory does not account completely for coextensive names with different meanings—Frege's problem. It is quite possible, for example, that the two names have only one bearer each. As far as I know, this is true for 'Archie Leach' and 'Cary Grant'. Since these two terms have the same referent, there seems to be just one intension to be the value of their character functions on a Millian theory. Moreover, the Pelczar–Rainsbury theory has the same difficulty with

Russell's problem as other modal Millian theories. Since Pegasus does not exist, it is not the value of any function. Since 'Pegasus' has no intension, it has no character.

## NOTES

¹ See e.g., Mill 1879: Ch. 1.2; Frege 1892b: 58; 1918: 11–2; Russell 1910–11; 1912: Ch. 5; Burks 1951; Ryle 1957: 247–8; Ziff 1960: 102–4, 173–6; Zink 1963: 482–6; Vendler 1972: 74–82, 142; Loar 1976a: esp. 360–1; Lyons 1977: 202–4, 215–23; Castañeda 1977: 172–3; 1985; Burge 1977: 351–2, 354–62; McKinsey 1978: 180, 188–90; 1984: 506–7; 1999: 519–20, 527; 2002: 203, 206; Kaplan 1977: 485, 506, fn. 31; 1978: 22–3; Katz 1977a; 1986a: 74–6; 1990; 2001; Kripke 1979: 244, 246–8; Schwarz 1979: xii–xiii; Boër and Lycan 1980: 435–7; Chisholm 1981: 57–60; Searle 1983: Ch. 9; Barwise and Perry 1983: 197; Peacocke 1983: 196–8; Lycan 1984: 98; Luntley 1984: esp. 266, 279; Bertolet 1984a: 214; Salmon 1986: 1–9, 63–76, 125–6; 1989c: 444–5; 450–2; Allan 1986: 70–2; Laurier 1986: 43; Bach 1987a: Chs. 7–8; Fitch 1987: 70–7; 1993: 480–1; Perry 1988: 1; Pendelbury 1990: 527–9; Recanati 1990: 698;1993: 398; Braun 1991a; 294; 1998: 558; Wettstein 1991: esp. 20, 28; Pagin 1992: 28–9; Lehrer 1992a; 1992b: 126–7; Bealer 1993a: 19; Rosenberg 1993: 516; Adams and Stecker 1994; D. Sosa 1996: 396–9; Adams, Fuller, and Stecker 1997: 129, 131; Stalnaker 1997: 541; Wreen 1998: 325; Justice 2002; Soames 2002: 102, 161, 236. Reimer 2002 combines the two theories in a unique way, but still endorses the basic dichotomy.

² E.g., Marcus 1961: 11; 1993: xiii; Alston 1964a: 12; Heath 1967: 179; Katz 1977a: 12; 1979: 112; 1986a: 77–8; Algeo 1973: 44–6; Almog 1981: 366–8; Unger 1983: 4–5; Allan 1986: 71–100, 244; Lehrer 1992a: 395; 1992b: 126, 138; Bealer 1993a: 40; Napoli 1997: 188; Adams, Fuller, and Stecker 1997. According to Katz (1994: 32), Kripke held that proper names are 'as senseless as nonsense words like Bandersnatch' (in the unpublished Shearman lectures and the 1973 John Locke Lecture); cf. Kripke 1980: 32. Contrast Husserl 1900: §1.1.16; Katz 1977a: 58ff; 1979: 118–0; 1986a: 82–6; 1990; 1994; and Napoli 1997: 189–90.

³ Cf. Sainsbury 2000: 57–61.

⁴ There is also an idiomatic use of proper names as general terms denoting 'temporal parts' of the referent of the proper name, as in 'The Bill that my mother loved years ago is very different from the Bill that I know today'. And there are some specialized conventions whereby particular names become general, as illustrated by 'This is Bordeaux', in which 'Bordeaux' can be interpreted either as a proper name of a certain city or region of France or as a mass noun denoting the sort of wine produced in that region. In 'He bought a Picasso', the name would most naturally be interpreted as meaning 'a painting by Picasso'. Finally, there is a parallel convention, limited to the vocative, whereby common nouns are used as singular terms, as in 'Boy, look out!' (Thomsen 1997: 98). And in some cases, words are independently lexicalized as proper and common nouns (e.g., *Mother/mother*).

⁵ Katz 1977a: 12; 1979: 112. See also Rundle 1979: 71–2; Allan 1986: 71. Contrast Zink 1963: 494–5 and Linsky 1977: 7–8, 75.

⁶ Katz 1977a: 13; 1979: 112; 1986a: 77–8; 1990: 49; 1994: 18; 2001: 147. See also Algeo 1973: 44–6; Loar 1976a: 372; Bach 1987a: 34–5, 137, 144; 2002: 82; Napoli 1997: 188. Contrast Allerton 1987, who freely describes proper names as 'polysemous'; Geach 1962: 71, who uses 'equivocal'; Perry 1997b: 11; Soames 2002: 98.

⁷ The same confusion can be found in Almog 1981: 366–8 and Katz 1990: 49. Cf. Nelson (1992: 248), whose argument is considerably more plausible because he is concerned with a supposedly innate language.

⁸ See also *Meaning, Expression, and Thought* §10.6, where I argue that complex expressions with ambiguous components may well have thousands of senses.

[9] See also Allan 1986: 72; Lehrer 1992a: 395; 1992b: 126, 138; and H. H. Clark 1993: 302; Katz 2001: 148.

[10] The argument originates with Rundle 1979: 72–3, 79. See also Salmon 1986: 54; Yagisawa 1993a:141; Napoli 1997: §2; and Katz 2001: 148.

[11] See also Strawson 1950: 190; Ryle 1957: 247–8; Ziff 1960: 86, 93; Vendler 1967: 38; Katz 1977: 13; 58ff; 1979: 118–20; 1986a: 77–8; 1990: 49; 1994: 18; Evans 1982: 373; Lycan 1984: 99; McKinsey 1984: 511; 1994: 317; Marcus 1985/86: 203–4; Bach 1987a: 143; 2002: 76, 82; Castañeda 1989a: 53; 1990a: 197. Contrast Reid 1785: 465; Geach 1962: 27; Algeo 1973: 62–63; Lyons 1977: 222–3; Recanati 1993: 138, 144–6, 164; Perry 1997b: 11; Stroll 1998: 528; Pelczar 2001: 134.

[12] It is also unclear whether '8' or even 'eight' is properly classified as a name.

[13] Webster's *Encyclopedic Unabridged Dictionary* has an entry for '3-D' before 'three-dimensional', though, perhaps because it is never written 'three-D'.

[14] Sources: *Wikipedia, Nationmasater.com, Microsoft Encarta*.

[15] See also 'pitch names' in *The Norton/Grove Concise Encyclopedia of Music*.

[16] See e.g., Smullyan 1947: 140; Salmon 1986: 8, 21; Fitch 1987: 71; Recanati 1993: 137; Adams and Stecker 1994: Perry 1997b: §2; Soames 2002: 55ff.

[17] See e.g. Salmon 1989c: 444; Yagisawa 1993a: 142–3.

[18] Bolton 1996: 149; Sainsbury 2000: 62.

[19] I give this as 'Russell's Problem' because it is an instance of the general problem for the referential theory bearing his name. But in fact, Russell thought (at least on one occasion) that names were special, and held the Millian view that a name without a bearer was simply devoid of meaning (1938: 178–9).

[20] Cf. Sainsbury 2000: 60; 2001: 215.

[21] Sainsbury (1999) provides a careful and in depth rebuttal of Evans's argument that empty names have no meaning. See also Sainsbury 2000; and Ch. 11, fn. 33, below.

[22] See also Miller 1975: 345; Peacocke 1975: 221; Crimmins and Perry 1989: 704. Currie's actual view is more complex. He holds that names are synonymous with definite descriptions only in meta- and trans-fictional discourse. In fiction itself, Currie maintains that they are 'bound variables' (1990: 180–1), which resembles the view of Adams, Fuller, and Stecker 1997.

[23] See also Reimer 2002 and Sainsbury 2002: 68.

[24] See also Currie 1990; Adams and Fuller 1992; Adams and Stecker 1994: 390; Adams, Fuller, and Stecker 1997: 130. Cf. Yagisawa's (1998: 453) view that '*semantically* names are indistinguishable from variables.' Note the use-mention confusion in the passage quoted. The variable 'x' is a 'place-holder' for *terms*, not their referents.

[25] This is not to deny that open sentences can be used in derivations in many logical systems. Such derivations are sequences of sentences, not psychological processes.

[26] Contrast Salmon 1998: 307; Reimer 2001: 494ff.

[27] Cf. Benacerraf 1965; Wetzel 1989.

[28] Sources: Greenaway 1966: 146, 176; A. Thackray, 1972: 76, 86.

[29] Contrast Marcus 1975: 107–9.

[30] Cf. Richard 1990; 1993; 1995; Larsen and Ludlow 1993, esp. 1002. Contrast Sider 1995; Rieber 1997b; Saul 1999a; Soames 2002: 144–5, 155–9, 166–71.

[31] Similar cases were described by Geach 1980: 85, Salmon 1986: 75, and Heck 1995: 95–6. See also Burge 1977: 355; Kaplan 1990b: 107–9, 115; and Wettstein 1991: 176. Soames's (2002: 98–100) account of ambiguity overlooks this possibility. Castañeda (1985: 97) erroneously concluded that contradiction could be avoided in such cases only if the two tokens could not have the same referent. He thus ended up with a needlessly mysterious notion of a referent.

[32] Compare and contrast Heck 1995.

[33] Recanati (1993: Ch. 8) sketched a similar theory, and Pelczar 2001 responds to objections by Perry 1997b. See also Moore's (1999b) contextualist theory of belief sentences, and his view that different 'guises' or semantic entities are selected in different contexts to interpret names in belief sentences.

[34] Cf. Perry 1997b.

[35] Cf. Perry 1997b. Contrast Pelczar 2001: 150. Pelczar (2001: 134) argues against the thesis that names are ambiguous by claiming that names are not given multiple meanings in dictionaries. This reasoning was criticized in §10.3.

# Defenses of Millianism

Devitt (1989a, 1989b) has observed that the main reasons for the recent enthusiasm for Millian theories of meaning for names are the following theses: the falsity of the description theory, and the implication that names refer directly; the rigidity of names; and the causal theory of reference. All four, for example, are cited by Kripke (1979: 246–7).

These reasons provide little support for Millianism. The falsity of the description theory (Chapter 12) does not support Millian theories without the groundless Frege–Mill dichotomy. Standard names are rigid designators, but so are many definite descriptions (e.g., 'the square root of 4'), which have a sense distinct from their reference on anyone's view. We saw in §8.3 that the causal theory of reference is false. The most we can say is that a name has the meaning and reference it has in virtue of expressing a particular link in the typical causal chain connecting utterances of a name to its bearer (§13.5).

The arguments against Millianism, in contrast, are very powerful. We reviewed the reasons for thinking that the meaning of an expression is a property distinct from its reference in Chapter 9, and we saw in Chapter 10 that the same reasons tell against identifying the meaning of a name with its referent. Despite the lack of sound arguments for Millianism, and what seems to be an open and shut case against it, Millians have expended considerable energy and ingenuity in an effort to explain away the counterevidence. We will review the attempts in this chapter, and show that they are unsuccessful.

## 11.1 EXISTENCE FAILURES

Soames (2002: 91–5) tries to evade Russell's problem by saying that just as 'Socrates' refers to an object that existed in the past, so 'Vulcan' refers to an object existing in some other possible world (a hypothetical planet), and 'Sherlock Holmes' refers to a person existing in novels (a fictional detective).[1] Soames is here either (i) adopting radical modal realism or Meinongianism, or (ii) using an intentional sense of reference. Radical modal realism is the view that objects existing in other possible worlds are just as real as actual objects. On this view, 'Santa Claus exists' is just as true as 'George Bush exists'. In my view, radical modal realism is absurd. There is no sense in English in which 'Santa Claus exists' is true, or in which it follows from 'It is possible that Santa Claus exists'. Just as to run is to actually run, so to exist is to actually exist. Existing *in* a story, scenario, hypothetical case, or possible world does not prove existence. Any theory entailing the existence of Santa Claus is empirically unacceptable. To save the Millian theory from Russell's objection by adopting radical modal realism is to give up one of the principal strengths of the referential theory: its ontological economy and conservatism. Many have questioned whether ideas exist in general, and there are many unanswered questions about their nature. Many have questioned specifically whether a name like 'George Bush' expresses an idea, even if in general ideas exist. But there is no question that the name has a referent, and no serious questions about the nature of its referent. This advantage of the referential theory is lost if it is insisted that Santa Claus is just as real as George Bush.

Moreover, even radical modal realism does not completely eliminate Russell's problem. For there are meaningful names that could not possibly have a referent. Let us stipulate, for example, that ρ is the Russell set: the set of all sets that are not members of themselves. We know that ρ cannot possibly exist because if it did, it would have to be true that $\rho \in \rho$ iff $\rho \notin \rho$, which is a contradiction. So '$\Box - \exists x(x = \rho)$' is true. This means that 'ρ' is meaningful even though it does not have even a possible referent. Kripke (1972: 253, 763–4) suggested the thesis that '$\Box - \exists x(x = \mu)$' is true whenever 'μ' is the name of a mythical object. On his view, there is no such thing in any possible world as Pegasus. While I think Kripke's view is false at least for logically possible worlds, I see no grounds for dismissing it as meaningless or incoherent. But if the referential theory were true, '$\Box - \exists x(x = \text{Pegasus})$' would have to be false if it were meaningful. To avoid these problems, the Millian would have to adopt not just radical modal realism, but full-blown Meinongianism about the referents of names.

Alternatively, and much more plausibly, Soames could be shifting to an *intentional* sense of reference, making word reference more like speaker reference in one respect (cf. §8.2, §9.1). This is easy for an ideational theorist to do, for he can say that a name 'N' refers to Φ iff 'N' conventionally expresses the idea of Φ. But if 'refers' were taken intentionally in 'The meaning of a name is the object it refers to', it would no longer express the referential theory. It would not locate meaning in the language–world link. For in the intentional sense, reference is not a relation, and referents may be non-existent objects. If Soames accepted the definition of reference just offered, he would in essence be claiming that meanings are *objects of ideas*, and so adopting a form of the ideational theory. The only other alternative in sight is to rely on the fact that any meaningful term means something, and adopt the Meinongian view that what any term means counts as an object (see Edwards, Alston, and Prior 1967: 239–40). But meaning "Pegasus" cannot be treated as a relation to Pegasus (§2.8, §8.2). If referents are defined as objects of meaning, the referential theory can no longer be offered as an account of meaning.

Soames also points to some sentences in which names like 'Sherlock Holmes' do have a referent.[2] Thus we can truly say

(1) Sherlock Holmes is a fictional character.

Characters are real and important components of novels, which are brought into existence by the authors. They may be well developed, or poorly developed. Characters may be based on real people, or completely made up. We refer to characters when we are talking about literature. But in the first sentence of *The Hound of the Baskervilles* (2), the name is not referring to a component of a novel.

(2) Mr. Sherlock Holmes... was seated at the breakfast table.

The name has a perfectly good meaning in this sentence; indeed, that is its primary meaning. It has the same meaning in (3), a true statement made seriously outside the world of fiction.

(3) Sherlock Holmes does not exist.

The problem for the referential theory is that while Sherlock Holmes exists in stories, he does not exist in reality. This is what it means to say that he is a *merely* fictional character. Hence the name has no referent in the first sentence of Conan Doyle's most famous story, despite having a meaning.[3]

Soames might also point to the intuitive truth of sentences like (4), which seems to say that in some sense Vulcan does exist.[4]

(4) There are some things that do not exist, such as Vulcan.

On such an interpretation, however, (4) would be self-contradictory. In sentences like (4), however, 'There are some things that' does not represent the objectual existential quantifier '∃x'. Instead, it represents a substitutional quantifier. Thus (4) is equivalent to

(5) There are true substitution instances of statements of the form 'Φ does not exist'; an example is 'Vulcan does not exist'.

A claim like (5) is obviously true, and not at all self-contradictory. It in no way claims that Vulcan exists, and provides no support for the referential theory.

## 11.2 SUBSTITUTIVITY FAILURES

Stalnaker suggested an argument from common sense in favor of Millianism.

> If we ask, what does one have to know to understand a name? the naive answer is that one must know who or what it names—nothing more. (In contrast, no-one would be tempted to give this answer to the analogous question, of what one must know to understand a definite description.)
>
> (Stalnaker 1997: 544).[5]

The exact import of Stalnaker's knowledge condition can be questioned. Do we know who 'Deep Throat' names? There are many contexts in which we would not count as knowing this (e.g., those in which we are speculating on Deep Throat's identity). But there are others in which we would count as knowing who Deep Throat is (imagine a question on a history test in which important names from the Watergate era are listed and the student is to identify the person named; the answer 'Woodward and Bernstein's secret source' should be marked correct).[6] There is a clear sense in which we all know who 'Santa Claus' is the name of (Santa Claus, of course). But if that knowledge suffices to understand the name, then Stalnaker's commonsense principle provides no support for the Millian theory. If this knowledge does not seem sufficient, then Stalnaker's principle fails for a large class of standard names.

More importantly, a speaker knowing only who 'Carlos' and 'Ilich Ramirez Sanchez' name will not be able to grasp the large semantic difference between 'Carlos is Carlos' and 'Carlos is Ilich Ramirez Sanchez'. The speaker will not understand how 'Ilich's mother believes that Carlos is a terrorist' could be true while 'Ilich's mother believes that Ilich is a terrorist' is false. The speaker will also not understand why the CIA and other organizations had such a difficult time proving that 'Carlos is Sanchez' is true. In short, Stalnaker's thesis about names has all the difficulties of Davidson's thesis that all there is to knowing the meaning of a sentence is knowing its truth conditions (§9.3).[7]

In §10.5, we used examples like the following to argue that the coreferential names like 'Clark Kent' and 'Superman' do not have the same meaning. We use these sentences to express different thoughts, one of which is true in the Superman story, while the other is false.

(6) Lois Lane believes that Clark Kent is Clark Kent.
(7) Lois Lane believes that Clark Kent is Superman.

Soames (1995a: 519–21) and Braun (1998: 559) concede the force of these linguistic intuitions, but try to take the offensive, arguing that 'some of our intuitions about belief reports actually support' Millianism. Suppose Linda meets a politician, and quickly concludes that he is drunk, without learning who it is. I might say any of the following:

> (8) Linda believes that Gingrich is drunk [addressing someone who knows as well as I do that the man is Gingrich].
> (9) Linda believes that he is drunk [pointing at Gingrich].
> (10) Linda believes that you are drunk [addressing Gingrich himself].

In this case, the fact that 'Gingrich', 'he', and 'you' differ markedly in meaning does not matter at all. But this is clearly a case in which the belief ascriptions are intended *transparently*. It is on the *opaque* interpretation that substitutivity fails (§2.8). While there is an interpretation on which (8) is true (because the man happens to be Gingrich), there is another interpretation on which it is false (because Linda does not realize that it is Gingrich). Furthermore, some opaque constructions have no transparent interpretation at all.

> (11) Oedipus thought of Jocasta as his wife, not as his mother.
> (12) Johnny possesses the concept "water" but not the concept "$H_2O$".

In (11), the context occupied by 'Jocasta' is most naturally interpreted transparently, but the contexts occupied by 'his wife' and 'his mother' can only be opaque. The same is true of the contexts occupied by 'water' and '$H_2O$' in (12).

When defending the principle that substitution of synonyms in belief contexts results in synonymous sentences (§2.5), I observed that apparent exceptions arise when one of the terms is used metalinguistically or quotationally. Thus when we hear (14) as meaning "Henry believes that eye-doctors *are called 'oculists'* ", we may take it to be false even though (13) is true.

> (13) Henry believes that eye-doctors are eye-doctors.
> (14) Henry believes that eye-doctors are oculists.

We might say in that case "Henry didn't realize that eye-doctors are 'oculists' ". Rieber (1997b) suggested that substitutional failures involving co-designative singular terms be handled in the same way. In some cases, this is plausible. For example, when we hear (15) as true and (16) as false, we are most likely interpreting (15) as meaning "Ann did not realize that John Fitzgerald Kennedy was called 'JFK' ".

> (15) Ann did not realize that John Fitzgerald Kennedy was JFK.
> (16) Ann did not realize that John Fitzgerald Kennedy was John Fitzgerald Kennedy.

But not all substitutivity failures can be handled in this way, such as those involving 'water' and '$H_2O$', 'Jacosta' and 'his mother', and 'Superman' and

'Clark Kent'. It is true that Lois Lane does not believe that Clark Kent is called 'Superman'. But her ignorance is not merely linguistic. She knows who Clark Kent and Superman are, but thinks they are two different individuals.

J. Saul has suggested an ingenious counterargument for the Millian.[8] Even though the following sentences contain no psychological verbs or intensional contexts at all, they do not appear to be equivalent. Sentence (17) could well be true, it seems, while (18) is false.

> (17) Clark Kent went into the phone booth, and Superman came out.
> (18) Clark Kent went into the phone booth, and Clark Kent come out.

Any Fregean who insists that (17) and (18) are actually equivalent 'owes us a reason for supposing that one set of intuitions deserves to be taken so much more seriously than the other' (1997a: 107). How can we maintain that (17) and (18) are equivalent if we insist that pairs like (6) and (7) are not?

I believe we all recognize that something special is going on in the case of (17) and (18). While we understand the difference speakers would be communicating, we would acknowledge—at least after a little reflection—that the two statements are literally equivalent. For we know that Clark Kent and Superman are the same person. Hence if Superman came out of the phone booth, then it was Clark Kent who came out of the phone booth, even if he was coming out as Superman. A similar argument cannot be given in the case of (6) and (7) because beliefs can be false and incomplete. Hence what we believe about an object, in the opaque sense, cannot be validly inferred from facts about that object. Moreover, we can see that (18) follows from the stronger statement (19), which is obviously true in the case imagined.

> (19) Clark went into the phone booth and Clark came out, but he came out as Superman, not as Clark Kent.

Superman has two different public images or 'identities'. Superman can 'be himself', or he can put on his disguise and be Clark Kent. 'As' creates an opaque context. So even though Clark Kent is Superman, doing something as Clark Kent is not the same as doing it as Superman.

Once we reflect on what makes (19) stronger than (18), we realize what (17) and (18) are commonly used to communicate besides their literal meaning. In the most natural context of use, the user 'in the know' would use (17) to express the thought that the man who is both Clark Kent and Superman went into the phone booth as Clark Kent and came out as Superman. Knowledgeable speakers would similarly use (18) to say that the man went in as Clark Kent and came out as Clark Kent. Hence knowledgeable speakers would mean something true by (17) in the scenario imagined, and would meaning something false by (18).[9] This non-literal usage of (17) and (18) represents a common figure of speech, which I would classify as a type of *synecdoche*. In an attempt at humor I might similarly say, 'Kathy's husband takes out the garbage, Prof. Davis does not'. What I meant was true (I take out the garbage as part of my domestic responsibilities, not as part of my professorial responsibilities). What I said was false (the person who takes out Kathy's garbage, her husband, is me, Prof. Davis). Nunberg (1993: §3) noted that similar figures of speech are involved in 'The Founding Fathers gave me the power' (said by the president) and 'I am traditionally allowed...' (said by a prisoner). The non-literal interpretation of (17) and (18) is especially natural given that they are about a fictional character one of whose most salient traits is his dual identity.

Braun and Saul object to the sort of pragmatic explanation given above on the grounds that it lacks psychological reality.

> So, if these accounts were correct, you would surely have paused to consider whether the authors were thinking about aspects, before passing judgement on the truth-values of [(17) and (18)]; and you would have withheld judgment if you did not know, or were not sure, whether the authors were focused on aspects. But these predictions are incorrect. You did not pause to consider the knowledge and interests of the authors before making your judgments, and you did not withhold judgment on the sentences. On the contrary, you quickly and confidently made your judgments without any consideration of such matters.
>
> (Braun and Saul 2002: 10)

This objection falsely assumes that when we read display sentences like (17) and (18), we take them to be the utterances of a real speaker, and are concerned with what the sentences meant on the occasion of utterance, for which we would need to know what the speaker meant by them. On the contrary, when we read a display sentence, one or more propositions that it expresses simply come to mind. This is an associative process (§3.6), not the inferential 'working out' Grice had in mind. When evaluating the sentence as true or false, we interpret it as expressing one of those propositions (see Definition 9.1 in §9.4). In the case of (17) or (18), at least two propositions will come to mind: one is the proposition the sentence literally expresses, and another is the proposition the sentence would naturally be used to implicate. If we interpret the sentence as expressing the latter proposition, we might judge (18) to be false even though we would judge it to be true on its literal interpretation. So the fact that speakers in the know about Superman and Clark Kent would be most likely to interpret (17) and (18) non-literally explains why they would take them to be inequivalent, at least initially.[10]

Saul would also respond that if we appeal to pragmatics to explain why (17) and (18) appear to have different truth values, why not do the same for (6) and (7)? The short answer is that a pragmatic explanation is plausible for the one case but not the other. We believe that (7) is *literally* false even though (6) is true, and we continue to believe that (7) is false even when any implicatures are cancelled. If (7) were literally true, the story of Lois and

Superman would not make sense. Moreover, we can confirm the pragmatic account of the difference between (17) and (18) by noting that similar factors are at play when we interpret sentences that have no singular terms in them at all. As Predelli (2001) observed, we might say 'No one in this room is successful with women' if the Kryptonian were there in his Clark Kent disguise, but not if he were there in his Superman uniform. We might say it in the first case even though we know the statement to be literally false in order to implicate that the man of steel is not successful with woman when he is acting as Clark Kent. We might similarly use 'No one in this room is believed by Lois to be Clark Kent' in the second case but not the first. For we would implicate that she does not believe Superman to be Clark Kent in the second case, while implicating that she does not believe Clark Kent to be Clark Kent in the first case. We will devote §11.4 through §11.6 to showing that the most plausible pragmatic explanations of intuitive difference between sentences like (6) and (7) are unsuccessful.

## 11.3   THE KRIPKEAN DEFENSE

Kripke (1979) sought to defend the Millian theory against Frege's problem by undermining one argument for substitutivity failures.[11] He took the conclusion that substitution of one co-referential name for another in a belief context may change the truth value of the belief statement to depend on a generalization that relates what people believe to the sentences they use. The basic idea is that when a woman uses a sentence to make a statement, and takes it to be true, we can normally infer that she believes the proposition it expresses.[12] We can equally well infer that she is thinking that thought. The process is aptly called '*disquotation*'. We might try formulating the principle as follows.

> (20)   If S believes that 'p' is true, then S believes that p, provided S is a
>          normal speaker of the language to which 'p' belongs, and pro-
>          vided 'p' is nonindexical and unambiguous.

The nonindexicality clause keeps (20) from ruling that a woman believes that I am a woman from the fact that she utters 'I am a woman' with an affirmative nod. The requirement that 'p' be unambiguous is designed to protect (20) from cases in which S interprets 'The river rose over the bank' to mean that the river rose over the river bank while we (the speakers) use it to mean that the river rose over the savings bank. In that case, S can take the sentence to be true even though S is not thinking that the river rose over the savings bank. It is hard to find a sentence of any natural language that does not contain some indexicality or ambiguity. So the applicability of (20) is at best limited.

Moreover, the disquotation principle can fail for reasons not covered by the provisos. Even highly competent speakers make linguistic mistakes on occasion, or are ignorant of some vocabulary. Thus the normal speaker clause does not assure that S understands 'p'. Suppose a zoologist tells John that 'Tayra are oviparous' is true. John will undoubtedly take the sentence to be true. But like most other normal speakers of English, John does not know what either 'tayra' or 'oviparous' means. Hence he will not think that tayra are oviparous. And if he uses the sentence, he will express a different belief.

*Kripke's Puzzle*[13] demonstrates the possibility of a deeper class of exceptions. Kripke imagines that Pierre grows up in France as a native French speaker. He learns second hand about the city called 'Londres', and forms the opinion that it is pretty. Later, Pierre moves to a city in England, and picks up English from his neighbors. He learns first hand about the city they call 'London', and forms the opinion that it is ugly. He does not realize that it is the city he calls 'Londres'. He comes to think that 'Londres est jolie' and 'London is not pretty' are both true. Pierre does not seem guilty of self-contradiction, inconsistency, or any other lapses of rationality, even if these beliefs are occurrent at the same time. So we cannot characterize him as believing (in the opaque sense) both that London is and that London is not pretty. We must therefore conclude that the disquotation principle fails in at least one of the two cases. We can draw the same conclusion in the case of Peter (§7.7), despite the unambiguity clause. While Peter uses 'Ronald W. Reagan' equivocally, the name does not have a relevant ambiguity in English.

Kripke found the case of Pierre profoundly puzzling because he could not see any basis for deciding which application of the disquotation principle fails and which succeeds. I believe this was partly because Kripke assumed a causal theory of reference that validates both applications (see §8.3). That is one more argument against the causal theory. Kripke was also puzzled because he assumed that 'as an English speaker', Pierre 'does not differ at all' from his neighbors (1979: 120). This conflicts with Kripke's assumption that before Pierre moved to England, he 'differed not at all' from his French neighbors. Pierre's English neighbors were not native French speakers who learned English as a second language. If Pierre were like his French neighbors, then he had beliefs about London (in the intentional sense of 'about' as well as the relational), and used 'Londres' to express the concept of London. But then Pierre would have differed markedly from his English neighbors because he did not recognize that the English city he lived in was London. That is, he did not apply his previously acquired concept to his new home. In that case, when he eventually learned the English term 'London', he would have to have used it to express a concept other than the concept of London. Kripke's assumption that Pierre differed not at all from his French neighbors is itself false. If Pierre were a typical Frenchman, then he would have learned that 'London' refers to the same city that 'Londres' does when visiting London and learning English, and would have ended up using both 'London' and 'Londres' to express the same concept. The fact that Pierre used 'London' and 'Londres' to express different concepts enabled him to believe that 'Londres is London' is false. Pierre believes the negation of the identity proposition in which the two individual concepts are those he expresses using 'Londres' and 'London'. Since that proposition contains two different individual concepts, its negation is consistent and Pierre could rationally believe it. Pierre is again like Peter, who mistakenly believes that there are two different people named 'Ronald W. Reagan', an actor and a president. So Pierre must differ in significant respects from both his English speaking neighbors and his French neighbors. This is obvious in the case of Peter.

Kripke said that by a 'normal speaker' he meant one who 'uses all words in the sentence in a standard way, combines them according to the appropriate syntax, etc.: in short, *he uses the sentence to mean what a normal speaker should mean by it*' (1979: 113, my emphasis). This understanding avoids the problems I noted with (20). But if Pierre *were* a normal speaker in *this* sense, then it *would* follow that he has contradictory beliefs. For a normal French speaker uses 'Londres est jolie' to mean *"London is pretty"*, and a normal English speaker uses 'London is not pretty' to mean *"London is not pretty"*. If Pierre believes both sentences to be true *with these meanings*, then he believes both that London is pretty and that it is not. Since Kripke's description of Pierre made it evident that Pierre does not have contradictory beliefs, he must not be a normal speaker in Kripke's sense. That is, he must use one or both of those sentences to mean something different from what people normally mean. It is very clear that Peter is not a normal speaker in Kripke's sense. He cannot always mean by 'Ronald W. Reagan' what we mean by it.[14]

Kripke took the argument against substitutivity to depend on disquotation principles together with plausible consistency assumptions.

Since a normal speaker—normal even in his use of 'Cicero' and 'Tully' as names—can give sincere and reflective assent to 'Cicero was bald' and simultaneously to 'Tully was not bald', the disquotational principle implies that he believes that Cicero was bald and believes that Tully was not bald. Since it seems that he need not have contradictory beliefs..., and since a substitutivity principle for coreferential proper names in belief contexts would imply that he does have contradictory beliefs, it would seem that such a substitutivity principle must be incorrect.

(Kripke 1979: 115)[15]

Kripke constructs the case of Pierre to show that the combination of disquotation and consistency is itself problematic, and so cannot be used to argue against substitutivity. However, formulations of the disquotation principle apply in the case of 'Cicero' and 'Tully' that are weaker than (20) in critical respects. Whereas we cannot assume that Pierre means by both 'Londres' and 'London' what normal speakers mean by them (viz., *"London"*), we can assume that someone who does not realize that Cicero is Tully means by 'Cicero' and 'Tully' what normal speakers mean by them. Hence (21) applies to the Cicero/Tully case but not the Londres/London case.

> (21) If S believes that 'p' *interpreted as meaning that p* is true, then S believes that p.[16]

If S believes that 'The bank is grassy' is true on the interpretation in which it means that the river bank is grassy, then S must believe that the river bank is grassy. If S believes that the same sentence is true when meaning that the commercial bank is grassy, then S must believe that. Even with no provisos restricting its applicability, it is hard to imagine any exceptions to (21). The problems with (20) therefore do not impugn the argument against substitutivity because it can rely on a different form of the disquotation principle.[17]

Furthermore, no such *general principle* of disquotation is needed in the argument against substitutivity. All one needs is the assumption that a *particular* individual's use of appropriately related sentences 'p' and 'q' in *particular contexts* provides some inductive *evidence* that that person believes p without believing q. That evidence can and should be supplemented by evidence about the person's nonlinguistic behavior and emotions. Since few people these days know much about Cicero or Tully, let us change to the story of Superman. There is abundant evidence in the story that Lois Lane believes that Superman is wonderful, without believing that Clark Kent is. The fact that she often says 'Superman is wonderful!' with great sincerity, and would deny the same claim about Clark, is one piece of evidence. Further evidence is provided by the following: her claims that Superman is so strong and talented, while Clark is so weak and klutzy; her willingness to accept the claim that she believes Superman is wonderful, and her rejection as ridiculous the claim that she believes Clark to be wonderful; her efforts to be with Superman and avoid Clark; her excitement when she is with Superman in his Superman outfit, and disappointment when she is with Superman disguised as Clark Kent; and so on and on. We have very little understanding of Lois as a person if we do not know that she has different attitudes to Clark Kent and Superman. We know furthermore that there is nothing self-contradictory or irrational about her attitudes. She is simply ignorant of a key empirical fact.

There are other Frege cases, moreover, in which we do not rely on disquotation at all. I have observed that ascriptions of speaker reference are like ascriptions of belief in being ambiguous, with a sense in which substitutivity of proper names holds (the transparent) as well as the one in which it fails (the opaque). Suppose Lois says 'I love him!' Then in one sense (22) and (23) are equivalent, but in another they are not.

> (22) Lois is referring to Superman.
> (23) Lois is referring to Clark.

(22) is true in both senses because Lois used 'him' to express the idea of Superman. Sentence (23) is false in the opaque sense because Lois did not use 'him' to express the idea of Clark Kent. Sentence (23) is nevertheless true in the transparent sense because she expressed the idea of Superman, who disguises himself as Clark Kent. The reader should be able to hear the ambiguity in (23), and should recognize that on the interpretation in which it is true it does not enable us to fully appreciate Lois's statement.

Arguments against substitutivity may also start with facts we know by *introspection*. Many of us can recall cases in our own lives in which we were in situations like Lois's. We remember later something that we knew by introspection earlier. At no time did we infer what we believed from what we said or believed about sentences. Similarly, I know directly by introspection that (24) is true while (25) is false. Since I do not infer this from what I say or from what I believe about sentences, I do not rely on any disquotation principle.

> (24) I believe that Lois believes that Clark Kent is not Superman.
> (25) I believe that Lois believes that Superman is not Superman.

From the fact that (24) and (25) differ in truth value, we can infer that they differ in meaning. But if the Millian theory were true, then (24) and (25) would be synonymous.

I also know directly by introspection that I myself believe that William Shakespeare was not Roger Bacon. I recognize, of course, that my belief might be wrong. That is, it is at least possible that historical evidence will be discovered establishing that Bacon was Shakespeare. If this turned out to be true, and if co-referential names were synonymous, then 'I believe that Shakespeare was not Bacon' could not now be true. For that would mean the same thing as 'I believe that Shakespeare was not Shakespeare' and 'I believe that Bacon was not Bacon', which are both false. So the substitutivity principle would imply that I cannot know what I believe by introspection, which is absurd. Note finally that if Bacon was Shakespeare, then it would not be possible to find historical evidence establishing that fact if Millianism were true. For 'Bacon was Shakespeare' would mean the same thing as 'Bacon was Bacon', which does not state something that could be established by historical evidence.

In conclusion, Kripke's defense of Millianism was unsuccessful. The case against substitutivity does not depend on independently questionable disquotation principles. Moreover, Frege's problem was only one of many problems with referential theories.

## 11.4 The Gricean Defense: Metalinguistic Implicatures

Others have attempted to explain away the evidence against the Millian theory by appealing to *pragmatic* factors, most commonly, *implicatures*.

Grice's (1975) theory of conversation has been widely adopted in pragmatics, and Grice himself used it to defend semantic analyses in the face of strong linguistic counter-evidence.[18] Generally, when a man uses 'Someone died in the accident' he not only *says* that at least one person in the accident died, he *implies* that not everyone died. The phenomenon of implying that one thing is the case by saying something different is what Grice called *implicature*. While some implicatures are part of the conventional meaning of the expression used (e.g., those associated with 'but' as opposed to 'and'), most are not. Grice referred to implicatures that are not part of the meaning of the sentence used as *conversational* implicatures, since they need to be inferred from facts about the conversational context, and can be *'canceled'* by the same. The implication associated with 'some' cannot be part of its meaning, because 'Some died, indeed everyone did' is not self-contradictory or infelicitous in any way, and 'Everyone died therefore someone did' is logically valid. Moreover, when we are engaging in deliberate understatement, we are not implying that not all died. As this example illustrates, the implicatures of a sentence are generally not among its truth conditions.

The first move in the Gricean defense is to find differences in the implicatures of sentences containing co-referential terms compatible with their having the same meaning. The implicatures will therefore have to be special in one respect. For Grice observed that implicatures are generally attached to the meaning of the expressions used, so that 'it is not possible to find another way of saying the same thing, which simply lacks the implicature in question' (1975: 39). Grice thus used *'non-detachability'* as a test of implicature. He allowed exceptions to the rule, though, 'where some special feature of the substituted version is itself relevant to the determination of an implicature (in virtue of one of the maxims of Manner).' Metalinguistic implicatures—those that refer to the particular words the speaker used—are clearly detachable, and they are what McKay and Berg cite.[19] When we use '*S believes that p*' opaquely, we not only say that S believes that p, we also commonly implicate that *S believes (or would accept) that the sentence 'p' is true* and that *S would be prepared to assert 'I believe that p'*. The fact that belief ascriptions generally do not have these implicatures on the transparent interpretation supports the Gricean strategy. For it is only in opaque contexts that the substitutivity of coreferential terms fails (§7.7). What the Millian must say here is that using a belief sentence opaquely (or transparently) consists in using it with (or without) the metalinguistic implicatures.[20]

That these metalinguistic implicatures are not part of the meaning of 'S believes that p' becomes evident when the implicatures are canceled. These implicatures depend on the speaker's assumption that the subject being described understands the language and words used, and thus would realize both that the clause 'p' used to express the content of the belief ascribed is true, and that the predicate 'believes that p' applies to himself. The metalinguistic implicature will be canceled when it is evident in the context that the speaker is using a language not known by the subject being described. If I say, 'Boris Yeltsin believes that the Pacific Ocean is larger than the Atlantic', I would not imply or be taken to have implied that Yeltsin believes any English sentence to be true. When we ascribe beliefs to a prelinguistic child or an animal, we do not implicate that the subject would believe any sentence at all to be true.

Since the metalinguistic implicatures of a sentence are not part of its meaning, the way is clear for the Millian to claim that the intuitive differences between sentences with coreferential names are due entirely to differences in implicature, and not to any difference in meaning. The key move in the Gricean defense against substitutivity arguments is to claim that even though (26) and (27) say the same thing and are both true, (27) may be misleading or inapt because it implicates something that is false.

> (26) Lois Lane believes that Clark Kent is Clark Kent.
> (27) Lois Lane believes that Clark Kent is Superman.

McKay and Berg maintain that we are unwilling to assert or accept (27) because we would then falsely implicate that Lois Lane believes that the sentence 'Clark Kent is Superman' is true, and that she would be willing to say 'I believe that Clark Kent is Superman'. Lois would not say these things because she does not realize that the names 'Superman' and 'Clark Kent' are co-referential.

The Gricean defense enables the Millian to make some progress with Russell's problem as well as Frege's. The theory implies that 'Jimmy believes Santa Claus brings lots of presents' does not *say* anything, and has no truth value, because one of its constituents is meaningless. The sentence may nevertheless *implicate* something that is true, since Jimmy will typically believe that sentences saying that Santa brings presents are true. Hence the Millian can claim that our pragmatic purpose in using sentences with empty names is to communicate the information that the subject we are talking about believes that certain sentences containing them are true.

The Gricean defense cannot account for all the evidence on which the objections to Millianism are based, however. It is no help accounting for vagueness or Fine terms, or the fact that reference depends on meaning (§9.2). Concerning Russell's problem, reference to implicatures does not explain how, when its subject term has no meaning, 'Pegasus does not exist' could be true, or why competent and knowledgeable speakers of English believe that it is true. Nor does the Gricean strategy explain away the fact that " 'God exists' is meaningful, therefore it is true" seems to be an invalid argument. Reference to metalinguistic implicatures also provides no explanation as to how a sentence with a meaningless subject term could express a belief or thought specifically about Santa Claus, or how we could explain the actions and emotions of children at Christmas time if they do not have any beliefs about Santa Claus but only have beliefs about sentences with meaningless subject terms.

Concerning Frege's problem, the Gricean defense is clever but unsatisfying. We often use literally false statements to implicate something that is true. Hyperbole and irony are paradigm examples. If we say hyperbolically 'That limousine is a block long', we would not disagree with someone who says 'That is literally false, of course'. And if some hearer says 'You're wrong, it is less than two hundred feet long', we might speculate on whether she is a pedant, or a comedian, or just obtuse. But we would not dispute the fact she cites. In contrast, if we say 'Lois Lane does not realize that Clark Kent is Superman', we would strenuously disagree with anyone who says 'That is literally false'. Anyone who has read and understood a Superman comic book or seen the movies knows that the sentence is literally true (in the story) because Superman disguises himself as Clark Kent well enough so that Lois was unable to recognize him.[21] Its truth is critical to understanding the story, explaining why Lois Lane is so indifferent to Clark Kent despite her infatuation with Superman, why she does not expect Clark to come to the rescue, why she does not write stories about Clark, and so on. The essential fact is that she does not believe that Clark is Superman. What Lane believes or fails to believe about sentences is not important in explaining any of the central elements of the story.

As the Millian explains it, Lois would deny that sentence (27) is true even though she knows that Clark Kent is Superman because she does not realize that the names 'Superman' and 'Clark Kent' are co-referential. But we need to ask how Lois could fail to realize this if, as the Millian maintains, the names are synonymous. The Millian cannot claim that Lois fails to understand one of these names. For it is obvious that the following sentences are true (in the story).

(28) Lois knows that 'Superman' refers to Superman.
(29) Lois knows that 'Clark Kent' refers to Clark Kent.

But on the Millian theory, if these are true, then (30) and (31) are just as true, since they result from (28) and (29) by substituting co-referential names after the word 'to'.

(30) Lois knows that 'Superman' refers to Clark Kent.
(31) Lois knows that 'Clark Kent' refers to Superman.

So if Lois knows that 'Superman' and 'Clark Kent' both refer to Superman, how can she fail to know that the names are co-referential?[22] We want to say that there is a sense in which Lois does not know that 'Superman' refers to Clark Kent (the opaque sense). But the Millian must deny this. If Millianism were true, we could not understand even the metalinguistic facts of the story of Lois and Superman.

Soames (1989: 220) and Berg (1998: 468–9) maintain that people think 'Lois Lane believes that Clark Kent is Superman' (27) is false only because they are insufficiently aware of the distinction between semantically encoded and pragmatically imparted information. People are fooled by the fact that the sentence implicates something that is false (namely, that Lois believes that the sentence 'Clark Kent is Superman' is true).[23] This condescending claim would be hard to defend, I think, given the skill with which even youngsters use and consume a wide spectrum of figures of speech. Surely those of us working in pragmatics are not insensitive to the distinction. Right now we have the distinction at the forefront of our attention. It still seems that (27) explicitly says something that is false, while implicating some things that are true.

Saul (1998: 385) makes a more plausible point: 'It is very easy to mistake a generalized pragmatic implicature for semantic content.' The experience of many of our logic students with 'some' will attest to this, and we grappled with the problem at the theoretical level in §5.4. But it is hard to believe that no one noticed such a confusion with belief statements before McKay and others saw that hypothesizing it could be used to defend the Millian theory against objections. Moreover, if speakers are guilty of any confusion, it is not the one Saul identified. For most people who use sentences like (26) and (27) will insist that they are not talking about sentences at all: they are describing Lois's beliefs about Superman and Clark Kent. What the metalinguistic theory must claim is that *competent speakers of English mistake implying something concerning beliefs about sentences for saying something concerning beliefs about things other than sentences.* There is no plausibility in this claim at all. The Gricean defense is ultimately unsatisfying because 'Lois Lane believes that Clark Kent is Superman' still seems literally false even when we are focusing on the distinction between what the sentence says and what it implicates, and recognize that belief sentences implicate something about sentences. (We can also acknowledge that the sentence may seem true to those like Urmson who are focused on the transparent interpretation.)

Recanati (1993: 245, 248) observed that there is an internal difficulty with the Gricean defense of the Millian theory. Grice (1975: 31) held that an implicature must be 'calculable', and that the calculation of an implicature starts from a knowledge of what the sentence uttered means and what the speaker said. While Grice is not explicit about who must be able to calculate an implicature, it seems clear that he had in mind competent speakers in general. But Millians adopting the Gricean defense claim that even competent speakers are generally unaware of what they or others say when they use belief sentences. Speakers confuse what the sentences mean with what they implicate. Since I have argued that Grice's calculability assumption is too strong, I do not take Recanati's objection to be decisive as presented.[24] But judging from clear cases of implicature, it must at least be true that the speaker intended to convey what he implicated *by* saying what he did, and is so understood by hearers. This implies that the speaker and hearer do know what the speaker said. So a weaker form of Recanati's objection still goes through.

Saul (1998) correctly observed that in some of Grice's most important applications of his theory of implicature, speakers have what Grice takes to be an implicature firmly in mind, but are not clearly aware of what Grice claims they have said. For example, people who say 'They fell in love and got married' would normally mean 'They fell in love *and then* got married', which Grice takes to be an implicature. Grice claims that what they said is merely 'They both fell in love and got married'—a simple conjunction. Yet few people think that this is what they said, and so few people intended to convey the thought that they fell in love and then got married by saying that they both fell in love and got married. Most hearers, furthermore, do not take the speaker to have said what Grice thinks they said. So hearers are in no position to work out or recognize the implicature. But precisely because it is not clear that speakers mean 'p and then q' by saying that both p and q, it is not clear that we have here a case of implicature rather than ambiguity (cf. §5.4).[25]

If the apparent failures of substitutivity were an illusion due to differences in implicature, they should disappear when the implicatures are canceled. Many people who knew Archie Leach as a young man in Bristol, England, before World War I never realized that he was Cary Grant. If I claim that Yeltsin probably does not know that Archie Leach was Cart Grant, the main point I would be trying to communicate is not simply the likelihood that Yeltsin probably does not know that the English sentence 'Archie Leach was Cary Grant' is true. Similarly, when we use a secret code to describe someone's beliefs, the metalinguistic implicature is canceled by the very fact that we are using a code. Suppose I have a code in which 'Babe Ruth' means "Cary Grant", 'Lou Gehrig' means "Clark Gable", and 'Joe DiMaggio' means "Archie Leach". I might say and mean 'Jane believes that Lou Gehrig rather than Babe Ruth is Joe DiMaggio'. The fact that what I said may well appear to be true could not be attributed to the evident truth of the metalinguistic implication my utterance would normally carry. For I did not imply that Jane knew anything about the sentences in my code, and I certainly was not implying that she believes that 'Lou Gehrig rather than Babe Ruth is Joe DiMaggio' is true in English.

The Millian could plausibly maintain that when it is clear in the context that S does not speak the language we are using, then what 'S believes that p' implicates is *"S believes that the translation of 'p' in S's language is true"*.[26] While Jane does not have any beliefs about the sentences in my code, she will presumably have beliefs about their translations into her own language, which we may presume to be English. The Yeltsin case is problematic, however. For while 'Cary Grant' surely has a translation into Russian, it is not at all clear that 'Archie Leach' does, as 'translation' is normally understood.[27] Worse yet, on Millianism, any translation of 'Cary Grant' would also be a translation of 'Archie Leach'. For on Millianism, co-referential names are strictly synonymous. So *as understood by the Millian*, the relevant implicature of 'Yeltsin does not know that Cary Grant was Archie Leach' would be obviously true because Yeltsin surely believes the translation of 'Cary Grant is Cary Grant' is true, and that translation is also a translation of 'Cary Grant is Archie Leach'. Saul (1998: 275) observed, furthermore, that the traditional metalinguistic theory wrongly implies that Kripke's Pierre would implicate that he does *not* believe 'Londres est jolie' to be true when he says 'London is not pretty'. Finally, apparent failures of substitutivity do not disappear even when we cancel the presupposition that S knows *any* language. Since Superman looks, sounds, and acts very differently in his two identities, we could perfectly well accept 'Lois does not realize that Clark Kent is Superman' even when the story made it clear that Lois did not know Superman's name(s), or any language at all. Lois's deception does not depend on her linguistic competence.

The metalinguistic implication may be canceled if there is even one word used by the speaker that the subject does not understand. Thus we can cancel the metalinguistic implicature of 'Mary believes that Cary Grant is Archie Leach' by adding 'even though she did not know Archie's last name'. In that case, there will be no implication that she would recognize the truth of 'Cary Grant is Archie Leach'. 'Mary believes that Cary Grant is Archie Leach but she does not know Archie's last name' does not even appear to follow from 'Mary believes that Cary Grant is Cary Grant although she does not know Archie's last name'. Yet the inference should appear to be valid if Millianism were correct.

Belief ascriptions are not the only psychological statements for which substitutivity appears to fail. When 'believes' is replaced by 'is thinking the thought' in (26) and (27), for example, the resulting sentences seem to differ in meaning just as much. In the case of occurrent thought, the metalinguistic implicature would be *S is thinking the thought that sentence 'p' is true*. This implicature can be cancelled simply by saying that the subject is not at the moment thinking about sentences. Even if competent speakers have beliefs about the sentences we use (or translations thereof), they may well not be thinking about them.

(32) Lois is not thinking about sentences at all; what she is thinking is the thought that Clark Kent is Clark Kent.
(33) Lois is not thinking about sentences at all; what she is thinking is the thought that Clark Kent is Superman.

We can now note that (32) and (33) seem to differ just as much as (26) and (27) even though the corresponding metalinguistic implicatures have been canceled.

Finally, if the differences between co-referential terms were due entirely to differences in the metalinguistic implicatures of sentences containing them, then co-referential terms should never seem interchangeable in opaque belief contexts. But 'S believes Mars has two moons' has exactly the same meaning as 'S believes Mars has 2 moons'. The fact that the metalinguistic implications of these two sentences are clearly about different sentences is irrelevant. And if I have stipulated that 'Cal Ripken' also means "Cary Grant" in my code, then it will be impossible for me to assert 'Jane believes that Babe Ruth is Joe DiMaggio' while denying 'Jane believes that Cal Ripken is Joe DiMaggio' (recall §2.5).

We will say more about attempts to account for the differences between proper names in terms of metalinguistic differences in §12.5.

## 11.5   The Gricean Defense: Mode Implicatures

*Russellians* are referential theorists who take belief to be a relation between individuals and *situations* (or *states of affairs*), construed as complex entities composed of individuals and properties. The Russellian takes 'S believes that *a* is *F*' to assert that S stands in the belief relation to the situation *a's being F*, which is identified with the ordered pair ⟨*a*, *being F*⟩ (see §14.2). Since Superman = Clark Kent, ⟨Superman, being strong⟩ = ⟨Clark Kent, being strong⟩. Hence on the Russellian view, 'Lois believes that Superman is strong' and 'Lois believes that Clark Kent is strong' assert that Lois stands in the belief relation to the same situation.[28]

A problem for the Russellian view is that if belief statements are interpreted this way, then they do not have the explanatory power we generally take them to possess. For example, we cannot explain why Lois Lane gets so excited when she is with Superman in his superhero guise but not when she is with him in his klutzy reporter guise by saying that in the first situation she believes she is with Superman while in the later she believes she is with Clark Kent. For on the Russellian view, these two beliefs are the same. To explain the behavior we ordinarily explain in terms of beliefs, many Russellians introduce the notion of a *way of believing*.[29] On this *triadic relation theory of belief*, people can believe one situation in different ways. Because Lois believes ⟨Superman, being strong⟩ in one way, she gets excited when she is around Superman in his cape and tights. Because Lois does not believe ⟨Superman, being strong⟩ in another way, she does not get similarly excited when she is around Superman in his business suit and spectacles. It is often said that the different ways of believing a situation involve different *modes of presentation* of the situation, which are composed of the different modes of presentation of the constituents of the situation. Thus the different ways of believing ⟨Superman, being strong⟩ are said to involve different modes of presentation of Superman. Modes of presentation are also ways of desiring, intending, hoping, and so on.

Using the triadic relation theory, Salmon and Soames attempt to explain away apparent substitutivity failures in terms of implicatures not about sentences, but about modes of presentation.[30] Thus 'Lois believes that Superman is strong' may implicate that Lois believes ⟨Superman, being strong⟩ in one way, while 'Lois believes that Clark Kent is strong' implicates that Lois believes ⟨Superman, being strong⟩ in another way. Letting '⟨p⟩' designate the situation described by 'p,' the triadic theorist claims that 'S believes that p' generally implicates: *S believes ⟨p⟩ under a certain mode of presentation (the one associated with 'p').* The italicized formula could be construed as expressing a metalinguistic implicature—as talking about the mode expressed by 'p', whatever mode it happens to be. But then the proposal would be subject to many of the objections raised in the previous section. We get a completely different version of the Gricean defense by taking the italicized formula to be talking about the mode of implicature associated with a sentence without talking about the sentence. Another virtue of the mode implicature theory is that the extra information conveyed is more clearly relevant to common conversational purposes (explanation and prediction), making Grice's maxim of quantity ('Make your contribution as informative as required') more readily applicable.

Triadic relation theorists generally say little about what these ways of believing or modes of presentation are. Without knowing what they have in mind, we cannot assess whether ordinary language users mean, imply, or understand anything about ways of believing or modes of presentation. Hence the widespread belief that sentences like (26) and (27) differ in meaning and truth value cannot not be attributed to the fact that people commonly confuse what the sentences mean with what they are used to implicate about modes.

Another problem for the triadic relation theorist is to explain what the association is between sentences and modes, and how different sentences get associated with different modes of presentation. Why is 'Clark Kent is here' associated with a way of believing that explains Lois's lack of excitement when she is with Superman in his reporter outfit? It is especially problematic that the triadic relation theorist must hold that *synonymous* sentences have different mode implicatures. Since the postulated mode implicatures are not metalinguistic, this runs afoul of Grice's rule that conversational implicatures are non-detachable. Salmon and Soames hold that the mode of presentation is *like* the sentence used. They do not specify the respect of similarity. It is hard to see what the respect could be given that sentences with the same meaning according to the Millian theory need not be like the same mode, while translations of a sentence must not be like different modes.

Given the explanatory and descriptive purposes to be served by ways of believing, it seems clear that they must stand in a one to one correspondence to what we believe in the opaque sense. I would therefore explain these notions as follows. First, though, note that while the triadic relation theorist uses the term 'proposition' to denote situations, I use it to denote declarative thoughts (Definition 2.4).[31] Let us introduce a *situational extension function* $\mathrm{sx}\{P\} = A$ that takes us from propositions (declarative thoughts) to the situations (n-tuples of individuals and properties) that would make them true. If M is the thought that the morning star is bright and E is the thought that the evening star is bright, then $\mathrm{sx}\{M\} = \mathrm{sx}\{E\}$ = ⟨Venus, being bright⟩. Let us say that the situational extension of a singular concept is its extension, and that the situational extension of a general concept is the property defining its extension. Let 'c(w)' designate the concept "w." Then $\mathrm{sx}\{c(\text{bright})\}$ is the property of being bright, and $\mathrm{sx}\{c(\text{the morning star})\} = \mathrm{sx}\{c(\text{the evening star})\} = $ Venus. The situational extension of a simple subject-predicate proposition is the situation consisting of the situational extensions of its subject and predicate concepts: $\mathrm{sx}\{c(a \text{ is } F)\} = \langle \mathrm{sx}\{c(a)\}, \mathrm{sx}\{c(F)\} \rangle$. We can now define ways of believing and modes of presentation as follows.

11.1    **Definition:** *P is a mode of presentation of $A$* iff $A = \mathrm{sx}(P)$.

11.2    **Definition:** *P is a way in which S believes $A$* iff (i) S believes P; and (ii) $\mathrm{sx}(P) = A$.[32]

Ways of thinking, desiring, intending, and so on, can be defined in the same way. If concepts are similarly defined as modes of presentation of their extensions, it follows that ways of believing are composed of modes of presentation. It is then true on Definition 11.2 that John Dalton believed ⟨water, being HO⟩ in one way but not another, the former involving the concept "water," the later involving the concept "$H_2O$".

If we explain what ways of believing and modes of presentation are in this way, then the association problem confronting the triadic relation theory is solved. There are two ways in which sentences get associated with ways of believing: intention and convention. Individual speakers use sentences to express certain thoughts (Chapter 4), and speakers conventionally use sentences to express certain thoughts (Chapter 5). The objection that speakers do not have the concept of ways of believing or modes of presentation is also mitigated, for everyone has concepts of thoughts and ideas. The claim that when we are talking about beliefs, desires, intentions and the like we are concerned with thoughts and ideas is platitudinous. The conception problem is not completely eliminated, however. For it is not at all clear that when ordinary speakers say 'S believes that p', they mean or imply anything about a triadic relation between S, a situation, and a thought.[33]

The triadic relation theorist's attempt to avoid problems with Millianism in terms of mode implicatures is not completely successful: Russell's problem still looms. First, if the triadic relation theory is correct, then 'Johnny believes that Santa Claus brings presents' cannot be true, and does not mean or implicate anything either. Since 'Santa Claus' has no referent, it is meaningless. As a result, '⟨Santa Claus, bringing presents⟩' is also meaningless, as is 'S believes ⟨Santa, bringing presents⟩ under a certain way of believing'. The way of believing exists, but there is no corresponding situation.[34] The situational extension function is undefined for that mode of presentation. *A fortiori*, the triadic relation theory really provides no account of the semantic difference between 'x believes Superman is strong' and 'x believes Clark Kent is strong'. On the Millian theory, both predicates are actually meaningless.

Second, even when there is a situation corresponding to the thought expressed by 'p', S's relationship to the situation is not essential to the truth of 'S believes that p' as it is understood in English. Thus 'S believes that Homer was Greek' could be true even though Homer, and therefore the situation ⟨Homer, being Greek⟩, does not in fact exist. S's relationship to situations is in this way irrelevant to the truth of most psychological explanations. When S answers 'Yes' to a question because he believes that Homer was Greek, the situation ⟨Homer, being Greek⟩ is relevant to the extent (if any) that it caused the observations that led people in general and S in particular to believe that Homer was Greek. But given that belief, S would act the same way even if Homer did not actually exist and the observations leading people to believe in Homer had other causes. The fact that it is the modes of presentation that do all the explanatory work, not the situations, is further shown by the fact that we can explain why Lois is happy in terms of her believing and desiring ⟨Superman, being here⟩ only if the ways of believing and desiring 'match' (Braun 2001).

The triadic relation theorist takes 'S believes that *a* is *F*' to *mean* "S believes ⟨*a, being F*⟩" and to *implicate* "S believes ⟨*a, being F*⟩ under a certain mode of presentation (the one associated with '*a* is *F*')". This implicature, as noted, is not metalinguistic: it is about the mode, not the sentence. So let us now stipulate that 'S believes$_0$ that *a* is *F* *means* "S believes ⟨*a, being F*⟩ under a certain mode of presentation (the one associated with '*a* is *F*')". That is, let 'S believes$_0$ that *a* is *F*' mean what the triadic theorist thinks 'S believes that *a* is *F*' merely implicates. Even if substitutivity does hold for the latter, it will fail for the former.

The triadic relation theorist might respond that the opaque form we just introduced is not an expression of any natural language. But we are considering the Millian theory as telling us not just what name meaning is in natural languages, but what name meaning is in general. More importantly, why should we not take 'S believes that *a* is *F*' in English to mean what the triadic relation theorist thinks it merely implicates? The triadic relation theorist grants that competent users of English think that (26) and (27) mean something different, and generally use them to mean what the triadic relation theorist thinks they merely implicate. Since meaning is determined by conventional usage (Chapter 5), it seems we should instead conclude that the triadic relation theorist is simply wrong about what English belief sentences mean. In fact, the theory of belief ascriptions we are entertaining is very close to the theory developed by Crimmins and Perry (1989).[35] Because 'Superman' and 'Clark Kent' differ in meaning, (26) and (27) 'specify' (to use Crimmins and Perry's term) that different modes of presentation (specifically, 'notions') are involved in the beliefs they ascribe to Lois. This does not mean that the semantic value (i.e. referent) of these terms is anything other than the man who is both Superman and Clark Kent. But it does imply that the different meanings of the terms cannot be identified with their common referent.

One reason not to take belief sentences to mean what the triadic relation theorist thinks they merely implicate is Russell's problem. Even on the Crimmins–Perry theory, 'Young children believe that Santa brings presents' is false or truth-valueless, as they note (1989: 702). The mode of presentation exists[36] (we do have a concept or notion of Santa), but there is no situation to believe under it. Russell's problem can easily be solved, though, by taking belief to be a relation to modes of presentation that implies a relation to situations if they exist. On this revision, 'S believes that *a* is *F*' is used to mean *S believes a certain mode of presentation (the one associated with 'a is F,' whose situational extension is⟨a, being F⟩if it exists)*. This gives precisely the truth conditions to the belief ascription that we would expect on its opaque interpretation (cf. 3.7). Of course, the theory gives up Millianism entirely, and is similar or identical to the ideational theory, depending on what modes of presentation are taken to be.

We can take a similar approach to Braun's (1998: 571–7; 2002) attempt to explain away the fact that competent, rational, and reflective speakers of English can think that 'Water is HO' and '$H_2O$ is HO' differ in meaning and express different propositions. Braun's hypothesis is that speakers do this because they have different modes of presentation for the situation ⟨$H_2O$ is HO⟩. When they believe the situation under one mode, they think 'Water is HO' is true, but when they believe it under another mode, they think 'Water is HO' is false. We get a simpler theory of meaning, however, and do not have to jump through hoops explaining things away, by saying that 'Water is HO' and '$H_2O$ is HO' differ in meaning because speakers conventionally use them to express different modes of presentation, both of which have as their situational extension ⟨$H_2O$ is HO⟩.

Crimmins and Perry give two reasons for taking the objects of propositional attitudes to be situations:

The first, *direct reference*, is that the utterance of a simple sentence containing names or demonstratives normally expresses a 'singular proposition'—a proposition that contains as constituents the individuals referred to, and not any descriptions of or conditions on them; the second, *semantic innocence*, is that the utterances of the embedded sentences in belief reports express just the propositions they would if not embedded, and these propositions are the contents of the ascribed beliefs.

(Crimmins and Perry 1989: 686)[37]

Unlike the Fregean theories Crimmins and Perry reject, my view is semantically innocent too: in 'Bill believes that John F. Kennedy was a democrat', the embedded sentence 'John F. Kennedy was a democrat' expresses the proposition (declarative thought) that Kennedy was a democrat, and the whole belief sentence asserts that that proposition is the object of Bill's belief. 'John F. Kennedy was a democrat' thus expresses the same proposition when embedded in the belief ascription that it does when uttered as a free-standing sentence. I have described this use as *ideo-reflexive* (§2.5, §3.7). My view also shares much with the direct reference view: while the name 'John F. Kennedy' refers to Kennedy only because it expresses the concept of John F. Kennedy, that concept refers directly to Kennedy. The concept does not refer to Kennedy through any descriptive content, the way the concept of the 35th president does. Direct reference theories are tenable if they maintain that names and indexicals have no *descriptive* sense. They go too far if they try to maintain that words refer to things without expressing a concept. There has to be enough indirectness to allow for Frege cases and Russell cases. So I suggest redefining directly referential terms as those whose reference is determined by a directly referential concept. Then as intended, standard names and simple indexicals like 'I' will be classified as directly referential.

## 11.6 THE GRICEAN DEFENSE: DESCRIPTIVE ASSERTIONS

The versions of Grice's defense discussed so far have identified specific implicatures as responsible for the appearance of substitutivity failures. McKay and Berg focused on metalinguistic implicatures, and Salmon and Soames focused on mode implicatures. In rejecting these defenses, we observed that substitutivity failures still appear when such implicatures are canceled, and appear even to those who are focused on the distinction between what a sentence says and what it implicates. In his most recent attempt to explain away substitutivity failures, Soames (2002: Ch. 8) drops the focus on specific implicatures. He allows that the appearance may be due to fact that speakers use sentences like (34) and (35) to *assert* different propositions, which may *vary* from occasion to occasion. He suggests that we mistakenly think (34) and (35) differ in meaning because we know they can be used to assert propositions like those listed under them, which differ in descriptive content.

> (34) Lois believes that Clark Kent can fly.[38]
>> (a) Lois believes that the reporter Clark Kent can fly.
>> (b) Lois believes that the bespectacled reporter Clark Kent can fly.
> (35) Lois believes that Superman can fly.
>> (a) Lois believes that the Kryptonian Superman can fly.
>> (b) Lois believes that the caped Kryptonian Superman can fly.

We might question whether (34) *asserts* (34)(a) rather than *implicating* it, but this would probe a vagueness in the concepts that is unimportant for our purposes. It is obvious at least on reflection that (34) differs in meaning from (34)(a), (b), etc., and that (35) differs in meaning from (35)(a), (b), etc. But even when these differences are at the forefront of my attention, as they are now, it seems just as clear that (34) and (35) themselves differ in meaning. In thinking that (34) could be true while (35) is false, I am not making the mistake of thinking that (34)(a) could be true while (35)(a) is false (*pace* Soames 2002: 214). I could assert (34) and deny (35) even if I believed that Lois did not realize that Superman is from Krypton or Clark Kent a reporter. According to Soames,

> When speakers say that [(34)] and [(35)] mean different things, what they are really telling us is that competent speakers may use them to assert and convey different information, which is true.                     (Soames 2002: 228)

This is not what I mean. Like most other competent language users, I am well aware of the distinction between what a sentence means and what it can be used to assert and convey. I know, for example, that (34) can be used to assert and convey the information that Lois believes *someone* can fly without meaning "Lois believes someone can fly"; (34) is more specific than that. I am talking about what (34) and (35) *mean*.

We can bypass the distinction between meaning and asserting altogether by asking: Is asserting that the Kryptonian Superman can fly the same as asserting that the Kryptonian Clark Kent can fly? Soames has to say 'Yes', but that seems contrary to the truth.

Soames (2002: 230–5) himself derives a particularly implausible consequence from the Millian theory: asserting (A) that Mary just learned that Clark Kent is Superman is the same as asserting (B) that Mary just learned that Superman is Superman. Soames concedes that people who assert (A) are likely to deny that they asserted (B), which would imply that Mary had been ignorant of a self-evident truth. Soames argues that people might well not know that they have asserted something, and might be convinced that they have asserted (B) by an argument that he presents. The argument presupposes the truth of the Millian theory,[39] and so begs the question at issue. But let us grant that people might be convinced by it. Does it follow that they did make the assertion in question? Not necessarily, because we have no privileged access to what we assert. Assertion is governed by external conditions that are not introspectible, such as the literal meaning of the words uttered. For the same reason, the fact that people do not recognize they have asserted (B) is no guarantee that they did not. So let us change examples. An even more implausible consequence of Millianism is that *thinking* (A) is the same as *thinking* (B). We know introspectively that when we are thinking (A) are not thinking (B). The Millian would have to claim that we do not know what we are thinking (cf. §8.4).

Given that Soames thinks competent speakers confuse the meaning (or 'semantic content') of a sentence with what it is used to assert and convey, we might wonder how he rises above this ignorance to determine that the meaning of a sentence 'Fn' is the Russellian proposition ⟨n, F-hood⟩. He infers this conclusion from his general theory of meaning.

In Chapter 3, I presented an account of the meaning, or semantic content, of nonindexical sentences. The account recognizes that despite being nonindexical, such sentences are routinely used by speakers to assert and convey different information in different contexts of utterance. Nevertheless, if x is such a sentence, typically there is some common core of information that is asserted and conveyed by utterances of x across different contexts. The meaning of an unambiguous, noncontext-sensitive sentence s—the proposition p that it semantically expresses— is this common information; that is, it is the information that would be asserted and conveyed by an assertive utterance of s in any context in which s is used with its literal meaning by competent speakers who understand it (provided that s is used nonmetaphorically, nonironically, nonsarcastically, and without any conversational implicature defeating the presumption that the speaker intends to be committed to p).

(Soames 2002: 204)

Soames's account of meaning has problems independent of Millianism. As Soames himself acknowledges, it fails for all ambiguous sentences—and that includes nearly every sentence of a natural language. It also unclear how this account rules that the meaning of 'Superman can fly' is the singular proposition that *Superman* can fly rather than the existential proposition that *someone* can fly. The latter would seem to be asserted and conveyed in any context in which the former is. But the important problem for us is this: if competent speakers confuse the meaning of a sentence with what it conveys, how could Soames have established that this theory is true? His ignorance claim precludes the possibility of establishing inductively that the meaning of a sentence is the proposition speakers use it to convey in any context. Soames cannot gather any data about the meanings of particular sentences to generalize and explain. In addition, there is a key provision in

Soames's thesis that makes it circular as a definition of meaning, and useless for establishing the Millian theory. That is the provision that 's is used with its literal meaning'. If (34) is used to mean what (35) means, is (34) used with its literal meaning? That is just to ask whether (34) has the same meaning as (35). So we cannot use Soames's theory of meaning to argue that (34) and (35) have the same meaning without begging the question.

## 11.7 Conclusion

Although this chapter and the preceding were devoted to refutation, we have established a positive conclusion: a standard name does have a meaning that is distinct from its reference and is a determinant thereof. What we need is a positive account of standard name meaning.

### Notes

[1] See also Lewis 1973: 86–7; Salmon 1986; 1987: 94; 1998; Forbes 1989b: Ch. 2. Contrast Marcus 1983/86, 1997; Soames 2002: 30, 109; Brock 2002.

[2] See also Salmon 1998: 294; 302; Forbes 1989b: 21. Compare and contrast Van Inwagen 2003: 137ff; Reimer 2001: 501.

[3] On my view, 'Sherlock Holmes' has the meaning it has in (2) and (3) because it expresses an idea, one that has no referent in reality. It expresses a different though related idea in (1), which has a referent. The character 'Sherlock Holmes' refers to in (1) is, or is represented by, a system of thoughts (propositions) containing that idea, including the thought that Sherlock Holmes is a detective, the thought that Sherlock Holmes is brilliant at deduction, etc. Conan Doyle created the character by thinking up the thoughts and putting them to paper. The story, in turn, is, or is represented by, a large system of thoughts containing the character. When we say something like 'The central character of *The Hound of the Baskervilles* is a detective', we are not of course claiming that a novel component or system of thoughts is a detective. Such a claim is interpreted as saying that the system of thoughts contains the thought that its object is a detective. See Van Inwagen (2003) for an excellent introduction to the problems an adequate theory of literary characters must resolve.

[4] Cf. Forbes 1989b: 20ff.

[5] Cf. Rundle 1979: 75, 80; Stanley 1999: 15; Soames 2002: 101ff. This is in essence the 'Hermeneutic Principle' criticized effectively by D. Sosa 1996. Contrast also Heck 1995.

[6] For more on the context-relativity of knowing who, see Chisholm 1976: 173–4; Boër and Lycan 1975; 1986; and Davis 2003: §16.5.

[7] Cf. McDowell 1977.

[8] See Saul 1997a; 1997b; 1999c; and responses by Forbes 1997b; Moore 1999b; Predelli 1999; Barber 2000; and Braun and Saul 2002.

[9] Cf. Forbes (1997b: 111–2; 1999). Contrast Saul 1997b; Barber 2000: 304–5 ; Moore 1999b. See also the discussion of Forbes's (1990; 1993) agent centered analysis of belief statements in *Meaning, Expression, and Thought*, §13.4.

[10] Braun and Saul (2002) observe that some readers may judge (17) and (18) to be inequivalent on their literal interpretations just because they fail to recall at the moment of judgment that Clark Kent is Superman and thus make a mistake. I have been concerned solely with why (17) and (18) strike those of us who do recall the identity as expressing inequivalent thoughts.

[11] He accepts others. See Kripke 1980: 20–1.

[12] See e.g., Kripke 1979: §2; Over 1983: 253; D. Sosa 1996; Frances 1998b; Moore 1999a; Feit 2001: 30–1. Kripke and others suggest that the disquotation principle can be strengthened to a biconditional. The converse of (20), however, has the unacceptable implication that a speaker who believes a proposition must have an opinion about and recognize to be true every sentence that expresses that proposition in his or her language (cf. Soames 2002: 12). The analog for thought is particularly implausible: people thinking about sex, for example, are normally not thinking about sentences.

[13] See Kripke 1979; Pollock 1980: 489; Noonan 1980–81; Lewis 1981a; Linsky 1983: 144; Over 1983; Barwise and Perry 1983: 252; Castañeda 1985; Travis 1985: 87ff; Salmon 1986: 120–1; 1995: 4ff; Böer and Lycan 1986: §4.2; Loar 1987: 1988; Taschek 1988; 1995a: 277–9; Crimmins and Perry 1989; Owens 1989; Devitt 1989a: 91–2; Forbes 1990: 557–62; McCulloch 1991: 76–8; Goldstein 1993; D. Sosa 1996; Frances 1998a; 1998b; 1999; Pelczar and Rainsbury 1998: 307–8; Braun 1998: 580; Moore 1999a; Feit 2001; Soames 2002: 10–11. For a precursor, see Vendler 1976: 42.

[14] Elsewhere Kripke gives a weaker formulation of what a normal speaker is: 'I am supposing that Pierre satisfies all criteria for being a normal French speaker, in particular, that he satisfies whatever criteria we usually use to judge that a Frenchman (correctly) uses *'est jolie'* to attribute pulchritude and uses *'Londres'*—standardly—as a name of London' (1979: 119). This formulation requires the speaker to use words with their normal *reference*, but does not assure that they are used with their normal *meaning* (cf. Over 1983; Laurier 1986: 41; Taschek 1988: 103). The assumption that Pierre is a normal speaker thus defined would not imply that he has contradictory beliefs. But the problems with (20) would not be entirely avoided.

[15] Cf. Soames 1989: 212–13.

[16] The *oratio recta* form would read: *If S believes that 'p' interpreted as meaning "p" is true, then S believes that p, provided 'p' is non-indexical* (cf. §3.7). No unambiguity clause is needed on (21) because of the general rule that substitutions for different occurrences of 'p' must be uniform, the same sentences with the same meaning.

[17] The disquotation principle is generally formulated using the obscure notion of 'assenting to a sentence': (21)′ *If S assents to 'p', then S believes that p.* I believe this would most naturally be interpreted as meaning (21), but its application to the case of Pierre suggests that Kripke and others take it to mean (20). "Assenting to 'p'" might also be taken to mean *sincerely asserting that p*. In that case (21)′ would be tautologous. But then the disquotation principle could not be used to establish what someone's beliefs are: we would have to know what his beliefs are to know what he assents to.

[18] For example, Grice 1967; 1969b. See my *Implicature* (1998) for critical discussion of extant theories of implicature, and for a bibliography on the subject.

[19] McKay 1981: 293, 296; Berg 1988; 1998. Cf. Peacocke 1975: 218; Barwise and Perry 1981b: 394; 1983: 196–200, 258–264; Salmon 1986: 117–8; 1989b; Soames 1987a: §7, §9; 1989: §5; 1995: 523; Saul 1997a: 106–7. Contrast Schiffer 1987b: §4; Devitt 1989a: 84–88; Crimmins 1992: Ch. 1; Recanati 1993; Heck 1995: 80, fn. 4; Bezuidenhout 1997a: 207; Jacob 1997: §2.2; Green 1998; Saul 1998: 363–79; Predelli 1999: 115. Compare and contrast Richard 1987: §2; 1990: Ch. 3. Urmson (1968: 115–22) provided the theoretical and empirical tools for the Gricean strategy, although he was not concerned to defend Millianism. He seemed, moreover, so focused on the transparent interpretation of propositional attitude reports that he could not hear the opaque.

[20] Compare and contrast McKinsey 1999: 523ff. Because he thinks implicatures must be calculable, McKinsey assumes that the opaque/transparent distinction must be independently characterized. I reject the calculability assumption (Davis 1998).

[21] Schiffer (1987b: 470) has observed that when we say something false in order to implicate something that is true, we generally count on our audience's recognizing the obvious falsity of what we said, and taking that as a clue to look for an implicature. Thus when we use irony, it is

no good using a falsehood that the audience might think we think is true. The fact that Salmon insists that we all believe the negative belief statements in question to be true thus undermines his claim that we are asserting a falsehood in order to communicate the true implicature.

[22] Braun 2002: 71–2 developed a similar argument.

[23] Cf. Peacocke 1975: 218; McKay 1981: 294–5; Barwise and Perry 1981b: 394; 1983: 262–4; Soames 1987a: 123; 2002: 228–35; Berg 1988: 356, 358; Braun 1998: 562–3. Contrast Braun 1998: 570–1; Reimer 2001: 502, 505; and Spencer 'Do Conversational Implicatures Explain Substitutivity Failure?' (forthcoming). Recanati (1993: 343), Bezuidenhout (1997a: 207), Jacob 1997: §2.2; and Green (1998: 73) criticize the implicature theory on the grounds that conversational implicatures do not generally fall within the scope of logical operators or connectives. But McKay and Berg could claim that 'It is not the case that S believes that p' implicates that S does not believe 'p' to be true even if it does not inherit this implicature from the implicature of its that-clause. They might similarly maintain that 'If Lois does not realize that Clark Kent is Superman then she is an idiot' is literally true while implicating something false, namely "If Lois does not realize that 'Clark Kent is Superman' is true, then she is an idiot".

[24] Davis 1998: Ch. 3. I thus agree with Green (1998: 69–72) that the postulated metalinguistic implicatures are not calculable, but do not take that to be a criticism of the McKay–Berg theory.

[25] In the same vein, Crimmins (1992: 23) attacked the implicature theory by questioning whether cancelability proves implicature. As Recanati (1993: 330) notes, 'What looks like the contextual cancellation of an implicature may also be seen as the contextual disambiguation of an ambiguous sentence.' Contrast Braun and Saul (2002: 9–10), who ran an argument like Recanati's for the implicature account of 'simple sentences' discussed in §11.2.

[26] Cf. Soames 1987a: 119; Braun 1998: 564.

[27] Cf. Saul 1999b: 36–8.

[28] Recall that we are using this example as representative of real-life cases in which an identity is unknown, and thus are pretending that Superman really exists.

[29] Cf. Kaplan 1977: 532; Perry 1979: 18–9; Schiffer 1978; 179; 1981: 71, 81; 1987b: 459–60; 1990; Böer and Lycan 1980; Salmon 1986: Chs. 8–9, esp. pp. 119–20; 1995: 6–10; McKay 1981; Barwise and Perry 1981a: 687; Richard 1983: 173–4; Soames 1987a: 125; 1995: 522; Fitch 1987: 131–52; 1993: 475; Levine 1988; Crimmins and Perry 1989: 696–9; D. F. Austin 1990: 112–5; Fodor 1990a: 68–70; Recanati 1990: 701; 1993: Ch. 2; Braun 1991a: 294–7; 1998; 2000; 2001; 2002; Corazza and Dokic 1992; Crimmins 1992: 41, 100–1, 152. 204–5; 1995a: 465; Adams, Stecker, and Fuller 1993a; McKinsey 1994: 309, 315, 317; Forbes 1997c; Jacob 1997; Frances 1998b: 344; 1999: 204; Peacocke 2000: 330–31; Predelli 2000. Contrast Schiffer 1992; 1995; Saul 1993; McKinsey 1999: 543–5; and Spencer 'Do Conversational Implicatures Explain Substitutivity Failures?' (forthcoming).

[30] Salmon 1986: 1989b; 1990; Laurier 1986: 48; Soames 1987a; 1987b; 1995; Saul 1998.

[31] Situations are often called 'singular' or 'Russellian' propositions. Declarative thoughts might similarly be called 'conceptual' or 'Fregean' thoughts (although the latter is liable to evoke specific tenets of Frege's views that I reject).

[32] Cf. Levine 1988; Crimmins and Perry 1989: 696–9; Forbes 1989a: 474–5; 1990, 1993, 1997b, 1997c; Adams, Stecker, and Fuller 1993a; 1993b; Crimmins 1995a: 465; 1998: 31; Clapp 1995: 535–6. See especially Crimmins (1992: 152, 204–5), who identifies ways of believing with 'thought maps', structured types of representations containing ideas and notions. Contrast Chisholm (1989) and Fitch (1987: Chs. 4–5; 1993: 475), who identify ways of believing ('cognitive states') with the self-attribution of properties (see my *Indexicals*); and Schiffer (1978), who concluded, most curiously, that I believe ⟨Wayne Davis, being a man⟩ when I believe that I am a man, but not when I believe that Wayne Davis is a man! Schiffer's view is usefully discussed in Austin 1990: Ch. 3.

[33] Compare and contrast Braun 1998: 567–8.

[34] Cf. Laurier 1986:47; Tomberlin 1989b: 524–5; 1991: 242–4. This problem has inspired a number of desperation measures. See, for example, Fitch 1987: 163–9; 1993: 476, 483; and Crimmins 1992: 195. Given a sufficiently Platonistic ontology, the situation consisting of Santa Claus's bringing presents could be treated as an abstract object that exists even though Santa Claus and the ordered n-tuple ⟨Santa, bringing presents⟩ do not (see Forbes 1993, 1997). Situations so-conceived would *exist* in all worlds even if they do not *obtain* in all worlds, just as properties exist even in worlds in which they are not instantiated. This Platonistic theory gives up the key Russellian tenet that the objects of propositional attitudes literally contain the people, places, and things that we think about.

[35] See also Crimmins 1992. One important difference is that for Crimmins and Perry, modes of presentation are cognitive *particulars* that are *possessed by the subject*. For some of the problems this creates, see Saul 1993; Clapp 1995: 546–60.

[36] Evans (1985: 74–9, 90) denies this, taking 'mode of presentation of y' and 'way of thinking of y' relationally rather than intentionally (see §8.2). As a result, Evans cheerfully swallows the absurd claim that fictional names really have no sense, and are used at best to express 'mock thoughts', an idea Frege himself at least entertained (1979: 130). See also Russell 1912: Ch. 4; McDowell 1977: 173–5; Chisholm 1981: 74; McGinn 1982: 249; Travis 1985; Fitch 1987: 163, 167–8; Boër 1989: 191; Crimmins 1992: 83, 89; Wiggins 1999. Contrast Sainsbury 1999; and §10.4 above.

[37] See also Clapp 1995; Braun 1998: 558–61.

[38] Soames uses 'Peter Hempel' and 'Carl Hempel'. Carl Hempel, the famous philosopher of science, was known as Peter Hempel to his friends and colleagues. Newcomers to Princeton were often surprised to learn that Peter Hempel was Carl Hempel. Since few readers will have known Peter Hempel as Peter Hempel, this example is not very effective for producing intuitions of substitutivity failure (see §10.5).

[39] By using a quantificational variable in a belief clause, making it extensional. Alternatively, the argument assumes the transparent interpretation of belief sentences, which is not the interpretation on which substitutivity failures appear to arise.

# Fregean Theories

The failure of Mill's way shows that proper names have a meaning, and that their sense must be distinguished from their reference. Proper names conform to the general rule that the meaning or sense of a term is a factor which, together with nonlinguistic facts, determines what if anything the term denotes. But it is commonly assumed that if proper names have a sense, they must have a descriptive sense. What we shall call 'Fregean' theories hold that the meaning of a proper name can in principle be defined using general terms or descriptions. On the ideational theory, this means that the concept expressed by a proper name is complex, containing general or descriptive concepts as parts. The classical Fregean theory was the description theory, according to which proper names are 'disguised' definite descriptions. The classical description theory holds that the meaning of every proper name 'N' can be given specifically by a definite description of the form *'the (unique) F'*, for some general term *'F'* that is purely descriptive. To say that a term is 'purely' descriptive is to say that it contains no indexical elements and no ineliminable proper names. Nonclassical theories allow that proper names might be defined using descriptions that are not purely descriptive. We will review arguments that show, conclusively I believe, that no Fregean theory is plausible for standard proper names. Frege's horn of the dichotomy is as untenable as Mill's.

## 12.1 THE CLASSICAL DESCRIPTION THEORY

The description theory works very well for proper names such as 'May 9th', 'New Year's Eve', 'page 10', and 'Superbowl XXI'. These terms have descriptive conditions of application: 'May 9th' applies to an object if and only if 'the ninth day of May' applies to it. Indeed, 'May 9th is the ninth day of May' expresses a self-evident *a priori* truth, known to everyone who has considered the proposition.[1] 'May 9th' and 'the ninth day of May' appear to be completely intersubstitutable even in that-clauses. 'Mary believes that May 9th is tomorrow' seems to be just a reformulation of 'Mary believes that the ninth day of May is tomorrow'. Even though it has descriptive conditions of application, 'May 9th' is a proper name rather than a definite description. It must be capitalized. It cannot be pluralized or modified by articles, quantifiers, or restrictive clauses, except when used as a general term ('a May 9th', 'the May 9th that made history', 'all May 9ths'). It can be used as the subject of a sentence without a determiner ('May 9th is finished' versus '*day is finished'), to refer to a single definite object. It is very plausible that 'May 9th' and 'the ninth day of May' differ syntactically but not semantically. I will call such names *logically descriptive*.[2]

Since it fits logically descriptive names well, and easily accommodates referentless names with meaning and coreferential names with different meanings, the description theory has considerable prima facie plausibility. But logically descriptive names are decidedly atypical, differing in several respects from what I shall call *standard names* like 'Aristotle', 'Johannes Brahms', 'The United States', and 'Mt. Everest'. First, 'That is N' *describes* the object when 'N' is a definite description or descriptive name, but *merely identifies* it when 'N' is a standard proper name.[3]

Second, a standard name cannot be used to refer to a particular object unless it or an etymological antecedent was at some point *given* to that object. While 'John Smith' could conceivably be given to any individual, it cannot be used to refer to Joe's son in particular unless and until he has been so named. The English name 'Aristotle' was never given to Aristotle, but the Greek term from which it has evolved was given to him. The giving of the name need not be a formal baptism or official registry. But somehow the connection between that name and the particular object must have been *stipulated*. In contrast, if a student submits a paper with unnumbered pages, we can still refer to the tenth page as 'page 10'. If the student adds two pages, what was formerly page 10 may automatically become page 12. The connection between name and page is not made by stipulation. Instead, the connection is determined by the meaning of the name's components and its syntactic structure.[4]

Third, exhaustive searches fail to discover *any* descriptions synonymous with standard names.[5] What turns up instead is compelling evidence that no description 'F' would make 'N is the F' a good definition of the meaning of 'N' if 'N' is a standard name. As a typical example, consider:

(1) Aristotle is the author of *De Anima*.

In this case, the proposed analysis is at least true. But if 'Aristotle' and 'the author of *De Anima*' were completely synonymous, then the proposition expressed by (1) should be an *a priori* and necessary truth, one that is not only common knowledge but self-evident. Indeed (1) should have the same semantic properties and express the same proposition as (2) and (3).

(2) The author of *De Anima* is the author of *De Anima*.
(3) Aristotle is Aristotle.

But these three sentences seem far from synonymous. Sentence (1) tells us who wrote *De Anima*; (2) and (3) do not. And whereas everyone who considers the proposition expressed by either (2) or (3) is likely to believe it, the same is not true for (1). Moreover, while it is possible that (1) is false, it makes no sense to suggest that (2) or (3) is false. And whereas (2) and (3) are self-evident logical truths, historical evidence is needed to establish (1). Some individuals may come to know (1) by testimony, of course, based on the authority of others who have historical evidence. But both constitute empirical evidence. (1) cannot be known without such evidence; knowledge of (2) and (3) requires no evidence.[6] Note that unlike (2) and (3), (1) implies that Aristotle is an author. Similarly, (1) implies that Aristotle and *De Anima* exist, whereas (2) lacks the former implication and (3) lacks the latter. In general, (1)–(3) are used to communicate different things, and to express different thoughts and beliefs. All these facts show that 'Aristotle' is not synonymous with 'the author of *De Anima*'.

Because (1) does not express a necessary truth, the terms 'Aristotle' and 'The author of *De Anima*' would denote different things if the world were different, even if their meanings remain unchanged. For example, if Plato rather than Aristotle were the author of *De Anima*, 'The author of *De Anima*' would denote Plato, but 'Aristotle' would not. If we ask, 'Who is the author of *De Anima* in that world?' the answer is 'Plato.' If we ask 'Who is Aristotle in that world?' the answer can only be 'Aristotle.' Names are thus said to be *rigid designators* (Kripke 1972). Descriptions are generally nonrigid, unless they are about abstract objects (an example is 'the square root of 4', which designates 2 in every possible world). A rigid name cannot be synonymous with any nonrigid description. For terms with the same meaning have the same referent in every possible world.[7]

The statistical predicates suggested by Strawson (1963: Ch. 6) and Searle (1958) produce analyses with all of the problems discussed:

(4) Aristotle is the thing with most of the properties people believe Aristotle to possess.

Sentence (4) has the virtue of expressing something that might be believed even by people who know very little about Aristotle. Furthermore, while it is easy to imagine Aristotle lacking any *one* of the properties we believe him to possess, it is harder to imagine that he lacks most of them. Still, what (4) expresses is far from self-evident, and seems decidedly contingent. Cynics or elitists who think that 'most people' are wrong about most things might doubt what (4) expresses in principle. What assurance do any of us have that the beliefs of most people would be consistent and accurate enough for there to be a unique person with most of the properties they believe Aristotle to possess? Are the properties of an object even countable, so that it makes sense to speak of 'most' properties? Do all properties count equally when determining whether something is Aristotle, or are some more important than others? Finally, the two occurrences of 'Aristotle' in (4) are intended to have the same meaning. But then the predicate of (4) cannot tell us what the subject means. Moreover, the descriptive predicate in (4) has to have more semantic structure than the proper name, because the name expresses a proper part of what the description expresses.

It might be argued that 'male' and 'person' provide at least part of the meaning of 'Cary', since it is a boy's rather than a girl's name.[8] 'Carrie' is the feminine form. But we must distinguish conventions regulating *naming*, which involves the *introduction* of names, from conventions governing their subsequent *usage*. Usage conventions determine whether a given expression *has* a particular meaning, and thus whether the name can correctly be used on any given occasion to refer to a given object. Naming conventions determine whether a particular meaning and reference is *appropriate* for a given linguistic expression.[9] It would be unconventional to name a female dog, building, or body of water 'Cary'. Hence 'Cary' would be an inappropriate name for such things. But if someone did unconventionally name a female dog 'Cary', and everyone picked up the name and used it to refer to that dog, then on one interpretation 'Cary is male' would be false, 'Cary hurt herself' would be grammatical, and so on. An unconventional naming act would have given rise to a conventional meaning. Even when by 'Cary' we mean "Cary Grant", 'Cary is male' is not analytic. Nothing in the meaning of the name rules out the possibility of a sex change operation, for example, or the possibility of discovering that Cary Grant was really a woman all along, who perpetrated an enormously profitable hoax on the entire world. Nothing in the meaning of the name rules out the possibility of Cary Grant being a mutant chimpanzee or Martian indistinguishable from a human being except upon microscopic examination, in which case even 'Cary is a person' would be false.

The etymological sense in which the meaning of 'Cary' is "from the castle" (since the name derives from a Welsh word with that meaning) is irrelevant to both the sense of the term and its appropriateness.[10] To say that the star is Cary Grant is not to say or imply that the star is from the castle. Note that it would be possible, though unconventional, to give an individual the name 'Bormang', a made-up expression completely devoid of descriptive appropriateness conditions or etymological meaning. Algeo (1973: 6, 58) provides references to actual cases of this sort. Once such a name is established, it would have meaning in the sense we are interested in, and sentences like 'Bormang is a dog' would be true or false depending on whether the individual named is a dog. Note finally that the distinction between meaning, etymological meaning, and appropriateness conditions is not unique to proper names. For example, the common name 'hippopotamus' does not mean "river horse" even though etymologically it comes from Greek words meaning "river horse". And it would be inappropriate to call a newly discovered species of slime mold 'F-23 Lightning'.

The descriptive condition for the application of 'page 10' is not just an appropriateness condition. It would of course be eccentric to name a child 'page 10,' and perverse to paginate a manuscript '1, 3, 10, 9, 2, 5, ...'. But when it is used in the conventional manner with reference to a manuscript whose pages are not numbered, 'page 10' necessarily applies to the tenth page. Someone who uses 'Page 10 has a footnote' with its regular meaning, but is referring to the twentieth page, has made a mistake, and will have said something false if the tenth page has no footnote. In contrast, an ostensibly similar name like 'Tenth Street' has being the tenth street as an appropriateness condition only. We cannot walk into a town with streets arranged perfectly in a grid and automatically refer to the tenth street as Tenth Street.

Finally, it should be noted that standard names are not the only names that fail to fit the description theory. Two classes are too descriptive to be classified as standard and yet not descriptive enough to be classified as logically descriptive. The first class includes 'Monday' and 'Christmas' when used as singular terms, along with '$\pi$' and the gravitational constant 'G'. These resemble standard names in lacking structure and therefore compositional meaning. They nevertheless have descriptive conditions of application. Monday is necessarily the day before Tuesday and the day after Sunday. $\pi$ is defined as the ratio of the circumference of a circle to its diameter. It is doubtful, however, that these descriptions are strictly synonymous with the names. It is arguable that someone might know that $\pi$ is approximately 3.14, and that its more exact value can be obtained by punching a key on any standard calculator, without knowing that $\pi$ is the exact ratio of circumference to diameter. 'Monday' stands in the same relation to 'the day after Sunday' and 'the day before Tuesday', but it cannot be synonymous with both. The second class includes 'Springfield Virginia' or 'Aristotle of Stagira'. These are syntactically structured, and have a descriptive condition as part of their meaning (being in Virginia, or being from Stagira). But the descriptive condition is only a necessary condition. Hence the name is not synonymous with any purely descriptive phrase.

## 12.2   THE MODAL ARGUMENT: SCOPE DEFENSE

The modal argument concludes that 'N' does not mean 'the F' from the fact that 'N is the F' does not express a necessary truth. Given that Plato could have written *De Anima*, 'Aristotle is the author of *De Anima*' is not true in every possible world. If not, then 'Aristotle' and 'the author of *De Anima*' cannot mean the same thing.

The modal argument is commonly dismissed on the grounds that 'names are normally read as having wider scope than modal operators'.[11] The truth of 'Aristotle need not have been the author of *De Anima*' does not suffice to show that 'Aristotle' is not synonymous with 'the author of *De Anima*'. For 'The author of *De Anima* need not have been the author of *De Anima*' is also true, despite the fact that the very same description was used in both the subject and the predicate. What makes it true is that the first occurrence of the description is outside the scope of the modality operator, while the second is inside. Hence the first is said to have 'wide' scope, the second 'narrow' scope. The suggestion, then, is that names are disguised descriptions with wide scope.

However, both names and descriptions can also have narrow scope. If 'N' and 'the F' were synonymous, then modal sentences containing them should also be synonymous when both terms are given narrow scope. They are not. Compare the following:

(5) Necessarily, the author of *De Anima* is the author of *De Anima*. (narrow)
(6) The author of *De Anima* is such that necessarily, he is the author of *De Anima*. (wide)
(7) Necessarily, Aristotle is the author of *De Anima*. (narrow)
(8) Aristotle is such that necessarily, he is the author of *De Anima*. (wide)

Let the scope of the terms and modal operators be indicated by the commas, so that the singular terms 'The author of *De Anima*' and 'Aristotle' have narrow scope in (5) and (7), wide scope in (6) and (8). Using some technical notation, (5) would be '□(The author of *De Anima* is the author of *De Anima*)' whereas (6) would be 'The author of *De Anima* is such that □(he is the author of *De Anima*)'. (5) says that if you go to any world and find out who is the author of *De Anima* in that world, then that individual will be the author of *De Anima* in that world. (6) says that if you find the author of *De Anima* in the actual world and then pick this individual out in any other world, he will be the author of *De Anima* in that world too. (7) says '□(Aristotle is the author of *De Anima*)': if you go to any world and find out who is Aristotle in that world, then that individual will be the author of *De Anima* in that world. (8) says 'Aristotle is such that □(he is the author of *De Anima*)': if you find the individual who is Aristotle in the actual world and pick that individual out in any other world, he will be the author of *De Anima* there.

I hope it is clear both how I am interpreting (5)–(8), and that these sentences *can* be so interpreted in English.[12] Now observe that on the intended interpretation (5) is true, whereas (7) is false. Moreover, (7) and (8) are equivalent, while (5) and (6) differ in truth value.[13] If 'Aristotle' and 'the author of *De Anima*' had the very same meaning, these differences would not be possible. Related differences show up in other modal sentences.

> (9) The author of *De Anima* might not have been the author of *De Anima*.
>
> (10) Aristotle might not have been the author of *De Anima*.
>
> (11) Aristotle might not have been Aristotle.

Let the three occurrences of 'Aristotle' and 'the author of *De Anima*' have the same meaning. Even with this constraint, (9) is markedly ambiguous, representing either the denial of (5) or the denial of (6). Hence (9) can be heard either as true or as false. In contrast, (10) and (11) do not seem ambiguous. (10) can only be heard as true, and (11) only as false.[14] If some theoretical reason would lead us to say that (10) is structurally ambiguous, representing the denial of either (7) or (8), we would still get the result that (10) is true on both its interpretations, whereas (9) is true only on one. Under the parallel assumption, (11) would be false on both interpretations, whereas (9) is false on only one. Either way, (9)–(11) differ, proving that 'Aristotle' and 'the author of *De Anima*' are not synonymous.

The scope defense is particularly problematic for the Fregean because descriptive names exhibit scope ambiguity as freely as definite descriptions. For example, 'Page 11 might not have been page 11' is ambiguous, with one interpretation that is false and a more common interpretation that is true. Being false for logically descriptive names, the descriptivist's claim is at best *ad hoc* for standard names. If the description theory were true, one would expect all names to behave like logically descriptive names in modal contexts. When all the evidence is considered, I believe the conclusion to draw is not that standard names normally have wide scope, but that they differ from descriptions and descriptive names in that their meaning is such that it normally does not matter which scope they have.

This can be confirmed by noting that names of objects known to be non-existent are normally given narrow scope in certain contexts. Consider the hypothetical planet Vulcan, once thought to lie closer to the Sun than Mercury.

> (12) Vulcan could have been observed.

On its most natural interpretation, (12) would be interpreted as saying that scientific results could have shown that Vulcan existed, even though in fact they did not. (12) is thus the true narrow-scope statement that the object denoted by 'Vulcan' in some world was observed there. On its wide-scope interpretation, (12) would state that the object denoted by 'Vulcan' in the actual world was observed in some world. It would thus be false or truth-valueless because it falsely presupposes that Vulcan exists. For similar reasons, 'If Vulcan existed, there would be a tenth planet' cannot be interpreted with 'Vulcan' given wide scope without turning a plausible truth into something with a false presupposition.[15]

A final piece of evidence that the modal argument does not rest on over-looking scope distinctions comes from the fact that modal differences be-tween names and descriptions arise even when there are no scope distinctions.[16] There are two distinct ways in which a subject-predicate proposition 's is P' can be evaluated as true or false in a hypothetical case, imagined situation, or possible world w: find the individual that is s in w, and then determine whether that individual is P in w; or: find the individual that is s in the actual world, and then determine whether that individual is P in w. As a result, both (13) and (14) are ambiguous:

(13) 'The author of *De Anima* wrote *De Anima*' is true in that case.
(14) 'Aristotle wrote *De Anima*' is true in that case.

Let 'that case' refer to a case in which Plato wrote *De Anima*. Then (13) is true on one interpretation and false on another, while (14) is false on both interpretations. The sentences *mentioned* in (13) and (14) are both to be understood as having a fixed interpretation, the one that has been standard in this discussion ('Aristotle' means Aristotle the philosopher rather than Aristotle Onassis, etc.). And the two occurrences of the demonstrative 'that' should have the same referent.[17] The ambiguity of (13) and (14) therefore lies solely in the predicate *true in that case* when applied to a subject-predicate sentence. We can see that scope distinctions are not somehow being smuggled in via the reference to possible worlds or cases by observing that the same differences show up when we ask whether the sentences mentioned in (13) and (14) are true in a particular *story* or *account*.

The difference between (13) and (14) is due not to a difference in the scope of their subject terms, but instead to a difference in their *rigidity*. (14) is false on both interpretations because 'Aristotle' denotes the same person in every possible world. (13) is true on one interpretation and false on another because 'the author of *De Anima*' denotes Aristotle in one world, Plato in another. The same difference in rigidity accounts for why differences in scope typically matter for definite descriptions but not names, as illustrated in (5)–(8).

## 12.3 THE MODAL ARGUMENT: RIGIDITY DEFENSE

The description theorist might therefore be able to avoid the modal objec-tion by finding a *rigid description* that is synonymous with a standard name. Several authors have suggested 'rigidifying' descriptions with the word *actual*.[18] I do not believe 'actual' produces a rigid description on its conven-tional meaning. 'Actual' would produce rigid descriptions if the indexical theory of actuality were true (cf. Lewis 1973: 86). But that theory is untenable, in my view, in large part because it presupposes Lewis's idea that individuals are world-bound (see §14.6). Note first that replacing 'author' with 'actual author' does not eliminate the marked difference between (9) and (11). Consider:

(15) The actual author of *De Anima* might not have been the actual author of *De Anima*.
(16) Aristotle might not have been Aristotle.

(16) is unequivocally true. (15) is ambiguous, since either occurrence of 'the actual author of *De Anima*' may have wide or narrow scope with respect to the modal operator expressed by 'might'. On an interpretation in which the first occurrence of the description has wide scope and the second has narrow scope, (15) is false. The referent of 'the actual author of *De Anima*' in the actual world is Aristotle. In a world in which Plato wrote *De Anima*, Plato actually wrote *De Anima*. Hence 'Aristotle' and 'the actual author of *De Anima*' designate different individuals in that world; the latter designates Plato there. Hence (17) is true.

(17) 'The actual author of *De Anima*' designates Plato in a world in which Plato actually authored *De Anima*.

'The actual world' itself may seem like a rigid description. But if a world $w_p$ in which Plato wrote *De Anima* were the actual world, then 'the actual world' would denote $w_p$.

Adding 'actual' to 'the author of *De Anima*' does not produce a rigid description. What it does is produce a description that we normally read as having wide scope. One way to rigidify descriptions in the way these authors had in mind is to introduce '@' as a *proper name* for the actual world. Then assuming that possible worlds have their contents essentially, 'the author of *De Anima* in @' is a rigid designator.[19] Even in $w_p$, the author of *De Anima* in @ is Aristotle. But in $w_p$, @ is not the actual world: $w_p$ is.

Descriptions rigidified with '@' are of little use for the description theorist, for four reasons. (i) Aside from some philosophers and modal logicians, few of the billions of users of proper names world wide have concepts like '@' or 'the author of *De Anima* in @'. A word cannot mean something in a natural language that few users have ever meant or even conceived. (ii) People who do have such concepts need not have any beliefs about @. Hence someone could well believe "Aristotle is Aristotle", in a close world as well as a remote one, without believing "Aristotle is the F in @" no matter what "F" is (cf. Soames 1998: 15). (iii) Any description rigidified by reference to the actual world @ will be inappropriate for names of nonexistent objects. Analyzing "Pegasus" as meaning "the white flying horse named 'Pegasus' in @" would entail that there is no such thing as Pegasus not only in the actual world, but in any possible world—implying that Pegasus is not only nonexistent but impossible. If that implication should strike you as correct, compare the following sentences.

(18) The F in @ exists in @ if it exists in any world.
(19) Pegasus exists in @ if it exists in any world.

For any 'F', (18) is trivially true, self-evident, and indubitable. (19) is not. Consequently (18) cannot be *synonymous* with (19). We might try to resolve this problem by rigidifying the description by reference to some other possible world (one in which the Pegasus myth is true). But in addition to exacerbating the first problem, this suggestion would imply that the very meaning of a name like 'God' could not be settled until the existence of a referent is settled, even though reference is determined by meaning. (iv) Even if all *other* proper names could be defined in terms of descriptions containing '@', we would still have to account for the sense of '@'. All we need is *one* proper name with a nondescriptive sense to show that the Frege–Mill dichotomy is false. And if we have one such name, what would be the point of insisting on implausible descriptive senses for other proper names?

Another rigidifier is the indexical *'this world'*, said while pointing or looking at the world around us. 'The author of *De Anima* in this world' is as rigid as 'the author of *De Anima* in @'. The use of 'this world' as the rigidifier avoids some of the problems noted above, principally the problem of explaining the meaning of one name in terms of the meaning of another. But other problems hold *mutatis mutandis*. It is questionable whether people who can think about Aristotle must have the concept of a possible world, or any beliefs containing the concept *"this world"*. Furthermore, descriptions rigidified by 'this world' will be inappropriate for names of nonexistent objects. A new problem is that 'the author of *De Anima* in this world' can be used, without change of sense, to refer to Plato, as when the speaker points to the description of a world in which Plato wrote Aristotle's books. 'Aristotle' cannot be so used.

## 12.4   THE INDEXICAL DESCRIPTION THEORY

Burks (1951) showed that if 'F' is a *purely* descriptive predicate, containing no proper names or indexical elements, then a proper name such as 'Aristotle' could not be synonymous with 'the F'. For no matter how far-fetched, it is at least logically possible that there is a 'mirror universe' containing an object descriptively indistinguishable from Aristotle.[20] In that case, 'Aristotle is *the* F' would be false (or truth valueless). But if there is a logically possible case in which 'A is B' is false, then 'A' and 'B' cannot be synonymous.

Burks concluded that proper names must abbreviate *'indexical* definite descriptions', like 'this man' (said while pointing at Aristotle) or 'that philosopher' (said while listening to a lecture on Aristotle). (To maintain the letter of the classical description theory, we could even let the definite description be something like 'the man who is this man'.) With Kripkean hindsight, we can observe another advantage of Burks's theory: indexical descriptions resemble proper names in being rigid designators. Just as Aristotle might not have been a philosopher, so that philosopher could have had a different profession. Similarly, 'Necessarily, that man is that man' and 'That man is such that necessarily, he is that man' are equivalent (assuming that the terms are given the same interpretation), in marked contrast to what we found with pure descriptions.

Despite these advantages, Burks's indexical description theory shares many of the defects of the pure. A radical feminist might speculate, for example, that Aristotle was really a woman forced to act like a man by a sexist society. While fanciful, such speculation is not self-contradictory, as it would be to conjecture that this man is really a woman. If we posit a sortal general enough to express part of the meaning of this name (§13.4), it will be too general for the indexical reference to succeed. It might be analytic that Aristotle is a concrete object, but 'This concrete object' said while pointing at Aristotle does not have a unique reference. The descriptive element in indexical descriptions still causes problems.

Moreover, Burks's theory has a defect of its own. 'Aristotle' cannot really be *synonymous* with anything as simple as 'this man'. If it were, then I should be able to refer to the president by pointing to him and saying 'Aristotle is an American'. I should also be able to refer to Aristotle's twin by saying the same thing while pointing at a picture representing him in his mirror universe. But I cannot use 'Aristotle' in this way, at least not if I am speaking English correctly. As we noted in criticism of Pelczar and Rainsbury (§10.6), the referent of a name is determined completely by the meaning of the name on that occasion together with the identities of objects in the world, whereas the referent of an indexical is determined by an additional contextual factor. In a crucial respect, proper names do not behave like indexical descriptions of the sort Burks suggested. In defense of Burks, one might suggest that 'Aristotle' has the meaning of 'this man' said while pointing at Aristotle, although not the meaning of 'this man' said while pointing at the president. But 'this man' has the same meaning in both contexts. One of the distinctive facts about indexicals is that their reference varies from context to context even though their meaning does not. Burks's theory may be adequate to fix the reference of a proper name, but not to identify its sense.

Burge (1973; 1977; 1983) has defended a version of the indexical description theory according to which the singular sense of a name is defined in terms of its sense as a general term. Suppose someone said 'Which Aristotle is the philosopher?' The reply might be 'That Aristotle', said while pointing at the cover of a philosophy text rather than the style section. According to Burge, the singular term 'Aristotle' has the meaning of 'that Aristotle', making the following sentences synonymous:

(20) Aristotle was a student of Plato.
(21) That Aristotle was a student of Plato.

At least to my ear, these sentences do not sound synonymous. To back up this linguistic intuition, imagine that a knowledgeable speaker uttered one of these sentences with apparent sincerity while pointing at Aristotle Onassis. If the speaker uttered (20), we would have a hard time figuring out what he said. The fact that he was pointing at Onassis is evidence that by 'Aristotle' he meant Aristotle Onassis rather than Aristotle of Stagira. But the predicate of the sentence together with his evident sincerity and knowledge of famous people is evidence that he meant Aristotle of Stagira. In a case like this, the rules of English make what the speaker said dependent on what he meant. We would be confused for exactly the same reason if the speaker said 'The bank is a tree lined grassy slope' while pointing at Riggs National Bank. In contrast, if the speaker uttered (21), we would have no trouble figuring out what he said: whether he meant to or not, he said that the Aristotle he was pointing at was a student of Plato.[21] The semantic rules governing (20) and (21) are quite different.

Two other differences between 'Aristotle' and 'that Aristotle' are subtler and harder to characterize.

(i) Imagine a young child who first hears the name 'Aristotle' when someone says, 'A long time ago there was a philosopher named Aristotle who lived in Greece'. It would be perfectly natural for the child to utter (20); but (21) would be completely unexpected. For (21) is appropriately used only if the speaker realizes that there are several Aristotles, and wishes to select one for discussion. In contrast, (20) could appropriately be used by someone who had never even considered the possibility that there was another Aristotle besides the one he has in mind.

(ii) In any speech context, something overt must indicate which Aristotle the speaker has in mind when (21) is used. Otherwise 'that' was used improperly. If the overt context did not make it clear which Aristotle an utterer of (20) had in mind, we will not know who he was referring to. To that extent, his utterance will be infelicitous. But he would not have used any word improperly. In short, proper names behave like indexicals in some respects, but are not as context dependent.

As a result of these differences, extended dialogues that are completely natural turn into utter gibberish when every proper name 'N' is replaced by 'that N'. For a demonstration (plus some further semantic differences), see

Castañeda (1983: 359–65). This would not happen if 'N' had the same meaning as 'that N'.

Linsky suggested a slightly different variant on the classical view. Following Dummett (1973: 112–16), Linsky claims that our 'criterion of identification' for the referent of the name 'St. Anne' is given by the description 'the mother of Mary'. Linsky concludes that the meaning of that description is a constituent of the sense of the name. This constituent cannot be the whole of the meaning, Linsky observes (as against Dummett), for the name is not *synonymous* with the description, as the rigidity of the former and the nonrigidity of the latter proves. Linsky concludes that 'Another constituent of its sense accrues to it solely by virtue of the fact that it is a proper name. It is by virtue of this constituent of its sense that we know that any proper name is a rigid designator' (1977: 84).[22] The view is that the sense of a presumably standard name has a descriptional component and a rigidifying component. This generalizes the suggestion of Plantinga and others discussed in §12.3 by dropping the requirement that the rigidifying element be part of descriptional element.

A formal model of Linsky's rigidifier is provided by the 'operator' interpretation of *dthat* (Kaplan 1977).[23] On this specification, Linsky's view is that 'St. Anne' means "dthat (the mother of Mary)". Since the latter expression is rigid, Kripke's modal objections are avoided. As the relevance of Kaplan's work suggests, Linsky's view also generalizes Burks's and Burge's theories. The latter focus on *demonstrative* forms of indexicality, which, as noted, require that some overt element of the context (such as the act of pointing) indicate which object the speaker has in mind. Other forms of indexicality, such as found in 'now' and 'I' as opposed to 'this' or 'that', are nondemonstrative, directly selecting certain elements of the context as referents no matter what the speaker has in mind. By emphasizing nondemonstrative indexicality, the principal objections to Burge's and Burks's theories are avoided.

There are several lines of evidence that a standard proper name 'N' does not mean "dthat (the F)" for any descriptive term 'F'. First, if the sense of 'the mother of Mary' is part of the sense of 'St. Anne', then 'St. Anne is the mother of Mary' should be self-evident, 'St. Anne was childless' should be self-contradictory, and so on. Linsky believes these semantic predictions are correct.

I remember the occasion upon which I learned the name. I was looking at Leonardo's famous painting of the Virgin and St. Anne and I asked my wife, 'Who is St. Anne?' The reply was, 'St. Anne is the mother of the Virgin Mary.' To this day that is *all* I know about St. Anne. For me, the suggestion that St. Anne existed but was not the mother of Mary is simply unintelligible. . . .					(Linsky 1977: 55)

I myself learned about St. Anne from Dummett and Linsky. But I do not find the suggestion unintelligible at all. Indeed, let us suppose that I asked one of my Jesuit colleagues, 'Who is St. Anne? Leonard Linsky and Michael Dummett say she is the mother of Mary. Are they right?' And suppose the reply is, 'No. That is a common confusion. St. Anne is the Virgin Mary's aunt, who raised her after the Virgin Mother's mother died in childbirth.' Would I be in any position to say that my Jesuit colleagues must be mistaken? In contrast, suppose I asked my colleagues whether dthat (the mother of Mary) is the mother of Mary. If they said no, I would fail them on their Kaplan exam.

Second, someone might well learn the name 'St. Anne' without ever having heard of the Virgin Mary. Someone with only the slightest knowledge of the Christian religion might have learned that St. Anne is the grandmother of Jesus Christ well before learning that Mary is the mother of Jesus, and therefore the daughter of St. Anne. And Linsky, despite what he said, knew that St. Anne was the woman in Leonardo's painting before he knew that she was the mother of Mary. Hence the sense of 'Mary' cannot be part of the sense of 'St. Anne'.

To see the third reason, we need to change examples. Boër (1978) imagined that the members of a drug ring do not know who their leader is, but call him 'Mr. Heroin'. Boër suggests that the name 'Mr. Heroin' is just 'shorthand' for 'the leader of the ring'. Linsky's suggestion would be that 'Mr. Heroin' has the same meaning as 'dthat (the leader of the ring)'. It would have the sort of meaning 'the King' has in Great Britain. But suppose Bob says 'Mr. Heroin was born in Grosse Point' on Monday, and Tom says 'Mr. Heroin was not born in Grosse Point' on Tuesday. Then Bob and Tom have made contradictory claims if 'Mr. Heroin' is a standard name. But they would not have made contradictory claims if either Boër or Linsky were right about what the name means. If either were right, then Bob's and Tom's claims would both be true if the ring got a new leader on Tuesday.

## 12.5 THE METALINGUISTIC THEORY

Many argue that the objections to classical descriptivism can be avoided by selecting a metalinguistic description. According to this proposal, a name 'N' is semantically equivalent to *"the (unique) bearer of the name 'N.'"*[24] Bach argued that the metalinguistic theory must be true because 'there is nothing else for a name to mean!' (1987a: 136). Bach is presumably suggesting that all other possibilities have been ruled out, which may seem plausible given that all description theories we have reviewed so far have failed. But Bach's argument falsely assumes the Frege–Mill dichotomy. There is something else for a name to mean: 'Aristotle' can and does mean "Aristotle". The question is whether such a meaning is descriptive. The fact that no other description has proven to be synonymous with a name is better taken as inductive evidence against the metalinguistic theory than as a proof by elimination of all possible alternatives.

Algeo cited as an advantage of the metalinguistic theory the fact that 'In effect it says that Thomases are individuals who can be recognized by the fact that people apply the name Thomas to them' (1973: 85). 'Thomases' and 'a Thomas' are clearly metalinguistic: a Thomas is someone named 'Thomas'. Consequently, Thomas Jefferson would not have been a Thomas if he had not been named 'Thomas'. But in this sense, 'Thomas' is a *general* term. We are concerned with names, which are *singular* terms. The subject and predicate of (22) have very different meanings.

> (22)  Thomas is a Thomas.

We hear (22) as referring to an individual and claiming that he has a certain name. We do not hear (22) as having meaning of 'A Thomas is a Thomas' or 'Thomas is Thomas'. The latter express (different) logical truths. (22) expresses a contingent truth: Thomas need not have been a Thomas.

Burge's indexical theory (§12.4), according to which 'Thomas' means "that Thomas", is also a metalinguistic theory. For in 'that Thomas', 'Thomas' is the general term meaning "person named 'Thomas' "—or in other words, "bearer of 'Thomas' ". Segal (2002) observed that using 'the' as the determiner rather than 'that' would avoid the problem for Burge's theory described in §12.4. Someone who says 'Thomas was a slave owner' in the presence of Thomas Kuhn has not automatically made a claim about the Thomas before him, as he would have if Burge were right about the meaning of 'Thomas'. Despite this advantage of the nonindexical metalinguistic theory, the fact is that we do not hear 'Thomas was a slave owner' as meaning "The Thomas was a slave owner". Nor do we hear (22) as meaning "The Thomas is a Thomas" or "The bearer of 'Thomas' is a bearer of 'Thomas' ".[25] The name differs from the description in that we hear it as referring to Thomas directly. Note that 'Necessarily Thomas is a Thomas' does not have the scope ambiguity that 'Necessarily the Thomas is a Thomas' has.

Metalinguistic theorists also point to cases in which proper names are used as singular terms to convey metalinguistic information.[26] Suppose someone says (23) when introducing himself to a group of people he has not met before.

> (23)  I am Aristotle.

In many cases, the information the speaker would be most intent on conveying is that his name is 'Aristotle'. But general terms can be used the same way. Suppose I am helping a foreigner learn English. I might point to a horse and say 'That is a horse'. My main concern is to convey what the animal is called, not what kind of animal it is, which I presume he already knows. The linguistic information is in both cases conveyed pragmatically. Moreover, when the speaker can presume that his audience has heard of him before, his main interest in saying (23) may well be to identify himself. Indeed, the speaker can explicitly cancel the metalinguistic implicature of (23) by adding "but I am called 'Joe Jones' now". Similarly, Bach (2002: 85) observes that we could naturally hear (24) as expressing a truth:

> (24) If his parents had named him 'Aristocrates', Aristotle would have been Aristocrates instead of Aristotle.

We can use common nouns the same way: "If such things had been named 'walkie-talkies', this cell phone would be a walkie-talkie rather than a cell phone". When (24) is heard as expressing a truth, the two occurrences of 'Aristotle' are heard as having different meanings. The same goes for 'cell phone'. Note well that (24) can also be heard as expressing a patent false-hood. When 'Aristocrates' and the second occurrence of 'Aristotle' are used literally rather than metalinguistically, (24) says that a different name would have made Aristotle a different person—which is absurd.

The metalinguistic theory does have two significant virtues. Compare 'Aristotle is the author of *De Anima*' (1) with (25).

> (25) Aristotle is the bearer of 'Aristotle'.

Whereas it is not widely known that Aristotle is the author of *De Anima*, it is common knowledge among competent speakers of English that Aristotle bears the name 'Aristotle'. Furthermore, sentence (25) is in some way trivially true. It is thus much more plausible that (25) is analytic than any of the other proposals to define 'Aristotle' that we have seen.

These considerations cannot be good evidence for the metalinguistic theory, however. For metalinguistic statements involving common nouns have the same features. The fact that *"Horses are denoted by 'horse'"* is similarly trivial does not imply that being denoted by 'horse' is part of the meaning of 'horse'.[27] Metalinguistic theorists have provided no reason to think that a proper name differs from a common noun in expressing the property of bearing itself. Without such a reason, it is arbitrary and *ad hoc* to make the claim for one but not the other. Bach attempts to provide one, without success:

> there is a relevant difference: whereas Socrates is called 'Socrates' because he has the property of bearing the name 'Socrates' (a property he acquired on being so named), horses are called 'horses' because they each have the property of being a horse.
>
> (Bach 2002: 83)

It is true that no one gave the common name 'horse' to horses; the word 'horse' had a gradual evolution. But televisions and telephones were given their names, even though 'television' and 'telephone' are not proper names.

And no one ever gave the Atlantic Ocean that name; it's name evolved from the Greek name 'Atlantikos' via Latin. On the other hand, it is just as true that Aristotle is called 'Aristotle' because he has the property of being Aristotle (i.e., because he is Aristotle) as it is that horses are called 'horses' because they have the property of being horses (i.e., because they are horses).

Furthermore, *"Aristotle is the referent of 'the bearer of "Aristotle"'"* is also trivially true, as are all higher order iterations. So the fact cited provides no reason to think that 'Aristotle' is synonymous with the first order metalinguistic description rather than any of the higher order descriptions. Indeed, the triviality of (25) cannot be used to show anything about the meaning of the name involved, since substituting a different name with the same meaning for the subject term will eliminate the triviality. For the same reason, "Horses are denoted by 'equus'" is nontrivial despite the fact that 'equus' means "horse".

The triviality of (25) can be explained without assuming that 'Aristotle' is synonymous with "the bearer of 'Aristotle'". Even if 'Aristotle' meant "the author of *De Anima*", the speaker used 'Aristotle' properly and literally in the subject of (25) only if he used it to refer to the conventional referent of 'Aristotle'. Since the conventional referent of a name is its bearer, the speaker had to have spoken truly if he used language properly and literally. That is, the speaker cannot fail to assert a truth. As for the hearer, she cannot possibly learn anything about Aristotle from the utterance of (25). For if the hearer does not already know the fact expressed by (25), she will not be able to understand (25). This distinguishes (25) markedly from 'Aristotle is still living'. A similar explanation can be given for the triviality of "Horses are denoted by 'horse'" and all its higher order iterations. Any theory postulating different explanations for phenomena as similar as the truth in every context of "Aristotle is the bearer of 'Aristotle'" and "Horses are denoted by 'horse'" has, *ipso facto*, a strike against it.

The metalinguistic theory wrongly predicts that the truth of (25) has the same *kind* of guarantee as the truth of (26) and (27), which are supposed to have exactly the same meaning.

> (26)  Aristotle is Aristotle.
> (27)  The bearer of 'Aristotle' is the bearer of 'Aristotle'.

There is an important distinction between a sentence which can, in virtue of its meaning, be used in any context to assert a truth, and a sentence which can be used to assert a necessary truth.[28] 'I am here' is an example of the former, but not the latter (I am here at my desk right now, but could have been elsewhere). All three sentences have the former property. Only (26) and (27) have the latter property. No one has to bear any particular name—or any name at all. But if (25) had exactly the same meaning as (26) or (27), then (25) would have to express a necessary truth because (26) and (27) do. The scope and rigidity defenses against Kripke's modal objection have the same inadequacies when employed by the metalinguistic theory (§12.2, §12.3).

Since the connection between names and things depends on convention, sentence (25) expresses an *a posteriori* truth. Sentences (26) and (27), in contrast, express *a priori* truths. The metalinguistic theory wrongly predicts that (25) also expresses an *a priori* truth. The knowledge that the *sentences* are true is of course *a posteriori* in all three cases: we cannot know that any English sentence is true without empirical evidence about the English language. It is what the sentences express whose epistemological status differs.

To see additional semantic differences between any name 'N' and the definite description "the bearer of 'N'", compare the following sentences:

(28) *De Anima* was written by the bearer of 'Aristotle'.
(29) *De Anima* was written by an Aristotle.
(30) *De Anima* was written by Aristotle.

First, sentence (28) explicitly mentions the word 'Aristotle,' and (29) implicitly mentions it (in one of its senses). (30) seems to contrast markedly with them by using the word without mentioning or talking about it.[29] Consequently, a translation of (30) into German would contain 'Aristoteles' in place of 'Aristotle', but a strict translation of (28) or (29) would not: (28) and (29) are about an English word, not a German word.[30] Second, since (28) mentions the name, it entails "The name 'Aristotle' exists", "Someone bears the name 'Aristotle'", and so on.[31] Since (30) is not about words, it has no such implications. Of course, the existence of the sentence marked (28) entails the existence of the name 'Aristotle'; but what the sentence expresses does not. Similarly, the fact that the *sentence* (30) is true implies that (28) and (29) are true. But the *proposition (30) expresses* does not entail the propositions expressed by (28) and (29). Third, (28) differs from (30) in presupposing that only one person bears the name 'Aristotle.' In a context in which both Aristotle of Stagira and Aristotle Onassis are salient bearers of 'Aristotle', (28) will be false or truthvalueless. But (30) will still be true as long as the speaker means 'Aristotle of Stagira' by 'Aristotle'. On any occasion of use, however, (30) differs from (29) in referring to a particular person named 'Aristotle'. Given these differences in implications, it is quite possible for someone to believe what (30) expresses without believing what (28) or (29) expresses. Indeed, contemporaries who knew that *De Anima* was written by Aristotle could not have known that *De Anima* was written by the bearer of 'Aristotle', since that name did not exist in Ancient Greek.[32]

One of the three problems just detailed—the false uniqueness presupposition of (28)—could be eliminated if we individuated names by their senses. That is, instead of taking the quoted name "'Aristotle'" to refer to a letter (or sound) sequence, as has been our practice, we could take it to refer to a letter sequence with a given meaning.[33] The tokens of these name types would all be tokens of the letter sequence 'Aristotle' produced when the name is used with the same meaning. This move is unavailable to the metalinguistic theory, however, for it is trying to explain what it is for names to have a meaning.

The false uniqueness presupposition could also be eliminated by individuating names according to their bearers, taking a name to be a letter sequence with a given referent.[34] For clarity, let us use 'name$_1$' to denote names as letter sequences, and 'name$_2$' to denote names as letter sequences with referents. Ambiguity is typical of names$_1$, homonymy of names$_2$. The letter sequence 'Aristotle' is a name$_1$ because many people have that name$_1$, among them Aristotle Onassis and Aristotle of Stagira. We cannot talk about *the* name$_2$ 'Aristotle', however. For "'Aristotle'" refers to different names$_2$ on different occasions, depending on the referent of 'Aristotle'. Let "'Aristotle$_S$'" and "'Aristotle$_O$'" designate the two names$_2$. The metalinguistic theorist can now account for the ambiguity of the name$_1$ 'Aristotle' by saying that it means either ''the bearer of 'Aristotle$_S$' '' or ''the bearer of 'Aristotle$_O$' ''.

Individuating names by their bearers does not, however, enable the metalinguistic theory to provide a satisfactory account of the meaning of names. First, names without bearers obviously cannot be individuated by their bearers. So we cannot in the way suggested account for the ambiguity of 'St. Nick', which means either ''Santa Claus'' (the mythical bringer of Christmas gifts) or ''St. Nicholas'' (the real Bishop of Myra, AD 300). For in one of the senses, the name has no bearer.[35] Second, it is possible for an ambiguous name$_1$ to have the same referent on both of its meanings. Suppose, for example, that unbeknownst to everyone, Aristotle Onassis was Aristotle of Stagira, reincarnated after two thousand years. In that case, the name$_2$ 'Aristotle$_S$' would be identical to the name$_2$ 'Aristotle$_O$,' and the metalinguistic theory would provide no account of the ambiguity of the name$_1$ 'Aristotle'. In short, the process of individuating names by bearers would import the limitations of Millian theories into the metalinguistic theory. Unless otherwise indicated, 'names' for us will mean letter or sound sequences.

Besides incorrectly predicting the synonymy of (28) and (30), the metalinguistic theory also wrongly predicts the nonsynonymy of (31) and (32).

(31) Delta Airlines may declare bankruptcy.
(32) Delta may declare bankruptcy.

"The bearer of 'Delta'" and "The bearer of 'Delta Airlines'" differ in meaning because they mention different names, one longer than the other. But the two names are used rather than mentioned in the sentences displayed, and are used with the same meaning. I hope it will at least be conceded that (31) and (32) are a lot more similar in meaning than either is to its metalinguistic counterpart.

There is a general rule behind the synonymy of (31) and (32), called the 'namehead' rule (Carroll 1985: 144–52). Names of the form '*(The) $N_1N_2$*' (where '$N_1$' and '$N_2$' are nouns) can generally be abbreviated '*(The) $N_1$*', as in the following:

The Capitol Building → The Capitol
The Marriott Hotel → The Marriott
The New York Yankees → New York
The Philosophy Department → Philosophy
Princeton University → Princeton

In all these cases, '*(The) $N_1$*' has the same meaning as '*(The) $N_1N_2$*'. The exceptions to the rule are instructive because they are in comparison so markedly nonsynonymous. For example, 'The Philosophy' does not mean 'The Philosophy Department' (or anything else). Note that since the namehead rule operates by deletion, multiple application can produce ambiguous names. Thus 'New York' can have the meaning of 'New York City' and 'New York State' as well as 'The New York Yankees'. We relied on other synonymy rules for names in §10.2. One is that any name of the form *(Given Name) (Middle Names) (Surname)* can be abbreviated as *(Surname), (Given Name), (Given Name) (Surname)*, or even *(Given Name)(Middle Name)*. We also noted that a person's nickname means the same thing as his name.

In support of the implication that no two proper names are synonymous, Katz cites pairs like 'Mark Twain' and 'Samuel Clemens'.[36] His sample was nonrepresentative. The whole point of pen names and aliases would be destroyed if they were synonymous. Bach (1987a: 142–4) argued similarly from the premise that we do not translate 'Johann' as 'John'. That is probably because in English we do not consider those two names to be synonyms: I cannot call my son 'Johann' even though his name is 'John'. We do translate 'Deutschland' as 'Germany' just as we translate 'Deutsch' as 'German'. And 'transliteration' or 'transcription', the process whereby many names in Greek, Russian, and other languages with different alphabets and sound systems are rendered into English, is for our purposes a form of translation: the result is a pairing of distinct symbol sequences that have the same meaning.[37] Standard names formed from one or more general terms present a difficult choice for translators rendering them for the first time into a new language.[38] The translator can maximize fidelity to the source language in one respect (look and sound) by transliterating all or part (which gave us 'Pravda' rather than 'Truth'), or in another (appropriateness conditions and non-Millian connotations) by using a 'word-for-word' translation (which produced 'La Maison Blanche' in French and 'Weißhaus' in German for 'the White House'). Once the choice becomes conventionalized, the result is the same: a distinct name in the second language with the same meaning as one in the source language.

Since the claim that 'New York' in one sense does in fact mean the same thing as 'New York City' is an empirical statement about a natural language, it could conceivably be refuted by evidence we have overlooked. But the metalinguistic theory implies not only that synonymous names *do* not exist in natural languages, but that they *cannot* exist in any language. We can falsify this new prediction at will by devising codes or artificial languages in which new symbols are *stipulated* to have exactly the same meaning and syntactic properties as some familiar names. Indeed, such codes exist. For example, '– – •   •   – –   • – •   – – •   •   – •••   •• –   •••   ••••' can be used in Morse code to mean "George Bush". And 'Orgegay Ushbay' can be used in Pig-Latin to mean the same thing. Alternatively, I can simply stipulate that henceforth 'G' is to be understood as an abbreviation for 'George Bush'. If this stipulation became conventional among users of English, the letter 'G' would come to have "George Bush" as one of its meanings in English.

I have focused on linguistic objections to the claim that the sense of any name 'N' is given by the description "the bearer of 'N'". Let me now present a more metaphysical objection: *The metalinguistic theory of names makes the reference of a name a determinant of itself, thereby violating the irreflexivity of the determination relation.*[39] This objection is based on the premise that *the object bearing a standard name is the object the name refers to.* As Frege observed, the reference of a term depends on (at least) two factors: its sense, and 'the facts'—i.e., the history of the world. 'The 35th president' refers to Kennedy because the expression means "the 35th president" and because in fact Kennedy was the 35th president. Neither factor alone suffices to determine the referent. If the expression had had a different meaning (say "the tallest man") or if the historical facts had been different (say Nixon had won the 1960 election) the referent would have been different as a result. Now let us suppose that 'Aristotle' means "the bearer of 'Aristotle'". Then what is the other, historical, factor that determines the bearer of the name 'Aristotle'? Obviously, the determinant is the fact *that Aristotle is the bearer of 'Aristotle'*, which is the very state of affairs whose determinants we are seeking. This means that the fact that Aristotle bears a certain name is determined by two factors, one of which is the very fact that Aristotle bears that name, violating the asymmetry and irreflexivity of determination. Some sorts of determination are not asymmetric, such as the purely functional kinds discussed in mathematics. But the causal-explanatory dependence of reference on sense is.

Geurts's (1997: §4) strategy is to avoid the irreflexivity problem by finding a metalinguistic property that is not simply the logical converse of the reference relation.[40] Consider, for example, the speech act of naming a baby, boat, or whatever. This act is also called 'dubbing' or 'baptism' (without religious overtones). If the metalinguistic theorist says that 'N' means *"the individual who was named 'N' "* in this sense of naming, the irreflexivity problem will not arise. This suggestion is untenable for a different reason: the name 'N' need not be coextensive with *"*the individual who was named 'N' *"*. Aristotle, for example, was never named 'Aristotle', in this sense of naming. His parents gave him a Greek name, not an English name. It is doubtful that the Moon was ever baptized 'the Moon'. Standard names differ markedly in this respect from a logically descriptive name like 'Invoice #1735'. 'Invoice #1735' generally refers to the invoice with the number 1735 stamped on it in a designated location. If no invoice was so stamped, or if more than one was so stamped, the use of 'Invoice #1735' would have false presuppositions. The name 'N' may fail to be coextensive with *"the individual people have called 'N'"* for the opposite reason: in cases of mistaken identity, people may be called 'N' by mistake.

The mistake problem can be avoided by taking a name 'N' to mean *"the individual called 'N' by the people who were the sources of the usage of 'N' ".*[41] But it is a contingent and *a posteriori* fact that linguistic usage has sources. Children have to learn that language is not just there, that it is conventional as opposed to natural, that it changes and evolves, and so on. Consequently "N is the individual called 'N' by its sources" is in no way analytic or trivially true. A separate problem for this suggestion is that the sources themselves will not have used the name with this meaning. So this version of the metalinguistic theory would wrongly predict that the Kennedy family means something different by 'Jack Kennedy was the 35th president' than the rest of us do, and that the meaning of the sentence varies from occasion to occasion depending on whether they use it or we. This last version of the metalinguistic theory is close to the truth, I believe, because it resembles the neo-Gricean analysis of meaning (Chapter 5). What is true is that 'N' *has the meaning it has because* 'N' *is conventionally used to refer to* N—that is, to express the idea of N. It follows that 'N' has the meaning it has because the people who were the sources of the usage of 'N' used it to refer to N. But the property in virtue of which a term has its meaning is not part of what the term means.

Recanati has tried to defend the metalinguistic description theory by arguing that the meaning of a name is not sufficient to determine its referent.

> [W]hat a competent user of the language knows (and has to know, in order to be a competent user of the language) is merely that a proper name NN refers to an entity called NN. It is an essential characteristic of proper names that they can be used by people who do not know the name-conventions pairing the names with their bearers. (Recanati 1993: 160–1)

But surely no one can be a competent user of 'Aristotle' without having the concept of Aristotle, without knowing that 'Aristotle' expresses that concept, and without knowing that 'Aristotle' refers to Aristotle. To know that 'Aristotle' refers to Aristotle is to know the name convention pairing the name with its bearer. I think Recanati's point is that someone can be a competent user of 'Aristotle' without knowing who Aristotle is. A competent user might not know enough about Aristotle to be able to identify him in a useful way. The standards for 'knowing who $\Phi$ is' are contextually variable.[42] If the standard requires more than merely possessing the concept of $\Phi$, then knowing who Aristotle is is not necessary for using or understanding the term 'Aristotle.'[43] Merely possessing the concept "bearer of 'NN'" is definitely not sufficient for knowing the meaning of 'NN'. Consider the name 'John Xavier Smith'. I just made it up, but given what I know about naming customs among English-speaking peoples, I am confident that it has at least one bearer, and suspect that it has many. I thus have the concept "bearer of 'John Xavier Smith'". But I have no idea whatsoever who the name refers to, and do not have the concept it expresses (although I presume some people do). I can think about the name, but not about any of the people it names. I do know that the sentence "'John Xavier Smith' refers to John Xavier Smith" is probably true, but I do not know the fact it expresses. In the same way, a Korean might know enough English to infer that "'Potato' denotes potatoes" is true, without understanding the term 'potato', and thus without knowing that 'potato' denotes potatoes.

Katz also responds to the irreflexivity problem by abandoning the principle that sense is a determinant of reference.[44] Senses, on Katz's view, as on mine, are the properties of words in virtue of which they have semantic properties like meaningfulness and ambiguity and stand in sense-relations like synonymy and antonymy. He wonders why he needs to hold that senses so defined determine reference. The answer has two or three parts. (i) Tautologically, 'cat' has the sense "cat". That is, 'cat' means "cat". (ii) Any term meaning "cat" applies to an object if and only if the object is a cat. We can add (iii) that if 'cat' has the sense "feline animal", then 'cat' applies to an object iff 'feline animal' applies; hence by (ii), 'cat' applies to an object iff it is a feline animal. The same answer can be given for names. Tautologically, 'Aristotle' means "Aristotle". And any term meaning "Aristotle" applies to an object iff it is Aristotle.[45] If 'Aristotle' has the sense "the bearer of 'Aristotle'", then 'Aristotle' applies to an object iff it is the bearer of 'Aristotle'. These principles are consequences of the Tarskian truth postulate for ideas (Postulate 9.2). Ergo, we cannot hold that sense determines synonymy relations without holding that sense determines reference.

Geurts (1997: 325) and Bach (2002: 83) avoid the irreflexivity problem by combining the description theory with the Russellian theory of definite descriptions, which implies that names are not referring terms. I regard this as a *reductio ad absurdum*. "'Aristotle' refers to Aristotle" seems more evidently true than any claim made by the metalinguistic theory. It describes the paradigm case of reference (recall §9.1). If names do not refer, I have no idea what word reference is. Besides, the claim that names are non-referential implies that they do not have bearers. In that case, "the bearer of 'Aristotle'" will be referentless, and (25) will come out false rather than trivial on a Russellian analysis.

## NOTES

¹ I will ignore complications arising from the existence presupposition of subject-predicate propositions. If 'p' represents all the presuppositions of 'q,' let us say that 'q' is *a priori* in a broad sense iff 'q if p' is *a priori* in the strict sense (knowable without empirical evidence). Similar definitions can be given for the conditional senses of *self-evident, logically true,* and related notions. Then 'Chapter 11 is the eleventh chapter' is *a priori* in the broad sense because 'Chapter 11 is the eleventh chapter if there is one' is *a priori* in the strict sense.

² Names like 'Springfield, Virginia' and 'Fairfax County' (or 'The County of Fairfax') are partially descriptive. Compare Soames (2002: 86–9), who misidentified many examples (e.g., 'Princeton University'). See also McKinsey's (1999: 537) discussion of 'Jack the Ripper'. For detailed attempts to characterize the class of proper names, see Algeo 1973 and Allerton 1987. The logically descriptive nature of names like 'Chapter 11' led Algeo (1973: 26) to classify them as common nouns, and Soames (2002: 115) to classify them as descriptions.

³ Cf. Searle 1967: 488; Burge 1973: 426; and Lyons 1977: 214.

⁴ Compare and contrast Pendlebury (1990), who thinks that 'arbitrariness' is definitive of proper names. It should be noted that 'page n' can be used in two different ways: (i) to denote the nth page counting consecutively from the first; or (ii) to designate the page numbered 'n' by the author or publisher. 'Page 2A' can only be used with the second meaning. Both uses of the name are descriptive, although the second makes it look more like a standard name. Cf. §12.5 below. In complex manuscripts, a decision may have to be made as to what counts as the first page.

⁵ See Mill 1879: §1.2.5; Marcus 1961; Putnam 1970b, 1975; Kripke 1971, 1972; Donnellan 1972; Salmon 1981, 1989c: 445–9; Devitt and Sterelny 1987: Ch. 3; Larson and Segal 1995: 175–9; and Margolis and Laurence 1999: 21–23.

⁶ Jeshion (2002) rebuts many formulations of the epistemological argument against descriptivism, but as far as I can see nothing she says undermines this formulation.

⁷ Contrast Shieh 2001: 370. Stanley (1997a: 571, 574–8; 1997b) argues that a name and a description could have the same 'assertoric content' even though only one is rigid. Given that his notion of assertoric content concerns what is *said* and truth conditions rather than what is *meant* and synonymy, identity of assertoric content is compatible with differences in 'ingredient sense'.

⁸ Cf. Chomsky 1975: 44–6; Algeo 1973: 55–8; Carroll 1985: xvi–xvii, 163–87; and Katz 2001: 157–8. Contrast McCawley 1968: 139; Lyons 1977: 221; Rundle 1979: 73.

⁹ The importance of appropriateness as an object of linguistic study was stressed by Lehrer 1992b: 'Speakers of any language make judgements about the appropriateness of names for things that are analogous to judgments about grammatically, semantic well-formedness, and pragmatic acceptability.'

¹⁰ Contrast Stroll 1998: 528.

¹¹ See Loar 1976a: 373. Cf. Smullyan 1948; Lewis 1968: 119; Dummett 1973: 127–8; 1981: 574–84; Katz 1977a: 62–3; 1986a: 87, fn. 4; 1990: 43–5; Brody 1977; Donnellan 1977: 13–5; Schiffer 1979: 63–4; 1981: 58; Rundle 1979: 78–9; Schwarz 1979: Ch. 21; Burge 1979a: 412–4; Yu 1980; Geurts 1997: 323. Contrast Boër 1975: §3; Kaplan 1977: 517; Linsky 1977: Chs. 3–4; Ackerman 1979b: 9; Kripke 1980: 10–5; Cook 1980; Hudson and Tye 1980; A. D.

Smith 1984; Fitch 1987: 50–1; Bach 1987a: 149–53; Gale 1989: 296ff; Stanley 1997a: §6; Soames 1998; 2002: 25–31.

¹² Many other examples where names can very naturally be given narrow scope can be found in Soames's (2002: 24–39) refutation of Dummett.

¹³ Sentence (7) might be true if we are concerned with *epistemic* necessity: suppose Aristotle were introduced to you as the author of *De Anima*. Cf. Dummett 1973: 112–51 and Linsky 1977: 54–63, 96–7. For epistemic necessity, the difference is this: (5) would be true for everyone, (7) only for people in special epistemic circumstances. We will be concerned with logical necessity.

¹⁴ Bach (2002: 84–5) observes that (11) can be heard as false. But on that reading, the two occurrences of 'Aristotle' have different meanings. See the discussion of (24) in §12.5.

¹⁵ Cf. Soames 2002: 39.

¹⁶ Cf. Brody 1977; Kripke 1980: 12, 61–2; A. D. Smith 1984; Soames 1995b: 201. This was overlooked in Stanley's (1997a: 573, 578) and Soames's (2002: 34–5) rebuttals of Dummett's scope argument.

¹⁷ Note that 'the author of *De Anima* in w' differs from 'the author of *De Anima*' in being ambiguous. The former can be interpreted either as a noun phrase in which the prepositional phrase 'in w' is a restrictive modifier of the head noun 'author', or as a sentence fragment in which the adverbial phrase 'in w' modifies a yet to be presented verb phrase (such as 'wrote nothing'). Using parentheses and ellipsis marks, the two interpretations can be represented as 'the (author of *De Anima* in w) ...' or as '(the author of *De Anima*) ... in w'. 'Aristotle in w' can only be understood as a sentence fragment.

¹⁸ Salmon 1981: 27, 32–41; Almog 1986: 227 fn. 14, 223; Fodor 1987: 86; Kaplan 1989: 577; Larson and Segal 1995: 174–5; Braun 1995a: §3; Stanley 1997a: 574–6; 1997b: 137; Soames 1998: 13–7; 2002: 40; Shieh 2001: 381. Contrast Cook 1980: 116–7.

¹⁹ Cf. Plantinga (1978a, 1985), whose version of the description theory is criticized by Ackerman 1979a, 1979b, 1985; Fitch 1987: 52–8; and Austin 1990: Ch. 4. See also Kaplan 1979: 23–5; Burge 1979a: 419–20; Searle 1983: 258; Gale 1989; Ackerman 1989; and Soames 1998: 14; 2002: 43. 'The F in @' is to be interpreted here as a noun phrase, meaning 'the (F in @)'; see fn. 17.

²⁰ Cf. Black 1952; Strawson 1963: 7–10; Schiffer 1978: 194–6; Schwarz 1979: 7; Adams 1979: 13–9; Searle 1983: 253–5; Fitch 1987: 57; and Yourgrau 1990: 100.

²¹ Recall Kaplan's (1978: 30) famous example of the man who said, 'That is a picture of the greatest philosopher who ever lived', pointing inadvertently at a portrait of Spiro Agnew that had recently replaced one of Rudolf Carnap. I discuss this example in *Indexicals*. See also Higginbotham 1988: 36; Segal 2001: 550; 2002.

²² See also Linsky 1977: 62–3, 86; 1983: 130–1; Recanati 1993: Ch. 10; Bertolet 2001; Jeshion 2001. In the more ordinary case in which no single description expresses our criterion of identification for the referent, Linsky concludes that the name has no fixed sense—it is vague and ambiguous (1977: 99, 104–5, 111; 1983: 134–8). Here he follows Dummett 1973: 136 and Wittgenstein. A similar theory is presented by Almog 1981, and generalized to natural kind and color terms.

²³ See also Kaplan ; 1978; 1989: 579–82; Soames 2002: 49.

²⁴ Cf. Russell 1910–11: 221–3; Church 1956a: 5 fn 10; Kneale 1962: 630; Zink 1963: 491; Sloat 1969: 29; Algeo 1973: Ch. 6; Burge 1973: 432; 1977; 1983: 84; Plantinga 1974: 159–63; 1978a: 134–5; Loar 1976a: 364, §9; 1980; Katz 1977a: 61; 1979: 120–2; 1986a: 85–91; 1990; 1994; Schiffer 1978: 195–198; Lewis 1979a: 542; Schwarz 1979: Ch. 10; Ingber 1979: 737; Chisholm 1981: 65; Allan 1986: 244; Tienson 1986; Fodor 1987: 85–6; Fitch 1987: 164–8; Castañeda 1985; 1989a: §2.9; 1990a: 197–8; Bach 1987a; 2002; Kaplan 1989: 599; Seager 1990: 409; Geurts 1997; Justice 2001; 2002; 2003; Elugardo 2002. Compare and contrast Ackerman 1979a; 1979b; 1980a: esp. 481–3; Evans 1982: Ch. 11; Barwise and Perry 1983: 165–8; Rieber 1992; Recanati 1993: Chs. 8–10, §20.3; Braun 1995a; Newen 2001: 138; Abbott 2002: 196. MacBeth's (1995: fn. 4) theory that 'N' has the 'cognitive content' of "the one I refer

to as 'N'" has all the same defects, while in addition wrongly making proper names indexicals and making their reference differ from individual to individual.

²⁵ Contrast Bach 2002: 77.

²⁶ Cf. Geurts 1997: 322–3; Bach 2002: 79–81. Contrast Abbott 2002: 198.

²⁷ Cf. Kripke 1972: 283–4; Geach 1980: 84–5; and Wreen 1989. Contrast Tienson 1986; Recanati 1993: 163; Bach 2002: 76. In a textbook *ignoratio elenchi*, Katz dismisses this objection by arguing that "Horses are called 'Horse'" is false: "Some horses might have the name 'Horse' just as Tarzan's young son has the name 'Boy', but few if any, do" (1990: 53; see also 2001: 141, fn. 11). "Horses are denoted by 'horse'" says that the general term 'horse' is truly predicable of all horses, not that the proper name 'Horse' is the name of every horse.

²⁸ Cf. Lewy 1976: 12; Kaplan 1977: 507–10; 1990a; Donnellan 1977: §2; P. T. Smith 1985: 159–63; Forbes 1989b; Chierchia and McConnell-Ginet 1990: 277; Nelson 1992: 103; Recanati 1993: 156; Katz 2001: 145.

²⁹ Contrast Bach 2002: 75. Bach correctly notes that in (29) there is no *explicit mention* of the name, as there is in (28); but still, (29) does refer to and talk about the name in a way (30) does not.

³⁰ Katz (1994: 36–7) thinks he can deny this, without saying how. Contrast Rieber 1992. To see that a translation of (29) that replaces 'Aristotle' with 'Aristotles' is not strict, note that a similar translation of 'Is every Aristotle an Aristoteles?' would turn a legitimate question into triviality.

³¹ Cf. Lewy 1976: Chs. 1, 2, 6. Contrast Castañeda's (1985: 101) existential generalization rule for names; and Bach 1987a: 142.

³² Contrast Zemach 1985: 183 and Seager 1990: 409, who may have had in mind the *transparent* reading of "S knew that *De Anima* was written by the bearer of 'Aristotle'" (§2.8).

³³ Cf. The notion of a 'mode of expression' used in §5.1.

³⁴ Cf. Kripke 1980: 8; Reimer 2002: 457. Compare and contrast Braun 1995a: 555; Justice 2002: 574–5; 2003. Contrast Katz 2001: 150; Bach 2002: 88–9.

³⁵ The 'Santa Claus' example shows how names can have more than one bearer even on Justice's view that names are individuated by their origins, and that even if a name has a unique bearer it may not be the referent in one of its senses.

³⁶ Cf. Katz 1977a: 12–3; 1979: 112–3; 1986a: 87–91; 1990: 33; D. J. Clark 1995. Contrast Braun 1995a: 574.

³⁷ Cf. Algeo 1973: 59–2; Allerton 1987: 82–6; and Castañeda 1990a: 197; 1990b: 219.

³⁸ Bantas and Manea 1990; Kingscott 1990; Lehrer 1992a: 396; Bantas 1994.

³⁹ This argument was suggested by Kripke 1972: 283–4; Devitt 1980: 275–8, and Fitch 1987: 44, who observed that a metalinguistic theory of *reference* would be circular. See also Dummett 1981: 589–90. Algeo (1973: 70–2) correctly observed that definitions of the form "N is the bearer of 'N'" are not circular, but that is not the objection I am leveling.

⁴⁰ Compare and contrast Bach 2002: 83, who does not clearly distinguish between bearing a name and being given a name nor (on the page cited) between speaker and word reference (elsewhere Bach is very clear about this distinction).

⁴¹ Cf. Ingber 1979: 731; Noonan 1980–81; and Loar 1980: 87. Compare and contrast Evans 1982: Ch. 11.

⁴² For more on the context-relativity of knowing who, see Chisholm 1976: 173–4; Boër and Lycan 1975; 1986; and Davis 2003: §16.5.

⁴³ Cf. Stanley (1999), who argues that 'full understanding' of a term, in contrast to 'minimal linguistic competence', requires nontrivial uniquely identifying knowledge. See §12.1.

⁴⁴ See Katz 1990: 40; 1994: 4, 7; 1997; 2001.

⁴⁵ Segal (2002: 551) uses such principles as axioms in a T-theory for names.

# 13
# Standard Name Meaning

The Frege–Mill dichotomy is the thesis that proper names must have descriptive meanings or no senses at all. The classical corollary adds that names must be definable if they have meanings. If the Frege–Mill dichotomy is accepted, standard proper names will surely seem problematic. But there is no good reason to accept that dichotomy. The arguments against Mill's way support the thesis that proper names have a sense distinct from their reference. The evidence against Frege's way indicates standard names do not have a descriptive sense. The alternative to the Frege–Mill dichotomy follows directly: *standard names have nondescriptive senses.*[1] That is, standard names have senses that differ from the senses of descriptive terms like common nouns, adjectives, verbs, or definite descriptions. The evidence presented against Frege's way supports an even stronger conclusion: *standard names have undefinable senses.* The sense of a standard name is different from the sense of any combination of nonsynonymous terms. On an ideational theory, this implies that *standard proper names express basic concepts.* Basic concepts are either atomic or contain an atomic component that is not lexicalized. We also presented evidence that proper names have *nonindexical* senses. Standard proper names can therefore be characterized as the primitive singular nonindexical words in a language. The subject concepts they express are typically acquired by abstraction or through communication. The concepts represent their objects directly and rigidly. While concepts expressed by standard names could be atomic, there is evidence that they consist of a general sortal concept combined with a nondescriptive, nonindexical individuating concept. In this chapter, we will explain these conclusions, and defend them against a variety of objections.

## 13.1  NONDESCRIPTIVE, UNDEFINABLE SENSES

We observed in §10.1 that some names are *logically descriptive*, like 'May 9th' and 'Super Bowl XXI'. Such names do have descriptive meanings, and are synonymous with definite descriptions. Thus 'May 9th' means 'The 9th day of May', and 'Super Bowl XXI' means 'The 21st Super Bowl'. Some names are *partially descriptive*, such as 'Denver Colorado' and 'the Potomac

River'. Denver Colorado is necessarily in Colorado, and the Potomac River is necessarily a river. In contrast, standard proper names, such as 'Aristotle' and 'Paris', have *nondescriptive* senses. We presented evidence that standard proper names are not synonymous with any definite description formed from purely descriptive general terms.

Standard names are not unique in being nondescriptive. Articles ('a', 'an', and 'the'), logical constants ('if', 'or', 'all'), pronouns ('this', 'he', 'I', 'who') and interjections ('Ouch!', 'Damn!') also have nondescriptive meanings. But standard names do have a unique kind of nondescriptive meaning. They differ from interjections in expressing ideas (thought parts). They are like pronouns rather than articles and logical constants in being singular terms. They are thus grammatically and semantically suited to appear in sentences as subjects, direct objects, or indirect objects, and to have referents. Standard names differ from pronouns in that their meaning determines a referent independently of the context. We may have to rely on contextual evidence to determine whether 'Roosevelt' means "Theodore Roosevelt" or "Franklin Roosevelt" on a given occasion. But once that is decided, the referent of 'Roosevelt' is fixed.

Logically descriptive names are *syntactically structured*, and have *compositional meanings*. The meaning of 'Super Bowl XXI' is determined by the meaning of 'XXI' and 'Super Bowl' together with the fact that expressions of the form 'Super Bowl N' are used to mean 'The Nth Super Bowl' (cf. §5.6). Standard proper names, in contrast, are syntactically unstructured. This is obvious for the large number of standard names that consist of a single morpheme, such as 'Aristotle', 'Detroit', 'Europe', and 'Mars'. It is evident on reflection for countless compound proper names: 'John Stuart Mill', 'New Jersey', 'West Virginia', 'General Dynamics', 'Daimler-Benz', and so on. Lacking syntactic structure, their meaning cannot be compositional. That is, the meaning of a standard proper name is in no sense composed of the meanings of its components.

The sense of a term might be analyzable even though the analysis is not reflected in the structure of the term. 'Vixen' and 'bachelor' are standard illustrations. Even though they themselves are syntactically unstructured, they are synonymous with phrases whose meanings are fully compositional, 'female fox' and 'unmarried man' respectively. The evidence presented in Chapter 12 supports the conclusion that standard proper names cannot be semantically defined. They are not synonymous with any complexes of terms that do not themselves contain proper names. Consequently, standard proper names have senses that are not only nondescriptive but unanalyzable. Put positively, they are *primitive* and *irreducibly nominal*. The fact that not every term can be defined may be reformulated as saying that some senses must be unanlyzable. The conclusion to draw from the evidence presented against classical and indexical description theories is that standard names should be assigned some of the unanalyzable senses. Given that typical standard names are syntactically unstructured, and are introduced ostensively rather than by definition, it is hard to imagine any more plausible candidates for the possession of unanalyzable senses.

Focusing on general terms like 'cat', 'kill', and 'know', Fodor has argued that most syntactically unstructured expressions in a language are undefinable.[2] The basic argument is familiar: Any attempt to fill in the 'G' in 'A cat is a G' will be either too broad, too narrow, not necessarily true, not *a priori*, not common knowledge, not uninformative, or else circular. Moreover, unstructured terms are generally introduced by ostension rather than by explicit definition. While we might wonder whether Fodor was right that *most* unstructured general terms are undefinable, he is surely right that *some* are, indeed *many*. The notion that 'cat' either has a definable sense or no sense at all is not widely accepted.[3] Whether 'cat' is definable or not, it has a sense. While numerous semantic and syntactic differences are evident between proper names and common names, none seem to support the claim that they differ in addition in regard to definability. So the arguments above serve to generalize Fodor's thesis to proper names, and Fodor's arguments with other terms serve to support by analogy the argument given for names.[4]

'But', it might be objected, 'if the sense of a standard name cannot be equated with the sense of some combination of descriptive terms, we will have no idea what the sense of a standard name is'. Such an objection would be misguided for a variety of reasons. First, there is no good reason to accept the principle that something does not exist or should not be posited unless we have a philosophically satisfactory account of what it is. Not everything can be explained or analyzed. Second, the objection assigns a conceptual priority to descriptive senses that has no evident rationale. A common noun like 'man' cannot be defined in terms of a disjunction of standard names like 'Aristotle or Brahms or Clinton or...'. Indeed, the meaning of a common noun generally differs from that of any combination of terms containing names. The thesis that standard proper names have nondescriptive senses should be no more surprising than the thesis that standard common nouns have nonnominal senses. I hope few will argue that if the sense of a common noun cannot be equated with the sense of some combination of standard names, we will have no idea what the sense of a common noun is. To my knowledge, however, no one has even tried to show that the Frege–Mill dichotomy is any more plausible than the claim that common nouns have a nominal sense or no sense at all.[5]

Third, the description theory itself must posit at least one nondescriptive sense. For the theory needs to account for the singularity of proper names. What can be added to a combination of general senses to produce a singular sense? The answer provided by the classical description theory is the sense of 'the'. The answer from the indexical description theory is the sense of 'that' or something similar. If we do not know what the senses of these nondescriptive terms are, the description theory will never be able to define anything but general terms. The description theory also helps itself to logical constants and other syncategorematic terms, which themselves have nondescriptive meaning.

Fourth, and most importantly, we have developed a pretty substantial idea of the sort of sense standard names possess. We have observed that the senses of proper names resemble those of other words and phrases in being subsentential: the meaning of a proper name is not the meaning of any sentence, although it is a component or determinant of sentence meanings (§10.2). The senses of standard names are nondescriptive, resembling those of pronouns and logical particles and differing from those of common nouns, adjectives, and verbs (§12.1). Standard names are nonindexical in meaning (§10.6, §12.4). The senses of proper names, like those of common nouns, are reference determining factors that do not stand in a one-to-one correspondence with either referents or words (§10.4, 10.5). Consequently, the sense of a proper name contributes to determining the truth conditions of any sentence containing it just as the sense of a common noun, adjective, or definite description does. Thus T-sentences of the form '*x is N' is true iff x is N* hold for each sense of 'N' whether it is a proper name or other kind of term. Having unanalyzable senses, standard names are *directly* referential: their reference is not determined by which object satisfies a particular complex description (§11.5). Consequently, names are *rigid* in their reference: they denote the same object in every possible world (§12.3).

In short, we can characterize standard proper names as having *singular, directly and rigidly referential meanings that are nondescriptive, nonindexical, and undefinable*. This characterization might be criticized on the grounds that it is largely negative. But no more positive characterization is possible for basic general terms like 'cat' or 'red' (general, directly and rigidly referential meanings that are nonnominative, nonindexical, and undefinable). Furthermore, negative descriptions can be highly informative. Consider 'foreign' (not from the home country), 'axiom' (not proven as a theorem), 'element' (not composed of atoms of another kind of matter), and 'odd' (not divisible by 2). The positive fact is that standard names have a distinctive kind of meaning, which differs from the meaning of any other kind of expression. This fact is fundamentally important for semantic theory.

## 13.2 BASIC CONCEPTS

Many fundamental issues have not been settled, of course. For example, the conclusion that names have nondescriptive senses does not tell us what it is for proper names to have a sense. But neither does the claim that they have descriptive senses. Neither the description theory nor the nondescription theory are *foundational* theories of meaning. The Millian thesis that the meaning of a proper name is its referent is not a foundational theory of meaning either unless it is supplemented by a theory telling us what it is for a name to have a referent. It might be thought, however, that a foundational theory of meaning is possible for names only if Millianism or Fregeanism is true. The remainder of this chapter and the next will show that such an argument for the Frege–Mill dichotomy is unsound.

The expression theory I have developed is a mentalistic theory in which ideas play the central role (Chapter 5). Recapitulating, for a word to have a meaning is for it to express an idea or other mental state. Ideas are event-types of a certain sort, specifically, thoughts or parts of thoughts. Hence ideas are mental representations, distinct from images or conceptions. The change in a woman who is thinking about cats one minute and dogs the next is a change in the ideas that are occurring to her. Both ideas are occurring to someone who is thinking the thought that cats are not dogs. To express an idea is to perform an observable action with a certain intention, roughly, the intention of providing an indication that the idea is occurrent. What speakers mean by a word on a given occasion is determined by what idea or other mental state they are using the word to express. What a syntactic-ally unstructured word means in a natural language is determined by what idea speakers of the language conventionally use the word to express. 'Horse' means "horse" because it is conventionally used to express the concept of a horse. What a syntactically structured expression means is determined by what ideas its components express together with what con-ceptual structure speakers conventionally use the linguistic structure to express.

Since we are able to think about Aristotle, we have to have the concept of Aristotle (§3.4). The thought that Aristotle was a philosopher, that Aristotle was the author of *De Anima*, that Plato lived longer than Aristotle, and so on, all have a common component. Since that thought component is ex-pressed by the word 'Aristotle', the component can be referred to as 'the concept of Aristotle' (§3.7). It is because 'Aristotle' expresses that particular thought component that the word refers to the philosopher Aristotle. The idea of Aristotle is associated with the ideas of Plato, Ancient Greece, and philosophy, but not with the ideas of nuclear power, Hitler, or music. People have acquired the concept in two of the standard ways (§3.5): those who knew Aristotle personally acquired the concept through observation and abstraction; the rest of us have acquired the concept through communica-tion. Because the proper name 'Aristotle' is conventionally used to indicate that the speaker is thinking of Aristotle, it means "Aristotle", and as a result refers to Aristotle. The idea of Aristotle is distinct from the idea of the author of *De Anima*, as proven by the fact that one of the ideas can occur to us when the other does not, by the fact that someone might not realize that Aristotle was the author of *De Anima*, and so on. Hence 'Aristotle' does not mean "the author of *De Anima*". Being philosophers, we also have an elaborate conception of Aristotle, and can form a pretty good visual image of him. But that is irrelevant to the meaning of 'Aristotle'.

The expression theory has no difficulty with referentless names. We are able to think about Pegasus even though Pegasus does not exist. Hence we have an idea of Pegasus, which is expressed by the name 'Pegasus'. The expression theory also has no difficulty with coreferential but nonsynonymous names. Since people can wonder or doubt whether Archie Leach and Cary Grant are the same person, the ideas expressed by 'Cary Grant' and 'Archie Leach' must be different. As a result, the names have different meanings. The same goes for 'Aristotle' and 'the author of *De Anima*'.

What the failure of the description theory shows is that *the ideas expressed by standard names are not analyzable as complexes of descriptive concepts*. Searle's argument that the foundational questions of semantics could be answered for names only if the description theory were true is therefore mistaken.

[I]f the utterance of the expressions communicated no descriptive content, then there could be no way of establishing a connection between the expression and the object. 'What makes *this* expression refer to *that* object?' (Searle 1969: 93)

What makes the expression 'Aristotle' refer to a certain man is the fact that the word expresses the concept of Aristotle together with the fact that the man is Aristotle. The word expresses the concept because it is conventional for speakers to use the word to indicate that the idea is occurring to them. Whether the concept of Aristotle is analyzable as a complex of descriptive concepts is an independent issue that does not bear on the foundational question Searle raised. We can therefore follow the evidence and abandon the description theory without having to give up providing a foundational theory of meaning.

The evidence presented in Chapter 12 supports an even stronger conclusion: the concept expressed by a proper name like 'Aristotle' is not the concept expressed by any complex noun phrase. Hence standard names cannot be defined. We may say that standard names express *basic singular concepts*. The concepts are basic in the sense that the terms that express them are primitive or indefinable, and get their meaning from the base clause of the definition of word meaning rather than the recursion clause (see §5.6). 'Vixen' is not a basic general concept even though it means what it does because it is conventionally used to express the idea of a vixen. For 'vixen' can be defined as meaning "female fox". The concept expressed by 'vixen' is complex, and all of its components are expressed by other words in the language.

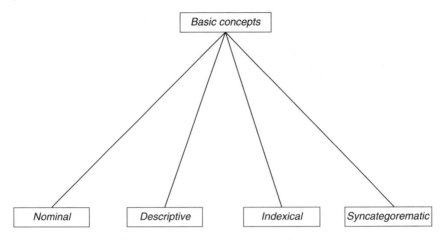

**Fig. 13.1** Atomic or basic concepts

Burge (1979a: 425) rejected as 'thin and implausible' the idea that proper names express 'special' concepts, by which he meant 'concepts not expressed by other expressions in the language.' But there is no reason to believe that every term *must* have a synonym in any given language, and conclusive reason to deny that every term must be synonymous with a compound expression in the language.[6] *A fortiori*, there is no reason to expect that every term can be defined in terms of a complex of terms from the descriptive portion of the vocabulary. On the contrary, there appear to be several fundamentally different kinds of atomic or at least basic concepts, which are classified in Fig. 13.1.

The category of syncategorematic concepts was discussed in §6.2, and includes most notably the logical connectives and operators. It is completely implausible that all syncategorematic concepts are complexes of general concepts, especially since such complexes generally contain logical concepts. I will show the irreducibility of indexical concepts to nonindexical concepts in *Indexicals*.

### 13.3 THE ATOMIC SUBJECT CONCEPT THEORY

From the premise that syntactically unstructured expressions are undefinable, Fodor drew the conclusion that they expressed concepts without constituents. On this hypothesis, the idea of Aristotle is not composed of *any* other ideas. It is an *atomic subject concept*. This hypothesis is compatible with the claim that Aristotle himself is complex, as are our images and conceptions of Aristotle. There are no metaphysical problems with the notion that some ideas cannot be described as compounds of other ideas.

Indeed, the familiar 'regress or circle' argument shows that *if there are any ideas at all, some of them must be atomic* (§3.9). Just as not every term can be analytically defined, nor every proposition proven, so not every idea can be analyzed into simpler ideas.

Even if the thesis that some ideas *have* to be atomic is somehow rejected, it is surely plausible that some *are* atomic (Postulate 3.17). Given that there is no reason whatsoever to assume that only complex ideas are expressed by words, nor that descriptive concepts are the only atomic concepts, the Frege–Mill dichotomy seems completely groundless. Given that standard names are syntactically unstructured, and introduced ostensively rather than by definition, they are plausible candidates for the expression of simple ideas. If you are still left with the nagging feeling that proper name concepts just have to be analyzed into descriptive concepts, it may help to ask yourself, 'Why shouldn't I be just as convinced that descriptive concepts have to be analyzed into proper name concepts?' I think you will be hard pressed to answer.

We distinguished between *mereological* and *logical* containment in §2.6. The claim that certain concepts are atomic is mereological: they are not made up of other concepts. It may still be true that simple concepts contain or exclude other concepts in the logical sense. For example, the premise that a certain number is 37 logically contains the proposition that it is a prime number even though the concept of 37 does not mereologically contain the concept of a prime number. So the claim that certain concepts are simple should not be rejected on the basis of logical evidence concerning entailments. Even if the concept of red does not have the concept of a color as a constituent, it is undeniable that being red entails being colored.

Section 3.5 distinguished four different processes by which concepts are acquired: observation or abstraction, communication, constructive thought, and abstractive thought. Since constructive thought is the process of putting simpler concepts together to form complex concepts, it cannot be responsible for the acquisition of standard name concepts if they are atomic. But the other three processes can produce atomic concepts. Indeed, we also observed in §3.5 that abstraction generally produces undefinable concepts, and that communication often does. These are the typical sources of standard name concepts. I acquired the concept of Kathryn Olesko (my wife) when I met her back in graduate school. I acquired the concept as a result of observing her. I acquired the concept of David Lewis (the philosopher) when I heard about him and read his work as an undergraduate. I acquired the concept as a result of communication. Some proper name concepts are acquired through abstractive thought. Thus Leverrier's reflections on the perturbations in the orbit of Uranus led him to postulate a planet beyond Uranus that influenced its orbit. As a result of thinking about the hypothesized planet beyond Uranus, he acquired the concept of Neptune, that planet.[7] The conclusion that standard names express atomic concepts does not require positing any special processes of concept formation.

The theory that standard names express atomic subject concepts is similar in one key respect to the 'direct reference' theory, according to which 'names denote objects directly, and not *via* a descriptive sense'.[8] The big difference, of course, is that on any ideational theory, words refer to things because they express ideas which represent those things. So the reference of words is always indirect in one way. But on the atomic subject concept theory, the concepts expressed by standard names, in contrast to definite descriptions, are such that when they occur to us, we think of the referent 'directly'. Since standard name concepts are simple, they have no other concepts as parts. Hence we do not think of their referents in virtue of thinking of certain other things that happen to pick out their referents. In contrast, to conceive of the author of *De Anima*, we must think of *De Anima*, of being an author, and so on. We think of the author of *De Anima* by thinking of *De Anima*. If the concept of Aristotle is atomic, any word expressing it must be rigid, designating the same individual (viz., Aristotle) in any possible world, hypothetical case, or imagined situation in which it exists. Since Aristotle cannot be anyone other than Aristotle, the concept of Aristotle must have Aristotle as its referent in any possible world. The atomic concept theory therefore ascribes enough directness to the reference of proper names to account for their rigidity and avoid the faulty predictions of the description theory (e.g., the nontriviality of certain identity statements), while also ascribing just enough indirectness to their reference to account for the linguistic data that is inexplicable on the direct reference theory (the existence of meaningful names without bearers, nontrivially true identity statements, failures of substitutivity, etc.).

As Perry (1997b: 3–4) puts it, to say that names are directly referential is to say that sentences containing names 'express' singular propositions, the names 'contributing' the objects to which they refer, rather than a 'mode of presentation', to those propositions. 'Singular propositions' are taken to be situations, ordered n-tuples of objects and properties. Thus 'Aristotle was a man' is said to express ⟨Aristotle, being a man⟩, which is true in a world iff Aristotle is a man in that world. Nothing Perry has said so far is incompatible with the view I am developing, although the terminology is different. Perry does not define 'express' for situations. As I have defined the term in Part I, sentences express thoughts, which are composed of concepts. To express a thought is to provide an indication that one is thinking it. I am using the term 'proposition' to denote declarative thoughts, which are capable of being believed or disbelieved. For the sake of comparison, the thought that Aristotle is a man can be represented by an ordered n-tuple of concepts, specifically, ⟨c(Aristotle), c(man)⟩. The proposition is singular, in my sense, because its subject concept is the concept of an individual object, Aristotle. This proposition is true in a world iff Aristotle is a man in that world. The concept of Aristotle is a 'mode of presentation' of Aristotle in my sense, because thinking of someone as Aristotle differs from thinking of him as the author of *De Anima* or as the husband of Xantippe. The concept is not a mode of presentation in Perry's sense because it is not a descriptive concept, and is not the concept 'the F' for any general description 'F'. It is true on both our views that 'Aristotle' is true of x iff x is Aristotle. What Perry calls a singular proposition is what I call the 'situational extension' of a singular proposition in my sense. Perry cites the arguments of Marcus, Donnellan, Kripke, and Kaplan as showing that names are directly referential. What these arguments show is that standard names do not have descriptive senses, and are rigid designators. Both conclusions are compatible with the view that names express atomic concepts. Thus the view of names I have been developing gets us all the genuine advantages of the sort of theory Perry favors without running afoul of Frege's and Russell's problems.

'In virtue of what', it will undoubtedly be asked, 'is the idea of Aristotle of Aristotle rather than Plato?' And it will be suggested, no doubt, that the theory presented is incomplete and therefore defective until such questions are answered. But the question may well have a false presupposition (§3.9). Since no word has its meaning by necessity, as part of its intrinsic nature, it makes sense to ask why the word 'Aristotle' happens to mean "Aristotle" rather than "Plato". The content of an idea, in contrast, is part of its identity. The idea of Aristotle could not possibly have been of Plato, and it makes no sense to ask why that idea happens to be of Aristotle. Ideas do not 'come by' their content. To explain why an idea has a particular content, we would have to refer to its intrinsic properties, specifically, its components. If standard name concepts are atomic, then there will be no way to explain why they have their content in terms of component concepts. Since that is the only way we know of to explain why concepts have a particular content, we currently have no way to explain why atomic concepts have their contents. The thesis that standard names express atomic concepts is thus supported by the fact that the question 'In virtue of what is the concept of Aristotle about Aristotle rather than Plato?' seems as unanswerable as parallel questions about descriptive concepts, such as 'What makes the concept of color of color rather than shape?' It does make sense, of course, to ask different questions, such as 'In virtue of what do people think of Aristotle rather than Plato?' or 'What makes it true that the idea of Aristotle is occurring to someone rather than the idea of Plato?' But these are fundamental psychological questions, which a linguistic theory is not called upon to answer. Progress has been made on answering the psychological question. Given current evidence, it is much more likely that people think of Aristotle in virtue of their neural activity than their muscular activity. If ideas are neural processes, than the idea of Aristotle is of Aristotle rather than Plato in virtue of having a particular neural identity.

Burge suggested that if individual concepts were nondescriptive, then they would be unshareable and incommunicable.[9] There is no reason to accept either implication.

(i) The concept of Aristotle is nondescriptive, as the refutation of the description theory shows. It is also communicable and shareable, as the conventionality of the meaning of 'Aristotle' shows. I am sure that you and I are both now conceiving the concept of Aristotle, and that I have succeeded in communicating some thoughts about Aristotle.

(ii) Communicability and shareability cannot entail that a concept can be analyzed into simpler concepts. For that would mean that all simple concepts are incommunicable and unshareable. It would then seem to follow that all concepts are incommunicable and unshareable. It is obviously impossible for complexes of unshareable concepts to be shareable. And it is hard to see how communicability could be an emergent property.

(iii) Finally, if our inability to analyze individual concepts in terms of descriptive concepts proves the obscurity of individual concepts, then by parity of reasoning our inability to analyze descriptive concepts in terms of individual concepts should prove the obscurity of descriptive concepts.[10]

Burge had another objection.

It is not clear what one is being told when it is said that the sense of "Aristotle" is the concept of being Aristotle. The expression "the concept of being Aristotle" does not suffice to convey what is intended, for it is just as context-dependent as the proper name. This insufficiency takes two forms. In the first place, there are lots of Aristotles— which one is intended? We seem to rely on the context to pick out the "right" one. But intuitively we do not—at least not always—rely on some contextually associated complete sense or concept which eternally determines the referent. In the second place, the name "Aristotle" may carry—even for a given Aristotle, a given speaker or thinker, and a given time—different cognitive values. "Aristotle is Aristotle," as used at a given time, may express a surprising discovery rather than a triviality.

(Burge 1979a: 428)

For the record, the concept of *being Aristotle* is not the concept of *Aristotle*. The former is the concept expressed by the *predicate* 'is Aristotle'. The latter is the concept expressed by the *name* 'Aristotle'. Aristotle is a man. Being Aristotle is a property possessed by that man.[11] Furthermore, concepts are not senses, although words have senses because they express concepts (§5.2). Now for the reply: despite the fact that Burge is criticizing the idea that proper names have special features, he overlooks one of the features names share with other terms, namely *ambiguity* (see §10.2). One could not reject the idea that 'bank' has a sense by noting that it is used to express different concepts in different contexts, and that as a result, the singular term 'the concept of a bank' is as ambiguous as 'bank' is. Despite the ambiguity, "'bank' expresses the concept of a bank" can be used to assert a truth in every context. For in any context, 'the concept of a bank' can be used to designate the concept expressed therein by 'bank' (§3.7). The sense a non-indexical term has in a context determines its reference there; its sense on any occasion is determined contextually. That is, contextual factors such as the speaker's intentions determine what sense a nonindexical term has when it is used on a given occasion, and observable features of the context usually enable us to figure out what the speaker's intention was. Like 'bank', the word 'Aristotle' is used to express several different concepts. As a result, the phrase 'the concept of Aristotle' is ambiguous, designating either the concept of Aristotle the philosopher or the concept of Aristotle the shipping magnate. Which concept the name expresses on any given occasion determines whether the name refers to the philosopher or the shipping magnate. Furthermore, because the name is ambiguous, there is an interpretation of 'Aristotle is Aristotle' on which it is not logically true, just as there is an interpretation of 'banks are banks' on which it is false.

## 13.4  THE SORTAL PLUS INDIVIDUATOR THEORY

The hypothesis that standard names express atomic subject concepts is plausible and simple. There is some evidence, however, favoring a slightly more complex hypothesis. The argument against the description theory supported the conclusion that for any standard name 'N', there are few if any general terms 'G' true of N whose meaning is plausibly part of the meaning of 'N'. If the concept expressed by 'G' were part of the concept expressed by 'N', then the sentence 'N is a G' would have to express a logically necessary, analytic, *a priori*, and even self-evident truth. Since 'Aristotle was a man' could conceivably be false, and cannot be known without empirical evidence, the concept of a man cannot be part of the concept of Aristotle. It is harder to imagine a case in which 'Aristotle was an animal' or 'Aristotle was a living being' would be false, but Putnamian cases are conceivable. We can even imagine that 'Aristotle was a material object' is false by imagining that Aristotle was really a god who made it appear to others that he had a material body. If we consider even more general concepts, however, I believe we can find some that are plausibly part of the concept of Aristotle. Consider the extremely general concept "individual thing" or "particular object". It makes no sense to suppose that Aristotle was not an individual thing. Since no one can think of Aristotle without thinking of an individual thing, and since thinking of something as Aristotle implies thinking of it as an individual thing, it is plausible that the general concept "individual thing" is part of the concept of Aristotle. 'Aristotle was a concrete object' also seems analytic, where 'concrete' means "existing in time and occupying space". If a woman does not know that 'Aristotle' denotes a concrete object rather than a number, place, time, or event, then surely she does not understand the term at all.

What holds for names of concrete objects seems even more clearly true for other names. It is plausible that different classes of proper names fall under different 'sortals' or 'categories'.[12]

| | |
|---|---|
| CONCRETE OBJECT: | *Aristotle* |
| EVENT: | *The Big Bang* |
| PLACE: | *Virginia* |
| TIME: | *10:00* |
| NUMBER: | *9* |

The hypothesis that the concept "Virginia" contains the concept "place" not only logically but mereologically is supported by the fact that no one can think of Virginia unless they are thinking of something as a place. If they are thinking of a woman or a boat, then they are thinking of a different Virginia. The fact that the concept of Virginia contains the general concept of a place is of little help to the description theory. For the term 'place' is much too general to define 'Virginia', and any descriptive terms that might serve as differentia do not appear to express concepts that are contained in the concept of Virginia.

If a standard name concept contains a general sortal concept, then it must contain at least one other concept too. Otherwise the singular name concept would be identical to the general concept. The other nonsortal component would serve to individuate that particular name concept and distinguish it from all other name concepts containing the same sortal. The fact that names express complex concepts is compatible with the conclusion that standard names are indefinable as long as the individuating, nonsortal component is not expressed by any words. This hypothesis would differ minimally from Fodor's if it were assumed in addition that the individuating and sortal components of name concepts are atomic.[13] What the evidence against the description theory shows is that the concept expressed by a standard name contains as a proper or improper part an atomic concept that is not expressed by any word that is not synonymous with the name. On the two-component theory, individual concepts have a syncategorematic component (the individuating concept) as well as a general component (the sortal), and are therefore nonatomic.

A similar theory can be used to explain semantic data concerning some general terms too.[14] For example, 'Red is a color' seems to be a paradigm example of a self-evident, analytic truth. This can be explained by the hypothesis that the concept of red contains the sortal concept of a color. No explanation is forthcoming on the one-factor theory.[15] But Fodor and others have observed that 'red' does not appear to be definable. We cannot find any other general term 'F' such that 'red' means "F color" is true and noncircular. We can only give a partial definition for 'red', because we can only specify a necessary condition of application that is not a sufficient condition. Fodor (1998a: 109) calls this the 'residuum problem'. However, it follows that the concept of red does not contain the concept of color only if it is assumed that the nonsortal component must be a descriptive concept expressed by some general term. That assumption is groundless. The nonsortal component could be a nondescriptive concept that combines with a sortal concept to form a more specific descriptive concept. Since the resulting concept is general rather than singular, the nonsortal component of a concept like that of red would more aptly be termed a *specifier* rather than an individuator. It could also be called a *determiner*, since it combines with the 'determinable' concept "color" to form the 'determinate' concept "red".

For Margolis and Laurence, the 'problem of completers' is a problem because it leaves us without an account of reference determination.

> Either partial definitions are fleshed out or they are not. If they are, then the problems associated with the Classical Theory return. If they are not, then we are left without an account of how concepts apply to their instances. What makes it the case that DOG applies to all and only dogs? The fact that the concept incorporates the feature ANIMATE may place a constraint on an explanation—DOG can only apply to animates—but it is a constraint that is far too weak to answer the question.
>
> (Margolis and Laurence 1999: 55).

If there is a problem here, it favors the two-component theory over the atomistic theory. For the latter does not provide even a partial definition as a constraint. But the problem is not genuine. What makes it the case that the concept of a dog applies to dogs is (i) dogs are dogs, and (ii) the concept of a dog is the concept of a dog. A concept is the concept of a dog, on the two-component theory, because it contains a specific sortal and individuator concept. A concept therefore applies to dogs if and only if it has those two components arranged properly. We cannot in this case say that the concept applies to certain objects because its components do. For one of the hypothesized components is neither a subject nor a predicate concept, and therefore is not the sort of concept that applies to objects. But we knew in advance that the reference of a concept cannot always be determined by the reference of its components, because supposing otherwise leads to an impossible infinite regress (§3.9).

The sortal plus individuator (or specifier) theory provides a plausible hypothesis concerning the details of the abstraction process. Abstraction begins when we observe that a sortal concept we already possess applies to an object of perception, and that the object is different from other objects to which the sortal applies. The hypothesis is that this causes the mind to produce an individuator concept, which combines with the sortal to form an individual concept. Communication could work similarly. We observe that someone is talking about an object to which a sortal concept we already possess applies, and conclude that the object is different from other objects to which that sortal applies. This causes the mind to produce an individuator concept, which combines with the sortal to form an individual concept. On both the two component and the one component theory, abstraction and communication cause the formation of new atomic concepts. The difference is that on the two-component theory, the newly formed atomic concept is combined with a general concept to form a new singular concept.

A question arises on the two-component theory that does not arise on atomic concept theory: why isn't the individuating, non-sortal part of a standard name concept expressed in any language? One might expect some language to lexically distinguish the two components if they existed. If no language does, then there is a nontrivial linguistic universal that needs to be explained. I can see two possible reasons why the individuating concepts might not be lexicalized. First, by hypothesis, the individuating component of a standard name concept does not appear in any concept that does not contain the whole name concept. There is thus little point in having a separate word for the component in addition to the name that expresses the whole concept. Second, a term expressing the nondescriptive individuating component in an individual concept would not fit into any of the grammatical categories of our language. The term would not be a proper name since it could not serve as the subject of a sentence; and it would not be an adjective since it could not serve as a predicate or combine freely with nouns. Thus 'reddish color' cannot provide the desired analysis of 'red', not only because of circularity (we understand 'reddish' in terms of 'red'), but also because 'reddish' is an adjective and therefore expresses a descriptive concept, not the hypothesized individuator.

I do not believe the evidence currently available is sufficient to decide whether a standard name expresses an atomic concept or rather a concept with an individuating nondescriptive component that is not lexicalized. While we have conclusive reason to believe that names express *basic* concepts, the theory that names express *atomic* concepts is just the simplest way of explaining why they are basic. The hypothesis that a name expresses a concept with a general descriptive component and an individuating nondescriptive component is slightly more complex, but explains some data the simple theory does not predict.

## 13.5  ALTERNATIVE APPROACHES TO NONDESCRIPTIVE MEANING

Frege said that the sense of a sentence was a thought, and regarded the senses of referring terms in sentences as ways in which objects are presented in thoughts. We may think of Venus *as* the morning star or *as* the evening star. These different 'modes of presentation' are the senses of 'The morning star' and 'The evening star', respectively. With regard to standard names, there is really no reason why Frege had to take Frege's way. Thinking about Venus *as Venus* differs from thinking of it as either the morning star or the evening star. So there is a third 'mode of presentation', fit to be the meaning of 'Venus'.[16] Similarly, we can think of Pegasus as Pegasus, as Bellerophon's horse, or as the horse that flies around in myths. All three modes of presentation exist even though Pegasus does not. The first mode of presentation would be the meaning of 'Pegasus'. Nothing in the Fregean framework compels him to say that all modes of presentation are descriptive or compound. Thinking of Venus as Venus is no less real or more mysterious than thinking of water as water, which is distinct from thinking of water as $H_2O$ or as the liquid covering two-thirds of the world.

There are at least three different kinds of mode of presentation: images, conceptions, and ideas (concepts, thought parts). We have a 'presentation' of Venus when we are forming an image of Venus, a different sort of 'presentation' when we have a system of beliefs about Venus, and a third type when we are thinking about Venus. I have argued that senses are correlated with ideas rather than images or conceptions. Given that Frege took thoughts to be the senses of sentences, and took the senses of words to be modes of presentation *in thought*, it is natural to interpret Frege as identifying senses with ideas in the sense of thought parts. Frege himself denied emphatically that senses were 'ideas,' but it seems clear that by 'idea' he meant images rather than thought parts—particular occurrences unique to each subject, rather than general types of mental occurrence. When ideas are understood as thought parts, Frege's theory may be understood as an ideational theory. I have also argued that senses cannot be *identified* with ideational modes of presentation, but that identification is a dispensable feature of Frege's theory (§5.2).

Anduschus (1997) has argued that a Fregean mode of presentation theory has a fatal defect. He assumes that a mode of presentation is a *conception*, and argues that the Fregean analysis cannot get the truth conditions of attitude statements right because of the intersubjective variation in conceptions. Anduschus correctly observes that every individual has a slightly different conception of Aristotle or Napoleon, and takes Kripke's arguments to show that there is no conception that all competent users of 'Aristotle' or 'Napoleon' must share. There is no reason why a Fregean has to define a mode of presentation as a conception rather than as a concept, however, where concepts are defined as *thought parts* (§3.3). *There is* a concept conventionally associated with the name 'Aristotle', possessed by everyone who can think of Aristotle.

On Loar's view (1976a; 1981), words have meaning because there are conventions that associate them with aspects or types of communicative intentions, which are intentions to produce beliefs or actions in one's hearer. Thus 'The largest planet is Jupiter' means what it does because it is used to produce the belief that the largest planet is Jupiter. The intentions of people who use sentences containing 'the largest planet' all have a common feature, which Loar calls the concept of the largest planet. 'The function of a singular term', he proposes, 'is to introduce an *individual concept* into what is meant or expressed on its particular uses' (1976a: 354). Given this framework, there is no basis for Loar's additional assumption that all individual concepts are descriptive. The intentions of people who use sentences containing 'Jupiter' also have a common feature, which Loar should call the concept of Jupiter. Loar should say 'Jupiter' means what it does because it is associated conventionally with that intention feature. On my view, intentions have this feature if their propositional object has a certain part, which is what I call the concept of Jupiter.

Devitt suggests that the causal theory of reference can be modified to provide a theory of sense as well. His specific suggestion is that the sense of a name is 'the type of causal chain linking uses of the name to its bearer.'[17] Specifically, the sense of a term is a 'd-chain,' which is "generated by 'groundings in an object' and by 'reference borrowings' in communities"; it also involves 'file accessing'. Thus 'Archie Leach' and 'Cary Grant' have different meanings because the terms are involved in different causal networks, one beginning in the common bearer's youth and involving his parents, the other beginning in the bearer's adulthood and involving the movies. This theory must be modified to account for fictional names like 'Pegasus', which are not linked causally to their nonexistent bearers, and to account for coreferential names like 'five' and '5', which are synonymous despite the fact that their use has very different causal histories, neither anchored in the existent but abstract referent of the terms. What these names suggest is that the sense of a name is a particular *medial link* of the typical causal chain.[18] That is, the sense of 'Aristotle' is not the whole causal chain connecting the name to Aristotle, but just a certain critical part of the chain, one involved in the production of synonymous names like 'Aristoteles' whose causal chain differs in other respects. While this sort of segment is typically caused by perception of a physical object, 'Pegasus' and 'five' show that the link can occur independent of such a cause. Thus one can without contradiction grant that 'Aristotle' is meaningful while arguing that Aristotle never existed. The theory of meaning I have presented identifies several medial links in the typical causal chain as critical to words having the meaning they do, principally an idea and the intention to provide an indication that that idea is occurrent. The idea of Aristotle originated in a familiar way in the perception of Aristotle, was transmitted from generation to generation as people used Aristotle's name, and is the idea people around the world today use the name 'Aristotle' to express. We cannot say that this link in the causal chain *is* the sense of the term 'Aristotle'; for example, senses are possessed by words, and do not have the causes and effects those mental states do (§5.2).[19] But the name has the sense it does because it is associated in the right way with that link. Given Devitt's (1989a: §3) belief that the critical property of linguistic expressions is that they express thoughts together with his sketchy comments about 'files', which look like metaphorical descriptions of concepts, he should have no objection to identifying ideas as the 'medial links' in virtue of which names have senses.

## 13.6 THE ARGUMENT FROM ACQUAINTANCE

I have argued that the Frege–Mill dichotomy is false and groundless. It is natural to wonder, then, why it has been so widely accepted. Surprisingly few arguments have been presented, or can be reconstructed from the literature. One can be found in Russell (1912: 46–59). Russell defined *acquaintance* as direct awareness of an object. By 'direct' he meant 'without the intermediary of any process of inference or any knowledge of truths' (1912: 46). Two theses about the objects of acquaintance led Russell to the Frege–Mill dichotomy.

The meaning we attach to our words must be something with which we are acquainted. We are acquainted with universals, sense-data, memories, feelings, thoughts, and probably ourselves, but not physical objects or other minds. Hence the meaning of a proper name could only be a description composed wholly of universals and particulars with which we are acquainted (except for names for sense-data and the like, and ourselves).[20]

Russell claimed that "when, for example, we make a statement about Julius Caesar, it is plain that Julius Caesar himself is not before our minds, since we are not acquainted with him. We have in mind some *description* of Julius Caesar: 'the man who was assassinated on the Ides of March', 'the founder of the Roman Empire', or, perhaps, merely 'the man whose name was *Julius Caesar*'" (1912: 58). As the possible exception that proves the rule, Russell noted that only the bearer of a personal proper name would be in a position to give it 'the direct use which it always wishes to have, as simply standing for a certain object, and not for a description of the object' (1912: 54). For only the bearer is directly acquainted with its referent.

I rehearse Russell's argument only to illustrate how confused the sources of the Frege–Mill dichotomy are. The premises have been sufficiently dissected in the last ninety years for me to dismiss them briefly. The thesis that we are not directly aware of physical objects has been seriously questioned, if not thoroughly refuted (see, e.g., Dretske 1969). But even if it is true, there is no reason why the *referent of a word* must be an object of direct awareness; if there were, modern physics would be in serious trouble. Nor need the referent be an object of any sort of awareness. People have to be able to *think of* the object to be sure; but thinking of something is not a form of awareness, as fantasy and delusion proves abundantly. If by 'the meaning we attach to our words', Russell meant their *sense* rather than their reference, then his first premise is thoroughly untenable. We can know what a word means, of course. But that is knowledge of a truth. And since the meaning of a word depends on conventional usage, it could hardly be known directly. Individual speakers can know directly what they mean by an expression at the moment of utterance. But this is true whether someone means "the king" or "Julius" by 'Caesar'. Similarly, we can be directly aware of the thoughts and ideas we use words to express; but this too is true whether someone uses 'Caesar' to express the idea of the king or the idea of Julius. It is doubtful that we can be described as 'aware' of universals like 'whiteness, diversity, and brotherhood' in the same sense in which we can be described as aware of physical objects, thoughts, feelings, or sense-data. Russell defined awareness of universals as 'conceiving' a concept (1912: 52). Since conceiving is not an inferential process, the term 'direct' would apply automatically. But we can conceive the concept of Julius Caesar as well as we can conceive the concept of the first emperor of Rome (§3.3).

## 13.7 THE ARGUMENT FROM IDENTIFICATION

Another argument for the Frege–Mill dichotomy used to be quite popular among description theorists, and derives its inspiration from Wittgenstein. It was still seen as recently as Dummett (1993: 40–1), and has been resurrected in a new form by Stanley (1999). I call it *the argument from identification*.

A speaker knows the meaning of a term only if he knows a criterion for applying the term. A criterion for applying a name 'N' must be a description 'D' by which the speaker can identify N. So a speaker does not know the meaning of a name 'N' unless he knows that 'N' applies to the D, for some identifying description 'D.' Therefore, either a name has no meaning, or its name is given by a definite description.[21]

I believe the first premise of this argument is acceptable unless the second premise is true. For example, a speaker knows the meaning of the adjective 'red' if he has the concept of red and knows that 'red' means "red", and therefore knows that 'red' applies to an object iff it is red. It is not necessary for him to know any *description* by which he can recognize red objects. It suffices if he can 'just tell' perceptually that an object is red, or if he can rely on others to tell him whether it is red. Moreover, knowledge of the meaning of the term 'red' does not entail that we are able to identify any red objects. A skeptic who shows that none of our methods for identifying red objects are reliable has not thereby shown that we do not even know the meaning of the word 'red'. The existence of semantic knowledge does not suffice to refute skepticism about the nonlinguistic world. Consider next a description. It suffices for a speaker to know the meaning of 'the murderer of Jones' if he knows that it means "the murderer of Jones", and knows that the description applies to an object iff that object is the murderer of Jones. It is not necessary for a speaker to know any *further* description by which he can recognize the murderer of Jones. Indeed, it may be impossible for anyone ever to know who the murderer of Jones is.

The same goes for a proper name like 'Aristotle'. A speaker knows the meaning of the name 'Aristotle' if he has the concept of Aristotle and realizes that 'Aristotle' means "Aristotle", knowing as a result that the name refers to an object iff that object is Aristotle. Aristotle's friends and family surely were able to recognize him perceptually without inferring that he must be Aristotle because he is perceived to satisfy some description uniquely true of Aristotle. Others may in fact not be in a position to determine which individual actually is Aristotle. So one of the two premises of the argument is unwarranted.

The conclusion, moreover, does not follow. Let us suppose for the sake of argument that anyone who knows the meaning of 'Aristotle' has to know that Aristotle is the D, for some identifying description 'D'. It does not follow that 'D' will be the same for any two individuals who know the meaning of 'Aristotle'. The premises of the argument from identification would be satisfied if one speaker knew that Aristotle was Plato's best pupil, another knew that Aristotle was the author of *De Anima*, and so on. Since 'Plato's best pupil' and 'the author of *De Anima*' differ in meaning, we cannot conclude that 'Aristotle' means the same as both. Furthermore, the premises give us no reason to think that the meaning of 'Aristotle' is given by either of these descriptions. We are supposing that each speaker must know something about Aristotle. This assumption describes the speaker's *conception* of Aristotle, saying that among the things the speaker knows about Aristotle is that he is the D, for some 'D'. It does not follow that the *concept* of Aristotle is identical with the concept of the D, for any 'D'. Let us suppose, as an analogy, that no one knows the meaning of 'one meter', or acquires the concept it expresses, unless one knows that one meter is the length of the standard meter. Then no one can have the concept of a meter without having a rudimentary conception of a meter. But it does not follow that 'one meter' *means* "the length of the standard meter", or that the concepts are identical.

Loar's (1976a: 360–1) argument for the view that individual concepts must be descriptive is a variant of the above. He assumes, plausibly, that a speaker who means something by a singular sentence 't is G' must have a grasp of what would verify what he meant. Loar then asserts that either the speaker takes the H's being G to verify what he meant when he said 't is G', for some description 'H,' or else the speaker did not know what he meant when he said 't is G'. But if S says 'Aristotle was Greek', it would suffice for him to mean something if he took Aristotle's being Greek to verify what he meant. There is no evident reason why, in addition, he should have to take the H's being G to verify what he meant, for some general term 'H'.

In defense of the description theory, Stanley (1999) has argued that 'full understanding' of a term requires knowing a non-trivial uniquely identifying description of what it refers to. He assumes that understanding a term requires knowing who or what it refers to, and observes that knowing who or what is highly context relative (see §11.2). Stanley defines full understanding as a level of understanding sufficient to converse with experts. He grants that 'minimal linguistic competence' does not require knowing a uniquely identifying description. In the terms of §3.3, we may say that minimal competence with the term 'N' requires the knowledge that 'N' expresses the concept of N, which entails possession of that concept. Full understanding of 'N' requires a full understanding or mastery of the concept. It is highly likely that mastery of the concept of N requires knowing a nontrivial uniquely identifying description of N. Stanley's thesis is therefore plausible. But it does not support the description theory we have been criticizing. Stanley is concerned with what it is to understand a term; we are concerned with what it is for a term to have meaning. It does not follow from Stanley's thesis that a standard proper name 'N' means "D", where 'D' is a nontrivial identifying description of what 'N' denotes. The expert knowledge required for fully understanding a term is not generally part of its meaning for the sorts of reason we have discussed: it is typically *a posteriori*, contingent, not known by everyone who can use 'N' to mean "N", and so on. As Stanley grants, the knowledge is not a minimum requirement of linguistic competence.

A final relative of the argument from identification focuses on the idea that sense *determines* reference. What is it for sense to determine reference, it might be asked, except to provide an identifying description which, given the facts, uniquely fits the referent? The answer is simple. To say that sense determines reference is to say that the word has the reference it does because it has the meaning it does. For example, the word 'Aristotle' refers to the man Aristotle because the name means "Aristotle". If the word had meant something like "blue" instead, it would not have referred to Aristotle. If any other word had the meaning 'Aristotle' has, it too would refer to Aristotle. The same goes for indefinable general terms like 'color'. It denotes the class of colors because it means "color". If it had meant "shape", it would not have denoted the class of colors. If any other term meant "color", it too would denote colors. The thesis that sense determines reference does not entail that senses are analyzable or composite, and holds for primitive terms as well as defined terms.

## 13.8 THE ARGUMENT FROM ABSTRACTION

With the ideational theory as background, a third argument can be constructed whose premises are familiar theses about concept acquisition with roots in Aristotle that were widely accepted in both scholastic and modern philosophy.[22] While I have never seen the argument in print, it might be in the back of the minds of those who accept the Frege–Mill dichotomy. I call it *the argument from abstraction*.

All basic empirical concepts are derived from experience by a process of abstraction. Only concepts of universals (properties, relations, kinds) can be acquired by abstraction. Therefore, only concepts of universals are basic empirical concepts.

Abstraction was traditionally thought of as a process whereby repeated perception of particulars leads the mind to focus on similarities and ignore differences, producing a concept. Thus as a result of perceiving red apples, red strawberries, red shirts, and the like, children acquire the concept of redness. *Abstraction* was Locke's term. Aristotle's was *intuitive induction*. If abstraction essentially involves repetition and recurrence, it is natural to conclude that it necessarily yields general ideas. It is also natural to associate *abstraction* with *abstract objects* (like properties and unlike the stereotypical bearers of standard names).

The other classical process of concept formation is 'definition,' which involves putting previously formed concepts together to form new concepts. Given the argument from abstraction, it follows that if there are any individual concepts, then they are either *a priori* or defined. Since typical name concepts are not *a priori*, they must be definable in terms of universal concepts. Assuming that only descriptive concepts are universal, the semantic Frege–Mill dichotomy follows directly given an ideational theory of meaning.

My short way with the argument from abstraction is this. The theory of abstraction behind the argument is a speculation based on the anecdotal observations of philosophers from their armchairs. There is more evidence that people are able to think about individuals, and that our concepts of Tom, Dick, and Harry cannot be defined exclusively in terms of general concepts, than there is that only concepts of universals can be acquired by abstraction. Concept formation is undoubtedly a complex cognitive process. We may know its products by introspection, but not its laws. Since we have reviewed abundant evidence that the conclusion of the argument is false, one or both of its premises must also be false.

Moreover, there is independent reason to think that the traditional assumptions about abstraction are unwarranted. First, people can acquire concepts on the basis of a single experience. We would not have to see an animal as unusual as an octopus more than once to acquire the concept. Second, just as universals are recurrent features of particulars, so particulars are recurrent elements of situations.[23] The child perceives his mother giving him breakfast in the morning, and putting him to bed at night. He differentiates such situations from those in which his father gives him breakfast in the morning and puts him to bed at night. So even if concept formation does require repeated perception, selective attention, and differentiation, it does not follow that only concepts of universals are acquired by abstraction.

### 13.9   CONCEPTUAL DESCRIPTIVISM

I shall refer to the doctrine that all basic nonlogical and nonindexical concepts are universal as *conceptual descriptivism*.[24] The thesis is that nothing goes through a person's mind except purely or indexically descriptive thoughts. Given an ideational theory of meaning, conceptual descriptivism is equivalent to linguistic descriptivism. The usual argument for conceptual descriptivism is that it is the only way to avoid Frege's and Russell's problems. But as we have seen, there is an alternative. The concepts expressed by proper names could be atomic or basic, just like the concepts expressed by primitive descriptive terms.

Millians have assumed conceptual descriptivism as well as Fregeans.

Suppose Tom, Dick, and Harry, who have never met one another, agree to think some simple thought. Their instructions are 'Think to yourself that Ted Kennedy is tall', and each complies. Surely what goes on in each thinker's mind will differ considerably from one thinker to the next, varying with the thinker's political ideology and his familiarity with Kennedy's physical appearance, achievements, deeds, and so on. Tom thinks something along the lines of "That famous senator from Massachusetts is tall", while Dick thinks "That handsome brother of Jack and Bobby is tall", while Harry thinks "That good-for-nothing !@%!@ is tall."

(Salmon 1986: 2)

But, Salmon adds,

these various thoughts, though different in content, are not completely and utterly dissimilar; otherwise the thinkers in our experiment could hardly be said to be unanimously complying with their instruction to think that Ted Kennedy is tall.

(Salmon 1986: 3)

Evidently the only similarity Salmon could see is that these three different thoughts all correspond to the single objective situation consisting of Ted Kennedy's being tall.

There is another more pertinent similarity. If Tom, Dick and Harry followed instructions, then all three were *also* thinking *"Ted Kennedy is tall."* They were not just forming images of the *words* 'Ted Kennedy is tall,' which is something a foreigner might do without thinking the thought that Kennedy is tall, or a native might do while thinking about some obscure person who happens to have the same name as the senator. The men were all thinking *the* thought *expressed* by those words in our discussion. The thought that Ted Kennedy is tall differs from the thought that the senior senator from Massachusetts is tall. Even if Tom inevitably thinks one when he thinks the other, it is possible to think the former thought without thinking the latter, and vice versa, as Dick and Harry illustrate. To comply with their instructions, it is not enough that the three men all think *of* Ted Kennedy that he is tall. They might all do that, for example, while looking at a man too far away for them to recognize. What they must do is think of Ted Kennedy *as Ted Kennedy*. Castañeda's thesis that 'proper names do not reveal how we think of the objects denoted by them' is just as false as the parallel claim for definite descriptions.[25]

Conceptual descriptivism underlies a second argument Salmon offers for Millianism.

The sense theory's claim that the matter of which object a name refers to is due in part to the extralinguistic fact of which object uniquely fits the particular associated concept yields an implausible account of what makes it true that a name names what it does.... When my wife befriends yet another stray or abandoned cat, it is usually left up to me to name it. When I do, I do not first assign some sort of conceptual description (say, *the calico cat that Eileen just adopted, whichever cat that turns out to be*) and then allow this concept to probe the universe seeking whatever fits it uniquely (crossing my fingers in hopes that I got things right). I choose a name, and I begin referring to the cat by that name. I look the cat straight in the eye and I say 'You will be Sonya'. I have thereby stipulated that 'Sonya' will be the name for *this very cat*, irrespective of her color or breed or how she became a member of the household.

(Salmon 1986: 54)[26]

Salmon is overlooking the fact that he has a concept of Sonya, the very cat he is naming. In saying 'You will be Sonya,' he makes it true that the name 'Sonya' expresses the concept of Sonya in his and his wife's idiolect. The name 'Sonya' thus refers to x only if x 'fits' the concept of Sonya. It is neither an accident nor a matter of stipulation that Sonya 'fits' the concept of Sonya uniquely (assuming, as we are, that Sonya exists). It is similarly neither an accident nor a matter of stipulation that the property of being a cat, and the class of all cats, 'fit' the general concept of a cat. Whether the concept is descriptive or not is irrelevant.

Let us finally return to the Twin Earth case. I argued in §8.6 that the usual Twin Earth examples do not refute a purely mentalistic theory of meaning because they are either incompletely or incoherently described. One thing the case does demonstrate is that conceptual descriptivism is false.

> Suppose that in a far corner of the universe there is a planet on which there is a perfect duplicate of a particular earthly woman. Each lives a life on her own planet qualitatively identical to the other's. Even their streams of consciousness are qualitatively identical. Moreover, each has a husband named 'Hubert', and the two Huberts are dead ringers for one another, except that the earthly Hubert weighs exactly 165 pounds whereas his alien counterpart weighs exactly 165.000000001 pounds. Now, suppose that both wives simultaneously utter, assertively and sincerely, the string of symbols 'Hubert weighs exactly 165 pounds' in conversation, each talking about her own husband. The speakers are in exactly the same (purely psychological) state of consciousness.... Hence, by the first assumption, the purely conceptual content that each associates with her use of the name 'Hubert' is exactly the same. But the information encoded by the sentence uttered, as used on these two occasions, is different. This is evident because the information asserted by the earthly woman concerns her husband and is true whereas the information asserted by the alien woman concerns her husband and is strictly false.
>
> (Salmon 1986: 67)[27]

Salmon's stipulation that there are two Huberts implies that the proper name 'Hubert' has two meanings and two referents (Ch. 10). Let us use subscripts for disambiguation, so that '$Hubert_1$' names the earthly Hubert, and '$Hubert_2$' his twin. Then while both women utter the same sentence out loud or to themselves, the earth woman thinks "$Hubert_1$ weighs 165 pounds," while her twin thinks "$Hubert_2$ weighs 165 pounds." This is why each is thinking and talking about her own husband. These thoughts differ because their components differ. The concept of $Hubert_1$ differs from the concept of $Hubert_2$. One is occurring to the earth woman and applies to $Hubert_1$. The other is occurring to her twin and applies to her husband. Both concepts occur in the true thought that $Hubert_1$ weighs a fraction of a pound less than $Hubert_2$. Because the Earth woman lacks the concept of $Hubert_2$, she is incapable of thinking about $Hubert_2$. She could conceivably acquire that concept, however, in which case the thought that $Hubert_1$ is a lot like $Hubert_2$ might well cross her mind. It cannot consistently be maintained, therefore, that the two women associate the same concept with the name 'Hubert,' or that their states of consciousness are exactly the same. If the alien *were* thinking *exactly* the same thoughts as the earthling, then *both* would be thinking about $Hubert_1$ (§8.6). It cannot even be maintained that the two women's thoughts are qualitatively identical. For thinking of someone as $Hubert_1$ differs qualitatively from thinking of someone as $Hubert_1$ just as surely as thinking of someone as Theodore Roosevelt differs from thinking of someone as Franklin Roosevelt.

The Twin Earth case therefore shows that proper name concepts and the thoughts containing them are not purely descriptive.[28] It also shows that they are not indexically descriptive (cf. §12.4). If the Earthling thinks 'This Hubert weighs 165 pounds' while looking at Hubert$_1$, and the alien thinks 'This Hubert weighs 165 pounds' while looking at Hubert$_2$, the earthling's thought will be true, the alien's false. If the two women now miraculously trade places without noticing it or changing thoughts, the alien's indexical thought will now be true (for she is now looking at Hubert$_1$) while the earthling's indexical thought will be false (for she is now looking at Hubert$_2$). Trading places would not prevent the women from thinking about their own husbands, however, who remain behind. Indeed, assuming the switch went unnoticed, the earth woman would presumably continue thinking 'That is Hubert$_1$,' the alien 'That is Hubert$_2$.' While *these* thoughts were both true before the switch, both are false after. Ergo 'Hubert' cannot mean anything like "this Hubert" or "that man".

### 13.10 CONCLUSION

Names are not a hard case for everyone. They are problematic for semantic theories that insist without reason that names have either a definable descriptive sense or no meaning beyond their reference. The massive quantity of evidence that has accumulated shows, I believe, that standard names are semantic primitives with nondescriptive, nonindexical senses. The challenge is to say that it is to have such a sense, and to provide a formal theory accounting for the contribution of names to the meanings and referential properties of the sentences and other compounds names appear in. The expression theory, sketched in the first part of this book and developed at greater length elsewhere, provides a ready answer to the foundational question. Even if the evidence against Millian and Fregean theories is not conclusive, the thesis that names express nondescriptive, nonindexical concepts should at least be considered a viable alternative. We will see in Chapter 14 how a formal semantics can be provided for names within the ideational framework.

### NOTES

[1] A few authors briefly suggest the possibility of nondescriptive senses: Schwarz 1979: xvii–xviii; C. A. Anderson 1984: 380; Evans 1985: 79–80; Boër and Lycan 1986: 80; Taschek 1988: 100, fn. 3; Forbes 1989a: 471; 1990: 540; Peacocke 1990: 57; Wettstein 1991: 116; Yagisawa 1993a; and Horwich 1998a: §3.8; §5.4; 1998c: 376. See also Philipse (1994), who observes that Peacocke's (1992) 'informativeness criterion' implies that proper names express concepts if any terms do; and Stalnaker (1993: 311), who is concerned with 'content' representation. Dummett (1973: 111–2, 130), Linsky (1977: 6, 43, 68, 75, 83–4; 1983: 12, 126, 129, 132–3), and Burge (1979: 412, 420, 427) insist that Frege himself did not, and did not need to, identify the sense of a name with that of a definite description; see also Geach 1957a: Ch. 16; 1980: 87–9. But Dummett (1973: 135–43; 1981: 585, 588, 595–6), Linsky (1977: 8, 48, 75, 81–2, 111; 1983: 42, 120–1, 134–8, 146–7), and Burge (1979a: 427–8) still seem to conceive of senses as essentially descriptive. Lockwood (1975) and Ackerman (1979a; 1979b; 1980a; 1980b; 1985;

1989) argue for nondescriptive 'connotations' in the Millian sense of property expressed; but connotations cannot be equated with senses. Pollock (1980) argues that we all have nondescriptive mental representations of the referents of names; but then he argues that no two people have the same nondescriptive representations, which would make them ill-suited to provide the conventional senses of common proper names. Only D. W. Smith (1981: 105; 1982a: 196; 1982b: 183) and Devitt (1980: 278; 1989a, 1989b, 1990), to my knowledge, argue rigorously that there may be nondescriptive senses. Their theories are very different. Segal (2002: 551) has briefly sketched a theory with key elements of mine, but he still calls it a 'quasi-descriptive' theory. Larson and Segal (1995: 181–4, 191) did the same, but ended up with a Davidsonian theory of meaning and a causal theory of reference.

² Cf. Fodor 1975: 124–56; 1981: Ch. 10; 1987: 161; 1994: Chs. 2–3; 1998a: Chs. 3, 4, 5A. See also Wittgenstein 1953: 31–2; Bambrough 1961; Putnam 1970a; 1973; 1975; Fodor et. al. 1980; Smith and Medin 1981: Ch. 3; Unger 1983: 39ff; Jackendoff 1983: Ch. 7; 1989: 97–8; Lakoff 1987; E. E. Smith 1988: 21; Sterelny 1989: §5; Boghossian 1997b: 346–7; Margolis 1998: §3; Millikan 1998b; Horwich 1998a: §5.4; Malt 1999: 332–6; and Margolis and Laurence 1999: §2. The opposing view that unstructured terms are definable, and therefore do express structured concepts, has come to be known as the 'classical theory,' and became part of 'generative semantics.' See Katz and Fodor 1963; Katz 1964b; 1966: 72–3; 1972; 1974; 1977b: 14ff; 1990; McCawley 1968; 1994; Miller and Johnson-Laird 1976; and Fodor 1990a: 111. Katz (1997: 1) has recently tried arguing that terms might have analyzable senses even if they are undefinable. Authors like Schank and Abelson (1977: §1.4) and Wierzbicka (1992a) provide a very different argument for 'breakdown,' one based, I believe, on a completely different notion of 'analysis.' For an introduction to the whole issue, see Lyons 1977: §9.9 and Chierchia and McConnell-Ginet 1990: 350–66.

³ Katz appears to be an exception: 'If the Putnam–Kripke argument is sound, it refutes the possibility of intensional semantics insofar as this kind of semantics is based on the notion of definitional properties and thus depends on the existence of a class of sentences expressing explicative predications' (1977a: 14). Katz is right if he is saying that the Putnam–Kripke argument refutes a certain sort of intensional semantics, wrong if he is saying that the argument refutes all sorts of intensional semantics. Cf. §14.1.

⁴ Cf. Husserl 1900: 495–8 and Lampert 1992: 71–2. The conclusion that the sense of a proper name is unanalyzable provides a simple explanation for some of the data Katz (1972: 381–2; 1977a: 13; 1979: 113) cites in favor of the hypothesis that they have no sense at all, namely: (i) it is difficult or impossible to find analytic sentences with names as subjects; and (ii) proper nouns in construction with nonrestrictive relative clauses are rarely if ever redundant.

⁵ James Mill (1829: Ch. 8) attempted a nominalist definition of general terms. Contrast James 1890: 477.

⁶ Cf. Devitt 1990: 82.

⁷ Compare and contrast Harman 1977b: 174; Marcus 1975: 107–9.

⁸ See especially Kripke 1979: 244, 246–8; also Husserl 1900: 684; Kaplan 1977: 483; 1989: 368–9; D. W. Smith 1982a: 201; Barwise and Perry 1983; Fitch 1985: 208; Salmon 1986; Soames 1989: 402; Pendelbury 1990: 526–33; Recanati 1993: 130; Braun 1993: 44; Stalnaker 1997: §4; Adams, Fuller, and Stecker 1997; Perry 1997b; Yagisawa 1998; Pelczar and Rainsbury 1998. Contrast Ackerman 1987: 505–7; Stroll 1998: 533.

⁹ Burge 1977: 353; 1979a: 428; 1983: 82–3. Cf. Ackerman 1979a: 65; 1980a: 475 and Pollock 1980: 498.

¹⁰ Burge's main target seems to be indexical concepts, which many have thought to be unshareable and incommunicable (I will examine this view in *Indexicals*). The theory that 'it' expresses a special concept, the concept if it, which all by itself determines 'it's' reference, would certainly be 'thin and implausible.' But names are not indexicals.

[11] On Ackerman's theory, the property of being Aristotle is the 'connotation' of the name as well as, presumably, the predicate.

[12] Cf. Zink 1963: 485; Geach 1980: 83–4; Wiggins 1980: 48; Cocchiarella 1984: 335–7; 2002: 358–60; Soames 2002: 122.

[13] Fodor (1998a: 58–9) objected to Pinker's (1989) suggestion to the effect that the concept of a snail contains the concept of an agent, on the grounds that he does not tell us what 'agent' means, and therefore does not tell us what mental state is being attributed to people with the concept of a snail. But Pinker can use the line Fodor (1998a: 53–6) developed earlier. Pinker can say that 'agent' cannot be defined because it expresses an atomic concept. Inability to define a term does not mean that it is meaningless or that we do not know which concept it expresses.

[14] Cf. Jackendoff 1983: 121; 1989; Pinker 1989: 68; Margolis and Laurence 1999: §5. Contrast Recanati 1993: §10.2.

[15] Fodor correctly observed that RED might entail COLORED without containing it. He goes on to assert without any warrant I can see that "Meaning postulates allow one to give up [constituency] claims while holding onto both '"red" means *color* is analytic' and 'you don't have RED unless you know that red is a color'"(1998a: 110–1). To *postulate* that RED entails COLORED is not to explain anything, and the fact postulated does not explain why anything is or appears to be analytic and self-evident. Many entailments are neither. Cf. Rey 1993; Margolis and Laurence 1999: 65–7.

[16] Cf. Philipse (1994: 228–9), who is criticizing Peacocke 1992a: 32. Contrast also Schiffer 1978: 181; 1990: 260–1; 1992: 507; Peacocke 1983: 198; 1986: 102; Recanati 1993: §10.3, §10.5; McKinsey 1994: 317; Larson and Segal 1995: 180.

[17] See Devitt 1981: §5.1, §5.5; 1989a; 1989b; Devitt and Sterelny 1987: 56; Fitch 1987: 70; Nelson 1992: 195, 183, 204–5; Larson and Segal 1995: 191; Sainsbury 2001: 216 ff. Contrast Devitt 1980: 274; 1981: §6.4; Heck 1995: 6–7.

[18] This appears to be Devitt's opinion even though it conflicts with his 'official thesis' that the sense of a name is a d-chain linking uses of a name to its bearer. See e.g., Devitt 1989a: 76–7.

[19] See *Meaning, Expression, and Thought*, §21.1 for the full argument.

[20] This argument is distilled from Russell 1912: 46–59. See also Russell 1910–11; 1956; Hacking 1975: Ch. 7, Ackerman 1987, and even Locke 1690: §3.2.2. Contrast Lyons 1977: 330; and Donnellan 1990. For a related discussion, see Crimmins 1992: §3.3.

[21] See also Zink 1963: 489–91; Searle 1967: 489–90; and Luntley 1984: 279. Contrast Plantinga 1973: 154. Compare and contrast Geach 1962: §34; 1980; Dummett 1973: 110; Linsky 1977: Ch. 4; 1983: 120, 131–7; Cocchiarella 1984: 336–9; Fitch 1987: 150–1.

[22] See Woozley 1967; Heath 1967: 179; Burks 1977: 608–13; and perhaps Vendler 1972: 74–5.

[23] This was stressed by Barwise and Perry 1983: 7–9 and Nelson 1992: 203, 233–4.

[24] Cf. Leibniz as described in Mates 1986: 88; Burge 1977: 351–2; 1979a: 421–3, 425; 1983: 82–3; Castañeda 1977: 172–3, 178–9; 1987: 418, 440, 444; Schiffer 1978: 58, 84; Schwarz 1979: xii; Noonan 1980–81: 99–100; Chisholm 1986b: 199; Laurier 1986; Fitch 1987: 71–7, 138–41, 151, 164; Ryckman 1988: 244; Pape 1990: 187; Dummett 1991: 127–30; Nelson 1992: 178; Crimmins 1992: 48–52; Rosenberg 1993: 516; Kvart 1993; 1994; and Frances 1998b: §3. Wettstein (1991: Ch. 8) has a nice comparison of Russell and Frege, both of whom held conceptual descriptivism. Wettstein himself insists that we have irreducibly singular thoughts because of the failures of the description theory, but appears to affirm conceptual descriptivism anyway (1991: 5, 6, 9, 152, 155, 157–8, 171, 175–6). Chisholm (1976: 44–5) attributes a similar thesis to Kant, according to which we have a concept of x only if 'x' is a 'predicate.' Chisholm (1981: 16) later attributed to Brentano the related thesis that the only properties we grasp are those capable of being exemplified by many individuals. Austin (1990: Ch. 1) rejects conceptual descriptivism, but concludes that 'the fate is rather gloomy' for individual propositions, which he takes to have individuals as constituents (cf. §14.2).

A corollary of conceptual descriptivism would be the view that all propositions are either purely descriptive or else singular in Kaplan's sense. Contrast McDowell 1977: 173–4; Crimmins 1992: 79; Stalnaker 1997: 545–8; Millikan 1998b: §4.

[25]  See Castañeda 1977: 172 and Pape 1990: 187.

[26]  See also Wettstein 1991: 140.

[27]  See also Noonan 1984: 220–1.

[28]  See also Burks's (1951) mirror universe argument discussed in §12.4.

# 14

## Formal Semantics

I have argued that standard proper names have unanalyzable, nondescriptive, non-indexical senses, and therefore express a distinctive class of atomic concepts (or concepts with distinctive atomic components). Names are meaningful, and have the particular meanings they do, in virtue of the base clause of the recursive definition of word meaning: speakers conventionally use them to directly express concepts of individuals. Like basic logical concepts and atomic descriptive concepts, standard name concepts (or their distinctive atomic components) are cognitive elements. Standard names are not directly referential in an absolute sense, because, like all other words, their reference is determined by a sense. Consequently names with the same referent are not necessarily synonymous, and meaningful names need not have a referent. But a standard name is directly referential in a relative sense in that the reference of the concept it expresses, and therefore its reference, is not determined compositionally by the reference of the concept's components. For this reason, standard names are rigid designators.

The final stage in defending this thesis is to show that it does not preclude a powerful formal semantics. In particular, we need to show how the referential properties of names can be treated formally without identifying the meaning of a name with its reference. To this end, I will provide a brief sketch of how names can be handled within an ideational semantics.

I will also indicate how proper names can be handled by situation semantics and possible worlds semantics. These theories do not, I believe, explain what it is for words to have a sense. But they do provide a powerful formal framework for describing and predicting the semantic properties of, and relations among, the infinity of expressions in a language. In particular, they are to date the most highly developed attempts to represent the semantic compositionality of languages: how the sense and reference of a compound expression depends on the senses and referents of its components. Some may view the success of these frameworks as providing a powerful argument for Millianism. I will show how the frameworks can accommodate proper names while rejecting both Millianism and Fregeanism. The key to avoiding both Russell's and Frege's problems is to drop the assumption that the elements of the ordered n-tuples representing situations, or the values of intension functions representing meanings, are the referents of the terms whose meanings are being represented, and to rely on the formal character of formal semantics.

## 14.1 IDEATIONAL SEMANTICS

On an ideational theory, the referential properties of expressions, along with their logical properties, are derived from those of the ideas they express. An expression e is true on interpretation i iff i is true (Def. 9.1). Expression e denotes object x on interpretation i iff x is, or is in, the extension of i. A formal semantics for a language must therefore begin by assigning thoughts and ideas to the sentences and words of the language. The semantics of the ideas can be formulated by a Tarski-style recursive theory. As sketched in §9.5, such a theory provides a structural description of ideas, an assignment of referents to simple ideas, rules assigning referents to complex ideas given the referents of the atomic ideas composing them, rules assigning truth conditions to simple thoughts on the basis of the referents of the ideas composing them, and finally, rules assigning truth conditions to complex thoughts on the basis of the truth values of the thoughts composing them. The rudimentary rules (9.3, 9.4) used as illustrations of a Tarskian theory of thought contained:

*PRED* → M, F.
*SUB* → j, m.
*ex{j} = John.*
*ex{m} = Mary.*
*ex{M} = {x:x is male}.*
*ex{F} = {x:x is female}.*
*ex{PRED(SUB)} = T iff ex{SUB} ∈ ex{PRED}.*

M is the concept of a male, F is the concept of a female, j is the concept of John, and m is the concept of Mary. The first rule therefore says that two general, descriptive concepts may be predicate concepts, and the second says that two singular nondescriptive concepts may be subject concepts. Neither rule requires that the concepts involved can be analyzed. The determination that John is the extension of the concept of John is no more difficult than the determination that the set of all males is the extension of the concept of a male. So nothing in a Tarskian ideational semantics requires that proper name concepts be descriptive or analyzable.

To convert a Tarskian theory of ideas into a semantic theory for words, we need to assign ideas to morphemes, the elementary meaningful units of the language.

'*male*': M
'*female*': F
'*John*': j
'*Mary*': m

As a serious theory of English, this lexical rule would be inadequate, because it would falsely predict that the four terms are unambiguous. A complete theory would have more than one entry for each word, plus Tarskian reference rules for each entry. A complete semantic theory would also have to have a formal mechanism for assigning idea structures to the syntactic structures that express them (§5.6).[1] If any of the ideas M, F, j, or m is analyzable, the Tarskian theory will contain a definition identifying it with one of the complex ideas generated by the theory's rules. If the ideas are atomic, there will be no such principle. Any Tarskian theory will contain a finite stock of atomic concepts. Nothing prevents their assignment to proper names.

## 14.2 SITUATION SEMANTICS

Situation semantics represents the senses of sentences and words by assigning them types or elements of situations. Simplifying, a *situation* (or equivalently, *state of affairs*) may be defined as a number of individuals standing in a given relation at a given spatio-temporal location. Properties are conceived of as monadic relations. Situations are represented by set-theoretic compounds of individuals, properties or relations, and locations. Thus the ordered triple $\langle a, P, t \rangle$ might be used to represent *a's being P at t*. Some situation types are *actual* (or *obtain*), such as my working now: $\langle me, working, now \rangle$. Other situation types are nonactual, such as my sleeping now: $\langle me, sleeping, now \rangle$. In general, $\langle a, P, t \rangle$ is actual iff a has P at t. The identity conditions for situations follow directly from the set-theoretical nature of their representatives: $\langle a, P, t \rangle = \langle a', P', t' \rangle$ iff $a = a'$, $P = P'$, and $t = t'$. Existence conditions follow just as directly: $\langle a, P, t \rangle$ exists iff a, P, and t exist.

These conditions present a problem when our concern is the semantics of proper names. Situation semantics takes the sense of a sentence to be a situation type. Thus the sense of 'Cary Grant was alive in 1993' would be something like $\langle Cary\ Grant, being\ alive, 1993 \rangle$. Given that the sense of a sentence is determined by the senses of its components, it is natural to take the sense of 'alive' to be the property of being alive, of '1993' to be the year 1993, and of 'Cary Grant' to be Cary Grant. But this has all the defects of Millianism: 'Cary Grant' comes out synonymous with 'Archie Leach,' and 'Cary Grant was alive in 1993' comes out synonymous with 'Archie Leach was alive in 1993.' Worse, 'Pegasus was alive in 1993' comes out meaningless. Since Pegasus does not exist, $\langle Pegasus, being\ alive, 1993 \rangle$ does not exist. These problems can be ameliorated in the manner of Plantinga (1974; 1978a; 1985) by replacing individuals in situation-types with individual properties like *being Pegasus*, which Plantinga calls 'essences.' For this move to solve Frege's problem as well as Russell's, the property of being

Cary Grant must be distinct from the property of being Archie Leach. Plantinga must similarly conclude that the property of being water is distinct from the property of being $H_2O$, given that 'water' and '$H_2O$' differ in meaning. While not obviously false, these metaphysical claims are implausible, in my opinion. Another task for the Plantinga solution is to differentiate the meaning of the name 'N' from that of descriptions like 'the thing that is N,' and from predicates like 'is N' and 'is N himself,' all of which would appear to connote the same individual property.

An innovation introduced by Barwise and Perry (1983) provides another solution to both problems, with no such difficulties. In order to represent *types* of situation like *someone's kissing Mary* and *Jack's kissing someone*, Barwise and Perry introduced an additional set of objects called *indeterminates*. These can be anything, as long as they are distinct from the individuals, relations, and locations used in the theory. Let $\iota$ be the general individual indeterminate. Then $\langle \iota, P, t \rangle$ represents a situation type whose tokens are situations in which someone has P at t. Then my working now and your working now are both instances of $\langle \iota, \text{working}, \text{now} \rangle$. In order to represent more specific types of situations, Barwise and Perry introduced a variety of *constraints* on indeterminates. The constraint on $\rho$, for example, might be *x is a musician*. This would mean that x's having P at t is an instance of $\langle \rho, P, t \rangle$ iff x is a musician. Hence $\langle \rho, P, t \rangle$ would represent the type of situation in which a musician has P at t.

Situation semantics can now handle the semantics of proper names as follows. Introduce a unique individual indeterminate into the theory for each sense of each proper name. Thus 'Roosevelt' must be assigned at least two indeterminates $\phi$ and $\theta$. Constrain each indeterminate so that it can be instantiated only by the referent determined by the sense it represents. The constraints on $\phi$ would be *x is Franklin Roosevelt* and on $\theta$ would be *x is Theodore Roosevelt*. 'Cary Grant' and 'Archie Leach' would be assigned two different indeterminates, both anchored in the same individual by equivalent constraints. 'Pegasus' would be assigned a unique indeterminate $\pi$ subject to the constraint *x is Pegasus*. Since Pegasus does not exist, $\langle \pi, \text{flying}, \text{now} \rangle$ represents a nonactual type of situation. No situation is a token of that type. It is therefore an appropriate meaning for 'Pegasus is flying now.'

Given their indeterminate nature, indeterminates could consistently be taken to be concepts or simple intensions. Thus $\pi$ could be the concept of Pegasus, or the rigid intension function which associates Pegasus with every world $W$ in which Pegasus exists. On either interpretation, the constraints on an indeterminate would be determined by its identity. I believe a consideration of empirical property and location identities[2] would lead to the use of property and location indeterminates to represent the senses of the words expressing properties and locations too. If this were done, and all indeterminates were taken to be concepts or intensions, the resulting situation semantics would be an ideational or possible worlds semantics, respectively.

In short, if the n-tuple assigned to a sentence consists of the extensions of the expressions in the sentence, then a situational semantics cannot represent meaning adequately. A situation semantics can represent meaning adequately if the n-tuple assigned to a sentence consists of entities other than the referents of terms in the sentence. A generalized situation semantics is defined by its form only. It could be combined with an ideational theory of meaning by letting the n-tuples be sequences of concepts.

Situation semantics can be combined with ideational semantics in another way. As sketched in §14.1, the meanings of expressions can be represented by an assignment of ideas to the words of the language on the basis of linguistic and ideational structure. The semantics of the ideas in turn can be represented formally by an assignment of referents to the ideas. When the referents in question are situations and their constituents, the result is a situation semantics. John F. Kennedy would be assigned to the concept of John F. Kennedy, the property of being a man would be assigned to the concept of being a man, and the state of affairs consisting of Kennedy's being a man would be assigned to the thought that Kennedy is a man. The concept of Pegasus might be assigned an indeterminate, as in Barwise and Perry; alternatively, it might be assigned individual essences, as Plantinga suggests. The fact that the concept of Cary Grant and the concept of Archie Leach are assigned the same referent would not predict that 'Cary Grant' and 'Archie Leach' are synonymous. For their difference of meaning is represented by the assignment of different concepts to the names. Nothing in this procedure requires that proper name concepts be descriptive or analyzable.

### 14.3  POSSIBLE WORLDS SEMANTICS: PROBLEMS

A possible worlds semantics seeks to represent the senses of standard names by assigning them *intensions* and *characters*.[3] A simple intension is a function associating possible worlds with extensions. A character is a function from contexts to intensions. The intension of a standard name would be a function associating possible worlds with individuals existing in those worlds. The character of a standard name would be a constant function, since, unlike pronouns, the referent of a standard name does not vary from context to context when the sense is held fixed. Thus the intension of 'Aristotle' would be the function $a(w)$ associating Aristotle with any world in which Aristotle exists. The character of 'Aristotle' would be the function $a'(c)$ whose value for any context is the intension function $a(w)$. The distinction between rigid and non-rigid designators is easy to draw in such a framework. Whereas the intension of 'Aristotle' associates the same object—Aristotle—with every world, the intension of 'The author of *De*

*Anima*' associates different objects with different worlds: Aristotle with the actual world, Plato with any world in which Plato wrote *De Anima*, and so on.

A complication for possible worlds semantics is that names for numbers have the same intensions and characters as countless nonsynonymous definite descriptions. For example, 'seven,' 'the square root of forty nine,' and 'the cube root of three hundred and forty three' all have the same character and intension, since they all designate the number seven in every possible world. This problem can be solved by assigning to definite descriptions *structured intensions* in the manner of Lewis (1972: §5) and Cresswell (1985). Functions associating extensions with worlds are *simple* intensions. A structured intension is a set-theoretic object containing a number of simple intensions whose structure represents the structure of a meaning. The structured intension for 'The square root of forty nine' would be a set-theoretical object like $\langle SR(x, w), 49(w)\rangle$ whose ultimate components are the simple intensions for 'square root' and 'forty nine.' The structured intension for 'The cube root of three hundred and forty three' would then be $\langle CR(x, w), 343(w)\rangle$, with the simple intensions for 'cube root' and 'three hundred and forty three' replacing those for 'square root' and 'forty nine' in the same structure. What the arguments against the description theory show is that standard names do not have the sort of structured intensions that descriptions have. Standard names only have simple intensions. We will focus henceforth on simple intensions.

A more serious complication is that without unrealistic existence and identity assumptions, a possible worlds semantics using intensions whose values are referents cannot account adequately for the intensionality of meaning. A *function* is a set of ordered pairs satisfying the constraint that whenever the first member (or *argument*) is the same, the second member (or *value*) is the same. An ordered pair exists only if its members exist. Consequently the arguments and values of any function must exist: *If* $f(a) = b$, *then* $\exists x[f(x) = b]$ *and* $\exists y[f(a) = y]$. The requirement that the values of a function must exist makes it impossible for standard models to represent vacuous names. Since Pegasus does not exist, it cannot be the value of any intension function for any of its arguments. No *function* will take us from any argument to Pegasus as a value. When w is a possible world, 'f(w) = k' represents more than the fact that k exists *in* w. It also entails that k exists. This implication is false when 'k' is 'Pegasus.' Pegasus exists in many possible worlds, just as it exists in a familiar myth. But it is just an imaginary creature, not a real horse. If possible worlds semantics cannot represent the meaning of 'Pegasus' without the implication that $\exists x[x = \text{Pegasus}]$, then possible worlds semantics is unacceptable.

I do not believe, though, that the requirement that the arguments of intension functions exist poses any problem for a possible worlds semantics.

For on my view, possible worlds are *ways things could be*. In fact, things are a certain way: the sun rises in the east, the moon revolves around the earth, and so on; that is the actual world. But things could have been different. Hence there are other ways things could be—for example, the Moon could have revolved around Mars, and the Sun could have risen in the west. Since there are other ways things could be, it is literally true that there are non-actual worlds. 'World', in this sense, is a near synonym for *case, situation,* and *circumstance*. If we are tossing a die, there are two possible cases: one in which it falls heads, the other in which it falls tails. Who wins a bet often depends on which case is actual—which of the two is the way things actually turn out. 'World' is used to denote *complete* cases, which specify how everything turns out.[4]

Another aspect of intensionality is no less problematic for a possible worlds semantics in which the values of the intension functions are supposed to be the referents of the terms under investigation. The transitivity of identity entails that identical objects are the values of all the same functions: *If $f(x) = y$ and $y = z$, then $f(x) = z$.* Since Carlos is Ilich Sanchez, any intension whose value is Sanchez for a given argument is a function whose value is Carlos. Since 'Carlos' and 'Ilich Sanchez' are both rigid, their intensions must have the same value at every world. This means that a standard possible worlds semantics will assign the same intension to 'Carlos' and 'Ilich Sanchez,' and therefore rule that they have the same meaning. It also means that a standard possible worlds semantics will entail the principle of the necessity of identity: for names 'N' and 'M,' if 'N = M' is true, then it is true in all possible worlds. While this principle is plausible for natural and possibly metaphysical necessity, it fails for logical and epistemic necessity (Ch. 15). A sentence like 'Carlos is Ilich Sanchez' does not express a logical truth, and what it expresses had to be established by painstaking empirical investigation. A standard possible worlds semantics, however, assigns it the same meaning it assigns to 'Carlos is Carlos,' which does express a logical truth, requiring no empirical investigation to establish.[5]

Despite their name, if intensions are functions, then they are fully extensional objects. A possible worlds semantics using intensions whose values are extensions cannot avoid the Millian result that fictional names have no meaning, and that co-referential names have the same meaning. Despite identifying meanings with intensions (or characters) rather than extensions, standard possible worlds semantics still succumb to Russell's and Frege's problems.

The fact that we are dealing with proper names rather than common nouns is not the source of the problem. Consider common nouns like 'satyr' and 'nymph.' If the values of their intension functions are sets of satyrs and nymphs respectively, then both values must be the empty set no matter what worlds are the arguments of the function. For there are no satyrs or nymphs: these are mythical creatures. Since both intension functions take us to the empty set for any possible world, they are the same function. A standard possible worlds semantics would therefore rule that 'satyr' and 'nymph' have the same meaning, but they do not. Similarly, if the value of a function for any argument is the set of renates, then its value is the set of chordates, assuming that all renates are chordates and vice versa. But then 'renate' and 'chordate' would have the same intension, despite having different meanings.

## 14.4   WORLD MODELS

We have seen several reasons to conclude that if a possible worlds semantics is to provide an adequate representation of the meaning of names—overcoming Russell's and Frege's problems—then we must drop the assumption that the values of intension functions are the referents of the names whose meanings they represent. How can this assumption be avoided without abandoning possible worlds semantics? The answer lies in the very formality of formal semantics. Formal semantics is an application of mathematical modeling. When specifying a model structure, we specify sets of elements, and formal relationships among the elements. The exact identity of the elements is not important for the formal use of the model. Heuristically, we think of the elements as *representing* certain things. But they need not actually *be* those things. Thus any model structure used in a possible worlds semantics will contain some objects representing possible worlds, and other objects representing objects existing in those worlds. The mathematical and logical manipulation of the model, however, does not depend on the objects' actually being possible worlds, or even on the fact that they represent possible worlds. For all the mathematical logician cares, the elements in the model could be real numbers or points in the plane. In some of the most rigorous presentations, the basic component of a model structure is simply a non-empty *set*, whose members are not even specified.[6]

So the constant intension function $\pi$ used to represent the meaning of 'Pegasus' in a possible worlds semantics must have a value that we think of as *representing* Pegasus. The value need not, indeed can not, actually *be* Pegasus. For there is no such thing as Pegasus to serve as the value.[7] It is easy for us to think of real objects as representing non-existent objects. In a model of the solar system, for example, there might be a tenth ball that we think of as representing a tenth planet. We can do this even though there are in fact only nine planets.

There is a standard figure of speech whereby we refer to elements of a model as the things they represent. Thus in a model of the solar system, we can refer to the ball representing Jupiter as Jupiter. I might say 'Jupiter is out of place' in a discussion of the model. I would not mean literally that Jupiter is out of place. What I would mean is that the element representing Jupiter is out of place. It is natural to use this figure of speech when doing possible worlds semantics. As long as it is clear to us as well as our audience that we are not speaking literally, there is no harm in referring to a certain element of the model as Pegasus, the domain as the set of possible objects, and intensions as functions from worlds to the referents of the names whose meanings they represent. The practice verbally underscores the fact that we are thinking of the model elements as representing other things.

To represent the difference in meaning between 'Carlos' and 'Ilich Sanchez,' a possible worlds semantics must assign these terms different simple intensions $in_C$ and $in_S$ despite the fact that Carlos is Sanchez. This will be impossible if the values of the intensions are the referents of these names, but not if their values are different objects representing Carlos and Sanchez. A model cannot have distinct elements that *are* Carlos and Sanchez, but it can have distinct elements that *represent* them. What the values of $in_C$ and $in_S$ are does not matter as long as they are different (the terms are not synonymous) and constant (the names are rigid designators). There must be an argument representing worlds (including the actual world) in which Sanchez is Carlos. And there must be arguments representing worlds in which Sanchez is not identical to Carlos (their identity is logically contingent).

An intension may therefore associate possible worlds with extensions directly or indirectly. A *direct* intension is a function whose arguments are possible worlds and whose values are extensions. An *indirect* intension is a function whose arguments or values are different from the worlds or extensions they represent. Standard possible worlds semantics use direct intensions to represent meanings.[8] That is what makes it impossible for them to adequately represent the meanings of names. The solution is to use indirect intensions instead.

It might be objected at this point that if what I have been arguing is true, then a possible worlds semantics is valueless. Since intensions and character functions cannot actually *be* meanings, the semantics cannot tell us what meanings are. But we knew independently of the arguments of this section that meanings could not be functions—whether they are direct or indirect. For meanings are properties of words, not sets of ordered pairs of anything.[9] The objection can be extended by noting that if intensions and character functions are set-theoretical constructions of arbitrary elements satisfying merely formal constraints, then a possible worlds semantics cannot explain *what it is* for words to have meanings, or *why* expressions have the particular meanings they do. But that too we knew in advance. A formal semantics is not designed to explain such things. What a possible worlds semantics *is* designed to do, is provide a mathematically tractable finite representation of all the infinity of expressions in any natural language, along with all the semantic and referential properties of those expressions. Achieving this goal would be an intellectual advance of the highest order. None of the arguments I have presented show that a possible worlds semantics cannot succeed in this project. Finally, nothing impugns the literal truth of the truth condition statements provided by possible worlds semantics. They correctly rule, for example, that 'Santa Claus could be identical to the tooth fairy' is true iff there is a possible world in which Santa Claus is identical to the tooth fairy.

## 14.5   A MODEL STRUCTURE FOR STANDARD NAMES

Let me briefly suggest one sort of model structure that would support a semantics appropriate for standard names, which I shall call an *NC-structure*. 'NC' abbreviates 'nontransitive corepresentation,' the distinctive feature of such structures. An **NC** structure will consist of at least five elements: a set $\Omega$ of objects (world models) representing possible worlds; a set **D** whose members represent objects existing in the possible worlds; an inhabitants function **N** assigning to each element of $\Omega$ a subset of **D** representing all objects existing in the world represented by that element; a nontransitive corepresentation relation **S** defined on **D**; and an interpretation function **I** defined on expressions of the object language.[10] Beyond their formal properties, the only thing important about the elements of $\Omega$ and **D** is what they represent, which must be explicitly stipulated. To keep things straight, we will use lower case Greek letters as variables ranging over the elements of $\Omega$ and **D**.

The corepresentation relation is a reflexive and symmetric relation on the elements of **D**. 'S$\alpha\beta$' is to be interpreted as meaning that there is something $\alpha$ and $\beta$ both represent. That is, $\alpha$ and $\beta$ represent the same object.[11] In standard model structures, no corepresentation function is specified, but different elements of **D** are taken to represent different objects. Hence the implicit corepresentation relation is the identify function: S$\alpha\beta$ iff $\alpha = \beta$. This choice makes the relation transitive, and is therefore appropriate for modal logics in which the necessity of identity holds. What is distinctive about NC-structures, and the source of their name, is that the corepresentation relation is nontransitive, which entails that different elements of **D** may represent the same object. 'S$\alpha\beta$' may be true even though $\alpha \neq \beta$. To make this concrete, suppose that we are modeling different states of the solar system, constructing a number of three dimensional scale models with wooden balls representing the sun and the planets. Each model will contain a different set of ten wooden balls. Yet each model will contain one ball representing the sun. So a number of different balls (in different models) will represent the same heavenly body.

The fact that distinct objects associated with different world models can represent the same object, together with the nontransitivity of the corepresentation relation, allows logically contingent identities to be represented in

NC-structures. In models of the heavens representing the way the ancients viewed them, different balls η and φ will represent Hesperus and Phosphorus respectively. But in realistic models, one object $v$ will represent both Hesperus and Phosphorus. Then even though S$\eta v$ and S$v\phi$ are both true, S$\eta\phi$ is not. Similarly, we might have α and γ both representing Cary Grant, and α and δ both representing Archie Leach, without having γ and δ both representing the same person. This would represent the fact that Cary Grant and Archie Leach are the same person in one world but different people in another.

The interpretation function **I** is the semantic component of an **NC**-structure, assigning to each meaningful unit of the object language an intension (plus a character and a structured intension). Let 'Ps' represent a singular subject-predicate sentence in the object language. Let '$in_s$' denote the intension function assigned by **I** to the subject 's,' and let '$in_P$' denote the intension assigned by **I** to the predicate 'P.' Let $\omega_w$ be the element of $\Omega$ representing w, and let $\omega_@$ be the element representing the actual world. Then truth conditions for 'Ps' and related constructions can then be formulated as follows:

14.1　　'Ps' is true iff $in_s(\omega_@) \in in_P(\omega_@)$
　　　　'Ps' is true in w iff $in_s(\omega_w) \in in_P(\omega_w)$[12]
　　　　'$\forall x Px$' is true in w iff for every element α in $N(\omega_w)$, $\alpha \in in_P(\omega_w)$.
　　　　'$\exists x Px$' is true in w iff for some element α in $N(\omega_w)$, $\alpha \in in_P(\omega_w)$.
　　　　'$\Box Ps$' is true iff 'Ps' is true in every w iff $\forall\omega[in_s(\omega) \in in_P(\omega)]$
　　　　'$\Diamond Ps$' is true iff 'Ps' is true in some w iff $\exists\omega[in_s(\omega) \in in_P(\omega)]$

To accurately represent the semantics of a standard proper name, I must assign it a rigid intension. Logically descriptive names and definite descriptions will typically be assigned nonrigid intensions. An *intension* is a function from members of $\Omega$ to members of **D** satisfying the condition that $f(\omega) = \alpha$ only if α represents an object existing in the world represented by $\omega$. That is, $f(\omega) \in N(\omega)$. A *rigid intension* is an intension meeting the further condition that $Sf(\omega)f(\omega')$ for all $\omega$ and $\omega'$, meaning that all values of a rigid intension represent the same object. When S is the identity relation, as in standard models, rigid intensions have just one value. In an NC-structure, rigid intensions may have different values representing one object. The values of a nonrigid intension sometimes represent different objects: $-Sf(\omega)f(\omega')$ for some $\omega$ and $\omega'$. Let $e$ be the intension assigned to 'Earth,' $t$ the intension assigned to 'the third planet,' and $E$ the intension assigned to the predicate 'has an elliptical orbit.' Let σ represent world S and τ represent T. $E(\sigma)$, of course, will be the set consisting of all those members of **D** (wooden balls perhaps) representing planets with elliptical orbits in S. Then our semantics will rule that 'Earth has an elliptical orbit' is true in S provided $e(\sigma) \in E(\sigma)$, and true in T provided $e(\tau) \in E(\tau)$. If the sentence is true in both worlds, then the rigidity of $e$ implies that $Se(\sigma)e(\tau)$: $e(\sigma)$ and $e(\tau)$ must represent the same object, namely Earth. Similarly, 'The third planet has an elliptical orbit' is true in S provided $t(\sigma) \in E(\sigma)$ and true in T provided $t(\tau) \in E(\tau)$. But since $t$ is a nonrigid intension function, 'The third planet has an elliptical orbit' may be true in both S and T even though $t(\sigma)$ and $t(\tau)$ do not represent the same object. The former might be a wooden ball representing Earth, the latter a ball standing for Mars; then $-St(\sigma)t(\tau)$. This would be appropriate if S were the actual world and T a world in which Earth and Mars have changed places.

I will assign the same rigid intension to synonymous standard names. It will assign different rigid intensions to coreferential but non-synonymous standard names; some but not all of the values of these functions will be corepresentational. Expressions like '9' and '8' referring to objects that are necessarily distinct will be assigned intensions whose ranges have no corepresentational elements. In standard models, in which the corepresentation relation is identity, the values of different rigid intensions always represent different objects. So it is not possible to represent the difference in meaning between coreferential but nonsynonymous names by assigning them different intensions.

Let $in_A$ and $in_B$ be the intensions assigned by **I** to singular terms 'A' and 'B' respectively. In an **NC**-structure, I will assign 'A = B' an intension whose value at any member of $\mathbf{\Omega}$ is T (truth) when the values of $in_A$ and $in_B$ represent the same object. Otherwise its value is F (falsity). That is:

14.2   'A = B' *is true in w iff* $Sin_A(\omega_w)in_B(\omega_w)$.

Thus the intension assigned to 'Cary Grant = Archie Leach' will assign F to a world model $\omega^*$ where $-Sg(\omega^*)l(\omega^*)$, even though it assigns T to the world model $\omega_@$ representing the actual world, where $Sg(\omega_@)l(\omega_@)$. If the inhabitants function **N** assigns *nonredundant* sets to each world model, so that no two members of $\mathbf{N}(\omega)$ are related by **S**, then the truth conditions for identity will have the standard form:

14.3   'A = B' *is true in w iff* $in_A(\omega_w) = in_B(\omega_w)$.

With a non-redundant inhabitants function, the intension assigned to 'Cary Grant = Archie Leach' has the value T for any element $\omega$ iff $g(\omega) = l(\omega)$.

How can the truth conditions of quantified modal sentences of the form '$\exists x\Box(x = a)$' be formulated on the sort of possible worlds semantics I have sketched? Sentences of this form will inevitably be false when '$a$' is a nonrigid designator, but may be true when '$a$' is rigid, depending on the referent of '$a$' and the type of necessity involved. For example, let '$\Box$' represent mathematical necessity, and let '$\eta$' abbreviate 'the number of planets.' Whereas the numeral '9' is a rigid designator, 'η' is nonrigid, designating the number nine in the actual world, the number 7 in worlds in which Hegel's speculations proved true, and so on. Then '$\exists x\Box(x = 9)$' is true, while '$\exists x\Box(x = \eta)$' is false.

In accordance with 14.2, '$\exists x\Box Fx$' is true in world w iff for some $\alpha \in N(\omega_w)$, $\alpha \in in_{\Box F}(\omega_w)$, where $in_{\Box F}$ represents the intension of '$\Box Fx$.' How can that intension be defined? We cannot simply say that $\alpha \in in_{\Box F}(\omega_w)$ iff for every $\omega$, $\alpha \in in_F(\omega)$. For in an NC-structure, $\alpha$ need not be an element of $N(\omega)$ for more than one $\omega$. What we need to say is that $\alpha$ is in $in_{\Box F}(\omega_w)$ provided every object corepresentative with $\alpha$ in every world is in $in_F(\omega)$. That is: $\alpha \in in_{\Box F}(\omega_w)$ iff for every $\omega$ and for every $\alpha' \in N(\omega)$ such that $S\alpha\alpha'$, $\alpha' \in in_F(\omega)$. Let $in_9(\omega)$ and $in_\eta(\omega)$ be the intensions assigned to '9' and 'η' respectively. Since $in_9(\omega)$ is rigid, all of its values represent the same thing: $Sin_9(\omega)in_9(\omega')$. Since $in_\eta(\omega)$ is nonrigid, $in_\eta(\omega)$ and $in_\eta(\omega')$ will not always represent the same object; so in some cases, $-Sin_\eta(\omega)in_\eta(\omega')$. Consequently, the intension for '$\Box(x = \eta)$' will assign the empty set to every world element $\omega$, including $\omega_w$, making '$\exists x\Box(x = \eta)$' false in w. But $N(\omega_w)$ must contain an element representing the number 9, since $\omega_w$ is supposed to represent a mathematically possible world. Since $in_9(\omega)$ is a rigid intension, all of its values represent the same object. So '$\exists x\Box(x = 9)$' will be true in w.

A possible worlds semantics is not incompatible with the expression theory. Indeed, we can meld the two by saying that words have the characters and intensions they do *because* they are used to express certain ideas. Thus 'horse' has as its simple intension a function $in_h$ associating with possible world w the set of all horses existing in w because 'horse' is used to express the idea of a horse. Similarly, 'Aristotle' has as its intension the function $in_a$ associating Aristotle with each world in which Aristotle exists because 'Aristotle' is used to express the idea of Aristotle. The integration could be made tighter formally by letting the elements of **D** representing individuals be ordered pairs consisting of an idea of an individual and an element of $\Omega$, with the provision that all the members of $N(\omega)$ contain $\omega$ as their element of $\Omega$. We could stipulate that $\langle c, \omega \rangle$ represents Cary Grant iff c is the concept of Cary Grant, and that where $\omega \neq \omega'$, $S\langle c, \omega \rangle\langle c', \omega' \rangle$ iff $c = c'$. Thus we can think of $\langle c(CG), \omega_w \rangle$ as representing Cary Grant in world w. If c(CG) is the concept of Cary Grant and c(AL) the concept of Archie Leach, $S\langle c(CG), \omega_@ \rangle\langle c(AL), \omega_@ \rangle$ would represent the fact that Cary Grant is Archie Leach in the actual world. $-S\langle c(CG), \omega_w \rangle\langle c(AL), \omega_w \rangle$ would represent the fact that Cary Grant is not Archie Leach in w. And $S\langle c(CG), \omega_w \rangle\langle c(MR), \omega_w \rangle$ would represent the fact that Cary Grant is Mickey Rooney in w, making it a very far-fetched world. $\langle c(Santa), \omega_@ \rangle \notin N(\omega_@)$ would represent the fact that Santa Claus does not exist in the actual world.

In possible worlds semantics, there is one interpretation function **I** assigning intensions (plus characters and structured intensions) directly to expressions. In an ideational semantics, a deep interpretation function $I_1$ assigns intensions to ideas, and a surface interpretation function $I_2$ assigns ideas to expressions. $I_2$ would assign proper name concepts to proper names, and $I_1$ would assign rigid intensions to proper name concepts. There is no need for proper name concepts to be descriptive or analyzable.

## 14.6   The Counterpart Relation

The corepresentation relation is similar in some ways to the *counterpart* relation of D. Lewis's theory.[13] Both are nontransitive relations used to define the intensions assigned to proper names. Lewis's key metaphysical assumption is that individuals exist in only one possible world, while having counterparts in other worlds. When 'N' is a standard proper name, the value of $in_N$ at the actual world is N, the actual referent of 'N.' But for Lewis, the value of $in_N$ at any other world is the counterpart of N there (1972: 174–5). Lewis's semantics endorses most elements of 14.1, including (1), with worlds representing themselves:

(1)   '$\Diamond$Ps'is true iff $\exists w[in_s(w) \in in_P(w)]$.
       '$\Box$Ps'is true iff $\forall w[in_s(w) \in in_P(w)]$.

The same rule holds for both names and definite descriptions. The difference for Lewis is that the value of the intension assigned to a name must always be the counterpart of its actual referent, while the value of the intension assigned to a description need not be the counterpart of its actual referent. 'Mt. Everest is volcanic' is true in a world for Lewis only if the counterpart of Mt. Everest is volcanic in that world. In contrast, 'The tallest mountain is volcanic' may be true in one world because the counterpart of Mont Blanc is both the tallest mountain and volcanic in that world, while false in the actual world because Mt. Everest is not volcanic. For the time being, we will make the simplifying assumption that an object has exactly one counterpart in any other world. (It is not clear what Lewis would say about the value of the intension function for a proper name at a world in which its referent in the actual world has more than one counterpart)

   Despite these similarities, Lewis's counterpart relation is very different from the corepresentation relation, both conceptually and formally. Conceptually, the counterpart relation is supposed to relate objects existing in different possible worlds, whereas the corepresentation relation relates objects in models of possible worlds. I take Lewis to be working implicitly with a model structure in which the elements of $\Omega$ are the possible worlds themselves, and the elements of **D** are the objects existing in all of those worlds.[14] The intension function for a name takes us to the thing named in the actual world and to its counterparts in other possible worlds. This means that in Lewis's model structures, as in standard model structures, the intensions are direct, and corepresentation is the identity relation. The only element of Lewis's models that represents Aristotle is Aristotle. If Lewis proceeded more formally, and defined **D** as any non-empty set representing objects existing in worlds, then exactly one object would represent Aristotle; any object representing an Aristotle counterpart would represent an object different from Aristotle.

Lewis's model structures differ from standard structures in that his inhabitants function assigns *nonintersecting* subsets of **D** to members of **Ω**, reflecting his belief that individuals cannot exist in more than one possible world. It is unnecessary, but an NC-structure could have an inhabitants function $N(\omega)$ that assigns nonintersecting sets to the elements of **Ω**. The existence of an individual in more than one world would be represented by the fact that the corepresentation relation relates elements in different sets of inhabitants. To represent all the modal assumptions incorporated in Lewis's counterpart theory, we would need to add the further stipulation that the corepresentation relation does not link objects in different values of $N(\omega)$. To generate the same semantic results, we need to assign standard names non-rigid intension functions, whose values represent different counterparts of the same object rather than the same object in every world.

Simplifying Lewis's definition, the counterpart of individual N in any world w is the object existing in w that is most similar overall to N.[15] The counterpart relation is therefore non symmetric. X may be the object in its world that is most similar to Y even though Y is not the object most similar in its world to X. There may be another object Z in Y's world that is more similar to X than Y is. The corepresentation relation, in contrast, must be symmetric. For the elements it relates represent numerically the same object: if α represents the same object as β, then β must represent the same object as α. There is no requirement on Sαβ that the object α and β represent have the same or similar properties in different possible worlds.

Despite his view that individuals exist in only one possible world, Lewis does not take 'PN' to entail '□PN.' He allows, for example, that 'Aristotle might have been a mathematician' is true even though in fact Aristotle was a philosopher. According to Lewis, 'Aristotle might have been a mathematician' is true even though there is no possible world in which Aristotle is a mathematician, because his counterpart in some other possible world is mathematician. Thus even though Lewis uses the machinery of (1), he rejects the other standard formulations in 14.1 of the truth conditions for modal statements made with proper names, and replaces them with the following. Let '$c_w(N)$' designate the counterpart of N in w. If w is the actual world, $c_w(N) = N$. Otherwise, $c_w(N) \neq N$.

(2)  '◇PN' is true iff 'Pc_w(N)' is true in some w.
     '□PN' is true iff 'Pc_w(N)' is true in every w.

These 'translations', as Lewis calls them, conflict with our linguistic intuitions in a number of ways, as Kripke (1972: 267–8) and Plantinga (1973)
noted. When we use (3), we take ourselves to be saying something about a
particular person, namely Aristotle. Aristotle is the only person we are
talking about. Both conjuncts are about the same person. We would say
the same thing about the sentence; that is, we take our usage to be conventional.

(3)  Aristotle was not a mathematician, but might have been.

Lewis's view rules that we are mistaken. We are talking directly about
Aristotle in the first conjunct, but not the second. In the second we are
saying that someone related to Aristotle is a mathematician in some world.
Furthermore, 'There is no possible world in which Aristotle is a mathematician' strikes us intuitively as an overblown but equivalent way of saying
'Aristotle could not have been a mathematician'. Lewis's semantics rules that
the former does not imply the latter. 'Aristotle might have been a mathematician' does not strike us as entailing 'There is a possible world in which
someone else is a mathematician', but Lewis's semantics rules that it does.[16]
    The charge against Lewis's semantic hypothesis is not the question-beg-
ging claim that modal discourse does not mean what his theory says it
means, as Stalnaker (1986: 127) worries, but rather that his hypothesis
conflicts with the data provided by linguistic intuition. Failure to conform
perfectly with linguistic intuition is never a decisive consideration all by
itself, as Sider (2003: 198) notes, since that is often impossible and there are
always other considerations. But it is hard to see how a semantic theory
could be accepted when it is this far off. And there are other problems.
    The definition of a counterpart as the most similar object overall generates
further implausible modal and semantic consequences. It makes 'Aristotle
might have been a mathematician' true on Lewis's semantics provided there
is some world in which the object most similar to Aristotle overall is a
mathematician. It seems logically possible that Aristotle did few of the things
he actually did, while having an identical twin who did most of what
Aristotle actually did. But on Lewis's counterpart theory, the twin who
does most of what Aristotle actually did would be Aristotle's counterpart.
So counterpart theory does not allow such a possibility. Lewis's definition of
the counterpart relation embeds an objective version of the Searle-Strawson
form of the description theory discussed in §12.1, and is thus subject to
parallel modal objections.
    Plantinga (1973: 162–3) also objected that Lewis's semantics rules that
Aristotle is necessarily self-identical even though he is not necessarily iden-

tical to Aristotle. This does seem contradictory, and is not validated in the model structure I have sketched. To see the problem for Lewis's semantics, let us ask what truth value it assigns to 'Aristotle might not have been Aristotle'—i.e., to '$\Diamond(A \neq A)$.' The natural extension of (2) to dyadic predicates says that '$\Diamond R_{NM}$' is true iff 'Rc(N)c(M)' is true in some world. In terms of (1), this means that $\langle in_N(w), in_M(w)\rangle \in in_R(w)$ for some w. Letting '$R_{NM}$' be 'N $\neq$ M,' it follows that '$\Diamond(A \neq A)$' is false because there is no possible world in which 'c(A) $\neq$ c(A)' is true. But let '$P_N$' be 'x $\neq$ A.' Lewis holds that Aristotle exists only in the actual world, so that the counterpart of Aristotle in any nonactual world is not Aristotle. The counterpart is not even Aristotle in that world; otherwise Aristotle would exist and have properties in another world, which Lewis denies. Hence 'c(A) $\neq$ A' must be true in every nonactual world. Consequently (2) itself rules that '$\Diamond(A \neq A)$' is true. It is hard to see a principled way for Lewis to avoid this contradiction. If he insists that despite our linguistic intuitions, 'Aristotle's counterparts are not Aristotle in any world' really means that they are not counterparts of Aristotle, then he has to count his own motivating principle as false.

We also get inconsistent answers when we ask whether Lewis's semantics endorses the necessity of identity for names (Ch. 15) on the assumption that every object in the actual world has a unique counterpart in any other world. If N and M are one and the same individual, they have the same set of counterparts on Lewis's theory. Consequently the intension $in_N$ assigned to 'N' will be the same as the intension $in_M$ assigned to 'M.' When 'N = M' is taken to be an instance of 'Rxy,' '$\Box$(N = M)' comes out true. Using (1), since $in_N$ (w) and $in_M$(w) always have the same value, $\langle in_N(w), in_M(w)\rangle$ is always an element of the intension function assigned to '=.' But when 'N = M' is taken to be an instance of 'Px,' '$\Box$(N = M)' comes out false. For the value of $in_N$(w) is an element of the intension assigned to 'x = M' evaluated at w only when w is the actual world. At other worlds, the value of $in_M$(w) is a counterpart rather than M itself.

Lewis himself denies the necessity of identity, for reasons that have nothing to do with the issues we have been studying. Lewis allows that an object in the actual world may have more than one counterpart in some other possible world. This occurs, he thinks, when there is a tie for most similar object. When a and b each have more than one counterpart in some worlds, Lewis stipulates that 'Rab' must be true of *all* their counterparts in every world for '$\Box$Rab' to be true. Now suppose a and b are one and the same object in the actual world, which has two different counterparts c and d in some world w. Then 'x = y' will be false of c and d in w, making '$\Box$(a = b)' false even though 'a = b' is true in the actual world. Lewis's theory allows the necessity of self-identity, because no matter how many counterparts a (= b) has, 'x = x' will be true of each of them.

Whatever Lewis's theory says about the necessity of identity, his semantics does not enable us to represent the difference in meaning between coreferential but non-synonymous names like 'Carlos' and 'Ilich Sanchez.' Since Carlos is Sanchez, any counterpart of Carlos in any world is a counterpart of Sanchez, and vice versa. Hence the intension functions for 'Carlos' and 'Ilich Sanchez' will be identical, having the same values at every world, no matter what values they are assigned in worlds with more than one counterpart. Thus the difference in meaning between the terms will not be represented by a difference in intension. This is a consequence of the fact that, despite the nontransitivity of the counterpart relation, the corepresentation relation implicit in a Lewisian model structure is the transitive identity function, which is itself a consequence of the fact that Lewis's semantics uses direct intensions, whose values are the referents of the terms whose meanings they represent. We can represent coreferential but nonsynonymous names without the implausible metaphysical and semantic assumptions of counterpart theory simply by choosing a nontransitive corepresentation function and indirect intensions.

### 14.7 TRANSWORLD IDENTITY

The corepresentation relation must also be distinguished from the 'transworld identity' relation Lewis sought to avoid.[17] Corepresentation holds among elements of models, relating elements that are intended to represent the same thing in different possible worlds. The fact that different balls in different models of the solar system can both represent the Sun shows that there is nothing mysterious or problematic about the notion of corepresentation. Transworld identity, on other hand, is supposed to relate the objects in the different possible worlds being modeled. The term 'transworld identity statement' is sometimes intended to denote statements with the general form *x in w = y in z*, describing a *quadratic* relation. I believe that such statements are grammatically ill-formed and therefore uninterpretable.

(4) Lee Harvey Oswald in w is identical to John Wilkes Booth in the actual world.

Sentence (4) is ungrammatical because the adverbial clauses 'in world w' and 'in the actual world' modify nouns rather than verbs. Either of the adverbial clauses could grammatically modify the verb 'is identical to,' but both cannot at the same time. The sentence literally makes no sense. Sentence (4) makes no sense whether w is a possible world, a theory, a novel, or a myth. Even though Perry Mason was the main character in both stories, a sentence like 'Perry Mason in *The Glamorous Ghost* is identical to Perry Mason in *The Terrified Typist*' is uninterpretable.

Many identity statements making reference to two different possible worlds do make sense. In (5), for example, the adverbial phrases modify verbs in appositive clauses.

(5) Lee Harvey Oswald, who exists in w, is identical to John Wilkes Booth, who exists in the actual world.

Statements like (5) are perfectly well formed, but the references to possible worlds are not part of the claim being made. The identity they assert is a *dyadic* relation (or triadic when the implicit reference to the actual world is counted). What (5) claims is simply that Oswald is identical to Booth. It is false even if w is a remote world in which Oswald is Booth (who resisted aging for over a century, carrying on his cause against northern presidents who promote civil rights). That Oswald is identical to Booth in w does not entail that Oswald is identical to Booth, and so does not entail (5). Similarly, the stipulation that z is a world in which Archie Leach is not Cary Grant does not conflict with the fact that Archie Leach (who exists in z) is identical to Cary Grant (who exists in the actual world).

Statements (6) through (8), in which the adverbial phrases modify verbs in restrictive clauses, also assert a dyadic relation.

(6) The man who shot Kennedy in w is identical to the man who shot Lincoln in the actual world.

(7) The man who is Booth in w is identical to the man who is Booth in the actual world.

(8) The Booth in w is identical to the Booth in the actual world.

Sentence (6) is well formed because the two adverbial clauses modify the verb phrases 'shot Kennedy' and 'shot Lincoln' respectively. Given that John Wilkes Booth shot Lincoln in the actual world, (6) asserts that the man who shot Kennedy in w was Booth. Sentence (6) will therefore be true or false depending on whether Booth shot Kennedy in w. Sentence (7) can be well formed as long as 'in w' and 'in the actual world' modify the two occurrences of 'is Booth.' Assuming that the speaker is referring to John Wilkes Booth in both cases, (7) will be true as long as Booth exists in w. In sentence (8), the names are being used as general terms rather than singular terms (§10.2). The definite descriptions in which they are embedded are understood as meaning "the person named 'Booth' who is in x" and "the person named 'Booth' who is in the actual world," respectively. Since there are many people named Booth in the actual world, the latter description introduces a false uniqueness assumption. But other than this, (8) is interpreted like (7). If transworld identity statements assert dyadic relations like (5) through (8), then they are well-formed and some seem obviously true.

Chisholm (1967) convinced many that transworld identity statements are problematic. Let x be an object existing in some other possible world w.

What purely descriptive properties of x in w would make it true or false that x is identical to an object in the actual world, such as Plato or Aristotle? Chisholm could not find any. The fact that x has all the purely descriptive properties in w that Plato has in the actual world, for example, does not entail that x is Plato nor that x is not Aristotle. Even though Aristotle was in fact born in 384 B.C., he could have been born in 427 B.C. (Plato's year of birth). Hence there is a logically possible world w in which Aristotle was born in 427 B.C. Ditto for all of Plato's other descriptive properties. Of course the property of being identical to Plato would entail that x is Plato, but that property is not purely descriptive. And the property of being older than Aristotle would entail that x is not Aristotle, but that property is not purely descriptive either. Chisholm presented the argument in the form of a sorites. Start with Aristotle as he is in the actual world, and imagine that one of his properties is different. That would take us to another possible world, and an object that must be Aristotle since the difference is so small. Then start with Aristotle in that world, and imagine that another one of his properties is different. Keep this up until you have a world with an object entirely different from Aristotle. By the transitivity of identity, the final object would have to be Aristotle too, despite being entirely different. Chisholm found this conclusion to be absurd, since he assumed that there would have to be a purely descriptive criterion of transworld identity. But Chisholm's sorites should be seen as reinforcing the modal argument (§12.2) that proper names cannot be defined in purely descriptive terms. That is why there is no purely descriptive criterion of identity. Possible worlds have nothing to do with it. Nothing makes Aristotle be Aristotle, even in the actual world.

Another way of putting the problem goes as follows. If there are any properties that make it true that x is identical to Aristotle, they would have to be essential properties. But how do we decide whether or not a property is essential? We would have to determine whether Aristotle could exist without the property. To do that is to determine whether anything could be Aristotle in a world in which it lacks that property. Is there a non-male in any world who is identical to Aristotle? This is just to ask whether Aristotle could have been nonmale. The problem is therefore a general problem concerning possibility and necessity, and is a problem for identity only by implication. If names had descriptive meanings, however, the logically essential properties of their referents should be readily available to us given our knowledge of the language. 'Aristotle could have been nonmale' should strike us the way 'Vixen could have been nonfemale' does if being male were part of the meaning of 'Aristotle'. The fact that it is at best unclear whether particular properties are essential to Aristotle thus supports the thesis that names are undefinable.

Chisholm's problem is what drove Lewis (1973: 39) to counterpart theory and the thesis that individuals exist in at most one possible world. In response to the suggestion that the counterfactual 'If Ripov had not bribed the judge, he would not have won' is true provided Ripov lost in worlds in which he did not bribe the judge, Lewis produced a dilemma.

> What makes the inhabitant of another world, who does not bribe and does not win, identical with our Ripov? I suppose the answer must be *either* that his identity with our Ripov is an irreducible fact, not to be explained in terms of anything else, *or* that his identity with our Ripov is due to some sort of similarity to our Ripov—he is Ripov because he plays much the same role at the other world that our Ripov plays here. Neither answer pleases me. The first answer either posits transworld identities between things arbitrarily different in character, thereby denying what I take to be some of the facts about *de re* modality, or else it makes a mystery of those facts by denying us any way to explain why there are some sorts of transworld identities but not others. The second answer at least is not defeatist, but it runs into trouble because similarity relations lack the formal properties—transitivity, for instance—of identity.
>
> (Lewis 1973: 39).[18]

The assumption that individuals exist in more than one world does not force us to posit 'identities between things arbitrarily different in character.' Given what we stipulated above, for example, we can say that *Aristotle* was <u>both</u> *born in 427 in w* and *born in 384 in the actual world*. It does not follow that anyone *born in 427* simpliciter is identical with someone *born in 384*.[19]

Lewis also claims that unless we can explain identities, their existence is mysterious. But even when we confine ourselves to the actual world, there is no explanation of the fact that N is identical to M when 'N' and 'M' are standard proper names. It makes no more sense to ask *why* Cary Grant was Archie Leach than it does to ask why Cary Grant was Cary Grant. Nothing *makes* Cary Grant be Archie Leach, and nothing makes them differ in worlds in which they are not the same person (§3.9). The fact that we cannot explain why Archie Leach is Cary Grant does not in any way make a mystery of the fact that they are one and the same person. There would be a mystery only if the fact had an explanation that we did not know. There would be an explanation if the names had descriptive meanings. We can explain why the morning star is identical to the evening star by explaining why one heavenly body (Venus) is both last out in the morning and first out in the evening.[20] The fact that there is no explanation when names are used is thus one more piece of evidence against the description theory.

## NOTES

[1] In the Katz's (1977a) terms, the symbols 'M,' 'F,' 'j,' and 'm' are the four 'semantic markers' of the Tarskian theory sketched above. The rules pairing them with names of words are 'dictionaries.' And the correlation of idea structures with syntactic structures is effected by 'projection rules.'

² Cf. Wolterstorff 1960 and Putnam 1970a. See also Plantinga 1985: 350–353; Beer (1988), who argues (essentially) that at 8:30, being now and being 8:30 are the same properties even though 'is now' and 'is 8:30' differ in meaning; and Perry 1990: 20. Contrast Ackerman 1985.

³ See e.g., Montague 1972; Lewis 1972; 1981b; Kaplan 1977; 1978; Anderson 1984; Cocchiarella 1984: 326–7; Cresswell 1985; Chierchia and McConnell-Ginet 1990: Chs. 5–6.

⁴ Cf. Hale 1997: 494–8. In another sense, 'world' means *"universe"*: the totality of concrete objects arrayed in space and time. The claim that there are other totalities of concrete things in addition to the totality of what actually exists is contradictory, I believe, despite the heroic efforts of Lewis (1968, 1973, 1986) to defend it. If it were not contradictory, it would require scientific evidence to support it, which would be unattainable given Lewis's hypothesis that the other universes are not in our space-time.

⁵ Contrast Kaplan (1977: 517, 562; 1989: 598) and Nelson (1992: 235), who assume that rigidity entails the necessity of identity, and infer that possible worlds semantics cannot handle coextensive but non-synonymous names without *ad hoc* devices. See Zalta 1989: 468 for a possible *ad hoc* device. Rigidity and the necessity of identity will be discussed at length in Ch. 15.

⁶ See e.g., Chellas 1980: 34–5; Bull and Segerberg 1984: §4; Cocchiarella 1984: 311; Anderson 1984: 358.

⁷ Cf. Plantinga 1976: 268; Kaplan 1978: 97; Stalnaker 1986.

⁸ Lewis (1972: 174) called direct intensions 'Carnapian' because Carnap (1947: §40) originated the idea of defining intensions as extension determining functions. But ironically, immediately after suggesting that intensions be defined as assignments of individuals to states, Carnap says that instead he is going to take intensions to be assignments of individual constants to state descriptions, since he assumes that there is a one-to-one correlation between the individuals and the individual constants. So Carnap actually works with non–Carnapian (i.e., indirect) intensions.

⁹ This is an instance of 'Cartwright's Problem' (§5.2, §9.2)

¹⁰ Model structures also contain an accessibility relation defined on $\Omega$, but its nature will have no bearing on any of our issues.

¹¹ While the two locutions I have used to give the interpretation of 'S$\alpha\beta$' are equivalent, the second formulation carries a uniqueness presupposition in some contexts that the primary formulation lacks. Hence 'Bob represents IBM' appears to follow from 'Alan represents IBM, and Bob and Alan represent the same company,' but not from 'Alan represents IBM, and there is a company Bob and Alan both represent.' Nevertheless, 'Alan and Bob both represent IBM' entails 'Alan and Bob represent the same company' as well as 'There is a company Alan and Bob both represent.' 'Both believe (want, hope for, imagine, etc.) the same thing' and 'There is something both believe (want, hope for, imagine)' are related similarly. As the text makes clear below, 'S$\alpha\beta$' is to have no uniqueness presupposition.

¹² This specifies the truth conditions of "'Ps' is true in w" on its 'narrow-scope' interpretation (see §12.2). On its 'wide scope' interpretation, it is true iff $in_s(\omega_@) \in in_P(\omega_w)$.

¹³ See Lewis 1968; 1971; 1972: 174–5; 1973: 39–43; 1986: 192 ff. See also Stalnaker 1986; 1997: §5; 2002.

¹⁴ We saw in §14.3 that this specification is problematic because it entails, among other things, that Santa Claus and golden mountains exist. Since the specific identities of the elements of $\Omega$ and D play no role in the formal development of a model structure, we shall ignore this problem.

¹⁵ 'In general: something has for *counterparts* at a given world those things existing there that resemble it closely enough in important respects of intrinsic quality and extrinsic relations, and that resemble it no less closely than do other things existing there. Ordinarily something will have one counterpart or none at a world, but ties in similarity may give it multiple counterparts. Two special cases: (1) anything is its own unique counterpart at its own world, and (2) the

abstract entities that exist alike from the standpoint of all worlds, but inhabit none, are their own unique counterparts at all worlds'(Lewis 1973: 39–40).

[16] Some of these consequences can be made to seem less unintuitive by interpreting 'world' to mean "universe," as Lewis does (cf. Lewis 1986: 196, 198), rather than "way things could be" ("case," "circumstance"). It is quite plausible, for example, that there is no universe other than the one we inhabit in which Aristotle is a mathematician. But it is just as implausible that there are other universes in which people like Aristotle are mathematicians. In general, (2) is even more unintuitive if 'w' is interpreted as ranging over universes.

[17] Cf. Marcus 1961: 11–12; 1985/86: 203–4; 1993: xiii; Chisholm 1967; Lewis 1968; 1973: 39–41; 1986; Kripke 1972: 266–73; Linsky 1977: 73–4, 143–52; Kaplan 1978: 93–109; 1979; Adams 1979: 22–3; Stalnaker 1986; Austin 1990: Chs. 1–2; Putnam 1992: 441; H. H. Clark 1993: 302; Yagisawa 1993a:142; Hintikka and Sandu 1995; Forbes 1997a: §3. Contrast Plantinga 1973 esp. 152; 1974: Ch.6; Plantinga 1985.

[18] Note that in 'our Ripov' and 'the Ripov in our world,' 'Ripov' functions as a general term rather than a proper name.

[19] Cf. Plantinga 1973: 148–53; 1985: 114. I think it becomes clear in Lewis (1986) that the fundamental source of Lewis's difficulty with transworld identity is his taking worlds to be universes. How could Humphrey, who exists in our universe and has five fingers, also exist in another universe and not have five fingers?

[20] Lewis may have wanted an explanation for why it was someone identical to Ripov who does things in the other possible worlds rather than someone identical to, say, Clinton. There is no explanation for this either. Since it is possible for Ripov to refrain from bribing and lose, that is a possible case. The fact that it is Ripov rather than someone else who refrains from bribing and loses is what makes it the case it is, but nothing makes it be a case in which Ripov has these properties. Cf. Kripke 1972: 267; Plantinga 1973: 152–54.

# 15

# Rigidity and Identity

Standard possible worlds semantics have as a theorem the principle of the necessity of identity. This principle is now widely thought to be self-evident or demonstrable. We have seen, however, that in order to provide an adequate semantics for proper names, a possible worlds semantics must allow contingent identities. This is one of the reasons why an adequate possible worlds semantics for names must drop the standard assumption that the values of intension functions are the referents of the terms whose meanings are being represented. Instead, the values must be objects representing the referents, and model structures must have a corepresentation relation specifying when two elements of a model represent the same object. As long as the corepresentation relation is nontransitive, and thus not the identity function, contingent identities will be allowed.

The necessity of identity is plausible for natural and on some definitions metaphysical necessity. I will argue, though, that the principle fails for logical and epistemic necessity. Given that coreferential proper names may have different meanings, some identity statements made using names are false in some logically or epistemically possible worlds. We will see that there is no sound argument from the rigidity of names to the necessity of identity, and that other well-known arguments for this principle are either invalid or question begging. This will require a deeper investigation of rigidity, and a review of different definitions. One under-appreciated semantic fact is that in being *de jure* rigid, standard names differ from other designators in referring to the same object in worlds that are mere logical or epistemological possibilities, in hypothetical situations that are impossible, and even in completely fictional stories. Another is that the rigidity that is characteristic of all standard names is intensional.

## 15.1 Contingent Identities

On the Millian theory that the meaning of a name is its referent, whenever names are used with the same meaning, they are used with the same referent. This holds even when the names are used to describe counterfactual situations. It follows immediately that if two names refer to the same object in the actual world, then they must refer to that object in every possible world.

Hence the Millian theory leads directly to the principle of the *necessity of identity*.[1] Let 'N' and 'M' be standard names.

(1) If 'N = M' is true, then 'N = M' is true in all possible worlds.

Or equivalently,

(2) If N = M, then $\Box(N = M)$.

We saw in Ch. 14, furthermore, that in any standard possible worlds semantics in which the values of intension functions are the referents of the terms whose meanings they represent, the rigidity of names would entail both the necessity of identity and the synonymy of coreferential names, a key element of Millianism. Frege's problem for such a semantics is that names like 'Deep Throat' and 'Henry Kissinger' are not synonymous even if they happen to be coreferential. Conversely, any reasons to think that some identities expressed using standard names are contingent are further objections to Millianism.

For some types of necessity, including *natural* and on some definitions *metaphysical*, the necessity of identity is eminently plausible, and not just for proper names. Let a natural necessity be something that is true in virtue of the nature things—that is, something true in all logically possible worlds in which things have the nature they have in the actual world. Then it is naturally necessary that water is $H_2O$. For it is the nature of water to be $H_2O$; that is what it is to be water. Similarly, if Deep Throat is in fact Henry Kissinger, then it is Deep Throat's nature to be Kissinger; that is what it is to be Deep Throat. In that case it is not naturally possible for Deep Throat to be anyone else. On the other hand, if Deep Throat is Alexander Haig, then it is not naturally possible for him to be anyone other than Haig. It is undeniably difficult in some cases to determine which properties of an object constitute its nature. But there is no question, I believe, that being identical to one individual rather than another is part of a thing's nature. We thus have a simple and sound argument for the natural necessity of identity.

(3) P is naturally necessary if P is true in virtue of the nature of things.
    If  'N = M' is true, it is true in virtue of the nature of N and M.
    ∴ If 'N = M' is true, then it is naturally necessary.

On some definitions, the notion of a metaphysical necessity coincides with that of a natural necessity (e.g., Fine 1994b: 9). On others, it is narrower. Fine (1995: 56; 2002: 254), for example, later defines a metaphysical necessity as one true in virtue of the identity of things. Peacocke (1997c: 540 ff) similarly says that a metaphysical possibility must respect what is constitutive of things—that which individuates them, and specifies what it is to be them. Arguably, the laws of nature are metaphysically necessary on the broader definition, but not the narrower. On either account, it is evident that true identities are metaphysically necessary.[2]

But for other types of modality, including the *epistemic* and the *logical*, the necessity of identity seems clearly false. Before it was known that water is $H_2O$, there were epistemically possible worlds in which 'Water is $H_2O$' was false. Epistemic possibilities are those that our evidence does not enable us to rule out. In the epistemic sense, 'Water might be HO' was true in John Dalton's day. It described a 'real' possibility. Since our evidence is not sufficient for us to determine who Deep Throat is, 'Deep Throat might or might not be Henry Kissinger' is true today. Both are real possibilities. Hence there is an epistemically possible world in which Deep Throat is Kissinger, and one in which he is someone else. This is the case no matter what Deep Throat's true identity is. The necessity of identity therefore presents difficulties for a possible worlds semantics not only for names, but for knowledge. The basic idea is that a believed proposition is known provided it is true in all epistemically possible worlds (see e.g., Hintikka 1969). If 'Water is $H_2O$' were epistemically necessary because true, it would follow absurdly that it was known before the crucial experiments were conducted.

Among empirical or *a posteriori* propositions (those which cannot be known to be true or false without empirical evidence), epistemic possibilities are logical possibilities. By a logically possible world I mean a world in which all logical truths hold. A logical truth is one that is true in virtue of its logical structure. Having that structure entails that it is true. Logical impossibilities are contradictory, incoherent, and inconceivable. A logical possibility has a consistent model. If logic alone is sufficient to determine that a proposition is true or false, it is not an empirical proposition. Since some empirical identity statements are epistemically possible even though they are actually false, the necessity of identity must fail for the logical modalities as well.

The conclusion that some identities expressed using standard names are logically contingent can be reached more directly. Let us assume that in fact, Deep Throat is Henry Kissinger. (If it turns out that Deep Throat is another well-known man, the argument can be run with his name in place of Kissinger's. We know there is such a name.) Then 'Deep Throat is not Kissinger' is false. But it is not self-contradictory or incoherent, and violates no law of logic.[3] Its logical form '$N \neq M$' has many true substitution instances. An argument like *Deep Throat was Woodward and Bernstein's informant, therefore Kissinger was Woodward and Bernstein's informant* is not logically valid, and the fact that someone can know that the premise is true without knowing that the conclusion is true does not prove that knowledge fails to be closed under logical entailment. Hence there is a logically possible world in which Deep Throat is not Henry Kissinger. 'Kissinger is Deep Throat' must therefore be false in that world even if it is true in the actual world. If we want to establish that Deep Throat is Kissinger, we need empirical evidence to rule out the possibility that Deep Throat is someone else. Such identities are *a posteriori*. They cannot be known to be true without empirical evidence. But while necessities that derive from the laws of nature are clearly *a posteriori*, it is hard to understand how a logical necessity could be. Experience can tell us which of all logical possibilities are actual, but it cannot establish what the set of logical possibilities is, or show that anything holds in all of them. In sum, some true identity statements are not logically necessary because (i) they are not true in virtue of their logical structure; and (ii) they are empirical. We saw in §14.5, furthermore, that (iii) instances of '□(N = M)' are false in some models even when 'N = M' is true.

When '□' expresses logical necessity, the only instances of '□(N = M)' that seem true are those in which 'N' and 'M' are completely synonymous, like 'Romania' and 'Roumania.' In that case, '□(N = M)' is synonymous with '□(N = N),' which does express a logical truth.[4] All propositions of the form 'N = N' are self-evidently true; their negations are self-contradictory. There is some debate as to whether '=' is a logical constant; if it is not, then not even self-identity is logically necessary. But I do not believe there are any clearer examples of logical structure. The necessity of identity fails for logical necessity because the fact that 'N' and 'M' have the same reference suffices to make the antecedent of (1) and (2) true, but not the consequent.

The distinction between sentences and the propositions (thoughts) they express needs to be stressed here (Chapter 2). The *sentence* 'Roosevelt is Roosevelt' has the same surface structure whether the two occurrences of the word 'Roosevelt' have the same meaning or not. The sentence differs syntactically from 'Roosevelt is Wilson' in virtue of the fact that the 'is' is flanked by different occurrences of the same word. But it is only when the two occurrences of the word 'Roosevelt' have the same meaning that the sentence expresses a logical truth. Only then does the *proposition* expressed by the sentence have a structure that guarantees its truth: the concept of identity is linked to two occurrences of the same concept. The proposition expressed by 'Roosevelt is Roosevelt' has the same structure as the proposition expressed by 'Roosevelt is Wilson' when the two occurrences of 'Roosevelt' have different meanings. In that case, the concept of identity is linked to occurrences of two different concepts. Whether positions in a proposition are occupied by different occurrences of the same concept or occurrences of different concepts is a key element of logical structure, just as whether two positions in a sentence are occupied by different occurrences of the same word or occurrences of different words is a key element of syntactic structure. We can now observe that while 'Roumania is Romania' has the same syntactic structure as 'Roosevelt is Wilson', it expresses a proposition with the same logical structure as is expressed by 'Roosevelt is Roosevelt' when the two occurrences of 'Roosevelt' have the same meaning.

I think the common distinction between analyticity and logical truth rests on a failure to properly distinguish between sentences and what they express. Whether *any* sentence is true depends on the meaning it has, which in turn depends on the meanings of its component words. No word or sentence has its meaning necessarily, whether we are talking about logical, metaphysical, or natural necessity. But given the meaning a sentence contingently has, it may express a necessary truth (that may have nothing to do with meaning).[5]

## 15.2 ARGUMENTS FOR THE NECESSITY OF IDENTITY

The argument (3) I have given for the natural or metaphysical necessity of identity is arguably implicit in the works of proponents. Their explicit arguments for the necessity of identity are different, though. Those arguments would, if sound, show that the principle holds for all kinds of necessity, including epistemic and logical necessity. I believe this indicates that the explicit arguments must be fallacious. If they were sound, then the necessity of identity would be a serious obstacle to providing a possible worlds semantics for names that avoids Frege's problem of substitutivity failure. So we need to examine each argument carefully.

Marcus (1961: 10) bases one of her arguments on the necessity of self-identity.

Now if 'N = M' is such a true identity, then N and M are the same thing. 'N = M' does not say that N and M are two things which happen, through some accident, to be one. True, we are using two different names for that same thing, but we must be careful about use and mention. If, then 'N = M' is true, it must say the same thing as 'N = N.' But surely 'N = N' is a tautology, and so 'N = M' must surely be a tautology as well.[6]

Since tautologies are one type of logical truth, '$\Box(N = M)$' must be true if 'N = M' is a tautology. The flaw in Marcus's argument is that unless 'N' and 'M' are *synonymous*, 'N = M' will not be *synonymous* with 'N = N'. They will not 'say the same thing' in the strictest sense, and will not express the same thought. But unless they are synonymous, the fact that one is a tautology cannot be inferred from the fact that the other is a tautology. The fact that in some weaker sense the two sentences say the same thing is not sufficient to make this inference.

Millianism, of course, entails that coreferential names are synonymous and consequently that 'N = M' is logically true if true.[7] But even if 'Deep Throat is Kissinger' happens to be true, it is not synonymous with 'Deep Throat is Deep Throat.' Among other things, the former expresses an *a posteriori* proposition that is far from evident, while the latter expresses a self-evident *a priori* proposition. This is an instance of Frege's problem for the Millian theory (§10.5). Since 'Deep Throat' and 'Henry Kissinger' differ in meaning, saying that someone is Deep Throat is different from saying that he is Henry Kissinger. Hence saying that Deep Throat is Deep Throat is different from saying that Deep Throat is Kissinger.

The necessity of identity would follow from the validity of arguments with the following form together with the obvious fact that their premises are necessarily true:

(4) $N = N$
∴ $N = M$.

In a valid argument, it is impossible for the conclusion to be false if the premise is true. Hence a valid argument with a necessarily true premise must have a necessarily true conclusion. However, argument form (4) is not itself valid. It has many substitution instances in which the premise is true but the conclusion is false (for example, 'Roosevelt is Roosevelt, so Roosevelt is Wilson'). And to assume that its instances are nonetheless valid when their conclusions are true is to assume what we are trying to prove, namely, that an identity statement is necessary if true.

Marcus bases another argument on the principle of substitutivity.

If 'N = M' expresses a true identity, then 'N' ought to be anywhere intersubstitutable for 'M.' If they are not so universally intersubstitutable—that is, if our decision is that they are not simply proper names for the same thing, then 'N = M' does not express an identity.[8]

The principle of substitutivity says we can infer '□(M = N)' from the axiomatic '□(N = N)' if N = M. Universal substitutivity (in nonmetalinguistic contexts) would be valid if the Millian theory that the meaning of a name is its referent were true. But as we have seen in Chs. 10 and 11, there is plenty of evidence against this implication of Millianism. Substitutivity of names fails in epistemic contexts and opaque propositional attitude contexts generally. 'We know that Deep Throat was Woodward and Bernstein's informant' may be true without 'We know that Kissinger was their informant' being true, for example, even if in fact 'Kissinger was Deep Throat' expresses a true identity. It is very clear that replacing just one of the names in 'It is knowable *a priori* that Kissinger is Kissinger' will turn a true statement false. It is possible that coreferential names are intersubstitutable specifically in modal contexts. But that cannot be assumed in an argument for the necessity of identity without begging the question.

Kripke (1980: 3) asserts that the Leibnizian principle of the indiscernibility of identicals 'is as self-evident as the law of contradiction,' and claims that the necessity of identity is clear from Leibniz's law (5) together with the necessity of self-identity (6). His formulation of the necessity of identity is (7).

(5)  $(x)(y)[(x = y \ \& \ Fx) \supset Fy]$
(6)  $(x)\square(x = x)$
(7)  $\therefore (x)(y)[x = y \supset \square(x = y)]$

We can agree with Kripke that Leibniz's Law (5) is a logically valid formula. The necessity of identity follows from (5), however, only if '$\square(x = x)$' and '$\square(x = y)$' are legitimate substitutions for 'Fx' and 'Fy' respectively on the intended interpretation of '$\square$.' We cannot, for example, argue that formula (5) is not valid because '$2 = 4/2$' and "'2' is a numeral" are true while "'4/2' is a numeral" is false. For "'x' is a numeral" and "'y' is a numeral" are not legitimate substitution instances of 'Fx' and 'Fy'. In quantification theory, 'Fx' and 'Fy' stand for extensional contexts, subject to the substitutivity of identity. If, as in §2.9, it is stipulated that any place in which 'x' or 'y' is used is to be subject to the substitutivity of identity, then (7) will follow from (6) by itself. But in that case, (6) could not be used to argue for (7) without begging the question.

Marcus (1985/86) later derived the necessity of identity from the premise that identical objects have all the same properties.[9] This formulation of the indiscernibility of identicals can be obtained from (5) by substituting 'has P' for 'F.' Her proof assumes that 'being necessarily identical to *a*' designates a property (i.e., that '$\square(x = a)$' determines a property; i.e., that $\lambda\square(x = a)$ exists). But this assumption too is dubious when we are dealing with logical necessity. Interpol has always believed that Carlos is a terrorist. Can we infer that being believed by Interpol to be a terrorist is a property of Carlos? This inference may seem trivial, but parallel reasoning leads to contradiction. For Carlos is Ilich Sanchez, who was not always believed by Interpol to be a terrorist. By parallel reasoning, Sanchez must also have the property of not being believed by Interpol to be a terrorist. If, as Marcus rightly assumes, 'N has property P' is extensional, then we get the absurd conclusion that Carlos has both the property of being and the property of not being believed by Interpol to be a terrorist. Parallel reasoning leads to similar contradictions in the modal case. From the self-evident premise that Carlos is necessarily identical to Carlos, it may seem to follow that Carlos has the property of *being necessarily identical to Carlos*. But Carlos is Ilich Sanchez, who is not necessarily identical to Carlos when we are talking about logical necessity.[10] Of course, it is self-evident that *Carlos is necessarily Carlos*. Hence it is obvious that the predicate 'is necessarily Carlos' can be correctly attached to the subject 'Carlos'. What is not self-evident, is that the following are both true: *(i) any verb phrase VP determines a property; and (ii) sentences of the form 'N has property P' are extensional*. Since these assumptions jointly lead to absurdity, one must be false. A variant of Russell's paradox provides independent reason to reject (i): the assumption that the verb phrase 'is a property that is not a property of itself' determines a property leads straightaway to contradiction. So Marcus's assumption that 'is necessarily N' determines a property is problematic. If it is nonetheless accepted, then the assumption that 'N has property P' is extensional in the 'N' position is question-begging.

Kripke gives a second argument for (7), this one relying solely on the necessity of self-identity.

What pairs ⟨x, y⟩ could be counterexamples? Not pairs of distinct objects, for then the antecedent is false; nor any pair of an object and itself, for then the consequent is true.                                                          (Kripke 1980: 3)[11]

Kripke is here relying on the objectual interpretation of the quantifier, on which (7) says that the open sentence 'x = y ⊃ □(x = y)' is satisfied by every sequence ⟨a, b⟩. Since the necessity of self-identity is *logical* necessity, if this argument were valid then the necessity of identity would be logical necessity too. Given that identities like 'Deep Throat is Kissinger' are clearly empirical, something must be amiss. The question we need to raise is this: *Is* '□(x = y)' *satisfied by sequences like* ⟨*Deep Throat, Kissinger*⟩ *assuming that Deep Throat is Kissinger?* I believe the answer has to be 'No' because '□(Deep Throat = Kissinger)' is false when the box expresses logical necessity.

The question is, what is it for a sequence ⟨a, b⟩ to satisfy an open sentence of the form '□Rxy'? Satisfaction is generally defined recursively so that satisfaction of a compound formula is related to satisfaction of its components the same way the truth value of an instance of the formula is related to the truth values of its components. Thus ⟨a, b⟩ satisfies 'x = y ∨ x > y' iff it satisfies either 'x = y' or 'x > y.' Given that '□p' is true iff 'p' is true in all possible worlds, satisfaction for '□Rxy' should satisfy the following condition:

(8) ⟨*a, b*⟩ satisfies '□Rxy' iff ⟨a, b⟩ satisfies 'Rxy' in every possible world.

Thus ⟨2, 1⟩ satisfies '□(x > y)' because it satisfies 'x > y' in every possible world. But even though Kerry is taller than (≻) Bush in the actual world, ⟨Kerry, Bush⟩ does not satisfy '□(x ≻ y)' because ⟨Kerry, Bush⟩ does not satisfy 'x ≻ y' in every possible world. ⟨Kerry, Bush⟩ does not satisfy 'x ≻ y' in worlds in which Bush is taller than Kerry. Similarly, ⟨Deep Throat, Deep Throat⟩ satisfies '□(x = y)' because it satisfies 'x = y' in every possible world. For every world is one in which Deep Throat is Deep Throat. But even if Deep Throat is Kissinger in the actual world, ⟨Deep Throat, Kissinger⟩ does not satisfy '□(x = y)' because it does not satisfy 'x = y' in worlds in which Deep Throat is not Kissinger. On this interpretation, 'α is satisfied by β' is intensional in the 'β' position when α contains operators expressing the logical (or epistemic) modalities. ⟨Deep Throat, Deep Throat⟩ and ⟨Deep Throat, Kissinger⟩ do not satisfy the same modal formulas even if they are in fact identical. It is natural to assume that identical sequences satisfy all the same formulas when the formulas are extensional. But when the formulas are intensional, we have to expect that satisfaction is either intensional or undefined.

It is generally assumed, however, that satisfaction is extensional. Kripke seems to be assuming extensionality when he argues that if a = b, then ⟨a, b⟩ satisfies '□(x = y)' because it is a 'pair of an object and itself'—i.e., it is ⟨a, a⟩, which obviously satisfies '□(x = y).' But the only way satisfaction could be taken to be extensional given the condition formulated above, is if it is assumed that there is no possible world in which a ≠ b when in fact a = b. Thus if Kripke is relying on the extensionality of satisfaction, he is either begging the question or defining satisfaction for open sentences with modal operators in a way that does not conform to the standard connections between necessity and truth in all possible worlds and between truth and satisfaction.[12] If these connections are broken, then the connection between satisfaction and substitution will be broken too. From the fact that '⟨a, b⟩' designates a sequence satisfying '□(x = y),' we will not be able to infer that '□(a = b)' is true. Hence even if (7) were true, it could not be used to prove (2).

On the substitutional interpretation, what (7) says is that all substitution instances of 'x = y ⊃ □(x = y)' are true. To decide whether (7) is true on this interpretation, we need to know what counts as a legitimate substitution instance. What range of terms do the individual variables 'x' and 'y' stand for? If they stand for any singular terms, then (7) is false. For it will then have many substitution instances that are false, such as:

(9)  Independence Day = July 4th ⊃ □(Independence Day = July 4th).

While 'Independence Day is July 4th' is true in the actual world, it is not true in all possible worlds. Independence Day could have been December 4th. This substitution fails, of course, because the names replacing the variables are nonrigid. Suppose then that we stipulate that the variables 'x' and 'y' are place-holders for standard proper names only. On this interpretation, (7) says that all substitution instances of (2) are true, and is thus the very principle whose truth or falsity we seek to establish. If we stipulate further that 'x' and 'y' mark extensional contexts subject to the substitutivity of identity, then we cannot assert (6) without assuming what we are trying to prove.

To avoid begging the question, let us use capital letters 'N' and 'M' as place-holders for names without stipulating substitutivity. Then the question is whether we can conclude that all instances of (12) are true from the premise that all instances of (10) and (11) are true.

(10)  If N = M and F(N), then F(M)
(11)  □(N = N)
(12)  ∴ If N = M, then □(N = M).

That will all depend on whether instances of (13) are legitimate substitution instances of (10).

(13) If N = M and □(N = N), then □(N = M).

If they are, then premise (10) is no more evident than the conclusion we seek to draw from it. Indeed, given the self-evidence of (11), it would beg the question to assume that (10) is true if we are trying to prove (12).

We noted in §14.7 that philosophers like Chisholm and Lewis assumed that if individuals can exist in different possible worlds, then there must be a quadratic transworld identity relation relating x in one world w to x in another world w'. If this relation is assumed to be transitive, then there is a simple proof of the necessity of identity. Let 'A' and 'C' abbreviate 'Cary Grant' and 'Archie Leach,' respectively. Let @ be the actual world, in which A = C. Given that A = C in @, it might seem obvious that A in @ = C in @. Now let z be any other possible world. From the fact that 'A' and 'C' are rigid designators, it might seem to follow that A in z = A in @ and that C in z = C in @. The transitivity of identity might then seem to entail that A in z = C in z, from which it might seem to follow that there is no possible world z in which Cary Grant is not Archie Leach. This argument for the necessity of identity only makes sense, however, if statements of the form 'x in w = y in z' are grammatical, and have the logical properties indicated. Neither assumption is warranted. As explained in §14.7, 'in w' and 'in z' are adverbial phrases, which modify verbs rather than nouns. Since 'x in w = y in z' has only one verb, it is uninterpretable. In contrast, a sentence like 'The x that is A in @ = the x that is C in @' employs only dyadic identity, and is both interpretable and true. Together with 'The x that is C in @ = the x that is C in w,' it does entail 'The x that is A in @ = the x that is C in w' and 'A = C.' But these say nothing about whether A = C in w.

## 15.3 THE ARGUMENT FROM RIGIDITY

The most influential argument for the necessity of identity is the classic argument from rigidity.

Let 'N' and 'M' be standard proper names. If 'N = M' is true, then 'N' and 'M' designate the same object in the actual world. Since they are rigid designators, they must designate the same object in every world. Therefore, 'N = M' must be true in every possible world.[13]

There is no question that this argument seems self-evidently valid, and that its premise that standard names are rigid designators is undeniable. But the very rigidity of names means that if this argument is sound, then the necessity of identity is not restricted to natural or metaphysical necessity.

The argument works just as well for epistemic and logical necessity. 'Aristotle' designates Aristotle in *every* world, hypothetical situation, or case, whether it is a metaphysical possibility or merely an epistemic or logical possibility. The fact that 'Deep Throat is Kissinger' does not express something that is logically true or known even if it is true, means that the necessity of identity does not hold for logical or epistemic necessity. Similarly, the argument works just as well for other rigid designators. Suppose someone points at a photograph, that, unbeknownst to anyone, is of me, and asks, 'Is that me? It is neither epistemically nor logically necessary that that is me. So something must be wrong with the argument from rigidity. It proves too much.

I submit that the argument from rigidity is invalid. The premise that 'N' and 'M' are rigid designators entails that they *each* designate the same object in every world. 'N,' of course, designates N in every world, and 'M' designates M in every world. So we have:

> (14) 'N' designates the same object, namely N, in every world.
> (15) 'M' designates the same object, namely M, in every world.

To these two premises are added the further premise that 'N = M' is true, which means that 'N' designates the same object as 'M' in the actual world. So we also have:

> (16) 'N = M' is true in the actual world.

The argument from rigidity moves from these three premises to:

> (17) 'N = M' is true in every possible world.

This inference seems valid. But what is there in (14)–(16) that rules out the following possibility?

> (18) There is a non-actual but possible world w in which 'N' designates N and 'M' designates M but in which N ≠ M.

Premises (14) and (15) are both satisfied by (18). And since (18) is talking about a nonactual world, it is compatible with (16). It thus seems evident on reflection that nothing in the premises of the argument from rigidity rules out (18). Since the premises are compatible with (18), they do not entail the necessity of identity.

It might be thought that (18) is impossible given (16), because if N and M are actually one and the same object, then it is not possible for 'them' to be different objects.[14] On the surface, this appears to beg the question. But the intended argument, presumably, is that (18) cannot be true given (16) because *it is impossible for one object to be two objects.* On one interpretation, the italicized sentence expresses a self-evident truth. But nothing in (18) conflicts with that principle. (18) entails neither 'N is two objects in w' nor 'M is two objects in w.' And it does not entail that any other single object in w is two objects. Of course, 'One object cannot be two objects' may also be heard as saying that if two things are one and the same object in the actual world, then it is not possible for them to be different objects. But on that reading, it is just a formulation of the identity of necessity, and cannot be invoked here without begging the question.

## 15.4 THE MISDESCRIPTION MANEUVER

Putnam allowed that before we discovered that water is $H_2O$, we might have said that it is possible that water is something other than $H_2O$—XYZ, perhaps. Indeed, Dalton hypothesized that water was HO. But after the discovery, Putnam says, "we ought to say that the 'hypothetical situation in which water is XYZ' is misdescribed, any such hypothetical situation is properly described as one in which XYZ plays the role of water (fills the lakes and rivers, etc.) ... " (1992: 435).[15] But the hypothesis that water is HO is not the hypothesis that HO plays the role of water. One does not entail the other; they are logically independent. Putnam presented no evidence for the claim that historians have misdescribed Dalton's hypothesis, or that Dalton misdescribed it himself. Putnam seems to be assuming that hypothetical situations are observed and described using the same methods we apply to actual material objects. As Kripke once quipped, we don't use powerful telescopes (or microscopes).

Of course, the fact that we can *imagine* scenarios in which water is not $H_2O$ does not prove that they are *possible* scenarios. The scenarios are not self-contradictory, but self-contradictions are not the only kinds of impossibility. The point made above is that nothing in (14)–(16) entails that such scenarios are impossible, so the argument from rigidity is invalid.

Kripke also tried to address the idea many had that if things had turned out differently, Hesperus and Phosphorus would have been two different planets, leading his opponents to conclude that empirical identities are contingent.

Now there are two things that such people can mean. First, they can mean that we do not know a priori whether Hesperus is Phosphorus. This I have already conceded. Second, they may mean that they can actually imagine circumstances that they would call circumstances in which Hesperus would not have been Phosphorus. Let us think what would be such a circumstance, using these terms as *names* of a planet. For example, it could have been the case that Venus did indeed rise in the morning in exactly the position in which we saw it, but that on the other hand, in the position which is in fact occupied by Venus in the evening, Venus was not there, and Mars took its place.... Now one can also imagine that in this counterfactual other possible world, the earth would have been inhabited by people and that they should have used the names 'Phosphorous' for Venus in the morning and 'Hesperus' for Mars in the

evening. Now, this is all very good, but would it be a situation in which Hesperus was
not Phosphorus?                                          (Kripke 1971: 155)

Kripke (1971: 145) distinguishes two different ways that claims of the
following form can be interpreted.

    (19) 'N' designates M in w.

On one interpretation, (19) means that *as people in w use 'N,'* its referent
would be M if w were the actual world. On this interpretation, 'Hesperus'
could designate Mars in the imagined circumstances c simply because the
meaning of 'Hesperus' is different in c than it is in the actual world. This
interpretation of (19) is therefore irrelevant to our concerns. For we are
concerned with the meaning of names in English as it is actually spoken. On
the interpretation we are interested in when talking about rigid designation,
what (19) means is that *as we use 'N' in the actual world*, its referent would
be M if w were the actual state of affairs. On this interpretation, Kripke has
not told us enough about the case to tell whether 'Hesperus' designates Mars
or not in the imagined circumstances. Nothing in his description of the case
entails that Mars is Hesperus, or that Venus is Phosphorus. It is compatible
with Kripke's description, for example, that Mars had the distinctive and
instantly recognizable color, size, and twinkle of Phosphorus, while Venus
had the same features of Hesperus; that Phosphorus was the first planet
visible in the evening, while Hesperus is the last visible in the morning; and
finally, that scientists determined that the orbit of Hesperus matches that of
Venus, while the orbit of Phosphorus matches that of Mars. Given these
extra details, it is at least likely that 'Hesperus' designates Venus in c, while
'Phosphorus' designates Mars. The fact that the extra details are contrary to
fact does not undermine this conclusion, of course, because it was given that
c is a counterfactual case.

   Kripke's opponents could proceed more directly. It suffices for them to
imagine a circumstance in which Phosphorus is last out in the morning and
Hesperus is first out in the evening just as they are in the actual world, but in
which Hesperus and Phosphorus had different orbits. Hence careful observation and calculation led scientists in that world to realize that the planets
are different. This is definitely a circumstance in which 'Hesperus is not
Phosphorus' is true. If this were the actual state of affairs, then 'Hesperus is
not Phosphorus' would be true.

   Judging from what he says elsewhere, Kripke might reply that *to imagine
that Hesperus is first out in the evening IS to imagine that Venus is first out in
the evening*, so that his opponents must be either not really imagining that
Phosphorus is not Hesperus or imagining something self-contradictory. But
this reply is true only on the transparent interpretation of 'imagines that N is
P' (§2.8). On the transparent interpretation, to imagine that the last planet

visible in the morning is not the first planet visible in the evening is to imagine that Venus is not Venus, and to know that Venus is Venus is to know that Hesperus is Phosphorus. Kripke did not have the transparent interpretation in mind when he claimed that we do not know *a priori* whether Hesperus is Phosphorus. Similarly, to fully understand what Kripke's opponents were imagining, we have to interpret 'imagines that N is P' opaquely. On the opaque interpretation, to imagine something about Hesperus or the first planet visible in the evening is not to imagine something about Venus. The substitutivity of identity fails.

One might imagine some of Kripke's descriptivist opponents asking how we can know we are imagining something about Hesperus rather than Venus. The simple answer I would give is 'by introspection.' We know directly, by introspection, what we are thinking about or imagining. This is particularly clear in the Superman and Deep Throat examples.[16] Kripke himself (1971: 147ff) observes that the question falsely presupposes that counterfactual situations have to be imagined or described purely qualitatively, with consequences about named individuals deduced from descriptive 'criteria of identity.' Such criteria do not exist for proper names, and there is no basis for the requirement (Chapter 12). We do not have to deduce from descriptive criteria that we are thinking about Hesperus any more than we have to deduce from descriptive criteria that we are thinking about planets or identity.

## 15.5  *De Jure* versus *De Facto* Rigidity

Another way to see that the necessity of identity does not follow from the rigidity of names is to observe that (14) and (15) hold even when the domain of worlds includes fictional and impossible worlds as well as possible worlds. The contrast between the proper name 'Joseph P. Kennedy' and the definite description 'the President in 1964' that is marked by calling the former a rigid designator and the latter nonrigid surfaces when we use the terms to describe novels just as clearly as when we use the terms to describe possible worlds. Thus in the novel *Fatherland* by Robert Harris, 'Joseph P. Kennedy' denotes the same person it denotes in the actual world, namely, Joseph P. Kennedy, father of John F. Kennedy (US president from 1960 to 1963). As a consequence, 'Joseph P. Kennedy became president' is true in *Fatherland* because in the novel Joseph P. Kennedy did become president. In contrast, 'the president in 1964' denotes a different person in that novel than it does in real life. In the actual world, it denotes Lyndon Johnson, John F. Kennedy's successor. In the novel, Joseph Kennedy was the president in 1964, so the description refers to him rather than Johnson.

The name 'Joseph P. Kennedy' designates the same person even in impossible worlds. If I say, 'Let us imagine a scenario in which Joseph P. Kennedy is

36 years old and his son John F. Kennedy is 56 years old', then I am asking you to imagine a scenario in which *Joseph P. Kennedy* has the impossible property of being younger than his son. In contrast, the description 'the elder of Joseph and John' designates a different person in this world than it does in the actual world.

It is often noted that definite descriptions like 'the cube root of eight' satisfy the definition usually given for rigid designators—designating the same object in all possible worlds—even though they are descriptions. They are said to be '*de facto*' rather than '*de jure*' rigid. Little effort has been made to define this this distinction.[17] It might be stipulated that a rigid designator is *de facto* rather than *de jure* rigid provided it refers descriptively rather than nondescriptively (i.e., 'directly'). But this would make the claim that no descriptions are *de jure* rigid trivial. I would define a *de jure* rigid designator as one that designates the same object in *all* worlds, possible or not, and a *de facto* rigid designator as one that designates the same object in all *possible* worlds even though it is not *de jure* rigid. On this account, 'Nondescriptive names differ from descriptions in being *de jure* rigid' is both informative and true. Suppose I said 'Let us imagine that 3 were the cube root of eight.' Then I have stipulated an imaginary case in which 'the cube root of eight' refers to 3. As usual, though, the numeral '3' has its same reference, as does '2'.

So (14) and (15) follow from the rigidity of 'N' and 'M' even when the domain of worlds includes impossible as well as possible worlds, and includes fictional and epistemically possible worlds. Note now that the inference from (14)–(16) to (17) still *seems* valid even when 'world' has this broad domain. But for the very same reason, so does the inference from (14)–(16) to the following:

(20) 'N = M' is true in every fictional, epistemically possible, or impossible world.

Since this conclusion is patently false for proper names, the inference from (14)–(16) to (17) must be invalid.

## 15.6 THE INTENSIONALITY OF RIGID DESIGNATION

Our conclusion that (17) does not follow validly from (14)–(16) implies that (14) and (15) are not extensional in the positions occupied by the names that are used but not mentioned. Substitutivity fails. *'Carlos' rigidly designates Ilich Sanchez* does not follow from *'Carlos' rigidly designates Carlos* even though Carlos is Ilich Sanchez. In a novel in which Carlos is Usama Bin Laden and Ilich Sanchez becomes an innocent coffee farmer, 'Carlos' designates Carlos but not Sanchez. As a consequence, 'Carlos is an Arab' is true in that novel while 'Carlos is a coffee farmer' is false. Moreover, existential generalization fails. Like any other standard name, 'Pegasus' is rigid, and thus designates the same object, namely Pegasus, in every world. It does not follow that Pegasus exists. I assume that 'Pegasus' designates Pegasus in any world (or story) w only if Pegasus exists in w. But that does not require Pegasus to exist in the actual world. Unlike the simple notion of word reference, which is fully extensional (§9.1), *the notion of rigid designation is intensional*. The intensionality of rigid designation should not be surprising given that it is defined in terms of a modal notion.

Because it occurs in an intensional context, the identity notion used in (14) and (15) is what Geach (1967) called *intentional identity*, and thus differs markedly from the relational concept of identity used in (16) and (17). If Tom is thinking of Deep Throat and Dick is thinking of Deep Throat, then it follows that they are thinking of the same person. This would follow even if in fact there were no such person as Deep Throat. In the opaque sense, it would not follow that either of them is thinking of Kissinger even if he is Deep Throat.

Kripke seems to have assumed that rigid designation is extensional.

> If names are rigid designators, then there can be no question about identities being necessary, because 'a' and 'b' will be rigid designators of a certain man or thing x. Then even in every possible world, a and b will both refer to this same object x, and to no other, and so there will be no situation in which a might not have been b.
>
> (Kripke 1971: 154)[18]

Putting a variable after 'rigidly designates' assumes that it is an extensional context, subject to the substitutivity of identity. If it is stipulated that rigid designation is extensional, then the argument from rigid designation is valid but begs the question. For in order to accept the premise that 'Carlos' is a rigid designator, we would have to know that a world in which Carlos is not Ilich Sanchez is an impossible world. In that world, 'Carlos' designates Carlos, but not Ilich Sanchez. If it is a possible world, then "'Carlos' rigidly designates Carlos" is false on an extensional interpretation of 'rigidly designates.'

## 15.7  ALTERNATIVE DEFINITIONS OF RIGIDITY

I have been using Kripke's (1971: 146) original definition of a rigid designator as a term that *designates the same object in every world in which the object exists* (and nothing in any other world). 'Pluto' has no referent in a world in which Pluto does not exist, just as 'the ninth planet' has no referent in a world in which there are only eight planets. Kaplan (1977: §4) gave a slightly different definition. A singular term is Kaplan-rigid provided it *designates its actual referent in every possible world*.[19] Thus 'Mt. Everest' is Kaplan-rigid assuming it designates Mt. Everest in every possible world, while 'the tallest mountain' is not Kaplan-rigid because it does not designate

Mt. Everest in a world in which Mont Blanc is taller.[20] Kaplan's definition differs from Kripke's in not applying to 'Pegasus,' which has no actual referent. Indeed, Kaplan-rigidity is fully extensional. Kaplan's definition also differs from Kripke's in not applying to 'the object identical to Mt. Everest,' which, being a description, has no referent in worlds in which Mt. Everest does not exist. The main difference is that for Kaplan, a name or a demonstrative differs from a definite description in designating its actual referent even in a world in which its actual referent does not exist. If Kaplan is right, then from the fact that 'Mt. Everest' designates its actual referent in every possible world, we cannot infer that Mt. Everest exists in all possible worlds.

We now need to ask, *Does 'Carlos' designate its actual referent even in a world δ (possible or impossible) in which Carlos is not Ilich Sanchez?* I do not think this question has an answer on Kripke's approach. To determine whether a name refers to an object in a counterfactual circumstance for Kripke, we have to determine whether the name would have that referent if the circumstance were actual. It seems impossible to say whether 'Carlos' would have its actual referent (Carlos = Sanchez) if the counterfactual circumstance in which Carlos is not Sanchez were actual. I believe Kaplan would definitely answer 'Yes,' however. For he holds that directly referential terms like names differ from descriptions in that '*The rules do not provide a complex which together with a circumstance of evaluation yields an object. They just provide an object*' (1977: 495). If Kaplan does answer 'Yes' for this reason, then the premise that 'Carlos' and 'Ilich Sanchez' designate their actual referent in every possible world provides no more reason to conclude that 'Carlos is Ilich Sanchez' is true in every possible world than it does to conclude that 'Carlos (or Sanchez) exists' is true in every possible world. Kaplan's direct reference rule assigns referents to terms *independently of the nature of the circumstance*, and thus independent of whether the circumstance is possible. To know whether 'Carlos = Sanchez' is true in a circumstance, though, we have to know more than that Kaplan's rule assigns 'Carlos' and 'Sanchez' the same referent;[21] we also have to know something about the circumstance, specifically, whether it is one in which Carlos is identical to Sanchez. In the same way, to know whether 'Carlos exists' is true in a circumstance, we have to know more than that Kaplan's rule assigns 'Carlos' a referent; we have to know whether the circumstance is one in which Carlos exists. There is no valid argument from rigidity to the necessity of identity given Kaplan's direct reference rule.

Suppose, then, that in answer to "Does 'Carlos' designate its actual referent in δ," Kaplan says 'No,' or 'It depends on whether δ is a possible world.' In that case, we cannot accept the premise that 'Carlos' and 'Ilich Sanchez' designate their actual referent in every possible world without assuming what we are trying to prove, namely, that a world in which Carlos is not Ilich Sanchez is an impossible world. So an argument from Kaplan-rigidity to the necessity of identity is either invalid or question begging.

Another argument from rigidity can be constructed on the basis of the definition Soames gives.

To say that *Aristotle* is a rigid designator is to say that it denotes the same thing in (or at, or with respect to) all possible worlds. The reason we think it does this is that we think the truth-values, at different worlds, of sentences containing the name always depend on the properties of one and the same individual at those worlds. For example, we take the sentence *Aristotle was a philosopher* to be true at a world (state) w iff a certain individual—the person who was actually Aristotle—was a philosopher in w.[22]                              (Soames 2002: 23ff)

The last sentence leads Soames to say that 's' is a rigid designator provided (21) is true.

(21)  $\exists x \forall w$('s is P' is true in w iff x is P in w).

This suggests that if 'N' and 'M' are both rigid, designating the same object in the actual world, then that object is the only one that will make statements containing 'N' and 'M' true in any world. It thus seems that 'N = M' must be true in every world.

While this reasoning also seems valid, a closer examination will again show that it is not. To prove the necessity of identity, we need to derive (22) from the assumption that 'N = M' is true in the actual world, where 'N' and 'M' are rigid.

(22)  $\forall w$('N = M' is true in w).

Suppose that 'N' is a rigid designator. Substituting 'N' for 's' and '= M' for 'is P' in (21), we get:

(23)  $\exists x \forall w$('N = M' is true in w iff x = M in w).

Supposing that 'M' is rigid, and substituting 'M' for 's' and '= N' for 'is P,' we similarly get:

(24)  $\exists x \forall w$('N = M' is true in w iff x = N in w).

Now suppose that 'N = M' is true in the actual world. Then there is just one object z in the actual world such that z = N and z = M. So in order for (23) and (24) to be true, we must have:

(25)  $\forall w$('N = M' is true in w iff z = M in w)
(26)  $\forall w$('N = M' is true in w iff z = N in w)

Hence 'N = M' is true in any world w iff z is identical to both N and M in w. Nothing we have said so far, however, guarantees either z = M or z = N in w, unless we beg the question and assume what we are trying to prove, namely that any identity holding in the actual world holds in every world w. Without the assumption that z is identical to either N or M in w, however, we cannot derive (22) from (25) and (26). We could derive (22) from (27):

(27)  $\forall$w('N = M' is true in w if z = z in w).

For it is self-evident that z is self-identical in every possible world (ignoring questions of existence). But we cannot derive (27) from (25) and (26). There is no reason to assume that if z = z in w, then z = N or z = M in w.

It should be noted that Soames started with Kripke's definition of rigidity, but ended with a formulation that fits Kaplan's definition better. As a result, Soames's definition fails for names of non-existent objects like 'Santa Claus' or 'Vulcan,' even though they do satisfy Kripke's definition. In contrast to an empty definite description like 'the man in a red outfit who brings all good children Christmas presents,' which designates different individuals in different possible worlds (in which there is such a person), the proper name 'Santa Claus' designates the same person (Santa) in every possible world (in which Santa exists). We cannot explicate this by saying that any sentence containing 'Santa Claus' is true at a possible world iff a certain individual— the person who is actually Santa Claus—has the property expressed by the predicate. Since Santa Claus does not exist, no one actually is Santa Claus. We have here another instance of Geach's (1967) intentional identity problem.

An entirely different derivation of the necessity of identity can be based on an alternative condition of rigidity found in the modal logic literature.[23] If 'N' is a rigid designator, then it designates the same object, namely N, in every possible world. This seems straightforwardly to imply:

(28)  $\exists x\Box(N = x)$.

Similarly, the claim that 'M' is a rigid designator seems evidently to imply

(29)  $\exists y\Box(M = y)$.

To derive (2), we assume 'N = M' and use (28) and (29) to derive '$\Box(N = M)$' in a conditional proof.

1. N = M          Assumption
2. $\Box(N = x)$     (28), Existential Instantiation
3. $\Box(M = y)$     (29), Existential Instantiation
4. N = x           2, Modal Subalternation
5. M = y           3, Modal Subalternation
6. x = y           1, 4, 5, Transitivity
7. $\Box(x = y)$     6, by (7)
8. $\Box(N = M)$     2, 3, 7, Modal Transitivity

Since we have already showed that (14) and (15) do not entail (2), this version of the argument from rigidity must also be invalid. One problematic step is 7, which assumes a form of the necessity of identity. We saw above that when '□' expresses logical (or epistemic) necessity, the substitutional interpretation of (7) is definitely false, and the objectual interpretation is either false or question-begging. If (7) is accepted, making the validity of the derivation 1–8 valid, then by that very fact the inference from the rigidity of 'N' and 'M' to (28) and (29) is made suspect. That inference is problematic even without (7). For (28) and (29) entail that N and M necessarily exist: that they exist in the actual world and all other possible worlds. As we have observed before, 'Pegasus' is a rigid designator even though Pegasus does not exist. And 'Aristotle' is a rigid designator even though Aristotle does not exist in all possible worlds.

As Kripke (1971: 145ff) realized, the existence problem also afflicts (6), his formulation of the necessity of self-identity. '$(x)\Box(x = x)$' entails that everything exists necessarily. This implication can be avoided by conditionalizing. Let 'E!x' mean "$(\exists y)(y = x)$."

(30) $(x)\Box[E!x \supset x = x]$.

This says that every object is such that it is self-identical in every world in which it exists. The conditionalized version of (7) is:

(31) $(x)(y)[x = y \supset \Box(E!x \supset x = y)]$.

Everything Kripke said can be recast using this more adequate formulation. So simplification was legitimate.

A similar conditionalization of (28) and (29) is still problematic, though, as a condition of rigid designation. Consider:

(32) $\exists x\Box[E!N \supset N = x]$.

This says that there is an object x such that if N exists in any world, N is x in that world. 'Pegasus' is a rigid designator. But there is no existing object that 'Pegasus' designates in every world in which Pegasus exists. The only object that 'Pegasus' designates in any world is Pegasus, which does not exist. Another suggestion (Cocchiarella 2002: 246) is to replace (28) with:

(33) $\Diamond\exists x\Box(N = x)$.

This condition seems far from sufficient for 'N' to be a rigid designator. It would seem to allow that 'N' is a rigid designator even though N is different individuals in different worlds as long as there is a possible world in which N is the same object in every world. Moreover, if (28) is replaced by (33), the derivation sketched above fails at step 6 because 4 and 5 are relativized to an unspecified possible world while 1 is relativized to the actual world.

## 15.8  STANDARD INTENSIONS

There is one valid argument from rigidity for the necessity of identity. It is based on the standard assumption that the values of the intension functions representing the meanings of names are the referents of the terms under investigation. Let n(w) be the intension function representing the meaning of 'N,' and let m(w) be the intension function representing the meaning of 'M.' Since names designate the same object in every possible world, n(w) and n(w) must be constant functions. Given the standard assumption, their constant values are N and M respectively. If in fact N = M, then it follows that n(w) = m(w) for all possible worlds w. It follows further that 'N = M' is true not only in the actual world, but in all possible worlds; hence '□(N = M)' is true. It really does not matter to the argument that N and M are assumed to be identical in the actual world rather than a nonactual world. The same assumptions yield the conclusion that if an identity statement is possibly true (true in some possible world), then it is necessarily true (true in all possible worlds). That is, there are no contingent identity statements expressible with names.

While valid, this argument cannot be considered a proof of 'If N = M, then □(N = M)' (2). For it was based on a nonapodeictic theoretical assumption—that *the meaning of a name can be represented by a function whose value is the referent of that name.*[24] The most the argument proves is that *if* the meaning of names can be so represented, then 'If N = M, then □(N = M)' is true for all names 'N' and 'M.' But we can just as well turn the argument around, and conclude that since the necessity of identity would preclude the proper representation of the meaning of a name in a standard possible worlds semantics, then the meaning of a name cannot be represented by a function whose value is the referent of that name. Furthermore, if the intension functions are to fully represent the semantics of names, they must represent what the name designates in fictional and impossible worlds. But then the argument from rigidity would yield the patently erroneous conclusion that if 'N = M' is true in the actual world, then it is true in all stories and in all epistemic possibilities.

We saw in Ch. 14 how to develop a possible worlds semantics that enables us to avoid Frege's problem. The key is to drop the assumption that the value of an intension function is the referent of the term whose meaning is represented. The elements of formal model must represent the meanings and referents of terms, but need not be the meanings and referents themselves. To secure the result that the necessity of identity holds for natural (or metaphysical) necessity but not logical (or epistemic) necessity, the corepresentation relation must be transitive over the set of naturally (or metaphysically) possible worlds but not over the set of logically (or epistemically) possible worlds.

## NOTES

[1] The necessity of identity has been affirmed in some form by Ramsey 1927: 170; Smullyan 1947: 140; Fitch 1949: 138; Marcus 1961: 9; 1985/86: 201–2; 1993: xiii; Prior 1967b: 10–11, 148; Kripke 1972: 306–308, 333–341; 1980: 3; Putnam 1973: 708–709; 1975: 150–151; 1992; Plantinga 1974: 81–87; Linsky 1977: 137–139, 141–142; 1983: 93–94, 141; M. Bennett 1978: 4; Almog 1981: 351, 371; Böer and Lycan 1980: 437; 1986: 78; Salmon 1981: 79; Devitt 1981: 152; Hughes and Cresswell 1968: 191; Cocchiarella 1984: 318–319, 332–334, 338–339; 2002; Anderson 1984: 356, 365; Stalnaker 1986: 137; Hirsch 1986: 248–9; Taschek 1987: 176; Beer 1988: 161, fn. 3; Forbes 1989a: 481; Nelson 1992: 235; Soames 1995a; 1998: fn. 6; 2002: 254; Burgess 1996: 22; Jubien 1996: 351; Bolton 1996: 146–9, 155; Crimmins 1998: 36; Barnett 2000: 108. For insightful analytical histories, see Soames 1995b and Burgess 1996.

[2] Both of Fine's definitions were inspired by Kripke (1972; 268–9, 304, 313, 319–20). Others, also inspired by Kripke (1972: 305), have characterized metaphysical necessity as 'necessity in the highest degree' (e.g., Sidelle 2002: 309–10), which would seem to make it equivalent to logical necessity (cf. Hale 1997: 489–90). But most think metaphysical necessity is broader than logical necessity (e.g., Plantinga 1974: 1–9; Sider 2003: 181 ff; 202–3). Some appear to contradict themselves, holding that metaphysical necessity is the strongest kind of necessity while allowing that something can be metaphysically necessary without being logically necessary (e.g., Shoemaker 1998: 60). Some, again following Kripke, define metaphysical necessity as truth in all possible worlds (e.g., Freddosso 1986: 217: 310–11; Shoemaker 1998: 60–61). But this distinguishes metaphysical necessity from logical, natural, and epistemological necessity only if the set of 'possible' worlds referred to is the set of metaphysically possible worlds; without an independent characterization of that set, the definition is unhelpful (cf. Peacocke 1997c: 524).

[3] Cf. Place 1956; Smart 1959; Lewis 1968: 122; Hintikka 1969: 100–1; Gibbard 1975; Chandler 1975; Cocchiarella 1984: 332–4, 338–9; 2002: 256–7, 261–2; P. T. Smith 1985; Stalnaker 1986; Fine 1989: 206, 241–5; Taschek 1995b: 76–7, 85; Hintikka and Sandu 1995: 268–9; Kaplan 1995: 48; Hawthorne 2003: 128–9. Contrast Putnam 1975: 175; 1992: 436–7; Salmon 1981: 219–29. The arguments of Gibbard and Chandler are very different from the ones we are considering, turning on puzzling issues concerning the temporally extended nature of things like statues and ships, as well as their possession of material parts. I argued in §14.6 that it is unclear whether Lewis rejects the necessity of identity.

[4] To avoid an immaterial complication, I am, as is customary, ignoring the fact that the identity holds only in worlds in which N and M exist. See §15.7.

[5] See Davis 1995. Contrast Shoemaker 1998: 60.

[6] In this paraphrase, I changed Marcus's constants and referred to the sentences directly rather than via numbers. Otherwise it is a direct quote. See also Smullyan 1947: 140; Marcus 1961: 12; Wiggins 1965: 47 ff, 50, 59; Hughes and Cresswell 1968: 191; Plantinga 1974: 84–5; Linsky 1983: 93; Frápolli 1992: 97–8, 104; and Bolton 1996: 147. Burgess (1996: §2) observes that the germ of the argument can be found in Russell 1918: 113–4. Contrast Gallois 1986: 72; Hugly and Sayward 1998: 158.

[7] Evidently taking Millianism for granted, Yablo (2002: 446) states that since 'Hesperus' and 'Phosphorus' both mean "Venus," 'Hesperus $\neq$ Phosphorus' has to mean "Venus $\neq$ Venus," which could not possibly be true. Nevertheless, he thinks it should be 'conceptually possible' that Hesperus $\neq$ Phosphorus. He proposes that 'It is conceptually possible that p iff some world w is such that it would have turned out that p, had w turned out to be actual.' But then it is not conceptually possible that Hesperus $\neq$ Phosphorus. For assuming Millianism, 'it would have turned out that Hesperus $\neq$ Phosphorus' just means "It could have turned out that Venus $\neq$ Venus."

[8] This is a paraphrase of Marcus 1961: 12–3 , using place-holders for her examples of names (which in fact were definite descriptions). See also Fitch 1949: 138; Soames 1995b: 195, 201; and Burgess 1996: 16, 24. Contrast Hughes and Cresswell 1968: 195; Kripke 1980: 20 ff.

⁹ See also Prior 1967b: 10; Kripke 1971: 137; Plantinga 1974: 83; Wiggins 1980: 109–11; 2001: 114–6; Travis 1985: 93; Soames 1995b: 211. Contrast Hugly and Sayward 1998: 152; Della Rocca 2002: 225.

¹⁰ This is a description free variant of Quine's famous argument against essentialism and quantified modal logic. See Quine 1943; 1947; 1961b; Smullyan 1947; 1948; Fitch 1949; Kripke 1971: 138; 1972: 265; 1976: 374–5; Fine 1989; Burgess 1996: 16; Stanley 1997b: 559–60.

¹¹ Cf. Ramsey 1927; Prior 1967b: 148. Contrast Hugly and Sayward 1998: 153.

¹² Fine (1989) gives two definitions of satisfaction for '□Rxy' that breaks these connections. ⟨a, b⟩ satisfies '□Rxy' on the first definition provided '(x)(y)Rxy' is a logical truth (206, 243), and on the second, provided '(x)(y)[x = y ⊃ □Rxy]' is a logical truth (210). Fine's first definition makes Kripke's second premise false: since '(x)(y)(x = y)' is not a logical truth, no sequence satisfies '□(x = y).' His second definition makes the same premise question-begging.

¹³ Cf. Kaplan 1969: 139; 1977: 517, 562; 1989: 598; Kripke 1971: 154; 1972: 306, 308, 334–5; Putnam 1973: 313–4; Linsky 1977: 61–65, 137–139, 141–142; 1983: 93–94, 141; Haack 1978: 60; Salmon 1981: 79–80, 88–9; Cocchiarella 1984: 334; 2002: 257; Steinman 1985: 439 ff; Hirsch 1986: 248–9; Gallois 1986: 60, 63, 68; Zalta 1989: 468; Nelson 1992: 235; Soames 1995b: 213, fn. 34; Burgess 1996: 22. Contrast Gallois 1986: 63, 66, 68, 70. Compare and contrast Gibbard (1975), who denies the necessity of identity, and concludes as a result that proper names cannot be rigid designators.

¹⁴ Cf. Stalnaker 1995: 21. Contrast Stalnaker 1986: 132–3.

¹⁵ See also Kripke 1980: 143; Sainsbury 2000: 63; Chalmers 2002: 158–9; 162; Sidelle 2002: 325 Della Rocca 2003: 235–40.

¹⁶ Recall my observation in §10.5 that 'Hesperus' and 'Phosphorus' are less than ideal examples of proper names with the same reference but different meanings.

¹⁷ Kripke (1980: 21n) says that a *de jure* rigid designator is one 'where the reference of a designator is *stipulated* to be a single object whether we are speaking of the actual world or of a counterfactual situation.' But standard names like 'Aristotle' and 'Earth' do not satisfy this definition because their meanings are not stipulated. Stanley (1997a: 557) says instead that "if ... the semantical rule for a term t takes the form of a stipulation that it denotes a certain object x, then it is de jure rigid." For reasons canvassed in Chs. 10–11, specifying a referent is never sufficient to describe the meaning of a term.

¹⁸ See also Kripke 1972: 306.

¹⁹ See Kaplan 1973: 503; 1977: §4; 1989: 569; Kripke 1980: 21n; Salmon 1981: 34–40, 78–9; A. D. Smith 1984: 180; Steinman 1985; Gallois 1986: 60, 63, 66, 70; Plumer 1989; Peacocke 1997c: 534; Stanley 1997a: ;556 ff; Sainsbury 2000: 62. Kaplan (1989: 569) reports that Kripke later wished to leave open whether a rigid designator designates anything in a world in which its referent does not exist. This fits Kripke 1972: 269–70.

²⁰ Recall from §12.2 that there are two ways of interpreting a sentence like "'The tallest mountain is 30,000 ft high' is true in w." We can interpret it as saying that the referent of 'The tallest mountain' in w is 30,000 ft. high in w, or as saying that the referent of 'The tallest mountain' in the actual world is 30,000 ft high in w. These interpretations would be equivalent for both Kripke and Kaplan only if 'the tallest mountain' were rigid.

²¹ Cf. Gallois 1986: 61. Contrast Salmon 1981: 79; Steinman 1985: 439.

²² Cf. Kripke 1980: 6; A. D. Smith 1984: 179.

²³ Cochiarella 1984: 318; 2002: 242; Hintikka and Sandu 1995: 251. Salmon (1981: 40) took (28) to be a formulation of Kaplan's definition of rigidity. But (28) requires N to exist in every possible world, whereas Kaplan's definition does not require N to exist in any world with respect to which 'N' designates N. We can say, though, that if sentence (28) is true, then 'N' is both Kaplan- and Kripke-rigid.

²⁴ Compare and contrast Hugly and Sayward 1998: 153–4.

# References

Aaron, R. I. (1967), *The Theory of Universals*, 2nd edn. Oxford: Oxford University Press.

Abbott, B. (2002), 'Definiteness and Proper Names: Some Bad News for the Description Theory', *Journal of Semantics*, 19: 191–201.

Ackerman, D. (1979a), 'Proper Names, Propositional Attitudes, and Non-Descriptive Connotations', *Philosophical Studies*, 35: 55–69.

Ackerman, D. (1979b), 'Proper Names, Essences, and Intuitive Beliefs', *Theory and Decision*, 11: 5–26.

Ackerman, D. (1980a), 'Natural Kinds, Concepts, and Propositional Attitudes', *Midwest Studies in Philosophy*, 5: 469–87.

Ackerman, D. (1980b), 'Thinking About an Object: Comments on Pollock', *Midwest Studies in Philosophy*, 5: 501–7.

Ackerman, D. (1985), 'Plantinga's Theory of Proper Names', in J. Tomberlin and P. van Inwagen (eds.), *Alvin Plantinga*. Dordrecht: D. Reidel, pp. 187–98.

Ackerman, F. (1987), 'An Argument for a Modified Russellian Principle of Acquaintance', *Philosophical Perspectives I, Metaphysics*: 501–12.

Ackerman, F. (1989), 'Content, Character, and Nondescriptive Meaning', in J. Almog, J. Perry, and H. Wettstein (eds.), *Themes from Kaplan*. Oxford: Oxford University Press, pp. 5–21.

Adams, F. and Fuller, G. (1992), 'Names, Contents, and Causes', *Mind and Language*, 7: 205–21.

Adams, F., Fuller, G. and Stecker, R. (1997), 'The Semantics of Fictional Names', *Pacific Philosophical Quarterly*, 78: 128–48.

Adams, F. and Stecker, R. (1994), 'Vacuous Singular Terms', *Mind and Language*, 9: 387–401.

Adams, F., Stecker, R. and Fuller, G. (1993a), 'Schiffer on Modes of Presentation', *Analysis*, 53: 30–4.

Adams, F., Stecker, R. and Fuller, G. (1993b), 'The Floyd Puzzle: Reply to Yagisawa', *Analysis*, 53: 36–40.

Adams, R. M. (1979), 'Primitive Thisness and Primitive Identity', *Journal of Philosophy*, 76: 5–26.

Adams, R. M. (1989), 'Time and Thisness', in J. Almog, J. Perry, and H. Wettstein (eds.), *Themes from Kaplan*. Oxford: Oxford University Press, pp. 23–42.

Algeo, J. (1973), *On Defining the Proper Name*. Gainesville: University of Florida Press.

Allan, K. (1986), *Linguistic Meaning, Vol. I*. New York: Routledge and Kegan Paul.

Allan, K. (1994), 'Moods, Clause Types, and Speech Acts', in R. E. Asher (ed.), *Encyclopedia of Language and Linguistics*. Oxford: Pergamon Press, pp. 2540–2.

Allerton, D. J. (1987), 'The Linguistic and Sociolinguistic Status of Proper Names', *Journal of Pragmatics*, 11: 61–92.

Almog, J. (1981), 'Dthis and Dthat: Indexicality Goes Beyond That', *Philosophical Studies*, 39: 347–81.

Almog, J. (1986), 'Naming Without Necessity', *Journal of Philosophy*, 83: 210–42.

Alston, W. P. (1963a), 'Meaning and Use', *Philosophical Quarterly*, 13: 107–24. Reprinted in *Readings in the Philosophy of Language*, ed. J. Rosenberg and C. Travis, pp. 403–19. Englewood Cliffs, NJ: Prentice-Hall, 1971.

Alston, W. P. (1963b), 'The Quest for Meanings', *Mind*, 72: 79–87.

Alston, W. P. (1964a), *Philosophy of Language*. Englewood Cliffs, NJ: Prentice-Hall.

Alston, W. P. (1964b), 'Linguistic Acts', *American Philosophical Quarterly*, 1: 138–46.

Alston, W. P. (1965), 'Expressing', in M. Black (ed.), *Philosophy in America*. London: George, Allen, and Unwin, pp. 15–34.

Alston, W. P. (1967), 'Meaning', in: P. Edwards (ed.), *Encyclopedia of Philosophy*, Vol. 5. London: Macmillan, pp. 233–40.

Alston, W. P. (1971), 'How Does One Tell Whether a Word Has One, Several, or Many Senses?', in D. Steinberg and L. Jakobovits (eds.), *Semantics: An Interdisciplinary Reader in Philosophy, Linguistics, and Psychology*. Cambridge: Cambridge University Press, pp. 35–52.

Alston, W. P. (1974), 'Semantic Rules', in M. K. Munitz and P. Unger (eds.), *Semantics and Philosophy*. New York: New York University Press, pp. 17–48.

Alston, W. P. (1977), 'Sentence Meaning and Illocutionary Act Potential', *Philosophical Exchange*, 2: 17–35.

Alston, W. P. (1994), 'Illocutionary Acts and Linguistic Meaning', in S. L. Tsohatzidis (ed.), *Foundations of Speech Act Theory: Philosophical and Linguistic Perspectives*. London: Routledge.

Alston, W. P. (2000), *Illocutionary Acts and Sentence Meaning*. Ithaca, NY: Cornell University Press.

Ameka, F. K. (1992), 'Interjections: The Universal Yet Neglected Part of Speech', *Journal of Pragmatics*, 18: 101–18.

Ameka, F. K. (1994), 'Interjections', in R. E. Asher (ed.), *Encyclopedia of Language and Linguistics*. Oxford: Pergamon Press, pp. 1712–15.

Anderson, C. A. (1984), 'General Intensional Logic', in D. Gabbay and F. Guenthner (eds.), *Handbook of Philosophical Logic, Vol. II*. Dordrecht: D. Reidel, pp. 355–85.

Anduschus, M. (1997), 'Variations of *Sinn*', in W. Kunne, A. Newen, and M. Anduschus (eds.), *Direct Reference, Indexicality, and Propositional Attitudes*. Stanford, CA: CSLI Publications, pp. 277–91.

Anscombe, G. E. M. (1975), 'The First Person', in S. Guttenplan (ed.), *Mind and Language*. Oxford: Oxford University Press, pp. 45–64. Reprinted in *Demonstratives*, ed. P. Yourgrau, pp. 135–53. Oxford: Oxford University Press, 1990.

Anttila, R. (1989), *Historical and Comparative Linguistics*. Philadelphia: John Benjamins.

Apel, W. and Daniel, R. T. (1960), *The Harvard Brief Dictionary of Music*. Cambridge, MA: Harvard University Press.

Aquinas, T. (1268), *A Commentary on Aristotle's De Anima*, tr. R. Pasnau. New Haven, CT: Yale University Press, 1999.

Aquinas, T. (1272), *Treatise on Man*, tr. J. F. Anderson. Englewood Cliffs, NJ: Prentice-Hall, 1962. *Summa Theologica*, I, Q: 75–90.

Åqvist, L. (1972), 'On the Analysis and Logic of Questions', in R. Olson and P. Anthony (eds.), *Contemporary Philosophy in Scandinavia*. Baltimore: Johns Hopkins Press, pp. 27–39.

Åqvist, L. (1983), 'On the 'Tell Me Truly' Approach to the Analysis of Interrogatives', in F. Kiefer (ed.), *Questions and Answers*. Dordrecht: D. Reidel, pp. 9–14.

Aristotle, '*De Anima*', in R. McKeon (ed.), *The Basic Works of Aristotle*. New York: Random House, 1941, pp. 535–606.

Armstrong, D. M. (1971), 'Meaning and Communication', *Philosophical Review*, 80: 427–47.

Arnauld, A. (1641), 'Objections to the *Meditations*', in E. Haldane and G. Ross (eds.), *The Philosophical Works of Descartes*. Cambridge: Cambridge University Press, 1969, pp. 79–95.

Arnauld, A. (1662), *The Art of Thinking: Port-Royal Logic*, ed. J. Dickoff and P. James. Indianapolis, IN: Bobbs-Merrill, 1964.

Arnauld, A. (1683), *On True and False Ideas*, ed. S. Gaukroger. Manchester: Manchester University Press.

Arnauld, A. and Lancelot, C. (1660), *General and Rational Grammar: The Port-Royal Grammar*, ed. and tr. J. Rieux and B. E. Rollin. The Hague: Mouton, 1975.

Asher, N. (2000), 'Truth Conditional Discourse Semantics for Parentheticals', *Journal of Semantics*, 17: 31–50.

Asher, R. E. (1994), 'Design Features', in R. E. Asher (ed.), *Encyclopedia of Language and Linguistics*. Oxford: Pergamon Press, pp. 875–7.

Ashworth, E. J. (1982), 'The Structure of Mental Language: Some Problems Discussed by Early Sixteenth Century Logicians', *Vivarium*, 20: 59–83.

Augustine (397), *On Christian Doctrine*, in R. M. Hutchins (ed.), *Great Books of the Western World, Vol. 18: Augustine*. Chicago: Encyclopedia Britannica Inc., 1952, pp. 621–98.

Aune, B. (1967a), 'Thinking', in P. Edwards (ed.), *Encyclopedia of Philosophy, Vol. 8*. New York: Macmillan, pp. 101–4.

Austin, D. F. (1990), *What's the Meaning of 'This'?: A Puzzle About Demonstrative Belief*. Ithaca: Cornell University Press.

Austin, J. L. (1961), 'The Meaning of a Word', in *Philosophical Papers*. Oxford: Oxford University Press, pp. 23–43.

Austin, J. L. (1962), *How To Do Things with Words*. Oxford: Oxford University Press.

Authier, J. M. (1998), 'On Presuppositions and (Non)Coreference', *Studia Linguistica*, 52: 244–75.

Avramides, A. (1989), *Meaning and Mind: An Examination of a Gricean Account of Language*. Cambridge, MA: MIT Press.

Avramides, A. (1997), 'Intention and Convention', in B. Hale and C. Wright (eds.), *A Companion to the Philosophy of Language*. Oxford: Oxford University Press, pp. 60–86.

Aydede, M. (1997), 'Has Fodor Really Changed His Mind on Narrow Content?' *Mind and Language*, 12: 422–58.

Ayer, A. J. (1952), *Language, Truth, and Logic*. New York: Dover Publications, Inc.

Bach, K. (1987a), *Thought and Reference*. Oxford: Oxford University Press.

Bach, K. (1987b), 'On Communicative Intentions: A Reply to Recanati's "On Defining Communicative Intentions"' *Mind and Language*, 2: 141–54.

Bach, K. (1994a), 'Conversational Impliciture', *Mind and Language*, 9: 124–62.

Bach, K. (1994b), 'Meaning, Speech Acts, and Communication', in R. Harnish (ed.), *Basic Topics in the Philosophy of Language*. Englewood Cliffs, NJ: Prentice-Hall, pp. 3–21.

Bach, K. (1995), 'Standardization vs. Conventionalization', *Linguistics and Philosophy*, 18: 677–86.

Bach, K. (1999), 'The Myth of Conventional Implicature', *Linguistics and Philosophy*, 22: 327–66.

Bach, K. (2002), 'Giorgione Was So-Called Because of His Name', *Noûs Supplement: Philosophical Perspectives*, 16, *Language and Mind*: 73–103.

Bach, K. and Harnish, R. (1979), *Linguistic Communication and Speech Acts*. Cambridge, MA: MIT Press.

Bambrough, R. (1961), 'Universals and Family Resemblances', *Proceedings of the Aristotelian Society*, 61. Reprinted in *The Problem of Universals*, ed. C. Landesman, pp. 119–30. New York: Basic Books, 1971.

Bantas, A. (1994), 'Names, Nicknames, and Titles in Translation', *Perspectives: Studies in Translatology*, 1: 79–87.

Bantas, A. and Manea, C. (1990), 'Proper Names and Nicknames: Challenges for Translators and Lexicographers', *Revue Romaine de Linguistique*, 35: 183–96.

Barber, A. (2000), 'A Pragmatic Treatment of Simple Sentences', *Analysis*, 60: 300–8.

Barker, S. J. (2000), 'Is Value Content a Component of Conventional Implicature?' *Analysis*, 60: 268–79.

Barnett, D. (2000), 'Is Water Necessarily Identical to $H_2O$?' *Philosophical Studies*, 98: 99–112.

Barwise, J. and Perry, J. (1981a), 'Situations and Attitudes', *Journal of Philosophy*, 78: 668–91.

Barwise, J. and Perry, J. (1981b), 'Semantic Innocence and Uncompromising Situations', *Midwest Studies in Philosophy*, 6: 387–404. Reprinted in *The Philosophy of Language*, ed. A. P. Martinich, pp. 392–404. Oxford: Oxford University Press, 1990.

Barwise, J. and Perry, J. (1983), *Situations and Attitudes*. Cambridge, MA: MIT Press.

Bealer, G. (1993a), 'A Solution to Frege's Puzzle', in J. Tomberlin (ed.), *Philosophical Perspectives*, 7: *Language and Logic*. Atascadero, CA: Ridgeview, pp. 17–60.

Bealer, G. (1993b), 'Universals', *Journal of Philosophy*, 90: 5–32.

Bealer, G. (1998a), 'A Theory of Concepts and Concept Possession', in E. Villanueva (ed.), *Philosophical Issues*, 9: *Concepts*. Atascadero, CA: Ridgeview, pp. 261–301.

Bechtel, W. (1988), 'Connectionism and the Philosophy of Mind: An Overview', in T. Horgan and J. Tienson (eds.), *Connectionism and the Philosophy of Mind*. Dordrecht: Kluwer, pp. 30–55. From *Southern Journal of Philosophy*, 26 supplement (1988): 17–42.

Beer, M. (1988), 'Temporal Indexicals and the Passage of Time', *Philosophical Quarterly*, 38: 158–64.

Bell, M. (1975), 'Questioning', *Philosophical Quarterly*, 25: 193–212.

Benacerraf, P. (1965), 'What Numbers Could Not Be', *Philosophical Review*, 75: 47–73.

Bennett, J. (1971), *Locke, Berkeley, Hume: Central Themes*. Oxford: Oxford University Press.

Bennett, J. (1973), 'The Meaning-Nominalist Strategy', *Foundations of Language*, 10: 141–68.

Bennett, J. (1976), *Linguistic Behavior*. Cambridge: Cambridge University Press.

Bennett, J. (1982), 'Even If', *Linguistics and Philosophy*, 5: 403–18.

Bennett, M. (1978), 'Demonstratives and Indexicals in Montague Grammar', *Synthese*, 39: 1–80.

Benson, J. (1967), 'Emotion and Expression', *Philosophical Review*, 76: 335–57.

Bentham, J. (1816), 'Universal Grammar', in J. Bowring (ed.), *The Works of Jeremy Bentham, Vol. VIII*. New York: Russell and Russell, 1962, pp. 184–91.

Bentham, J. (1843), 'Essay on Language', in J. Bowring (ed.), *The Works of Jeremy Bentham, Vol. VIII*. New York: Russell and Russell, 1962, pp. 297–338.

Berg, J. (1988), 'The Pragmatics of Substitutivity', *Linguistics and Philosophy*, 11: 355–70.

Berg, J. (1998), 'In Defense of Direct Belief: Substitutivity, Availability, and Iterability', *Lingua e Stile*, 33: 461–70.

Berg, J. (1999), 'Referential Attribution', *Philosophical Studies*, 96: 73–86.

Berkeley, G. (1710), *A Treatise Concerning the Principles of Human Knowledge*, 2nd edn., ed., C. M. Turbayne Indianapolis, IN: Bobbs-Merrill, 1957.

Bertolet, R. (1984a), 'Inferences, Names, and Fictions', *Synthese*, 58: 203–18.

Bertolet, R. (1984b), 'Reference, Fiction, and Fictions', *Synthese*, 60: 413–37.

Bertolet, R. (1987), 'Speaker Reference', *Philosophical Studies*, 52: 199–226.

Bertolet, R. (1990), *What Is Said: A Theory of Indirect Speech Reports*. Dordrecht: Kluwer.

Bertolet, R. (2001), 'Recanati, Descriptive Names, and the Prospect of New Knowledge', *Journal of Philosophical Research*, 26: 37–41.

Bezuidenhout, A. (1997a), 'The Communication of *de Re* Thoughts', *Noûs*, 31: 197–225.

Bezuidenhout, A. (1997b), 'Pragmatics, Semantic Underdetermination and the Referential/Attributive Distinction', *Mind*, 106: 375–407.

Bilgrami, A. (1992), *Belief and Meaning: The Unity and Locality of Mental Content*. Cambridge: Blackwell.

Bird, A. (2001), 'Necessarily, Salt Dissolves in Water', *Analysis*, 61: 267–74.

Biro, J. (1979), 'Intentionalism in the Theory of Meaning', *The Monist*, 62: 238–58.

Black, M. (1952), 'The Identity of Indiscernibles', *Mind*, 61: 153–64.

Black, M. (1972–3), 'Meaning and Intention: An Examination of Grice's Views', *New Literary History*, 4: 257–79.

Blackburn, S. (1984), *Spreading the Word*. Oxford: Clarendon Press.

Blakemore, D. (1992), *Understanding Utterances*. Oxford: Basil Blackwell.

Bloomfield, L. (1933), *Language*. New York: Halt, Rinehart, and Winston.

Boden, M. A. (1991), 'A Horse of a Different Color?' in W. Ramsey, S. P. Stich, and D. E. Rumelhart (eds.), *Philosophy and Connectionist Theory*. Hillsdale, NJ: Lawrence Erlbaum Associates, pp. 3–20.

Boehner, P. (1964), 'Introduction', in P. Boehner (ed.), *Ockham: Philosophical Writings*. Indianapolis, IN: Bobbs-Merrill, pp. ix–li.

Boër, S. (1975), 'Proper Names as Predicates', *Philosophical Studies*, 27: 389–400.

Boër, S. (1978), 'Attributive Names', *Notre Dame Journal of Formal Logic*, 19: 177–85.

Boër, S. (1986), 'Chisholm on Intentionality, Thought, and Reference', in R. J. Bogdan (ed.), *Roderick Chisholm*. Dordrecht: D. Reidel, pp. 81–111.

Boër, S. (1989), 'Neo-Fregean Thoughts', in J. Tomberlin (ed.), *Philosophical Perspectives*, 3: *Philosophy of Mind and Action Theory*. Atascadero, CA: Ridgeview, pp. 187–224.

Boër, S. (1995), 'Propositional Attitudes and Compositional Semantics', in J. Tomberlin (ed.), *Philosophical Perspectives*, 9: *AI, Connectionism, and Philosophical Psychology*. Atascadero, CA: Ridgeview, pp. 341–79.

Boër, S. and Lycan, W. (1975), 'Knowing Who', *Philosophical Studies*, 28: 299–344.

Boër, S. and Lycan, W. (1980), 'Who, Me?' *Philosophical Review*, 89: 427–66.

Boër, S. and Lycan, W. (1986), *Knowing Who*. Cambridge, MA: Bradford Books, MIT Press.

Boghossian, P. A. (1989), 'Content and Self-Knowledge', *Philosophical Topics*, 17: 5–26.

Boghossian, P. A. (1997a), 'What the Externalist Can Know A Priori', *Proceedings of the Aristotelian Society*, 97: 161–75.

Boghossian, P. A. (1997b), 'Analyticity', in B. Hale and C. Wright (eds.), *A Companion to the Philosophy of Language*. Oxford: Basil Blackwell, pp. 331–68.

Boghossian, P. A. (1998a), 'What the Externalist Can Know A Priori', in E. Villanueva (ed.), *Philosophical Issues*, 9: *Concepts*. Atascadero, CA: Ridgeview, pp. 197–211.

Boghossian, P. A. (1998b), 'Replies to Commentators', in E. Villanueva (ed.), *Philosophical Issues*, 9: *Concepts*. Atascadero, CA: Ridgeview, pp. 253–60.

Bohnert, H. (1945), 'The Semiotic Status of Commands', *Philosophy of Science*, 12: 302–15.

Bolinger, D. (1978), 'Yes-No Questions Are Not Alternative Questions', in H. Hiż (ed.), *Questions*. Dordrecht: Kluwer, pp. 87–105.

Bolinger, D. (1996), 'Oddments of English', *Journal of English Linguistics*, 24: 4–24.

Bolton, C. (1996), 'Proper Names, Taxonomic Names and Necessity', *Philosophical Quarterly*, 46: 145–57.

Bradshaw, D. E. (1991), 'Connectionism and the Specter of Representationalism', in T. Horgan and J. Tienson (eds.), *Connectionism and the Philosophy of Mind*. Dordrecht: Kluwer, pp. 417–36.

Brandom, R. (1994), *Making It Explicit: Reasoning, Representing, and Discursive Commitment*. Cambridge, MA: Harvard University Press.

Braun, D. (1991a), 'Proper Names, Cognitive Contents, and Beliefs', *Philosophical Studies*, 62: 289–305.

Braun, D. (1991b), 'Content, Causation, and Cognitive Science', *Australasian Journal of Philosophy*, 69: 375–89.

Braun, D. (1993), 'Empty Names', *Noûs*, 27: 449–69.

Braun, D. (1995a), 'Katz on Names Without Bearers', *Philosophical Review*, 104: 553–76.

Braun, D. (1998), 'Understanding Belief Reports', *Philosophical Review*, 107: 555–95.

Braun, D. (2000), 'Russellianism and Psychological Generalizations', *Noûs*, 34: 203–36.

Braun, D. (2001), 'Russellianism and Prediction', *Philosophical Studies*, 105: 59–105.

Braun, D. (2002), 'Cognitive Significance, Attitude Ascriptions, and Ways of Believing Propositions', *Philosophical Studies*, 108: 65–81.

Braun, D. and Saul, J. (2002), 'Simple Sentences, Substitution, and Mistaken Evaluations', *Philosophical Studies*, 111: 1–41.

Brentano, F. (1874), *Psychology from an Empirical Standpoint*, ed. L. L. McAlister. New York: Humanities Press, 1973.

Brock, S. (2002), 'Fictionalism About Fictional Characters', *Noûs*, 36: 1–21.

Brody, B. (1977), 'Kripke on Proper Names', *Midwest Studies in Philosophy*, 2: 64–9. Reprinted in *Contemporary Perspectives in the Philosophy of Language*, ed. P. French *et al.*, pp. 75–80. Minneapolis: University of Minnesota Press, 1979.

Brown, R. (1958), 'How Shall a Thing Be Called?' *Psychological Review*, 65: 14–21.

Brueckner, A. (1986), 'Brains in a Vat', *Journal of Philosophy*, 83: 148–67.

Brueckner, A. (1990), 'Scepticism About Knowledge of Content', *Mind*, 99: 447–52.

Bull, R. A. and Segerberg, K. (1984), 'Basic Modal Logic', in D. Gabbay and F. Guenthner (eds.), *Handbook of Philosophical Logic, Vol. II*. Dordrecht: D. Reidel, pp. 1–88.

Burge, T. (1973), 'Reference and Proper Names', *Journal of Philosophy*, 70: 425–39.

Burge, T. (1977), 'Belief *de Re*', *Journal of Philosophy*, 74: 338–62.

Burge, T. (1978), 'Belief and Synonymy', *Journal of Philosophy*, 75: 119–38.

Burge, T. (1979a), 'Sinning Against Frege', *Philosophical Review*, 88: 398–432.

Burge, T. (1979b), 'Individualism and the Mental', *Midwest Studies in Philosophy*, 4: 73–121. Reprinted in *The Nature of Mind*, ed. D. M. Rosenthal, pp. 536–67. Oxford: Oxford University Press, 1991.

Burge, T. (1982), 'Other Bodies', in A. Woodfield (ed.), *Thought and Object: Essays on Intentionality*. Oxford: Clarendon Press, pp. 97–120.

Burge, T. (1983), 'Russell's Problem and Intentional Identity', in J. Tomberlin (ed.), *Agent, Language, and the Structure of the World: Essays Presented to Hector-Neri Castañeda with His Replies*. Indianapolis: Hackett, pp. 79–110.

Burge, T. (1988), 'Individualism and Self-Knowledge', *Journal of Philosophy*, 85: 654–5.

Burge, T. (1996), 'Our Entitlement to Self-Knowledge', *Proceedings of the Aristotelian Society*, 96: 91–116.

Burgess, J. P. (1996), 'Marcus, Kripke, and Names', *Philosophical Studies*, 84: 1–47.

Burks, A. W. (1949), 'Icon, Index, and Symbol', *Philosophy and Phenomenological Research*, 9: 673–89.

Burks, A. W. (1951), 'A Theory of Proper Names', *Philosophical Studies*, 2: 36–45.

Burks, A. W. (1977), *Cause, Chance, and Reason: An Inquiry into the Nature of Scientific Evidence*. Chicago: University of Chicago Press.

Byrne, A. and Thau, M. (1996), 'In Defense of the Hybrid View', *Mind*, 105: 139–49.

Campbell, R. (1968), 'Proper Names', *Mind*, 77: 326–50.

Carey, S. (1991), 'Knowledge Acquisition: Enrichment or Conceptual Change?' in S. Carey and R. Gelman (eds.), *The Epigenesis of Mind: Essays on Biology and Cognition*. New York: Lawrence Erlbaum Associates, pp. 257–91. Reprinted in

*Concepts: Core Readings*, ed. E. Margolis and S. Laurence, pp. 459–87. Cambridge, MA: MIT Press, 1991.

Carnap, R. (1947), *Meaning and Necessity*. Chicago: University of Chicago Press.

Carnap, R. (1954), 'On Belief Sentences', in M. MacDonald (ed.), *Philosophy and Analysis*. New York: Philosophical Library, pp. 128–31.

Carr, C. R. (1978a), 'Expression, Meaning, Conversation, and Indirect Speech Acts', *Southwestern Journal of Philosophy*, 9: 89–100.

Carroll, J. M. (1985), *What's in a Name?* New York: W. H. Freeman.

Carruthers, P. (1989), *Tractarian Semantics*. Oxford: Basil Blackwell.

Carruthers, P. (1992), *Human Knowledge and Human Nature*. Oxford: Oxford University Press.

Cartwright, R. (1962), 'Propositions', in R. Butler (ed.), *Analytic Philosophy*. Oxford: Basil Blackwell, pp. 81–103.

Cartwright, R. (1963), 'Negative Existentials', in C. Caton (ed.), *Philosophy and Ordinary Language*. Urbana: University of Illinois Press, pp. 55–66.

Cassam, Q. (1986), 'Science and Essence', *Philosophy*, 61: 95–107.

Castañeda, H.-N. (1977), 'On the Philosophical Foundations of the Theory of Communication: I. Reference', *Midwest Studies in Philosophy*, 2: 165–86.

Castañeda, H.-N. (1983), 'Reply to Burge: Reference, Existence, and Fiction', in J. Tomberlin (ed.), *Agent, Language, and the Structure of the World: Essays Presented to Hector-Neri Castañeda with His Replies*. Indianapolis: Hackett, pp. 355–72.

Castañeda, H.-N. (1985), 'The Semantics and the Causal Role of Proper Names', *Philosophy and Phenomenological Research*, 46: 91–114.

Castañeda, H.-N. (1987), 'Self-Consciousness, Demonstrative Reference, and the Self-Ascription View of Believing', in J. Tomberlin (ed.), *Philosophical Perspectives, I: Metaphysics*. Atascadero, CA: Ridgeview, pp. 406–54.

Castañeda, H.-N. (1989), *Thinking, Language, and Experience*. Minneapolis: University of Minnesota Press.

Castañeda, H.-N. (1990a), 'Proper Names, Singular Reference, and Baptisms', in K. Jacobi and H. Pape (eds.), *Thinking and the Structure of the World*. Berlin: De Gruyter, pp. 195–201.

Castañeda, H.-N. (1990b), 'Proper Names, Variables, and Reference', in K. Jacobi and H. Pape (eds.), *Thinking and the Structure of the World*. Berlin: De Gruyter, pp. 218–29.

Castañeda, H.-N. (1990c), 'Indicators: The Semiotics of Experience', in K. Jacobi and H. Pape (eds.), *Thinking and the Structure of the World*. Berlin: De Gruyter, pp. 57–93.

Chalmers, D. (2002), 'Does Conceivability Entail Possibility?', in T. S. Gendler and J. Hawthorne (eds.), *Conceivability and Possibility*. Oxford: Oxford University Press, pp. 145–200.

Chandler, H. (1975), 'Rigid Designation', *Journal of Philosophy*, 72: 363–9.

Chastain, C. (1975), 'Reference and Context', in K. Gunderson (ed.), *Language, Mind, and Knowledge*. Minneapolis: University of Minnesota Press, pp. 194–269.

Chellas, B. (1980), *Modal Logic: An Introduction*. Cambridge: Cambridge University Press.

Chierchia, G. and McConnell-Ginet, S. (1990), *Meaning and Grammar: An Introduction to Semantics*. Cambridge, MA: MIT Press.

Chihara, C. (1976), 'Truth, Meaning, and Paradox', *Noûs*, 10: 305–11.

Chisholm, R. M. (1955–6), 'Sentences About Believing', *Proceedings of the Aristotelian Society*, 56: 125–48.

Chisholm, R. M. (1958), 'The Chisholm-Sellars Correspondence on Intentionality', in H. Feigl, M. Scriven, and G. Maxwell (eds.), *Minnesota Studies in the Philosophy of Science*. Minneapolis: University of Minnesota Press, pp. 529–39. Reprinted in *Intentionality, Mind, and Language*, ed. A. Marras, pp. 214–48. Urbana, IL: University of Illinois Press, 1972.

Chisholm, R. M. (1967), 'Identity Through Possible Worlds: Some Questions', *Noûs*, 1: 1–8. Reprinted in *The Possible and the Actual*, ed. M. J. Loux, pp. 80–7. Ithaca: Cornell University Press, 1979.

Chisholm, R. M. (1976), *Person and Object*. La Salle, Ill.: Open Court.

Chisholm, R. M. (1981), *The First Person*. Minneapolis: University of Minnesota Press.

Chisholm, R. M. (1986), 'Replies', in R. J. Bogdan (ed.), *Roderick M. Chisholm*. Dordrecht: D. Reidel, pp. 195–216.

Chisholm, R. M. (1989), 'Why Singular Propositions?' in J. Almog, J. Perry, and H. Wettstein (eds.), *Themes from Kaplan*. Oxford: Oxford University Press, pp. 145–50.

Chisholm, R. M. (1990), 'Referring to Things That No Longer Exist', in J. Tomberlin (ed.), *Philosophical Perspectives, 4: Action Theory and Philosophy of Mind*. Atascadero, CA: Ridgeview, pp. 545–56.

Chomsky, N. (1965), *Aspects of the Theory of Syntax*. Cambridge, MA: MIT Press, Ch. 1. Reprinted in *Readings in the Philosophy of Language*, ed. J. Rosenberg and C. Travis, pp. 324–64. Englewood Cliffs, NJ: Prentice-Hall, 1971.

Chomsky, N. (1975), *Reflections on Language*. New York: Pantheon Books.

Christensen, C. (1997), 'Meaning Things and Meaning Others', *Philosophy and Phenomenological Research*, 57: 495–522.

Church, A. (1950), 'On Carnap's Analysis of Statements of Assertion and Belief', *Analysis*, 10: 97–9.

Church, A. (1951), 'The Need for Abstract Entities in Semantics', in J. A. Fodor and J. J. Katz (eds.), *The Structure of Language*. Englewood Cliffs, NJ: Prentice-Hall, 1964, pp. 437–45. From *Contributions to the Analysis and Synthesis of Knowledge, Proceedings of the American Academy of Arts and Sciences*, 80, 1951: 100–12.

Church, A. (1954), 'Intensional Isomorphism and the Identity of Belief', *Philosophical Studies*, 5: 65–73.

Church, A. (1956a), *Introduction to Mathematical Logic, Vol. I*. Princeton, NJ: Princeton University Press.

Church, A. (1956b), 'Propositions and Sentences', in *The Problem of Universals*. Notre Dame, Indiana: University of Notre Dame Press, pp. 3–11. Reprinted in *Readings in the Philosophy of Language*, ed. J. Rosenberg and C. Travis, pp. 276–82. Englewood Cliffs, NJ: Prentice-Hall 1971.

Churchland, P. M. (1980), 'Plasticity: Conceptual and Neuronal', *Behavioral and Brain Sciences*, 3: 133–4.

Churchland, P. M. and Churchland, P. S. (1983), 'Stalking the Wild Epistemic Engine', *Noûs*, 17: 5–18. Reprinted in *Mind and Cognition*, ed. W. G. Lycan, pp. 300–11. Oxford: Basil Blackwell, 1990.

Churchland, P. S. (1980), 'Language, Thought, and Information Processing', *Noûs*, 14: 147–70.

Clapp, L. (1995), 'How to Be Direct and Innocent: A Criticism of Crimmins and Perry's Theory of Attitude Ascriptions', *Linguistics and Philosophy*, 18: 529–65.

Clark, A. (1991), 'Systematicity, Structured Representations, and Cognitive Architecture: A Reply to Fodor and Pylyshyn', in T. Horgan and J. Tienson (eds.), *Connectionism and the Philosophy of Mind*. Dordrecht: Kluwer, pp. 193–217.

Clark, D. J. (1995), 'The Transcription of Proper Names', *Bible Translator*, 46: 343–8.

Clark, H. H. (1983), 'Making Sense of Nonce Sense', in G. F. D'Arcais and R. J. Javella (eds.), *The Process of Language Understanding*. New York: Wiley, pp. 297–331. Reprinted in *Arenas of Language Use*, ed. H. H. Clark, pp. 305–40. Chicago: University of Chicago Press, 1993.

Clark, H. H. (1993), *Arenas of Language Use*. Chicago: University of Chicago Press.

Cocchiarella, N. B. (1984), 'Philosophical Perspectives on Quantification in Tense and Modal Logic', in D. Gabbay and F. Guenthner (eds.), *Handbook of Philosophical Logic, Vol. II*. Dordrecht: D. Reidel, pp. 309–53.

Cocchiarella, N. B. (2002), 'Philosophical Perspectives on Quantification in Tense and Modal Logic', in D. Gabbay and F. Guenthner (eds.), *Handbook of Philosophical Logic*. Dordrecht: Kluwer Academic Publishers, pp. 235–75.

Cohen, L. J. (1971), 'The Logical Particles of Natural Language', in J. Bar-Hillel (ed.), *Pragmatics of Natural Language*. Dordrecht: Reidel, pp. 50–68.

Cohen, S. (1986), 'Knowledge and Context', *Journal of Philosophy*, 83: 574–83.

Cohen, S. (1988), 'How To Be a Fallibilist', *Philosophical Perspectives*, 2: 581–605.

Collins, A. M. and Loftus, E. F. (1975), 'A Spreading Activation Theory of Semantic Processing', *Psychological Review*, 82: 407–28.

Cook, M. (1980), 'Rigid Designators and Disguised Descriptions', *Canadian Journal of Philosophy Supplement*, 6: 111–18.

Corazza, E. (2002), 'Description Names', *Journal of Philosophical Logic*, 31: 313–25.

Corazza, E. and Dokic, J. (1992), 'On the Cognitive Significance of Indexicals', *Philosophical Studies*, 66: 183–96.

Corbí, J. (1998), 'A Challenge to Boghossian's Incompatibilist Argument', in E. Villanueva (ed.), *Philosophical Issues, 9: Concepts*. Atascadero, CA: Ridgeview, pp. 231–42.

Cormack, A. and Kempson, R. (1991), 'On Specificity', in J. L. Garfield and M. Kiteley (eds.), *Meaning and Truth: The Essential Readings in Modern Semantics*. New York: Paragon Press, pp. 546–81.

Cowie, A. P. (1994), 'Phraseology', in R. Asher (ed.), *The Encyclopedia of Language and Linguistics*. Oxford: Pergamon Press, pp. 3168–71.

Cowie, F. (1999), *What's Within? Nativism Reconsidered*. Oxford: Oxford University Press.

Crane, T. (1990), 'The Language of Thought: No Syntax Without Semantics', *Mind and Language*, 5: 187–212.

Crane, T. (1991), 'All the Difference in the World', *Philosophical Quarterly*, 41: 1–25.

Cresswell, M. J. (1985), *Structured Meanings*. Cambridge, MA: MIT Press.

Crimmins, M. (1989), 'Having Ideas and Having the Concept', *Mind and Language*, 4: 280–94.

Crimmins, M. (1992), *Talking About Belief*. Cambridge, MA: MIT Press.

Crimmins, M. (1995), 'Notional Specificity', *Mind and Language*, 10: 464–77.

Crimmins, M. (1998), 'Hesperus and Phosphorus: Sense, Pretense, and Reference', *Philosophical Review*, 107: 1–47.

Crimmins, M. and Perry, J. (1989), 'The Prince and the Phone Booth: Reporting Puzzling Beliefs', *Journal of Philosophy*, 86: 685–711.

Cruse, D. A. (1986), *Lexical Semantics*. Cambridge: Cambridge University Press.

Cummins, R. (1979), 'Intention, Meaning, and Truth-Conditions', *Philosophical Studies*, 35: 345–60.

Cummins, R. (1996), 'Systematicity', *Journal of Philosophy*, 93: 591–614.

Currie, G. (1990), *The Nature of Fiction*. Cambridge: Cambridge University Press.

Danto, A. C. (1975), 'Preface', in J. Rieux, B. E. Rollin, and N. Kretzmann (eds.), *General and Rational Grammar: The Port-Royal Grammar*. The Hague: Mouton, pp. 11–17.

Davidson, D. (1967), 'Truth and Meaning', *Synthese*, 17: 304–23. Reprinted in *The Philosophy of Language*, ed. A. P. Martinich, pp. 79–90. Oxford: Oxford University Press, 1990.

Davidson, D. (1968), 'On Saying That', *Synthese*, 19: 130–46. Reprinted in *The Philosophy of Language*, ed. A. P. Martinich, pp. 337–46. New York: Oxford University Press, 1996.

Davidson, D. (1973), 'Radical Interpretation', *Dialectica*, 27: 313–28. Reprinted in *Truth and Interpretation*, ed. D. Davidson, pp. 125–39. Oxford: Clarendon Press, 1984.

Davidson, D. (1974), 'Belief and the Basis of Meaning', *Synthese*, 27: 309–23. Reprinted in *The Philosophy of Language*, ed. A. P. Martinich, pp. 456–64. Oxford: Oxford University Press, 1996.

Davidson, D. (1975), 'Thought and Talk', in S. Guttenplan (ed.), *Mind and Language*. Oxford: Oxford University Press, pp. 7–23. Reprinted in *The Nature of Mind*, ed. D. M. Rosenthal, pp. 363–71. Oxford: Oxford University Press, 1991.

Davidson, D. (1976), 'Reply to Foster', in G. Evans and J. McDowell (eds.), *Truth and Meaning: Essays in Semantics*. Oxford: Clarendon Press.

Davidson, D. (1977), 'Reality and Reference', *Dialectica*, 31: 247–53. Reprinted in *Inquiries into Truth and Interpretation*, ed. D. Davidson, pp. 215–25. Oxford: Clarendon Press, 1984.

Davidson, D. (1979), 'Moods and Performances', in A. Margalit (ed.), *Meaning and Use*. Dordrecht: D. Reidel, pp. 9–20. Reprinted in D. Davidson (ed.), *Inquiries into Truth and Interpretation*, pp. 109–21. Oxford: Clarendon Press, 1984.

Davidson, D. (1983), 'Communication and Convention', *Journal of Indian Council of Philosophical Research* 1: 13–25, in *Truth and Interpretation*. Oxford: Clarendon Press, 1984, pp. 265–80.

Davidson, D. (1986), 'A Nice Derangement of Epitaphs', in R. Grandy and R. Warner (eds.), *Philosophical Grounds of Rationality: Intentions, Categories, Ends*. Oxford: Oxford University Press, pp. 157–74.

Davies, E. (1986), *The English Imperative*. London: Croon Helm.

Davies, M. (1991), 'Concepts, Connectionism, and the Language of Thought', in W. Ramsey, S. P. Stich, and D. E. Rumelhart (eds.), *Philosophy and Connectionist Theory*. Hillsdale, NJ: Lawrence Erlbaum Associates, pp. 229–57.

Davis, S. (1994), 'The Grice Program and Expression Meaning', *Philosophical Studies*, 75: 293–9.

Davis, W. A. (1986), *An Introduction to Logic*. Englewood Cliffs, NJ: Prentice-Hall.

Davis, W. A. (1988), 'Expression of Emotion', *American Philosophical Quarterly*, 25: 279–91.

Davis, W. A. (1995), 'Analytic-Synthetic Distinction', in R. Audi (ed.), *The Cambridge Dictionary of Philosophy*. Cambridge: Cambridge University Press, pp. 23–4.

Davis, W. A. (1998), *Implicature: Intention, Convention, and Principle in the Failure of Gricean Theory*. Cambridge: Cambridge University Press.

Davis, W. A. (1999), 'Communicating, Telling, and Informing', *Philosophical Inquiry*, 21: 21–43.

Davis, W. A. (2003), *Meaning, Expression, and Thought*. New York: Cambridge University Press.

Della Rocca, M. (2002), 'Essentialism Versus Essentialism', in T. S. Gendler and J. Hawthorne (eds.), *Conceivability and Possibility*. Oxford: Oxford University Press, pp. 223–52.

Dennett, D. C. (1969), *Content and Consciousness*. London: Routledge and Kegan Paul.

Dennett, D. C. (1982), 'Beyond Belief', in A. Woodfield (ed.), *Thought and Object: Essays on Intentionality*. Oxford: Clarendon Press, pp. 1–95.

DeRose, K. (1995), 'Solving the Skeptical Problem', *Philosophical Review*, 104: 1–52.

Descartes, R. (1641), 'Replies to Objections', in E. Haldane and G. Ross (eds.), *The Philosophical Works of Descartes*. Cambridge: Cambridge University Press, 1969, pp. 1–380.

Deuchar, M. (1984), *British Sign Language*. London: Routledge and Kegan Paul.

Devitt, M. (1974), 'Singular Terms', *Journal of Philosophy*, 71: 183–205.

Devitt, M. (1980), 'Brian Loar on Singular Terms', *Philosophical Studies*, 37: 271–80.

Devitt, M. (1981), *Designation*. New York: Columbia University Press.

Devitt, M. (1989a), 'The Revival of "Fido"-Fido', in J. Heil (ed.), *Cause, Mind, and Reality*. Dordrecht: Kluwer Academic Publishers, pp. 73–94.

Devitt, M. (1989b), 'Against Direct Reference', *Midwest Studies in Philosophy*, 14: 206–40.

Devitt, M. (1990), 'Meanings Just Ain't in the Head', in G. Boolos (ed.), *Meaning and Method: Essays in Honor of Hilary Putnam*. Cambridge: Cambridge University Press, pp. 79–104.

Devitt, M. and Sterelny, K. (1987), *Language and Reality: An Introduction to the Philosophy of Language*. Cambridge, MA: MIT Press.

Donnellan, K. (1966), 'Reference and Definite Descriptions', *Philosophical Review*, 75: 281–304. Reprinted in *The Philosophy of Language*, ed. A. P. Martinich, pp. 235–47. Oxford: Oxford University Press, 1990.

Donnellan, K. (1972), 'Proper Names and Identifying Descriptions', in D. Davidson and G. Harman (eds.), *Semantics of Natural Language*. Dordrecht: D. Reidel, pp. 356–79.

Donnellan, K. (1974), 'Speaking of Nothing', *Philosophical Review*, 83: 3–31.

Donnellan, K. (1977), 'The Contingent *a Priori* and Rigid Designators', *Midwest Studies in Philosophy*, 2: 6–27.

Donnellan, K. (1983), 'Kripke and Putnam on Natural Kind Terms', in C. Ginet and S. Shoemaker (eds.), *Knowledge and Mind: Philosophical Essays*. New York: Oxford University Press, pp. 84–104.

Donnellan, K. (1990), 'Genuine Names and Knowledge by Acquaintance', *Dialectica*, 44: 99–112.

Downing, B. T. (1969), 'Vocatives and Third-Person Imperatives in English', *Papers in Linguistics*, 1: 570–92.

Dressler, W. U. (1996), 'Language Death', in R. Singh (ed.), *Towards a Critical Sociolinguistics*. Amsterdam: John Benjamins Publishing Co., pp. 195–210.

Dretske, F. (1969), *Seeing and Knowing*. Chicago: University of Chicago Press.

Dretske, F. (1970), 'Epistemic Operators', *Journal of Philosophy*, 67: 1007–23. Reprinted in K. DeRose and T. A. Warfield (eds.) *Skepticism: A Contemporary Reader*. Oxford: Oxford University Press 1999, pp. 131–44.

Dretske, F. (1981), *Knowledge and the Flow of Information*. Oxford: Basil Blackwell.

Dummett, M. (1956), 'Nominalism', *Philosophical Review*, 65: 491–505.

Dummett, M. (1973), *Frege: Philosophy of Language*. London: Duckworth.

Dummett, M. (1976), 'What is a Theory of Meaning? (II)', in G. Evans and J. McDowell (eds.), *Truth and Meaning: Essays in Semantics*. Oxford: Clarendon Press, pp. 67–137.

Dummett, M. (1981), *The Interpretation of Frege's Philosophy*. London: Duckworth.

Dummett, M. (1991), *The Logical Basis of Metaphysics*. Cambridge, MA: Harvard University Press.

Dummett, M. (1993), *Origins of Analytical Philosophy*, vol. 6. Cambridge, MA: Harvard University Press.

Edwards, P., Alston, W. P., and Prior, A. N. (1967), 'Russell, Bertrand Arthur William', in P. Edwards (ed.), *Encyclopedia of Philosophy*, vol. 6. New York: Macmillan, pp. 235–58.

Elugardo, R. (1997), 'Descriptions, Indexicals, and Speaker Meaning', *Protosociology*, 10: 155–89.

Elugardo, R. (2002), 'The Predicate View of Proper Names', in G. Preyer (ed.), *Logical Form and Language*. Oxford: Clarendon Press, pp. 467–503.

Emmett, K. (1988), 'Meaning and Mental Representation', in H. R. Otto (ed.), *Perspectives on Mind*. Dordrecht: Kluwer, pp. 77–84.

Evans, G. (1973), 'The Causal Theory of Names', *Proceedings of the Aristotelian Society, Supplementary Volume* 47: 187–208. Reprinted in *The Philosophy of Language*, ed. A. P. Martinich, pp. 295–307. Oxford: Oxford University Press, 1990.

Evans, G. (1982), *The Varieties of Reference*. Oxford: Oxford University Press.

Evans, G. (1985), 'Understanding Demonstratives', in *Collected Papers*. Oxford: Oxford University Press, pp. 291–321. Reprinted in *Demonstratives*, ed. P. Yourgrau, pp. 71–96. Oxford: Oxford University Press, 1990.

Evans, G. and McDowell, J. (eds.) (1976), *Truth and Meaning: Essays in Semantics*. Oxford: Clarendon Press.

Evans, J. (1989), 'Concepts and Inference', *Mind and Language*, 4: 29–33.

Facione, P. A. (1972), 'The Problem of Defining Utterer's Meaning', *Southwestern Journal of Philosophy*, 3: 75–84.

Facione, P. A. (1973), 'Meaning and Intending', *American Philosophical Quarterly*, 10: 277–87.

Falvey, K. and Owens, J. (1994), 'Externalism, Self-Knowledge, and Skepticism', *Philosophical Review*, 103: 107–37.

Farrell, R. (1981), 'Metaphysical Necessity is not Logical Necessity', *Philosophical Studies*, 39: 141–53.

Fasold, R. (1990), *The Sociolinguistics of Language*. Oxford: Basil Blackwell.

Feit, N. (2000), 'Self-Ascription and Belief *de Re*', *Philosophical Studies*, 98: 37–51.

Feit, N. (2001), 'Rationality and Puzzling Beliefs', *Philosophy and Phenomenological Research*, 63: 29–55.

Field, H. (1972), 'Tarski's Theory of Truth', *Journal of Philosophy*, 69: 347–75. Reprinted in *Meaning and Truth: Essential Readings in Modern Semantics*, ed. J. Garfield and M. Kiteley, pp. 271–96. New York: Paragon House, 1991.

Field, H. (1978), 'Mental Representation', *Erkenntnis*, 13: 9–61.

Fine, K. (1989), 'The Problem of De Re Modality', in J. Almog, J. Perry, and H. Wettstein (eds.), *Themes from Kaplan*. Oxford: Oxford University Press, pp. 197–272.

Fine, K. (1994), 'Essence and Modality', in J. Tomberlin (ed.), *Philosophical Perspectives, 8: Logic and Language*. Atascadero, CA: Ridgeview Press, pp. 1–16.

Fine, K. (1995), 'Senses of Essence', in W. Sinnott-Armstrong (ed.), *Modality, Morality, and Belief: Essays in Honor of Ruth Barcan Marcus*. Cambridge: Cambridge University Press, pp. 53–73.

Fine, K. (2002), 'The Varieties of Necessity', in T. S. Gendler and J. Hawthorne (eds.), *Conceivability and Possibility*. Oxford: Oxford University Press, pp. 253–81.

Fischer, R. (1993), 'Abbe de l'Epee and the Living Dictionary', in J. V. Van Cleve, (ed.), *Deaf History Unveiled*. Washington, DC: Gallaudet University Press, pp. 12–26.

Fitch, F. B. (1949), 'The Problem of the Morning Star and the Evening Star', *Philosophy of Science*, 16: 137–41.

Fitch, G. W. (1985), 'On the Logic of Belief', *Noûs*, 19: 205–28.

Fitch, G. W. (1987), *Naming and Believing*. Dordrecht: D. Reidel.

Fitch, G. W. (1990), 'Thinking of Something', *Noûs*, 24: 675–96.

Fitch, G. W. (1993), 'Non-Denoting', in J. Tomberlin (ed.), *Philosophical Perspectives, 7: Language and Logic*. Atascadero, CA: Ridgeview, pp. 461–86.

Fodor, J. A. (1975), *The Language of Thought*. New York: Thomas Y. Crowell.

Fodor, J. A. (1981), *Representations*. Cambridge, MA: MIT Press.

Fodor, J. A. (1987), *Psychosemantics*. Cambridge, MA: MIT Press.

Fodor, J. A. (1989), 'Substitution Arguments and the Individuation of Beliefs', in G. Boolos (ed.), *Method, Reason, and Language*. Cambridge: Cambridge University Press, pp. 63–78. Reprinted in *A Theory of Content*, ed. J. Fodor, pp. 161–176. Cambridge, MA: MIT Press, 1990.

Fodor, J. A. (1990a), *A Theory of Content*. Cambridge, MA: MIT Press.

Fodor, J. A. (1990b), 'Psychosemantics or: Where Do Truth Conditions Come From?' in W. Lycan (ed.), *Mind and Cognition*. Oxford: Basil Blackwell, pp. 312–37.

Fodor, J. A. (1994), *The Elm and the Expert: Mentalese and its Semantics*. Cambridge, MA: MIT Press.

Fodor, J. A. (1998a), *Concepts*. Oxford: Oxford University Press.

Fodor, J. A. (1998b), 'There Are No Recognitional Concepts: Not Even RED', in E. Villanueva (ed.), *Philosophical Issues, 9: Concepts*. Atascadero, CA: Ridgeview, pp. 1–14.

Fodor, J. A., Garrett, M., Walker, E., and Parkes, C. (1980), 'Against Definitions', *Cognition*, 8: 263–367. Reprinted in *Concepts: Core Readings*, ed. E. Margolis and S. Laurence, pp. 491–512. Cambridge, MA: MIT Press, 1999.

Fodor, J. A. and Katz, J. J. (eds.) (1964), *The Structure of Language: Readings in the Philosophy of Language*. Englewood Cliffs, NJ: Prentice-Hall.

Fodor, J. A. and Lepore, E. (1992), *Holism: A Shopper's Guide*. Oxford: Basil Blackwell.

Fodor, J. A. and Pylyshyn, Z. (1988), 'Connectionism and Cognitive Architecture: A Critical Analysis', in C. Macdonald and G. Macdonald (eds.), *Connectionism*. Oxford: Basil Blackwell, pp. 90–163.

Fodor, J. D. and Sag, I. A. (1982), 'Referential and Quantificational Indefinites', *Linguistics and Philosophy*, 5: 475–521. Reprinted in P. Ludlow (ed.), *Readings in the Philosophy of Language*, pp. 475–521. Cambridge, MA: MIT Press, 1997.

Follett, W. (1970), *Modern American Usage*. New York: Grosset and Dunlop.

Forbes, G. (1987), 'Indexicals and Intensionality: A Fregean Perspective', *Philosophical Review*, 96: 3–31.

Forbes, G. (1989a), 'Indexicals', in D. M. Gabbay and F. Guenthner (eds.), *Handbook of Philosophical Logic* vol. IV. Dordrecht: Kluwer, pp. 463–90.

Forbes, G. (1989b), *Languages of Possibility: An Essay in Philosophical Logic*. Oxford: Basil Blackwell.

Forbes, G. (1990), 'The Indispensability of *Sinn*', *Philosophical Review*, 99: 535–63.

Forbes, G. (1993), 'Solving the Iteration Problem', *Linguistics and Philosophy*, 16: 311–30.

Forbes, G. (1997a), 'Essentialism', in B. Hale and C. Wright (eds.), *A Companion to the Philosophy of Language*. Oxford: Basil Blackwell, pp. 515–33.

Forbes, G. (1997b), 'How Much Substitutivity?' *Analysis*, 57: 109–13.

Forbes, G. (1997c), 'Belief Reports and Speech Reports', in W. Kunne, A. Newen, and M. Anduschus (eds.), *Direct Reference, Indexicality, and Propositional Attitudes*. Stanford, CA: CSLI Publications, pp. 313–30.

Forbes, G. (1999), 'Enlightened Semantics for Simple Sentences', *Analysis*, 59: 86–91.

Forster, P. G. (1982), *The Esperanto Movement*. The Hague: Mouton.

Foster, J. (1976), 'Meaning and Truth Theory', in G. Evans and J. McDowell (eds.), *Truth and Meaning: Essays in Semantics*. Oxford: Clarendon, pp. 1–32.

Frances, B. (1998a), 'Defending Millian Theories', *Mind*, 107: 703–27.

Frances, B. (1998b), 'Arguing for Frege's Fundamental Principle', *Mind and Language*, 13: 341–6.

Frances, B. (1999), 'Contradictory Belief and Epistemic Closure Principles', *Mind and Language*, 14: 203–26.

Francescotti, R. M. (1995), 'Even: The Conventional Implicature Approach Reconsidered', *Linguistics and Philosophy*, 18: 153–73.

Frápolli, M. J. (1992), 'Identity, Necessity, and *A Prioricity*: The Fallacy of Equivocation', *History and Philosophy of Logic*, 13: 91–109.

Fraser, B. (1988), 'Motor Oil is Motor Oil: An Account of English Nominal Tautologies', *Journal of Pragmatics*, 12: 215–20.

Freddoso, A. J. (1986), 'The Necessity of Nature', *Midwest Studies in Philosophy*, Vol. 11: *Studies in Essentialism*: 215–42.

Frege, G. (1884), *The Foundations of Arithmetic*, 2nd edn., ed., J. L. Austin. Oxford: Basil Blackwell, 1959.

Frege, G. (1892a), 'On Concept and Object', in P. Geach and M. Black (eds.), *Translations from the Philosophical Writings of Gottlob Frege*. Oxford: Basil Blackwell, 1952, pp. 42–55. From *Vierteljahrsschrift für wissenschaftliche Philosophie*, 16: 192–205.

Frege, G. (1892b), 'On Sense and Reference', in P. Geach and M. Black (eds.), *Translations from the Philosophical Writings of Gottlob Frege*. Oxford: Basil Blackwell, 1952, pp. 56–78. From *Zeitschrift für Philosophie und philosophische Kritik*, 100: 25–50.

Frege, G. (1897), 'Logic', in: H. Hermes, F. Kambartel, and F. Kaulbach (eds.), *Gottlob Frege: Posthumous Works*. Chicago: University of Chicago Press, 1979, pp. 126–51.

Frege, G. (1918), 'Thoughts', in P. T. Geach (ed.), *Logical Investigations*. Oxford: Basil Blackwell, 1977, pp. 1–30.

Frege, G. (1919), 'Notes for L. Darmstädter', in H. Hermes, F. Kambartel, and F. Kaulbach (eds.), *Gottlob Frege: Posthumous Works*. Chicago: University of Chicago Press, 1979, pp. 253–7.

Frege, G. (1923), 'Compound Thoughts', in P. T. Geach (ed.), *Logical Investigations*. Oxford: Basil Blackwell, 1977, pp. 55–78.

Fries, C. (1940), *American English Grammar: The Grammatical Structure of Present-Day American English with Especial Reference to Social Differences or Class Dialects*. New York: Appleton-Century-Crofts.

Gale, R. M. (1967), 'Indexical Signs, Egocentric Particulars, and Token-Reflexive Words', in P. Edwards (ed.), *The Encyclopedia of Philosophy*, Vol. 4. New York: Macmillan, pp. 151–4.

Gale, R. M. (1989), 'Lewis' Indexical Argument for World-Relative Actuality', *Dialogue (Canada)*, 28: 289–304.

Gallois, A. (1986), 'Rigid Designation and the Contingency of Identity', *Mind*, 95: 57–76.

García-Carpintero, M. (2000), 'A Presuppositional Account of Reference Fixing', *Journal of Philosophy*, 97: 109–47.

Garson, J. W. (1991), 'What Connectionists Cannot Do', in T. Horgan and J. Tienson (eds.), *Connectionism and the Philosophy of Mind*. Dordrecht: Kluwer, pp. 113–42.

Gassendi, P. (1641), 'Objections to the *Meditations*', in E. Haldane and G. Ross (eds.), *The Philosophical Works of Descartes*. Cambridge: Cambridge University Press, 1969, pp. 135–203.

Gauker, C. (1994), *Thinking Out Loud: An Essay on the Relation Between Thought and Language*. Princeton, NJ: Princeton University Press.

Geach, P. T. (1957), *Mental Acts*. London: Routledge and Kegan Paul.

Geach, P. T. (1962), *Reference and Generality*. Ithaca, NY: Cornell University Press.

Geach, P. T. (1967), 'Intentional Identity', *Journal of Philosophy*, 64: 627–32.

Geach, P. T. (1980), 'Some Problems About the Sense and Reference of Proper Names', *Canadian Journal of Philosophy*, Supplement 6: 83–96.

Geurts, B. (1997), 'Good News About the Description Theory of Names', *Journal of Semantics*, 14: 319–48.

Gibbard, A. (1975), 'Contingent Identity', *Journal of Philosophical Logic*, 4: 187–221.

Gibbons, J. (1996), 'Externalism and Knowledge of Content', *The Philosophical Review*, 105: 287–310.

Gilbert, M. (1996), *Living Together: Rationality, Sociality, and Obligation*. Lanham, MD: Rowman and Littlefield.

Gillett, G. (1992), *Representation, Meaning, and Thought*. Oxford: Clarendon Press.

Ginnane, W. J. (1960), 'Thoughts', *Mind*, 49: 372–90.

Goldstein, I. (1986), 'Must There Be Indefinable Words?' *Metaphilosophy*, 17: 90–1.

Goldstein, L. (1993), 'The Fallacy of the Simple Question', *Analysis*, 53: 178–81.

Goodman, N. (1952), 'On Likeness of Meaning', in L. Linsky (ed.), *Semantics and the Philosophy of Language*. Urbana: University of Illinois Press, pp. 67–76.

Gordon, D. and Lakoff, G. (1975), 'Conversational Postulates', in P. Cole and J. L. Morgan (eds.), *Syntax and Semantics*, 3: *Speech Acts*. New York: Academic Press, pp. 83–106.

Grandy, R. (1977), 'Review of *Convention* by David Lewis', *Journal of Philosophy*, 74: 129–39.

Grandy, R. (1990), 'Understanding and the Principle of Compositionality', *Philosophical Perspectives*, 4: *Action Theory and Philosophy of Mind*: 557–72.

Green, M. S. (1997), 'On the Autonomy of Linguistic Meaning', *Mind*, 106: 217–44.

Green, M. S. (1998), 'Direct Reference and Implicature', *Philosophical Studies*, 91: 61–90.

Green, M. S. (2000), 'Illocutionary Force and Semantic Content', *Linguistics and Philosophy*, 23: 435–73.

Green, O. H. (1970), 'The Expression of Emotion', *Mind*, 79: 551–68.

Greenaway, F. (1966), *John Dalton and the Atom*. Ithaca, NY: Cornell University Press.

Greenbaum, S. (1996), *The Oxford English Grammar*. Oxford: Oxford University Press.

Grice, H. P. (1957), 'Meaning', *Philosophical Review*, 66: 377–88.

Grice, H. P. (1967), 'Indicative Conditionals', in *Studies in the Way of Words*. Cambridge, MA: Harvard University Press, 1987, pp. 58–85. A revised version of part of the William James Lectures entitled 'Logic and Conversation' presented at Harvard University in 1967.

Grice, H. P. (1968), 'Utterer's Meaning, Sentence Meaning, and Word Meaning', *Foundations of Language*, 4: 225–42. Reprinted in *Studies in the Way of Words*, ed. H. P. Grice, pp. 117–37. Cambridge, MA: Harvard University Press, 1989.

Grice, H. P. (1969a), 'Utterer's Meaning and Intentions', *Philosophical Review*, 78: 147–77. Reprinted in *Studies in the Way of Words*, ed. H. P. Grice, pp. 86–116. Cambridge, MA: Harvard University Press, 1989.

Grice, H. P. (1969b), 'Vacuous Names', in D. Davidson and J. Hintikka (eds.), *Words and Objections*. Dordrecht: D. Reidel, pp. 118–46.

Grice, H. P. (1975), 'Logic and Conversation', in P. Cole and J. Morgan (eds.), *Syntax and Semantics, 3: Speech Acts*. New York: Academic Press. Reprinted in *Studies in the Way of Words*, ed. H. P. Grice, pp. 22–40. Cambridge, MA: Harvard University Press, 1989.

Grice, H. P. (1981), 'Presupposition and Conversational Implicature', in P. Cole (ed.), *Radical Pragmatics*. New York: Academic Press, pp. 183–98. Reprinted in *Studies in the Ways of Words*, ed. H. P. Grice, pp. 269–82. Cambridge, MA: Harvard University Press 1989.

Grice, H. P. (1982), 'Meaning Revisited', in N. Smith (ed.), *Mutual Knowledge*. New York: Academic Press, pp. 223–43.

Grice, H. P. (1986), 'Reply to Richards', in R. Grandy and R. Warner (eds.), *Philosophical Grounds of Rationality: Intentions, Categories, Ends*. Oxford: Clarendon Press, pp. 45–106.

Grice, H. P. (1989), *Studies in the Way of Words*. Cambridge, MA: Harvard University Press.

Haack, S. (1978), *Philosophy of Logics*. Cambridge: Cambridge University Press.

Hacking, I. (1975), 'Why Does Language Matter to Philosophy?' Cambridge: Cambridge University Press.

Hajičová, E. (1983), 'Presuppositions of Questions', in F. Kiefer (ed.), *Questions and Answers*. Dordrecht: D. Reidel, pp. 85–96.

Hale, B. (1997), 'Modality', in B. Hale and C. Wright (eds.), *Companion to the Philosophy of Language*. Oxford: Blackwell, pp. 487–514.

Hall, R. A., Jr. (1962), 'Review of *Webster's Third New International Dictionary*', *The Quarterly Journal of Speech*, 68: 434–5.

Hamblin, C. L. (1987), *Imperatives*. Oxford: Blackwell.

Hamlyn, D. W. (1967), 'A Priori and A Posteriori', in P. Edwards (ed.), *The Encyclopedia of Philosophy*. New York: Macmillan, pp. 140–4.

Hamlyn, D. W. (1971), 'Epistemology and Conceptual Development', in T. Mischel (ed.), *Cognitive Development and Epistemology*. New York: Academic Press, pp. 3–24.

Hampshire, S. (1939–40), 'Ideas, Propositions, and Signs', *Proceedings of the Aristotelian Society*, 40: 1–26.

Han, C.-H. (2000), *The Structure and Interpretation of Imperatives: Mood and Force in Universal Grammar*. New York: Garland Publishing Co.

Hare, R. M. (1949), 'Imperative Sentences', *Mind*, 58: 21–39.

Hare, R. M. (1952), *The Language of Morals*. Oxford: Oxford University Press.

Hare, R. M. (1970), 'Meaning and Speech Acts', *Philosophical Review*, 79: 3–24. Reprinted in R. M. Hare *Practical Inferences*, pp. 74–93. London: Macmillan, 1971.

Harman, G. (1973), *Thought*. Princeton: Princeton University Press.

Harman, G. (1977), 'How To Use Propositions', *American Philosophical Quarterly*, 14: 173–6.

Harrah, D. (2001), 'The Logic of Questions', in D. M. Gabbay and F. Guenthner (eds.), *Handbook of Philosophical Logic,* 2nd edn., Vol. 8. Dordrecht: Kluwer Academic Publishers, pp. 1–60.

Harris, R. (1980), *The Language Makers*. Ithaca, NY: Cornell University Press.

Harris, Z. S. (1978), 'The Interrogative in a Syntactic Framework', in H. Hiż. (ed.), *Questions*. Dordrecht: D. Reidel, pp. 37–86.

Harrison, G. (1980), *Introduction to the Philosophy of Language*. New York: St. Martin's Press.

Hart, H. L. A. (1952), 'Signs and Words', *Philosophical Quarterly*, 27: 59–62.

Hartnack, J. (1972), 'On Thinking', *Mind*, 81: 543–52.

Hawthorne, J. (2003), 'Identity', in M. J. Loux and D. W. Zimmerman (eds.), *The Oxford Handbook of Metaphysics*. Oxford: Oxford University Press, pp. 99–130.

Heal, J. (1997), 'Indexical Predicates and Their Uses', *Mind*, 106: 619–40.

Heal, J. (1998), 'Externalism and Memory', *Proceedings of the Aristotelian Society,* Supplement 72: 95–109.

Heath, P. L. (1967), 'Concepts', in P. Edwards (ed.), *Encyclopedia of Philosophy*. New York: Macmillan, pp. 177–80.

Heck, R. (1995), 'The Sense of Communication', *Mind*, 104: 79–106.

Heil, J. (1988), 'Privileged Access', *Mind*, 97: 238–51.

Heil, J. (1995), 'Twin-Earth', in R. Audi (ed.), *The Cambridge Dictionary of Philosophy*. Cambridge: Cambridge University Press, p. 816.

Higginbotham, J. (1988), 'Contexts, Models, and Meanings: A Note on the Data of Semantics', in R. Kempson (ed.), *Mental Representations: The Interface Between Language and Reality*. Cambridge: Cambridge University Press, pp. 29–48.

Higginbotham, J. (1998), 'Conceptual Competence', in E. Villanueva (ed.), *Philosophical Issues, 9: Concepts*. Atascadero, CA: Ridgeview, pp. 149–62.

Hintikka, J. (1969), *Models for Modality*. Dordrecht: D. Reidel.

Hintikka, J. and Sandu, G. (1995), 'The Fallacies of the New Theory of Reference', *Synthese*, 104: 245–83.

Hirsch, E. (1986), 'Metaphysical Necessity and Conceptual Truth', *Midwest Studies in Philosophy*, Vol. 11: *Studies in Essentialism*: 253–6.

Hiż, H. (1978), 'Introduction', in H. Hiż (ed.), *Questions*. Dordrecht: D. Reidel, pp. ix–xvii.

Hobbes, T. (1655), '*Computation or Logic*', in I. C. Hungerland and G. R. Vick (eds.), *Thomas Hobbes: Part I of De Corpore*. New York: Abaris Books, 1981, pp. 171–331.

Hockett, C. F. (1958), *A Course in Modern Linguistics*. New York: Macmillan.

Hockett, C. F. (1966), 'The Problems of Universals in Language', in J. H. Greenberg (ed.), *Universals of Language*, 2nd edn. Cambridge, MA: MIT Press, pp. 1–29.

Hoepelman, J. (1983), 'On Questions', in F. Kiefer (ed.), *Questions and Answers*. Dordrecht: D. Reidel, pp. 191–227.

Hofstadter, A. and McKinsey, J. C. C. (1939), 'On the Logic of Imperatives', *Philosophy of Science*, 6: 446–55.

Holdcroft, D. (1978), *Words and Deeds: Problems in the Theory of Speech Acts*. Oxford: Clarendon Press.

Hornstein, N. (1984), *Logic as Grammar*. Cambridge, MA: MIT Press.

Horwich, P. (1998a), *Meaning*. Oxford: Oxford University Press.

Horwich, P. (1998b), 'Concept Constitution', in E. Villanueva (ed.), *Philosophical Issues, 9: Concepts*. Atascadero, CA: Ridgeview, pp. 15–19.

Horwich, P. (1998c), 'The Deflationary View of Reference', *Lingua e Stile*, 33: 367–81.

Hudson, J. and Tye, M. (1980), 'Proper Names and Definite Descriptions with Widest Possible Scope', *Analysis*, 40: 63–4.

Hughes, G. E. and Cresswell, M. (1968), *An Introduction to Modal Logic*. London: Methuen.

Hugly, P. and Sayward, C. (1995), 'What's So Special About Sentences?' *Communication and Cognition*, 28: 409–26.

Hugly, P. and Sayward, C. (1998), 'Kripke on Necessity and Identity', *Philosophical Papers*, 27: 151–9.

Hume, D. (1739), *A Treatise of Human Nature*, ed. L. A. Selby-Bigge. Oxford: Clarendon Press, 1888.

Humphrey, G. (1951), *Thinking: An Introduction to Experimental Psychology*. London: Methuen.

Hungerland, I. C. and Vick, G. R. (1981), 'Hobbes's Theory of Language, Speech, and Reasoning', in I. C. Hungerland and G. R. Vick (eds.), *Thomas Hobbes: Part I of De Corpore*. New York: Abaris Books, pp. 1–70.

Hunt, E. B. (1962), *Concept Learning: An Information Processing Problem*. New York: John Wiley and Sons.

Huntley, M. (1984), 'The Semantics of English Imperatives', *Linguistics and Philosophy*, 7: 103–33.

Husserl, E. (1900), *Logical Investigations*, tr. J. N. Findlay. New York: Humanities Press, 1970.

Ingber, W. (1979), 'The Descriptional View of Referring: Its Problems and Prospects', *Journal of Philosophy*, 76: 725–38.

Jackendoff, R. (1983), *Semantics and Cognition*. Cambridge, MA: MIT Press.

Jackendoff, R. (1989), 'What is a Concept, That a Person May Grasp It?' *Mind and Language*, 4: 68–101.

Jackson, F. (1998), 'Reference and Description Revisted', *Philosophical Perspectives*, 12: 201–18.

Jackson, F. and Pettit, P. (1998), 'A Problem for Expressivism', *Analysis*, 58: 239–51.

Jacob, P. (1997), 'Frege's Puzzle and Belief Ascription', in W. Kunne, A. Newen, and M. Anduschus (eds.), *Direct Reference, Indexicality, and Propositional Attitudes*. Stanford, CA: CSLI Publications, pp. 215–45.

James, D. (1978), 'The Use of Oh, Ah, Say, and Well in Relation to a Number of Grammatical Phenomena', *Papers in Linguistics*, 11: 517–35.

James, W. (1890), *The Principles of Psychology*. New York: Dover, 1950.

Janton, P. (1993), *Esperanto: Language, Literature, and Community*, tr. H. Tonkin, J. Edwards, and K. Johnson-Weiner. Albany, NY: SUNY Press.

Jeshion, R. (2001), 'Donnellan on Neptune', *Philosophy and Phenomenological Research*, 63: 111–35.

Jeshion, R. (2002), 'The Epistemological Argument Against Descriptivism', *Philosophy and Phenomenological Research*, 64: 325–45.

Jespersen, O. (1921), *Language: Its Nature, Development, and Origin*. London: Allen and Unwin.

Johnston, M. (1997), 'Manifest Kinds', *Journal of Philosophy*, 94: 564–83.

Jordan, D. K. (1992), 'What is Colloquial Esperanto?' *Esperantic Studies*, 2 (Winter): 3–4.

Joseph, H. W. B. (1916), *An Introduction to Logic*, 2nd edn. Oxford: Clarendon Press.

Jubien, M. (1993), 'Proper Names', in J. Tomberlin (ed.), *Philosophical Perspectives*, 7: *Language and Logic*. Atascadero, CA: Ridgeview, pp. 487–504.

Jubien, M. (1996), 'The Myth of Identity Conditions', in J. Tomberlin (ed.), *Philosophical Perspectives*, 10: *Metaphysics*. Atascadero, CA: Ridgeview, pp. 343–56.

Justice, J. (2001), 'On Sense and Reflexivity', *The Journal of Philosophy*, 98: 351–64.

Justice, J. (2002), 'Mill-Frege Compatibilism', *Journal of Philosophical Research*, 27: 567–76.

Justice, J. (2003), 'The Semantics of Rigid Designation', *Ratio*, 16: 33–48.

Kant, I. (1787), *Critique of Pure Reason*, tr. N. K. Smith. New York: St. Martin's Press, 1965.

Kaplan, D. (1969), 'Quantifying In', in D. Davidson and J. Hintikka (eds.), *Words and Objections: Essays on the Work of W. V. Quine*. Dordrecht: D. Reidel, pp. 206–42.

Kaplan, D. (1973), 'Bob and Carol and Ted and Alice', in J. Hintikka, J. Moravcsik, and P. Suppes (eds.), *Approaches to Natural Language*. Dordrecht: D. Reidel, pp. 490–518.

Kaplan, D. (1977), 'Demonstratives', in J. Almog, J. Perry, and H. Wettstein (eds.), *Themes from Kaplan*. Oxford: Oxford University Press, 1989, pp. 481–563.

Kaplan, D. (1978), 'Dthat', in P. Cole (ed.), *Syntax and Semantics*, 9: *Pragmatics*. New York: Academic Press, pp. 221–53. Reprinted in *The Philosophy of Language*, ed. A. P. Martinich, pp. 316–29. Oxford: Oxford University Press, 1990.

Kaplan, D. (1979), 'Transworld Heir Lines', in M. J. Loux (ed.), *The Possible and the Actual*. Ithaca, NY: Cornell University Press, pp. 88–109.

Kaplan, D. (1989), 'Afterthoughts', in J. Almog, J. Perry, and H. Wettstein (eds.), *Themes from Kaplan*. Oxford: Oxford University Press, pp. 565–614.

Kaplan, D. (1990a), 'Thoughts on Demonstratives', in P. Yourgrau (ed.), *Demonstratives*. Oxford: Oxford University Press, pp. 34–49.

Kaplan, D. (1990b), 'Words', *Proceedings of the Aristotelian Society*, Supplementary Volume 64: 93–119.

Kaplan, D. (1995), 'A Problem in Possible Worlds Semantics', in W. Sinnott-Armstrong (ed.), *Modality, Morality, and Belief: Essays in Honor of Ruth Barcan Marcus*. Cambridge: Cambridge University Press, pp. 41–52.

Karttunen, L. and Peters, S. (1979), 'Conversational Implicature', in C.-K. Oh and D. A. Dinneen (eds.), *Syntax and Semantics*, 11: *Presupposition*. New York: Academic Press, pp. 1–56.

Katz, J. J. (1964a), 'Analyticity and Contradiction in Natural Language', in J. A. Fodor and J. J. Katz (eds.), *The Structure of Language*. Englewood Cliffs, NJ: Prentice-Hall, pp. 519–43.

Katz, J. J. (1964b), 'Semantic Theory and the Meaning of 'Good'', *Journal of Philosophy*, 61: 739–66.

Katz, J. J. (1966), *Philosophy of Language*. New York: Harper and Row.

Katz, J. J. (1972), *Semantic Theory*. New York: Harper and Row.

Katz, J. J. (1974), 'Where Things Now Stand with the Analytic-Synthetic Distinction', *Synthese*, 28: 283–319.

Katz, J. J. (1977a), 'A Proper Theory of Names', *Philosophical Studies*, 31: 1–80.

Katz, J. J. (1977b), *Propositional Structure and Illocutionary Force*. New York: Thomas Y. Crowell.

Katz, J. J. (1979), 'The Neoclassical Theory of Reference', in P. French, T. Uehling, and H. Wettstein (eds.), *Contemporary Perspectives in the Philosophy of Language*. Minneapolis: University of Minnesota Press, pp. 103–24.

Katz, J. J. (1986a), 'Why Intensionalists Ought Not Be Fregeans', in E. LePore (ed.), *Truth and Interpretation: Perspectives on the Philosophy of Donald Davidson*. Oxford: Basil Blackwell, pp. 59–91.

Katz, J. J. (1986b), *Cogitations*. Oxford: Oxford University Press.

Katz, J. J. (1987), 'Descartes's *Cogito*', *Philosophical Quarterly*, 68: 154–81. Reprinted in *Demonstratives*, ed. P. Yourgrau, pp. 154–81. Oxford: Oxford University Press, 1990.

Katz, J. J. (1990), 'Has the Description Theory Been Refuted?' in G. Boolos (ed.), *Meaning and Method: Essays in Honor of Hilary Putnam*. Cambridge: Cambridge University Press, pp. 31–61.

Katz, J. J. (1994), 'Names Without Bearers', *Philosophical Review*, 103: 1–39.

Katz, J. J. (1997), 'Analyticity, Necessity, and the Epistemology of Semantics', *Philosophy and Phenomenological Research*, 57: 1–28.

Katz, J. J. (2001), 'The End of Millianism', *Journal of Philosophy*, 98: 137–66.

Katz, J. J. and Fodor, J. A. (1963), 'The Structure of a Semantic Theory', from *Language*, 39: 170–210, in J. A. Fodor and J. J. Katz (eds.), *The Structure of Language*. Englewood Cliffs, NJ: Prentice-Hall, 1964, pp. 479–518.

Kemmerling, A. (1986), 'Utterer's Meaning Revisited', in R. Grandy and R. Warner (eds.), *Philosophical Grounds of Rationality: Intentions, Categories, Ends*. Oxford: Clarendon Press, pp. 131–55.

Kempson, R. (1975), *Presupposition and the Delimitation of Semantics*. Cambridge: Cambridge University Press.

Kenny, A. (1963), *Action, Emotion, and Will*. New York: Humanities Press.

Kiefer, F. (1983), 'Introduction', in F. Keifer (ed.), *Questions and Answers*. Dordrecht: D. Reidel, pp. 1–14.

Kingscott, G. (1990), 'The Translation of Names and Titles', *Language International*, 2: 13–21.

Kneale, W. (1962), 'Modality, *de Dicto* and *de Re*', in E. Nagel, P. Suppes, and A. Tarski (eds.), *Logic, Methodology, and Philosophy of Science*. Stanford: Stanford University Press, pp. 622–33.

Kneale, W. and Kneale, M. (1962), *The Development of Logic*. Oxford: Clarendon Press.

Koch, P. J. (1983), 'Expressing Emotions', *Pacific Philosophical Quarterly*, 64: 176–89.

Kretzmann, N. (1967), 'History of Semantics', in P. Edwards (ed.), *Encyclopedia of Philosophy*, Vol. 8. New York: Macmillan, pp. 358–406.

Kretzmann, N. (1982), 'Syncategoremata, Exponibilia, Sophismata', in N. Kretzmann, A. Kenny, J. Pinborg, and E. Stump (eds.), *The Cambridge History of Later Medieval Philosophy*. Cambridge: Cambridge University Press, pp. 211–45.

Kripke, S. (1971), 'Identity and Necessity', in M. Munitz (ed.), *Identity and Individuation*. New York: New York University Press, pp. 135–64.

Kripke, S. (1972), 'Naming and Necessity', in D. Davidson and G. Harman (eds.), *Semantics of Natural Language*. Dordrecht: D. Reidel, pp. 253–355, 763–9.

Kripke, S. (1976), 'Is There a Problem About Substitutional Quantification?' in G. Evans and J. McDowell (eds.), *Truth and Meaning: Essays in Semantics*. Oxford: Clarendon Press, pp. 325–419.

Kripke, S. (1977), 'Speaker Reference and Semantic Reference', *Midwest Studies in Philosophy*, 2: 255–78.

Kripke, S. (1979), 'A Puzzle About Belief', in A. Margalit (ed.), *Meaning and Use*. Dordrecht: D. Reidel, pp. 239–83. Reprinted in S. Soames and N. Salmon (eds.), *Propositions and Attitudes*, pp. 102–48. Oxford: Oxford University Press, 1988.

Kripke, S. (1980), *Naming and Necessity*. Cambridge, MA: Harvard University Press.

Kripke, S. (1982), *Wittgenstein on Rules and Private Languages*. Cambridge, MA: Harvard University Press.

Kuhn, S. (1984), 'Stenius on Meaning', *Theoria*, 50: 165–77.

Künne, W. (1997), 'First Person Propositions: A Fregean Account', in W. Künne, A. Newen, and M. Anduschus (eds.), *Direct Reference, Indexicality, and Propositional Attitudes*. Stanford, CA: CSLI Publications, pp. 49–68.

Kvart, I. (1993), 'Mediated Reference and Proper Names', *Mind*, 102: 611–28.

Kvart, I. (1994), 'A Theory of Thinker Reference', *Philosophical Studies*, 1994: 291–323.

Labov, W. (1970), *The Study of Nonstandard English*. Champaign, IL: National Council of Teachers of English.

Lakoff, G. (1971), 'On Generative Semantics', in D. Steinberg and L. Jakobovits (eds.), *Semantics: An Interdisciplinary Reader*. Cambridge: Cambridge University Press, pp. 232–96.

Lakoff, G. (1987), *Women, Fire, and Dangerous Things: What Categories Reveal About the Mind*. Chicago: University of Chicago Press.

Lakoff, G. (1989), 'Some Empirical Results About the Nature of Concepts', *Mind and Language*, 4: 103–29.

Lampert, J. (1992), 'Husserl's Account of Syncategorematic Terms: The Problem of Representing the Synthetic Connections That Underlie Meanings', *Southern Journal of Philosophy*, 30: 67–94.

Lance, M. (1984), 'Reference Without Causation', *Philosophical Studies*, 45: 335–51.

Lance, M. and O'Leary-Hawthorne, J. (1997), *The Grammar of Meaning*. Cambridge: Cambridge University Press.

Landau, S. I. (1984), *Dictionaries: The Art and Craft of Lexicography*. New York: Charles Scribner's Sons.

Large, A. (1985), *The Artificial Language Movement*. Oxford: Basil Blackwell.

Larson, R. and Ludlow, P. (1993), 'Interpreted Logical Forms', *Synthese*, 95: 305–56. Reprinted in P. Ludlow, (ed.) *Readings in the Philosophy of Science*. Cambridge, MA: MIT Press, 1997.

Larson, R. and Segal, G. (1995), *Knowledge of Meaning: An Introduction to Semantic Theory*. Cambridge, MA: MIT Press.

Laurence, S. (1996), 'A Chomskian Alternative to Convention-Based Semantics', *Mind*, 105: 269–301.

Laurier, D. (1986), 'Names and Beliefs: A Puzzle Lost', *Philosophical Quarterly*, 36: 37–49.

Leech, G. (1983), *Principles of Pragmatics*. London: Longmans.

Lehrer, A. (1992a), 'Principles and Problems in Translating Proper Names', in B. Lewandowska-Tomazczyk and M. Thelen (eds.), *Translation and Meaning, II*. Rijkschogeschool Maastricht, pp. 395–402.

Lehrer, A. (1992b), 'Names and Naming: Why We Need Fields and Frames', in A. Lehrer and E. F. Kittay (eds.), *Frames, Fields, and Contrasts*. Hillsdale, NJ: Erlbaum, pp. 123–42.

Leibniz, G. W. F. (1676), 'What is an Idea?' in P. P. Wiener (ed.), *Leibniz: Selections*. New York: Charles Scribner's Sons, 1951, pp. 281–3.

Leibniz, G. W. F. (1709), *New Essays Concerning Human Understanding*, 2nd edn., tr. A. G. Langley. Chicago: Open Court.

Leonard, S. A. (1929), *The Doctrine of Correctness in English Usage 1700–1800*. New York: Russell and Russell.

Levine, J. (1988), 'Demonstrating in Mentalese', *Pacific Philosophical Quarterly*, 69: 222–40.

Levinson, S. C. (1983), *Pragmatics*. Cambridge: Cambridge University Press.

Lewis, D. (1968), 'Counterpart Theory and Quantified Modal Logic', *Journal of Philosophy*, 65: 113–26.

Lewis, D. (1969), *Convention*. Cambridge, MA: Harvard University Press.

Lewis, D. (1970), 'How to Define Theoretical Terms', *Journal of Philosophy*, 67: 427–46.

Lewis, D. (1971), 'Counterparts of Persons and Their Bodies', *Journal of Philosophy*, 68: 203–11.

Lewis, D. (1972), 'General Semantics', in D. Davidson and G. Harman (eds.), *Semantics of Natural Language*. Dordrecht: D. Reidel, pp. 169–218.

Lewis, D. (1973), *Counterfactuals*. Cambridge, MA: Harvard University Press.

Lewis, D. (1974), 'Radical Interpretation', *Synthese*, 27: 331–44.

Lewis, D. (1975), 'Languages and Language', in K. Gunderson (ed.), *Minnesota Studies in the Philosophy of Language*. Minneapolis: University of Minnesota Press, pp. 3–35. Reprinted in A. P. Martinich (ed.), *The Philosophy of Language*, 3rd edn., pp. 538–57. New York: Oxford University Press, 1996.

Lewis, D. (1976), 'Conventions: Reply to Jamieson', *Canadian Journal of Philosophy*, 6: 113–20.

Lewis, D. (1979), 'Attitudes *de Dicto* and *de Se*', *Philosophical Review*, 88: 513–43.

Lewis, D. (1981a), 'What Puzzling Pierre Does Not Believe', *Australasian Journal of Philosophy*, 59: 282–9.

Lewis, D. (1981b), 'Index, Context, and Content', in S. Kanger and S. Ohman (eds.), *Philosophy and Grammar*. Dordrecht: D. Reidel, pp. 79–100.

Lewis, D. (1986), *On the Plurality of Worlds*. Oxford: Basil Blackwell.

Lewis, D. (1992), 'Meaning Without Use: Reply to Hawthorne', *Australasian Journal of Philosophy*, 70: 106–10.

Lewis, D. and Lewis, S. (1975), 'Review of Olson and Paul, *Contemporary Philosophy in Scandinavia*', *Theoria*, 41: 39–60.

Lewy, C. (1976), *Meaning and Modality*. Cambridge: Cambridge University Press.

Liedtke, F. (1990), 'Meaning and Expression: Marty and Grice on Intentional Semantics', in K. Mulligan (ed.), *Mind, Meaning, and Metaphysics*. Dordrecht: Kluwer, pp. 29–49.

Linsky, L. (1963), 'Reference and Referents', in C. C. Caton (ed.), *Philosophy and Ordinary Language*. Urbana: University of Illinois Press, pp. 74–89.

Linsky, L. (1977), *Names and Descriptions*. Chicago: University of Chicago Press.

Linsky, L. (1983), *Oblique Contexts*. Chicago: University of Chicago Press.

Loar, B. (1972), 'Reference and Propositional Attitudes', *Philosophical Review*, 81: 43–62.

Loar, B. (1976a), 'The Semantics of Singular Terms', *Philosophical Studies*, 30: 353–77.

Loar, B. (1976b), 'Two Theories of Meaning', in G. Evans and J. McDowell (eds.), *Truth and Meaning*. Oxford: Oxford University Press, pp. 138–61.

Loar, B. (1980), 'Names and Descriptions: A Reply to Michael Devitt', *Philosophical Studies*, 38: 85–9.

Loar, B. (1981), *Mind and Meaning*. Cambridge: Cambridge University Press.

Loar, B. (1987), 'Names in Thought', *Philosophical Studies*, 51: 169–85.

Loar, B. (1988), 'Social Content and Psychological Content', in R. H. Grimm and D. D. Merrill (eds.), *Contents of Thought*. Tucson: University of Arizona Press, pp. 99–110. Reprinted in *The Nature of Mind*, ed. D. M. Rosenthal, pp. 569–75. Oxford: Oxford University Press, 1991.

Loar, B. (1991), 'Can We Explain Intentionality?' in B. Loewer and G. Rey (eds.), *Meaning in Mind: Fodor and His Critics*. Oxford: Basil Blackwell, pp. 119–35.

Locke, J. (1690), *An Essay Concerning Human Understanding*, ed. A. C. Fraser. New York: Dover Publications, 1959.

Lockwood, M. (1975), 'On Predicating Proper Names', *Philosophical Review*, 84: 471–98.

Loux, M. (ed.) (1979), *The Possible and the Actual*. Ithaca, NY: Cornell University Press.

Love, N. (1994), 'Correctness and Norms', in R. Asher (ed.), *Encyclopedia of Language and Linguistics*. Oxford: Pergamon Press, pp. 1398–403.

Ludlow, P. (1995), 'Social Externalism, Self-Knowledge, and Memory', *Analysis*, 55: 157–9.

Ludlow, P. and Neale, S. (1991), 'Indefinite Descriptions: In Defense of Russell', *Linguistics and Philosophy*, 14: 171–202.

Ludwig, K. (1992), 'Brains in a Vat, Subjectivity, and the Causal Theory of Reference', *Journal of Philosophical Research*, 17: 313–45.

Luntley, M. (1984), 'The Sense of a Name', *Philosophical Quarterly*, 34: 265–82.

Lycan, W. (1981), 'Toward a Homuncular Theory of Believing', *Cognition and Brain Theory*, 4: 139–59.

Lycan, W. (1984), *Logical Form in Natural Language*. Cambridge, MA: MIT Press.

Lycan, W. (1985), 'The Paradox of Naming', in B. K. Matilal and J. L. Shaw (eds.), *Analytical Philosophy in Comparative Perspective*. Dordrecht: D. Reidel, pp. 81–102.

Lycan, W. (ed.) (1990), *Mind and Cognition: A Reader*. Oxford: Basil Blackwell.

Lycan, W. (1991), '"Even" and "Even If"', *Linguistics and Philosophy*, 14: 115–50.

Lyons, J. (1971), *Introduction to Theoretical Linguistics*. Cambridge: Cambridge University Press.

Lyons, J. (1977), *Semantics*. Cambridge: Cambridge University Press.

MacBeth, D. (1995), 'Names, Natural Kind Terms, and Rigid Designation', *Philosophical Studies*, 79: 259–81.

Macdonald, C. (1998), 'Externalism and Authoritative Self-Knowledge', in C. Macdonald, B. Smith, and C. Wright (eds.), *Knowing Our Own Minds: Essays on Self-Knowledge*. Oxford: Oxford University Press, pp. 123–53.

Macdonald, C. and Macdonald, G. (eds.) (1995), *Connectionism: Debates in Psychological Explanation*. Oxford: Basil Blackwell.

MacKay, A. F. (1968), 'Mr. Donnellan and Humpty Dumpty on Referring', *Philosophical Review*, 77: 197–202.

Maloney, J. C. (1989), *The Mundane Matter of the Mental Language*. Cambridge: Cambridge University Press.

Malt, B. C. (1999), 'Word Meaning', in W. Bechtel and G. Graham (eds.), *A Companion to Cognitive Science*. Oxford: Blackwell Publishing, pp. 331–7.

Marconi, D. (1990), 'Dictionaries and Proper Names', *History of Philosophy Quarterly*, 7: 77–92.

Marcus, R. B. (1961), 'Modalities and Intensional Languages', *Synthese*, 13: 303–22. Reprinted with editorial corrections in *Modalities: Philosophical Essays*, pp. 5–23. Oxford: Oxford University Press, 1993.

Marcus, R. B. (1975), 'Does the Principle of Substitutivity Rest on a Mistake?' in A. R. Anderson, R. M. Martin, and R. B. Marcus (eds.), *The Logical Enterprise*. New Haven: Yale University Press, pp. 31–8. Reprinted in *Modalities*. Oxford: Oxford University Press, 1993, pp. 102–9.

Marcus, R. B. (1985/86), 'Possibilia and Possible Worlds', *Grazer-Philosophische Studien*, 25–26: 107–33. Reprinted in *Modalities: Philosophical Essays*, pp. 190–213. Oxford: Oxford University Press, 1993.

Marcus, R. B. (1993), *Modalities*. Oxford: Oxford University Press.

Marcus, R. B. (1997), 'Are Possible Non Actual Objects Real?' *Revue Internationale de Philosophie*, 2: 251–7.

Margolis, E. (1998), 'How to Acquire a Concept', *Mind and Language*, 13: 347–69. Reprinted in *Concepts: Core Readings*, ed. E. Margolis and S. Laurence, pp. 549–67.

Margolis, E. and Laurence, S. (1999), 'Concepts and Cognitive Science', in E. Margolis and S. Laurence (eds.), *Concepts: Core Readings*. Cambridge, MA: MIT Press, pp. 3–81.

Martinich, A. P. (1979a), 'The Attributive Use of Proper Names', *Analysis*, 37: 159–63.

Martinich, A. P. (1979b), 'Referring', *Philosophy and Phenomenological Research*, 40: 157–72.

Martinich, A. P. (1984), *Communication and Reference*. Berlin and New York: Walter de Gruyter.

Marty, A. (1908), *Untersuchungen Zur Grundlegung der Allgemeinen Grammatik und Sprach-Philosophie*. Halle: Niemeyer.

Mates, B. (1950), 'Synonymity', *University of California Publications in Philosophy*, 25: 201–26. Reprinted in *Semantics and the Philosophy of Language*, ed. L. Linsky, pp. 111–38. Urbana, IL: University of Illinois Press, 1952.

Mates, B. (1986), *The Philosophy of Leibniz*. New York: Oxford University Press.

McCawley, J. D. (1968), 'The Role of Semantics in a Grammar', in E. Bach and R. T. Harms (eds.), *Universals in Linguistic Theory*. New York: Holt, pp. 124–69.

McCawley, J. D. (1994), 'Generative Semantics', in R. E. Asher (ed.), *Encyclopedia of Language and Linguistics*. Oxford: Pergamon Press, pp. 1398–403.

McCulloch, G. (1991), 'Making Sense of Words', *Analysis*, 91: 73–9.

McDermott, M. (1988), 'The Narrow Semantics of Names', *Mind*, 97: 224–37.

McDowell, J. (1976), 'Truth Conditions, Bivalence, and Verificationism', in G. Evans and J. McDowell (eds.), *Truth and Meaning: Essays in Semantics*. Oxford: Clarendon Press, pp. 42–66.

McDowell, J. (1977), 'On the Sense and Reference of a Proper Name', *Mind*, 86: 159–85.

McDowell, J. (1978), 'Physicalism and Primitive Denotation: Field on Tarski', *Erkenntnis*, 13: 131–52, in J. L. Garfield and M. Kiteley (eds.), *Meaning and Truth*. New York: Paragon House (1991), pp. 297–315.

McDowell, J. (1980), 'Meaning, Communication, and Knowledge', in Z. van Straaten (ed.), *Philosophical Subjects: Essays Presented to P. F. Strawson*. Oxford: Clarendon Press, pp. 117–39.

McGinn, C. (1977), 'Semantics for Non-Indicative Sentences', *Philosophical Studies*, 32: 301–11.

McGinn, C. (1982), 'The Structure of Content', in A. Woodfield (ed.), *Thought and Object*. Oxford: Clarendon Press, pp. 207–58.

McGinn, C. (1989), *Mental Content*. Oxford: Basil Blackwell.

McGinn, C. (1997), *The Character of Mind*. Oxford: Oxford University Press.

McKay, T. (1981), 'On Proper Names in Belief Ascriptions', *Philosophical Studies*, 39: 287–303.

McKay, T. (1994), 'Names, Causal Chains, and *de Re* Beliefs', in J. Tomberlin (ed.), *Philosophical Perspectives*, 8: *Logic and Language*. Atascadero, CA: Ridgeview, pp. 293–302.

McKinsey, M. (1978), 'Names and Intentionality', *Philosophical Review*, 87: 171–200.

McKinsey, M. (1984), 'Causality and the Paradox of Names', *Midwest Studies in Philosophy*, 9: 491–516.

McKinsey, M. (1991), 'Anti-Individualism and Privileged Access', *Analysis*, 51: 9–16.

McKinsey, M. (1994), 'Individuating Beliefs', in J. Tomberlin (ed.), *Philosophical Perspectives*, 8: *Logic and Language*. Atascadero, CA: Ridgeview, pp. 303–29.

McKinsey, M. (1999), 'The Semantics of Belief Ascriptions', *Noûs*, 33: 519–57.

McKinsey, M. (2002), 'Forms of Externalism and Privileged Access', *Philosophical Perspectives*, 16: Language and Mind: 199–224.

McLaughlin, B. P. (1995), 'Philosophy of Mind', in R. Audi (ed.), *The Cambridge Dictionary of Philosophy*. Cambridge: Cambridge University Press, pp. 597–606.

McLaughlin, B. P. and Tye, M. (1998), 'Externalism, Twin-Earth, and Self-Knowledge', in C. Wright, B. Smith, and C. Macdonald (eds.), *Knowing Our Own Minds: Essays on Self-Knowledge*. Oxford: Oxford University Press, pp. 285–320.

Meggle, G. (1997), *Brundbegriffe de Kommunicakation*, 2nd edn. Berlin: Walter de Gruyter.

Meidner, O. M. (1994), 'Emotive Meaning', in R. E. Asher (ed.), *Encyclopedia of Languages and Linguistics*. Oxford: Pergamon Press, p. 1111.

Meinong, A. (1910), *On Assumptions*, ed. J. Heanue. Berkeley, CA: University of California Press, 1983.

Mellor, D. H. (1977), 'Natural Kinds', *British Journal for the Philosophy of Science*, 28: 299–312.

Mey, J. (1993), *Pragmatics: An Introduction*. Oxford: Basil Blackwell.

Mill, J. (1829), *Analysis of the Phenomenon of the Human Mind*, ed. J. S. Mill. London: Longmans Green Reader and Dyer, 1869.

Mill, J. S. (1879), *A System of Logic*, 10th edn. London: Longmans Green.

Miller, B. (1975), 'In Defense of the Predicate "Exists"', *Mind*, 84: 338–54.

Miller, G. and Johnson-Laird, P. (1976), *Language and Perception*. Cambridge, MA: Harvard University Press.

Millikan, R. (1984), *Language, Thought, and Other Biological Categories: New Foundations for Realism*. Cambridge, MA: MIT Press.

Millikan, R. (1990), 'The Myth of the Essential Indexical', *Noûs*, 24: 723–34.

Millikan, R. (1998), 'A Common Structure for Concepts of Individuals, Stuffs, and Real Kinds: More Mama, More Milk, and More Mouse', *Behavioral and Brain Sciences*, 21: 55–65. Reprinted in *Concepts: Core Readings*, ed. E. Margolis and S. Laurence, pp. 525–47. Cambridge, MA: MIT Press, 1999.

Montague, R. (1972), 'Pragmatics and Intensional Logic', in D. Davidson and G. Harman (eds.), *Semantics of Natural Language*. Dordrecht: D. Reidel, pp. 142–68.

Moore, G. E. (1942), 'A Reply to My Critics', in P. A. Schilpp (ed.), *The Philosophy of G. E. Moore*. La Salle, IL: Open Court, 1968, pp. 533–689.

Moore, J. G. (1999a), 'Misdisquotation and Substitutivity: When Not to Infer Belief from Assent', *Mind*, 108: 335–65.

Moore, J. G. (1999b), 'Saving Substitutivity in Simple Sentences', *Analysis*, 59: 91–105.

Moya, C. (1998), 'Boghossian's *Reductio* of Compatibilism', in E. Villanueva (ed.), *Philosophical Issues, 9: Concepts*. Ridgeview, pp. 243–51.

Napoli, E. (1997), 'Names, Indexicals, and Identity Statements', in W. Kunne, A. Newen, and M. Anduschus (eds.), *Direct Reference, Indexicality, and Propositional Attitudes*. Stanford, CA: CSLI Publications, pp. 185–211.

Neale, S. (1992), 'Paul Grice and the Philosophy of Language', *Linguistics and Philosophy*, 15: 509–59.

Neale, S. (1997), 'Context and Communication', in P. Ludlow (ed.), *Readings in the Philosophy of Language*. Cambridge, MA: MIT Press, pp. 415–74.

Nelson, R. J. (1992), *Naming and Reference*. London: Routledge and Kegan Paul.

Newen, A. (2001), 'Fregean Senses and the Semantics of Singular Terms', in A. Newen, U. Nortmann, and R. Stuhlmann-Laeisz (eds.), *Building on Frege: New Essays on Sense, Content, and Concept*. Palo Alto, CA: CSLI Publications, pp. 113–40.

Newman, J. (1962), 'Review of *Webster's Third New International Dictionary*', *The Quarterly Journal of Speech*, 68: 437–8.

Noonan, H. (1980–1), 'Names and Belief', *Proceedings of the Aristotelian Society*, 81: 93–108.

Noonan, H. (1984), 'Fregean Thoughts', *Philosophical Quarterly*, 34: 205–24.

Nozick, R. (1981), *Philosophical Explanations*. Cambridge, MA: Harvard University Press.

Nunberg, G. (1993), 'Indexicality and Deixis', *Linguistics and Philosophy*, 16: 1–43.

Ockham, W. (1325), '*Summa Logicae, Part I: On Terms*', in M. J. Loux (ed.), *Ockham's Theory of Terms: Part I of the Summa Logicae*. Notre Dame, IN: University of Notre Dame Press, 1974, pp. 49–221.

Over, D. E. (1983), 'On Kripke's Puzzle', *Mind*, 92: 253–6.

Owens, J. (1989), 'Contradictory Belief and Cognitive Access', in P. French, T. Uehling, and H. Wettstein (eds.), *Midwest Studies in Philosophy*, 14. Notre Dame, IN: University of Notre Dame Press, pp. 289–316.

O'Grady, W., Dobrovolsky, M., and Aronoff, M. (1993), *Contemporary Linguistics: An Introduction, 2nd edn.* New York: St. Martin's Press.

O'Leary-Hawthorne, J. (1990), 'A Note on "Languages and Language"', *Australasian Journal of Philosophy*, 68: 116–18.

O'Leary-Hawthorne, J. (1993), 'Meaning and Evidence: Reply to Lewis', *Australasian Journal of Philosophy*, 71: 202–12.

Pagin, P. (1992), 'Names In and Out of Thought', *Philosophical Studies*, 66: 27–51.

Pap, A. (1955), 'Belief, Synonymity, and Analysis', *Philosophical Studies*, 6: 11–15.

Pap, A. (1957), 'Belief and Propositions', *Philosophy of Science*, 24: 123–36.

Pape, H. (1990), 'What's in a Name', in K. Jacobi and H. Pape (eds.), *Thinking and the Structure of the World*. Berlin: De Gruyter, pp. 181–94.

Partee, B. (1972), 'Opacity, Coreference, and Pronouns', in D. Davidson and G. Harman (eds.), *Semantics of Natural Language*. Dordrecht: D. Reidel, pp. 415–41.

Patton, T. E. and Stampe, D. W. (1969), 'The Rudiments of Meaning: On Ziff on Grice', *Foundations of Language*, 5: 2–16.

Peacocke, C. (1975), 'Proper Names, Reference, and Rigid Designation', in S. Blackburn (ed.), *Meaning, Reference, and Necessity*. Cambridge: Cambridge University Press, pp. 109–32. Reprinted in *Definite Descriptions: A Reader*, ed. G. Osterling, pp. 201–34. Cambridge, MA: MIT Press, 1998.

Peacocke, C. (1981), 'Demonstrative Thought and Psychological Explanation', *Synthese*, 49: 187–217.

Peacocke, C. (1983), *Sense and Content: Experience, Thought, and Their Relations*. Oxford: Oxford University Press.

Peacocke, C. (1986), *Thoughts: An Essay on Content*. Oxford: Basil Blackwell.

Peacocke, C. (1990), 'Content and Norms in a Natural World', in E. Villanueva (ed.), *Information, Semantics, and Epistemology*. Oxford: Basil Blackwell, pp. 57–76.

Peacocke, C. (1992), *A Study of Concepts*. Cambridge, MA: MIT Press.

Peacocke, C. (1996), 'Can Possession Conditions Individuate Concepts?' *Philosophy and Phenomenological Research*, 56: 433–60. Excerpted in *Concepts: Core Readings*, ed. E. Margolis and S. Laurence, pp. 345–51. Cambridge, MA: MIT Press, 1999.

Peacocke, C. (1997a), 'Concepts Without Words', in R. Heck (ed.), *Language, Thought, and Logic: Essays in Honour of Michael Dummett*. Oxford: Oxford University Press, pp. 1–33.

Peacocke, C. (1997b), 'Metaphysical Necessity: Understanding, Truth and Epistemology', *Mind*, 106: 521–74.

Peacocke, C. (2000), 'Fodor on Concepts: Philosophical Aspects', *Mind and Language*, 15: 327–40.

Peirce, C. S. (1931–5), *Collected Papers*, ed. P. Hartshorne, P. Weiss, and A. W. Burks. Cambridge, MA: Harvard University Press.

Pelczar, M. W. (2001), 'Names as Tokens and Names as Tools', *Synthese*, 128: 133–55.

Pelczar, M. W. and Rainsbury, J. (1998), 'The Indexical Character of Names', *Synthese*, 114: 293–317.

Pendlebury, M. (1986), 'Against the Power of Force: Reflections on the Meaning of Mood', *Mind*, 95: 361–72.

Pendlebury, M. (1990), 'Why Names Are Rigid Designators', *Philosophy and Phenomenological Research*, 50: 519–37.

Perloff, M. (1995), 'Stit and the Imperative', *American Philosophical Quarterly*, 32: 71–81.

Perry, J. (1979), 'The Problem of the Essential Indexical', *Noûs*, 13: 3–21. Reprinted in *Meaning and Truth: The Essential Readings in Modern Semantics*, ed. J. Garfield and M. Kiteley, pp. 613–27. New York: Paragon House, 1991.

Perry, J. (1980), 'A Problem About Continued Belief', *Pacific Philosophical Quarterly*, 61: 317–32.

Perry, J. (1988), 'Cognitive Significance and New Theories of Reference', *Noûs*, 22: 1–18.

Perry, J. (1990), 'Self-Notions', *Logos*, 11: 17–31.

Perry, J. (1997), 'Reflexivity, Indexicality, and Names', in W. Künne, A. Newen, and M. Anduschus (eds.), *Direct Reference, Indexicality, and Propositional Attitudes*. Stanford, CA: CSLI Publications, pp. 3–19.

Peterson, P. (1999), 'On the Boundaries of Syntax: Non-Syntagmatic Relations', in P. Collins and D. Lee (eds.), *The Clause in English: In Honour of Rodney Huddleston*. Amsterdam: John Benjamins, pp. 229–50.

Pettit, P. (1987), 'Inference and Information', *Behavioral and Brain Sciences*, 10: 727–9.

Philipse, H. (1994), 'Peacocke on Concepts', *Inquiry*, 37: 225–52.

Pinker, S. (1989), *Learnability and Cognition: The Acquisition of Argument Structure*. Cambridge, MA: MIT Press.

Place, U. T. (1956), 'Is Consciousness a Brain Process?' *British Journal of Psychology*, 47: 44–50.

Plantinga, A. (1973), 'Transworld Identity or Worldbound Individuals?' in M. Munitz (ed.), *Logic and Ontology*. New York: New York University Press. Reprinted in *The Possible and the Actual*, ed. M. J. Loux, pp. 146–65. Ithaca, NY: Cornell University Press, 1979.

Plantinga, A. (1974), *The Nature of Necessity*. Oxford: Oxford University Press.

Plantinga, A. (1976), 'Actualism and Possible Worlds', *Theoria*, 42: 139–60. Reprinted *The Possible and the Actual* ed. M. J. Loux, pp. 253–73. Ithaca, NY: Cornell University Press, 1979.

Plantinga, A. (1978), 'The Boethian Compromise', *American Philosophical Quarterly*, 15: 129–38.

Plantinga, A. (1985), 'Self-Profile and Replies', in J. Tomberlin and P. Van Inwagen (eds.), *Alvin Plantinga*. Dordrecht: D. Reidel, pp. 3–97, 313–94.

Plato (360 BC), '*Cratylus*', in E. Hamilton (ed.), *The Collected Dialogues of Plato*. Princeton, NJ: Princeton University Press, 1961, pp. 421–74.

Plato (360 BC), '*Sophist*', in E. Hamilton (ed.), *The Collected Dialogues of Plato*. Princeton, NJ: Princeton University Press, 1961, pp. 957–1017.

Platts, M. (1979), *Ways of Meaning*. London: Routledge and Kegan Paul.

Plumer, G. (1989), 'Mustn't Whatever is Referred to Exist?' *Southern Journal of Philosophy*, 27: 511–28.

Pollock, J. L. (1980), 'Thinking About an Object', *Midwest Studies in Philosophy*, 5: 487–99.

Posner, R. (1980), 'Semantics and Pragmatics of Sentence Connectives in Natural Languages', in J. Searle, F. Kiefer, and M. Bierwisch (eds.), *Speech-Act Theory and Pragmatics*. Dordrecht: D. Reidel, pp. 169–203.

Predelli, S. (1999), 'Saul, Salmon, and Superman', *Analysis*, 59: 113–16.

Predelli, S. (2000), 'Who's Afraid of Substitutivity', *Noûs*, 34: 455–67.

Predelli, S. (2001), 'Art, Bart, and Superman', *Analysis*, 61: 310–13.

Price, H. H. (1953), *Thinking and Experience*. Cambridge, MA: Harvard University Press.

Priestley, J. (1762), *A Course of Lectures on the Theory of Language and Universal Grammar*. Menston, England: Scolar Press, 1970.

Prior, A. N. (1967), *Past, Present, and Future*. Oxford: Clarendon Press.

Prior, A. N. and Prior, M. (1955), 'Erotetic Logic', *Philosophical Review*, 64: 43–59.

Putnam, H. (1970a), 'On Properties', in N. Rescher *et al.*, (eds.), *Essays in Honor of Carl G. Hempel*. Dordrecht: D. Reidel. Reprinted in *Philosophical Papers*, ed. H. Putnam, pp. 305–22. Cambridge: Cambridge University Press, 1975.

Putnam, H. (1970b), 'Is Semantics Possible?' in H. Kiefer and M. Munitz (eds.), *Languages, Belief, and Metaphysics*. New York: SUNY Press. Reprinted in *Concepts: Core Readings*, ed. E. Margolis and S. Laurence, pp. 178–87. Cambridge, MA: MIT Press, 1999.

Putnam, H. (1973), 'Meaning and Reference', *Journal of Philosophy*, 70: 699–711. Reprinted in *The Philosophy of Language*, ed. A. P. Martinich, pp. 308–15. Oxford: Oxford University Press, 1991.

Putnam, H. (1975), 'The Meaning of "Meaning",' in K. Gunderson (ed.), *Language, Mind, and Knowledge*. Minneapolis: University of Minnesota Press, pp. 131–93.

Putnam, H. (1981), *Reason, Truth, and History*. Cambridge: Cambridge University Press.

Putnam, H. (1992), 'Is It Necessary That Water is $H_2O$?' in L. E. Hahn (ed.), *The Philosophy of A. J. Ayer*. La Salle, IL: Open Court.

Pylyshyn, Z. (1980), 'Computation and Cognition: Issues in the Foundations of Cognitive Science', *The Behavioral and Brain Sciences*, 3: 111–32, 154–69.

Quillian, M. R. (1968), 'Semantic Memory', in M. L. Minsky (ed.), *Semantic Information Processing*. Cambridge, MA: MIT Press, pp. 216–55.

Quine, W. V. O. (1943), 'Notes on Existence and Necessity', *Journal of Philosophy*, 60: 113–27.

Quine, W. V. O. (1947), 'The Problem of Interpreting Modal Logic', *Journal of Symbolic Logic*, 12: 43–8.

Quine, W. V. O. (1959), *Methods of Logic*. New York: Holt, Rinehart, and Winston.

Quine, W. V. O. (1960), *Word and Object*. Cambridge, MA: MIT Press.

Quine, W. V. O. (1961a), 'The Problem of Meaning in Linguistics', in *From a Logical Point of View*, 2nd edn., pp. 47–64. Cambridge, MA: Harvard University Press, 1961. Reprinted in J. A. Fodor and J. J. Katz (eds.), *The Structure of Language*. Englewood Cliffs, NJ: Prentice-Hall, 1964, pp. 21–32.

Quine, W. V. O. (1961b), 'Reference and Modality', in *From a Logical Point of View*. New York: Harper and Row, pp. 139–59.

Quine, W. V. O. (1963), *Set Theory and Its Logic*. Cambridge, MA: Harvard University Press.

Quine, W. V. O. (1972), 'Methodological Reflections on Current Linguistic Theory', in D. Davidson and G. Harman (eds.), *Semantics of Natural Language*. Dordrecht: D. Reidel, pp. 442–54.

Quintilian, M. F. (1997), '*Institutio Oratoria*', in R. Harris and T. J. Taylor (eds.), *Landmarks in Linguistic Thought, I*. pp. 60–75. London: Routledge.

Radutzky, E. (1993), 'The Education of Deaf People in Italy and the Use of Italian Sign Language', in J. V. Van Cleve (ed.), *Deaf History Unveiled*. Washington, DC: Gallaudet University Press, pp. 237–51.

Ramsey, F. P. (1927), 'Facts and Propositions', *Proceedings of the Aristotelian Society*, Supplement 8: 153–70.

Rand, A. (1969), *Introduction to Objectivist Epistemology*. New York: The Objectivist.

Read, S. (1994), 'Syncategoremata', in R. E. Asher (ed.), *Encyclopedia of Languages and Linguistics*. Oxford: Pergamon Press, pp. 4452–3.

Recanati, F. (1986), 'On Defining Communicative Intentions', *Mind and Language*, 1: 213–42.

Recanati, F. (1987), *Meaning and Force: The Pragmatics of Performative Utterances*. Cambridge: Cambridge University Press.

Recanati, F. (1989a), 'Referential/Attributive: A Contextualist Proposal', *Philosophical Studies*, 56: 217–49.

Recanati, F. (1989b), 'The Pragmatics of What is Said', *Mind and Language*, 4: 293–329.

Recanati, F. (1990), 'Direct Reference, Meaning, and Thought', *Noûs*, 24: 697–722.

Recanati, F. (1993), *Direct Reference: From Language to Thought*. Oxford: Basil Blackwell.

Reid, T. (1764), '*Inquiry into the Human Mind*', in K. Lehrer and E. Beanblossom (eds.), *Thomas Reid's Inquiry and Essays*. Indianapolis, IN: Bobbs-Merrill, 1975, pp. 3–125.

Reid, T. (1785), *Essays on the Intellectual Powers of Man*, ed. B. Brody. Cambridge, MA: MIT Press, 1969.

Reimer, M. (1998a), 'The Wettstein/Salmon Debate: Critique and Resolution', *Pacific Philosophical Quarterly*, 79: 130–51.

Reimer, M. (1998b), 'Donnellan's Distinction/Kripke's Test', *Analysis*, 58: 89–100.

Reimer, M. (2001), 'The Problem of Empty Names', *Australasian Journal of Philosophy*, 79: 491–506.

Reimer, M. (2002), 'Ordinary Proper Names', in G. Preyer (ed.), *Logical Form and Language*. Oxford: Clarendon Press, pp. 444–66.

Rey, G. (1993), 'The Unavailability of What We Mean: A Reply to Quine, Fodor, and Lepore', in J. A. Fodor and E. Lepore (eds.), *Holism: A Consumer Update*. Atlanta: Rodopi B. V., pp. 61–101.

Rey, G. (1994), 'Concepts', in S. Guttenplan (ed.), *A Companion to the Philosophy of Mind*. Oxford: Basil Blackwell, pp. 185–93.

Rey, G. (1995), 'A Not "Merely Empirical" Argument for a Language of Thought', in *Philosophical Perspectives, 9: AI, Connectionism, and Philosophical Psychology*, 1995: 201–22.

Rhodes, R. A. (1992), 'Interjections', in W. Bright (ed.), *International Encyclopedia of Linguistics*. New York: Oxford University Press, p. 222.

Richard, M. (1983), 'Direct Reference and Ascriptions of Belief', *Journal of Philosophical Logic*, 12: 425–52. Reprinted in *Propositions and Attitudes*, ed. N. Salmon and S. Soames, pp. 169–239. Oxford: Oxford University Press, 1988.

Richard, M. (1987), 'Attitude Ascriptions, Semantic Theory, and Pragmatic Evidence', *Proceedings of the Aristotelian Society*, 87: 243–62.

Richard, M. (1989), 'How I Say What You Think', *Midwest Studies in Philosophy*, 14: 317–37.

Richard, M. (1990), *Propositional Attitudes: An Essay on Thoughts and How We Ascribe Them*. Cambridge: Cambridge University Press.

Richard, M. (1993), 'Attitudes in Context', *Linguistics and Philosophy*, 16: 123–48.

Richard, M. (1995), 'Defective Contexts, Accommodation, and Normalization', *Canadian Journal of Philosophy*, 25: 551–70.

Rickford, J. (1992), 'Pidgins and Creoles', in W. Bright (ed.), *International Encyclopedia of Linguistics,* Vol. 2. Oxford: Oxford University Press, pp. 224–9.

Rieber, S. (1992), 'A Test for Quotation', *Philosophical Studies*, 68: 83–94.

Rieber, S. (1997a), 'Conventional Implicatures as Tacit Performatives', *Linguistics and Philosophy*, 20: 51–72.

Rieber, S. (1997b), 'A Semiquotational Solution to Substitution Puzzles', *Philosophical Studies*, 86: 267–301.

Rosch, E. (1978), 'Principles of Categorization', in E. Rosch and B. Lloyd (eds.), *Cognition and Categorization*. Hillsdale, NJ: Lawrence Erlbaum Associates, pp. 189–206.

Rosenberg, J. (1974), *Linguistic Representation*. Dordrecht: D. Reidel.

Rosenberg, J. (1993), 'Another Look at Proper Names', in J. Tomberlin (ed.), *Philosophical Perspectives, 7: Language and Logic*. Atascadero, CA: Ridgeview, pp. 505–30.

Ross, A. (1944), 'Imperatives and Logic', *Philosophy of Science*, 11: 30–46.

Ross, J. R. (1970), 'On Declarative Sentences', in R. A. Jacobs and P. S. Rosenbaum (eds.), *Readings in English Transformational Grammar*. Waltham, MA: Ginn.

Rundle, B. (1979), *Grammar in Philosophy*. Oxford: Clarendon Press.

Russell, B. (1905), 'On Denoting', in A. P. Martinich (ed.), *The Philosophy of Language*, 2nd edn. Oxford: Oxford University Press, 1990, pp. 203–11.

Russell, B. (1910–11), 'Knowledge by Acquaintance and Knowledge by Description', *Proceedings of the Aristotelian Society*, 11: 108–28. Reprinted in *Mysticism and Logic*, pp. 209–32. London: Allen and Unwin, 1917.

Russell, B. (1912), *The Problems of Philosophy*. Oxford: Oxford University Press.

Russell, B. (1919), 'Descriptions', in A. P. Martinich (ed.), *The Philosophy of Language*. Oxford: Oxford University Press, pp. 212–18.

Russell, B. (1938), *Introduction to Mathematical Philosophy*. London: Allen and Unwin.

Russell, B. (1940), *An Inquiry into Meaning and Truth*. London: Allen and Unwin.

Russell, B. (1948), *Human Knowledge: Its Scope and Limits*. New York: Simon and Schuster.

Russell, S. (1987), 'Rationality as an Explanation of Language', *Behavioral and Brain Sciences*, 10: 730–1.

Ryckman, T. C. (1988), 'The Millian Theory of Names and the Problem of Negative Existentials and Non-Referring Names', in D. F. Austin (ed.), *Philosophical Analysis: A Defense by Example*. Dordrecht: Kluwer, pp. 241–9.

Ryle, G. (1949), *The Concept of Mind*. New York: Barnes and Noble.

Ryle, G. (1951), 'Thinking and Language', from *Proceedings of the Aristotelian Society*, Supplementary Volume 25: 65–82, in *Collected Essays*. New York: Barnes and Noble, 1971, pp. 258–71.

Ryle, G. (1957), 'The Theory of Meaning', in C. A. Mace (ed.), *British Philosophy in the Mid-Century*. London: Allen and Unwin, pp. 239–64.

Ryle, G. (1958), 'A Puzzling Element in the Notion of Thinking', from *Proceedings of the British Academy*, 44: 129–44, in *Collected Essays*. New York: Barnes and Noble, 1971, pp. 391–406.

Sadock, J. M. (1974), *Toward a Linguistic Theory of Speech Acts*. New York: Academic Press.

Sadock, J. M. and Zwicky, A. M. (1985), 'Speech Act Distinctions in Syntax', in T. Shopen (ed.), *Language Typology and Syntactic Description*, Vol. 1: *Clause Structure*. Cambridge: Cambridge University Press, pp. 155–96.

Sainsbury, R. M. (1999), 'Names, Fictional Names, and "Really"', *Proceedings of the Aristotelian Society*, Supplement 73: 243–69.

Sainsbury, R. M. (2000), 'Empty Names', in A. Kanamori (ed.), *The Proceedings of the Twentieth World Congress of Philosophy*. Bowling Green: Philosophy Document Center, pp. 57–65.

Sainsbury, R. M. (2001), 'Sense Without Reference', in A. Newen, U. Nortmann, and R. Stuhlmann-Laeisz (eds.), *Building on Frege*. Palo Alto, CA: CSLI, pp. 211–30.

Salmon, N. (1981), *Reference and Essence*. Princeton: Princeton University Press.

Salmon, N. (1982), 'Assertion and Incomplete Definite Descriptions', *Philosophical Studies*, 42: 37–45.

Salmon, N. (1986), *Frege's Puzzle*. Cambridge, MA: MIT Press.

Salmon, N. (1987), 'Existence', in J. Tomberlin (ed.), *Philosophical Perspectives*, 1: *Metaphysics*. Atascadero, CA: Ridgeway, pp. 49–108.

Salmon, N. (1989a), 'How to Become a Millian Heir', *Noûs*, 23: 211–20.

Salmon, N. (1989b), 'Reference and Information Content: Names and Descriptions', in D. M. Gabbay and F. Guenthner (eds.), *Handbook of Philosophical Logic*, Volume IV. Dordrecht: D. Reidel, pp. 409–61.

Salmon, N. (1990), 'A Millian Heir Rejects the Wages of *Sinn*', in C. A. Anderson and J. Owens (eds.), *Propositional Attitudes*. Stanford, CA: CSLI Publications, pp. 215–57.

Salmon, N. (1995), 'On Being of Two Minds: Belief with Doubt', *Noûs*, 29: 1–20.

Salmon, N. (1998), 'Nonexistence', *Noûs*: 32: 277–319.

Saul, J. (1993), 'Still an Attitude Problem', *Linguistics and Philosophy*, 16: 423–35.

Saul, J. (1997a), 'Substitution and Simple Sentences', *Analysis*, 57: 102–8.

Saul, J. (1997b), 'Reply to Forbes', *Analysis*, 57: 114–18.

Saul, J. (1998), 'The Pragmatics of Attitude Ascription', *Philosophical Studies*, 92: 363–89.

Saul, J. (1999a), 'The Best of Intentions: Ignorance, Idiosyncrasy, and Belief Reporting', *Canadian Journal of Philosophy*, 29: 29–48.

Saul, J. (1999b), 'The Road to Hell: Intentions and Propositional Attitude Ascription', *Mind and Language*, 14: 356–75.

Saul, J. (1999c), 'Substitution, Simple Sentences, and Sex Scandals', *Analysis*, 59: 106–12.

Saul, J. (2001), 'Review of *Implicature: Intention, Convention, and Principle in the Failure of Gricean Theory* by Wayne Davis', *Noûs*, 35: 630–41.

Saul, J. (2002), 'Speaker Meaning, What is Said, and What is Implicated', *Noûs*, 36: 228–248.

Saussure, F. (1916), *Course in General Linguistics*, tr. W. Baskin. New York: McGraw-Hill, 1966.

Schank, R. and Abelson, R. (1977), *Scripts, Plans, Goals, and Understanding*. Hillsdale, NJ: Erlbaum.

Scheffler, I. (1955), 'On Synonymy and Indirect Discourse', *Philosophy of Science*, 22: 39–44.

Schein, J. D. and Stewart, D. A. (1996), *Language in Motion: Exploring the Nature of Sign*. Washington, DC: Gallaudet University Press.

Schelling, T. (1960), *The Strategy of Conflict*. Cambridge, MA: Harvard University Press.

Schiffer, S. (1972), *Meaning*. Oxford: Clarendon Press.

Schiffer, S. (1978), 'The Basis of Reference', *Erkenntnis*, 13: 171–206.

Schiffer, S. (1979), 'Naming and Knowing', in P. French, T. Uehling, and H. Wettstein (eds.), *Contemporary Perspectives in the Philosophy of Language*. Minneapolis: University of Minnesota Press, pp. 61–73.

Schiffer, S. (1981), 'Indexicals and the Theory of Reference', *Synthese*, 49: 43–100.

Schiffer, S. (1982), 'Intention-Based Semantics', *Notre Dame Journal of Formal Logic*, 23: 119–56.

Schiffer, S. (1987a), *Remnants of Meaning*. Cambridge, MA: MIT Press.

Schiffer, S. (1987b), 'The "Fido"-Fido Theory of Belief', in J. Tomberlin (ed.), *Philosophical Perspectives*, 1: *Metaphysics*. Atascadero, CA: Ridgeview, pp. 455–80.

Schiffer, S. (1990), 'The Mode-of-Presentation Problem', in C. A. Anderson and J. Owens (eds.), *Propositional Attitudes*. Stanford, CA: CSLI Publications, pp. 249–68.

Schiffer, S. (1992), 'Belief Ascription', *Journal of Philosophy*, 89: 499–521.

Schiffer, S. (1994), 'A Paradox of Meaning', *Noûs*, 28: 279–324.

Schiffer, S. (1995), 'Descriptions, Indexicals, and Belief Reports: Some Dilemmas (but not the ones you expect)', *Mind*, 104: 107–31.

Schiffrin, D. (1994), *Approaches to Discourse*. Oxford: Basil Blackwell.

Schmerling, S. (1982), 'How Imperatives Are Special, and How They Aren't', in R. Schneider, K. Tuite, and R. Chametzky (eds.), *Papers from the Parasession on Nondeclaratives*. Chicago: Chicago Linguistics Society, pp. 202–10.

Schwarz, D. (1979), *Naming and Referring: The Semantics and Pragmatics of Singular Terms*. New York: De Gruyter.

Schweizer, P. (1991), 'Blind Grasping and Fregean Senses', *Philosophical Studies*, 62: 263–87.

Seager, W. (1990), 'The Logic of Lost Lingens', *Journal of Philosophical Logic*, 19: 407–28.

Searle, J. (1958), 'Proper Names', *Mind*, 67: 212–18.

Searle, J. (1965), 'What is a Speech Act?' in M. Black (ed.), *Philosophy in America*. London: Allen and Unwin, pp. 221–39.

Searle, J. (1967), 'Proper Names and Descriptions', in P. Edwards (ed.), *Encyclopedia of Philosophy* vol. 6. New York: Macmillan, pp. 487–91.

Searle, J. (1969), *Speech-Acts*. Cambridge: Cambridge University Press.

Searle, J. (1979), *Expression and Meaning*. Cambridge: Cambridge University Press.

Searle, J. (1983), *Intentionality*. Cambridge: Cambridge University Press.

Searle, J. (1986), 'Meaning, Communication, and Representation', in R. Grandy and R. Warner (eds.), *Philosophical Grounds of Rationality: Intentions, Categories, Ends*. Oxford: Clarendon Press, pp. 209–26.

Segal, G. (2001), 'Two Theories of Names', *Mind and Language*, 16: 547–63.

Segal, G. (2002), 'Two Theories of Names', *Philosophy*, 51 (Supplement): 75–93.

Sellars, W. (1954), 'Presupposing', *Philosophical Review*, 63: 197–215.

Sellars, W. (1955), 'Putnam on Synonymity and Belief', *Analysis*, 15: 117–20.

Sellars, W. (1958), 'The Chisholm-Sellars Correspondence on Intentionality', in M. Feigl, M. Scriven, and G. Maxwell (eds.), *Minnesota Studies in the Philosophy of Science*. Minneapolis: University of Minnesota Press, pp. 529–39. Reprinted in *Intentionality, Mind, and Language*, ed. A. Marras, pp. 214–48. Urbana, IL: University of Illinois Press, 1972.

Sellars, W. (1963), 'Empiricism and the Philosophy of Mind', in *Science, Perception, and Reality*. London: Routledge and Kegan Paul, pp. 127–96.

Sellars, W. (1969), 'Language as Thought and as Communication', from *Philosophy and Phenomenological Research*, 29: 506–27, in *Essays in Philosophy and History*. Dordrecht: D. Reidel, 1974, pp. 93–117.

Sellars, W. (1979), *Naturalism and Ontology*. Reseda, CA: Ridgeview.

Shieh, S. (2001), 'Meaning, Rigidity, and Modality', in J. Floyd (ed.), *Future Pasts: The Analytic Tradition in Twentieth Century Philosophy*. New York: Oxford University Press, pp. 369–92.

Shoemaker, S. (1998), 'Causal and Metaphysical Necessity', *Pacific Philosophical Quarterly*, 79: 59–77.

Sidelle, A. (2002), 'On the Metaphysical Contingency of Laws', in T. S. Gendler and J. Hawthorne (eds.), *Conceivability and Possibility*. Oxford: Oxford University Press, pp. 253–81.

Sider, T. (1995), 'Three Problems for Richard's Theory of Belief Ascription', *Canadian Journal of Philosophy*, 25: 487–513.

Sider, T. (2003), 'Reductive Theories of Modality', in M. Loux and D. Zimmerman (eds.), *The Oxford Handbook of Metaphysics*. Oxford: Oxford University Press, pp. 180–208.

Siebel, M. (2001), 'William P. Alston: *Illocutionary Acts and Sentence Meaning*', *Glazier Philosophische Studien*, 62: 249–61.

Simpson, J. M. Y. (1994), 'Language', in R. E. Asher (ed.), *Encyclopedia of Language and Linguistics*. Oxford: Pergamon Press, pp. 1893–7.

Sirridge, M. (1974), 'William of Sherwood on Propositions and Their Parts', *Notre Dame Journal of Formal Logic*, 15: 462–4.

Skulsky, H. (1986), 'Metaphorese', *Noûs*, 20: 351–69. Reprinted in *Meaning and Truth*, ed. J. Garfield and M. Kiteley, pp. 582–98. New York: Paragon House, 1991.

Sloat, C. (1969), 'Proper Nouns in English', *Language*, 45: 26–30.

Smart, J. J. C. (1959), 'Sensations and Brain Processes', *Philosophical Review*, 58: 141–56.

Smith, A. D. (1984), 'Rigidity and Scope', *Mind*, 93: 177–93.

Smith, D. V. *et al.* (1952), *The English Language Arts*. New York: Appleton-Century-Crofts. Prepared by the Commission on the English Curriculum of the National Council of Teachers of English.

Smith, D. W. (1981), 'Indexical Sense and Reference', *Synthese*, 49: 101–28.

Smith, D. W. (1982a), 'Husserl on Demonstrative Reference and Perception', from *Husserl, Intentionality, and Cognitive Science: Recent Studies in Phenomenology*, ed. H. Dreyfus, pp. 193–214. Cambridge, MA: MIT Press.

Smith, D. W. (1982b), 'What's the Meaning of "This"?' *Noûs*, 16: 181–208.

Smith, E. E. (1988), 'Concepts and Thought', in R. J. Sternberg and E. E. Smith (eds.), *The Psychology of Human Thought*. Cambridge: Cambridge University Press, pp. 19–49.

Smith, E. E. and Medin, D. L. (1981), *Categories and Concepts*. Cambridge, MA: Harvard University Press.

Smith, M. (1987), 'The Humean Theory of Motivation', *Mind*, 96: 36–61.

Smith, P. T. (1985), 'Names, Identity, and Necessity', in I. Hacking (ed.), *Exercises in Analysis*. Cambridge: Cambridge University Press, pp. 147–69.

Smullyan, A. F. (1947), 'Review of Quine (1947)', *Journal of Symbolic Logic*, 12: 139–41.

Smullyan, A. F. (1948), 'Modality and Description', *Journal of Symbolic Logic*, 13: 31–7.

Soames, S. (1987a), 'Substitutivity', in J. J. Thompson (ed.), *On Being and Saying: Essays for Richard Cartwright*. Cambridge, MA: MIT Press, pp. 99–132.

Soames, S. (1987b), 'Direct Reference, Propositional Attitudes, and Semantic Content', *Philosophical Topics*, 15: 197–239.

Soames, S. (1989), 'Direct Reference and Propositional Attitudes', in J. Almog, J. Perry, and H. Wettstein (eds.), *Themes from Kaplan*. Oxford: Oxford University Press, pp. 393–419.

Soames, S. (1995a), 'Beyond Singular Propositions?' *Canadian Journal of Philosophy*, 25: 515–550.

Soames, S. (1995b), 'Revisionism About Reference: A Reply to Smith', *Synthese*, 104: 191–216.

Soames, S. (1998), 'The Modal Argument: Wide Scope and Rigidified Descriptions', *Noûs*, 32: 1–22.

Soames, S. (2002), *Beyond Rigidity: The Unfinished Semantic Agenda of Naming and Necessity*. Oxford: Oxford University Press.

Sosa, D. (1996), 'The Import of a Puzzle About Belief', *Philosophical Review*, 105: 373–402.

Sosa, E. (1970), 'Propositional Attitudes *de Dicto* and *de Re*', *Journal of Philosophy*, 67: 883–96.

Sosa, E. (1991), 'Between Internalism and Externalism in Consciousness', *Philosophical Issues*, 1 (Consciousness): 179–95.

Sosa, E. (1993), 'Abilities, Concepts, and Externalism', in J. Heil and A. Mele (eds.), *Mental Causation*. Oxford: Oxford University Press, pp. 309–28.

Sosa, E. (1995), '*De Re* Belief, Action Explanations, and the Essential Indexical', in W. Sinnott-Armstrong, D. Raffman, and N. Asher (eds.), *Modality, Morality, and Belief*. Cambridge: Cambridge University Press, pp. 235–49.

Sperber, D. and Wilson, D. (1986), *Relevance: Communication and Cognition*. Cambridge, MA: Harvard University Press.

Stalnaker, R. (1972), 'Pragmatics', in D. Davidson and G. Harman (eds.), *Semantics of Natural Language*. Dordrecht: D. Reidel, pp. 380–97.

Stalnaker, R. (1981), 'Indexical Belief', *Synthese*, 49: 129–52.

Stalnaker, R. (1986), 'Counterparts and Identity', *Midwest Studies in Philosophy*, Vol 11: *Studies in Essentialism*: 121–40.

Stalnaker, R. (1989), 'On What's in the Head', in J. Tomberlin (ed.), *Philosophical Perspectives*, 3: *Philosophy of Mind and Action Theory*. Atascadero, CA: Ridgeview, pp. 287–316. Reprinted in D. M. Rosenthal (ed.), *The Nature of Mind*, pp. 576–89. Oxford: Oxford University Press, 1991.

Stalnaker, R. (1993), 'Twin Earth Revisited', *Proceedings of the Aristotelian Society*, 93: 297–311.

Stalnaker, R. (1995), 'The Interaction of Modality with Quantification and Identity', in W. Sinnott-Armstrong (ed.), *Modality, Morality, and Belief: Essays in Honor of Ruth Barcan Marcus*. Cambridge: Cambridge University Press, pp. 12–28.

Stalnaker, R. (1997), 'Reference and Necessity', in B. Hale and C. Wright (eds.), *A Companion to the Philosophy of Language*. Oxford: Basil Blackwell, pp. 534–54.

Stampe, D. W. (1968), 'Towards a Grammar of Meaning', *Philosophical Review*, 77: 137–74.

Stampe, D. W. (1974), 'Attributes and Interrogatives', in M. K. Munitz and P. K. Unger (eds.), *Semantics and Philosophy*. New York: New York University Press, pp. 159–96.

Stampe, D. W. (1979), 'Towards a Causal Theory of Linguistic Representation', in P. French, T. Uehling, and H. Wettstein (eds.), *Contemporary Perspectives in the Philosophy of Language*. Minneapolis: University of Minnesota Press, pp. 81–102.

Stanley, J. (1997a), 'Names and Rigid Designation', in B. Hale and C. Wright (eds.), *A Companion to the Philosophy of Language*. Oxford: Basil Blackwell, pp. 555–85.

Stanley, J. (1997b), 'Rigidity and Content', in R. G. Heck (ed.), *Language, Thought, and Logic: Essays in Honour of Michael Dummett*. Oxford: Oxford University Press, pp. 131–56.

Stanley, J. (1999), 'Understanding, Context-Relativity, and the Description Theory', *Analysis*, 59: 14–18.

Steinitz, Y. (1994), 'Brains in a Vat: Different Perspectives', *The Philosophical Quarterly*, 44: 213–22.

Steinman, R. (1985), 'Kripke Rigidity Versus Kaplan Rigidity', *Mind*, 94: 431–42.

Stenius, E. (1967), 'Mood and Language Game', *Synthese*, 17: 254–74.

Sterelny, K. (1989), 'Fodor's Nativism', *Philosophical Studies*, 55: 119–41.

Sterelny, K. (1990), *The Representational Theory of Mind*. Oxford: Basil Blackwell.

Stich, S. (1983), *From Folk Psychology to Cognitive Science*. Cambridge, MA: MIT Press.

Stillings, N. A., Feinstein, M. H., Garfield, J. L., Rissland, E. L., Rosenbaum, D. A., Weisler, S. E., and Baker-Ward, L. (1987), *Cognitive Science: An Introduction*. Cambridge, MA: MIT Press.

Stillings, N. A., Weisler, S. E., Chase, C. H., Feinstein, M. H., Garfield, J. L., and Rissland, E. L. (1995), *Cognitive Science: An Introduction*, 2nd edn. Cambridge, MA: MIT Press.

Stine, G. (1978), 'Meaning Other Than What We Say and Referring', *Philosophical Studies*, 33: 319–37.

Strawson, P. F. (1950), 'On Referring', *Mind*, 59: 320–44.

Strawson, P. F. (1963), *Individuals*. New York: Anchor Books.

Strawson, P. F. (1964), 'Intention and Convention in Speech Acts', *Philosophical Review*, 73: 439–60. Reprinted in *Pragmatics: A Reader*, ed. S. Davis, pp. 290–302. Oxford: Oxford University Press, 1991.

Strawson, P. F. (1971), 'Meaning and Truth', in *Logico-Linguistic Papers*. London: Methuen, pp. 170–89.

Strawson, P. F. (1986), 'Direct Singular Reference: Intended Reference and Actual Reference', in V. Cauchy (ed.), *Philosophy and Culture*. Montreal: Édition du Beffroi, pp. 249–54.

Stroll, A. (1998), 'Proper Names, Names, and Fictive Objects', *Journal of Philosophy*, 95: 522–34.

Suppes, P. (1986), 'The Primacy of Utterer's Meaning', in R. Grandy and R. Warner (eds.) *Philosophical Grounds of Rationality: Intentions, Categories, Ends*. Oxford: Clarendon Press, pp. 109–29.

Taavitsainen, I. (1995), 'Interjections in Early Modern English: From Imitation of Spoken to Conventions of Written Language', in A. H. Jucker (ed.), *Historical Pragmatics: Pragmatic Developments in the History of English*. Amsterdam: John Benjamins, pp. 439–65.

Tarski, A. (1944), 'The Semantic Conception of Truth and the Foundations of Semantics', *Philosophy and Phenomenological Research*, 4: 341–75. Reprinted in *The Philosophy of Language*, ed. A. P. Martinich, pp. 48–71. Oxford: Oxford University Press, 1991.

Taschek, W. (1987), 'Content, Character, and Cognitive Significance', *Philosophical Studies*, 52: 161–89.

Taschek, W. (1988), 'Would a Fregean Be Puzzled by Pierre?' *Mind*, 97: 99–104.

Taschek, W. (1995a), 'On Belief Content and That-Clauses', *Mind and Language*, 10: 274–98.

Taschek, W. (1995b), 'Belief, Substitution, and Logical Structure', *Noûs*, 29: 71–95.

Taylor, C. (1980), 'Review of *Linguistic Behavior*, by J. Bennett', *Dialogue*, 19: 290–301.

Teichmann, R. (1991), 'Future Individuals', *The Philosophical Quarterly*, 41: 194–211.

Thackray, A. (1972), *John Dalton*. Cambridge, MA: Harvard University Press.

Thomsen, H. E. (1997), 'On the Proper Treatment of Proper Names', *Nordic Journal of Linguistics*, 20: 91–110.

Tienson, J. (1986), 'An Observation on Common Names and Proper Names', *Analysis*, 46: 73–6.

Tomberlin, J. (1989), 'Critical Notice of G. W. Fitch's *Naming and Believing*', *Philosophy and Phenomenological Research*, 49: 521–5.

Tomberlin, J. (1991), 'Belief, Self-Ascription, and Ontology', in E. Villanueva (ed.), *Philosophical Issues*, 1: *Consciousness*. Atascadero, CA: Ridgeview, pp. 233–59.

Tormey, A. (1971), *The Concept of Expression*. Princeton: Princeton University Press.

Travis, C. (1985), 'Are Belief Ascriptions Opaque?' *Proceedings of the Aristotelian Society*, 85: 73–99.

Tsohatzidis, S. L. (1994), 'Ways of Doing Things with Words', in S. L. Tsohatzidis (ed.), *Foundations of Speech Act Theory: Philosophical and Linguistic Perspectives*. London: Routledge, pp. 1–25.

Tye, M. (1998), 'Externalism and Memory', *Proceedings of the Aristotelian Society*, Supplement 72: 77–94.

Ullmann-Margalit, E. (1977), *The Emergence of Norms*. Oxford: Oxford University Press.

Unger, P. (1983), 'The Causal Theory of Reference', *Philosophical Studies*, 43: 1–45.

Urdang, L. (1996), 'The Uncommon Use of Proper Names', *International Journal of Lexicography*, 9: 30–4.

Urmson, J. O. (1967), 'Ideas', in P. Edwards (ed.), *Encyclopedia of Philosophy*. New York: Macmillan, pp. 118–21.

Urmson, J. O. (1968), 'Criteria of Intensionality', *Proceedings of the Aristotelian Society*, Supplementary Volume 42: 107–22.

Van Gelder, T. (1990), 'Compositionality: A Connectionist Variation on a Classical Theme', *Cognitive Science*, 14: 355–84.

Van Gelder, T. (1991), 'Classical Questions, Radical Answers: Connectionism and the Structure of Mental Representations', in T. Horgan and J. Tienson (eds.), *Connectionism and the Philosophy of Mind*. Dordrecht: Kluwer, pp. 355–81.

Van Inwagen, P. (1985), 'Plantinga on Trans-World Identity', in J. Tomberlin and P. van Inwagen (eds.), *Alvin Plantinga: A Profile*. Dordrecht: Reidel, pp. 101–20.

Van Inwagen, P. (2003), 'Existence, Ontological Commitment, and Fictional Entities', in M. J. Loux and D. W. Zimmerman (eds.), *The Oxford Handbook of Metaphysics*. Oxford: Oxford University Press, pp. 131–57.

Vanderveken, D. (1990), *Meaning and Speech Acts*. Cambridge: Cambridge University Press.

Vendler, Z. (1967), 'Singular Terms', in *Linguistics in Philosophy*. Ithaca, NY: Cornell University Press, pp. 33–69.

References 435

Vendler, Z. (1972), *Res Cogitans: An Essay in Rational Psychology*. Ithaca NY: Cornell University Press.

Vendler, Z. (1976), 'Thinking of Individuals', *Noûs*, 10: 35–46.

Vendler, Z. (1977), 'Words in Thought', *Philosophical Exchange*, 2: 55–66.

Vermazen, B. (1971), 'Semantics and Semantics', *Foundations of Language*, 7: 539–55.

Vogelin, C., Vogelin, F. *et al.* (1988), 'Languages of the World', in R. McHenry (ed.), *Encyclopaedia Britannica*. Chicago: Encyclopaedia Britannica, pp. 591–815.

Walker, R. (1975), 'Conversational Implicatures', in S. Blackburn (ed.), *Meaning, Reference, and Necessity: New Studies in Semantics*. Cambridge: Cambridge University Press, pp. 133–81.

Walton, K. (1990), *Mimesis as Make-Believe*. Cambridge, MA: Harvard University Press.

Walton, K. (1993), 'Metaphor and Prop Oriented Make-Believe', *European Journal of Philosophy*, 1: 39–56.

Weiskrantz, L. (ed.) (1988), *Thought Without Language*. Oxford: Clarendon Press.

Weiskrantz, L. (1997), 'Thought Without Language: Thought Without Awareness?' in J. Preston (ed.), *Thought and Language*. Cambridge: Cambridge University Press, pp. 127–50.

Wells, J. C. (1994), 'Esperanto', in R. Asher (ed.), *The Encyclopedia of Language and Linguistics*. Oxford: Pergamon Press, pp. 1143–5.

Wettstein, H. K. (1976), 'Can What Is Asserted Be a Sentence?' *Philosophical Review*, 85: 196–207. Reprinted in *Has Semantics Rested on a Mistake? And Other Essays*, ed. H. Wettstein, pp. 9–19. Palo Alto: Stanford University Press, 1991.

Wettstein, H. K. (1981), 'Demonstrative Reference and Definite Descriptions', *Philosophical Studies*, 40: 241–57. Reprinted in *Has Semantics Rested on a Mistake? And Other Essays*, ed. H. Wettstein, pp. 35–58. Palo Alto: Stanford University Press, 1991.

Wettstein, H. K. (1984), 'Did the Greeks Really Worship Zeus?' *Synthese*, 60: 439–49. Reprinted in *Has Semantics Rested on a Mistake? And Other Essays*, ed. H. Wettstein, pp. 59–68. Palo Alto: Stanford University Press, 1991.

Wettstein, H. K. (1986), 'Has Semantics Rested on a Mistake?' *Journal of Philosophy*, 83: 185–209.

Wettstein, H. K. (1991), *Has Semantics Rested on a Mistake? And Other Essays*. Palo Alto: Stanford University Press.

Wetzel, L. (1989), 'That Numbers Could Be Objects', *Philosophical Studies*, 56: 273–92.

Wetzel, L. (forthcoming), *Of Types and Tokens*. Cambridge, MA: MIT Press.

Whorf, B. (1956), *Language, Thought, and Reality*. Cambridge, MA: MIT Press.

Wierzbicka, A. (1992a), 'Semantic Primitives and Semantic Fields', in A. Lehrer and E. Kittay (eds.), *Frames, Fields, and Contrasts*. Hillsdale, NJ: Erlbaum, pp. 209–27.

Wierzbicka, A. (1992b), 'The Semantics of Interjection', *Journal of Pragmatics*, 18: 159–92.

Wiggins, D. (1965), 'Identity-Statements', in R. J. Butler (ed.), *Analytical Philosophy, Second Series*. Oxford: Blackwell, pp. 40–71.

Wiggins, D. (1980), *Sameness and Substance*. Oxford: Blackwell.

436 References

Wiggins, D. (1999), 'Names, Fictional Names and "Really"', *Proceedings of the Aristotelian Society*, Supplement 73: 271–86.

Wiggins, D. (2001), *Sameness and Substance Renewed*. Cambridge: Cambridge University Press.

Wilbur, R. B. (1987), *American Sign Language: Linguistic and Applied Dimensions*. Boston: Little, Brown.

Wilkins, D. P. (1992), 'Interjections as Deictics', *Journal of Pragmatics*, 18: 119–58.

Williams, C. J. F. (1991), 'You and She', *Analysis*, 51: 143–6.

Wilson, D. and Sperber, D. (1981), 'On Grice's Theory of Conversation', in P. Werth (ed.), *Conversation and Discourse*. New York: St. Martins Press, pp. 155–78.

Wilson, D. and Sperber, D. (1988), 'Mood and the Analysis of Non-Declarative Sentences', in J. Dancy (ed.), *Human Agency*. Stanford, CA: Stanford University Press, pp. 77–101.

Wittgenstein, L. (1953), *Philosophical Investigations*. Oxford: Oxford University Press.

Wolterstorff, N. (1960), 'Are Properties Meanings?' *Journal of Philosophy*, 57: 277–81.

Woodfield, A. (1982), 'On Specifying the Contents of Thought', in A. Woodfield (ed.), *Thought and Object*. Oxford: Clarendon Press, pp. 259–97.

Woodfield, A. (1991), 'Conceptions', *Mind*, 100: 547–72.

Woodfield, A. (1997), 'Social Externalism and Conceptual Diversity', in J. Preston (ed.), *Thought and Language*. Cambridge: Cambridge University Press, pp. 77–102.

Woodward, J. (1978), 'Historical Bases of American Sign Language', in P. Siple (ed.), *Understanding Language Through Sign Language Research*. New York: Academic Press, pp. 333–47.

Woozley, A. D. (1967), 'Universals', in P. Edwards (ed.), *Encyclopedia of Philosophy*. New York: Macmillan, pp. 194–206.

Wreen, M. (1989), 'Socrates is Called "Socrates"', *Linguistics and Philosophy*, 12: 359–71.

Wreen, M. (1998), 'Proper Names and the Necessity of Identity Statements', *Synthese*, 114: 319–35.

Yablo, S. (1998), 'Self-Knowledge and Semantic Luck', in E. Villanueva (ed.), *Philosophical Issues, 9: Concepts*. Atascadero, CA: Ridgeview, pp. 220–9.

Yablo, S. (2002), 'Coulda, Woulda, Shoulda', in T. S. Gendler and J. Hawthorne (eds.), *Conceivability and Possibility*. Oxford: Oxford University Press, pp. 441–92.

Yagisawa, T. (1984), 'The Pseudo-Mates Argument', *Philosophical Review*, 93: 407–18.

Yagisawa, T. (1993), 'A Semantic Solution to Frege's Puzzle', in J. Tomberlin (ed.), *Philosophical Perspectives, 7: Language and Logic*. Atascadero, CA: Ridgeview, pp. 135–54.

Yagisawa, T. (1998), 'Naming and Its Place in Reference', *Lingua e Stile*, 33: 445–58.

Yourgrau, P. (1986), 'The Path Back to Frege', in *Demonstratives*. Oxford: Oxford University Press, pp. 97–132.

Yourgrau, P. (ed.) (1990), *Demonstratives*. Oxford: Oxford University Press.

Yu, P. (1979), 'On the Gricean Program About Meaning', *Linguistics and Philosophy*, 3: 273–388.

Yu, P. (1980), 'The Modal Argument Against Description Theories of Names', *Analysis*, 40: 208–9.

Zadeh, L. A. (1983), *A Fuzzy-Set-Theoretic Approach to the Compositionality of Meaning: Propositions, Dispositions, and Canonical Forms*. Berkeley Cognitive Science Report No. 13.

Zalta, E. N. (1989), 'Singular Propositions, Abstract Constituents, and Propositional Attitudes', in J. Almog, J. Perry, and H. Wettstein (eds.), *Themes from Kaplan*. Oxford: Oxford University Press, pp. 455–78.

Zemach, E. (1976), 'Putnam's Theory on the Reference of Substance Terms', *Journal of Philosophy*, 73: 116–27.

Zemach, E. (1985), 'De Se and Descartes', *Noûs*, 19: 181–204.

Ziff, P. (1960), *Semantic Analysis*. Ithaca, NY: Cornell University Press.

Ziff, P. (1964), 'On Understanding "Understanding Utterances"', in J. A. Fodor and J. J. Katz (eds.), *The Structure of Language*. Englewood Cliffs, NJ: Prentice-Hall, pp. 390–9.

Ziff, P. (1967), 'On H. P. Grice's Account of Meaning', *Analysis*, 28: 1–8.

Ziff, P. (1977), 'About Proper Names', *Mind*, 86: 319–32.

Zink, S. (1963), 'The Meaning of Proper Names', *Mind*, 72: 481–99.

# Index

448

Rigidity (*cont.*)
  Soames rigidity, 389–90
  existence problem, 391
Roman numerals, 243
Ross, J. R., 127
Rundle, B., 240
Russell, B., 182, 183, 211, 337–8
Russellian theory of belief, 282, 287. *See also*
    Triadic relation theory of belief
  modes of presentation, 282–4, 293n35,
    335
  triadic relation theory, 282–6
  ways of believing, 282, 284
Russell's paradox, 211, 213ff, 265
Russell's problem, 7, 211, 213–4, 245–51,
    256, 260–1, 262n19, 302, 335, 349.
    *See* Referential theory
  Gricean defense, 277
  in formal semantics, 351, 354–5
  Millian defense, 264–6
  triadic relation theory, 285

Sadock, J. M., 134
Sainsbury, M., 247
Salmon, N., 283, 287, 342–5
Saul, J., 269–71, 279–81
Saying, 77, 133, 157n48, 162, 218, 288
  versus implicating, 276–9, 280, 288
  versus meaning, 288–9
Schiffer, S., 75, 195
Schwarz, D., 175
Searle, J., 173, 232, 325
Segal, G., 308
Semantic innocence, 70, 287
Self-perpetuation, 103–5. *See* Conventions
Sentential primacy thesis, 98–99. *See* Word
    meaning
Sider, T., 364
Singular terms, 209
Situational extension (function), 284–6,
    329
Situations, 293n34, 351
Situation semantics, 125, 349–50, 351–3
  assignment of indeterminates to names,
    352–3
  concepts as indeterminates, 353
  definition, 351
  essences, 351
  indeterminates, 352
  referentialist difficulties, 351–2
  situation semantics for ideas, 353

Soames, S., 232, 264–6, 267, 279, 283,
    287–90, 302, 389–90
Social utility, 103. *See* Conventions
Sortal plus individuator theory, 331–5
  account of abstraction, 333–4
  for names, 331–2
  for general terms, 332–3
  lexicalization question, 333
  reference determination, 333
Speaker expression, 4, 74, 77, 78, 81–84
  and indication, 82
  and intention, 74, 81–82.
  and occurrence, 83
  and public observability, 82
  definition, 83
  direct versus indirect, 76, 78–79, 149
Speaker implication, 76–7. *See* Speaker
    meaning
Speaker meaning, 5, 71–89, 164–166
  as species of intention, 74
  cogitative, 75ff, 77–81, 100, 149, 164–6
  cognitive, 75–77
  conventional, 74. *See also* Conventions
  definitions, 166
  Gricean analysis, 84
  inclusive versus exclusive, 76, 78, 164–5
  naive analysis, 72
  non-ideational, 80–81
  versus attempting to communicate, 84
  versus implication, 76–77,
  versus mentioning, 166–7
  versus word meaning, 71–75
  without audience, 84
Speaker reference, 5, 7, 161–9, 173–6
  ambiguities, 167–71
  and intention, 194, 202–3
  and predication, 162–4
  as opaque and intentional, 7, 176–87
  causal theory, 184–7, 187–91, 200–1,
    264
  Chierchia and McConnell-Ginet's
    definition, 174
  definition, 162,
  description theory, 191, 203
  dyadic versus triadic, 176
  Gricean definitions, 175–6
  Introspectibility, 179ff, 187–91
  Kripke's definition, 174
  oblique, 163, 165
  Searle's definition, 173
  semantic pretense, 180–1